Lecture Notes in Computer Science 1157

Edited by G. Goos, J. Hartmanis and J. van Leeuwen

Advisory Board: W. Brauer   D. Gries   J. Stoer

Springer
Berlin
Heidelberg
New York
Barcelona
Budapest
Hong Kong
London
Milan
Paris
Santa Clara
Singapore
Tokyo

Bernhard Thalheim   (Ed.)

Conceptual Modeling – ER '96

15th International Conference
on Conceptual Modeling
Cottbus, Germany, October 7-10, 1996
Proceedings

 Springer

Series Editors

Gerhard Goos, Karlsruhe University, Germany

Juris Hartmanis, Cornell University, NY, USA

Jan van Leeuwen, Utrecht University, The Netherlands

Volume Editor

Bernhard Thalheim
Institut für Informatik, Lehrstuhl Datenbanken und Informationssysteme
Technische Universität Cottbus
Postfach 10 13 44, D-03013 Cottbus, Germany
E-mail: thalheim@informatik.tu-cottbus.de

Cataloging-in-Publication data applied for

Die Deutsche Bibliothek - CIP-Einheitsaufnahme

Conceptual modeling : proceedings / ER '96, 15th International
Conference on Conceptual Modeling, Cottbus, Germany,
October 7 - 10, 1996. Bernhard Thalheim (ed.). - Berlin ;
Heidelberg ; New York ; Barcelona ; Budapest ; Hong Kong ;
London ; Milan ; Paris ; Santa Clara ; Singapore ; Tokyo :
Springer, 1996
  (Lecture notes in computer science ; Vol. 1157)
  ISBN 3-540-61784-1
NE: Thalheim, Bernhard [Hrsg.]; ER <15, 1996, Cottbus>; GT

CR Subject Classification (1991): H.2, H.4, F.1.3, F.4.1, I.2.4, H.1, J.1

ISSN 0302-9743
ISBN 3-540-61784-1 Springer-Verlag Berlin Heidelberg New York

© Springer-Verlag Berlin Heidelberg 1996
Printed in Germany

Typesetting: Camera-ready by author
SPIN 10525581   06/3142 – 5 4 3 2 1 0   Printed on acid-free paper

Preface

The papers published in these proceedings were contributed for presentation at the Fifteenth International Conference on Conceptual Modeling (ER '96), held in Cottbus, Germany, from October 7-10, 1996.

In response to the call for papers, approximately 110 papers were submitted for review, 29 of which were selected by the program committee for ten sessions covering the topics: advanced schema design, processes, query languages, representation, integration, principles of database design, transformation, enhanced modeling, capturing design information and last but not least, evolution. The program committee's outstanding job in refereeing the papers and composing a challenging program is acknowledged here with sincere thanks.

The invited speakers Heikki Mannila, Johann Makowsky, and Charlie Bachman presented their views respectively in the following talks: Schema Design and Knowledge Discovery, Translation Schemes and the Fundamental Problem of Database Design, Impact of Object Oriented Thinking on ER Modeling.

A tutorial program, coordinated by a dedicated Mike Papazoglou, began the week's event. Research themes presented by the experts were:
database cooperation: classification and middleware tools, modeling the enterprise with objects, objects and rules: an emerging synergy, and reuse at the conceptual design level: models, methods and tools.

Extending and complementing the main program were parallel events such as an internationial exhibition on ER CASE tools and four workshops, one on Business Process Modeling, another on ER concepts in Software Engineering, a third on Challenges of Applications and lastly, Challenges of Design.

We trust that ER '96 continues the well established and respected tradition in providing colleagues with an international forum for the understanding of current research in conceptual modelling, facilitating the exchange of experience gained in this field, and encouragement in the discussion of future research directions.

Our special thanks go to Bernhard Thalheim and his team in Cottbus for their enthusiasm and untiring efforts in organizing the conference on the banks of the Spree.

Finally, we would like to express our sincere thanks to all those who contributed to the success of ER '96, the authors, invited speakers, session chairs, tutors, industrial chairs, and participants.

Hamburg, October 1996   Joachim W. Schmidt

CONFERENCE ORGANIZATION

CONFERENCE CHAIR:
Joachim W. Schmidt
Hamburg University

PROGRAM CHAIR:
Bernhard Thalheim
Cottbus Technical University

ORGANIZATION COMMITTEE:
Cottbus Technical University
Chair: Bernhard Thalheim

Meike Albrecht
Wolfram Clauß
Rotraut Goebel
Karla Kersten

Günter Millahn
Manfred Roll
Hans-Jochen Schüler
Suzan Yigitbasi

PROGRAM COMMITTEE

Catriel Beeri, Israel
Janis A. Bubenko jr., Sweden
Sharma Chakravarthy, USA
Isabelle Comyn-Wattiau, France
Opher Etzion, Israel
David W. Embley, USA
Jean-Luc Hainaut, Belgium
Terry Halpin, USA, Australia
Igor Hawryszkiewycz, Australia
Hannu Kangassalo, Finland
Jacques Kouloumdjian, France
Alberto Laender, Brazil
Claus Lewerentz, Germany
Leonid Libkin, USA
Tok Wang Ling, Singapore
Ling Liu, Canada
Peri Loucopoulos, Great Britain
Florian Matthes, Germany
Heinrich C. Mayr, Austria
Leszek A. Maciaszek, Australia

Takao Miura, Japan
Robert Meersman, Belgium
Shamkant B. Navathe, USA
Erich Neuhold, Germany
Maria Orlowska, Australia
Peretz Shoval, Israel
Gunter Saake, Germany
Arne Sølvberg, Norway
August-Wilhelm Scheer, Germany
Bernd Scholz-Reiter, Germany
Graeme Shanks, Australia
Il-Yeol Song, USA
Stefano Spaccapietra, Switzerland
Eberhard Stickel, Germany
Markus Stumptner, Austria
Bernhard Thalheim, Germany
A Min Tjoa, Austria
Olga De Troyer, Netherlands
Yannis Vassiliou, Greece
Herbert Weber, Germany

Tutorials Chair:
Mike Papazoglou, Queensland University of Technology

Industrial Chairs:
Terry Halpin, Asymetrix
Gerhard Rodé, SAP

Workshop Chairs:

Business Process Modeling
Bernd Scholz-Reiter, Cottbus Technical University
Eberhard Stickel, European University Viadrina

ER-Modeling in Software Engineering
Claus Lewerentz, Cottbus Technical University
Herbert Weber, Fraunhofer Institute for Software
Engineering and Systems Engineering

CASE Tools
Bernhard Thalheim, Cottbus Technical University

Challenges
Erich Neuhold, GMD Darmstadt

Modeling of Industrial Information Systems
Bernd Scholz-Reiter, Cottbus Technical University

External Referees

Aberer, Karl
Albrecht, Meike
Altus, Margita
Arisawa, Hiroshi
de Barros, Roberto S. M.
Bastian, Dörte
Bax, Marcello
Bloesch, Anthony
Böhm, Klemens
Bonnet, Christine
Campbell, Linda
Claßen, Ingo
Clauß, Wolfram
Colby, Latha
Conrad, Stefan
Creasy, Peter
Düsterhöft, Antje
Eiter, Thomas
Erkollar, Alptekin
Ewald, Cathy
Fan, Wenfei
Fankhauser, Peter
Fellner, Klement J.
Filippidou, Despina
Fischer, Gisela
Georgalas, Nectarios
Heuser, Carlos
Hochin, Teruhisa
Hofstede, Arthur ter
Kardasis, Panos
Kaschek, Roland
Kavakli, Evagelia

Klar, Markus
Klas, Wolfgang
Klimathianakis, Polivios
Kop, Christian
Kottl, Claudia
Lee, Joseph
Lee, Mong Li
Leone, Nicola
Liddle, Stephen W.
Lieuwen, Daniel
Liu, Chengfei
Loos, Peter
McAllester, David
Medeiros, Claudia Bauzer
Millius, Frank
Mok, Yin Wai
Ng, Yiu-Kai
de Oliveira, José Palazzo M.
Ribeiro, Berthier A. N.
Riecke, John G.
Schewe, Klaus-Dieter
Schmitt, Ingo
Schrefl, Michael
Shioya, Isamu
Teo, Pit Koon
Türker, Can
Tzanaki, Anna
Waßeroth, Susanne
Wijsen, Jef
Woodfield, Scott
Wortmann, Jan

Contents

Keynotes

Impact of Object Oriented Thinking on ER Modeling 1
Charles W. Bachman

Translation Schemes and the Fundamental Problem of Database Design 5
Johann A. Makowsky, Elena V. Ravve

Schema Design and Knowledge Discovery 27
Heikki Mannila

Session 1: Advanced Schema Design
Chair: *Herbert Weber*

Decomposition of Relationships Through Pivoting 28
Joachim Biskup, Ralf Menzel, Torsten Polle, Yehoshua Sagiv

Understanding the Implementation of IS-A Relations 42
Jean-Luc Hainaut, Jean-Marc Hick, Vincent Englebert,
Jean Henrard, Didier Roland

Deductive Object Oriented Schemas 58
Dimitri Theodoratos

Session 2: Processes
Chair: *Arne Sølvberg*

Verification Problems in Conceptual Workflow Specifications................73
Arthur H. M. ter Hofstede, Maria E. Orlowska, Jayantha Rajapakse

Process Knowledge Modeling 89
Pierre Maret, Jean-Marie Pinon

The Conceptual Database Design Optimizer CoDO - Concepts,
Implementation, Application 105
Martin Steeg

Session 3: Query Languages
Chair: *Opher Etzion*

ConQuer: A Conceptual Query Language 121
Anthony C. Bloesch, Terry A. Halpin

Using Structural Recursion as Query Mechanism for Data Models
with References 134
Wolfram Clauß

Session 4: Representation
Chair: *Takao Miura*

A Modular Design Strategy for a Flexible Graphical Database
Design Environment: An Experimental Study 146
Margita Altus

Graph Based Modeling and Implementation with EER/GRAL 163
*Jürgen Ebert, Andreas Winter, Peter Dahm, Angelika Franzke,
Roger Süttenbach*

Session 5: Integration
Chair: *Florian Matthes*

On the Applicability of Schema Integration Techniques
to Database Interoperation 179
Mark W. W. Vermeer, Peter M. G. Apers

Integration of Inheritance Trees as Part of View Generation
for Database Federations 195
Ingo Schmitt, Gunter Saake

A Formal Basis for Dynamic Schema Integration 211
Love Ekenberg, Paul Johannesson

Session 6: Principles of Database Design
Chair: *Robert Meersman*

Graphical Entity Relationship Models: Towards a More
User Understandable Representation of Data 227
Daniel Moody

Benefits and Quality of Data Modelling - Results of an
Empirical Analysis 245
Ronald Maier

Normative Language Approach - A Framework for Understanding 261
Erich Ortner, Bruno Schienmann

Session 7: Transformation
Chair: *Heinrich C. Mayr*

Improving Quality in Conceptual Modelling by the Use
of Schema Transformations 277
Petia Assenova, Paul Johannesson

An Approach to Maintaining Optimized Relational
Representations of Entity-Relationship Schemas 292
Altigran Soares da Silva, Alberto H.F. Laender, Marco A. Casanova

Transforming Conceptual Models to Object-Oriented
Database Designs: Practicalities, Properties, and Peculiarities 309
Wai Yin Mok, David W. Embley

Session 8: Enhanced Modeling
Chair: *Gunther Saake*

Representing Partial Spatial Information in Databases 325
Thodoros Topaloglou, John Mylopoulos

Specification of Calendars and Time Series for Temporal Databases 341
Jae Young Lee, Ramez Elmasri, Jongho Won

View-Centered Conceptual Modelling - An Object Oriented Approach 357
Klaus-Dieter Schewe, Bettina Schewe

Session 9: Capturing Design Information
Chair: *Gerhard Rodé*

Reverse Engineering of Relational Database Physical Schema 372
Isabelle Comyn-Wattiau, Jacky Akoka

Extracting N-ary Relationships Through Database Reverse Engineering ... 392
Christian Soutou

Inheritance as a Conceptual Primitive 406
Roland Kaschek

iO2: An Algorithmic Method for Building Inheritance Graphs
in Object Database Design 422
Amina Yahia, Lofti Lakhal, Rosine Cicchetti, Jean-Paul Bordat

Session 10: Evolution
Chair: *Markus Stumptner*

Workflow Evolution 438
Fabio Casati, Stefano Ceri, Barbara Pernici, Giuseppe Pozzi

A Model for Classification Structures with Evolution Control 456
Moira C. Norrie, Andreas Steiner, Alain Würgler, Martin Wunderli

Integrating Versions in the OMT Models 472
Eric Andonoff, Gilles Hubert, Annig Le Parc, Gilles Zurfluh

Author Index 489

Impact of Objected Oriented Thinking on ER Modeling

Charles W. Bachman

Cayenne Software, Inc., A Bachman and Cadre Company
8 New England Executive Park
Burlinton, MA 08103, U. S. A.
bachmanc@cayennesoft.com

Entity Relationship modeling (ER modeling) defines a set of business entity types, attributes, relationships, roles, dimensions, roles and states of interest to the business.

The data model identifies, defines, and controls the structure, content and changes to the information for database data, message data, process-local variables, and constants and literals.

Data structure diagrams, the first published manifestation of ER model, were published in 1964. They were used in conjunction with the Integrated Data Store (IDS) database management system to provide a visual aid in database design and comprehension. From that starting point, these data structure diagrams have evolved to take into consideration new concepts as they were understood and integrated into the data modeling practice.

Object oriented concepts have effected analysis and design practice in the last few years as they have gained acceptance and wider usage. This paper has been constructed to illustrate how some of the major premises of the objected oriented concepts could be integrated into ER modeling to provide an enhanced modeling paradigm without loosing some of the existing power. One might call this enhanced ER model, "ER++". While object oriented systems focus closely in implementation issues, they also have much to say to those of use who use data modeling as an important element in the practice of model driven development.

The following major themes are listed as containing some of the major benefits of the object oriented concepts:

1. Objects (and their relationships)

2. Inheritance and Multi-Type Objects

3. Abstract Data Types and Operator Overloading

4. Encapsulation and Entity Methods

5. Tight Integration of Database and Programming Language

Each of these major themes will be examined to see how it might impact the conventional approach to ER modeling.

Authors of the various publications which have put forward the object oriented concepts are somewhat at variance as to the definition of the "object" which is the focal point of the object oriented methodology. One definition which seems to cover the major authors' views is as follows, "An object is an entity able to save a state (information) and which offers a number of operations (behavior) to either examine or affect the states."

One of the public speakers which I have heard speak with regard to this subject answered the question, "What is the difference between an 'entity' and an 'object'?" in the following manner. "An entity is an object that does not know how to behave!"

Inheritance is a major point of focus within the object oriented thinking. In its most elementary form, inheritance supports the closely related concepts of generalization and specialization. Horses and turtles are specializations of the "quadruped" concept, as mankind and apes are specializations of the "biped" concept. Both mankind and ape classes (entity types) inherit the properties of the biped class and thus they does not need to define all of the common properties directly for themselves.

For the purpose of classification and discussion, inheritances can be divided into four classes:

1. single inheritance,

2. multiple inheritance,

3. around-the-corner inheritance, and

4. mutual inheritance.

The first of these, "single inheritance" is directly supported by some programming languages and must data modeling systems. It is the easiest form of inheritance to explain and to understand. The way that plants and animals are classified by taxonomist is based on single inheritance.

Multiple inheritance, around-the-corner inheritance and mutual inheritance move into more difficult territory and can be logically combined with single inheritance when a slightly deeper analysis is undertaken. This concept might be categorized as "multi-typing." With multi-typing, it is said that a "real world" entity or a "business" entity may play many roles and that it is a composite of several entity instances, each of a different entity type, which collectively represent that which is known about an entity in the real world.

Rather than attempting to define a new entity type for each possible combination of elementary behaviors that might be witnessed in the real world, with multi-typing entity types are defined for each of the primitive behavior patterns and permitted to be combined in meaningful combinations.

Polymorphism is an other major feature of object oriented thinking. A short definition of Polymorphism says that "the sender of a stimulus does not need to know the receiving instance's class." Polymorphism may manifest itself in several forms in object oriented systems. One of these forms is that which is called a "complex relationship." Complex relationships support the idea that an entity may be associated with a set of entities whose exact nature is not fully known. All that is known is that they have a certain behavior pattern by which they are related to the first entity. In addition to the fact that a certain type of relationship might bind an instance of one entity type to instances of two or more second entity types, there is the ability to define additional constraints that apply to the various instances which are involved.

While complex relationships were first introduced into data modeling to support the view that a real world entity might play two or more roles (the multi-type concept) the associated methodology supporting these relationship quickly lost the distinction between 1) the association of entities representing a single real world entity, and 2) the association of entities representing different real world entities. This is an important issue to be resolved in the correct analysis of the world being modelled and should not be lost.

Abstract data types (dimensions) and operator overloading are strong issues in object oriented systems. Abstract data types define sets of homogeneous data values which can be used in a consistent manner. Real data types might be validly added or compared by the hardware instructions of a computer, but that computation might not make business sense. Adding two social-security-numbers (SSN) makes no business sense. Therefore, defining a dimension (abstract data type) for social-security-numbers and another for dates and another for financial data make sense. Thus an attempt to add or compare values taken from one dimension with the values of a second dimension would result in error condition being detected.

"Dimensions" at the logical level, define for those attributes which are classified within its scope, the type of operations that may be rationally executed. In contrast, "domains" operate at the physical level define for its dimension the physical realizations for its dimension. For example, MM-DD-YY may be the physical representation defined by one domain for the date dimension, while another domain might define a DD-MM-YY or YY-MM-DD representation.

The support of multiple representations (domains) for the values of a single dimension is another application of the polymorphism concept. "Encapsulation" is one of the words that has been used to state that a logical access to information such as a date value does not have to be constrained by the actual physical representation of that data as long as the entity methods which are responsible for providing logical access are capable of making the right kind of physical conversion at access time.

Object oriented analysis and design claim to be broader than just data modeling but also include process modeling. While this paper does not have time to discuss this issue in any detail, it is essential that a full complement of models, "data" model, and "process" model, and "logic" model and "event" model, etc., be defined and integrated in such a manner that the entirety, called the "business" model, or the "enterprise" model, may become a complete, understandable, executable functional specification of the business being modelled.

Translation Schemes and the Fundamental Problem of Database Design

J.A. MAKOWSKY* and E.V. RAVVE **

Department of Computer Science
Technion - Israel Institute of Technology
Haifa, Israel
e-mail: {cselena,janos}@cs.technion.ac.il

Invited Lecture[3]

Abstract. We introduce a new point of view into database schemes by applying systematically an old logical technique: *translation schemes*, and their induced formula and structure transformations. This allows us to re-examine the notion of dependency preserving decomposition and its generalization *refinement*.

The most important aspect of this approach lies in laying the groundwork for a formulation of the *Fundamental Problem of Database Design*, namely to exhibit desirable differences between translation–equivalent presentations of data and to examine refinements of data presentations in a systematic way. The emphasis in this paper is not on results. The main line of thought is an exploration of the use of an old logical tool in addressing the Fundamental Problem.

Translation schemes allow us to have a new look at normal forms of database schemes and to suggest a new line of search for other normal forms. Furthermore we give a characterization of the embedded implicational dependencies (EID's) using FD's and inclusion dependencies (ID's) and a basic class of refinements consisting of projections and natural joins.

---

* Partially supported by a Grant of the German-Israel Foundation and by the Fund for Promotion of Research of the Technion–Israeli Institute of Technology

** Partially supported by a Grant of the German-Israeli Foundation

[3] Given by the first author

1 Introduction

Some ten years ago a famous and influential American database researcher declared that dependency and design theory for relational databases was *passé*. The classification of various useful dependency classes had reached a satisfactory state [Var87, FV86]. Furthermore, the decision problem for the consequence relation of dependencies had been solved for all but one case, the embedded multivalued dependencies, which was finally solved by C. Herrmann, [Her95]. Work on normal forms of database schemes seemed to reach an end and it was time to proceed in different directions. Nevertheless, work in design theory continued to some extent, mostly in Europe, as witnessed in [PDGV89, MR92, Tha91], but the database community at large showed diminished enthusiasm for this kind of work, [AHV94].

In this paper we make a modest attempt to revive interest in design theory. We hope to do this with the help of the systematic use of *translation schemes* as the major logical tool to carry out research in design theory.

Traditional design theory of relational databases comprises the following steps:

- Identify a set of entities;
- Identify, for each entity, a fixed set of attributes;
- Identify a set of functional dependencies between those attributes;
- Check whether the entities are in BCNF;
- if not, decompose into BCNF, if possible, else into 3NF;
- Choose set of relationships;
- Identify weak entities;
- Introduce aggregations.

The steps are iterated, choices are modified, and ultimately some satisfactory design emerges, which can be specified with functional (FD's) and inclusion dependencies (ID's). For an excellent sound exposition cf. [MR92, PDGV89, Tha93] and for an encyclopedic view of dependency theory, cf [Tha91, Tha94].

In the process of modification, horizontal and vertical decompositions are used. Ideally, these decompositions should be information and dependency preserving. The requirement of preservation of information leads to join dependencies (JD's). The requirement of dependency preservation very quickly becomes complicated even in the case of FD's. In particular, not every database scheme specified by FD's can be decomposed into BCNF while preserving the dependencies.

In this paper we introduce a new notion of *information and dependency preserving refinements* of database schemes which is meaningful for arbitrary first order dependencies. The basic underlying notion is a *first order translation scheme*. It is based on the classical syntactic notion of interpretability from logic made explicit by M. Rabin in [Rab65]. More recently, translation schemes have been used in descriptive complexity theory under the name of first order reductions [Dah83] and [Imm87], and in descriptive graph theory [Cou94]. A systematic survey of their use to analyze complexities of logical theories, cf. [CH90]. The paper is organized as follows:

In section 2 we introduce in detail the notion of a translation scheme Φ and its derived maps Φ^* on database instances and $\Phi^\#$ on formulae expressing queries or dependencies. The *fundamental property* of translation schemes shows that these maps are dual to each other. We also introduce the notion of *reductions and weak reductions* between classes of instances defined by dependencies. This section is fairly abstract allowing arbitrary first order formulae or relational algebra expressions as dependencies. Although of purely logical character, it is written in the notation of databases.

In section 3 we review classical decomposition theory and show how its problems can be expressed in the framework of translation schemes. This allows us to give a general definition of *information preserving transformation* of database schemes in terms of the existence of a left inverse Ψ^* of a transformation given by a weak reduction Φ^*. Besides this, the purpose of this section consists also in helping the reader to absorb the material from section 2 in a familiar landscape.

In classical decomposition theory the notion of projections of functional dependencies plays an important role. In section 4 we lay the grounds for generalizing this to arbitrary transformations Φ^* induced by translation schemes and arbitrary sets of dependencies Σ.

The material presented in section 5 is central to our exploration. Here we consider several definitions of *dependency preserving transformations* involving the maps $\Phi^\#$ and $\Psi^\#$. We analyze their interrelationship and give complete characterizations in terms of (weak) reductions Φ^* and Ψ^*.

The characterizations of dependency preserving transformations leads us naturally to ask for which classes of translation schemes $TRANS$ a given dependency class DEP is closed under the syntactic transformations $\Phi^\#$ with $\Phi \in TRANS$. This is trivially true for domain independent (safe) dependencies and transformations. More surprisingly this gives us a characterization of the *Embedded Implicational Dependencies (EID)* as the smallest class of dependencies closed under $\Phi^\#$ for $\Phi \in BASIC$ and containing the functional and inclusion dependencies. Here $BASIC$ is the smallest class of translation schemes containing the projections and joins and closed under composition.

In section 7 we discuss several definitions of dependency preserving transformations where the class of dependencies DEP and of translation schemes $TRANS$ are restricted classes. This is needed to formulate precisely what we call the *Fundamental Problem of Database Design*. To state it precisely, we introduce in section 8 two relations between database schemes, dependency preserving *translation–refinement and translation–equivalence* . The first induces a partial pre-order on the set of database schemes, and second induces an equivalence relation. The Fundamental Problem of Database Design consists in identifying properties which distinguish translation–equivalent presentations of data represented by different database schemes, or, when this is not meaningful, to study the properties of the partial pre-order induced by translation–refinement. This leads us to the notion of *separability of a database scheme modulo a simple set of dependencies*. We show how the classical normal form theory of 3NF and BCNF fits in this framework, and discuss reasons for the failure of 4NF. Our view of BCNF, taken from [MR96] is new in its generality, although it may have been known as folklore before.

In the last section we draw our conclusions and sketch further research in progress.

The use of translation schemes can be extended to a full fledged design theory for Entity–Relationship design or, equivalently, for database schemes in ER-normal form, cf. [MR92]. It can also be used to deal with views and view updates, as views are special cases of translation schemes. These issues will be discussed in the full paper.

Acknowledgments

The material presented in this paper is an outcome of teaching database theory over the years. We would like to thank O. Shmueli, our co-teacher, for many valuable arguments, and our students for their questions and their commitment in projects. In particular, we would like to thank A. Goldin and M. Epstein, who checked the details of section 6. We are indebted to E. Rosen for patiently listening to our draft presentations and providing many valuable comments. We also thank B. Thalheim and C. Beeri for inviting the first author for the invited lecture. Both provided us with a great stimulus for writing this version of the paper.

2 Translation Schemes

In this section we introduce the general framework for syntactically defined translation schemes in terms of databases. The definition is valid for a wide class of logics or query languages, but in this paper we restrict ourselves to first order logic (FOL). The reader should be able to give corresponding definitions also for relational algebra. Note that the definition can be expanded to the parameterized case as well.

2.1 The basic definition

We use the following notations:

- $\bar{A}$ is a finite set of attributes;
- R is a relation name;
- $\mathbf{R}$ is a database scheme (i.e. a non empty set of relation names);
- $I(\mathbf{R})(A(\mathbf{R}), B(\mathbf{R}))$ is an instance of $\mathbf{R}$.
- Σ is a set of dependencies (first order unless specified otherwise).

Definition 1 (Translation schemes Φ).
Let $\mathbf{R}$ and $\mathbf{S}$ be two database schemes. Let $\mathbf{S} = (S_1, \ldots, S_m)$ and let $\rho(S_i)$ be

the arity of S_i. Let $\Phi = \langle \phi, \psi_1, \ldots, \psi_m \rangle$ be first order formulae over $\mathbf{R}$. Φ is $k-$
feasible for $\mathbf{S}$ *over* $\mathbf{R}$ if ϕ has exactly k distinct free first order variables and each
ψ_i has $k\rho(S_i)$ distinct free first order variables. Such a $\Phi = \langle \phi, \psi_1, \ldots, \psi_m \rangle$ is
also called a k–$\mathbf{R}$–$\mathbf{S}$–*translation scheme* or, in short, a *translation scheme*, if the
parameters are clear in the context. If $k = 1$ we speak of *scalar* or *non–vectorized*
translation schemes.

The formulae $\phi, \psi_1, \ldots, \psi_m$ can be thought of as queries. ϕ describes the
new domain, and the ψ_i's describe the new relations. Vectorization creates one
attribute out of a finite sequence of attributes.

Remark. In the logical tradition one also allows in translation schemes to redefine
equality. For our applications in databases this is not needed.

2.2 Transforming database instances

A (partial) function Φ^* from $\mathbf{R}$ instances to $\mathbf{S}$ instances can be directly associated
with a translation scheme Φ.

Definition 2 (Induced map Φ^*).
Let $I(\mathbf{R})$ be a $\mathbf{R}$ instance and Φ be k–feasible for $\mathbf{S}$ over $\mathbf{R}$. The instance $I(\mathbf{S})_\Phi$
is defined as follows:

(i) The universe of $I(\mathbf{S})_\Phi$ is the set $I(\mathbf{S})_\phi = \{\bar{a} \in I(\mathbf{R})^k : I(\mathbf{R}) \models \phi(\bar{a})\}$.
(ii) The interpretation of S_i in $I(\mathbf{S})_\Phi$ is the set

$$I(\mathbf{S})_\Phi(S_i) = \{\bar{a} \in I(\mathbf{S})_\phi{}^{\rho(S_i)} : I(\mathbf{R}) \models (\psi_i(\bar{a}) \wedge \phi)\}.$$

Note that $I(\mathbf{S})_\Phi$ is a $\mathbf{S}$ instance of cardinality at most $\mid \mathbf{R} \mid^k$.
(iii) The partial function $\Phi^* : I(\mathbf{R}) \rightarrow I(\mathbf{S})$ is defined by $\Phi^*(I(\mathbf{R})) = I(\mathbf{S})_\Phi$. Note
that $\Phi^*(I(\mathbf{R}))$ is defined iff $I(\mathbf{R}) \models \exists \bar{x} \phi$.

Φ^* maps $\mathbf{R}$ instances into $\mathbf{S}$ instances, by computing the answers to the
queries $\psi_1, \ldots, \psi_m$ over the domain of $\mathbf{R}$ specified by ϕ.

2.3 Transforming queries and dependencies

Next we want to describe the way formulae (query expressions) are transformed
when we transform databases by Φ^*. For this a function $\Phi^\#$ from first order
formulae over $\mathbf{S}$ to first order formulae over $\mathbf{R}$ can be directly associated with a
translation scheme Φ.

Definition 3 (Induced map $\Phi^\#$).
Let θ be a $\mathbf{S}$–formula and Φ be k–feasible for $\mathbf{S}$ over $\mathbf{R}$. The formula θ_Φ is defined
inductively as follows:

(i) For $S_i \in \mathbf{S}$ and $\theta = S_i(x_1, \ldots, x_l)$ let $x_{j,h}$ be new variables with $j \leq l$ and
$h \leq k$ and denote by $\bar{x}_j = \langle x_{j,1}, \ldots, x_{j,k} \rangle$. We make $\theta_\Phi = \psi_i(\bar{x}_1, \ldots, \bar{x}_l)$.

(ii) For the boolean connectives, the translation distributes,
i.e. if $\theta = (\theta_1 \vee \theta_2)$ then $\theta_\Phi = (\theta_{1\Phi} \vee \theta_{2\Phi})$ and if $\theta = \neg\theta_1$ then $\theta_\Phi = \neg\theta_{1\Phi}$, and similarly for $\wedge$.

(iii) For the existential quantifier, we use relativization, i.e. if $\theta = \exists y\theta_1$, let $\bar{y} = \langle y_1, \ldots, y_k \rangle$ be new variables. We make

$$\theta_\Phi = \exists\bar{y}(\phi(\bar{y}) \wedge (\theta_1)_\Phi).$$

(iv) The function $\Phi^\# : FOL$ over $\mathbf{S} \to FOL$ over $\mathbf{R}$ is defined by $\Phi^\#(\theta) = \theta_\Phi$.

(v) For a set of $\mathbf{S}$–formulae Σ we define

$$\Phi^\#(\Sigma) = \{\theta_\Phi : \theta \in \Sigma \text{ or } \theta = \forall\bar{y}(S_i \leftrightarrow S_i)\}$$

This is to avoid problems with Σ containing only quantifierfree formulae, as $\Phi^\#(\theta)$ need not be a tautology even if θ is.

Fig. 1. Translation scheme and its components

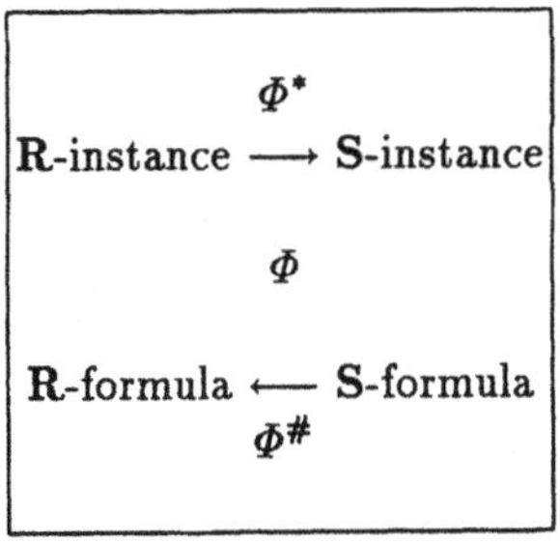

For both induced maps we have simple monotonicity properties:

Proposition 4. Let $\Phi = \langle \phi, \psi_1, \ldots, \psi_m \rangle$ be a k–$\mathbf{R}$–$\mathbf{S}$–translation scheme, K_1 be a set of $\mathbf{R}$–instances, K_2 be a set of $\mathbf{S}$–instances, Σ_1 be a set of $\mathbf{R}$–sentences and Σ_2 be a set of $\mathbf{S}$–sentences.

(i) If $K_1 \subseteq K_2$ then $\Phi^*(K_1) \subseteq \Phi^*(K_2)$.
(ii) If $\Sigma_1 \models \Sigma_2$ then $\Phi^\#(\Sigma_1) \subseteq \Phi^\#(\Sigma_2)$.

2.4 The fundamental property of translation schemes

The following fundamental theorem is easily verified, cf. [EFT94]. Its origins go back at least to the early years of modern logic, cf. [HB70, page 277 ff].

Theorem 5.
Let $\Phi = \langle \phi, \psi_1, \ldots, \psi_m \rangle$ be a k–$\mathbf{R}$–$\mathbf{S}$–translation scheme, $I(\mathbf{R})$ be a $\mathbf{R}$-instance and θ be a FOL–formula over $\mathbf{S}$. Then $I(\mathbf{R}) \models \Phi^\#(\theta)$ iff $\Phi^*(I(\mathbf{R})) \models \theta$.

Note that we now can define the composition of translation schemes:

Definition 6 (Composition of translation schemes).
Let $\Psi = \langle \psi, \psi_1, \ldots, \psi_{m_1} \rangle$ be a k_1–**R**–**S**–translation scheme, and let
$\Phi = \langle \phi, \phi_1, \ldots, \phi_{m_2} \rangle$ be a k_2–**S**–**T**–translation scheme. Then we denote by $\Psi(\Phi)$
the $(k_1 \cdot k_2)$–**R**–**T**–translation scheme given by $\langle \Phi^{\#}(\psi), \Phi^{\#}(\psi_1), \ldots, \Phi^{\#}(\psi_{m_1}) \rangle$.
$\Psi(\Phi)$ is called the composition of Φ with Ψ.

2.5 Weak reductions and reductions

Given a translation schemes Φ the function Φ^* may be a partial function. We
now define weak reductions over a specific domain K. In this case we shall always
require that Φ^* be total on K.

Definition 7 (Weak reduction and reduction).
Let $K_{\mathbf{R}}, K_{\mathbf{S}}$ be classes of **R**(**S**)-instances closed under isomorphism, and Φ be
a translation scheme. Φ^* is a *weak reduction (reduction)* of $K_{\mathbf{R}}$ to $K_{\mathbf{S}}$ if Φ^* is
total on $K_{\mathbf{R}}$ and for every **R**-instance $I(\mathbf{R})$ we have that, $I(\mathbf{R}) \in K_{\mathbf{R}}$ implies
that (iff) $\Phi^*(I(\mathbf{R})) \in K_{\mathbf{S}}$.

Let Σ be a set of first order sentences (i.e formulae without free variables)
for a relation scheme **R**. We denote by $Inst(\Sigma)$ the set of **R**–instances which
satisfy Σ. For $\Sigma^{\mathbf{R}}, \Sigma^{\mathbf{S}}$ sets of **R** (**S**) sentences we are often interested in (weak)
reductions with $K_{\mathbf{R}} = Inst(\Sigma^{\mathbf{R}})$ and $K_{\mathbf{S}} = Inst(\Sigma^{\mathbf{S}})$.

Proposition 8.

(i) The following are equivalent:
  (i.a) Φ is a weak reduction from $Inst(\Sigma^{\mathbf{R}})$ to $Inst(\Sigma^{\mathbf{S}})$;
  (i.b) $Inst(\Sigma^{\mathbf{R}}) \subseteq Inst(\Phi^{\#}(\Sigma^{\mathbf{S}}))$;
  (i.c) $\Sigma^{\mathbf{R}} \models \Phi^{\#}(\Sigma^{\mathbf{S}})$.
(ii) Furthermore, Φ^* is a reduction from $Inst(\Sigma^{\mathbf{R}})$ to $Inst(\Sigma^{\mathbf{S}})$ iff $\Sigma^{\mathbf{R}}$ is equivalent to $\Phi^{\#}(\Sigma^{\mathbf{S}})$.

Proof. Use the fundamental property of theorem 5.

3 Decomposing relation schemes

In this section we review the elementary material of database decomposition in
terms of translation schemes. Our main goal here is to motivate our further development and convince the reader that translation schemes are the appropriate
tool for this. We assume the reader is familiar with traditional database design
as given in [AHV94, PDGV89, MR92].

Proviso: From now in we consider only finite relations (structures) and equivalence of formulae is meant to be equivalence over finite structures.

3.1 Projections and Joins

The most popular transformations in Databases are: Projections and Joins. Let us give their definitions in terms of translation schemes:

Projection (π) :

In this case all the formulae ψ_i (see definition 1 on page 3) are in form

$\psi_i(\bar{x}_i) = \exists \bar{y}_i R_i(\bar{x}_i, \bar{y}_i)$,

where R_i is a relation symbol and $\bar{x}_i$ is a vector of free variables.

Note that if Φ consists of projections only, and Σ is a set of functional dependencies (FD's), then $\Phi^{\#}(\Sigma)$ is also a set of FD's.

Join ($\bowtie$) :

In this case all the formulae ψ_i are in form

$\psi_i(\bar{x}_i) = \exists \bar{y}_i \wedge_j R_{i_j}(\bar{x}_{i_j}, \bar{y}_{i_j})$,

where every R_{i_j} is a relation symbol, $\cup_j \bar{x}_{i_j} = \bar{x}_i$, $\cup_j \bar{y}_{i_j} = \bar{y}_i$ and for all $\bar{x}_{i_{j_1}}$ there is $\bar{x}_{i_{j_2}}$ such that $\bar{x}_{i_{j_1}} \cap \bar{x}_{i_{j_2}} \neq \emptyset$.

If there are no common variables, this just defines the Cartesian product.

Note that if Φ consists of a join, and Σ is a set of FD's, then $\Phi^{\#}(\Sigma)$ is not necessarily equivalent to a set of FD's.

3.2 Information preserving decomposition by projections

The classical decomposition theory can now be expressed via translation schemes.

Let $(\mathbf{R}, \Sigma^{\mathbf{R}})$ be a database scheme with $\mathbf{R} = \{R\}$. Let Φ be a $\mathbf{R} - \mathbf{S}$ translation scheme given by a sequence of projections $\langle \pi_1(R), \ldots, \pi_n(R) \rangle$ with $\mathbf{S} = (S_1, \ldots, S_n)$. Φ^* decomposes $\mathbf{R}$ into a set of projections. Let Ψ be given by $\bowtie_{i \leq n} \pi_i R$. Ψ is now a $\mathbf{S} - \mathbf{R}$ translation scheme. Ψ reconstructs the original database instance from a decomposition.

Φ^* is said to be *information preserving* or has the *lossless join property*, if $\bowtie_{i \leq n} \pi_i(I(R)) = I(R)$ for every instance of $(\mathbf{R}, \Sigma^{\mathbf{R}})$.

In our terminology of translation schemes this can be expressed as, Φ^* is said to be *information preserving* if $\Psi^*(\Phi^*(I(\mathbf{R}))) = I(\mathbf{R})$ for every instance of $(\mathbf{R}, \Sigma^{\mathbf{R}})$, or, in other words, $\Sigma^{\mathbf{R}} \models \bowtie_{i \leq n} \pi_i(R) = R$.

This definition is very restricted for the following reasons:

- $\Sigma^{\mathbf{R}}$ is usually restricted to FD's or some other restricted class of dependencies.
- Φ is of the very restricted form of projections.
- Ψ is of the very restricted form of joins.
- No set of dependencies is specified for the decomposed databases.

With the help of translation schemes we can give now a more general definition.

3.3 Information preserving translation schemes

Let $< \mathbf{R}, \Sigma^{\mathbf{R}} >$ be a database scheme. Using the function Φ^* derived from a $\mathbf{R} - \mathbf{S}$ translation scheme Φ we can transform database instances in a uniform way. We would like to make precise the notion of information preserving (lossless) transformation.

Definition 9. Φ^* is *information preserving for* $\Sigma^{\mathbf{R}}$ if there exists a $\mathbf{S} - \mathbf{R}$-translation scheme Ψ such that for every $I(\mathbf{R}) \models \Sigma^{\mathbf{R}}$ we have that

$$\Psi^*(\Phi^*(I(\mathbf{R}))) \cong I(\mathbf{R})$$

In other words, Ψ^* is a left inverse of Φ^* on $Inst(\Sigma^{\mathbf{R}})$.

Remark. We could have required also that the structures be equal, i.e $\Psi^*(\Phi^*(I(\mathbf{R}))) = I(\mathbf{R})$. This is often the case in the database context, but the weaker requirement seems more appropriate, as it allows also for vectorized translation schemes.

Proposition 10. *Let* $< \mathbf{R}, \Sigma^{\mathbf{R}} >$ *be a database scheme. Let* Φ *be a* $\mathbf{R} - \mathbf{S}$-*translation scheme and* Ψ *be a* $\mathbf{S} - \mathbf{R}$-*translation scheme. Then the following are equivalent:*

(i) Φ *is information preserving for* $\Sigma^{\mathbf{R}}$ *with left inverse* Ψ^*.
(ii) for every relation $R_i \in \mathbf{R}$ *we have that* $\Sigma^{\mathbf{R}} \models (R_i \leftrightarrow \Phi^\#(\Psi^\#(R_i)))$
(iii) for every $\mathbf{R}$-*formula* χ *we have that* $\Sigma^{\mathbf{R}} \models (\chi \leftrightarrow \Phi^\#(\Psi^\#(\chi)))$

Proof. (i) $\rightarrow$ (ii) follows directly from the fundamental property in theorem 5 applied to atomic formulae and $\Psi^*(\Phi^*(I(\mathbf{R}))) \cong I(\mathbf{R})$.
(ii)$\rightarrow$(iii) follows from the definition of $\Phi^\#$.
(iii)$\rightarrow$(ii) follows, as (ii) is a special case of (iii).
(ii)$\rightarrow$(i) follows by iterated use of theorem 5:
$I(\mathbf{R}) \models R(\bar{a})$ iff $I(\mathbf{R}) \models \Phi^\#(\Psi^\#(R(\bar{a}))$ iff $\Psi^*(\Phi^*(I(\mathbf{R})) \models R(\bar{a})$.

3.4 The decomposition theorem

For a single relation scheme $R(XYZ)$ with functional dependencies F the classical decomposition theorem states that $\Phi =< \pi_{XY} R, \pi_{YZ} R >$ is an information preserving decomposition with left inverse $\Psi =< R_1 \bowtie_Y R_2 >$ iff

(*) either $Y \rightarrow X$ or $Y \rightarrow Z$ follows from F.

Using proposition 10 Φ is information preserving iff

(**) $F \models (\Phi^\#(\Psi^\#(R))) \leftrightarrow R)$.

Writing this explicitly we get

(***) $F \models ((\pi_{XY} R \bowtie_Y \pi_{YZ}) \leftrightarrow R)$.

But $(Y \rightarrow Z$ or $Y \rightarrow X)$ is equivalent, if written in first order logic, to $((\pi_{XY} R \bowtie_Y \pi_{YZ}) \leftrightarrow R)$.

The general form of the decomposition theorem can now be stated, using proposition 10, as follows:

Theorem 11. *Let $< \mathbf{R}, \Sigma^{\mathbf{R}} >$ be a database scheme. Let Φ be a $\mathbf{R} - \mathbf{S}$-translation scheme and Ψ be a $\mathbf{S} - \mathbf{R}$-translation scheme. Then Φ is information preserving with left inverse Ψ iff $\Sigma^{\mathbf{R}} \models (\Phi^\#(\Psi^\#(R_i)) \leftrightarrow R_i)$ for each $R_i \in \mathbf{R}$.*

3.5 FD's preserving decompositions

For a single relation scheme $R(XYZ)$ with functional dependencies F and the decomposition $\Phi =< \pi_{XY} R, \pi_{YZ} R >$ one usually defines the projections F_{XY} and F_{YZ} of F as the functional dependencies which specify the decomposed relation. From the definition of Φ it follows that $\Phi^*(I(\mathbf{R})) \models (F_{XY} \cup F_{YZ})$, in other words Φ is a weak reduction from $Inst(F)$ to $Inst(F_{XY} \cup F_{YZ})$.

By abuse of notation, one says traditionally that Φ is a dependency preserving decomposition if

$(\#)$ $(F_{XY} \cup F_{YZ}) \models F$.

If we look instead at the FD's at their equivalent first order formulae we see why this *is an abuse of notation*. F_{XY} speaks about a binary relation, whereas F speaks about a ternary relation. The precise formulation of $(\#)$ can be stated as

$(\#\#)$ $\Phi^\#(F_{XY} \cup F_{YZ}) \models F$.

It is easy to see, cf. also the table 6 in section 6, that $\Phi^\#(F_{XY} \cup F_{YZ})$ is equivalent to a set of FD's, which indeed look the same, if written in the $X \rightarrow Y$ notation.

Note, that by proposition 5, we always have that $I(R) \models F$ iff $\Psi^*(\Phi^*(I(R))) \models F$ iff $\Phi^*(I(R)) \models \Psi^\#(F)$. In other words, as Φ^* and Ψ^* are mutual inverses, it would have been more natural to express preservation of FD's by $\Phi^*(I(R)) \models \Psi^\#(F)$. However, as one can easily compute, $\Psi^\#(F)$ is not a set of FD's.

4 Preserving general dependencies and the range of Φ^*

The notion of projection of a set of FD's is difficult to generalize for three reasons, all of which can be overcome using the framework of translation schemes.

- Its definition depends on the special choice of decomposition via projections;
- Its definition depends, furthermore, on the special character of the FD's, in as much as their meaning depends only on values of specific attributes.
- The class of FD's is not closed under $\Psi^\#$ for joins.

If $\Sigma^{\mathbf{R}}, \Sigma^{\mathbf{S}}$ and Φ are given, it is natural to study the relationship between $\Sigma^{\mathbf{R}}$ and $\Sigma^{\mathbf{S}}$. From the fundamental property in theorem 5 we get

Proposition 12. *If Φ^* is a reduction from $Inst(\Sigma^{\mathbf{R}})$ to $Inst(\Sigma^{\mathbf{S}})$ then*

$$Inst(\Sigma^{\mathbf{R}}) = Inst(\Phi^{\#}(\Sigma^{\mathbf{S}})),$$

in other words, $\Sigma^{\mathbf{R}}$ is equivalent $\Phi^{\#}(\Sigma^{\mathbf{S}})$.

It is also natural to ask if we can characterize $\Sigma^{\mathbf{S}}$ similarly in the case, where Φ is a (weak) reduction. For this we introduce the following

Definition 13. $(\Sigma^{\mathbf{R}})^{\Phi} = \{\theta \in FOL(\mathbf{S}) : \Sigma^{\mathbf{R}} \models \Phi^{\#}(\theta)\}$

Note that $(\Sigma^{\mathbf{R}})^{\Phi}$ is infinite as defined.

Problem 14. Find a characterization of the situation where $(\Sigma^{\mathbf{R}})^{\Phi}$ is equivalent to some finite set.

Returning to our example of the single relation scheme $R(XYZ)$ we note that $F^{\Phi} \models F_{XY} \cup F_{YZ}$. But F^{Φ} contains also some inclusion dependencies such as $\pi_Y(R_1) \subseteq \pi_Y(R_2)$ and $\pi_Y(R_2) \subseteq \pi_Y(R_1)$. In the design process the option of adding dependencies which are in F^{Φ} must be allowed.

Proposition 15. *Let $\Sigma^{\mathbf{R}}$ and Φ be given.*

(i) Φ is a weak reduction from $Inst(\Sigma^{\mathbf{R}})$ to $Inst((\Sigma^{\mathbf{R}})^{\Phi})$
(ii) If Φ is a weak reduction from $Inst(\Sigma^{\mathbf{R}})$ to $Inst(\Sigma^{\mathbf{S}})$ then $(\Sigma^{\mathbf{R}})^{\Phi} \models \Sigma^{\mathbf{S}}$.
(iii) If Φ is a reduction from $Inst(\Sigma^{\mathbf{R}})$ to $Inst((\Sigma^{\mathbf{R}})^{\Phi})$ then $\Sigma^{\mathbf{R}}$ is equivalent to $\Phi^{\#}((\Sigma^{\mathbf{S}})^{\Phi})$.

Proof. To see (i) assume $A(\mathbf{R}) \models \Sigma^{\mathbf{R}}$ and $B(\mathbf{S}) = \Phi^*(A(\mathbf{R}))$. Assume for contradiction that there is $\theta \in (\Sigma^{\mathbf{R}})^{\Phi}$ with $B(\mathbf{S}) \models \neg\theta$. Using the fundamental property of theorem 5 we get $A(\mathbf{R}) \models \Phi^{\#}(\neg\theta)$ which is equivalent to $A(\mathbf{R}) \models \neg\Phi^{\#}(\theta)$. But then $\Sigma^{\mathbf{R}} \not\models \Phi^{\#}(\theta)$ and $\theta \notin (\Sigma^{\mathbf{R}})^{\Phi}$ which is a contradiction.
(ii) follows from (i) and (iii) follows from (ii) and theorem 5.

Proposition 16. *Let $< \mathbf{R}, \Sigma^{\mathbf{R}} >$ be a database scheme. Let Φ be a $\mathbf{R} - \mathbf{S}$-translation scheme which is information preserving for $\Sigma^{\mathbf{R}}$ with left inverse Ψ^*. Then*

(i) $\Psi^{\#}(\Sigma^{\mathbf{R}}) \models (\Sigma^{\mathbf{R}})^{\Phi}$.
(ii) If additionally, Ψ is a weak reduction from $Inst(\Sigma^{\mathbf{S}})$ to $Inst(\Sigma^{\mathbf{R}})$ then $\Sigma^{\mathbf{S}} \models (\Sigma^{\mathbf{R}})^{\Phi}$.

Proof. (i) Use theorem 5 and proposition 15.
(ii) use (i) and proposition 8.

Conclusion: The meaning of $(\Sigma^{\mathbf{R}})^\Phi$ for the choice of $\Sigma^{\mathbf{S}}$ is as follows:

- If we require that Φ be a weak reduction from $Inst(\Sigma^{\mathbf{R}})$ to $Inst(\Sigma^{\mathbf{S}})$ then it follows that $(\Sigma^{\mathbf{R}})^\Phi \models \Sigma^{\mathbf{S}}$.
- If we require that Φ is information preserving for $\Sigma^{\mathbf{R}}$ and the left inverse Ψ is a weak reduction from $Inst(\Sigma^{\mathbf{S}})$ to $Inst(\Sigma^{\mathbf{R}})$ then $\Sigma^{\mathbf{S}} \models (\Sigma^{\mathbf{R}})^\Phi$.
- If Φ is information preserving and both Φ and Ψ are weak reductions, then $\Sigma^{\mathbf{S}}$ is equivalent to $(\Sigma^{\mathbf{R}})^\Phi$.

5 Dependency preserving translation schemes

5.1 Three options

Our general situation is now as follows:

[Assumption] $< \mathbf{R}, \Sigma^{\mathbf{R}} >$ and $< \mathbf{S}, \Sigma^{\mathbf{S}} >$ are database schemes. Φ is a $\mathbf{R} - \mathbf{S}$–translation scheme which is information preserving for $\Sigma^{\mathbf{R}}$ with left inverse Ψ^* and a weak reduction from $Inst(\Sigma^{\mathbf{R}})$ to $Inst(\Sigma^{\mathbf{S}})$. Additionally, $(\Sigma^{\mathbf{R}})^\Phi \models \Sigma^{\mathbf{S}}$.

We would like to formulate in general that Φ is dependency preserving. We have three options:

(A) For **R**-instances: $\Phi^\#(\Sigma^{\mathbf{S}}) \models \Sigma^{\mathbf{R}}$
(B) For **S**-instances: $\Sigma^{\mathbf{S}} \models \Psi^\#(\Sigma^{\mathbf{R}})$
(C) For **S**-instances: $(\Sigma^{\mathbf{R}})^\Phi \models \Psi^\#(\Sigma^{\mathbf{R}})$

The relationship between these options is given by the following

Proposition 17.

(i) Under the assumption above we have (C) → (B) and (B) → (A).
(ii) If Φ is also a left inverse of Ψ, we have also (A) → (B).
(iii) If Ψ is also a weak reduction from $Inst(\Sigma^{\mathbf{S}})$ to $Inst(\Sigma^{\mathbf{R}})$ then we have also (B) → (C).

Proof. (i) (C) → (B) follows as by our assumption $(\Sigma^{\mathbf{R}})^\Phi \models \Sigma^{\mathbf{S}}$.
(B) → (A) follows as, by proposition 4 $\Phi^\#(\Sigma^{\mathbf{S}}) \models \Phi^\#(\Psi^\#(\Sigma^{\mathbf{R}}))$ and hence by proposition 10 $\Phi^\#(\Sigma^{\mathbf{S}}) \models \Sigma^{\mathbf{R}}$.
(ii): Now assume Φ is also a left inverse of Ψ. Then $\Psi^\#(\Phi^\#(\Sigma^{\mathbf{S}})) \models \Psi^\#(\Sigma^{\mathbf{R}})$ and hence, $\Sigma^{\mathbf{S}} \models \Psi^\#(\Sigma^{\mathbf{R}})$.
(iii): If Ψ is a weak reduction from $Inst(\Sigma^{\mathbf{S}})$ to $Inst(\Sigma^{\mathbf{R}})$ then by proposition 8, $(\Sigma^{\mathbf{R}})^\Phi$ is equivalent to $\Sigma^{\mathbf{S}}$.

The next theorem shows that each of these variants of dependency preservation is equivalent to either Φ^* or Ψ^* being a (weak) reduction.

Theorem 18. Assume $< \mathbf{R}, \Sigma^{\mathbf{R}} >$ is a database scheme, Φ is lossless for $\Sigma^{\mathbf{R}}$ with left inverse Ψ.

(i) Ψ^* *is a weak reduction from* $Inst((\Sigma^{\mathbf{R}})^{\Phi})$ *to* $Inst(\Sigma^{\mathbf{R}})$ *iff (C) holds.*
(ii) Ψ^* *is a weak reduction from* $Inst(\Sigma^{\mathbf{S}})$ *to* $Inst(\Sigma^{\mathbf{R}})$ *iff (B) holds.*
(iii) Φ^* *is a reduction from* $Inst(\Sigma^{\mathbf{R}})$ *to* $Inst(\Sigma^{\mathbf{S}})$ *iff (A) holds.*

Proof. (i): Assume first that Ψ^* is a weak reduction from $Inst((\Sigma^{\mathbf{R}})^{\Phi})$ to $Inst(\Sigma^{\mathbf{R}})$. Using proposition 8 we have $Inst((\Sigma^{\mathbf{R}})^{\Phi}) \subseteq Inst(\Psi^{\#}(\Sigma^{\mathbf{R}}))$ and using proposition 16 we have $Inst(\Psi^{\#}(\Sigma^{\mathbf{R}})) \subseteq Inst((\Sigma^{\mathbf{R}})^{\Phi})$ and therefore $Inst(\Psi^{\#}(\Sigma^{\mathbf{R}})) = Inst((\Sigma^{\mathbf{R}})^{\Phi})$, which shows that Φ is dependency preserving. Now assume Φ is dependency preserving, i.e. $Inst(\Psi^{\#}(\Sigma^{\mathbf{R}})) = Inst((\Sigma^{\mathbf{R}})^{\Phi})$. Using only that $Inst((\Sigma^{\mathbf{R}})^{\Phi}) \subseteq Inst(\Psi^{\#}(\Sigma^{\mathbf{R}}))$ and proposition 8 we get that Ψ^* is a weak reduction from $Inst((\Sigma^{\mathbf{R}})^{\Phi})$ to $Inst(\Sigma^{\mathbf{R}})$.
(ii) is similar.
(iii) is just proposition 8.

5.2 Discussion

We have characterized three options for our definition of dependency preserving transformations. Each of them has been characterized within the terminology of translation schemes.

- The strongest version, (C), has the advantage of being independent of the choice of $\Sigma^{\mathbf{S}}$. The disadvantage of this approach is that $(\Sigma^{\mathbf{R}})^{\Phi}$ is in general infinite and not even recursively enumerable. It also contains first order formulae of arbitrary complexity. The structure of $(\Sigma^{\mathbf{R}})^{\Phi}$ deserves further studying, though.
- The remaining two versions, (A) and (B), reflect different perspectives, depending on whether we are more interested in the domain or range of Φ^*. Both approaches depend on the choice of $\Sigma^{\mathbf{S}}$, which is not uniquely determined and may depend on various extraneous design decisions. We use (B) to show, in [MR96] how to obtain dependency preserving transformations of database schemes with $\Sigma^{\mathbf{R}}$ consisting of FD's which are always in Boyce–Codd Normal Form, cf. theorem 27.
- So far we have generalized the functional dependencies in one big leap and allowed arbitrary first order dependencies. We would like to choose a more customary dependency class DEP, such as the full implicational or embedded implicational dependencies and develop a similar framework. For (A) we have to study whether $\Phi^{\#}(\Sigma^{\mathbf{S}})$ is also of this form, for (B) the analogue question for $\Psi^{\#}(\Sigma^{\mathbf{R}})$.

6 Embedded implication dependencies

In this section we study the closure of dependency classes under the function $\Phi^{\#}$ for translation schemes Φ. Obviously, if we allow all first order formulae to be used both as dependencies and in translation schemes, we get closed classes. Less obviously so, if we restrict the formulae both as dependencies and in translation schemes to domain independent (safe) formulae, cf. [AHV94], we get another closed class. We leave the proof of this last assertion as an exercise.

Dependency classes which are closed allow us to transfer specific dependencies via reductions. We first recall a classification of dependencies introduced in [BV84, MV86], cf. also [FV86, Var87, Tha91, AHV94].

Definition 19 (Dependencies).

(i) A first order formula over a set τ of relation symbols is a *full implicational dependency (FID)*, if it is of the form $\forall \bar{x}(\wedge_i R_i(\bar{x}) \rightarrow \varphi(\bar{x}))$,
where each R_i is an atomic formula not containing the equality symbol, φ is atomic possibly containing equality and each variable which occurs in φ also occurs in some R_i. Note that we do not allow the empty conjunction.

(ii) If φ is an equality we also speak of *equality generating dependencies (EGD)*, and if φ is an instance of a relation symbol we speak of *tuple generating dependencies (TGD)*. The *functional dependencies (FD)* are the EGD's with only two R_i's.

(iii) The classes $TFID$ of *typed full implicational dependencies*, *typed tuple generating dependencies (TTGD)* and *typed equality generating dependencies (TEGD)* are defined analogously for the case where τ is typed.

(iv) The class of *embedded implicational dependencies (EID)*, consists of first order formulae of the form $\forall \bar{x}(\wedge_i R_i(\bar{x}) \rightarrow \exists \bar{y} \wedge_j \phi_j(\bar{x}, \bar{y}))$,
where the R_i's are as for the FID and the ϕ_j's are atomic with all the variables from $\bar{x}$ occurring already in the R_i's.

(v) If every ϕ_j is an instance of a relation symbol we speak of an *embedded tuple generating dependency (ETGD)*.

(vi) The class of *embedded template dependencies (ETD)*, consists of the EID's with only one formula ϕ_j, which is not an equality. A special case of template dependencies are the *inclusion dependencies (IND)*, where there is also only one formula R_i.

(vii) The classes $TFID, TEID, TETD, TIND$ of typed embedded dependencies are defined similarly.

(viii) A dependency is a *projection generating dependency (PGD)* if it is of the form $\forall \bar{x}(\exists \bar{y} \wedge_i R_i(\bar{x}_i, \bar{y}_i) \rightarrow \exists \bar{z} \wedge_j R_j(\bar{x}_j, \bar{z}_j))$, where the R_i's are as for the FID and $(\cup_i \bar{x}_i) \cup (\cup_j \bar{x}_j) = \bar{x}, \cup_j \bar{z}_j = \bar{z}$.

(ix) A dependency is a *embedded multivalued dependency (EMD)* if it is of the form $\forall \bar{x} \bar{y}_1 \bar{y}_2 \bar{z}_1 \bar{z}_2 \bar{t}_1 \bar{t}_2 ((P(\bar{x}, \bar{y}_1, \bar{z}_1, \bar{t}_1) \wedge P(\bar{x}, \bar{y}_2, \bar{z}_2, \bar{t}_2) \rightarrow \exists \bar{t}_3 P(\bar{x}, \bar{y}_1, \bar{z}_2, \bar{t}_3))$.

Here all the $\bar{x}, \bar{y}, \bar{z}, \bar{t}$'s are vectors of variables.

In particular we define

Definition 20 (Basically closed dependency class). We denote by $PROJ$ $(JOIN)$ the set of translation schemes consisting of projections (joins). We denote by $BASIC$ the smallest set of translation schemes which contains projections and joins and is closed under composition. A class of dependencies D is *basically closed* if for every basic translation scheme Φ and every $\Sigma \subseteq D$ we have: $\Phi^{\#}(\Sigma) \subseteq D$.

Obviously $PROJ$ and $JOIN$ are closed under compositions. Furthermore every basic transformation can be written as $\Phi(\Psi)$ with $\Phi \in PROJ$ and $\Psi \in JOIN$.

The following table shows how different types of translation schemes change the types of dependencies:

Table 1. Changes of dependencies for different types of translation schemes

Φ :. Dependency Class	FD	EID	EGD	TGD	PGD	ETGD
PROJ	FD	EID	EGD	ETGD	ETGD	ETGD
JOIN		EID	EID	EGD	ETGD	ETGD	ETGD
BASIC		EID	EID	EGD	ETGD	ETGD	ETGD

From the table we can conclude that the FD's, TGD's and PGD's are not basically closed. On the other hand EID's, EGD's and $ETGD$'s are basically closed. Furthermore, we have

Theorem 21. *The EID's are the smallest basically closed dependency class which contains both the functional and inclusion dependencies.*

The proof is tedious but straightforward.

The theorem justifies the choice of EID's as a dependency class, inspite of the undecidability of its consequence problem, [CLM81]. For an Entity–Relationship diagram both FD's and IND's are used, so, by stepwise refinements which are dependency preserving, all the EID's have to be available.

7 Preserving dependencies from a class DEP

Let us fix a class of dependencies DEP. For a set of first order sentences Σ we say that $\Sigma \subseteq_{eq} DEP$ if there is a set of dependencies $D \subseteq DEP$ which is equivalent to Σ. In general, checking whether $\Sigma \subseteq_{eq} DEP$ is undecidable, by Trakhtenbrot's theorem, cf. [EFT94], but this is not the point here. We want to study dependency preserving transformations where the dependencies are restricted to DEP.

7.1 Many options

Our general situation is now as follows:

[Assumption] $< \mathbf{R}, \Sigma^{\mathbf{R}} >$ and $< \mathbf{S}, \Sigma^{\mathbf{S}} >$ are database schemes. Φ is a $\mathbf{R} - \mathbf{S}$–translation scheme which is information preserving for $\Sigma^{\mathbf{R}}$ with left inverse Ψ^* and a weak reduction from $Inst(\Sigma^{\mathbf{R}})$ to $Inst(\Sigma^{\mathbf{S}})$. Additionally, $(\Sigma^{\mathbf{R}})^{\Phi} \models \Sigma^{\mathbf{S}}$.

We would like to formulate in general that Φ is dependency preserving. We have various options:

(A-DEP) For R-instances: $\Sigma^{\mathbf{R}} \subseteq_{eq} DEP$, $\Phi^{\#}(\Sigma^{\mathbf{S}}) \subseteq_{eq} DEP$ and $\Phi^{\#}(\Sigma^{\mathbf{S}}) \models \Sigma^{\mathbf{R}}$.

(B-DEP) For S-instances: $\Sigma^{\mathbf{S}} \subseteq_{eq} DEP$, $\Psi^{\#}(\Sigma^{\mathbf{R}}) \subseteq_{eq} DEP$, $\Sigma^{\mathbf{S}} \models \Psi^{\#}(\Sigma^{\mathbf{R}})$.

(C-DEP) For S-instances: $\Psi^{\#}(\Sigma^{\mathbf{R}}) \subseteq_{eq} DEP$, $(\Sigma^{\mathbf{R}})^{\Phi} \cap DEP \models \Psi^{\#}(\Sigma^{\mathbf{R}})$.

(X^*-DEP) For X=A, B or C, $\Sigma^{\mathbf{R}} \cup \Sigma^{\mathbf{S}} \subseteq DEP$ and either (A-DEP), (B-DEP) or (C-DEP).

We leave it to the reader to formulate some basic interrelations between these definitions.

7.2 FD's revisited

For $DEP = FD$ (A^*-DEP) with $\Sigma^{\mathbf{R}} \cup \Sigma^{\mathbf{S}} \subseteq FD$ is the classical notion. But we could add to $\Sigma^{\mathbf{S}}$ some inclusion dependencies and still get (A-DEP). Returning to our example of the single relation scheme $R(XYZ)$ consider the inclusion dependencies $\pi_Y(R_1) \subseteq \pi_Y(R_2)$ and $\pi_Y(R_2) \subseteq \pi_Y(R_1)$. It is easy to see that $\Phi^{\#}(\pi_Y(R_1) \subseteq \pi_Y(R_2))$ and $\Phi^{\#}(\pi_Y(R_2) \subseteq \pi_Y(R_1))$ are tautologies.

The options (A-DEP) and (B-DEP) allow us to exploit this possibility when we want to transform a database scheme by an information and dependency preserving translation scheme.

We can use our definitions also to study dependency preserving horizontal decomposition, cf. [PDGV89]. We do not develop this further, due to lack of space.

Problem 22. Develop a theory of dependency preserving horizontal decompositions based on our approach. The *clean decompositions* and *clean normal form (CNF)* of [PDGV89] is a first step in this direction.

8 Making the Fundamental Problem precise

8.1 Equivalent presentations of data

Let DEP be a class of first order dependencies and $TRANS$ be a class of first order translation schemes with some closure properties to be identified in the sequel.

Definition 23 (Translation refinement and equivalence). Given $\Sigma^{\mathbf{R}} \cup \Sigma^{\mathbf{S}} \subseteq DEP$ and $< \mathbf{R}, \Sigma^{\mathbf{R}} >$ and $< \mathbf{S}, \Sigma^{\mathbf{S}} >$ two database schemes.

(i) We say that $< \mathbf{S}, \Sigma^{\mathbf{S}} >$ is a *translation–refinement of* $< \mathbf{R}, \Sigma^{\mathbf{R}} >$ if there is $\Phi \in TRANS$ which is a weak reduction which is both information and (A^*)-dependency preserving.

(ii) We say that $< \mathbf{R}, \Sigma^{\mathbf{R}} >$ and $< \mathbf{S}, \Sigma^{\mathbf{S}} >$ are *translation–equivalent* under transformations from $TRANS$ if one can be converted into the other by weak reductions $\Phi^*, \Psi^* \in TRANS$ which are information and (A^*)-dependency preserving.

Among the closure properties we will require that $TRANS$ is closed under composition and that DEP is closed under $\Phi^\#$ for $\Phi \in TRANS$. Examples for DEP and $TRANS$ are

- Safe (domain independent) dependencies and translation schemes;
- EID and $BASIC$.

Problem 24. Identify other closed pairs DEP and $TRANS$.

Under these closure properties, translation–refinement defines a partial pre–order on different data presentations via database schemes. Translation–equivalence defines an equivalence relation.

Proposition 25. *Let* $< \mathbf{R}, \Sigma^{\mathbf{R}} >$ *and* $< \mathbf{S}, \Sigma^{\mathbf{S}} >$ *two translation–equivalent database schemes over* DEP *with* $\Phi, \Psi \in TRANS$. *Then*

(i) Both Φ^* *and* Ψ^* *are reductions.*
(ii) Both Φ^* *and* Ψ^* *are* (B^*)-*information preserving.*

If $< \mathbf{S}, \Sigma^{\mathbf{S}} >$ *is only a translation–refinement of* $< \mathbf{R}, \Sigma^{\mathbf{R}} >$ *we still have that* Φ^* *is a reduction.*

Proof. Use theorem 18 and proposition 17.

8.2   Normal forms revisited

The Fundamental Problem of Database Design consists in identifying properties which distinguish translation–equivalent presentations of data represented by different database schemes. The classical study of normal forms was such an attempt with $DEP = FD$ and $TRANS$ extremely restricted. The synthesis algorithm for 3NF, cf. [PDGV89], can be paraphrased as follows:

Theorem 26. *Let* $< \mathbf{R}, F^{\mathbf{R}} >$ *be an FD-database scheme. Then there exists a translation–equivalent FD-database scheme* $< \mathbf{S}, F^{\mathbf{S}} >$ *which is in 3NF. Furthermore* Φ *can be chosen to consist of projections and* Ψ *of joins.*

Already for Boyce-Codd Normal Form the analogue statement is not true. This has two reasons: the class of transformations allowed is too restricted and translation-equivalence may be too strong a requirement.

In [MR96] we prove the following

Theorem 27. *Let* $< \mathbf{R}, F^{\mathbf{R}} >$ *be a relation scheme with* $F^{\mathbf{R}} \subseteq FD$. *There is database scheme* $< \mathbf{S}, \Sigma^{\mathbf{S}} >$ *with* $\Sigma^{\mathbf{S}} \subseteq FD \cup IND$ *which is a translation-refinement with weak reductions* Φ *and (left inverse)* Ψ *such that:*

(i) Both Φ and Ψ are compositions of projections and joins, but Ψ uses vector-ization.

(ii) Φ is dependency preserving in the sense of (A-DEP)

(iii) for $F^{\mathbf{S}} = \{f \in FD : \Sigma^{\mathbf{S}} \models f\} < \mathbf{S}, F^{\mathbf{S}} >$ is in Boyce-Codd Normal Form.

This theorem contrasts the fact that for Φ consisting only of projections, and Ψ consisting only of joins, Boyce–Codd Normal Form cannot be achieved in general with dependency preserving decompositions.

Attempts to find translation–refinements to other normal forms (4NF) including other dependencies than FD's have failed, cf. [AHV94], because the notion of dependency preservation was not well understood.

It may be more promising to study first the pre-order and equivalence relation of translation–refinement and translation–equivalence on database schemes for various classes DEP and $TRANS$. An inspiration for such a study, although the notion of translation–equivalence there is weaker, may be found in [MPS90]. The adhoc definition of nice properties of database schemes will not lead anywhere without a deeper understanding of translation–refinement and translation–equivalence.

8.3 The Fundamental Problem of Database Design

For a fixed dependency class DEP and a database scheme $< \mathbf{R}, \Sigma^{\mathbf{R}} >$ with $\mathbf{R} = \{R_1, \ldots R_n\}$ and $\Sigma^{\mathbf{R}} \subseteq DEP(\mathbf{R})$ we would like to find criteria for transparent design.

Our first requirement is data independence.

Definition 28 Data independence:. We say that $\mathbf{R}$ is independent over $\Sigma^{\mathbf{R}}$ if there is no first order query $\theta \in FOL(\mathbf{R} - \{R_i\})$ such that $\Sigma^{\mathbf{R}} \models (\theta \leftrightarrow R_i)$.

Our next requirement concerns $\Sigma^{\mathbf{R}}$. In the degenerate case $\Sigma^{\mathbf{R}}$ does not express any interaction between the relations.

Definition 29. Let $< \mathbf{R}, \Sigma^{\mathbf{R}} >$ be a database scheme.

(i) We say that $\Sigma^{\mathbf{R}}$ is *separable over* $\mathbf{R}$ if there exist for each i a $\Sigma_i \subset DEP(R_i)$ such that $\bigcup_i \Sigma_i$ is equivalent to $\Sigma^{\mathbf{R}}$.

(ii) $< \mathbf{R}, \Sigma^{\mathbf{R}} >$ *splits* if there exists a database scheme $< \mathbf{S}, \Sigma^{\mathbf{S}} >$ such that

(ii.a) $\mathbf{S}$ contains at least two relation symbols;

(ii.b) $\Sigma^{\mathbf{S}} \subseteq DEP(\mathbf{S})$;

(ii.c) $< \mathbf{S}, \Sigma^{\mathbf{S}} >$ is a translation–refinement of $< \mathbf{R}, \Sigma^{\mathbf{R}} >$;

(ii.d) $\mathbf{S}$ is independent over $\Sigma^{\mathbf{S}}$ and

(ii.e) $\Sigma^{\mathbf{S}}$ is separable over $\mathbf{S}$.

The following is immediate.

Proposition 30. For $< \mathbf{R}, \Sigma^{\mathbf{R}} >$ we define $\Sigma_i = \{\phi \in DEP(R_i) : \Sigma^{\mathbf{R}} \models \phi\}$. $\Sigma^{\mathbf{R}}$ is separable over $\mathbf{R}$ iff $\bigcup_i \Sigma_i$ is equivalent to $\Sigma^{\mathbf{R}}$.

Note that it is undecidable to check whether a given $\Sigma^{\mathbf{R}}$ is separable over $\mathbf{R}$ already for $DEP = FD \cup IND$, as the corresponding consequence problem is undecidable, cf. [AHV94].

Problem 31. Find deeper (model theoretic) criteria for separability and splitting.

Remark. In [MPS90] a related notion of *connected theories* is introduced. A theory is connected if there is no translation–equivalent theory which is separable. In general it is highly non–trivial to establish that a mathematical theory is connected. Such results have been proved by J. Mycielski and P. Pudlak for Linear Orders (without last element), Peano Arithmetic, Zermelo Fraenkel Set Theory. It is open whether the theory of Algebraic (Real) Closed Fields is connected.

If a database schemes is specified by FD's only, it always splits. But if the database scheme originates from an ER-scheme, the presence of inclusion dependencies will prevent, in general, splitting. The *universal instance* of [Ull82] is not necessarily a solution to the splitting problem, as the resulting translation scheme is not dependency preserving.

Splitting is, in general, too strong a requirement. What we really want is that the interaction between the relations be as simple to express as possible. To capture this notion we specify a class of simple formulae $SIMPLE$. A good candidate for $SIMPLE$ are the inclusion dependencies IND. We do not require that $SIMPLE \subseteq DEP$ as we could take for $DEP = FID$ and $SIMPLE = IND$. If $DEP \subseteq SIMPLE$ all the notions trivialize.

Definition 32. Let $< \mathbf{R}, \Sigma^{\mathbf{R}} >$ be a database scheme.

(i) We say that $\Sigma^{\mathbf{R}}$ is *separable over* $\mathbf{R}$ *modulo* $SIMPLE$ if there exist $\Sigma_i \subset DEP(R_i)$ and $D \subseteq SIMPLE$ such that $\bigcup_i \Sigma_i \cup D$ is equivalent to $\Sigma^{\mathbf{R}}$.

(ii) $< \mathbf{R}, \Sigma^{\mathbf{R}} >$ *splits modulo* $SIMPLE$ if there exists a database scheme $< \mathbf{S}, \Sigma^{\mathbf{S}} >$ such that

   (ii.a) $\mathbf{S}$ contains at least two relation symbols;
   (ii.b) $\Sigma^{\mathbf{S}} \subseteq DEP(\mathbf{S})$;
   (ii.c) $< \mathbf{S}, \Sigma^{\mathbf{S}} >$ is a translation–refinement of $< \mathbf{R}, \Sigma^{\mathbf{R}} >$;
   (ii.d) $\mathbf{S}$ is independent over $\Sigma^{\mathbf{S}}$ and
   (ii.e) $\Sigma^{\mathbf{S}}$ is separable modulo $SIMPLE$ over $\mathbf{S}$.

Clearly, every database scheme derived from an ER-scheme splits modulo IND. In this case we can choose the $\Sigma_i \subseteq FD$ and such that each $< S_i, \Sigma_i >$ is in BCNF, cf. [MR92]. Our theorem 27 shows that, modulo IND every database scheme $< \mathbf{R}, \Sigma^{\mathbf{R}} >$ with $\Sigma^{\mathbf{R}} \subseteq FD$ splits into BCNF.

Problem 33. Characterize the $\Sigma^{\mathbf{R}}$ for which a given database scheme $< \mathbf{R}, \Sigma^{\mathbf{R}} >$ splits modulo IND into BCNF.

It is not clear whether BCNF is the best choice. However, a general approach to normal forms should take into account splitting modulo IND.

The Fundamental Problem of Database Design Theory, as we see it, consists in the systematic study of non–splitting database schemes.

8.4 ER-schemes

If we restrict our translation schemes to compositions of projections and joins and our dependencies to EID's, the previous section showed that for X = A, B or C, (X) and (X^*-EID) are equivalent, because the EID's are basically closed, cf. theorem 21. This is the appropriate framework to compare transformations of ER-schemes and to address the Fundamental Problem of ER–Database Design. We plan to address this issue in our future work.

9 Conclusions and further research

We have introduced the use of translation schemes into database design theory. We have shown how they capture disparate notions such as information preservation and dependency preservation in a uniform way. We have shown how they relate to normal form theory and have stated what we think to be the Fundamental Problem of Database Design. Several resulting research problems have been explicitly stated in the paper.

We have shown that the Embedded Implicational Dependencies are all needed, when we deal with stepwise refinements of database schemes specified by Functional and Inclusion Dependencies.

As the material presented grew slowly while teaching database theory, its foundational and didactic merits should not be underestimated. Over the years our students of the advanced database theory course confirmed our view that traditional database design lacks coherence and that this approach makes many issues accessible to deeper understanding.

Our approach via dependency preserving translation–refinements can be extended to a full fledged design theory for Entity–Relationship design or, equivalently, for database schemes in ER-normal form, cf. [MR92]. It is also the appropriate framework to compare transformations of ER-schemes and to address the Fundamental Problem of ER–Database Design.

Translation schemes can also be used to deal with views and view updates, as views are special cases of translation schemes. The theory of *complementary views* from [BS81] can be rephrased elegantly in this framework. It is connected with the notion of translation schemes invariant under a relation and implicit definability, [Kol90]. Order invariant translation schemes play an important role in descriptive complexity theory, [Daw93] and [Mak94]. The theory of *independent* complementary views of [KU84] exhibits some severe limitations on the applicability of [BS81]. In spite of these limitations it seems worthwhile to explore the connection between independent views and transformation invariant for certain relations further.

The latter two applications are currently being developed by the authors and their students and will be included in the full paper.

References

[AHV94]   S. Abiteboul, R. Hull, and V. Vianu. *Foundations of Database.* Addison Wesley, 1994.

[BS81] F. Bancilhon and N. Spyratos. Update semantics of relational views. *ACM Transactions on Database Systems*, 6(4):557–575, 1981.

[BV84] C. Beeri and M. Vardi. Formal systems for tuple and equality generating dependencies. *SIAM Journal on Computing*, 13(1):76–98, 1984.

[CH90] K.J. Compton and C.W. Henson. A uniform method for proving lower bounds on the computational complexity of logical theories. *Annals of Pure and Applied Logic*, 48:1–79, 1990.

[CLM81] A. Chandra, H. Lewis, and J.A. Makowsky. Embedded implicational dependencies and their implication problem. In *ACM Symposium on the Theory of Computing 1981*, pages 342–354. ACM, 1981.

[Cou94] B. Courcelle. Monadic second order graph transductions: A survey. *Theoretical Computer Science*, 126:53–75, 1994.

[Dah83] E. Dahlhaus. Reductions to NP–complete problems by interpretations. In E. Börger et. al., editor, *Logic and Machines: Decision Problems and Complexity*, volume 171, pages 357–365. Springer Verlag, 1983.

[Daw93] A. Dawar. *Feasible Computation Through Model Theory*. PhD thesis, Department of Computer Science, University of Maryland, 1993.

[EFT94] H.D. Ebbinghaus, J. Flum, and W. Thomas. *Mathematical Logic, 2nd edition*. Undergraduate Texts in Mathematics. Springer-Verlag, 1994.

[FV86] R. Fagin and M. Vardi. The theory of data dependencies. In M. Anshel and W. Gewirtz, editors, *Proceedings of Symposia in Applied Mathematics*, volume 34 of *American Mathematical Society*, pages 19–71. RI, 1986.

[HB70] D. Hilbert and P. Bernays. *Grundlagen der Mathematik, I*, volume 40 of *Die Grundleheren der mathematischen Wissenschaften in Einzeldarstellungn*. Springer Verlag, Heidelberg, 2nd edition, 1970.

[Her95] C. Herrmann. On the ubdecidability of implication between embedded multivalued database dependencies. *Information and Computation*, 122:221–235, 1995.

[Imm87] N. Immerman. Languages that capture complexity classes. *SIAM Journal on Computing*, 16(4):760–778, Aug 1987.

[Kol90] P.G. Kolaitis. Implicit definability on finite structures and unambiguous computations. In *FOCS'90*, pages 168–180. IEEE, 1990.

[KU84] A. Keller and J.D. Ullman. On complementary and independent mappings. *Proc. ACM SIGMOD Symp. on the Management of Data*, pages 145–148, 1984.

[Mak94] J.A. Makowsky. Capturing complexity classes with Lindström quantifiers. In *MFCS'94*, volume 841 of *Lecture Notes in Computer Science*, pages 68–71. Springer Verlag, 1994.

[MPS90] J. Mycielski, P. Pudlák, and A.S. Stern. *A Lattice of Chapters of Mathematics*, volume 426 of *Memoirs of the American Mathematical Society*. American Mathematical Society, 1990.

[MR92] H. Mannila and K.J. Räihä. *The Design of Relational Databases*. Addison-Wesley, 1992.

[MR96] J.A. Makowsky and E. Ravve. Dependency preserving refinment of database schemes. Technical Report, April 1996, Department of Computer Science, Technion–Israel Institute of Technology, Haifa, Israel, 1996.

[MV86] J.A. Makowsky and M. Vardi. On the expressive power of data dependencies. *Acta Informatica*, 23.3:231–244, 1986.

[PDGV89] J. Paredaens, P. De Bra, M. Gyssens, and D. Van Gucht, editors. *The Structure of the Relational Database Model*, volume 17 of *EATCS Monographs on Theeoretical Computer Science*. Springer Verlag, Heidelberg, 1989.

[Rab65] M.A. Rabin. A simple method for undecidability proofs and some applications. In Y. Bar Hillel, editor, *Logic, Methodology and Philosophy of Science II*, Studies in Logic, pages 58–68. North Holland, 1965.

[Tha91] B. Thalheim. *Dependencies in Relational Databses*, volume 126 of *Teubner-Texte zur Mathematik*. B.G. Teubner Verlagsgesellschaft, Leipzig, 1991.

[Tha93] B. Thalheim. Foundation of entity-relationship modeling. *Annals of Mathematics and Artificial Intelligence*, 7:197–256, 1993.

[Tha94] B. Thalheim. A survey on database constraints. Reine Informatik I-8/1994, Fakultät für Mathematik, Naturwissenschaften und Informatik, 1994.

[Ull82] J.D. Ullman. *Principles of Database Systems*. Principles of Computer Science Series. Computer Science Press, 2nd edition, 1982.

[Var87] M. Vardi. Fundamentals of dependency theory. In *Trends in Theoretical Computer Science*, pages 171–224. Computer Science Press, 1987.

Schema Design and Knowledge Discovery

Heikki Mannila

Department of Computer Science
University of Helsinki
P.O. Box 26
FIN-00014 Helsinki
Finland

Heikki.Mannila@cs.helsinki.fi
http://www.cs.helsinki.fi/ mannila

Abstact

Knowledge discovery in databases (KDD), often also referred to as data mining, aims at the discovery of useful information from large masses of data. In this talk we review some issues in the intersection of schema design and knowledge discovery, both in the relational database design and in text databases.

Decomposition of Relationships through Pivoting

Joachim Biskup[1], Ralf Menzel[1], Torsten Polle[1] and Yehoshua Sagiv[2]

[1] Institut für Informatik, Universität Dortmund, Germany
[2] Department of Computer Science, Hebrew University of Jerusalem, Israel

Abstract. In the literature there are several proposals to map entity-relationship schemas onto object-oriented schemas, but they only treat relationship sets naïvely or restrict them to binary relationship sets. We follow a different approach in the treatment of relationship sets. Our goal is to let the designer specify relationships of any arity and then to employ semantic constraints to decompose relationships into smaller fragments. The semantic constraints in use are functional constraints, which are defined in the object-oriented framework. The decomposition process guided by functional constraints is similar to the decomposition process in the relational approach with functional dependencies, but it takes advantage of the features provided by the object-oriented data model. In object-oriented schemas it is possible to enforce a certain kind of functional constraints automatically, namely unary functional constraints.

1 Introduction

The Entity-Relationship approach (ER approach) to modelling data, as proposed by Chen [7], is a simple way of representing data in the form of entities and relationships among entities. Because of its simplicity, it has found a wide spread acceptance and serves as starting point for transformations into different data models. One of the target data models is the object-oriented model (OO model) [3, 1, 14], and there are numerous proposals to map ER-schemas, their variations or different conceptual schemas onto object-oriented schemas [12, 19, 11, 20, 15, 18, 4]. The basic idea of these transformations is to map entity sets onto (entity) classes in the object-oriented data model and relationship sets, also called associations, onto (relationship) classes. This mapping seems unnatural in the object-oriented framework, when it comes to n-ary relationships. Therefore the common approach is to restrict relationships to binary relationships as, e.g. in [15], or to nest relationships [18], which clears the path to represent these relationships by means of methods. Another way is to make relationships first class citizens of the object-oriented data model as it is done in the object-relation model [21]. But even there it is claimed that in practice only binary relationships or special ternary relationships occur. The difficulties to decompose ternary or even n-ary relationships into binary relationships is discussed by Thalheim [22].

We follow a different approach in the treatment of relationship classes. Our goal is to let the designer specify relationships of any arity in the conceptual model, i.e., the ER model, and then to employ semantic constraints given by the designer to decompose the corresponding relationship classes losslessly into smaller fragments in the object-oriented data model. For this decomposition we use mainly functional dependencies, which are defined in the object-oriented data model. The difference in the decomposition in this setting to the decomposition in the relational approach is that we use the features of the object-oriented data model. The decomposition relies heavily on a transformation called pivoting. This transformation is a special case of pivoting introduced in [4], and hence called *property pivoting*. Since we do not refer to (general) pivoting in this article, we use the term pivoting meaning property pivoting.

This paper is organised as follows. In Sect. 2 a simple object-oriented data model is introduced. The transformation pivoting used at the core of the decomposition is presented in Sect. 3. We start with briefly outlining the mapping from ER-schemas to OO-schemas and then give a simple definition of pivoting and later on extend it to recursive pivoting, leading to a transformation suitable to decompose relationships. Finally, we discuss the interplay between the behaviour of pivoting and the characteristics of semantic constraints, which guide the transformation process. Here we put special emphasis on the features of object-oriented models influencing the decomposition process.

2   Object-Oriented Data Model

2.1   Overview

In this section we present the basic terms relevant to our notion of an object-oriented data model, concentrating only on the *main* concepts that are important for our transformations. This is in particular the capability to reference objects. Therefore our type system is only rudimentarily developed. The data model does not even contain inheritance, although it is needed for the transformations. The reason is that inheritance is only required for technical purpose, and therefore we decided to leave it out to facilitate the presentation. This simplification shifts our data model closer to the network model and even to the relational model, but still these lack the concept of an object identifier, which is used for the reference mechanism, and hence essential for pivoting. In Sect. 2.2 we will give an good sized example for this model.

Our idea of a database is that it consists of two parts. One part, the database schema, is relatively stable over the time. It is used to describe the structural part of applications.

Definition 1. A *(database) schema* D consists of a finite set of *class schemes* of the form
$$c\{p_1 : c_1, \ldots, p_n : c_n\}F.$$
c is the name of the class scheme. Each *property name*[3] p_i is unique in a given class scheme. Its type, written $\mathrm{Ran}_D(c, p_i)$, is the name c_i of another class

---

[3] We will often use the terms property and class instead of property name and class name.

scheme. The set of names of class schemes in D is written Class(D), and the set of property names occurring in the definition of a particular class scheme with name c is written Props(c). The set F consists of

- *functional constraints* of the form $c(m_1 \cdots m_n \rightarrow m_{n+1} \cdots m_o)$ where $1 \leq n < o$ and where $m_i \in$ Props$(c) \uplus \{\text{Id}\}^4$, for $1 \leq i \leq o$ and,
- *(range) completeness constraints* of the form $c\{m\}$ where $m \in$ Props(c).

Functional constraints play a similar rôle in our data model as functional dependencies in the relational data model, where they ensure that tuples agree on the values of the attributes on the right-hand side, whenever they have the same values for the attributes on the left-hand side. So functional constraints ensure that objects agree on the values of the properties on the right-hand side, whenever they have the same values for properties on the left-hand side. Functional constraints correspond to Weddell's path functional dependencies [23], where the length of all paths is not greater than one. If the property Id occurs on the right-hand side of a functional constraint, this functional constraint is called a *key constraint*. If in the relational model a set of attributes forms a key, the values for these key attributes uniquely determine a tuple. Key constraints are used if a set of property values is to uniquely determine an object.

A (range) completeness constraint for a property states that all objects of the type of the property are referenced by an object through this property.

The other part of a database is a *database instance*. It describes the time-varying part of a database, and is used to understand formally that semantic constraints are satisfied. We found it natural and intuitive to think of objects as vertices and of property values as edges in a graph, following the approach of Beeri [3].

Definition 2. An *(database) instance* of a database schema D is a directed graph $G(V, E)$ with vertex and edge labelling as class and property names respectively. G must also satisfy the following constraints, where the class name label of a vertex v is denoted $l_{Cl}(v)$.

1. *(property value integrity)* If $u \xrightarrow{p} v \in E$, then $p \in$ Props$(l_{Cl}(u))$ and $l_{Cl}(v) =$ Ran$_D(l_{Cl}(u), p)$.
2. *(property functionality)* If $u \xrightarrow{p} v, u \xrightarrow{p} w \in E$, then $v = w$.
3. *(property value completeness)* If $u \in V$, then there exists $u \xrightarrow{p} v \in E$ for all $p \in$ Props$(l_{Cl}(u))$.

Property value integrity ensures that property values are of the type given in the corresponding database schema. Property functionality ensures that properties are scalar, i.e., single-valued. Property value completeness forbids *null values*, i.e., the property value for an object must always be defined. We can construct

---

[4] Id is the identity property. We assume that it does not correspond to the name of any property in D, and furthermore Ran$_D(c, \text{Id}) := c$ for all classes $c \in$ Class(D). It is used to refer to the object itself. This is necessary for so-called *key constraints*.

a database instance out of a database schema. For the schema depicted in Fig. 2 this is done in Fig. 3.

If we have an object, i.e., a vertex, in an instance, and a property that is defined for the class name label of the object, we can reach another object by following the edge labelled by the property. If the property is the identity property Id, we arrive at the original object again.

Definition 3. Let $G(V, E)$ be an instance of schema D, $u \in V$ be a vertex, and $p \in \text{Props}(l_{Cl}(u)) \cup \{\text{Id}\}$ be a property. Then $u.p$ denotes the vertex u if $p = \text{Id}$ and the vertex v, where $u \xrightarrow{p} v \in E$, if $p \in \text{Props}(l_{Cl}(u))$.

Definition 4. A functional constraint $c(p_1 \cdots p_n \rightarrow p_{n+1} \cdots p_o)$ over a schema D is *satisfied* by an instance $G(V, E)$ for D iff for any pair of vertices $u, v \in V$, where $l_{Cl}(u) = l_{Cl}(v) = c$, $u.p_i = v.p_i$, $1 \leq i \leq n$ implies $u.p_j = v.p_j$, $n < j \leq o$.

Definition 5. A completeness constraint $c\{p\}$ over a schema D is *satisfied* by an instance $G(V, E)$ for D iff for any vertex v, where $l_{Cl}(v) = \text{Ran}_D(c, p)$, there is an incoming edge $u \xrightarrow{p} v \in E$ and $l_{Cl}(u) = c$.

As in the relational data model, it is also possible to define the *logical consequences* of a set of functional constraints and give a sound and complete derivation system for the implication of functional and completeness constraints.

By means of this derivation system we can calculate for a class scheme the set of properties uniquely determined by a given set of properties. This set of properties is called the *closure of X under F*, denoted $\text{Cl}_F(X)$, for a given set X of properties and a given set F of functional constraints.

2.2 Example

A designer should be supported to focus on the essential parts of the applications in the conceptual design phase, i.e., he has to find out what are the vital things and associations among them that constitute the application and their abstractions. He should not be burdened to deal with restrictions or to take the characteristics of further steps into account, i.e., to break relationships into smaller ones.

We give in Fig. 1 an example of a conceptual schema an experienced designer would intuitively tend to model with smaller relationships. The ER-diagram reflects the Assignment from Teachers and Assistants to Courses in combination with the Date they take place at, and Rooms and Wings they are given in. The object-oriented database schema (displayed in Fig. 2) is obtained by the mapping sketched in Sect. 3. The semantic constraints are added later in a refinement of the original conceptual schema. They can already be declared in the conceptual schema, but we refrained from doing so because it would overload the diagram.

The semantic constraints declared for the class scheme Assignment are of main interest. For every Course there is exactly one Assistant and it takes place at only one Date. The functional constraint Assignment(course → assistant date) enforces

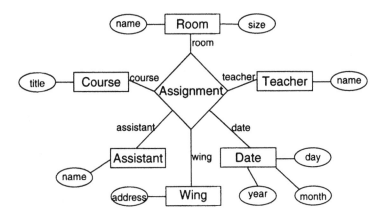

Fig. 1. ER-diagram

Course{title : String}{Course(title → Id)}
Teacher{name : String,...}{Teacher(name → Id)}
Assistant{name : String,...}{Assistant(name → Id)}
Date{year : Int, month : Int, day : Int}{Date(year month day → Id)}
Room{size : Int}{}
Wing{address : String}{}
Assignment{course : Course, assistant : Assistant, date : Date, teacher : Teacher,
          room : Room, wing : Wing}
          {Assignment(course → assistant date),
           Assignment(teacher → room),
           Assignment(room → wing),
           Assignment(course teacher → Id)}
Int{}{}   String{}{}

Fig. 2. Database schema

that this restriction is met. Imagine that in the application at hand a Teacher is assigned a fixed Room, then the semantic constraint Assignment(teacher → room) ensures just this requirement. Additionally, the constraint that a Room is situated in only one Wing is reflected in the functional constraint Assignment(room → wing).

An instance for the schema in Fig. 2 is depicted in Fig. 3. Here we took the approach to view the schema as an instance. This is quite easily accomplished by making every class scheme name an object of itself, yielding an abstract instance. Then for every property in a class scheme we introduce an edge labelled with the property going from the vertex corresponding to the class scheme to the vertex corresponding to the property type. Viewing schemas as instances helps us to display the schema as a graph. Therefore we will subsequently present schemas as instances in this paper. To simplify the representation further, we displayed some of the vertices several times instead of once, e.g., the vertex with label String.

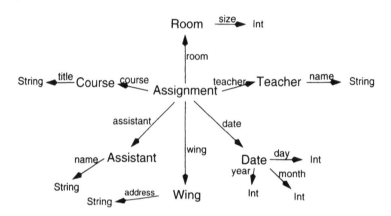

Fig. 3. Database instance

3 Object-Oriented Formalisation of Relationships

3.1 Mapping from ER to OO

For the design of object-oriented schemas, entity sets are simply formalised as (entity) classes the basic types of which are determined by the pertinent properties of the entities. In order to formalise a relationship set, we can always canonically simulate the relational approach [12, 11, 18, 21]. For every individual relationship we construct an object that is counterpart to the corresponding tuple in the relational approach. Then these objects are understood as instances of a (relationship) class. As objects correspond in this case to tuples we also need *canonical semantic constraints* to ensure that they behave as such. These constraints require that the property values of a relationship object uniquely represent the relationship, i.e., there is at most one object for any value combination. This kind of constraint is formalised as a key constraint for the class. The constraint usually accommodates all properties for this class. For example, the ER diagram that leads to the database schema in Fig. 2 is depicted in Fig. 1. In this example the key constraint for the relationship class Assignment is Assignment(course teacher → Id). Here the application-dependent constraints allowed a reduction of the left-hand side of the constraint to the properties course and teacher.

3.2 Pivoting

Our goal is to decompose (relationship) classes into smaller fragments. Roughly speaking, we cut properties from (relationship) classes (e.g., introduced by the canonical formalisation) and graft these properties onto (entity) classes participating in the relationship.

The effect of the transformation can be redundancy reducing and that constraints are implicitly enforced. We call this implicit enforcement *natural enforcement of constraints*. The classes chosen to receive new properties are called *pivot classes*.

Now we present (property) pivoting in detail, i.e., we define how we can obtain the target schema and transformation rules from a given source schema. The effect of pivoting is concentrated in one class scheme. So we suppose we consider a class scheme with the form

$$\text{RelCl}\{\text{PivPr} : \text{PivCl}, \underbrace{p_1 : c_1, \ldots, p_n : c_n,}_{\substack{\text{pivoted prop.} \\ \text{with types}}} \ldots\}F_{\text{RelCl}}$$

where PivPr is called the *pivot property*, PivCl is the *pivot class* and properties p_i are the *pivoted properties*.

- We add now the class scheme $p\{\text{RelCl\_PivPr\_}p_1 : c_1, \ldots, \text{RelCl\_PivPr\_}p_n : c_n\}$ to the database schema, remove $p_1 : c_1, \ldots, p_n : c_n$ from the class scheme RelCl, replace PivCl with p in the class scheme RelCl and finally make the class p a subclass of class PivCl. In this process we introduce new property names for the class scheme p, assuming that this prevents name clashes with already existing property names.
- Then we adjust the semantic constraints of the classes RelCl and p to the new class schemes. Basically, this means for class scheme RelCl that we project the semantic constraints on the altered set of property names, and for class p this is a kind of projection, too, taking the newly introduced property names into account. Finally, we add a completeness constraint RelCl{PivPr} for the class scheme RelCl.

The relationship between the original schema and the transformed schema is described by a notion of *schema equivalence* [2, 5, 13]. It is based on transformations on instances, i.e., an instance of one schema is transformed into an instance of a different schema. These transformations are defined by so-called *transformation rules*. For example to transform instances of a schema into instances of its pivoted schema, we give the following transformation rules.

- If u is an object of class RelCl ($l_{Cl}(u) = \text{RelCl}$), the property value for the pivot property is v ($u \overset{\text{PivPr}}{\to} v \in E$) and the property value for some pivoted property p_i is w ($u \overset{p_i}{\to} w \in E$), we add the property value w for property RelCl_PivPr_p_i to the object v and make v an element of class p ($l_{Cl}(v) := p$).
- Finally we remove the property value v for property p_i from object u.

We say two schemas are *equivalent* if there are transformation rules, such that the transformation rules define a one-to-one and onto function that maps instances of one schema onto instances of the other.

Now we can make the following observation.

Theorem 6. *A database schema and its pivoted schema are equivalent in the above sense iff*

1. *each pivoted property is uniquely determined by the pivot property, i.e, the property values for the pivoted properties agree for two objects, whenever they hold the same property value for the pivot property, and*
2. *for all property sets M for RelCl, $M \subset$ Props(RelCl), the following conditions hold with $\mathcal{M} := \{p_1, \ldots, p_n\}$ the set of pivoted properties:*
   (a) $\mathrm{Cl}_{F_{\mathrm{RelCl}}}(M) = \mathrm{Cl}_{F_{\mathrm{RelCl}}}(M \backslash \mathcal{M}) \cup \mathrm{Cl}_{F_{\mathrm{RelCl}}}(M \cap \mathcal{M})$,
   (b) $\mathrm{Cl}_{F_{\mathrm{RelCl}}}(M \backslash \mathcal{M}) \subset$ Props(RelCl)$\backslash \mathcal{M}$ *or* PivPr $\in \mathrm{Cl}_{F_{\mathrm{RelCl}}}(M \backslash \mathcal{M})$, *and*
   (c) $\mathrm{Cl}_{F_{\mathrm{RelCl}}}(M \cap \mathcal{M}) \subset \mathcal{M}$.

We merely give a brief motivation for the above conditions omitting the formal proof. The first condition is necessary because the transformation shifts properties from the relationship class to the pivot class. This means on the instance level that we cut the property values from a relationship object and graft them onto the property value of the corresponding pivot property. Thus the pivot property value must uniquely determine the pivoted property values otherwise we get a violation of property functionality for instances. So what has to be enforced in the original schema by means of functional constraints is naturally enforced in the pivoted schema due to the property functionality. Therefore we speak of a *natural enforcement* of functional constraints in the pivoted schema. The reason for the second condition is that, although we are interested in dropping specific constraints, namely those enforced naturally, this condition is necessary to preserve the effect of semantic constraints. Condition 2a ensures that the effect of constraints of the form that the left-hand side has attributes both in $\mathcal{M}$ and in $M \backslash \mathcal{M}$ are not lost because such constraints are dropped in the transformation process. The same line of argumentation is used for the conditions 2b and 2c. Basically, they ensure that there is not a constraint whose left-hand side is a subset of $\mathcal{M}$ or $M \backslash \mathcal{M}$ and the right-hand side is a subset of $M \backslash \mathcal{M}$ or $\mathcal{M}$ respectively. The reason for the more complex treatment of condition 2b is that sets of attributes that have the pivot attribute PivPr in their closure have to be dealt with in a special way.

That these conditions are sufficient indeed can be shown be lifting the whole consideration onto a level where we look solely at the semantic constraints.

In Fig. 4 the pivoted instance of the instance in Fig. 3 is presented. In the transformation property course was used as pivot property and properties assistant and date played the rôle of pivoted properties. To simplify the presentation we did not introduce new cryptic method names rather reusing the old ones and we dispense with the introduction of a subclass of Course. The graphical display of the pivoted instance in Fig. 4 lacks the representation of semantic constraints, which are part of a schema. Pivoting alters merely the semantic constraints for the relationship class and the pivot class, so it suffices to exhibit them. As the semantic constraint Assignment(course → assistant date) is naturally enforced in the pivoted schema, the semantic constraints for the pivot class Course are not affected by the transformation. This means that the semantic constraints remaining for class scheme Assignment are Assignment(teacher → room), Assignment(room → wing) and Assignment(course teacher → Id).

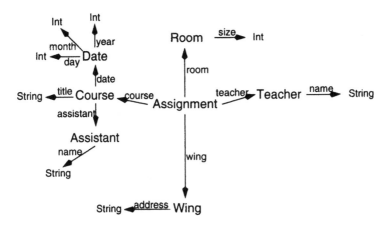

Fig. 4. Pivoted instance

Before we continue in our task to define a decomposition for relationships, we concern ourselves with special properties and their subsequent treatment, i.e., properties the closures of which are equal. The crucial point is that they are not treated equally by pivoting, namely if we want to make one a pivoted property for the other, we get a violation of condition 2c. This can be remedied by introducing a new property for the type of the pivoted property and stating that the pivoted property and the newly introduced property are inverses of each other [6]. Therefore we assume in the sequel that for all properties occurring in a class scheme the closures are different.

3.3 Natural Enforcement of Functional Constraints

Our goal is to transform a schema such that all original functional constraints are naturally enforced except for functional constraints being key constraints. In order to reach this goal, we have to consider two things. First of all, it is in general impossible to discard all functional constraints in one transformation step. This leads to a recursive application of the transformation as shown in Fig. 5. We first chose teacher as pivot property with room and wing as pivoted properties. Then we performed pivoting on the resulting schema with pivot property room and pivoted property wing. We get the same outcome if we take first room as pivot property and wing as pivoted property and afterwards choose **teacher** as pivot property and room as only pivoted property.

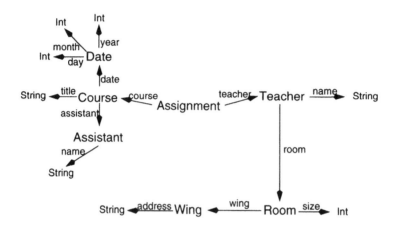

Fig. 5. Recursive pivoted instance

This example indicates that the outcome of recursive pivoting is in a sense independent of the order in which the single pivoting steps are performed. This interesting feature of recursive pivoting is captured in the following theorem.

Theorem 7. *If we choose pivot properties with appropriate pivoted properties, such that the application of pivoting with each of the pivot properties leads to an equivalent pivoted schema, we can apply pivoting recursively and the outcome is independent of the order in which we chose the pivot properties*[5].

Secondly, not all kinds of functional constraints can be naturally enforced and the second condition of Theorem 6 imposes further restriction on the set of semantic constraints. The natural enforcement of functional constraints works only for those the left-hand side of which is a singleton because pivoting can be applied only with one pivot property at a time. Functional dependencies of this form are called *unary functional dependencies* [16]. We follow this notation and call functional constraints the left-hand side of which are singletons *unary functional constraints*.

Unfortunately the restriction to unary functional constraints is not sufficient in order to eliminate all functional constraints by recursive pivoting. To achieve that we further have to make the set of pivoted properties comprise the complete

---

[5] In the recursive pivoting the originally chosen set of pivoted properties has to be adapted to the new context, namely the properties for the class in which the pivot property is declared in.

closure of the pivot property in each transformation step. If we select as pivoted properties the whole closure of the pivot property, we call the underlying pivoting *maximal pivoting*. Now what thwarts maximal pivoting? The obstacle is a possible violation of the conditions given in Theorem 6 referring to the equivalence of schemas. The first condition is fulfilled due to the confinement to the closure of the pivot property. The second condition has to be investigated in more depth. Conditions 2a and 2c are satisfied since we limit the use to unary functional constraints. Having only sets of unary functional constraints means that their closures are *topological* [9]. Therefore the equation

$$\mathrm{Cl}_F(X) = \bigcup_{A \in X} \mathrm{Cl}_F(A) \tag{1}$$

holds for sets F of unary functional constraints, ensuing the fulfilment of conditions 2a and 2c.

Condition 2b is harder to deal with. Here we consider a selection of a pivot property PivPr with a corresponding set $\mathcal{M}$ of pivoted properties such that the selection violates condition 2b. This means that there is a set of properties or to be more precise due to equation (1) a property $m \in \mathrm{Props}(\mathrm{RelCl})\backslash\mathcal{M}$ such that $\mathrm{Cl}_{F_{\mathrm{RelCl}}}(m) \not\subset \mathrm{Props}(\mathrm{RelCl})\backslash\mathcal{M}$ and PivPr $\notin \mathrm{Cl}_{F_{\mathrm{RelCl}}}(m)$. To describe this situation in a better way, we build a *constraint graph* for the set F_{RelCl} of functional constraints. The set of vertices is the set of properties occurring in F_{RelCl}. For each $L \to R_1 \cdots R_n \in F_{\mathrm{RelCl}}$ we add the edges (L, R_i) to the graph. An example for this graph can be found in Fig. 6, which uses the functional constraints of the class scheme Assignment in Fig. 2.

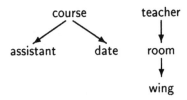

Fig. 6. Functional constraint graph

The graph describing the situation with the violation of condition 2b above is as depicted in Fig. 7. There is a path from m to a property $m' \in \mathcal{M}$ and due to the fact that $m' \in \mathcal{M}$ there is a path from PivPr to m'. In addition there is no path from m to PivPr and vice versa. This kind of structure can be forbidden if we say that the graph has to form a forest, i.e., whenever there is one vertex reachable from two other nodes, one of these two nodes must be reachable by the other.

We can make the following observation.

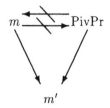

Fig. 7. Constraint graph describing the violation of condition 2b

Theorem 8. *The two statements below concerning a class scheme are equivalent.*

- *The set of functional constraints consists merely of unary functional constraints and the corresponding graph forms a forest.*
- *Maximal recursive pivoting leads to a natural enforcement of all functional constraints occurring in the class scheme.*

4 Conclusion

In this paper we introduced a method to decompose relationship classes in an object-oriented data model that stem originally from a relationships in the ER model, and thereby improving already existing mappings from ER models to OO models. Therefore we support a user in the design process since he can concentrate on identifying the essential things of the application and their associations (later on modelled as relationships), without burdening with the task to break associations into smaller ones at this phase of the design process.

Comparing pivoting with the decomposition of a relational scheme into Boyce-Codd normal form based on the work of Delobel and Casey [8], we find a strong resemblance between both transformations. This is not astonishing as both transformation consider mainly sets of attributes and sets of functional dependencies. In fact we can even simulate pivoting in the relational model. Then it comes really close to the decomposition into Boyce-Codd normal form. In this case we use foreign keys in relations that represent relationship sets in order to access represented entities participating in a relationship. A subtle difference between both transformations is that pivoting uses object identifiers for the reference mechanism whereas the relational model uses foreign keys, which are value oriented. Often, in the modelling process using the relational model, foreign keys are introduced that comprise only one attribute, e.g. a student number to uniquely identify a student. This can be seen as an attempt to simulate object identifiers. Using this approach throughout the modelling process shifts pivoting even closer to the decomposition into Boyce-Codd normal form. Now Theorem 6 gives conditions for pivoting to be *lossless* and *dependency preserving* [17]. Condition 2a guarantees the lossless property and conditions 2b and 2c guarantee dependency preservation. Theorem 7 gives as result that dependency preservation leads to the fact that the transformation process is independent of the order in which pivot attributes are chosen. Theorem 8 underlines the importance of unary constraints as these constraints can be naturally supported. As a by-product we know that if a set of functional dependencies consists only of unary functional dependencies, the corresponding Armstrong relation can be found in polynomial time [16].

The effect of the decomposition is not only to break relationship classes into smaller fragments but also to discard a certain kind of functional constraints, so-called unary functional constraints. What remains to be investigated is the trade-off between discarding a functional constraint and introducing a new completeness constraint with respect to costs for updates.

References

1. S. Abiteboul and P. C. Kanellakis. Object identity as a query language primitive. In *Proceedings of the 1989 ACM SIGMOD International Conference on Management of Data*, pages 159–173, 1989.

2. P. Atzeni, G. Ausiello, C. Batini, and M. Moscarini. Inclusion and equivalence between relational database schemata. *Theoretical Comput. Sci.*, 19:267–285, 1982.

3. C. Beeri. Formal models for object-oriented databases. In W. Kim, J.-M. Nicolas, and S. Nishio, editors, *Proceedings of the 1st Deductive and Object-Oriented Databases (DOOD '89)*, pages 405–430, Kyoto, Japan, 1989. North-Holland.

4. J. Biskup, R. Menzel, and T. Polle. Transforming an entity-relationship schema into object-oriented database schemas. In J. Eder and L. A. Kalinichenko, editors, *Advances in Databases and Information Systems, Moscow 95*, Workshops in Computing. Springer-Verlag, 1996.

5. J. Biskup and U. Räsch. The equivalence problem for relational database schemes. In *Proceedings of the 1st Symposium on Mathematical Fundamentals of Database Systems*, number 305 in Lecture Notes in Computer Science, pages 42–70. Springer-Verlag, 1988.

6. R. G. G. Cattell and T. Atwood, editors. *The object database standard: ODMG-93; release 1.1*. Morgan Kaufmann, 1994.

7. P. P.-S. Chen. The entity-relationship-model — towards a unified view of data. *ACM Trans. Database Syst.*, 1(1):9–36, Mar. 1976.

8. C. Delobel and R. G. Casey. Decomposition of a data base and the theory of boolean switching functions. *IBM J. Res. Dev.*, 17(5):374–386, 1973.

9. J. Demetrovics, L. O. Libkin, and I. B. Muchnik. Functional dependencies in relational databases: a lattice point of view. *Discrete Applied Mathematics*, 40:155–185, 1992.

10. R. A. Elmasri, V. Kouramajian, and B. Thalheim, editors. *Proceedings of the 12th International Conference on Entity-Relationship Approach*, Arlington, Texas, USA, 1993.

11. M. Gogolla, R. Herzig, S. Conrad, G. Denker, and N. Vlachantonis. Integrating the ER approach in an OO environment. In Elmasri et al. [10], pages 376–389.

12. R. Herzig and M. Gogolla. Transforming conceptual data models into an object model. In G. Pernul and A. M. Tjoa, editors, *Proceedings of the 11th Interna-*

tional Conference on Entity-Relationship Approach, number 645 in Lecture Notes in Computer Science, pages 280–298, Karlsruhe, Germany, 1992. Springer-Verlag.

13. R. Hull. Relative information capacity of simple relational database schemata. *SIAM J. Comput.*, 15(3):856–886, 1986.

14. M. Kifer, G. Lausen, and J. Wu. Logical foundations of object-oriented and frame-based languages. *J. ACM*, 42(4):741–843, 1995.

15. Y. Kornatzky and P. Shoval. Conceptual design of object-oriented schemes using the binary-relationship model. *Data & Knowledge Engineering*, 14(3):265–288, 1995.

16. H. Mannila and K.-J. Räihä. Practical algorithms for finding prime attributes and testing normal forms. In *Proceedings of the Eighth ACM SIGACT-SIGMOD-SIGART Symposium on Principles of Database Systems*, pages 128–133, 1989.

17. H. Mannila and K.-J. Räihä. *The Design of Relational Databases*. Addison-Wesley, Wokingham, England, 1992.

18. R. Missaoui, J.-M. Gagnon, and R. Godin. Mapping an extended entity-relationship schema into a schema of complex objects. In M. P. Papazoglou, editor, *Proceedings of the 14th International Conference an Object-Oriented and Entity Relationship Modelling*, pages 205–215, Brisbane, Australia, 1995.

19. B. Narasimhan, S. B. Navathe, and S. Jayaraman. On mapping ER and relational models into OO schemas. In Elmasri et al. [10], pages 403–413.

20. P. Poncelet, M. Teisseire, R. Cicchetti, and L. Lakhal. Towards a formal approach for object database design. In R. Agrawal, editor, *Proceedings of the 19th International Conference on Very Large Data Bases*, pages 278–289, Dublin, Irland, 1993.

21. J. Rumbaugh. Relations as semantic constructs in an object-oriented language. In N. Meyrowitz, editor, *Object-Oriented Programming Systems, Languages and Applications OOPSLA '87*, pages 462–481, Orlando, Florida, 1987. acm Press.

22. B. Thalheim. *Fundamentals of Entity-Relationship Modeling*. Springer-Verlag, 1996.

23. G. E. Weddell. Reasoning about functional dependencies generalized for semantic data models. *ACM Trans. Database Syst.*, 17(1):32–64, Mar. 1992.

Understanding the Implementation of *IS*-A Relations[1,2]

J-L. Hainaut, J-M. Hick, V. Englebert, J. Henrard, D. Roland

Institut d'Informatique, University of Namur, rue Grandgagnage, 21 - B-5000 Namur
jlhainaut@info.fundp.ac.be

Abstract. Generalization/specialization hierarchies (IS-A relations for short) are basic semantic constructs proposed in most information system conceptual models. At the other side of design methodologies, where standard DBMSs are used, and will still be used for several years, there is no explicit representation of these IS-A relations. As a consequence, all the current methodologies include rules through which these semantic constructs are transformed into standard structures. However, it quickly appears that the translation rules proposed are most often incomplete, and sometimes incorrect. This fact has been experienced by many practitioners, who are faced with complex translation problems, but who do not find satisfying help neither in modern text books, nor in CASE tools. The aim of this paper is to analyze IS-A relations in some detail, and to propose a wide range of correct techniques to express IS-A relations into standard constructs. Understanding these techniques has also proved essential in reverse engineering processes.

Keywords ER model, conceptual modelling, supertype/subtype hierarchy, IS-A relation, schema transformation, implementation, logical design, physical design, reverse engineering

1. Introduction

Semantic models commonly include generalization/specialization abstraction mechanisms to structure knowledge according to taxonomic or subsetting structures. Originated in the SIMULA language, the concept was quickly adopted by the artificial intelligence and database communities, then appeared again as a basic programming language paradigm, in Smalltalk [8] and C++ for instance. In the database realm, it was mentioned in [6] then discussed in [23]. This common concept was the origin of some attempts to merge these three domains (e.g. [3] and OODBMS).

Though their names (generalization, specialization, subset, supertype/subtype, inheritance hierarchy, *is-a* relation, etc) and the symbols used to denote them (directed arcs, triangles, inclusion symbols, etc) vary considerably, most methodologies and CASE tools propose some variants of this construct that will be called *IS-A relation* in this paper.

However, most current DBMS do not provide corresponding logical constructs. Hence the need for translation rules to express them into plain data structures such as columns, keys and generic constraints, to be coded into SQL `check` predicates or `triggers`. The problem has been recognized as early as 1976 [6]. Since then, numerous papers and text books have proposed translation rules for IS-A relations, in such a way that this problem can be though to be solved, and therefore considered as out of interest by the scientific community. Fig. 1 shows a simple, but representative example of the way subtypes are implemented according to many text books.

As far as the authors know however, there is no scientific articles, no text books and no CASE tools which propose a complete set of rules that can translate all kinds of specialization hierarchy into equivalent operational data structures. Indeed, they are based on an incomplete IS-A model which ignores useful configurations, or they propose incorrect transformations, or ignore some standard techniques (proposed by others or found in implemented databases through reverse engineering techniques), or they do not translate IS-A relations completely, ignoring important integrity constraints.

---

[1] This study has been carried out in the DB-MAIN project, partially supported by the *Région Wallonne*, the *European Union*, the *Communauté Française de Belgique*, and by the industrial: ACEC-OSI (Be), ARIANE-II (Be), Banque UCL (Lux), BBL (Be), Centre de recherche public H. Tudor (Lux), CGER (Be), Clin. Univ. St Luc (Be), Cockerill-Sambre (Be), CONCIS (Fr), D'Ieteren (Be), DIGITAL, EDF (Fr), EPFL (CH), Groupe S (Be), IBM, OBLOG Software (Port), ORIGIN (Be), Ville de Namur (Be), Winterthur (Be), 3 Suisses (Be).

[2] This paper is an abstract of [16].

This situation must be interpreted as an evidence that IS-A relations are much more complex than generally estimated, and that they deserve some more effort from the scientific community before practitioners can use them reliably.

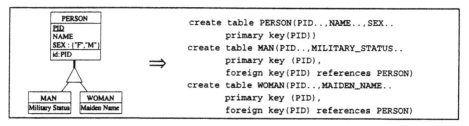

create table PERSON(PID..,NAME..,SEX..
    primary key(PID))
create table MAN(PID..,MILITARY_STATUS..
    primary key (PID),
    foreign key(PID) references PERSON)
create table WOMAN(PID..,MAIDEN_NAME..
    primary key (PID),
    foreign key(PID) references PERSON)

Figure 1 - Standard SQL translation of a subtype structure.

The purpose of this paper is to analyze in some detail the properties of the standard IS-A model, the translation rules that eliminate IS-A relations, and SQL mapping rules. Though we intend to keep the presentation as simple and intuitive as possible, we will try to propose a generic and fairly rigourous treatment of the problem. In this paper, we will use the notation **B is-a A** to state that

> *entity type (or entity set, or object class, etc) B is a subtype (or subset, or specialization, or subclass, etc) of entity type (...) A, that in turn is the supertype (or superset, or generalization, or superclass, etc) of B.*

We will also say that an *IS-A relation* holds from B to A.

In order to make the proposals as general as possible, we will develop a three-step framework for processing the IS-A relation, as illustrated in Fig. 2. First, we propose a set of techniques to replace IS-A relations with standard, DBMS-independent, ER constructs, such as relationship types, attributes and constraints, then we propose techniques to translate these standard constructs into DBMS-specific structures and constraints (e.g. relational), and finally we suggest coding patterns to express the latter into the DDL of the DBMS (e.g. SQL). This structure, which can be found in popular database development methods [1], provides a powerful approach to analyze IS-A relation translation according to various DBMS models and to different strategies. By reversing the transformation processes, we are also provided with a generic framework to elicit IS-A relations in existing database schemas, specially if non standard rules were applied when it was developed [11]. It should be clear that this framework is intended to analyze design and reverse engineering practical situations in a rigourous way, and that it is in no way a proposal to deal with IS-A relations in actual DB design methodologies. Indeed, the latter often propose more straighforward mapping schemes.

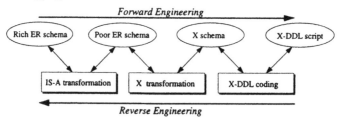

Figure 2 - General framework to analyse the translation of a schema with IS-A relations (rich ER schema) into the DDL of a DBMS based on data model X, and conversely (X = relational in this paper).

The paper is organized as follows. Section 2 describes the IS-A model underlying most semantic modeling approaches. Section 3 presents the notion of schema transformation. In Section 4, we present neutral IS-A transformation techniques, i.e. translation rules that replace IS-A relations with standard ER constructs, independently of the target DBMS. Section 5 describes how standard ER constructs can be expressed into relational data structures, and Section 6 proposes some coding rules to express relational data structures into SQL.

2. An extended Entity-relationship model

2.1 Main concepts

In the discussion that follows we will make use of the DB-MAIN extended ER model, which is a wide spectrum formalism that supports both standard and non standard processes, such as conceptual, logical and physical design, schema optimization, normalization and integration, database reverse engineering, system migration, conversion, maintenance and evolution. This model has been described in several recent papers [11, 12, 13, 14], so that we can limit its presentation to mentioning the constructs that will be used in this paper (Fig. 3).

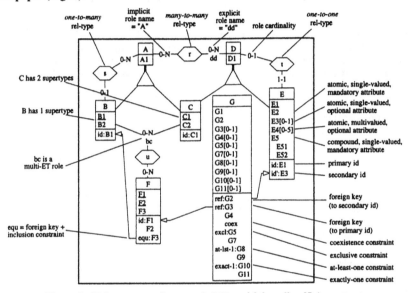

Figure 3 - Main concepts of an extended ER model that offers IS-A constructs.

A **conceptual schema** comprises mainly entity types, entity type attributes and relationship types. A collection of one or more entity types can be declared the subtypes of one or several entity types. An entity type can have one primary identifier (noted id, and generally underlined), and any number of secondary (or alternate) identifiers (id'). An identifier comprises attributes and/or roles. A relationship type, or *rel-type*, has two or more roles and any number of attributes; integrity constraints, such as identifiers can be associated with a rel-type. A role is generally defined on one entity type. It can also be defined on the union of several entity types (multi-ET role). In this case, in each relationship, this role is taken by an entity from one of the entity types. A role is characterized by cardinality constraints that specify through an interval in how many [min-max] relationships each entity plays this role. An attribute can be atomic or compound. It is characterized by cardinality constraints, stating how many [min-max] attribute values are associated with each parent object. Cardinality [1-1] is default, and is not represented. A group of attributes (and/or roles) can be constrained by one or several integrity constraints. A *coexistence* constraint (coex:G3,G4) states that either all the attributes have a definite value, or none have a value. An *exclusive* constraint (excl:G5,G7) states that at most one of the attributes has a definite value. An *at-least-one* constraint states that at least one of the attributes has a definite value. An *exactly-one* constraint (exact-1:G10,G11) means both *exclusive* and *at-least-one*.

A schema can also include **logical** (i.e. DBMS-dependent) constructs, a feature that is needed in logical design, but also in reverse engineering projects. For instance, a relational logical schema comprises (logical) entity types, to be interpreted as tables, (logical) attributes, to be interpreted as columns, identifiers (primary or alternate keys). In addition, a group of attributes can be used to reference a target entity (ref:G3,G4), and is to be interpreted as a foreign key. Such a key can reference either a primary id (ref:G3,G4), or a secondary id (ref:G2). If a reference group is associated with an inverse inclusion constraint, it is noted *equality* (equ:F3). Such a combined constraint specifies that the F3 value of each F entity must be the value of B1 of some B entity, *and conversely*.

Additional constraints will be described where they first appear in the discussion.

2.2 Semantics and typology of IS-A relations

The semantics of IS-A relations can vary from one model to another. Before going further, we have to define which semantics we will adopt in this paper. We consider first the two functions char(E) (returning the set of structural characteristics of E) and pop(E) (that returns the set of entities of E). Now, we consider the assertion B is-a A where A and B are two entity types of the same database. In the database realm, following Brachman's recommendation [2], the prevailing interpretation of this assertion is pop(B) ⊆ pop(A). We consider the property char(A) ⊆ char(B) as a mere consequence of this assertion. Hence the relations:

$$B \text{ is-a } A \quad \Rightarrow \quad \text{pop(B)} \subseteq \text{pop(A)} \quad \Rightarrow \quad \text{char(A)} \subseteq \text{char(B)}$$

Finally we consider the time-independent properties of *totality* and *disjunction* that apply on the set of subsets of a supertype, and that follow the standard definition (Fig. 4).

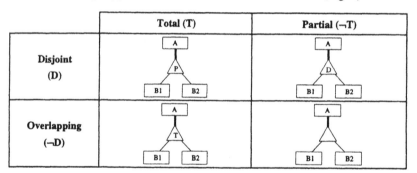

Figure 4 - *Graphical notation of subtype constraints. Two combinations have been given specific names: partition = total + disjoint, free = partial + overlapping.*

In the models proposed in the literature, the concept of IS-A relation has been refined in several ways. For instance, *predicate-based*, or qualified, *subtyping* [17, 25] consists in deriving subtypes from a predicate that states to which subtype each supertype entity must belong. Generally, this predicate defines a partition according to the values of an attribute of the supertype. According to another extension found in some ER models, a supertype can be given more than one collection of subtypes, sometimes called a *cluster*. Finally, we mention the *category* concept, introduced in [7], that generalizes the IS-A relation.

3. Schema transformations

A schema transformation is an operator that applies on a construct C of a schema S, and that replaces it with other constructs C', leading to new schema S'. C' is the target of source construct C through T, i.e. C' = T(C). Fig. 5 represents a popular example through which a binary relationship type, say PURCH, is replaced with an entity type PURCH and two one-to-many relationship types CP and SP.

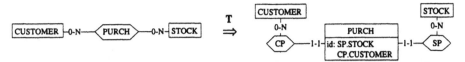

Figure 5 - A standard transformation: expressing a relationship type as an entity type.

To define transformations more precisely, we need a second mapping t, that specifies how valid instances of construct C are translated into C' instances: if c is an instance of C, then c' = t(c) is an instance of C'. We can denote a transformation by: $\Sigma = <T,t>$

There is a special class of transformations which satisfy the criterion of *semantics preservation*. Intuitively, a transformation is *semantics-preserving*, or *reversible*, if schemas S and S' describe the same real world portion. More precisely, if $\Sigma1=<T1,t1>$ is a reversible transformation, there must exist a transformation $\Sigma2=<T2,t2>$ such that:

for any construct C, and any valid instance c of C: [T2(T1(C))=C] $\wedge$ [t2(t1(c))=c]

There exists a higher-order kind of reversibility. S1 and S2 are called symmetrically reversible transformations, or SR-transformations, *iff*:

for any construct C, and any valid instance c of C: [T2(T1(C))=C] $\wedge$ [t2(t1(c))=c]

for any construct C', and any valid instance c' of C': [T1(T2(C'))=C'] $\wedge$ [t1(t2(c'))=c']

A more detailed presentation of the concept of transformation and of its properties can be found in [9, 14] for instance. Several authors have proposed schema transformations as basic building blocks for database engineering. We will mention [1, 11, 13, 22] as some representative examples.

4. Neutral transformations to eliminate IS-A relations

We will concentrate on reversible transformations that cope with IS-A relations, and more specifically that express IS-A relations through standard constructs such as relationship types, attributes and constraints. These techniques are called *neutral*, in that they do not target any specific DBMS. We will discuss relational expressions later on, as the relational translation of the result of neutral transformations. Traditionally, three basic techniques have been proposed [1]:

- *IS-A materialization*, through which each subtype is represented by an independent entity type related to the supertype by a *one-to-one* relationship type (Fig. 6.1);
- *upward inheritance*, that represents the supertype only (Fig. 6.2);
- *downward inheritance*, that represents the subtypes only (Fig. 6.3); entity type A collects the entities that do not belong to subtypes B or C, if any.

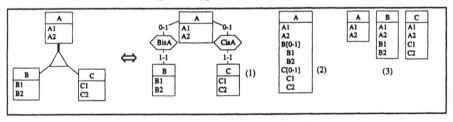

Figure 6 - The three standard techniques to replace IS-A relations.

In techniques (1) and (2), some authors include a *type* attribute (with domain { 'B', 'C'}) in the new version of A, in order to indicate to which subtype(s) each A entity belongs. We have omitted such an attribute in this discussion since it would be redundant. Indeed, its value(s) could be deduced from the presence/absence of BisA and CisA relationships in which each A entity is involved (1), or of values of attributes B and C (2).

Generally, the authors who propose a general introduction to database design have to stop their presentation here, due to space limit. Generally too, here begin the problems of practitioners who use IS-A relations to structure their models, and who try to retrieve IS-A structure in legacy systems. Indeed, addressing subtype constraints (T, ¬T, D, ¬D), roles played by supertypes and subtypes, and constraints such as identifiers, leads to much more complex schemas.

We will analyse these three aspects in some detail in the following. To keep the presentation simple, these constructs will be discussed independently. The rules for combined structures can be derived easily. Due to space limits, some special patterns have been discarded from this discussion; they are addressed in [16].

4.1 Expressing subtype constraints

The absence of constraints, i.e. *free* or (¬T & ¬D), leads to the three schemas of Fig. 6. Enforcing the D and T constraints in the *IS-A materialization* and *Upward inheritance* techniques is fairly straighforward: they translate into *exclusive* and *at-least-one* constraints holding among the representations of the subtypes (Fig. 7). The partitioning constraint translates naturally into *exclusive* and *at-least-one*, i.e. an *exactly-one* constraint.

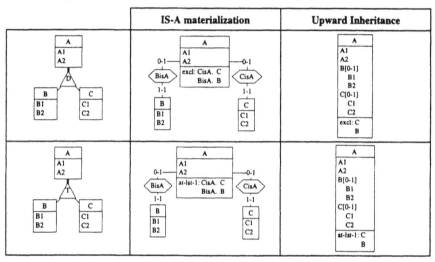

Figure 7 - Expression of D and T subtype constraints (techniques 1 and 2).

Let us observe that the *Downward inheritance* technique is valid for **disjoint** subtypes only. The other cases provide no means to identify the entities that belong to both B and C types, and therefore are not semantics-preserving. If ¬D holds, then A must have an identifier. On the other hand, the T constraint implies that only entity types B and C remains, while ¬ T leads to a schema including A, B and C. To summarize, constraints (¬T & D) are translated into Fig. 6.3 and constraint (T & D = P) are translated into the same schema, where A has been discarded; the two other cases require that A have an identifier, and will be discussed in the next section.

4.2 Expressing identifiers

There are two cases to consider: supertype A has an identifier (say A1) and subtype B has an identifier (say B1).

4.2.1 Supertype A has an identifier (A1)

The first two techniques preserve the supertype as well as its identifier A1. The third technique induces complex patterns that are illustrated in Fig. 8. The **D** constraint between subtypes must be expressed as a *disjoint* constraint among the identifier value sets: no A entity can have the same A1 value as any B or C entity, and so on for B and C. In addition, in the overlapping (¬D) situations, we have to state that whenever a B entity and a C entity agree on A1, they must have the same A2 value as well, since they represent a single entity in the source schema. Hence the functional dependency holding in the union of the entity type populations.

¬T & D	T & ¬D	T & D	¬T & ¬D
A | **B** | **C** A1 | A1 | A1 A2 | A2 | A2 id: A1 | B1 | C1 | B2 | C2 | id: A1 | id: A1 **constraints** disjoined(A.A1,B.A1,C.A1)	**B** | **C** A1 | A1 A2 | A2 B1 | C1 B2 | C2 id: A1 | id: A1 **constraints** (B U C): A1 --> A2	**B** | **C** A1 | A1 A2 | A2 B1 | C1 B2 | C2 id: A1 | id: A1 **constraints** disjoined(B.A1,C.A1)	**A** | **B** | **C** A1 | A1 | A1 A2 | A2 | A2 id: A1 | B1 | C1 | B2 | C2 | id: A1 | id: A1 **constraints** (B U C): A1 --> A2 disjoined(B.A1,A.A1) disjoined(C.A1,A.A1)

Figure 8 - Propagation of supertype identifier A1 (Downward inheritance).

4.2.2 Subtype B has an identifier (B1)

Techniques 1 and 3 preserve entity type B, so that its identifier B1 is preserved as well. Through technique 2, entity type B is replaced with attribute B, whose component B1 is made an optional identifier of A (Fig. 9).

¬T & D	T & ¬D	T & D	¬T & ¬D
A A1 A2 B[0-1] B1 B2 C[0-1] C1 C2 id: B.B1 excl: C B	**A** A1 A2 B[0-1] B1 B2 C[0-1] C1 C2 id: B.B1 at-lst-1: C B	**A** A1 A2 B[0-1] B1 B2 C[0-1] C1 C2 id: B.B1 exact-1: C B	**A** A1 A2 B[0-1] B1 B2 C[0-1] C1 C2 id: B.B1

Figure 9 - Propagation of subtype identifier B1 (Upward inheritance).

4.3 Expressing roles

Here too, we have two cases to consider: supertype A plays a role in R (Fig. 10a) and subtype B plays a role in R (Fig. 10b).

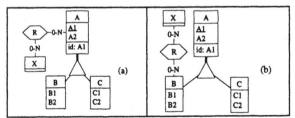

Figure 10 - The supertype and/or subtypes can play roles.

4.3.1 Supertype A plays a role in R

Techniques 1 and 2 preserve the supertype A as well as its roles. When technique 3 is applied, the role R.A is replaced with multi-ET role R.bac taken by A, B and C if the subtypes overlap, and by B and C if they don't (Fig. 11).

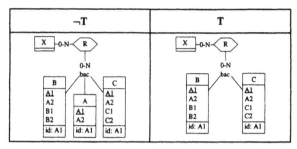

Figure 11 - Expression of role R.A by multi-ET role R.abc (constraints of Fig. 8 omitted)

4.3.2 Subtype B plays a role in R

Techniques 1 and 3 preserve subtype B as well as its roles. Following technique 2, the role R.B migrates to supertype A (Fig. 12). This migration induces an implication constraint stating that whenever an A entity is associated with X entities, then it must have a B attribute value.

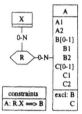

Figure 12 - Through Upward inheritance, *role R.B is replaced with role R.A.*

5. Relational representation techniques

The transformations proposed in Section 4 provide us with a rigourous way to get rid of IS-A relations, but they keep, and introduce several ER constructs which cannot be explicitly expressed into, e.g., relational structures. In particular, they produce *one-to-one rel-types, complex constraints on rel-types, optional compound attributes, multi-ET roles* and *implication constraints*. We will examine how each of these constructs can be transformed into pure relational structures. Standard ER structures (e.g. entity type, rel-type, all kinds of attributes) have long been given relational expressions [1, 24], and can be ignored.

5.1 Translation of one-to-one relationship types

We first note that such a relationship type is optional for the supertype (A) and mandatory for the subtype (say B). We mention three popular techniques.

(a) The most obvious translation of R consists in adding to B a mandatory, identifying, foreign key A1 referencing A, *provided A has an identifier* (Fig. 13a).

(b) If A has no identifier, but *B has one*, then R can be translated into an inverse foreign key B1 (Fig. 13b). This is a more complex technique, since it produces an optional, identifying foreign key + an inverse inclusion constraint (every B.B1 value must be the B1 value of some A entity), denoted by the equ clause.

(c) A third technique consists in merging B into A (Fig. 13c). There is no preconditions on identifiers. The result is the same as that of *Upward inheritance*, and will be studied in Section 5.3.

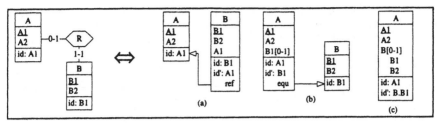

Figure 13 - *Three standard transformations of a one-to-one relationship type.*

5.2 Translation of *exclusive, at-least-1* and *exactly-1* constraints on relationship types

We must distinguish two situations, according to whether the relationship types translate into foreign keys in subtypes B and C (Fig. 13a) or in supertype A (Fig. 13b), which the constraint holds in.

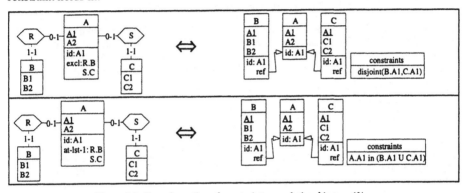

Figure 14 - *Transformation of constraints on relationship type (1).*

In the first case (Fig. 14), these constraints on rel-types are translated into constraints on subtype identifiers. Their interpretation is as follows:

- *exclusive* $\Rightarrow$ disjoint(B.A1,C.A1): the set of A1 values of B entities and the set of A1 values of C entities are disjoint;
- *at-least-1* $\Rightarrow$ A.A1 in (B.A1 $\cup$ C.A1): the A1 value of any A entity must belong to the union of the set of A1 values of B entities and the set of A1 values of C entities;
- *exactly-1* = *exclusive* $\wedge$ *at-least-1*.

The second case makes it possible to avoid these derived inter-entity constraints (Fig. 13b). Since these keys belong to the supertype, the source constraints are easier to assert.

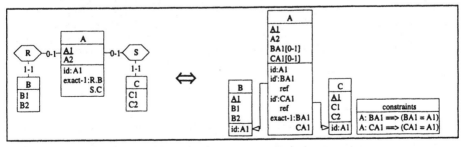

Figure 15 - *Transformation of constraints on relationship type (2).*

However, other constraints must be defined to garantee that each foreign key (BA1, CA1), when it has a value, is a copy of the identifier of A (Fig. 15)[3].

Another solution, based on foreign keys from the subtypes to the supertype, as in Fig. 14, consist in making these foreign keys reference *secondary identifiers* instead. The source constraints apply on the latter (Fig. 16).

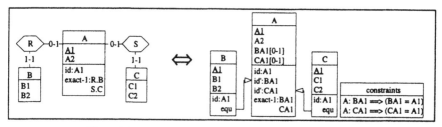

Figure 16 - Transformation of constraints on relationship type (3).

Predicate-based subtyping, based on discriminating attributes, has also been proposed by many authors. In [1] for instance, the supertype includes a subtyping attribute, say TYPE, that indicates to which subtype(s) each super-entity belongs. The cardinality of this attribute translates the subtype constraints as follows (n is the number of subtypes):

- disjoint $(D \wedge \neg T)$ $\Rightarrow$ TYPE[0-1]
- total $(\neg D \wedge T)$ $\Rightarrow$ TYPE[1-n]
- partition $(D \wedge T)$ $\Rightarrow$ TYPE[1-1]
- free $(\neg D \wedge \neg T)$ $\Rightarrow$ TYPE[0-n]

In order to simplify the implementation, the authors also propose to replace the multivalued versions by a single-valued attribute in which the subtype names are coded as a single value. Other authors propose to implement TYPE as a sequence of boolean attributes, each dedicated to one subtype. However, most authors ignore the constraints holding between the values of TYPE and the existence of referencing subtypes:

$\forall a \in$ pop(A) : (a.TYPE="B") $\Leftrightarrow$ ($\exists$b $\in$ pop(B) : b.A1=a.A1)
$\forall a \in$ pop(A) : (a.TYPE="C") $\Leftrightarrow$ ($\exists$c $\in$ pop(C) : c.A1=a.A1)

5.3 Translation of optional compound attributes

The optional compound attribute B can be extracted to form an individual entity type and a one-to-one relationship type. This technique has no particular interest since it produces a non relational construct, which is precisely the source schema of Fig. 13. Two specific techniques can be proposed.

(a) The first one consists in disaggregating B, replacing it with its components, and adding a coexistence constraint (Fig. 17a).

(b) The other is simpler but far less elegant. It consists in representing B by atomic attribute B', whose values are made of the concatenation of the values of the components of B (Fig. 17b). The lost structure of B can be recovered in a relational view, or in the application programs by storing B' values in variables with adhoc decomposition structures[4]. This technique is not applicable if individual components of B are involved in some integrity constraints, such as identifiers.

---

[3] When the subtypes are disjoint, some authors propose to merge all the foreign keys into a single one, and to add one or several discriminating boolean attributes indicating to which subtype(s) the entity belongs [18]. Such multi-target foreign keys can be translated into a series of SQL foreign keys defined on the same colomns.

[4] This technique is very frequent in actual files and databases, and makes one of the major problems in database reverse enginering [10, 15].

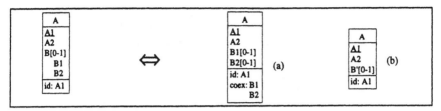

Figure 17 - Transformation of an optional compound attribute.

The problem is a bit more complex for compound attributes among which another constraint holds. Fig. 18 shows two translations of an *exclusive* constraints based on the same approaches as above. We observe that the source exclusive constraint `excl:B,C` should have been translated into `excl:{B1,B2},{C1,C2}`. However, thanks to the coexistence constraints, it has been simplified into `excl:B1,C1`.

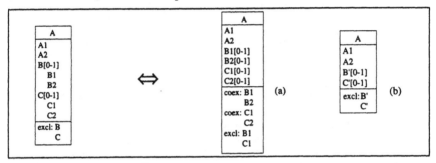

Figure 18 - Transformation of optional compound attributes with an exclusive constraint.

5.4 Translating multi-ET roles

Multi-ET role bc is eliminated by splitting its relationship type R, so that it is distributed among the entity types B and C on which it is defined (Fig. 19). This leads to plain ER structures which are easy to translate into relational structures.

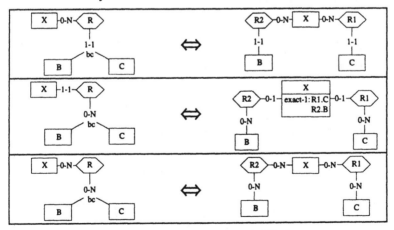

Figure 19 - Distribution of a multi-ET role.

5.5 Translating implication constraints

We consider the translation of two typical situations in which R is one-to-many from X to A (Fig. 20) and R is one-to-many from A to X (Fig. 21). In the left-side schema on Fig. 20, the constraint states that an A entity can be linked to an X entity only if it has a B value. The right-side schema translates this constraint for foreign key X1.

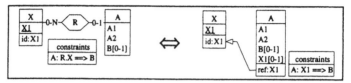

Figure 20 - *Expression of an implication constraint from a relationship type to an attribute (1).*

In Fig. 21, the constraint in the right-side schema tells that an A1 value in some X entity is the A1 value of an A entity only if this entity has a B value. More complex versions of R (many-to-many, N-ary, etc) can be coped with by applying transformation of Fig. 5 first.

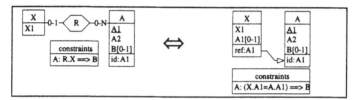

Figure 21 - *Expression of an implication constraint from a relationship type to an attribute (2).*

6. SQL translation of relational structures

Expressing entity types, single-valued and atomic attributes, primary, secondary and foreign keys in SQL is straighforward. However, the transformations proposed in Section 5 introduced some non standard constraints whose SQL expression can be delicate. In this section, we assume that the target RDBMS offers some variant of the check predicate as well as the trigger mechanism. Whenever possible, we will propose a translation into a check predicate. However, some RDBMS offers only a weak form of this mechanism, limited to local columns only. In this case, triggers will be used instead.

6.1 Translation of non standard keys

Some special cases of primary, secondary and foreign keys deserve special attention.

- Let us first consider *optional identifiers*. The first idea that comes to mind is to define a unique constraint or a unique index on the optional (nullable) columns. However, many RDBMS manage optional unique keys in an inadequate way: only one row is allowed to have a null value for this key. Therefore the programmer is forced, either to split the table or to resort to a trigger clause to express the uniqueness constraint (Fig. 22)
- The SQL expression of plain foreign keys is straighforward. That of Fig. 13b is less simple due to the inverse *inclusion constraint* (Fig. 22). This technique is not applicable in RDBMS that do not accept check predicates which mention other tables.

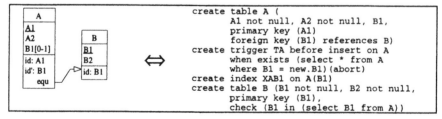

Figure 22 - *SQL expression of optional identifiers and inclusion constraints.*

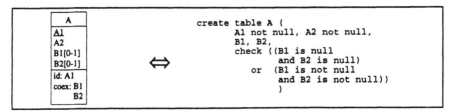

Figure 23 - Expression of a simple coexistence constraint.

6.2 Translation of *coexistence*, *exclusive* and *at-least-1* constraints on attributes

There is no problem to express these constraints into `check` or `trigger` clauses that are proposed by most current RDBMS. Fig. 23 and 24 illustrate the expression of simple and complex *coexistence* and *exclusive* constraints. *At-least-one* constraints will be translated in a similar way. *Exactly-one* constraints are formed by *exclusive* + *at-least-one* constraints.

```
create table A (
     A1 not null, A2 not null,
     B1, B2, C1, C2,
     check ((B1 is null and B2 is null)
     or   (B1 is not null
           and B2 is not null)),
     check ((C1 is null and C2 is null)
     or   (C1 is not null
           and C2 is not null)),
     check ((B1 is null and C1 is not null)
     or   (B1 is not null and C1 is null))
     )
```

Figure 24 - Expression of complex constraints.

6.3 Translation of constraints on identifiers

These constraints involve the identifier value sets of several entity types. They are fairly easy to translate into `check` predicates, provided the RDBMS accept multi-table predicates. Otherwise, `triggers` will be used instead.

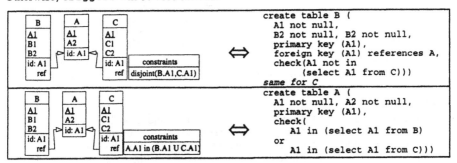

```
create table B (
     A1 not null,
     B2 not null, B2 not null,
     primary key (A1),
     foreign key (A1) references A,
     check(A1 not in
           (select A1 from C)))
same for C
```

```
create table A (
     A1 not null, A2 not null,
     primary key (A1),
     check(
          A1 in (select A1 from B)
     or
          A1 in (select A1 from C)))
```

Figure 25 - Expression of constraints on identifiers.

6.4 Translating FD among entity types

Any attempt to normalize the schema by factoring the common {A1,A2} fragments of A, B and C would produce the result of *IS-A materialization* technique, and therefore is not worth being considered. The proposed technique, applied to table C for example, is as follows: the row (a1,a2, ...) can be inserted into C if no other tables include a row (a1,a2',

...) such that a2 ≠ a2'. This technique is not applicable in RDBMS that do not accept check predicates which mention another table.

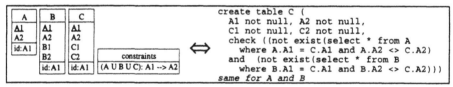

Figure 26 - Expression of distributed functional dependencies.

6.5 Translating implication constraints

Using the logical definition of the implication operator $((P \Rightarrow Q) = (\neg P \lor Q))$, we can propose the translation of the two schemas of Section 5.5 (Fig. 27 and 28).

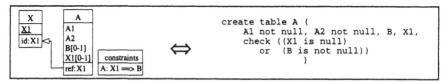

Figure 27 - Expression of an implication constraint involving an internal foreign key.

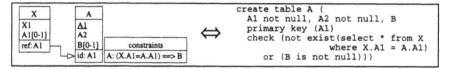

Figure 28 - Expression of an implication constraint involving an external foreign key.

The implication constraint in Fig. 15 and 16 can be expressed as in Fig. 29.

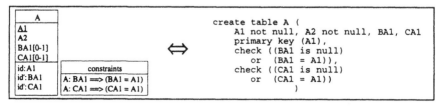

Figure 29 - Expression of a conditional equality constraint.

7. Conclusions

Through a precise analysis of IS-A relations translation techniques, we have shown that the problem is far more complex than generally presented in the literature, and that most proposed translation rules are too weak to provide reliable databases. We mention some of these proposals. Few of them include the four combinations of Fig. 4; [1, 26, 24] are some examples. [1] proposes the three basic implementation techniques, but with incomplete structure propagation and without derived constraints. [5] proposes the three implementation techniques, but for two combinations only, namely partition and free, and ignores derived constraints. [4] mention the first two techniques, but without any constraints. [24] and [21] propose the first technique without constraints.

The analysis performed in this paper can also translate into the following two conclusions.

1. When we compare the simplicity of the IS-A relations with the complexity of their complete translation into standard database structures, it appears that the availability of

built-in supertype/subtype constructs (e.g. in SQL-3) will simplify database design and programming considerably.

2. Understanding how IS-A relations can be translated into standard structures is essential, not only in database design, but also in database reverse engineering. Indeed, traces of IS-A implementation have been found in most legacy databases. However, these implementations often use more complex translation techniques than those assumed in reverse engineering methodologies [10, 15]. In particular, all the techniques proposed so far are limited to the *foreign key + unique key* pattern illustrated in Fig. 1 and Fig. 13a. Not only this technique is only one of the possible translation approaches, but such a key pattern can be the translation of a mere one-to-one relationship type as well, in which case most published algorithms fail.

It is needless to explain why CASE support of IS-A relations is particular weak. Indeed, at best, these tools implement the uncomplete translation processes proposed in the literature. Even when the OO paradigm is included in the target implementation system (OO languages, OODBMS, AI shells), the developer has to cope with severe limitations. For instance, the subtype constraints often are weaker than those presented in Section 2.2 (e.g. the disjoint hypothesis is often assumed), leading the developer to transform natural semantic structures into an artificial ones.

To be complete from the methodological viewpoint, this analysis should include further development such as the following.

1. What SQL techniques can be used to recover the source supertypes and subtypes ? For instance, what are the virtues and the limitations of (1) *Upward inheritance* complemented by views that extract subtypes through selection/projection, and of (2) *IS-A materialization* complemented by views that rebuild subtypes through joins ?

2. What is the best way to translate an arbitrarily complex IS-A hierarchy into plain SQL structures ? Such a heuristics should address the problem of multiple supertypes, multiple clusters, the satisfaction of definite design requirements (simplicity, space efficiency, time efficiency, evolutivity) and the specific features of the target DBMS (for instance, some RDBMS accept local check predicates only). These issues are partially addressed in [20] for example.

3. Which heuristics can be used to elicit the complex integrity constraints developed in this paper from the source code of legacy application programs ?

8. References

[1] Batini, C., Ceri, S., Navathe, S., *Conceptual Database Design - An Entity-Relationship Approach*, Benjamin/Cummings, 1992

[2] Brachman, R., J., What IS-A Is ans Isn't: An Analysis of Taxonomic Links in Semantic Networks, *IEEE Computer*, Oct. 1983

[3] Brodie, M., Mylopoulos, J., Schmidt, J., W., (Ed.), *On Conceptual Modelling*, Springer-Verlag, 1984

[4] Casanova, M., Tucherman, L., A., Laender, A., H., F., Algorithms for designing and maintaining optimized relational representations of entity-relationship schemas, in *Proc. of the 9th Int. Conf. on ERA*, 1990, North-Holland, 1991

[5] Catarci, T., Ferrara, F., M., OPTIM-ER: an Automated Tool for Supporting the Logical Design a Complete CASE Environment, in *Proc. of the 7th Int. Conf. on ERA*, 1988, North-Holland, 1989

[6] Chen, P., P., The Entity-Relationship Model - Towards a Unified View of Data, *ACM TODS*, Vol. 1, No. 1, 1976

[7] Elmasri, R., A., Weeldryer, J., Hevner, A., The Category Concept: An Extension to the Entity-Relationship Model, *J. of Data & Knowledge Engineering*, Vol. 1, No. 1, 1985

[8] Goldberg, A., Robson, D., *Smalltalk-80: The language and its Implementation*. Addison-Wesley, 1983

[9] Hainaut, J-L., Entity-generating Schema Transformation for Entity-Relationship Models, in *Proc. of the 10th ERA*, San Mateo (CA), North-Holland, 1991

[10] Hainaut, J-L., Chandelon M., Tonneau C., Joris M., Contribution to a Theory of Database Reverse Engineering, in *Proc. of the IEEE Working Conf. on Reverse Engineering*, Baltimore, May 1993, IEEE Computer Society Press, 1993.

[11] Hainaut, J-L, Chandelon M., Tonneau C., Joris M., Transformational techniques for database reverse engineering, in *Proc. of the 12th Int. Conf. on ER Approach, Arlington-Dallas*, E/R Institute and Springer-Verlag, LNCS, 1993

[12] Hainaut, J-L, Englebert, V., Henrard, J., Hick J-M., Roland, D., Evolution of database Applications: the DB-MAIN Approach, in *Proc. of the 13th Int. Conf. on ER Approach*, Manchester, Springer-Verlag, 1994.

[13] Hainaut, J-L., *Transformation-based database engineering*, Tutorial notes, VLDB'95, Zürich, Switzerland, Sept. 1995 (available at jlh@info.fundp.ac.be)

[14] Hainaut, J-L., Specification Preservation in Schema transformations - Application to Semantics and Statistics, *Data & Knowledge Engineering*, Vol. 19, pp. 99-134, Elsevier, 1996.

[15] Hainaut, J-L, Roland, D., Hick J-M., Henrard, J., Englebert, V., Database Reverse Engineering: from Requirements to CARE tools, *Journal of Automated Software Engineering*, Vol. 3, No. 2, 1996.

[16] Hainaut, J-L, Hick J-M., Englebert, V., Henrard, J., Roland, D., *Representation of IS-A Relations*, Research Report, DB-MAIN Project, Institut d'Informatique de Namur, March 1996 (available at jlh@info.fundp.ac.be)

[17] Halpin, T.A., Proper, H.A., Subtyping and Polymorphism in Object-role Modeling, *Data & Knowledge Engineering*, Vol. 15, pp. 251-281, Elsevier, 1995

[18] Hohenstein, U., Automatic Transformation of an Entity-Relationship Query Language into SQL, in *Proc. of the 8th Int. Conf. on ERA*, North-Holland, 1989

[19] Jajodia, S., Ng, P., Translation of Entity-Relationship Diagrams into Relational Structures, *Journal of System and Software*, Vol. 4, 1984

[20] Laender, Casanova, Carvalho, Ridolfi, An Analysis of SQL Integrity Constraints from an Entity-Relationship Model Perspective, *Information System Journal*, Vol. 19, No. 4, 1994

[21] Markowitz, V., M., Shoshani, A., Abbreviated Query Interpretation in Extended Entity-Relationship Oriented Databases, in *Proc. of the 8th Int. Conf. on ERA*, 1989, North-Holland, 1990

[22] Rosenthal, A., Reiner, D., Tools and Transformations - Rigourous and Otherwise - for Practical Database Design, *ACM TODS*, Vol. 19, No. 2, 1994

[23] Smith, J., M., Smith, D., C., P., Database Abstractions: Aggregation and Generalization, *ACM TODS*, Vol. 2, No. 2, 1977

[24] Teorey, T. J., *Database Modeling and Design: the Fundamental Principles*, Morgan Kaufman, 1994

[25] Tucherman, L., Casanova, M., A., Gualandi, P., M., Braga, A., P., A Proposal for Formalizing and Extending the Generalization and Subset Abstractions in the Entity-Relationship Model, in *Proc. of the 8th Int. Conf. on ERA*, North-Holland, 1989

[26] Wagner, C., W., Implementing Abstraction Hierarchies, in *Proc. of the 7th Int. Conf. on ERA*, 1988, North-Holland, 1989

Deductive Object Oriented Schemas

Dimitri Theodoratos*
University of Ioannina, Greece
dth@cs.uoi.gr

Abstract

Current Object Oriented (OO) Database schema structures allow *isa* relationships and multiple inheritance. We extend these structures with features from semantic modelling that are not traditionally supported by OO schemas: disjointness of classes and class intersection inclusion into other classes as well as negations of these statements. Formally we represent schemas as sets of first order monadic formulas. We provide a formal system for schemas that is sound and complete both for finite and unrestricted implications. Based on it and on well known algorithms we show that checking formula deduction is polynomial. Consistency is characterized completely in two alternative ways in terms of formula deduction. We show that these results allow us to deal efficiently with the issues of incremental/intelligent consistency checking, redundancy removal, minimal representation and updating in OO schemas.

Keywords: Object class structures, First order theory, Axiomatization, Deduction, Consistency

---

*Research carried out as part of the ERCIM Fellowship Program and financed by the Commission of the European Communities while the author was visitor at the INRIA, Rocquencourt.

1 Introduction

Object Oriented (OO) Database systems distinguish two notions on the model: the schema and the instances of the schema [18]. Another (orthogonal) distinction concerns the structural and the behavioral part of an OO Database System [2]. The structural part is quite similar to semantic modelling [17, 1]. The behavioral part deals with methods [18]. The main components of the schema are the class hierarchy and the method signatures. This paper does not deal with behavioral aspects or instances. Rather, we combine the OO paradigm with the Deductive one in a study of structural properties of OO schemas.

Usually OO schemas allow *isa* hierarchies and multiple inheritance [5]. We extend these schemas with features from semantic modelling which are not traditionally supported by Object-Oriented systems. In this direction our model supports the disjointness of classes, class intersection inclusion into other classes, and negations of these statements: that is the intersection of classes, and the possibility for common objects of some classes to be excluded from the intersection of other classes.

In practice a schema designer has to deal with several issues:
(1) Intelligent consistency checking: when performing consistency checking, take into account the particular properties of the schema.
(2) Incremental consistency checking: in checking a new schema for consistency, avoid redundant computations with respect to the previous schema checking. Thus, when a new statement is to be added to a schema, detect a part of the schema which does not contribute to a potential inconsistency of the schema after the modification. Then perform consistency checking only on the remaining part.
(3) Detecting redundant statements and finding minimal representations of the schema. A statement is redundant if, when removed from the schema, the resulting schema is equivalent to the initial.
(4) (Incremental) schema updating: when a new statement is to be added to a schema, find the maximal subsets of the schema that do not imply (the refusal of) the new statement. Incremental schema updating proceeds in a fashion similar to issue (2).

Our approach formalizes schema structure using first-order logic. Logic provides the semantics for the schema statements and allows notions such as consistency, implication, equivalence or minimality to be well-defined. Moreover, it provides methods for testing implication. More specifically, in formalizing schemas, we use a restriction of first order logic to a language having only unary predicate symbols (monadic logic). Monadic logic is decidable [14]. The class of formulas considered here for schemas (schema formulas) is not arbitrary: a schema is logically equivalent to a set of Horn clauses. Restricting a set of sentences to Horn clauses has proved in many cases, to have resulted in considerably lowering the computational complexity of the satisfiability problem. This fact has been recognized for some time now and a lot of research has been devoted to this direction. The approach of [19] and others is that of trying to approximate a knowledge base by a set of Horn clauses.

In order to deal with the real world problems stated above, two theoretical problems must be resolved efficiently in the formal model: the consistency problem (checking if a schema is consistent) and the implication problem (checking if a schema formula is logically implied by a schema). These two problems are two sides of the same coin. Checking implication of a schema formula from a schema can be done by adding the negation of the formula to the schema and testing the resulting schema for consistency. Checking inconsistency of a schema can be done by testing implication of an unsatisfiable formula from the schema. Let us concentrate on logical implication.

Formal systems and algorithms provide two alternative approaches for testing logical implication. Roughly speaking, the existence of a finite set of axioms and inference rules for logical formulas is a stronger property than the existence of an algorithm for testing implication: the existence of the first implies the existence of the second but the converse is not necessarily true.

In the context of schema formulas, the algorithmic approach is a general purpose algorithm based on resolution [13] for testing consistency of a schema [20]. Nonetheless, it does not take explicitly into account the particular properties of the schema nor the type of the formula we want to test for implication. Thus it cannot provide a suitable answer to all the practical issues.

In contrast, the information provided by a formal system allows for taking into consideration both the properties of the schema and the type of the formula. Therefore it is suitable for solving the practical problems mentioned before.

The main contributions of this paper consists in:

(a) providing a formal system for schema formulas that is sound and complete both for finite and unrestricted logical implication.

(b) characterizing schema formula deduction and providing polynomial methods for testing implication by constructing ad-hoc deductions of schema formulas.

(c) characterizing completely schema consistency in two alternative ways in terms of formula deduction.

Contribution (b) allows us to deal with with problems (3) and (4). Contribution (c) solves problem (1) and (2).

The paper is organized as follows: the next section is an example that highlights the issues we are tackle here. Section 3 contains preliminary definitions. In Section 4 we present a formal system for schema structures and we prove that it is sound and complete. Section 5 deals with the deduction of schema formulas. In Section 6 the consistency problem is addressed. Section 7 compares our work with related work. The last section contains concluding remarks and suggestions for further work. Because of lack of space, the proofs are omitted.

2   Example

We give in this section a simple example in order to provide some motivation about the issues we tackle. Consider a part of a university database schema involving the following entities (and the corresponding non-empty object classes): employees (*employee*), high income employees (*high_inc*), executives (*executive*), female people (*women*), students (*student*), fellowship receiving students (*fellow*) people belonging to an ethnic minority and veterans (*minority* and *veteran*) and people having a residence subsidized by the university (*sub_res*).

The following (intersection)class isa relationships hold over these classes and thus they are kept in the schema (called full schema rules in our model)

(1) $fellow \subseteq student$,
(2) $executive \subseteq high\_inc$,
(3) $high\_inc \subseteq employee$,
(4) $veteran \cap student \subseteq fellow$

For instance, (2) states that every executive has a high income. (4) states that every veteran who studies at the university has a fellowship (as a result, for instance, of an *ad hoc* fund from the ministry of defence).

The politics of the university concerning financial aspects and the status of executives is expressed by the following class disjointness relationships of the schema (called negative schema rules):

(5) $executive \cap student = \emptyset$,
(6) $high\_inc \cap sub\_res = \emptyset$,

For instance, (6) says that no one can have a high income and a subsidized residence at the same time. This does not prevent someone from enjoying one of these advantages.

The politics of the university towards women and minority groups is shown by the next class intersection statements (called positive schema facts).

(7) $women \cap fellow \neq \emptyset$,
(8) $minority \cap fellow \neq \emptyset$,
(9) $women \cap student \neq \emptyset$.

For instance, (8) says that some fellowships are attributed necessarily to people belonging to a minority group.

The same politics dictate the presence of (intersection)class non-inclusion statements in this university schema (called full schema facts in the model):

(10) $women \cap fellow \not\subseteq minority$.

Statement (10) says that there are fellowships attributed to women that do not belong to an ethnic minority.

Other schema statements can be deduced from the ones explicitly stated in the University schema. For instance from (1) and (8) we can deduce that some students belong to minority groups. This is expressed by the positive schema fact $minority \cap student \neq \emptyset$. The full schema rule $executive \subseteq employee \cap high\_inc$ says that every executive is an employee and has a high income. It can be deduced from (2) and (3).

By another elementary deduction from (1) and (7) we can obtain the positive fact $women \cap student \neq \emptyset$ stating that there are female students. This is exactly statement (9). Thus (9) is redundant in the sense that it can be removed from the schema without changing the meaning of the schema.

Suppose now that one inserts into the schema the positive fact $executive \cap sub\_res \neq \emptyset$ asserting that some of the executives live in residences subsidized by the university. By (2) and (6) we can deduce the negative rule $executive \cap sub\_res = \emptyset$. Then the schema is inconsistent in the sense that it asserts contradictory statements. In order to keep the consistency of the schema one needs to modify it prior to this insertion, which provides extra advantages to executives. This can be done for instance by removing (2) or (6) from the university schema.

3 Preliminaries

Monadic logic is a restriction of first order logic to a language which has only unary predicate names and no constant or function names. We consider a monadic language $\mathcal{L}$ with a set of predicate names $\mathcal{P}$. Small Latin letters from the beginning of the alphabet $a, b, c, \ldots$ (with or without subscripts) denote unary predicate names in $\mathcal{P}$. Intuitively, predicate names are object class names. A *(schema) fact* is a formula of the type
$\exists x[a_1(x) \wedge a_2(x) \wedge \ldots \wedge a_n(x) \wedge \neg(b_1(x) \wedge \ldots \wedge b_m(x))]$, $n \geq 1, m \geq 0$. For $m = 0$ we obtain a *positive fact*: $\exists x[a_1(x) \wedge a_2(x) \wedge \ldots \wedge a_n(x)]$. Otherwise ($m \geq 1$) the fact is called a *full fact*.

A *(schema) rule* is the negation of a schema fact. Thus a *(schema) rule* is a formula of the type $\forall x[\neg a_1(x) \vee \neg a_2(x) \vee \ldots \vee \neg a_n(x) \vee (b_1(x) \wedge \ldots \wedge b_m(x))]$, $n \geq 1, m \geq 0$. For $m = 0$ we obtain a *negative rule*: $\forall x[\neg a_1(x) \vee \neg a_2(x) \vee \ldots \vee \neg a_n(x)]$. Otherwise ($m \geq 1$) the rule is called a *full rule*. Full rules are negations of full facts and negative rules are negations of positive facts. Rules are universally quantified formulas while facts are existentially quantified ones. Variables range over objects. A *schema formula* is a schema fact or rule. Intuitively, schema formulas express relationships among object classes.

A *Schema* is a finite set of schema formulas. We use the letter S to denote it. Given a schema S, $FACTS$ is the set of its facts and $RULES$ is the set of its rules: $S = FACTS \cup RULES$. Given a set of facts $FACTS$, FF are the full facts and PF are the positive facts: $FACTS = FF \cup PF$; while given a set of rules $RULES$, FR are the full rules and NR are the negative rules: $RULES = FR \cup NR$. It is easy to see that if we put a schema in clausal form we obtain a set of Horn clauses (with Skolem constants) of a monadic language. Nevertheless, a schema is not restricted to Horn clause representation.

A set of predicate names $\{a_1 \ldots a_n\}$ is denoted by the juxtaposition of its elements as $a_1 \ldots a_n$. Small Latin letters $p, q, s, t, u, \ldots$ from the end of the alphabet denote sets of predicate names. If s, t are sets of predicate names, st denotes their union. The letters f and r are used for schema formulas. $pred(f)$ $(pred(r))$ is the set of predicate names in f (r). We extend this function to sets of schema formulas in the obvious way.

We use the following notation for facts and rules: the fact
$\exists x[a_1(x) \wedge \ldots \wedge a_n(x) \wedge \neg(b_1(x) \wedge \ldots \wedge b_m(x))]$ is denoted by $a_1 \ldots a_n \neg b_1 \ldots b_m$;
the positive fact $\exists x[a_1(x) \wedge \ldots \wedge a_n(x)]$ by $a_1 \ldots a_n$;
the rule $\forall x[\neg a_1(x) \vee \ldots \vee \neg a_n(x) \vee (b_1(x) \wedge \ldots \wedge b_m(x))]$ by $a_1 \ldots a_n \to b_1 \ldots b_m$
and the negative rule $\forall x[\neg a_1(x) \vee \ldots \vee \neg a_n(x)]$ by $a_1 \ldots a_n \to$.
Note that for positive facts the negation symbol is omitted. Notice also that with the notation introduced, syntactically different logically equivalent formulas may be denoted identically; for instance, the positive facts $\exists x[a(x) \wedge a(x) \wedge b(x)]$ and $\exists x[b(x) \wedge a(x)]$ can both be denoted as ab or ba.

Given a structure $\mathcal{S}(\mathcal{D}, \mathcal{I})$ where $\mathcal{D}$ is the interpretation domain and $\mathcal{I}$ is the interpretation function, the satisfaction of the schema formulas can be expressed in terms of simple set-theoretic relations: the full fact
$a_1 \ldots a_n \neg b_1 \ldots b_m$ is true in $\mathcal{S}$ iff $\mathcal{I}(a_1) \cap \ldots \cap \mathcal{I}(a_n) \not\subseteq \mathcal{I}(b_1) \cap \ldots \cap \mathcal{I}(b_m)$.
The positive fact $a_1 \ldots a_n$ is true in $\mathcal{S}$ iff $\mathcal{I}(a_1) \cap \ldots \cap \mathcal{I}(a_n) \neq \emptyset$. The negative rule $a_1 \ldots a_n \to$ is true in $\mathcal{S}$ iff $\mathcal{I}(a_1) \cap \ldots \cap \mathcal{I}(a_n) = \emptyset$. Finally, the full rule $a_1 \ldots a_n \to b_1 \ldots b_m$ is true in $\mathcal{S}$ iff $\mathcal{I}(a_1) \cap \ldots \cap \mathcal{I}(a_n) \subseteq \mathcal{I}(b_1) \cap \ldots \cap \mathcal{I}(b_m)$.
Intuitively, $\mathcal{I}(a)$ is an object class extension and structures are object bases.

The full fact $a_1 \ldots a_n \neg b_1 \ldots b_m$ where $b_1 \ldots b_m \subseteq a_1 \ldots a_n$ is an unsatisfiable formula while the full rule $a_1 \ldots a_n \to b_1 \ldots b_m$ where $b_1 \ldots b_m \subseteq a_1 \ldots a_n$ is a tautology. In the following we consider that a schema does not contain unsatisfiable formulas or tautologies. Note also that despite the notation we are not in the propositional case; for instance $\{a, b\} \not\models ab$.

4 A formal system for schemas

We present in this section a formal system for schema facts and rules and we prove that it is sound and complete both for finite and unrestricted implication. The formal system gives us an insight into schemas and allows us to see how schema facts and rules are deduced from those explicitly stored in S. This information enables us to show that polynomial algorithms for checking the implication of facts and rules comes directly from the form of deductions (next section). It also enables us to cope with the schema consistency problem (section 6).

The formal system comprises one axiom and ten inference rules. Let s, t, u be non-empty strings of predicate names. We consider that expressions as ss and s as well as st and ts represent the same syntactic object. Thus s, t, u can be thought of as sets of predicate names and their concatenation as their union. The formal system is depicted in figure 1.

Inference rules $IR8 - IR10$ can result from $IR5 - IR7$ if we allow u to be the empty set. Formal systems for subclasses of formulas can be derived easily from the one in Figure 1. For instance, axiom A and inference rules IR1 and IR5 form a formal system for full rules. Intuitively, with this subclass of formulas we can express that the objects of a class or the common objects of some classes multiply inherit from other classes.

Axiom

(A) $st \to s$ (axiom)

Inference rules

General

(IR1) $s \to t \;\vdash\; su \to tu$ (rule augmentation)

(IR2) $s \neg t \;\vdash\; s$ (fact right cut)

(IR3) $st \neg su \;\vdash\; st \neg u$ (fact right reduction)

(IR4) $s \to \;\vdash\; s \to t$ (rule generation)

Transitivity

(IR5) $s \to t, \; t \to u \;\vdash\; s \to u$ (rule transitivity)

(IR6) $s \neg u, \; s \to t \;\vdash\; t \neg u$ (fact right transitivity)

(IR7) $s \neg u, \; t \to u \;\vdash\; s \neg t$ (fact left transitivity)

Specialized transitivity

(IR8) $s \to t, \; t \to \;\vdash\; s \to$ (negative rule transitivity)

(IR9) $s, \; s \to t \;\vdash\; t$ (pos. fact right transitivity)

(IR10) $s, \; t \to \;\vdash\; s \neg t$ (pos. fact left transitivity)

Figure 1: A formal system for schema formulas

Deductions are defined as trees as usual. If there is a deduction of a schema formula f from S we write $S \vdash f$.

Lemma 4.1 (soundness of the deduction of schema formulas)
Let f be a schema formula. If $S \vdash f$ then $S \models f$.   □

Proposition 4.1 *The formal system of figure 1 is minimal.*   □

We can now prove the completeness of the formal system. One way of doing so would be to provide a procedure that constructs, given a consistent schema, a model of it which satisfies among schema formulas exactly those deduced from the schema using the formal system. By the previous lemma, this is a model which satisfies among schema formulas exactly those implied by the schema. Such a model is called an Armstrong model (relation) in the dependency theory of relational databases. It is not difficult to see that such a model does not exist for every consistent schema. Nevertheless there exists an Armstrong model for positive facts and an Armstrong model for rules. Thus we split the proof in two parts. We design two algorithms for model construction. The completeness of the formal system is then shown by induction on the steps of these algorithms. The proof is quite involved and the details are omitted here.

Theorem 4.1 (soundness and completeness of the deduction of schema formulas)
Let S be a consistent schema and f be a schema formula. $S \models f$ if and only if $S \vdash f$.   □

So far we have not restricted the interpretations of the predicate names: they can be finite or infinite sets. Correspondingly the notions of satisfaction and implication involved are those of unrestricted satisfaction and implication as opposed to finite ones. In the context of Object Oriented databases, class extensions generally contain a finite number of objects. Thus finite satisfiability and implication can be of great interest. It is well known that finite and unrestricted satisfiability coincide for a class of formulas (called an initially extended Bernays-Scönfinkel class) containing the class of schema formulas [14]. Therefore, finite and unrestricted implication coincide for schema formulas. The following theorem is a direct consequence of this fact. We write $S \models_{fin} f$ if a schema S finitely implies a schema formula f.

Theorem 4.2 (soundness and completeness of the deduction of schema formulas for finite implication)
Let S be a consistent schema and f be a satisfiable schema formula. $S \models_{fin} f$ if and only if $S \vdash f$. ☐

5 Deduction of schema formulas

5.1 Theoretical aspects

In this section we treat the implication problem for schema formulas. By the results of the previous section, this amounts to testing the deduction of a schema formula from a schema. We show therefore how, by using our formal system, schema facts and rules can be deduced from a schema. Then checking deduction becomes straightforward by using these results and well-known algorithms. Initially we treat an elementary case: the deduction of a positive fact from another positive fact and a set of full rules. We then provide a sequence of propositions that successively reduce the general case to the elementary one.

First, let us think of predicate names as attribute names, sets of predicate names as relation schemas, and full rules as functional dependencies in the relational model. Then notice that the axiom (A), IR1 and IR5 are precisely Armstrong's axioms [4, 23]. Moreover, no other inference rule is applicable in the particular case where only rules are involved. A functional dependency $s \to t$ is deduced from a set of functional dependencies FR if and only if the schema t is contained in the closure of the schema s under the set of functional dependencies FR [4, 23]. Now notice that $\{s\} \cup FR \vdash t$ if and only if $FR \vdash s \to t$ (proposition 5.1). Thus $\{s\} \cup FR \vdash t$ if and only if the schema t is contained in the closure of the schema s under FR. Functional dependencies have been studied extensively. A linear time algorithm for computing the closure of a relational schema under a set of functional dependencies can be found in [11, 23]

Remember that $S = FACTS \cup RULES$; $FACTS = FF \cup PF$ (full and positive facts); $RULES = FR \cup NR$ (full and negative rules). Let s, t, u, v be non empty sets of predicate names.

The following proposition reduces the deduction of a full rule from a set of full rules to the deduction of a positive fact from a positive fact and a set of full rules:

Proposition 5.1 $FR \vdash s \to t$ *if and only if* $\{s\} \cup FR \vdash t$ □

The deduction of a negative rule from a negative rule and a set of full rules can be reduced to the deduction of a positive fact from a positive fact and a set of full rules:

Proposition 5.2 $\{s \to\} \cup FR \vdash t \to$ *if and only if* $\{t\} \cup FR \vdash s$ □

The following proposition reduces the deduction of a positive fact from a full fact and a set of full rules to the deduction of a positive fact from a positive fact and a set of full rules.

Proposition 5.3 $\{s \neg t\} \cup FR \vdash u$ *if and only if* $\{s\} \cup FR \vdash u$ □

Only one fact from a set is involved in every deduction of a positive fact from this set of facts and a set of full rules:

Proposition 5.4 $FACTS \cup FR \vdash s$ *iff* $\exists f \in FACTS$ *s.t.* $\{f\} \cup FR \vdash s$ □

A similar result holds for negative rules.

Proposition 5.5 $RULES \vdash s \to$ *iff* $\exists t \to \in NR$ *s.t.* $\{t \to\} \cup FR \vdash s \to$ □

The proposition below reduces the deduction of a full rule from a set of rules to the deduction of a full rule from a set of full rules or the deduction of a negative rule from a set of rules:

Proposition 5.6 $RULES \vdash s \to t$ *iff* $FR \vdash s \to t$ *or* $RULES \vdash s \to$. □

Next we reduce the deduction of a rule from S to the deduction of this rule from the set of rules of S. Thus facts are irrelevant in the deduction of rules:

Proposition 5.7 *(a)* $S \vdash s \to$ *if and only if* $RULES \vdash s \to$
(b) $S \vdash s \to t$ *if and only if* $RULES \vdash s \to t$ □

The deduction of a positive fact from S can be reduced to the deduction of this positive fact from the facts and the full rules of S. Thus negative rules are irrelevant in the deduction of positive facts:

Proposition 5.8 $S \vdash s$ *if and only if* $FACTS \cup FR \vdash s$ □

Finally, the deduction of a full fact from S can be reduced to the deduction of a positive fact and a negative rule from S:

Proposition 5.9 $S \vdash s \neg t$ *if and only if* $(\exists u \neg p \in FACTS$ *such that* $\{u\} \cup FR \vdash s$ *and* $S \vdash ut \to)$ *or* $(\exists u \neg v \in FF$ *such that* $\{u\} \cup FR \vdash s$ *and* $\{ut\} \cup FR \vdash v)$
(p can be the empty set) □

It should be clear now how a schema fact or rule is deduced from a schema and that this checking can be performed efficiently. The following procedure summarizes how the deduction checking can be performed:

Procedure 5.1 checking deduction of a schema formula f from S

1. Use propositions 5.1 - 5.9 to express the existence of a deduction of f from S in terms of the existence of elementary deductions (deduction of a positive fact from a positive fact and a set of full rules).

2. Use linear algorithms in [11, 9, 23] to check the existence of elementary deductions. □

Remark 5.1 Clearly the above procedure can be performed in polynomial time since the existence of elementary deductions can be checked in linear time. □

For instance, in order to examine if $S \vdash s$, by propositions 5.8, 5.4 and 5.3, it suffices to check if there is a positive fact u or a full fact $u \neg t$ in S such that $\{u\} \cup FR \vdash s$. This test can be performed by computing in linear time the closure of u under FR for every positive or full fact $u \neg t$ in S and checking whether it includes s.

5.2 Practical aspects. Minimality and updating issues.

We address now the redundancy, minimal representation and updating issues from a syntax-based point of view. In this sense formulas are seen as objects to be removed from or left into the schema as a whole.

Equivalence of schemas is defined in terms of logical equivalence and *minimality* with respect to set inclusion. A formula is redundant in a schema, if when removed from it the resulting schema is equivalent to the initial one. A redundant formula can be detected by checking if it can be deduced by the rest of the schema. A minimal equivalent schema of a given schema can be found by removing redundant formulas until no more redundant formulas are left.

Syntax-based approaches for updating logical theories [16, 15, 21] are very popular because of their conceptual simplicity. When updating a schema S with a schema formula (update formula) with respect to these approaches, the minimal subsets of S that imply a schema formula f (the update formula or its negation) need to be computed. This allows for invalidating the implication of f from S. The results in this section allow for determining all these minimal subsets:

- Determine a specific sound and complete deduction depending on the type of f (i.e whether it is a negative rule or a full fact etc). This is done to reduce the number of deductions constructed in the next step.

- Construct all the specific deductions of f from S in a top-down way.

- Choose among them the deductions using minimal subsets of S.

Updating is not treated further here and it is the subject of a forthcoming paper.

6 Consistency checking

6.1 Theoretical aspects

In this section, we address the consistency problem. The following proposition gives us a characterization of the consistency of a schema in terms of schema formulas implication.

Proposition 6.1 *Let S be a schema that does not contain unsatisfiable formulas. Then S is inconsistent if and only if there exists a rule $s \to t \in S$ such that $S \vdash s \neg t$ (t may be empty).* ☐

Corollary 6.1 *Let S be a schema that does not contain unsatisfiable formulas. S is consistent if one of the following conditions hold.*
(a) S does not contain rules $(RULES = \emptyset)$
(b) S does not contain full rules $(FR = \emptyset)$ and there is no negative rule $s \to$ in S and fact $u \neg t$ in S such that $s \subseteq u$. ☐

The following proposition provides, as does proposition 6.1, a complete characterization of schema satisfiability.

Proposition 6.2 *A schema S is inconsistent if and only if there exists a fact $s \neg t \in S$ such that $S \vdash s \to t$ (t may be empty).* ☐

Corollary 6.2 *A schema S is consistent if one of the following conditions hold.*
(a) S does not contain facts $(FACTS = \emptyset)$
(b) S does not contain full facts and negative rules $(FF = NR = \emptyset)$ ☐

6.2 Practical aspects. Intelligent consistency checking and incrementality issues.

Consistency control can also be done by using a general purpose algorithm based on resolution which would attempt to derive the empty clause from a schema in clausal form. Though propositions and corollaries 6.1 and 6.2 along with the results of the previous section allow for *intelligent consistency checking* i.e. taking into account properties (the form) of the schema.

Example 6.1 Let S contain a small number of facts. In this case it is preferable to use proposition 6.2 and to check (using the results of the previous section) if a small number of rules can be deduced from S. To use another example, if S does not contain full rules but a small number of negative rules, it is preferable to use proposition 6.1 and to check if a small number of positive facts can be deduced from S. If S satisfies one of the conditions of the corollaries, the answer is immediate. ☐

When doing *Incremental consistency checking*, besides the form of the schema S, the type of the formula to be added into S is taken into account. The goal is to determine, given a consistent schema and a satisfiable formula to insert into it, a part of the schema which does not contribute to a potential inconsistency of the new schema. Consistency checking is then performed only on the remaining part. Again the propositions of the present and previous sections can be used here.

Example 6.2 Suppose that the positive fact s is to be added to the consistent schema S. By proposition 6.2 we need only checking if $s \rightarrow$ is deduced from S. By proposition 5.7(a), the subset of S, $RULES$, suffices for performing this checking. The remaining part of S (the set $FACTS$) is useless and can be ignored. Furthermore, if it is known that S does not contain any negative rules the whole schema is useless for performing consistency checking. Indeed, in this case, by proposition 5.5, $s \rightarrow$ cannot be deduced from $RULES$ and the answer comes without checking. The whole schema can be ignored. If an update is to be performed by adding s into S, modifications concern only the subset $RULES$, the subset $FACTS$ remaining unaltered (*incremental updating*). □

We are not going into the details of describing intelligent/incremental consistency checking for different forms of schemas and types of formulas to be inserted since they can be deduced easily from the results of the present and the previous sections.

7 Relevant work

Formal systems have been studied in database theory mainly in the domain of dependency theory [23], for different classes of dependency constraints. Axiom (A) and inference rules IR1 and IR5,presented in section 5, correspond to Armstrong's axioms for functional dependencies in the relational model [4, 23].

In [6] *isa* relationships and disjointness constraints are considered in the context of knowledge representation schemes based on semantic networks *Isa* relationships and disjointness constraints correspond in this context to binary (having at most two predicate names) schema full rules and binary schema negative rules, respectively. Thus the class of schema formulas strictly contains those statements and our formal system subsumes the formal system presented there. In [7] the same authors consider a more general class of binary constraints called containment constraints involving also complements of classes. It can be shown though that if constraints involving complements of classes are not considered, there is a correspondence between containment constraints and the restriction of the class of schema formulas to binary ones. In this restricted case the two formal systems are equivalent in satisfiable schemas. Nevertheless, the containment constraints studied cannot express statements involving more than two classes, as is the case with schema formulas. In [8] polynomial algorithms for the implication problem of containment constraints are provided.

In [20] a class of statements broader than schema formulas is considered to have first order logic semantics. A satisfiability checking algorithm is given for this class. Nevertheless, no formal system is provided and the algorithm is a general purpose one based on resolution that cannot take advantage of the properties of the schema. In our paper the information provided by the formal system allows for intelligent incremental consistency checking and update performance. The work in [20] is extended in [10] to consider non-unary predicates in the context of deductive Entity Relationship modelling. A satisfiability checking algorithm is provided but only for binary constraints. Here we do not restrict the number of predicate names involved in a schema formula.

In [3] different classes of statements having set-theoretic semantics are studied in the context of semantic modelling. Formal systems are presented for each of them. Schema formulas strictly contain all the classes of statements considered except those involving union operations. These classes cannot express non-binary schema facts and rules, negative rules and full facts. Thus no class considered contains schema formulas. Finally, in [22] a class of monadic formulas with equality is considered in the context of Knowledge bases and a formal system is provided. This class intersects without including schema formulas.

8 Conclusion

We have considered OO Database schema structures extended with features that are not supported by current OO Database systems. In this context, we have addressed the issues of incremental/intelligent consistency checking, redundancy removal, minimal representation and updating. In order to deal with these issues, we have formalized schemas as sets of formulas of a first order monadic language (schema formulas). When put in clausal form, schema formulas are Horn formulas (conjunctions of Horn clauses). A sound and complete formal system is presented for this class of formulas and a polynomial procedure for checking schema formula deduction is provided. Consistency is characterized completely in terms of schema formula deduction.

We are currently working on the issue of updating schemas with respect to syntax-based approaches. As explained in Section 5, the formal system and the deductions of schema formulas presented in this paper allow us to design improved procedures for schema updating. Nevertheless, the problem is still intractable. It is thus important to find conditions under which it becomes polynomial. Extension of the present work concerns the study of schemas that express, in addition, unions of classes. Then schema formulas are no longer Horn formulas. As it is shown in [7] the consistency problem for schemas becomes NP-complete. Further in this direction, it would be interesting to study more expressive Object Oriented schemas comprising non-binary relations and cardinality constraints [12] when consistency is decidable.

References

[1] S. Abiteboul and R. Hull. IFO: A formal semantic database model. *ACM Trans. Database Systems*, 12(3):525–565, 1987.

[2] S. Abiteboul and P. C. Kanellakis. The two facets of object-oriented data models. *Data & Knowledge Engineering*, 14(2):3–7, 1991.

[3] H. Arisawa and T. Miura. On the properties of extended inclusion dependencies. In *Proc. of Intl. Conf. on Very Large Data Bases*, pages 449–456, 1986.

[4] W. W. Armstrong. Dependency structures of database relationships. In *Proc. IFIP 74, North Holland, Amsterdam*, pages 580–583, 1974.

[5] M. Atkinson, D. DeWitt, D. Maier, F. Bancilhon, K. Dittrich, and S. Zdonik. The object-oriented database system manifesto. In *Proc. of 1st Intl. Conf. on Deductive and Object Oriented Databases*, pages 40–57, 1989.

[6] P. Atzeni and D. S. Parker. Formal properties of net-based knowledge represenation schemes. *Data & Knowledge Engineering*, 3:137–147, 1988.

[7] P. Atzeni and D. S. Parker. Set containment inference and syllogisms. *Theoretical Computer Science*, 62:39–65, 1988.

[8] P. Atzeni and D. S. Parker. Algorithms for set containment inference. In F. Bancilhon and P. Buneman, editors, *Advances in Database Programming Languages*, pages 43–65. ACM Press, Frontier Series, 1990.

[9] G. Ausiello, A. D'Atri, and D. Saccà. Graph algorithms for functional dependency manipulation. *Jour. of the ACM*, 30(4):752–766, Oct. 1983.

[10] G. D. Battista and M. Lenzerini. Deductive entity relationship modeling. *IEEE Transactions on Knowledge and Data Engineering*, 5(3):439–450, 1993.

[11] C. Beeri and P. Berstein. Computational problems related to the design of normal form relational schemas. *ACM Trans. Database Syst*, 4(1):30–59, Mar 1979.

[12] D. Calvanese and M. Lenzerini. Making object-oriented schemas more expressive. In *Proc. of the Intl. Conf. on Principles of Database Systems*, pages 243–254, 1994.

[13] C.-L. Chang and R. C.-T. Lee. *Symbolic Logic and Mechanical Theorem Proving*. Academic Press, New York, 1973.

[14] S. B. Dreben and D. W. Goldfarb. *The Decision Problem: Solvable Classes of Quantificational formulas*. Addison-Wesley, Reading, MA, 1979.

[15] R. Fagin, G. M. Kuper, J. Ullman, and M. Vardi. Updating logical databases. In P. Kanellakis and F. Preparata, editors, *Advances in computing Research*, volume 3, pages 1–18. JAI Press, Greenwhich, CT, 1986.

[16] R. Fagin, J. Ullman, and M. Vardi. On the semantics of updates in databases. In *Proc. Second ACM Symp. on Principles of Database Systems,* Atlanta, GA, pages 352–365, 1983.

[17] R. Hull and R. King. Semantic Database Modeling: Survey, Applications and Research issues. *ACM Computing Surveys,* 19(3):201–260, 1987.

[18] P. Kanellakis, C. Lécluse, and P. Richard. Introduction to the data model. In F. Bancilhon, C. Delobel, and P. Kanellakis, editors, *Building an Object Oriented Database system, the story of O2.* Morgan Kaufmann Publishers, 1992.

[19] H. A. Kautz, M. J. Kearns, and B. Selman. Horn approximations of empirical data. *Artificial Intelligence,* 74(1), mar 1995.

[20] M. Lenzerini. Class hierachies and their complexity. In F. Bancilhon and P. Buneman, editors, *Advances in Database Programming Languages,* pages 43–65. ACM Press, Frontier Series, 1990.

[21] B. Nebel. Belief revision and default reasoning: syntax based approaches. In *Proc. of the Second Intl. Conf. on Principles of Knowledge Representation and Reasoning,* pages 417–428, 1991.

[22] D. Theodoratos. Monadic databases with equality. In *Proc. of the Intl. Symp. on Mathematical Fundamentals of Database and Knowledge Base Systems,* pages 74–88. Springer-Verlag, LNCS 495, 1991.

[23] J. D. Ullman. *Principles of Database and Knowledge-Base Systems,* volume 2. Computer Science Press, 1989.

Verification Problems
in
Conceptual Workflow Specifications

A.H.M. ter Hofstede[1], M.E. Orlowska[1,2], J. Rajapakse[2]

[1]Department of Computer Science
The University of Queensland
Brisbane, Qld 4072
Australia
e-mail: {arthur,maria}@cs.uq.oz.au

[2]Distributed Systems Technology Centre
The University of Queensland
Brisbane, Qld 4072
Australia
e-mail: jb@dstc.edu.au

Abstract

Most of today's business requirements can only be accomplished through integration of various autonomous systems which were initially designed to serve the needs of particular applications. In the literature workflows are proposed to design these kinds of applications. The key tool for designing such applications is a powerful conceptual specification language. Such a language should be capable of capturing interactions and cooperation between component tasks of workflows among others. These include sequential execution, iteration, choice, parallelism and synchronisation. The central focus of this paper is the *verification* of such process control aspects in conceptual workflow specifications. As it is generally agreed upon that the later in the software development process an error is detected, the more it will cost to correct it, it is of vital importance to detect errors as early as possible in the systems development process. In this paper some typical verification problems in workflow specifications are identified and their complexity is addressed. It will be proven that some fundamental problems are not tractable and we will show what restriction is needed to allow termination problems to be recognized in polynomial time.

1   Introduction

Information systems integration may be considered a key theme for the 1990s since it is a prerequisite for running businesses cost-effectively. Most of today's business requirements can only be accomplished through the integration of various autonomous systems which were initially designed to serve the needs of particular applications. In designing such integrated systems we use pre-existing systems as components of the new system. As a result, we now see some complex applications which span across several pre-existing systems. Workflows have been identified as a good candidate for designing such applications [ASSR93, BGS93, FKB95, GHS95, RS94]. In a workflow, a set of operations performed to achieve some basic business process on one pre-existing system is usually described as a task. A set of tasks constitute a workflow where these tasks may be interrelated in some way reflecting business application needs. The tasks are either existing information processes in a pre-existing system or they may be implemented on request by the workflow designer.

Workflow management systems (WFMS) have been developed to implement work-flows as a whole. Analoguously to other systems, WFMSs have conceptual and phys-ical levels. It is important to capture all the details of tasks and their interactions at a *conceptual* level in order to prevent premature implementation decisions which may lead to suboptimal solutions later on. As validation is of crucial importance, workflow specifications should be comprehensive as this facilitates communication with domain experts. One way of achieving *comprehensibility* is by offering graphical representa-tions of modelling concepts. In order to be capable of adequately capturing a workflow problem, the workflow specification language should have sufficient *expressive power*. In particular this means that constructs for various forms of process control should be offered. Finally, a workflow specification language should have a *formal founda-tion* in order to allow for formal reasoning and prevent interpretation ambiguities. The formal foundation should include both syntax and semantics. Summarizing: A conceptual workflow specification language should be comprehensive, have sufficient expressive power and should have a formal foundation.

Workflow management research has received much attention in recent years. In [GHS95] an up-to-date high-level overview of the current workflow management methodolo-gies and software products is provided. Research prototypes, such as e.g. described in [MSKW96, KS95], concentrate on concurrency, correctness, and recovery of work-flows while commercial products pay more attention to user friendly workflow speci-fication tools leaving aspects like recovery and correctness to designers. Some WFMS have not given much attention to the conceptual level [RS94]. As identified in [GHS95], workflow management needs a complete framework starting from the conceptual level. In [CCPP95] a good review of current work at the conceptual level is provided and a conceptual level language to describe workflows is presented. Its implementation model is based on active database technology. Necessary active rules are semi-automatically generated from the conceptual level language. In this reference it is claimed that the work described in [BGS93, FKB95] lacks expressive power concerning the possibility of specifying task interactions and the mapping from workflow specification to work-flow execution, in particular with regard to exception handling. However, in [CCPP95] a formal semantics of the language presented is not given. Hence, it is not possible to reason about the correctness of the conceptual specifications.

Workflow modelling is similar to process modelling [GHS95]. In a workflow context, tasks are basic work units that collectively achieve a certain goal. The collective nature shows various types of process dependencies. Therefore, whatever language is used to specify workflows, it should be sufficiently powerful to capture those dependencies: sequential order, parallelism, iteration, choice, synchronisation etc.

The central focus of this paper is the identification of verification issues in conceptual workflow specifications, as far as process control is concerned, and their complexity. Clearly, verification at the conceptual level is crucial as it is a well-known fact that the later in the development process an error is detected, the more expensive it is to correct it. As mentioned above it is desirable to have sufficient expressive power in specification languages. However, there is an obvious trade-off between expressive power and complexity of verification. In this paper, we will prove that some verification problems in the context of workflow specifications are not tractable or even undecidable. In addition to that, we will focus on a restriction of expressive power which allows terminations considerations to be performed in polynomial time.

The paper is organised as follows. In the next section, core concepts for specifying process dependencies are introduced and an example of a workflow specification is given using these concepts. In section 3, a number of verification problems are defined and their complexity is determined. In section 4, a necessary and sufficient condition for detecting termination in a *restricted* workflow specification language is given and its correctness is proved. Section 5 concludes the paper and identifies topics for further research.

2   Essential Workflow Concepts

The specification of workflows in general is known to be quite complex and many issues are involved. Workflow specifications should be capable of expressing at least:

- Properties of tasks, such as compensatability (i.e. can the result of the task be undone), pre- and postconditions (which might involve complex time aspects), redo-ability (can a task be redone) etc.

- Information flows between tasks and information of a more persistent nature (e.g. external databases).

- Execution dependencies between tasks (also referred to as control flow). These dependencies can be based on conditions (value based or failure/successful) or temporal, parallel/sequential etc.

- Capacities of tasks. Capacities might e.g. refer to storage, to throughput, or to numbers of active instances.

Generally speaking, workflow specifications need not pay attention to task functionality as focus is on the coordination of tasks.

In this paper, focus is solely on *control flow* in workflow specifications. Any conceptual workflow specification language should at least be capable of capturing moments of choice, sequential composition, parallel execution, and synchronization. In the next section, task structures are presented which are capable of modelling these task dependencies. For a definition of their formal semantics the reader is referred to [HN93].

It should be stressed here that task structures serve as a means to an end. They might be viewed upon as a *kernel* for workflow specification concepts and are used in this paper to study verification problems. The results extend to any language offering concepts for choice, sequential composition, parallel execution, and synchronization.

2.1 Informal Explanation of Task Structures

Task structures were introduced in [Bot89] to describe and analyze problem solving processes. In [WHO92] they were extended and used as a meta-process modelling technique for describing the strategies used by experienced information engineers. In [HN93] they were extended again and a formal semantics in terms of Process Algebra was given [BW90].

In figure 1, the main concepts of task structures are graphically represented. They are discussed subsequently.

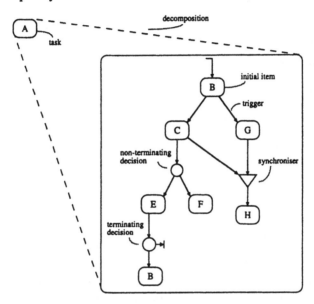

Figure 1: Graphical representation of task structure concepts

The central notion in task structures is the notion of a *task*. In a workflow context, tasks are basic work units that collectively achieve a certain goal. A task can be defined in terms of other tasks, referred to as its *subtasks*. This *decomposition* may be performed repeatedly until a desired level of detail has been reached. Tasks with the same name have the same decomposition, e.g. the tasks named *B* in figure 1. Performing a task may involve choices between subtasks, *decisions* represent these moments of choice. Decisions coordinate the execution of tasks. Two kinds of decisions are distinguished, *terminating* and *non-terminating* decisions. A decision that is terminating, may lead to termination of the execution path of that decision. If this execution path is the only active execution path of the supertask, the supertask terminates as well.

Triggers, graphically represented as arrows, model sequential order. In figure 1 the task with name *G* can start after termination of the top task named *B*. *Initial items* are those tasks or decisions, that have to be performed first as part of the execution of a task that has a decomposition. Due to iterative structures, it may not always be clear which task objects are initial. Therefore, this has to be indicated explicitly. Finally, *synchronisers* deal with explicit synchronisation. In figure 1 the task named *H* can only start when the tasks with names *C* and *G* have terminated.

As we use task structures as a generic language for workflow specifications, in the rest of the paper we refer to them as *workflow structures*.

2.2 Syntax of Workflow Structures

In this section the syntax of workflow structures is defined using elementary set theory.

A workflow structure consists of the following components:

1. A set $\mathcal{X}$ of workflow objects. $\mathcal{X}$ is the (disjoint) union of a set of synchronisers $\mathcal{S}$, a set of tasks $\mathcal{T}$ and a set of decisions $\mathcal{D}$. In $\mathcal{D}$ we distinguish a subset $\mathcal{D}_t$ consisting of the terminating decisions.

2. A relation $\mathsf{Trig} \subseteq \mathcal{X} \times \mathcal{X}$ of triggers.

3. A function $\mathsf{Name} \colon \mathcal{T} \to \mathcal{V}$ yielding the name of a task, where $\mathcal{V}$ is a set of names.

4. A partial decomposition function $\mathsf{Sup} \colon \mathcal{X} \rightarrowtail \mathcal{V}$. If $\mathsf{Sup}(x) = v$, this means that workflow object x is part of the decomposition of v. Names in the range of this function are called *decomposition names*. The set $\mathcal{Q} \equiv \mathsf{ran}(\mathsf{Sup})$ contains all these names. The complement $\mathcal{A} \equiv \mathcal{V} \setminus \mathcal{Q}$ is the set of *atomic actions*.

5. A partial function $\mathsf{Init} \subseteq \mathsf{Sup}$ yielding the initial items of a task.

Workflow structures are required to have a unique task, in the top of the decomposition hierarchy. For this task the decomposition function should be undefined, i.e. $\exists!_{t \in \mathcal{T}} [\mathsf{Sup}(t)\!\uparrow]$. In the remainder, we call this unique task, the *main* task and refer to it as t_0. Using the terminology of graph theory, this requirement stipulates that the decomposition hierarchy of task structures should be rooted. Contrary to [WHO92], we do not require the decomposition hierarchy to be acyclic, but allow recursive decomposition structures. They allow for recursive specification of workflows.

Decomposition allows for the modularization of workflow specifications. Typically, modules should be loosely connected and hence, triggers should not cross decomposition boundaries:

$$x_1 \mathsf{Trig} x_2 \Rightarrow \mathsf{Sup}(x_1) = \mathsf{Sup}(x_2)$$

Finally, each workflow object should be reachable from an initial item. This implies that there should be a trigger path from such an initial item to the workflow object in question:

$$\forall_{x \in \mathcal{X} \setminus \{t_0\}} \exists_{i \in \mathcal{X}} [\mathsf{Init}(i) = \mathsf{Sup}(x) \wedge i \mathsf{Trig}^* x]$$

In this requirement, Trig^* is the reflexive transitive closure of Trig.

3 Complexity of some Verification Problems

In this section focus is on the definition of verification problems in workflow specifications and their complexity. These problems solely concern process control issues and assume that specifications may use the core workflow concepts as presented in the previous section.

In a workflow specification it can be relevant to be able to determine whether a certain task can be invoked. This is particularly true if the task involved is critical, i.e. without its execution the workflow cannot be considered successful.

Definition 3.1

    The initiation problem for a workflow object x in a workflow structure $\mathcal{W}$ is to determine whether a sequence of events exists leading to the execution of x.

□

Theorem 3.1 The initiation problem is NP-complete (= NTIME(poly)-complete).

Proof:

    For this proof we describe a polynomial time transformation of SATISFIABIL-ITY to the initiation problem. SATISFABILITY, or SAT for short, is known to be NP-complete (see e.g. [GJ79]) and formally corresponds to the question whether there is a truth assignment to a set K of clauses over U, a set of boolean variables. Each clause is a set of literals, which are either boolean variables from U or negations of boolean variables from U. The proof given here is inspired by the proof given in [JLL77], where a comparable translation was used for proving the fact that determining liveness in a Free Choice Petri Net is an NP-complete problem.

    Let K be an instance of SAT. The workflow structure $\mathcal{W}_K$ resulting from the transformation consists of a main task t_0 with for each boolean variable $u \in U$ a decision D_u as initial item. This set of decisions is to capture all possible truth assignments to the boolean variables in U. Hence, each decision D_u has an output trigger to a task with name u and an output trigger to a task with name $\sim u$ (to avoid confusion, the symbol $\sim$ is used for logical negation in this proof).

    Let t be a task with name x, where x is a literal. For each clause C in K for which $\sim x \in C$ a trigger from t to a task with name $\langle \sim x, C \rangle$ exists (where it is assumed that $\sim\sim x \equiv x$). Further, for each C a synchroniser S_C exists which has as input all tasks with names of the form $\langle x, C \rangle$. Finally, each synchroniser S_C has an output trigger to a task with name K. Note that the construction implies that a synchroniser S_C will only be triggered if every one of its input tasks will be executed, which means that each of the literals in C evaluates to false in a particular truth assignment.

    The construction guarantees that K can be initiated if and only if K is not satisfiable. Suppose K is not satisfiable, then in any truth assignment T there is a clause $C = \{x_1, \ldots, x_n\}$ that evaluates to false under T. Hence, all literals x_i evaluate to false under T. Synchroniser S_C depends on the tasks with names $\langle \sim x_1, C \rangle, \ldots, \langle \sim x_n, C \rangle$. All these tasks will be started as a task with name $\langle \sim x_i, C \rangle$ will be started by a task with name $\sim x_i$. As x_i evaluates to false under T, decision d_{u_i}, where u_i is the boolean variable in literal x_i, will trigger the task with name $\sim x_i$. Synchroniser S_C will then trigger the task with name K. By analogous reasoning, if K is satisfiable, then none of the synchronisers S_C will be started.

Clearly this construction is a polynomial time transformation. Finally, to prove that the problem is in NP, it is sufficient to observe that the verification of an execution scenario (leading to the execution of a workflow object) can be done in polynomial time. Note that the translation will never result in loops and that decomposition is not used (except for the main task). □

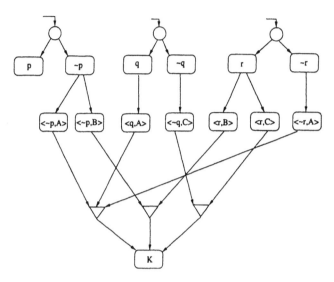

Figure 2: Workflow structure for $K = A \wedge B \wedge C = (p \vee \sim q \vee r) \wedge (p \vee \sim r) \wedge (q \vee \sim r)$

Example 3.1 The construction of the previous proof is illustrated in figure 2, where the result of the translation of the formula $K = A \wedge B \wedge C = (p \vee \sim q \vee r) \wedge (p \vee \sim r) \wedge (q \vee \sim r)$ to a workflow structure is presented. □

A *state* of a workflow structure may be defined as a multiset of its workflow objects. If a workflow object occurs n times in the multiset, n instances are active. The formal semantics of a workflow structure might be defined as its set of associated states and possible transitions between these states (see also section 4.3). The initial state then corresponds to the multiset containing the inital items of the main task exactly once. A state is *terminal* if it solely consists of terminating decisions and tasks without output triggers. As infinite workflow specifications are not desirable, it is imperative to be able to detect them statically.

Definition 3.2

The termination problem is to determine whether a workflow structure can reach a terminal state. □

Unfortunately, any algorithm solving the termination problem will require at least an exponential amount of storage space.

Theorem 3.2 The termination problem is DSPACE(exp)-hard.

Proof:

By a reduction of the reachability problem for Ordinary Petri Nets to the termination problem. In [JLL77] it is proven that the reachability problem is DSPACE(exp)-hard. Ordinary Petri Nets are Petri Nets where the multiplicity of any place is limited to be less than or equal to one. In [Pet81] it is shown that the reachability problem for Ordinary Petri Nets can be reduced to the reachability problem for Petri Nets.

The reachability problem has as input an Ordinary Petri Net $\mathcal{P}$ and markings μ and μ' of $\mathcal{P}$. A marking assigns a finite number of tokens to each place. The question is whether marking μ' can be reached from marking μ (see e.g. [Pet81]).

An Ordinary Petri Net is a four tuple $\langle P, T, I, O \rangle$, where P is a set of places, T is a set of transitions, $I : T \to \wp(P)$ is the input function, a mapping from transitions to sets of places, and $O : T \to \wp(P)$ is the output function, also a mapping from transitions to sets of places.

Let $\mathcal{P} = \langle P, T, I, O \rangle$ be an Ordinary Petri Net and μ and μ' markings of $\mathcal{P}$. The corresponding workflow structure $\mathcal{W}_{\mathcal{P}(\mu,\mu')}$ has a task T_p for each place p and a synchroniser S_t for each transition t. If p is a place with exactly one arrow to a certain transition t, then there is a corresponding trigger between T_p and S_t. If p is a place with more output arrows, this means that there is a choice between these transitions. Hence, a decision D_p is introduced and a trigger from T_p to D_p as well as for each arrow from p to a transition t, a trigger from D_p to S_t. Finally, each arrow from a transition t to a place p results in a trigger from S_t to T_p.

The initial marking μ determines the initial items of the workflow structure $\mathcal{W}_{\mathcal{P}(\mu,\mu')}$. For each place p with n tokens in marking μ ($n > 0$), we create n synchronisers, without input triggers, but with exactly one output trigger to task T_p. All such synchronisers are initial item of $\mathcal{W}_{\mathcal{P}(\mu,\mu')}$. Note that because of the fact that the trigger relation Trig is a set, we cannot create a single synchroniser for p with n arrows to task T_p.

Marking μ' is reachable from marking μ iff a state containing each task T_p exactly $\mu'(p)$ times (and no other workflow objects) is reachable in $\mathcal{W}_{\mathcal{P}(\mu,\mu')}$. □

Remark 3.1

In the previous proof it is necessary to use Ordinary Petri Nets instead of unrestricted Petri Nets as this would require the trigger relation Trig to be a multiset. In unrestricted Petri Nets there may be several arrows from a place to the same transition, or several arrows from a transition to the same place. This latter situation is not problematic in terms of the current definition of workflow structures, as it can be simulated by a "misuse" of the synchronizer: if a workflow object v should activate n instances of a workflow object w, then n intermediate synchronisers with one input trigger from v and an output trigger to w capture this behaviour. The former situation, however, cannot be captured. It would correspond to a situation where a synchroniser would have to await completion of a certain number of instantiations of the same workflow object. In the context of capacities (discussed later on in this section) it might be desirable to adapt the definition of workflow structures and to allow Trig to be a multiset. □

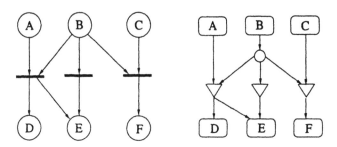

Figure 3: Translating Petri Nets to Workflow Structures

Example 3.2 In figure 3 an example of a Petri Net and its corresponding Workflow Stucture is shown. □

Definition 3.3
A workflow structure is safe if and only if from every reachable state a terminal state can be reached. □

Corollary 3.1 Determining safeness is a DSPACE(exp)-hard problem.

As capacities may play an important role in workflows, it may be important to know how many active copies of a workflow object may come into existence at a certain point of time. For example, the execution of a certain workflow object may be the responsibility of a certain department with only n members. If case of more than n invocations of that workflow object, the department is overloaded.

Definition 3.4
A workflow object w is n-bounded if and only if in every reachable state w does not occur more than n times. □

Theorem 3.3 Determining if a workflow object w is n-bounded is a DSPACE(poly)-complete problem.

Proof:
Follows immediately from the translation of Ordinary Petri Nets to Workflow Structures and the fact that determining n-boundedness in a Petri Net is DSPACE(poly)-complete (see e.g. [JLL77]). The reader is reminded of the inclusion NTIME(poly) ⊆ DSPACE(poly). □

Often it is desirable to determine whether two specifications are equivalent, i.e. whether they express the same workflow. This might be relevant e.g. in the context of execution optimization.

Formally, two workflow specifications are equivalent iff they can generate exactly the same set of traces. A trace corresponds to a list of atomic actions (see section 2.2) in an order as performed in a complete execution of a workflow specification. Atomic actions correspond to basic functionality in a workflow structure. For a formal definition of a trace refer to [HN93].

Theorem 3.4 The equivalence problem for workflow structures is undecidable.

Proof:

For context-free grammars G_1 and G_2 to determine whether $L(G_1) = L(G_2)$ is undecidable (see e.g. [Sal73]). Formally, a context-free grammar G is a tuple $\langle N, \Sigma, \Pi, S \rangle$, where N is a finite set of nonterminal symbols, Σ is a finite set of terminal symbols, $S \in N$ is the initial symbol and Π is a set of production rules of the form $A \rightarrow \omega$ where $A \in N$ and $\omega \in (N \cup \Sigma)^*$ (see e.g. [GJ79]).

A context-free grammar G can be translated to a workflow structure $\mathcal{W}_G$ such that $w \in L(G)$ if and only if w is a trace of $\mathcal{W}_G$. For every nonterminal t there will be a decomposition with name t, having a decision D_t as initial item. This decision is terminating iff G contains a rule of the form $t \rightarrow \varepsilon$. Let P be a production rule of the form $t \rightarrow s_1, \ldots, s_n$. For every s_i $(1 \leq i \leq n)$ there is a task T_{P_i} with name s_i in the decomposition of name t. Furthermore, there is a trigger from D_t to the task with name s_1. Hence production rule P results in a sequence of tasks in an order corresponding to the order of the nonterminals and terminals s_i in its righthand side. As P might be one of more production rules for t, decision D_t is introduced allowing a choice for P. The main task has a decision D_S as initial item (recall that S is the initial symbol of the grammar). This completes the construction of $\mathcal{W}_G$.

If $w \in L(G)$, then the corresponding trace simply follows a (!) derivation of w by choosing in each decision associated with each nonterminal the production rule chosen in that derivation. The other way around is identical. Hence, we achieved a one-to-one correspondence between context-free grammars and workflow structures.

Finally, note that this proof does not require the use of synchronisers, but makes substantial use of the fact that recursive decomposition structures are allowed.

$\square$

Corollary 3.2 Detecting whether a workflow specification is more generic than another workflow specification is undecidable.

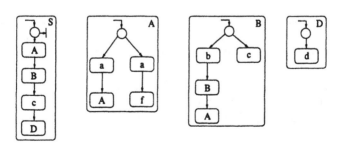

Figure 4: Workflow structure for context-free grammar G

Example 3.3 In figure 4, the workflow structure $\mathcal{W}_G$ for a context-free grammar G

is given. This grammar is defined by the following production rules:

$$
\begin{array}{llll}
S & \rightarrow & ABcD & \qquad S \rightarrow \varepsilon \\
A & \rightarrow & aA & \qquad A \rightarrow af \\
B & \rightarrow & bBA & \qquad B \rightarrow c \\
D & \rightarrow & d
\end{array}
$$

□

Theorem 3.4 implies that we have a situation similar to query optimization. Equivalence of first order queries for example is not decidable, hence focus is on the application of equivalence-preserving transformations. For workflow specifications, also desirable transformations could be defined, supporting the "optimization" of their execution.

4   Termination in Restricted Workflow Structures

In this section termination in Restricted Workflow Structures is studied and it is shown that safeness can be verified in polynomial time.

4.1   Restriction of Workflow Structures

When studying the proofs of the previous section it becomes clear that the expressive power of workflow structures is to a large extent due to the concept of synchroniser. Unrestricted use of this construct causes the non-polynomial complexity of termination verification.

On the other hand, obviously, disallowing all forms of synchronisation leads to an undesired loss of expressive power. Hence, it is necessary to focus on a more controlled form of synchronisation. This controlled form should guarantee that determining *local* correctness of synchronisation is sufficient for *global* correctness.

In workflow structures without synchronisers it is still possible to express some forms of synchronisation. One may refer to this form of synchronisation as *synchronisation through decomposition*: workflow objects after a decomposed task may only start if all execution paths in that task have terminated.

Another source of complexity is the fact that so far decomposition structures are allowed to be cyclic. This is heavily used in the proof of the undecidability of determining equivalence of workflow specifications. Hence, in Restricted Workflow Structures cyclic decomposition is not allowed.

Formally, Restricted Workflow Structures are workflow structures without synchronisers and without cyclic decomposition structures. The former requirement simply translates to $\mathcal{S} = \varnothing$ in terms of the syntax presented in section 2.2. To formally capture the latter requirement a relation Super $\subseteq \mathcal{V} \times \mathcal{V}$ has to be defined which defines decomposition relations between decomposition *names*:

$$
x\mathsf{Super}y \equiv \exists_{t \in \mathcal{T}} [\mathsf{Name}(t) = y \wedge \mathsf{Sup}(x) = y]
$$

The requirement that decomposition structures should be acyclic can now be formally stated by requiring that the reflexive transitive closure of this relation is asymmetric:

$$
x\mathsf{Super}^*y \Rightarrow \neg y\mathsf{Super}^*x
$$

4.2 Termination in Restricted Workflow Structures

Having defined a restriction of workflow structures it is important to find a computationally tractable rule that guarantees safeness, i.e. each execution scenario will lead to succesful termination. To provide some intuition, in figure 5 some workflow structures with termination problems are shown. The right most workflow structure represents a trivial example of deadlock: a "decision" with no outgoing triggers. The other two workflow structures are examples of livelocks: tasks are to be performed continuously, there is no execution path leading to termination.

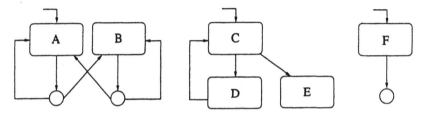

Figure 5: Livelock and deadlock in workflow structures

The solution starts with the observation that as decomposition is acylic, it is sufficient to look at each decomposition individually. In the rest, we therefore focus on a single supertask s and its decomposition. Sets such as $\mathcal{X}, \mathcal{T}, \mathcal{D}$ etc. are from now on restricted to this decomposition.

A workflow object may be considered *terminating* if and only if after its execution it is possible to terminate (in zero or more steps). For non-terminating decisions this means that at least one of the possible subsequent workflow objects is terminating. For tasks this means that all subsequent workflow objects have to be terminating as well (as they will all be started in parallel).

Formally, the notion of a terminating workflow object can be captured by the unary predicate Term, which is defined via the following set of derivation rules:

[T1] $d \in \mathcal{D}_t \vdash \text{Term}(d)$

[T2] $d \in \mathcal{D} \wedge d\text{Trige} \wedge \text{Term}(e) \vdash \text{Term}(d)$

[T3] $t \in \mathcal{T} \wedge \forall_{x \in \mathcal{X}} [\text{Term}(x)] \vdash \text{Term}(t)$

As will be shown in section 4.3.3, supertask s will always terminate succesfully if and only if every workflow object in its decomposition satisfies the predicate Term. Before these proofs can be given, however, it is necessary to define a formal semantics for Restricted Workflow Structures.

4.3 Semantics of Restricted Workflow Structures

Restricted Workflow Structures are workflow structures without synchronisers or cyclic decomposition structures. As the Process Algebra translation presented in [HN93] would be an overkill for the safeness proofs to be presented, we will assign a simple trace semantics to Restricted Workflow Structures. The basic observation is that each workflow structure state is completely determined by the workflow objects and their respective number of active instances. Formally, such a state can be seen as a multiset on $\mathcal{X}$.

4.3.1 Multisets

In this section the notation used for multisets and some definitions as far as they are needed in the rest of this paper are briefly introduced.

Multisets differ from ordinary sets in that a multiset may contain an element more than once. A multiset can be denoted by an enumeration of its elements, e.g. $\{\!\{a, a, a, b, c, c\}\!\}$. If X is a multiset, then $\#(a, X)$ denotes the number of occurrences of a in X. The membership operator for multisets takes the occurrence frequency of elements in a multiset into account: $a \in^n X \Leftrightarrow \#(a, X) = n$. In the remainder of this paper, $a \in X$ is used as a shorthand for $\#(a, X) > 0$.

Bag comprehension is the bag-theoretic equivalent of set comprehension. Let $C(a, n)$ be a predicate such that for each a exactly one n exists, such that $C(a, n)$. A multiset can then be denoted by means of the bag comprehension schema: $\{\!\{a\!\uparrow^n \mid C(a, n)\}\!\}$. This set is an intensional denotation of the multiset X that is determined by: $C(a, n) \Leftrightarrow a \in^n X$. The set of all *finite* multisets over a domain $\mathcal{X}$ is denoted as $\mathcal{M}(\mathcal{X})$.

4.3.2 Trace Semantics for Workflow Structures

The semantics of a workflow structure is the set of possible traces, i.e. possible action sequences. These traces can be captured by the introduction of a one step transition relation between states. This transition relation $\longrightarrow$ is a subset of $\mathcal{M}(\mathcal{X}) \times \mathcal{M}(\mathcal{X}) \times (\mathcal{A} \cup \{\varepsilon\})$, where $\mathcal{A}$ is the set of all task names of tasks occurring in the decomposition of supertask s (such names correspond to atomic actions in this context, even though they may have an associated decomposition), and ε represents the empty string. If $X \xrightarrow{a} Y$, then state X may change to state Y by performing a task with name a or by performing a decision in which case no action is performed and $a = \varepsilon$. Formally this one step transition relation may be defined by the following set of derivation rules:

[D1] $\quad C \in \mathcal{M}(\mathcal{X}) \wedge d \in \mathcal{D}_t \cap C \vdash C \xrightarrow{\varepsilon} C \setminus \{d\}$

The above rule states that executing a terminating decision may lead to the removal of that decision from the state. The following rule states that executing a decision (either terminating or not) may lead to the replacement of that decision in the state by one of its successors.

[D2] $\quad C \in \mathcal{M}(\mathcal{X}) \wedge d \in \mathcal{D} \cap C \wedge d\,\mathsf{Trig}\,e \vdash C \xrightarrow{\varepsilon} \{e\} \cup C \setminus \{d\}$

Execution of a task leads to its replacement by its successor workflow objects:

[D3] $\quad C \in \mathcal{M}(\mathcal{X}) \wedge t \in \mathcal{T} \cap C \vdash C \xrightarrow{\mathsf{Name}(t)} \{\!\{x\!\uparrow^1 \mid t\,\mathsf{Trig}\,x\}\!\} \cup C \setminus \{\!\{t\}\!\}$

The reflexive transitive closure of $\longrightarrow$ is $\longrightarrow^*$. Now we can define reachability of states. Formally, a state $m \in \mathcal{M}(\mathcal{X})$ is reachable, notation $\mathsf{reach}(m)$, if and only if it is reachable from the set of initial items by performing some sequence σ of actions:

$$\exists_{\sigma \in \mathcal{A}^*} \left[\{ x \uparrow^1 \mid \mathsf{Init}(x) = \mathsf{Name}(s) \} \xrightarrow{\sigma}{}^* m \right]$$

The semantics of supertask s is the set of all possible traces leading to termination, i.e. the set of $\sigma \in \mathcal{A}^*$ such that:

$$\{ x \uparrow^1 \mid \mathsf{Init}(x) = \mathsf{Name}(s) \} \xrightarrow{\sigma}{}^* \varnothing$$

As traces as such do not play an important role in the context of this paper, the notation $C \longrightarrow^* C'$ will be used as an abbreviation for $\exists_{\sigma \in \mathcal{A}^*} \left[C \xrightarrow{\sigma}{}^* C' \right]$.

4.3.3 Proving Correctness

In this section it is proved that the condition $\forall_{x \in \mathcal{X}} [\mathsf{Term}(x)]$ is a *necessary* and *sufficient* condition for guaranteeing safeness. Although this might seem rather trivial at first, the proofs are not. The reason for this is the fact that although workflow objects might be terminating, their execution might increase the number of workflow objects in the state. The sufficiency proof deals with this problem by defining a partial order on states and showing that for each state there is a monotonously decreasing series of states with as final state the empty state. This proof technique might be of interest for other conceptual workflow specification considerations.

Theorem 4.1 (*Suffiency*) $\forall_{x \in \mathcal{X}} [\mathsf{Term}(x)] \Rightarrow \forall_{Y \in \mathcal{M}(\mathcal{X})} [Y \longrightarrow^* \varnothing]$

Proof:
Assume $\forall_{x \in \mathcal{X}} [\mathsf{Term}(x)]$. A partial order $\prec$ on $\mathcal{X}$ can be defined as follows: $x \prec y$ if and only if the number of derivation steps needed to prove that $\mathsf{Term}(x)$ is less than the number of derivation steps needed for $\mathsf{Term}(y)$. From this partial order on workflow objects a partial order $\prec$ on states can be derived:

$$\alpha \prec \beta \text{ iff } \#(x, \alpha) > \#(x, \beta) \Rightarrow \exists_{y \succ x} [\#(y, \alpha) < \#(y, \beta)]$$

Informally one may think of this definition as: $\alpha \prec \beta$ if and only if α is closer to termination than β.

Now suppose $Y \in \mathcal{M}(\mathcal{X})$. If $Y = \varnothing$, then we are ready as $\varnothing \longrightarrow^* \varnothing$. Hence assume $Y \neq \varnothing$. We prove that we can find a $Z_0 \in \mathcal{M}(\mathcal{X})$ such that $Z_0 \prec Y$ and $Y \longrightarrow^* Z_0$. As there can only be finitely many Z_i such that $Y \succ Z_0 \succ Z_1 \succ \ldots \succ Z_m \succ \varnothing$, we have proven the result.

Let $w \in Y$ be a maximal element in Y. The following three cases can be distinguished:

- If $w \in \mathcal{D}_t$ then choose $Z_0 = Y \setminus \{ w \}$. In that case $Y \longrightarrow^* Z_0$ and $Z_0 \prec Y$.

- If $w \in \mathcal{D} \setminus \mathcal{D}_t$, then choose $v \in \mathcal{X}$ such that $v \prec w$ and $w \mathsf{Trig} v$ (such a v exists!). Define $Z_0 = \{ v \} \cup Y \setminus \{ w \}$. In that case we also have $Y \longrightarrow^* Z_0$ and $Z_0 \prec Y$.

- Finally, if $w \in \mathcal{T}$, $\forall_{x \in X, w \mathsf{Trig}x} [x \prec w]$.
  Hence by defining $Z_0 = \{x \uparrow^1 \mid w \mathsf{Trig}x\} \cup Y \setminus \{w\}$ again $Y \longrightarrow^* Z_0$ and $Z_0 \prec Y$.

$\square$

Note that the above theorem is a bit stronger than we actually need. It states that from *every* possible state, not only the reachable ones, the empty state can be reached.

The following theorem states that if not every workflow object in a decomposition is terminating, the workflow specification is not safe.

Theorem 4.2 (*Necessity*) $\exists_{x \in X} [\neg \mathsf{Term}(x)] \Rightarrow \exists_{Y \in \mathcal{M}(X), \mathsf{reach}(Y)} [\neg(Y \longrightarrow^* \varnothing)]$

Proof:
  By proving that if $Z \longrightarrow^* Y$:

$$\exists_{z \in Z} [\neg \mathsf{Term}(z)] \Rightarrow \exists_{y \in Y} [\neg \mathsf{Term}(y)],$$

which, informally speaking, captures the fact that it is not possible to get rid of nonterminating workflow objects in a state.

Assume $Z \longrightarrow^* Y$ and $z \in Z$ such that $\neg \mathsf{Term}(z)$. The following cases can now be distinguished:

1. $z \in \mathcal{D} \setminus \mathcal{D}_t$, in which case $\forall_{x \in X, z \mathsf{Trig}x} [\neg \mathsf{Term}(x)]$.

2. $z \in \mathcal{T}$, in which case $\exists_{x \in X, z \mathsf{Trig}x} [\neg \mathsf{Term}(x)]$. Executing z will then lead to the addition of such a workflow object x to Y.

Note that it is essential for this proof that the non-terminating workflow object is reachable from one of the initial items. $\square$

5 Conclusions

In this paper verification problems in workflow specifications were addressed. Focus was on control aspects only. Even then, however, it turns out that many interesting questions are not tractable. These may serve as "facts of life" for workflow specialists and may prevent fruitless searches for efficiency. A restriction of the synchronisation concept and decomposition structures has been proposed that allows for termination verification in polynomial time.

References

[ASSR93] P. Attie, P. Singh, A. Sheth, and M. Rusinkiewicz. Specifying and Enforcing Intertask Dependencies. In R. Agrawal, S. Baker, and D. Bell, editors, *Proceedings of the 19th VLDB Conference*, pages 134–145, Dublin, Ireland, August 1993.

[BGS93]   Y. Breibart, D. Georgakopoulos, and H. Schek. Merging Application-centric and
           Data-centric Approaches to Support Transaction-oriented Multi-system Work-
           flows. *SIGMOD Record*, 22(3):23–30, September 1993.

[Bot89]   P.W.G. Bots. *An Environment to Support Problem Solving.* PhD thesis, Delft
           University of Technology, Delft, The Netherlands, 1989.

[BW90]   J.C.M. Baeten and W.P. Weijland. *Process Algebra.* Cambridge University
           Press, Cambridge, United Kingdom, 1990.

[CCPP95]   F. Casati, S. Ceri, B. Pernici, and G. Pozzi. Conceptual Modeling of Workflows.
           In M.P. Papazoglou, editor, *Proceedings of the OOER'95, 14th International
           Object-Oriented and Entity-Relationship Modelling Conference*, volume 1021 of
           Lecture Notes in Computer Science, pages 341–354. Springer-Verlag, December
           1995.

[FKB95]   A. Forst, E. Kuhn, and O. Bukhres. General Purpose Workflow Languages.
           Distributed and Parallel Databases, 3(2):187–218, April 1995.

[GHS95]   D. Georgakopoulos, M. Hornick, and A. Sheth. An Overview of Workflow Man-
           agement: From Process Modelling to Workflow Automation Infrastructure. *Dis-
           tributed and Parallel Databases*, 3(2):119–153, April 1995.

[GJ79]   M.R. Garey and D.S. Johnson. *Computers and Intractability: A Guide to NP-
           Completeness.* W.H. Freeman and Company, San Francisco, California, 1979.

[HN93]   A.H.M. ter Hofstede and E.R. Nieuwland. Task structure semantics through
           process algebra. *Software Engineering Journal*, 8(1):14–20, January 1993.

[JLL77]   N.D. Jones, L.H. Landweber, and Y.E. Lien. Complexity of Some Problems in
           Petri Nets. *Theoretical Computer Science*, 4:277–299, 1977.

[KS95]   N. Krishnakumar and A. Sheth. Managing Heterogenous Multi-system Tasks
           to Support Enterprise-wide Operations. *Distributed and Parallel Databases*,
           3(2):155–186, April 1995.

[MSKW96]   J.A. Miller, A. Sheth, K.J. Kochut, and X. Wang. CORBA-Based Run-Time
           Architectures for Workflow Management Systems. *Journal of Database Man-
           agement*, 7(1):16–27, 1996.

[Pet81]   J.L. Peterson. *Petri Net Theory and the Modelling of Systems.* Prentice-Hall,
           Englewoods Cliffs, New Jersey, 1981.

[RS94]   M. Rusinkiewicz and A. Sheth. Specification and execution of transactional
           workflows. In W. Kim, editor, *Modern Database Systems: The Object Model,
           Interoperability, and Beyond.* ACM Press, Cambridge, Massachusetts, 1994.

[Sal73]   A. Salomaa. *Formal Languages.* ACM Monograph Series. Academic Press, New
           York, New York, 1973.

[WHO92]   G.M. Wijers, A.H.M. ter Hofstede, and N.E. van Oosterom. Representation
           of Information Modelling Knowledge. In V.-P. Tahvanainen and K. Lyytinen,
           editors, *Next Generation CASE Tools*, volume 3 of *Studies in Computer and
           Communication Systems*, pages 167–223. IOS Press, 1992.

Process Knowledge Modeling

Pierre Maret, Jean-Marie Pinon

LISI, INSA-LYON
Bât 502, F-69621 Villeurbanne Cedex - France.

Abstract. Knowledge is connected to a subject (a theory, a lesson) but Process Knowledge is connected to an object and to its production process. This leads to the need for a specific approach to the actual use of process knowledge models while carrying out processes. Models may then be constructed to guide, support and provide advice or instructions to users.

1 Introduction

The need for lean management and production and for concurrent engineering is a major concern in enterprises and organizations world-wide. They go hand in hand with an ever increasing demand for integrated computer-aided solutions (cf. office automation and computer-integrated manufacturing). Both a thorough understanding of and sufficient computer-support for business processes are considered necessary to meet current managerial challenges [36]. The terms "business process engineering" and "workflow management" indicate the trend towards corresponding concepts from the business administration and computer science fields. The more concurrent, lean, and thereby cooperative an organization, the less flow-oriented and hierarchical are the processes, and the less transform-type are the individual tasks (e.g. "take input from I, apply activity A and forward the result via output O"). Process knowledge becomes a critical value and important productivity factor. Process knowledge engineering is a problem domain which differs significantly from knowledge and expert systems based on "facts and rules". Moreover process knowledge modeling differs from process modeling because it emphasises the knowledge acquired by people while carrying out processes (their experience, their « way of working »). On the other hand, process knowledge is centered on the process description.

The importance of process knowledge for organizations today is recognized and the lack of means for the modeling and for computer-supported application of this knowledge cannot be stressed enough. An application domain which is particularly concerned with the understanding and optimization of business processes - which is a highly intellectual and creative activity - was selected : business consultancy. Based on the modeling of process knowledge applied to this domain, our aim is to adapt computer-support during the application of this knowledge. A review of relevant software tools used in the consulting business [4, 7, 11, 13, 22] reveals a key problem associated with the modeling of and computer-support for process knowledge, applied in domains such as consultancy : processes are so individual and "artistic" that a single, consistent, widely applicable (and thereby sufficiently detailed) model cannot be found [20, 24, 30]. The aim of this paper is to provide a flexible and open-ended approach for process knowledge modeling.

Firstly, modeling principles are described. Secondly, the process knowledge meta-model at the heart of this paper is described. Thirdly, an illustration/evaluation of this approach is given. Finally, a process knowledge support system which implements the meta-model based approach is described and illustrated. Two important points, however need to be made :

1. *Computer-support for human process execution* was favored over autonomous intelligent support. In this way the intellectual properties emerging from sophistica-ted processes e.g. those arising in business consultancy, are given a high priority.

2. Knowledge is connected to a subject (a theory, a lesson), as opposed to *process knowledge* which is connected to an *object* and to its *production processes*. This implies that process knowledge must be considered (formalized and used) while carrying out these production tasks. It cannot be disconnected from the activity.

2   Modeling Principles

2.1   Systemic Approach for Process Knowledge

A systemic analysis consists in describing a system as sub-systems and interactions. This approach has been depicted by Winograd [39] using the human body as a metaphor : a systemic analysis considers the body as composed of interconnected systems (blood circulation, respiration, etc.) and describes organs as parts of each system. Notice that the term "systemic" is also used to characterize an interrogative and open analysis, as opposed to a normative one. Process knowledge consists in methodological knowledge, that is to say, in generic models that one (he/she is generally called an Expert) has mastered while carrying out an activity in a specific domain [26, 28]. A systemic analysis leads to a description of process knowledge in business consultancy in terms of three components : Process Models, Cognitive Models and Document Structures.

Process models address the dynamic aspects of experts' tasks : methodological steps, associated actions, inputs, outputs, etc. *Cognitive models* address the knowledge and reasoning of experts : mental models, mental reference marks and cognitive plans. *Document structures* address the information lay out given by experts (documents as a means of communication and/or as a legal object, etc.). Document structures may be connected to steps and actions as well as reasoning models.

Each of these three components is considered as a system and is represented on a plane (Fig. 1). Following from this, experts' process knowledge will be taken as belonging to these three planes and as inter-planes references. Note that other dimensions (i.e. new planes) may be added to this open-ended framework. This is a consequence of the systemic approach we have chosen.

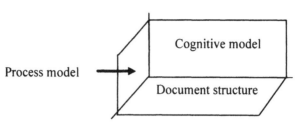

Fig. 1. The three components of process knowledge.

2.2 The Need of Specific Models

Process knowledge is connected to an object and to its production task. Consequently, a process knowledge model is practical if use can be make of it during a task, meaning it can be put into practice while carrying out the task. Therefore modeling process knowledge consists of two steps : formalizing and then supplying tools. The aim is to propose a general model which enables the design of tools to help users in the (re-)use of process knowledge. These tools consist in support and guide systems. Existing approaches to the modeling activity emphasize different aspects of process knowledge. Some of these models will be examined in order to estimate their capacity to capture and implement process knowledge. (These approaches will not be described in detail here because they are relatively well-known and due to limited space in this paper.)

Process models : Process modeling is a rather new research area and there is no consensus as to what constitutes a good model to represent processes [2, 30]. However, process models may be made using Petri nets [25] or using other dynamic models such as Calisto [32] or models proposed in the software development domain [2, 10, 34]. These models enable the visualization of a process, but not the actual *use* of the visualized representations while executing this process. A process model proposed by Rolland (in the field of Information system design) [30] considers representation re-use aspects by including didactic elements and explanations with the representations. Moreover, this approach takes into account the evolution of these representations and their management. This last point is particularly interesting because process knowledge must be considered as a developing and individual competence.

Cognitive models : Semantic nets have a central position in the field of cognitive models [27, 5, 1], and more generally in modeling. However, they are not capable of a generic approach (including re-use and evolution of knowledge and process knowledge representations). Frames [23], Prototype-like models [31, 12] and KADS (Knowledge Acquisition and Design Support) models [38, 14] propose *classes* and *elements* which are class instances. The re-use aspect of already developed representations consists in this two level approach providing on the one hand a model (classes) and on the other hand specific elements which are class instances.

Structured document norms : SGML (Standard Generalized Markup Language) [17] and ODA (Open Document Architecture) [16] both provide generic structures which are used in the description of specific document structures. Process knowledge concerning the document writing process benefit from these capabilities.

To sum up, this approach is similar to Rolland's, and provides a two level approach : generic model → specific elements. They provide a high representation level (meta-level) which firstly enables models to be described and managed, and secondly, enables them to be used as guidelines for specific issues. However, neither of them provides a widely applicable meta-model for the modeling of process knowledge in our domain of interest.

2.3 Object-Oriented Meta-modeling

In our approach, process knowledge (associated with an object and its production task) is represented with a model. In order to create models and to manipulate them a higher level of modeling -which is called meta-level- is needed. The meta-model is composed of meta-concepts which describe the concepts of the process knowledge models. A concept is an instance of a meta-concept, and a model is an instance of the meta-model. While carrying out an activity concerned by a process knowledge model, experts apply this model, that is, they create instances of the model concepts. In the object-oriented terminology, concepts are classes. Their instances are objects and they correspond to the experts' task data. Consequently, meta-concepts (where instances are concepts) are considered as meta-classes. A meta-class is shown as a double rectangle, a class as a simple rectangle and an objet as an oval (Fig. 2). Object-orientation provides the encapsulation feature [19]. Functions are associated with classes in order to implement actions associated with process knowledge models.

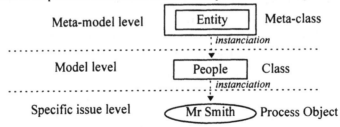

Fig. 2. Example of meta-class, class and process object.

2.4 Conceptual Framework

A three-dimensional approach is used, which combines dynamics (processes), cognitive aspects (knowledge) and documents (data structures), combining the individual strengths of the concepts found in each of these domains. Meta-model and model are clearly distinguished, supporting the customization of process knowledge to "classes" of process and domains, and also to particular issues in a second, instanciation-like step. Re-use and "individualization" of concepts is thus emphasized.

3 Process Knowledge Meta-model

3.1 Introduction

The purpose of this section is to focus on a detailed description of the meta-model for, and concept of, modeling process knowledge. As mentioned in the preceding section, this meta-model aims at computer-aid for human-centered processes and is founded on two further key approaches :

✓ The three-dimensional approach :

Dynamic	↔	Cognition	↔	Information structures
(processes)		(knowledge/reasoning)		(documents/data)

✓ The three-layer approach :

Meta-model	→	Model	→	Instanciation
		(individual concept)		(particular usage)

More precisely, all three dimensions of the meta-model will be based on the extended entity-relationship concept [8, 35], and the object-oriented approach will be used to interrelate the three levels (using meta-classes, classes, and instances). Our approach was strongly influenced by relevant issues and concepts close to some modeling approaches discussed in section 2.

3.2 Process Meta-model

The dynamics dimension is mainly founded on semantic Petri nets which is the most well known model [25]. The aim of the processes meta-model is to make it possible to undertake a description of processes (a process model). A meta-model based on the meta-concepts Stage and Action is suggested. A Stage (named a "Place" in Petri terminology) is made up of a Composed or Elementary Stage, an Elementary Stage is an Action. An Action is a coherent and non-decomposable task unit. Stages are described with a name, objectives, inputs and outputs (typed "Marks"). The input of a stage may be connected to the output of a second stage ("Transition"). A model and its concepts (Stages, Actions, Objectives, etc.) may be associated with explanatory comments and functions. These elements are intended to provide the "user" of the process model with support features (see below).

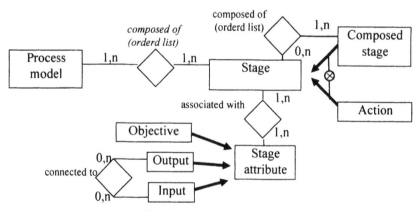

Fig. 3. Processes meta-model.

3.3 Reasoning Meta-model

The cognition dimension is mainly founded on semantic networks and hypertext [6, 9]. Indeed, the reasoning meta-model includes the meta-concepts Node, Link and Attribute (the latter may be associated to nodes or links). Similar to process models, a reasoning model and its concepts (Nodes, Links or Attributes) may be associated with help features (explanatory comments and functions).

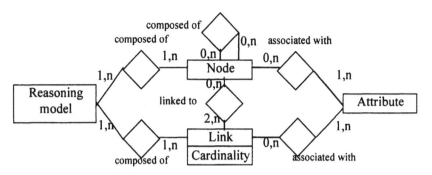

Fig. 4. Reasoning (cognitive) meta-model.

3.4 Document Meta-model

The information structure dimension is mainly founded on document norms (SGML and ODA). More specifically, the concept of document logical structure is used in order to capture process knowledge associated with document writing process. The ODA terminology was chosen because it is more adapted to a conceptual description : a "Document structure" is associated with a "Generic logical structure". "Logical objects" are either composed or elementary. The latter may either be common or parametric. "Contents" are composed of "Content portions" which are texts, graphs or images. Similar to the two previous meta-models, the document meta-model and its concepts may be associated with help features (explanatory comments and functions).

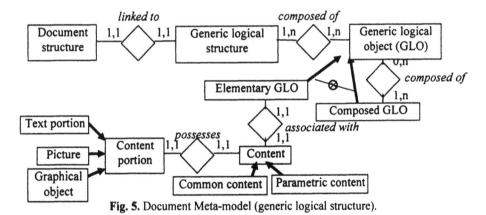

Fig. 5. Document Meta-model (generic logical structure).

3.5 Inter Plane Relations

Having considered a single dimension of our three dimensional conceptual framework, the relations which may be established in-between these planes are discussed below. Two types of inter-plane links are distinguished : reference links and similarity links. *Reference links* enable entities to be connected, as described in table 1. A reference link provides the origin entity with access to the target entity, i.e. the latter is proposed (and may be used with its support features and may be instanciated) while instanciating the origin entity. A reference link may be established for instance between a Stage of a Process and a Cognitive model. This means that this cognitive model is proposed while carrying out the Stage.

	Process Model	Stage	Stage Attribut	Reasoning Model	Node	Document Structure	GLO
Process Model							
Stage							
Stage Attribut							
Reasoning Model							
Node							
Document Structure							
GLO							

Table 1. Authorized reference links.

Similarity links are introduced to establish links between Generic Logical Objects (GLO) and Nodes when a reasoning model is associated to a document structure through a reference link. Similarity links are intended to set up "semantic bridges" in-between data included in both a reasoning model (Nodes) and a document (Logical objects). These semantic bridges make it possible to carry out document composition starting with a reasoning model, and also to establish links between documents (they are means of communication but key information is mainly "diluted") and formalized data (key information appears directly but is not detailed) (see § 4.2). This second point is interesting in view of information searching and document reuse. Moreover similar links can be established between process models, reasoning models and document structures for the same use (Fig. 6).

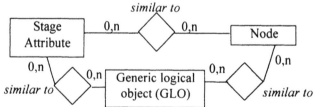

Fig. 6. Similarity links.

This section focused on the description of the process knowledge meta-model. The meta-model plays a central role because it aims at modeling process knowledge in a three dimensional approach (process, reasoning and document structure). Inter-plane relations and two types of links which may be established in-between several classes were considered : reference links and similarity links.

4 Illustration and Evaluation

The purpose in this section is to illustrate the meta-model instanciation described above. This illustration concerns studies currently carried out by consultants : enterprise diagnosis. The process knowledge described here was collected and formalized with our consultancy partner S2Com (Paris).

4.1 Illustration : Enterprise Diagnosis

Carrying out a diagnosis of an enterprise consists in examining - with a critical eye - the firm or a part of it (it may be an organizational, financial, or departmental diagnosis, etc.). The study points out the shortcomings or the strong points of the company / organization. It also points out the objectives of the organization and its resources. The latter is listed in order to be used to implement suggested changes. The illustration in this paper will specifically focus on a sub-part of our diagnosis methodology : information collection (collected through interviews) and writing questionnaires intended for interviews. Information collection is described using a reasoning model which covers preparing (which conduce to the writing of questionnaries), carrying out and exploiting interviews. This model is illustrated in Fig. 7 and can be read as follows : a study is structured in investigation axes. Each direction leads to questions which will be asked during interviews. People participate in interviews. An interview enables information to be collected. This helps conclusions to be drawn and may induce new questions. The structure of the conclusions depend on the direction the interview takes.

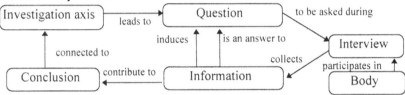

Fig. 7. Cognitive model : Study of the existing situation.

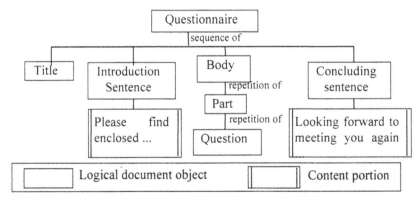

Fig. 8. Document logical structure : Questionnaire

A questionnaire is described as a logical document structure (Fig. 8). It is made up of elementary or composed logical objects. The objects Title, Introduction sentence, Concluding sentence and Question are elementary. Composed objects are Body and Part. The Body of the document is structured into Parts. Parts contain Questions. An elementary object such as an Introduction sentence may be associated with a text portion which may be partially parameterized for each questionnaire (as opposed to common to each questionnaire).

4.2 Meta-model Instanciation

Fig. 9 illustrates the instanciation of the meta-model. The meta-model level is composed of meta-concepts (meta-classes). Composition links aggregate these meta-concepts. The latter is instanciated into concepts (classes) at the lower level. The lower level represents a sub-part of the diagnosis model described before. It is composed of a reasoning model and a document structure. The reasoning model is proposed for the stage. A study of the existing situation and the document structure is proposed for writing questionnaires. The reasoning model is composed of concepts (People, Question, Interview, etc.) and links (Participate in to, To be asked during, ...). The questionnaire document structure is not detailed in the figure. It is composed of documentary objects (parts of documents).

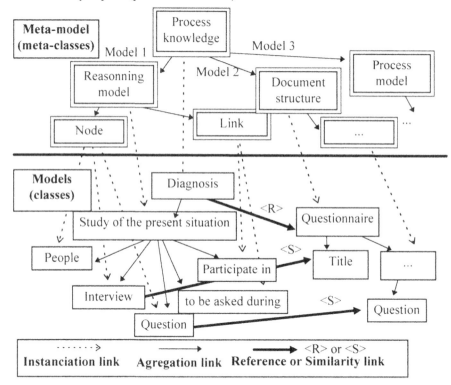

Fig. 9. Example of the meta-model instanciation.

The conception of the support tool based on the developed model is associated with the meta-model instanciation. Then, functions are associated with classes and their role is to operate on class instances. These functions are either generic or specific to a given task. Specific functions cannot appear in the meta-model because of their task-dependent nature. However, generic functions are associated with meta-classes and can easily be implemented into classes. They are parameterized using class names. Examples of generic functions are : Select objects of a given class, select objects of a given class connected to objects of a second given class, select objects of a given class which are not connected to a second given class using a given link class, etc.

The help and support functions can be classified (generic or specific) in the four categories listed below. The following table gives some examples of functions associated with the diagnostic model. Categories of help and support functions (generic or specific) :

- *User help (help)* : Explanatory comments are connected to each class of every model. Users can consult these comments to find, for instance, the description of the use of a reasoning model or to which type of node a "question" may be connected, etc.
- *Control functions (ctrl)* : Cardinality controls are often described by authors of process knowledge models. These constraints restrain (and guide) the user of the model. Some controls may be automatically called by the system to prevent users from making mistakes. Incoherence and incompleteness due to considerable data can then be detected.
- *Views (view)* : Clarity may be hindered because of considerable data and of inter-relation links. View functions provide users with pertinent and programmed filters which help them to read and complete data.
- *Automated tasks (auto)* : We favored computer-support for human process. The tasks proposed for automation are not intellectual but mechanical tasks. Here, the aim is to take advantage of inter-plane links and generate, for instance, a document based on a reasoning model (see Fig. 10).

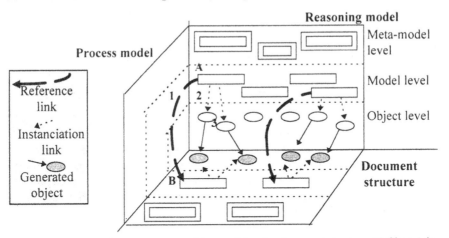

Fig. 10. Semantic bridge in-between a cognitive model and a document structure. (1.Class A is connected to Class B with a reference link. 2.While carrying out the supported task, reasoning objects are built. 3.Document objects are generated, based on reasoning objects.

In the object-oriented approach, user help tools are described as class variables. Control functions, views and automated tasks are methods attached to classes.

4.3 Evaluation

Several process knowledge models were elaborated with consultants, using the proposed meta-model as a basis. Consultants showed a great deal of interest in this because the approach aims at a self-description of their own process knowledge. The advantage is that this approach is based on a powerful and open-ended conceptual meta-model. Consultants enjoy modeling their own "tricks" and designing tools supporting these tricks. Presentations of the approach systematically leads to ideas and propositions for new problem domains. Moreover, our meta-model always fits these propositions ! Other meta-model instanciations were more especially carried out for the *Enterprise diagnosis* (previously described), for the *Writing of commercial proposals* and for the *Enterprise-wide management project*. These tree tasks were chosen for several reasons : they are currently carried out by S2Com consultants, S2Com developed specific methods for these tasks, and these tasks offer a variety of sample heterogeneous applications which illustrate the expressive power of the meta-model.

5 Process Knowledge Support System

Having decided on *computer-support* for *human process execution* led to a focus on *process knowledge support systems*, as opposed to process knowledge *illustration systems* and to process knowledge *autonomous intelligent systems* [40, 3, 15, 20].

5.1 Actors

Model developments are carried out by experts called *Application designers*, while customized process executions are carried out by experts called *Users* (Fig. 11). This terminology was proposed in the ITHACA Esprit Project [21]. Note that it only identifies different roles : an Application designers may be a User too!

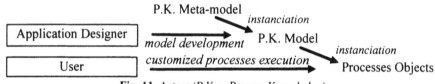

Fig. 11. Actors (P.K. = Process Knowledge)

5.2 Process Knowledge Management

Process knowledge management is carried out by Application Designers. In our approach, process knowledge is represented by classes. Process knowledge models are aggregations of classes. A process knowledge model possesses a root class which is necessarily an instance of one of the following meta-classes "Process model", "Reasoning model" and "Document structure".

As is the case with the object-oriented approach, classes may inherit other classes. Managing process knowledge models consists in building and managing an enterprise-wide process knowledge tree. Tree nodes correspond to roots of process knowledge models, and links between nodes are inheritance links (Fig. 12). This tree management in particular enables :

- Enterprise-wide models : models may be stipulated for the whole enterprise in order to share single process knowledge models and to improve communication.
- Customized models : each actor (or group of actors) may build individual models which correspond to his/her "way of doing things". Multiple versioning is then provided.

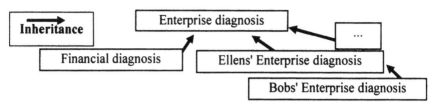

Fig. 12. Process knowledge tree

5.3 Process Knowledge Re-use

Re-use of process knowledge is the economic argument for this approach. Indeed, formalized process knowledge models can be shared and used within the organization. Non-formalized process knowledge models cannot be shared nor stored. They cannot be used during their owners' absence (sick, retired, resigned, transferred, etc.). Two levels for re-using process knowledge models are identified. The first one which is the direct consequence of the object oriented approach, appears while modeling and concerns Application Designers. The second achieves the goal of this modeling approach, and favors computing tools for human process execution. It appears during the effective process execution, i.e. the use of the process knowledge models.

Re-use during the modeling process. As a consequence of the object oriented approach and of the management facilities, a process knowledge model may inherit another process knowledge model. For instance, Bob builds his Diagnostic model starting with a model previously built by Ellen. Bob re-uses Ellen's model and adds features to it (classes, functions, etc.). Bobs' model is a specialization of Ellen's. Moreover, inheritance may be implemented on model classes (and not only on model root classes). In this case, there is no global model specialization, but a local class specialization.

Fig. 13 illustrates the two inheritance cases. On the left side, Bob's model inherits Ellen's model. This means that the model is provided with all the features of the first one (classes, functions, etc.). Both root classes are instances of the same meta-model root. On the right side of the figure, Class_j inherits class_i. The two root-classes may be instances of different meta-model roots.

Re-use During the Process Execution. The effective re-use of process knowledge appears during the carrying out of tasks (to which process knowledge is associated). The user (in fact the re-user) implements the process knowledge model while carrying out a task : he/she instanciates concepts of the model (Fig. 14) and makes calls to help and support features.

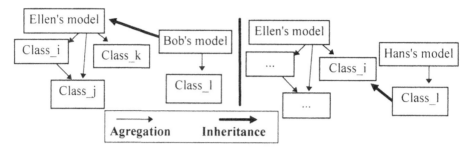

Fig. 13. Inheritance cases for process knowledge models.

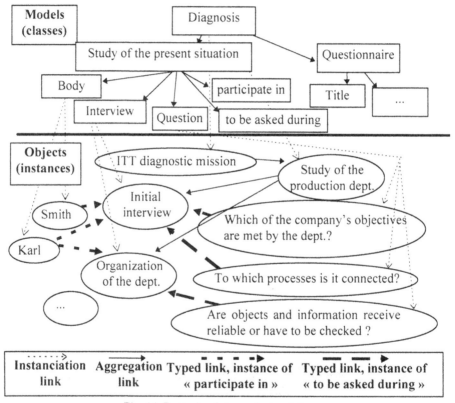

Fig. 14. Example of classes instanciation.

6 Conclusion

The subject of capitalization and re-use of experience concerns all human organizations : companies, administrative institutions, etc. In this paper it has been approached within the perspective of reusing process knowledge. The application domain chosen, business consultancy, is a non-trivial candidate for process knowledge modeling and this approach can be easily generalized to other contexts and domains. The competence of consultants is progressively built on the experience that they accumulate and it materializes into methods, reasoning models and document structures. In order to assist consultants in the re-use of their experience - while carrying out tasks - a process knowledge management approach was designed. This approach also aims at enabling a group of consultants to communicate their individual experience and then to improve productivity and quality. A comprehensive yet easy-to-manage concept was developed, based on an ER-based meta-model and object-oriented approach to the mapping onto concrete models and specific instances. In this approach, the three following relevant aspects - dynamics, cognition, and information structures - were adopted, combined, and harmonized. Our research findings have been implemented as a prototype (GraphTalk generator [29]) and applied to a variety of sample applications. The application domain chosen, consultancy, is a non-trivial candidate for process knowledge modeling.

Capitalization of process knowledge may prevent information availability problems (resignation, illness, retirement, etc.), but it may also play an important role for the purpose of setting up an enterprise-wide knowledge base. Enterprise-wide knowledge management may lead to an exchange dynamic which automatically leads to progress in an organization. The aim of this type of management is to promote individuals and to implement quality in the organization. People promotion may be carried out by creating copyrights for the re-use of process knowledge models. The concept of Process Knowledge Management System is connected with a wide range of research fields : hypermedia [33, 7], groupware [18], decision support system, active document base management [37], consultants' common sense knowledge, etc. Our aim is to work on a model to develop assistance for the functions of information collection and analysis carried out by consultants during their surveys and to connect these functions to process knowledge models.

References

1. John Anderson and G. Bower. *Human associative memory.* Winston-Wiley, Washington D.C., 1973.
2. P. Armenise, S. Bandinelli, C. Ghezzi and A. Morzenti. *A survey and assessment of software process representation formalisms.* In : Int. Journal of Software Engineering and Knowledge Engineering, 3 (3), 1993.
3. Larry Bielawski and Robert Lewand. *Intelligent systems design : integrating expert systems, hypermedia and databases.* New-York : Willey. 1991. 302p.
4. Gary Born. *Apache : a pictorial CASE tool for business process engineering.* In : Software assistance for business re-engineering. Kathy Spurr, Paul Layell, Leslie Jennison, Neil Richards. Chichester : John Wiley and Sons, 1993. pp.65-79.
5. Michael L. Brodie, John Mylopoulos and Joachim W. Schmidt. *On conceptual modelling.* New-York : Springer-Verlag, 1984. 510p.
6. V. Bush. *As we may think.* The Atlantic monthly, 176(1), July 1945, pp.101-108.
7. David Carlson, Sudha Ram. *Hyperintelligence : the next frontier.* In : Communication of the ACM. vol.33, n.3. March 1990, pp.311-321.
8. P. P. Chen. *The entity-relationship model. Toward a unified view of data.* ACM Trans. Database Syst. V.1, N.1 (March 1976), pp.9-36.

9. J. Conklin. *Hypertext: An introduction and survey.* IEEE Computer, September 1987, Vol.2, N.9, pp.17-41.

10. Bill Curtis, Marc I. Kellner and Jim Over. *Process Modeling.* In : Communication of the ACM. Sept 1992, V.35, N.9, pp.75-90.

11. Laura DeYoung. *Hypertext challenges in auditing domain.* In : Hypertext'89 proceedings, November 1989. pp169-180.

12. Scott E. Fahlman. *NETL : a system for representing and using real-world knowledge.* MIT press, Cambridge, MA, 1979.

13. Faramarz Farhoodi. *Caddie : an advanced tool for organisational design and process modelling.* In : Software assistance for business re-engineering. Kathy Spurr, Paul Layell, Leslie Jennison, Neil Richards. Chichester : John Wiley and Sons, 1993. pp.119-135.

14. Franck R. Hickman and al. *Analysis for knowledge-based systems, A practical guide to the KADS methodology.* New-York : Ellis Horwood, 1989. 190p.

15. Koichi Hori. *A system for aiding creative concept formation.* In : IEEE Transaction on systems and cybernetics. Vol.24, N.6, June 1994, p.882-894.

16. ISO. *Information Processing - Text and office systems - Standard Generalized Markup Language* (SGML), ISO 8879, 1986, 155p.

17. ISO. *Information Processing - Text and office systems - Office Document Architecture* (ODA) and Interchange format. ISO 8613, 1989, Parts 1-8.

18. S. Khoshasfian, A. Brad Baker, R. Abnous and K. Shepherd. *Intelligent offices.* New-York : Willey, 1991. 424p.

19. Tim Korson and John D. McGregor. *Understanding object-oriented : a unified paradigm.* In : Communication of the ACM Sept 90, Vol33, N.9, pp40-60.

20. Pierre Maret. Process knowledge modeling and re-use. PhD Thesis (in French). National Institute of Applied Sciences (INSA). October 1995. 227p.

21. V. deMey, O. Nierstrasz. *The ITHACA application development environment.* In : Visual objects, Tsichritzis (ed.) : Genève University, 1993. pp.265.278.

22. Michael Mills and Clive Mabey. *Automating business process re-engineering with the Business Design Facility.* In : Software assistance for business re-engineering. Kathy Spurr, Paul Layell, Leslie Jennison, Neil Richards. Chichester : John Wiley and Sons, 1993. pp.153-176.

23. M. Minsky. *A framework for representing knowledge.* In : P. Winston Ed. The psychology of computer vision, NYC Mc Graw Hill, 1975.

24. Chris Moss. *The development environment for business process re-engineering.* In : Software assistance for business re-engineering. Kathy Spurr, Paul Layell, Leslie Jennison, Neil Richards. Chichester : Wiley and Sons, 1993. pp.137-147.

25. C. A. Petri, *Kommunikation mit Automaten,* Schriften des Rheinisch. Westfalischen Institutes für Instrumentelle Mathematik, Universität Bonn, 1962.

26. J. Piaget. *Understanding causality.* New-York : Norton. 1974.

27. Ross Quillian. *Semantic memory.* In : Semantic information processing (Minsky Ed.). MIT Press, Cambridge, MA. 1968.

28. Arkalgud Ramaprasad. *Cognitive process as a basis for MIS and DSS design.* In : Management Science. V.33, N.2, February 1987, pp.139-148.

29. Rank Xerox France. *GraphTalk, Metamodeling.* Reference manual and Programming Interface, December 1993. 670p.

30. Colette Rolland, C. Souveyet and M. Moreno M. *An approach for defining ways-of-working.* In : Information Systems. Vol.20, N.4, pp337-359. 1995.

31. E. Rosch. *Cognitive representation of semantic categories.* Journal of experimental psychology: general. N.104, pp.192-233.

32. Arvind Sathi, Mark S. Fox and Michael Greenberg. *Representation of activity knowledge for project management.* In : IEEE Transactions on pattern analysis and machine intelligence. V.7, N.5, September 1985. pp531-552.

33. Patricia Search. *Computer graphics : changing the language of visual com.* In : Journal of the society for technical com., vol.40, n.4, Nov 1993, pp.629-637.

34. D. B. Simmons, N. C. Ellis and T. D. Escamilla. *Manager associate.* In : IEEE Transaction on knowledge and data engi.. V.5, N.3, June 1993, pp.426-438.

35. J. M. Smith and D.C.P. Smith. *Database abstraction : aggregation and generalization.* ACM Trans. Database Syst. V.2, N.2 (1977). pp.105-133.

36. Kathy Spurr, Paul Layell, Leslie Jennison, Neil Richards. *Software assistance for business re-engineering.* Chichester : Wiley and Sons. 1993. 224p.

37. Jason T. L. Wang and Peter A. Ng. *Texpros : an intelligent document processing system.* In : International Journal of Software Engineering and Knowledge Engineering. V.2, N.2, 1992. pp.171-196.

38. Bob Wielinga, Walter Van de Velde, Guus Schreiber and Hans Akkermans. *Towards a unification of knowledge modelling approaches.* 1993 : Simmons (eds.), Spring Verlag.

39. Terry Winograd. Langage as a cognitive process. Vol.1 Syntax. Addison Wesley. 1983.

40. L. Young. *Knowledge-based systems for idea processing support.* In : Data Base Fall 1990, pp.27-33.

The Conceptual Database Design Optimizer CoDO – Concepts, Implementation, Application

Martin Steeg

Magdeburger Straße 22*, 63110 Rodgau-Niederroden (Germany)

msteeg@t-online.de

Abstract. Traditional database design does not consider operational behavior in detail. In this way, tuning is a frequent requirement after conceptual, logical and physical design has been finished. The intension of tuning is to make database transactions run more quickly, which often results in redesigning and/or denormalizing internal data schemata. This, however, can become a crucial part of database life cycles whenever internal views are not represented externally anymore– and vice versa. This document introduces a data modeling and behavior specification technique that allows to observe the database schema for inconsistencies and probable bottlenecks already in the phase of conceptual design. The conceptual schema is here used to (a) derive internal database representations, (b) compute on the internal representation behavior and performance properties of transactions, and (c) gain aspects for more advantageous conceptual schema design, in order to omit these problems. The target is to develope a conceptual database schema that derives an efficient database application, such that logical/physical tuning measures of after work phases can be farreaching avoided. A prototype conceptual database optimizer (CoDO) which has been developed in this research will be presented.

1 Introduction

Traditional database design is based on waterfall approaches. The designer starts with requirement analysis, designs the conceptual schema and translates it to the logical schema. In this way, traditional data-driven approaches to information system design do not consider operational behavior. Most often, operational behavior is just then looked at when the database schema is implemented with the help of a chosen database management system (DBMS), the database is filled with a large amount of data, and, transactions are running and their response time behavior is inappropriate. Then, logical and physical database tuning actions are applied. But, normally these do not adapt the conceptual representation.

So, this traditional approach is not sufficient. The reason for internal schema tuning is that possible derivations for the implementation schema and transactions are not acquired and not prototyped during first phases. But, *most important transactions are often known in advance of system implementation and*

---

*This work has been carried out supported by DFG Bal185/1; Th465/10.

should be specified at an early stage [10]. So, type associations and integrity constraints of the conceptual schema already imply later transformation decisions such that complex or critical transactions of the database implementation can be identified. In this way, also critical parts of the conceptual schema can be detected, analysed, and improved. Examples for critical parts are on-delete-cascade rules which, under certain circumstances, empty the whole database, triggering actions which do not terminate or generate different results depending on the order of invoked actions [1], or certain update procedures which generate database states far away from the desired result [16, 17]. Sometimes, hand-made procedures are used for such purposes of integrity-enforcement too. But, using and maintaining them many times is more critical than using facilities provided by the DBMS. E.g., table, page or record locks cause suspension of applications and unsynchronized transactions can damage production databases.

This document introduces a data model such that conceptual and implementation concepts can be mapped to, and database behavior can be specified in terms like on-delete-cascade rules or insertion and retention options as well. Cardinality constraints of the conceptual schema and behavior specifications together make it possible to apply rigid transformation techniques to the conceptual schema. Then, the derived internal representation's operational fitness is used to reflect bottlenecks to the conceptual schema and external view. In this way, databases can already be optimized at the time of conceptual design. The conceptual database optimizer, CoDO, which was developed in this research uses an extensible repository of database design rules which serve for database schema transformation, transaction extensions, and schema tuning as well.

Related Work. *Conceptual schema transaction support* is covered by [14] who presuppose that structures of the Entity-Relationship schema are mapped to analogous structures of the implementation. *Su* [20] introduces *data profiles,* which relate assumed population aspects, such as numbers of tuples, to transaction frequencies. The data profile approach is also used by *van Bommel* [3, 4] who applies a *fitness function* to determine goodness properties for the schema. However, the term *conceptual schema tuning,* as it is used in [4, 5, 11], focusses rather on transforming the conceptual schema (*NIAM* schema) to a representation which is closer to the internal database implementation. Conceptual schema transactions and conceptual schema tuning, in this context, have a different meaning. Here, it focusses on improving the conceptual data schema. This work has profitted by the author's experience using and improving commercial databases running under *Informix, Ingres* and *Oracle,* and, by literature on database tuning ([18]), principles and backgroud of database implementations, and the effort and effect of different storage organizations influencing the maintenance cost ([12, 23]).

The paper is organized as follows. Section 2 illustrates database tuning by a sample entity-relationship schema and its relational database representation. Section 3 introduces the Entity-Relationship and Behavior Model (ERBM) that is used for the conceptual representation, and the mappings in form of logical/internal schema as well. Section 4 presents the model for database transaction and transaction cost evaluation. The Entity-Relationship and Behavior Model is used together with the evaluation model to determine transactions' consistency and performance. These properties are then used to improve the conceptual schema with the help of the database design rule repository EC^2A [19] and the generic cost model (Section 5). Section 6 presents an application scenario of the Cottbus cOnceptual Database Optimizer (CoDO), and Section 7 gives the conclusion.

2 Conceptual Schema Design and Tuning

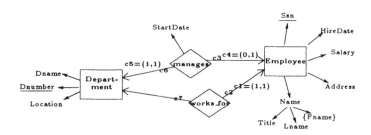

Fig. 1. Example Conceptual Schema (HERM+ data model, see Section 3.1).

We consider now a typical conceptual schema implementation. The Entity-Relationship schema in Fig. 1 shows an Employee-Department schema with asscociations *works_for* and *manages*. (For illustration purposes, the constraints/references are labeled here: c1 for the cardinanilty constraint (*works_for,Employee*), c2 for the reference from *works_for* to *Employee*, and so on.) If we group the structures associated with the (1,1) cardinalities– basis are the constraints labeled (c1,c2) and (c5,c6) which specify 1:1 associations –then we get a schema with {(Employee,works_for),(Department,manages)}). This schema can be used for a relational database implementation. So, let us take a look at the following SQL code, where table *Emp* and table *Dept* correspond to structures (Employee,works_for) and structures (Department,manages), respectively.

```
(1)
CREATE TABLE Dept
( dnumber    INTEGER PRIMARY KEY,
  dname      VARCHAR(20) NOT NULL,
  location   VARCHAR(20),
  manages    NUMBER(9) NOT NULL,
  startDate  DATE
) ;


CREATE TABLE Emp
( ssn        NUMBER(9) PRIMARY KEY,
  title      CHAR(8),
  fname      VARCHAR(30) NOT NULL,
  lname      CHAR(15) NOT NULL,
  hiredate   DATE
    CHECK (hiredate >= SYSDATE),
  salary     NUMBER(10,2)
    CHECK (salary > 5000),
  address    VARCHAR(25),
  worksfor   INTEGER NOT NULL
    CONSTRAINT emp_dept REFERENCES Dept
) ;

ALTER TABLE Dept ADD CONSTRAINT dept_mgr
  FOREIGN KEY (manages) REFERENCES Emp ;
```

```
(2a)
ALTER TABLE Emp MODIFY worksfor NULL ;

(2b)
ALTER TABLE Emp DISABLE CONSTRAINT emp_dept ;

(2c)
ALTER TABLE Emp DROP CONSTRAINT emp_dept ;

CREATE TRIGGER emp_dept
  AFTER INSERT OR UPDATE OF worksfor ON Emp
  FOR EACH ROW
  WHEN ( NOT new.worksfor IN
                (SELECT dnumber FROM Dept) )
BEGIN
  INSERT INTO Dept
    (dnumber,dname,location,manages)
  VALUES ( new.worksfor,
           concat(new.lname,"'s Dept"),
           concat(new.worksfor,"' Loc"),
           new.ssn ) ;
END ;
```

The following can be obtained from the SQL-implementation:

- Paragraph (1) shows how the database schema is realized when relating strictly to the demands of the conceptual schema (Fig. 1). One can easily recognize that this way a tuple can neither be inserted into *Dept* nor be inserted into *Emp*.

- Paragraph (2) shows how the database schema can be repaired. The alter statement of (2a) drops *Emp.worksfor*'s NOT NULL constraint. Alternatively, (2b) can be used to disable the referential constraint *emp_dept*. It can be re-enabled after the Department managers and Departments have been inserted successfully. Paragraph (2c) shows how the referential constraint *emp_dept* is substituted by a trigger. The trigger generates automatically the Department as soon as an Employee *emp* is inserted where *emp.worksfor* doesn't already exist in *Dept.dnumber*.

```
(3a)
ALTER TABLE Emp
  ADD CONSTRAINT emp_dept_del
    FOREIGN KEY (worksfor)
    REFERENCES Dept ON DELETE CASCADE ;

(3b)
CREATE TRIGGER emp_1mgr
  AFTER INSERT OR UPDATE OF manages ON Dept
FOR EACH ROW
  WHEN ( (SELECT count(*) FROM Dept
              WHERE manages = new.manages) > 1)
  BEGIN
    raise_application_error( -20477,
     'A Department Manager must manage
        at most (exactly) one Department !' ) ;
  END;

(3c)
DROP TRIGGER emp_dept ;

ALTER TABLE Dept
    REMOVE ( manages, startDate ) ;
```

```
(3c, continued)
ALTER TABLE Emp ADD startDate DATE ;

CREATE TRIGGER emp_dept
  AFTER INSERT OR DELETE
      OR UPDATE OF worksfor,startDate ON Emp
  BEGIN
    IF (SELECT worksfor,count(*) FROM Emp
          WHERE startDate IS NOT NULL
          GROUP BY worksfor HAVING count(*)<>1)
    THEN
      raise_application_error( -20478,
       'Violated Constraint:
        Each Department must have exactly one
        Manager in the Employee Relation !' ) ;
    END IF ;
  END ;

CREATE VIEW Department AS
  SELECT
    Dept.*,Emp.worksfor manager,Emp.startDate
    FROM Dept,Emp
    WHERE Dept.dnumber=Emp.worksfor
      AND Emp.startDate IS NOT NULL ;
```

- Paragraph (3) continues on (1) and the changes of (2c). (3a) adds a constraint that causes automatic delete of Employees whose Department has been deleted. (3b) adds a trigger that ensures that the inserted or updated Employee who is Department manager does really manage only one Department (constraint c4 in Fig. 1). Paragraph (3c) shows how the table schemata of *Dept* and *Emp* are restructured. The *manages* attribute is removed from the *Dept* table and the attribute *startDate* is moved as an optional one to the *Emp* table. The view *Department* substitutes the old *Dept* table. The integrity maintenance w.r.t. Department managers is then controlled by the new trigger *emp_dept* which ensures that the first Employee who is inserted to work for the new Department must be the manager (i.e., *Emp.startDate* must be NOT NULL).
- The later SQL schema is not represented anymore by the conceptual schema of Fig. 1. Further, the actions (2c) and (3c) gently presuppose that the Department manager must work for the same Department, which is not represented by the conceptual schema.

In accordance to the database schema resulting from (1), (2c) and (3c), the conceptual schema should be modified such that it is easier to find a good implementation schema. On basis of the given schema which is represented by the SQL-code in paragraph (1), we must additionally generate (remove) Employee (Department) items on insert (delete) of Department (Employee). Under these circumstances, the 'transaction cost' of *insert into/delete from Employee*, *insert into/delete from works_for*, *insert into/delete from Department*, and *insert into/delete from manages* can be assumed 'high'. This is caused by the required/generated 'co-transactions', also in case of partial user controlled integrity maintenance– for reason of problem (1). These may result in operation cycles, especially on deletes. To remedy this drawback let us consider the following tuning rule for conceptual schemata, which is taken from [19]:

```
When high complexity(delete(r1,?))
 And high complexity(delete(r2,?)):
  IF exists r3 and r4: (dcycle(r1,r3,r2,r4)
         or dcycle(r1,r4,r2,r3))
      and compatible(r3,r4)
   THEN group(r3,r4) FI;
```

I.e., if the delete complexity has to be optimized for the current schema and this complexity results mainly from a 'delete-cycle', then the relationship (the non-entity) structures in this cycle are inspected. If the relationships are 'compatible in structure' then they can be grouped to one relationship.

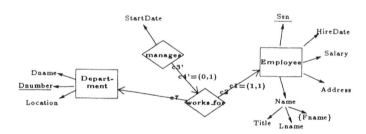

Fig. 2. Modified Concpetual Schema.

The relationships *manages* and *works_for* are compatible such that they can be grouped to one relationship– in case of the physical/internal view. The conceptual database optimizer must therefore group the relationship structures to one relationship. This results in a new relationship with an optional (nullable) attribute *startDate*. Subsequently, it must try to regenerate the old relationship structures from the new relationship. In our case, this results in the extraction of *manages(startDate)* from the grouped relationship (works_for,manages) such that the optimized conceptual schema looks like presented in Fig. 2.

To preserve the semantics of schema 1, we need additionally to add the following constraint to the new schema:

card(*Department*,
$$manages_{works\_for_{Employee}})=(1,1)$$

I.e., each Department number (*works_for*) in the *Emp* table must have exactly one tuple for which *startDate* is NOT NULL. In the following, we refer to this constraint as c5'– as the modified constraint c5 (of Fig. 1). Such new constraints must be (are) generated automatically by a (the) conceptual database optimizer (and are visualized to the database designer).

The optimized conceptual schema (Fig. 2) and the adapted constraints c3', c4', and c5' correspond to the implemented database schema that has been generated by the SQL-fragments (1), (2c), and (3c). The referential constraint– or in other words, the component structure Department of relationship *manages* –c6 completely disappears from the conceptual schema. It is not hard to see, that:

1. The new schema provides a consistent and efficient implementation (new tuples can always be inserted into Department), and more important:
2. The new schema is modeling the discourse completely. (The Employee who manages the Department usually also works for the same Department!)

But, unfortunately a restructured data schema cannot be taken automatically, but must be discussed with the conceptual database designer. However, the conceptual database optimizer should support the designer with proposals how it can be modeled in a better way, especially whenever obvious bottlenecks/untidynesses of the conceptual schema are recognized.

3   The Entity-Relationship and Behavior Model

The conceptual data model of this work bases on the Higher-order Entity-Relationship Model (HERM) of Thalheim [21] and extends the HERM+ model of [22]. We give now an overview on the HERM+ concepts and outline then the additional features of the Entity-Relationship and Behavior Model (ERBM).

3.1   The Higher-order Entity-Relationship Model HERM+

The Higher-order Entity Relationship Model HERM+ models structures and integrity constraints in a nearly exhaustive way– also w.r.t. object-oriented design issues. In HERM+, the following are considered as structures:

Attributes are identified by a name and are either of usual flat type like *string, numeric, int, float, date, bool* or of complex type like *record, set, list*.

Entities consist of a name, a non-empty set of attributes A, and a non-empty set of key-attributes K that must be a subset of A, $K \subseteq A$.

Relationships consist of a name, a set of attributes A, a set of component structures R (referenced structures, parent structures)– which are *Entity, Relationship, Cluster*, respectively –, and a non-empty set of key-attributes K that must be a subset of the union of A and the key-attributes of the component structures R. References are indicated in the graphical representation by an arrow from the child structure (subtype) to the parent structure (supertype, component structure). The reference to a component structure can also be nullable *(NULL, WITH NULL)*. A relationship is said *order-1* if all component structures are entities (entities can be looked at as order-0 relationships), otherwise the order must be greater than the order of all component structures, respectively.

Clusters consist of an at least two-elementary set of *Entities* and *Relationships*. The semantics of a cluster $C = \{s_1, ..., s_n\}$ is that each element of the occurence set is either s_1 or ... or s_n. I.e., the cluster C forms a union type of the $s_1, ..., s_n$.

Attribute, Entity, Relationship, and Cluster are considered as *structure*, respectively. The following surveys on the HERM+ definable constraints:

Cardinality Constraints (CC) are defined as participation constraints, i.e. **card**$(s_1, s_2)=(m, n)$ with structures s_1, s_2 expresses that each member of the occurence set $s_2{}^t$ has at least m and at most n related objects in $s_1{}^t$. E.g., **card**$(manages, Employee)=(0, 1)$ specifies that an Employee manages at least 0 (none) and at most 1 Department, such that a Department manager (represented by the relationship *manages*) manages exactly one Department.

Functional, Inclusion, and Exclusion Dependencies (FD,ID,ED) are specified in the usual way as known from the relational data model(s).

Key Dependencies (KD), as special case of Functional Dependencies, are already attached to the structure definitions of Entity and Relationship.

Path Dependencies state a more general kind of the above dependency types (CC,FD,ID,ED). The generalisation is that the objects of the dependency (left-hand-side and/or right-hand-side) do not only state a single structure, like Entity or Relationship, but can be a *join-path* over several structures.

For a detailed formal description the interested reader is directed to [22].

3.2 The Entity-Relationship and Behavior Model (ERBM)

The Entity-Relationship and Behavior Model (ERBM) enriches the HERM+ data model for behavior properties and behavior specifications.

Behavior Properties allow the conceptual designer to informally specify for the transaction behavior of the running database:

1. *RESTRICT*. Rollback of the transaction whenever a data inconsistency appears.

2. *CASCADE*. Invoking *repair actions* at appearance of data inconsistencies. (E.g., missing or deleted items of the parent structure.)

3. *SET NULL*. If the item of a parent structure for which still child items exist is deleted (or updated), then the corresponding child references are set to null (if nullable).

4. *SET DEFAULT*. On insert of some child item use a default as reference to the occurence set of the parent structure. If the item of a parent structure is deleted (or updated) for which still child items exist, then set the corresponding child references to the default.

Behavior Specifications are allowed with the help of user-defined database functions and IF-THEN-ELSE statements, such that transactions can also be specified in a programmatical way.

Moreover, we have *default behavior rules* which are compiled into CoDO, and, in the user's specification frame, *general rules* which are identified by a 'General' section, and *special rules* for special integrity constraints ('Special' section):

```
General:
  On insert restrict;
  On delete cascade;
  On update parent
   IF nullable(child) THEN set null
                      ELSE set default FI;
  On update child cascade;
```

```
Special:
  On insert("manages",m)
   IF Not (m.Employee in "Employee")
    THEN insert("Employee",s) FI;
  For Reference "manages" TO "Employee":
   On delete restrict;
```

3.3 Additional Features and Implementation of the ERBM

The Entity-Relationship and Behavior Model (ERBM) has some additional features in compare to the HERM+. These are:

1. Attributes can have the following type: *char(l)*, *varchar(l)* where $l = -1$ indicates infinitary (var)char fields– like the datatypes *long varchar* or *long raw* of Oracle [13] –, *smallint, integer, smallfloat, float, date, time, bool, binary,* and, *record, set, bag, list, vector,* and *array* as nested types. In addition, attributes can also be referential attributes (e.g. foreign-keys).
2. Entities may have empty attribute sets, or non-empty attribute sets and empty key sets. CoDO's transformation algorithm adds missing identifier attributes on the internal representation, like primary keys or object-identifiers. Entities are implemented as order-0 Relationship structures.
3. Relationship references can be added behavior specifications at the time of conceptual schema design, as illustrated above. Relationships may also (transitively) reference themselves. (The rule on the relationship *order* is deleted for the internal representation.)
4. Clusters may have also Clusters as referenced structures (parent structures, component structures). As well as Relationship references, Cluster references can be accomplished with behavior specifications.
5. All constraint types can– analogously to behavior specifications of the Relationship/Cluster references –be enriched at conceptual schema design time by behavior options/specifications.

In this way, ERBM provides more freedom than HERM+. However, to guarantee correct conceptual design of the user, CoDO contains a data schema verifier which ensures that the input schema actually preserves the requirements of the HERM+ conceptual model. This is also a foundation of the restructured HERM+ schema which can be generated (output schema).

4 The Transformer and the Behavior Evaluator

4.1 Transformation Foundations of CoDO

The internal representation is defined by a new structure set and a new constraint set. For the transformed, internally generated structures we use a set of *preceder references*, that are references to the structures which the internally evaluated structures are generated from:

Definition (Preceder). Preceder describes (one of) the object(s)– structure or integrity constraint – of the conceptual/internal data schema that precedes the actual object in the current schema. E.g., if a new structure Emp is generated by grouping Employee and works_for (Fig. 1 and its relational representation, Section 2) then structures Employee and works_for are Preceders of Emp.

Actually, we do not differentiate between types for conceptual and internal structures. This implies that conceptual structures contain always an empty Preceder set. E.g., a cardinality constraint $\mathbf{card}(p_1, p_2) = (m, n)$ is specified by a term $c = CC(p_1, p_2, \{m, n\}, B, P)$ such that B is the set of Behavior options and P is the set of Preceders. In case of a conceptual schema cardinality constraint c, the P is empty, and in case of an internal schema cardinality constraint c the P is empty if and only if the constraint and its (de)referenced structures p_1, p_2 have not been changed during the transformation.

4.1.1 Attribute Transformations. In the case of transformation to hierarchical and relational schemata, structured attributes in sense of record are substituted by flat attributes. These types of DBMS do also not support nested domains, like list, set and bag. E.g., we would have to create a separate relation for the attribute "{Fname}" (Fig. 1 and 2). But for a relational or hierarchical internal schema derivation, the Conceptual Database Optimizer, in such cases, typically generates repeated or flat, but 'long' attributes. Whether CoDO generates flat attributes or repeated attributes for its internally used schema depends upon how the transformation algorithm is configured (by predefined rules, or user's transformation options).

4.1.2 Structure and Constraint Transformations. As Fig. 1 and the SQL-implementation actions of Section 2 show, there are constraints that have been dropped from the implementation schema, e.g. c1,c2,c5,c6, for reason of resolving 1:1 associations. Here, on the basis of the new schema with the grouped structures we generated also a new constraint set such that the resulting schema consists of a new structure set (Emp,Dept) and a new constraint set (i3,i4,i7), that has to be only considered by the SQL-implementation– and so, whenever determining behavior properties of the derivable implementation.

But for reasons of space we cannot present the transformation procedure at this place. We direct the reader who is interested in this procedure to [19].

4.2 Transaction Extensions and Transaction Graphs

If operations, like insert, delete and update, are specialized under integrity maintenance, e.g. *insert of the subtype manages* requires/ or triggers *insert of the supertype Employee,* this is commonly denoted as *Transaction Extension.* (Refer also to [6, 15, 17].) We use Transaction Extensions in conjunction with design and operation rules. So-called EC^2A rules (event-constraint-condition-action) [19] have been developed to use the operations to be analyzed *(events)* in connection with the *constraint set* to be maintained. This way, *condition-action* pairs can be derived directly from the data schema. Then, the condition-action pairs are used for the data schema cost analysis.

The rule model EC^2A comprises several rules for transformation actions and tuning actions, and 14 RESTRICT, 16 CASCADE, and 14 SET NULL/SET DEFAULT rules for transaction extensions. An example of an EC^2A transformation/tuning rule is already found at the end of Section 2.

Also, we use *transaction graphs* to represent the content of transactions internally. Fig. 3 shows what the Transaction Graphs (Trees) look like, and intimates how the internal transactions/ transaction costs (double lined nodes and solid, rectilinear arrows) are remapped to the transactions the conceptual database designer is looking at (dashed nodes and dashed arrows). So, according to the content of the Transaction Graphs, the following will be presented to the conceptual designer:

- Insert(Employee) comprises (only):

    Insert(Employee); that is internally Insert(Emp)
- Insert(works_for) comprises:

    Insert(works_for) which is internally Update(Emp), and
    Retrieve(Department)/Insert(Department) which are internally
    Retrieve(Dept)/Insert(Dept)

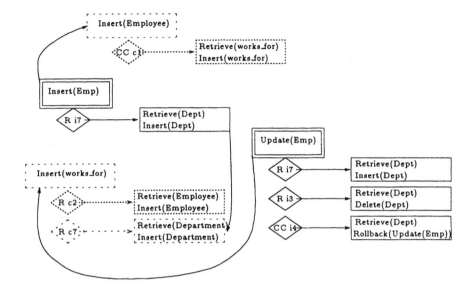

Fig. 3. Transaction Graphs mapping Conceptual and Internal Transactions– and their Costs

The Conceptual Database Optimizer has also an integrity checker which ensures that the behavior options specified by the conceptual designer are not in conflict with other behavior options, and also, not in conflict with operational behavior of the derived database system.

5 The Conceptual Database Optimizer's Generic Cost Model

In [7] an approach has been presented to compute optimal indices for relational databases. This approach uses basic operations; that are basic complexities for sub-operations necessary to perform inserts, deletes, updates or selects in a relational database. We use a similar evaluation frame for operation complexities. The Cost Model comprises Basic Operation Costs, which are used to evaluate complexities of retrieves, inserts, deletes and updates. The Basic Operation Costs are then used in Equation Systems to determine time and performance of transactions.

5.1 Basic Operation Costs

Basic Operation Costs use Cost Primitive Functions (1) and Cost Parameter Functions (2). For adaption of these functions to different storage models and to different other factors, e.g. knowledge on a certain DBMS's behavior and performance, we are applying Balancing Parameters (3). The model of the Basic Operation Costs is assembled as follows.

5.1.1 Cost Primitive Functions. Cost Primitive Functions describe costs of actions in general sense, e.g. tuple locating, fetching, storing, a.s.o. . But for reason to provide an abstract evaluation model, we do not consider costs of actual internal actions like read,write,lseek and disk management operations [23] here, such that Cost Primitive Functions state a couple of terms which are used to assemble a general framework. This general framework can be adapted according to different issues.

5.1.2 Cost Parameter Functions. The Basic Operation Costs are evaluated on the basis of a parameter function which relates to the type of physical data organization. This way, different storage organizations can be considered. Cost Parameter Functions for pointer access, Heap, Isam, sparse clustering/dense non-clustering Btrees, linear/extensible Hashing, and WiSS [8] data organization have been realized.

5.1.3 Balancing Parameters. Specific criteria for cost approximations on the basis of data manipulations are provided by a range of Balancing Parameters. These are initially set to default values and can be configured by startup files. In this way, the evaluation schema may also be adjusted according to whatever are the user's desires.

The following is a survey on the realized evaluation schema:

1. The approximation function for pointer semantics, e.g. Lists, assumes that the average cost is in general linear to the associated tuple number (or the population size). Here, we use the parameter n_p.

2. For Isam organized databases we assume the cost logarithmic with $log_{fanout}{}^N$, where N is the number of tuples (of the considered structure) and $fanout$ is the basis.

3. Btree databases perform accesses that are logarithmic according to the number of tuples and the fraction of the *blocksize* (e.g. 8192) and key-length *keylen*. In case of tuple storage, removal, modification, fetch, and secondary storage reorganization the approximation substitutes the key-length *keylen* by the record-length *reclen* of the according structure.

4. In the case of Hashing we make further assumptions, especially on some parameter function $p_{collision}()$. We assume that $p_{collision}()$ is dependent upon the chosen bucket size bc, the frequency of modification requirements fm(,) and some uniformity uf() of key data according to the (maximal) hash prefix:

$$p_{collision}(R^t) = \frac{fm(op,R^t) * uf(R^t)}{bc}$$

where fm(,) itself depends upon the operation type - e.g., on Retrieve it is 0 - and the occurence set, uf() depends on the number of tuples $uf(R^t) = n_h{}''' * tuple\#(R^t)$, and bc is set to some default bucket size.

Example:

– For a Btree organized (relational) database we assume the cost to retrieve one data item as follows:

$$C^b(retrieve_{R^t}) = p_{loc}(R^t) + p_{fet}(R) =$$
$$b_{lr} * n_b * (1 + log_{blocksize/keylen(R)}^{tuple\#(R^t)}) + b_f * reclen(R)$$

where $p_{loc}(R^t)$ is the time to locate the item and $p_{fet}(R)$ is the time to transfer the item to main memory *(fetch)*.

The *numbers of tuples* are acquired by a user interface that interactively asks for the 'Tuple number' corresponding to the structures of the HERM+ schema.

5.2 Cost Evaluation

The cost of the basic data manipulation operations, i.e. insert, delete, update, retrieve, are then simply evaluated by adding and multiplying the above terms. The cost of transactions, however, states a more severe problem. For this purpose we are using so-called Plausibilities.

Definition (Plausibility). A Plausibility $\beta_{o_1 o_2}$ specifies the probability we expect a data manipulation operation o_1 to trigger– or to pre-require –another data manipulation operation o_2.

Example. Let o_1, o_2 be data manipulation operations, $o_1 \in$ {insert, delete, update}, $o_2 \in$ {insert, delete, update, retrieve}. R_1, R_2 are the parameter types (structures) of o_1, o_2 respectively. Furthermore, R_2 is a subtype of R_1, e.g. R_2 is a relationship and R_1 is an entity referenced by R_2. Then, on basis of $\mathbf{card}(R_2, R_1) = (m, n)$ we assume:

$$\beta_{o_1 R_1 o_2 R_2} = \frac{avg(m,n) * \sqrt{m}}{\sqrt{n}} * \frac{\sqrt{tuple\#(R_1)}}{\sqrt{tuple\#(R_1)} + \sqrt{tuple\#(R_2)}}$$

In the opposite case, i.e. o_2 triggers/requires o_1, the term is inverted:

$$\beta_{o_2 R_2 o_1 R_1} = \frac{\sqrt{n+1}}{avg(m,n) * \sqrt{m+1}} * \frac{\sqrt{tuple\#(R_2)}}{\sqrt{tuple\#(R_2)} + \sqrt{tuple\#(R_1)}}$$

Further information on the Cost Evaluation is found in [19]. Especially explanations how special cases are treated in the evaluation schema are given there; e.g. usage of a cardinality constraint referencing structures from which one is transformed to an internal set-attribute.

5.3 Cost Equation Systems

The transaction graphs are used to construct equation systems. The root node (the operation that was invoked) and its first level children nodes are mapped to a cost equation. Consider the insert operation for Emp (Fig. 2 and 3). The complexity for this operation is evaluated by

$$C(insert_{Emp}) =$$
$$C^b(insert_{Emp}) + C(retrieve_{Dept}) +$$
$$\beta_{insert_{Emp} insert_{Dept}} * C(insert_{Dept})$$

The set of all cost equations is then used to construct an equation system. This equation system is solved, and the costs for the Transaction Graphs are determined and attached to the according nodes. Fig. 3 intimates how the different cost terms of the internal representation are mapped to conceptual schema transactions. For their cost determination, equations are used as well.

6 The Conceptual Database Optimizer

The application scenario of this section shows how the Conceptual Database Optimizer (CoDO) interacts with the conceptual designer and supports him in improving his data schema (and modeling the correct semantics).

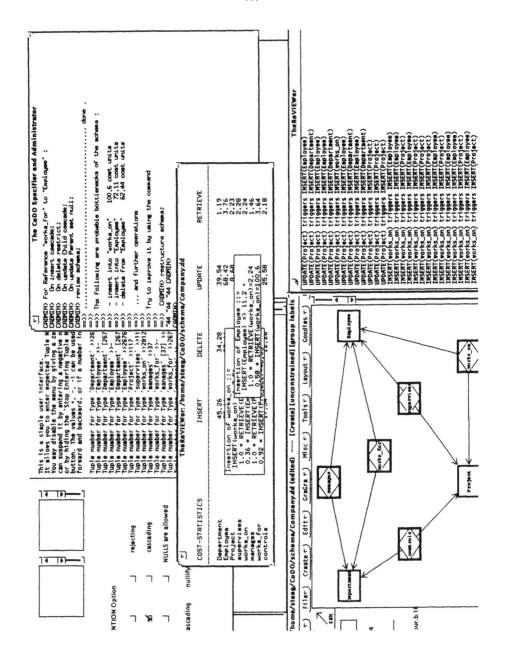

118

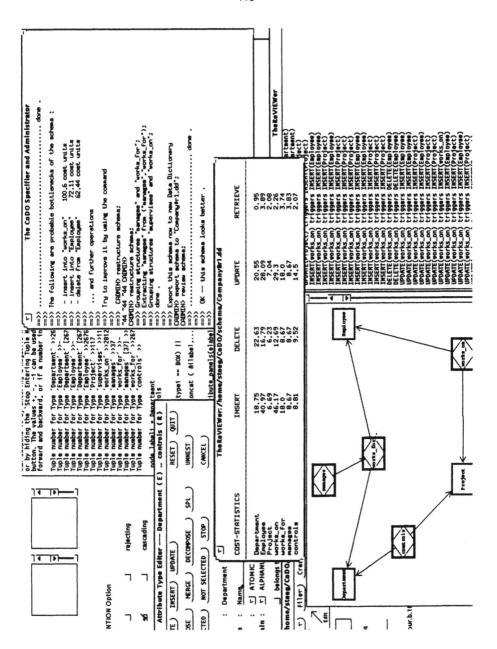

The page before the previous page shows how the given data schema (in the lower left corner) is 'reviewed' by CoDO. The CoDO Specifier and Administrator (in the upper right corner) hints the conceptual designer that the schema has possible bottlenecks. These are then observed by the database designer by popping up the transaction costs (in the middle of the screen, the 'TheReVIEWer: ...' frame). He can ascertain that, for example, *insert into Employee* triggers *insert into works_on* and reversally, *insert into works_on* also can trigger *insert into Employee* (for this schema, he defined a cardinility constraint **card**(*works_on, Employee*)=(1, 3)).

The previous page shows then how the optimized schema looks like (in the lower left corner). W.r.t. the operations which CoDO detects as 'Probable Bottlenecks' of the given schema, this schema has lower 'cost units' on the insert, delete, and update operations. This latter schema can therefore be looked at as the optimal conceptual schema for the considered discourse. But, it is clear that not all operation types can be optimized by restructuring the conceptual data schema, and also, schema equivalence (view integration, [9]) is in general undecidable and depends upon the context. Therefore, the 'optimized' schema cannot be taken automatically, but must be discussed with the conceptual database designer. In this way, the final task to decide whether to take the given or the optimized conceptual data schema always remains up to the database designer.

But, CoDO generates alternative representations for the data modeling context and helps so to improve conceptual data schemata.

7 Conclusion

The tool presented in this paper supports database design according to practical issues. Practical issues, however, are performance and consistency of database applications, and performance is not only reaction time of selects, inserts, deletes and updates, or, reaction time of database access in certain user menus, but also, easy-usability of the application. This requires, for example, non-normalizing (or denormalizing) relational database schemata, which sometimes causes problems of inconsistent or subsumption-free transactions. The Cottbus cOnceptual Database Optimizer (CoDO) considers these criteria of (internal) database design and supports the design of correct and reliable conceptual schemata which can be used for database implementation. In this way, requirements of restructuring the semantics of the database schema can be omitted in subsequent phases.

Storing the History of the Database Design and Transformation Process. The main idea of the Conceptual Database Optimizer is to preserve, store, maintain, and reuse historical aspects during the database design and transformation process. CoDO evaluates the conceptual schema on the basis of a rule-driven mechanism to support:

- Schema Transformation,
- Operational Cost Evaluation, and
- Bottleneck Detection and Visualization.

The results of CoDO's evaluation can then be used to optimize the conceptual schema in interaction with the database designer.

The Conceptual Database Optimizer CoDO is part of the Cottbus University toolbox for *Rapid Application and Database Development* (RADD) [2].

Acknowledgements. I like to thank Prof. Thalheim of Cottbus Tech University who initiated this work. I also like to thank some anonymous referees who carefully read this paper and helped to improve it.

References

1. A. Aiken, J.M. Hellerstein, and J. Widom. Static analysis techniques for predicting the behavior of active database rules. *ACM ToDS*, 20(1):3 – 41, March 1995.
2. M. Albrecht, M. Altus, E. Buchholz, A. Düsterhöft, and B. Thalheim. The rapid application and database development (RADD) workbench – A comfortable database design tool. In J. Iirari, K. Lyytinen, and M. Rossi, editors, *7th Int. Conf. on Advanced Information System Engineering, CAiSE'95*, number 932 in LNCS, Jyväskÿlä, Finland, June 14 - 16 1995.
3. P.van Bommel. Experiences with EDO: An Evolutionary Database Optimizer. In *Data & Knowledge Engineering*, 13, pages 243 – 263, 1994.
4. P.van Bommel. *Database Optimization - An Evolutionary Approach.* PhD thesis, Katholieke Universiteit Nijmegem, 1995.
5. L. Campbell. Adding a New Dimension to Flat Conceptual Modeling. In *First International Conference on Object-Role Modelling ORM-1*, July 1994.
6. S. Ceri, P. Fraternali, S. Paraboschi, and L. Tanca. Automatic Generation of Production Rules for Integrity Maintenance. *ACM ToDS*, 19(3):367 – 422, September 1994.
7. S. Choenni, H. Blanken, and T. Chang. Index selection in relational databases. In *Computing Surveys*, pages 491 – 496. IEEE, 1993.
8. H. Chou, D. DeWitt, R. Katz, and T. Klug. Design and Implementation of the Wisconsin Storage System (WiSS). In *Software Practice and Experience*, 15(10), 1985.
9. B. Convent. Unresolvable problems related to the view integration approach. In *Proc. ICDT 86*, number 243 in LNCS, pages 141 – 156, 1986.
10. R. Elmasri and S.B. Navathe. *Fundamentals of Database Systems.* Benjamin/Cummings, 1989.
11. T.A. Halpin. Conceptual schema optimization. *Australian Computer Science Communications*, 12(1):136 – 145, 1990.
12. H.F. Korth and A. Silberschatz. *Database System Concepts.* McGraw-Hill, 1991.
13. Brian Linden. *Oracle - Server SQL Reference. Release 7.2*, April 1995.
14. J.A. Pastor-Collado and A. Olivé. Supporting Transaction Design in Conceptual Modelling of Information Systems. In *LNCS 932*, 1995.
15. A. Rosenthal and D. Reiner. Tools and Transformations – Rigorous and Otherwise – for Practical Database Design. *ACM ToDS*, 19(2):167 – 211, June 1994.
16. K.-D. Schewe and B. Thalheim. Computing consistent transactions. Technical Report CS-08-92, University of Rostock, December 1992.
17. K.-D. Schewe and B. Thalheim. Achieving consistency in active databases. In S. Chakravarthy and J. Widom, editors, *Proc. RIDE-ADC*, Houston, 1994.
18. D.E. Shasha. *Database Tuning - A Principled Approach.* Prentice Hall, 1992.
19. M. Steeg. CoDO – The Cottbus Conceptual Database Optimizer – and its Extensible Rule Model EC^2A. Technical Report I - 2/1995, Cottbus Tech University, July 1995.
20. S.S. Su. Processing-Requirement Modeling and Its Application in Logical Database Design. In S.B. Yao, editor, *Principles of Database Design*, volume 1: Logical Organization, pages 151 –173, 1985.
21. B. Thalheim. The Higher-order Entity-Relationship-Model and $(DB)^2$. In *LNCS*, volume 364, pages 382 – 397. Springer, 1989.
22. B. Thalheim. *Fundamentals of Entity-Relationship Modeling.* Springer, 1994.
23. G. Wiederhold. *File Organization for Database Design.* McGraw-Hill, 1987.

ConQuer: A Conceptual Query Language

A. C. Bloesch and T. A. Halpin[1]

Asymetrix Corporation
Bellevue WA, USA
email: anthonyb@asymetrix.com; terryh@asymetrix.com
[1]on leave from Dept of Computer Science, University of Queensland

Abstract: Relational query languages such as SQL and QBE are less than ideal for end user queries since they require users to work explicitly with structures at the relational level, rather than at the conceptual level where they naturally communicate. ConQuer is a new conceptual query language that allows users to formulate queries naturally in terms of elementary relationships, and operators such as "and", "not" and "maybe", thus avoiding the need to deal explicitly with implementation details such as relational tables, null values, and outer joins. While most conceptual query languages are based on the Entity-Relationship approach, ConQuer is based on Object-Role Modeling (ORM), which exposes semantic domains as conceptual object types, thus allowing queries to be formulated in terms of paths through the information space. This paper provides an overview of the ConQuer language.

1   Introduction

It is now widely recognized that information systems are best designed first at the conceptual level, before mapping them to an implementation target such as a relational database. A conceptual schema expresses an application model in terms of concepts familiar to end users of the application, thus facilitating communication between modeler and subject matter experts when determining the schema. Once declared, a conceptual schema can be mapped in an automatic way to a variety of DBMS structures. Although use of CASE tools for conceptual modeling and mapping is widespread, very little use is currently made of tools for querying the conceptual model directly. Instead, queries are typically formulated either at the external level using forms, or at the logical level using a language such as SQL or QBE.

Form-based queries are typically very limited in expressibility, and can rapidly become obsolete as the external interface evolves. SQL queries, and to a lesser extent QBE queries, can be more expressive, but quickly become too complex for the average end user to formulate once non-trivial queries are considered. Even queries that are trivial to express in natural language (e.g. who does not drive more than one car?) can be difficult for non technical users to express in these languages. Moreover, an SQL or QBE query often needs to be changed if the relevant part of the conceptual schema or internal schema is changed, even if the conceptual version of the query still applies. Finally, commercial query optimizers for relational languages basically ignore the further semantic optimization opportunities arising from knowledge of conceptual constraints. Query languages for object-oriented DBMSs suffer the same problems, and languages for pre-relational systems are even lower-level.

For such reasons, considerable research has been undertaken to provide a conceptual query language that enables users to formulate queries directly on the conceptual schema itself. For example, the SUPER project [1] has a graphical conceptual query language based on ERC+ (a variant of Entity Relationship (ER) modeling) [14]. Essentially, users copy the relevant portions of a conceptual schema into the SUPER query editor. They may then add further conditions to the query in a first-order like language. The principal advantage of the SUPER query editor is that essentially the same graphical language is used to both model and query a database. Unfortunately, the query language would be hard to grasp, for naïve users, without significant training.

SUPER's query editor keeps the schema browser separate from the query editor. By contrast the Hybris project [16] integrates the query editor and schema browser. Hybris's approach reduces the user's cognitive load but at the cost of reducing the expressivity of the query language.

ERQL [11] is a conceptual query language for an EER (extended ER) conceptual modeling language. It differs from Super and Hybrid's query language in that it is textual. Essentially, ERQL is an SQL-like language modified to support EER. ERQL has the advantage over SQL in that relational details are hidden from the user.

Not all conceptual query languages are based on ER. ConceptBase models a deductive object database with a semantic net like modeling language Telos [13]. CBQL is a first-order like query language where users specify the attributes they wish to know and then constrain the result set with logical constraints. Like ERQL, ConceptBase's [10] query language CBQL [17] is textual. Unlike many conceptual query languages, CBQL supports the useful notion of parameterized queries. But once again, the language would be hard to grasp for naïve users.

Object-Role Modeling (ORM) is a generic term for a conceptual modeling approach which pictures the application world in terms of objects that play roles (individually or in relationships), thus avoiding the notion of attribute. It originated as a semantic modeling approach in the 1970s and has a number of closely related versions (e.g. NIAM [18], FORM [5], NORM [4] and PSM [9]). ORM facilitates detailed information modeling since it is linguistically based, is semantically rich and its notations are easily populated. An overview of ORM may be found in [6], a detailed treatment in [5] and formal discussions in [7; 8].

The use of ORM for conceptual and relational database design is becoming more popular, partly because of the spread of ORM-based CASE tools, such as Asymetrix's InfoModeler. However, as with ER, the use of ORM for conceptual queries is still in its infancy. The first ORM-based query language was RIDL [12], a hybrid language that combined both declarative and procedural aspects. Although RIDL is very powerful, its advanced features are not easy to master, and while the modeling component of RIDL was implemented in the RIDL* tool, the query component was not supported. Another ORM query language is LISA-D [9], which is based on PSM and has recently been extended to Elisa-D [15] to include temporal and evolutionary support. LISA-D is very expressive but it is technically challenging for end users, and is currently supported only as an academic prototype.

Since InfoAssistant is a commercial product, more care has been taken with its user interface than would be normal in a research tool. As well as complying with Microsoft's user interface standards, InfoAssistant provides an intuitive interface for constructing queries that has met with positive industry reviews and user feedback. Typical queries can be constructed by just clicking on objects with the mouse. User interface deficiencies in the current version have been identified and will be corrected in the next version. For example, it is planned to make queries appear more like English sentences and provide support for unlimited undo/redo.

The rest of this paper provides an overview of ConQuer (CONceptual QUERy), a new ORM conceptual query language designed for ease of use, an early version of which has been released in the InfoAssistant product from Asymetrix (see Figure 1). Section 2 explains how the language is based on ORM, and illustrates how queries are formulated and mapped to SQL. Section 3 discusses the formal semantics. Section 4 summarizes the main contributions and outlines future research.

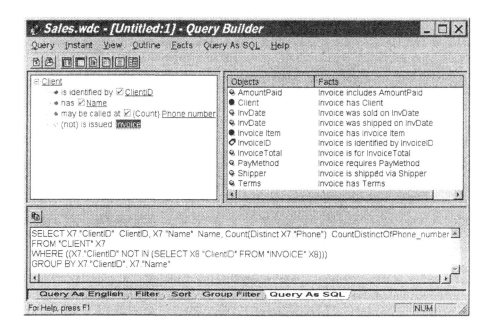

Fig. 1. Screen snapshot of InfoAssistant's query editor.

2 ORM-based Conceptual Queries

Figure 2 is a simple ORM schema. Object types are shown as named ellipses. Entity types have solid ellipses with their simple reference schemes abbreviated in parenthesis (these references are unabbreviated in queries). For example, "Employee (nr)" abbreviates "Employee is identified by EmployeeNr".

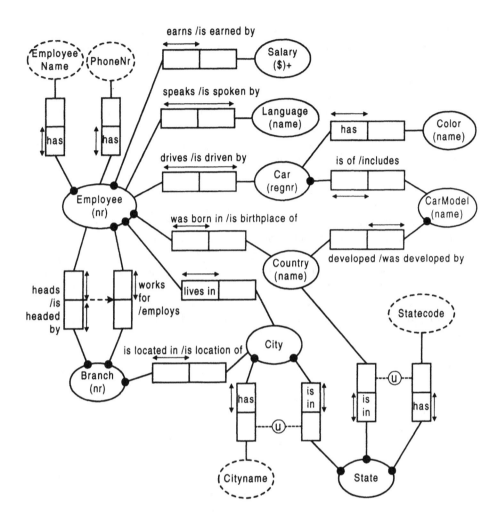

Fig. 2: An ORM conceptual schema

If an entity type has a compound reference scheme, this is shown explicitly using an external uniqueness constraint (circled "u"). For example, a state is identified by combining its country with its statecode (e.g. Washington state is in the country named "United Sates of America" and has the statecode "WA", whereas Western Australia is in the country named "Australia" and has the statecode "WA"). Value types have dotted ellipses (e.g. "Statecode"). For simplicity we assume that cities may be identified by combining their name and state (apologies to inhabitants of Stockbridge Massachusetts USA).

Predicates are shown as named role sequences, where each role is depicted as a box. In the example all the predicates are binary (two roles). In the ORM version on which ConQuer is based, predicates may have any arity (number of roles) and may be written in mixfix form. A relationship type not used for reference is a fact type. An *n*-ary relationship type has *n!* readings but only *n* are needed to guarantee access from any object type. Figure 2 shows forward and inverse readings (separated by "/") for several binaries.

An arrow-tipped bar across a role sequence depicts an internal uniqueness constraint. For example, each employee earns at most one salary, but an employee may speak many languages and vice versa. A black dot connecting a role to an object type indicates that the role is mandatory (i.e. each object in the database population of that object type must play that role). The dotted arrow from the heads predicate to the works-for predicate is a pair-subset constraint (each employee who heads a branch also works for that branch). ORM has many other kinds of constraint, but these are not germane to our discussion.

Notice that no use is made of attributes. This helps with natural verbalization, simplifies the framework, and avoids arbitrary or temporary decisions about whether some feature should be modeled as an attribute. Moreover, since ORM conceptual object types are semantic domains, they act as semantic "glue" to connect the schema. This facilitates not only strong typing but also query navigation through the information space. We give an example later. When desired, attributes (e.g. birthplace) can be introduced as derived concepts, based on roles in the underlying ORM schema.

2.1 An Informal Discussion of ConQuer

ConQuer queries may be represented as outline queries, schema trees or text. Currently the InfoAssistant tool requires ConQuer queries to be entered in outline form, and automatically generates a textual verbalization. In this paper we discuss only the outline form, including some minor changes to the current version of the tool.

On opening a model for browsing, the user is presented with an object pick list. When an object type is dragged to the query pane, another pane displays the roles played by that object in the model. The user drags over those relationships of interest. Highlighting an object type within one of these relationships causes its roles to be displayed, and the user may drag over those of interest, an so on. In this way, a user may quickly declare a query path through the information space, without any prior knowledge of the underlying data structures.

Items to be displayed are indicated with a tick "☑": these ticks may be toggled on/off as desired. The query path may be restricted in various ways by use of operators and conditions. As a simple example, consider the query: Who lives in the city in which branch 10 is located? This may be set out as the following ConQuer outline:

Q1 ☑Employee
    └── lives in City
       └── is location of Branch 10

This implicit form of the query may be expanded to reveal the reference schemes (e.g. EmployeeNr, BranchNr). Its verbalized form is: "List the employeenr of each employee who lives in the city that is location of a branch that is identified by branch nr 10". Notice how City is used as a join object type for this query. If attributes were used instead, one would typically have to formulate this is a more cumbersome way. For example, if composite attributes are allowed we might use: List Employee. employeenr where Employee.city = Branch.city and Branch.branchnr = 10. If not, we might resort to: List Employee.employeenr where Employee.cityname = Branch.cityname and Employee.statecode = Branch.statecode and Employee.country = Branch.country and Branch.branchnr = 10.

Avoidance of attributes also helps to lengthen the usable lifetime of a conceptual query. For example, suppose that after storing the previous query, we change the schema to allow an employee to live in more than one city (e.g. a contractor might live in two cities). The uniqueness constraint on Employee lives in City is now weakened, so that this fact type is now many:many. With most versions of ER, this would mean the fact can no longer be modeled as an attribute of Employee.

Moreover, suppose that we now decide to record the population of cities. In ER or OO this would require that City be remodeled as an entity type instead of as an attribute. Hence an ER or OO based query would need to be reformulated. With ORM based queries however, the original query can still be used, since changing a constraint or adding a new fact type has no impact on it. Of course, the SQL generated by the ORM query may well differ with the new schema, but the meaning of the query is unchanged.

The previous query formed a linear path. Tree-shaped queries may be formulated by use of the logical operators "and" and "or". When two or more predicates stem from the same object type occurrence, an "and" operator is implicitly assumed. For example, consider the query: List the employee number and salary of each employee who has a salary above $90000 and either speaks more than one language or drives a red car. This may be set out as Q2. Notice also the simple treatment of functions, which often prove difficult in SQL [2].

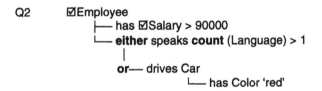

```
Q2      ☑Employee
        ├── has ☑Salary > 90000
        └── either speaks count (Language) > 1
            │
            or── drives Car
                 └── has Color 'red'
```

Unless qualified by a "not" or "maybe", predicates are interpreted in the normal, positive sense. For example, the following query asks: "Who has a phone and drives a car?"

```
Q3      ☑Employee
        ├── has PhoneNr
        └── drives Car
```

On our ORM schema it is optional for an employee to have a phone or to drive a car. To issue queries on optional roles in a relational language like SQL, we need to know where the facts are stored and to cater for null values. Neither of these needs has anything to do with conceptualizing the query. Null values and relational outer joins can prove very confusing for SQL users [3]. One of the benefits of ORM is that all its base fact types are elementary, and hence cannot have null values at all.

If we wish to exclude employees who play a given role, we add the "not" operator to that role. If we don't care whether they play a given role, we add the "maybe" operator to that role. For example, query Q4 asks "Who does not have a phone and does not drive a car?".

Q4   ☑Employee
              ├── **not** has PhoneNr
              └── **not** drives Car

and query Q5 asks: List the employee number, employee name, phone (if any) and cars (if any) of each employee.

Q5   ☑Employee
              ├── has ☑EmployeeName
              ├── **maybe** has ☑PhoneNr
              └── **maybe** drives ☑Car

As the next section shows, the SQL code generated for the these two "maybe"s differs since the underlying uniqueness constraints are different for each predicate, so the relational columns appear in different tables. Conceptually however, the user should not have to be concerned with these issues.

ConQuer is capable of far more complex queries than cited here. However in this paper we are more concerned with a clear exposition of our basic approach and its rationale rather than with providing a complete coverage of the language.

2.2 Mapping to SQL

Using the Rmap algorithm [5], our conceptual schema maps to the relational schema shown in Figure 3 (domains are omitted). Keys are underlined, using a double underline for the primary key where more than one key exists. Optional columns are shown in square brackets (as in BNF). Subset constraints (e.g. foreign key constraints) are shown as dotted arrows.

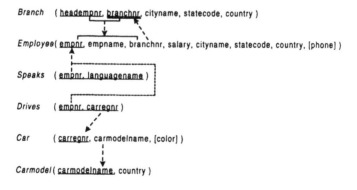

Fig. 3. The relational schema mapped from the ORM conceptual schema in Figure 2

InfoAssistant maps ConQuer queries to SQL for a variety of DBMSs, in the process performing semantic optimization where possible by accessing the constraints in the ORM schema. The SQL code for the earlier queries is shown below, S1 being the SQL for query Q1, and so on. A comparison with the ConQuer queries highlights the difference between the relational and the conceptual levels.

```
S1      select X1.empnr
        from   Employee as X1, Branch as X2
        where X1.cityname = X2.cityname and X1.statecode = X2.statecode
          and X1.country = X2.country
          and X2.branchnr = 10
```

```
S2      select X1.empnr, X1.salary
        from   Employee as X1, Drives as X2, Car as X3
        where X1.salary > 90000
          and (X1.empnr in
                    (select empnr from Speaks
                     group by empnr
                     having count(*) > 1)
              or (X1.empnr = X2.empnr and X2.carregnr = X3.carregnr
                  and color = 'red'))
```

```
S3      select X1.empnr
        from   Employee as X1, Drives as X2
        where X1.empnr = x2.empnr
          and X1.phone is not null
```

```
S4      select X1.empnr
        from   Employee as X1
        where X1.phone is null
          and X1.empnr not in
                    (select empnr from Drives)
```

```
S5      select X1.empnr, X1.empname, X1.phone, X2.carregnr
        from   Employee as X1 left outer join Drives as X2 on X1.empnr = X2.empnr
```

The mapping algorithms automatically determine the appropriate join type (e.g. inner versus outer) or subquery and grouping action by exploiting the ORM constraints. The software can also reverse-engineer an existing relational schema to an ORM schema, so that at no stage does the user have to decide how relational tables are to be related in a query.

As a simple example of semantic optimization, consider the following query: "Who works for a branch that is located in a city?". In ConQuer this is formulated as Q6:

```
Q6      ☑Employee
            └── works for Branch
                    └── is located in City
```

Using ORM mandatory role constraints, this query is automatically transformed into the simpler query "List all employees" and hence the following SQL is generated:

```
S6        select empnr from Employee
```

While the examples discussed here are simple, the benefits of the conceptual approach should now be clear. The reader interested in more complicated queries may wish to use the supplied ORM schema to formulate some harder queries first in ConQuer and then determine the corresponding SQL. It will become apparent that it is very easy to compose ConQuer queries that lead to extremely complicated SQL.

In section 2.1 we noted that ConQuer queries are minimally impacted by schema evolution. As a trivial example, suppose that originally our schema in Figure 2 required that employees drive at most one car. Query Q3 would now generate the following SQL:

```
S3'       select X1.empnr
          from   Employee as X1
          where X1.carregnr is not null
            and X1.phone is not null
```

Suppose that the schema now evolves into that of Figure 2, so that employees may drive many cars. The ConQuery query Q3 remains the same, even though the SQL generated changes from S3' to S3.

3   Formal Semantics

In this section, two alternative semantics are given for ConQuer queries: firstly a semantics based on conceptual versions of relational operators and, secondly, a semantics based on bag comprehension. The treatment is necessarily brief but it should be clear how the semantics could be completely formalized.

3.1 Conceptual Join Based Semantics

There is a certain similarity between relational tables and ORM fact types that can be capitalized on to give a relational model for ConQuer queries. In ORM, fact types such as 'Person works for Department' correspond to a *set* of tuples. In a well designed ORM model all fact types will be elementary (that is they cannot be split into simpler fact types without loss of information). However, in a well designed relational model the tables will not necessarily be elementary. Each row of a relational table corresponds to one or more facts. In general, each ORM fact type will correspond to a null free projection of certain columns in a relational table.

If we view fact types as relational tables then the *conceptual join* of two fact types in an ORM model corresponds to a relational join of the fact types (when viewed as tables). In general, a conceptual join of two fact types may or may not correspond to an actual relational join of tables in the relational schema to which the ORM schema maps. For example, if the two fact types map to the same table then an equijoin between the two fact roles will not require a relational join since, in a sense, the join has already been made. However, if two fact types map to different tables then an equijoin between the two fact roles will require a relational join. Note that if an object is compositely identified (e.g. a city may be identified by the combination of its name, state code and country) the fact roles it plays will correspond to more than one column in a table and conceptual joins involving it will correspond to relational joins over several columns.

Working from the root of a ConQuer query down, the query can be seen as a sequence of conceptual joins and conceptual operations forming a series of conceptual paths through the ORM model. Where the path passes through "and" and "or" nodes, conceptual inner equijoins are made between fact types and conceptual intersections or unions are made between the paths; where the path passes through "not" nodes the child role is conceptually subtracted from the parent role (here it is understood that the conceptual path below the "not" is evaluated first); where the path passes through "maybe" nodes conceptual left-outer equijoins are made between fact types (here also here it is understood that the conceptual path below the "maybe" is evaluated first).

Restrictions such as "Sales > 1 000 000" are placed on the population in fact roles before joins are computed. Conceptual selections (ticks) correspond to relational selections. Where an object type is compositely identified, a single conceptual selection will result in several relational selections.

There are however several complicating factors. Firstly, the population of the root object may not correspond to a single table column. If all the roles it plays are optional then the population may correspond to the union of several columns. Thus, for example, the query "What are the names of all the countries?" (see Q7) would require a conceptual union of all the fact roles that Country plays.

Q7   Country
          └── has ☑ Country Name

Secondly, there are two plausible ways of handling conditions on object types within the scope of a "maybe"—ignore them or do not ignore them. If they are not ignored then all the queries that can be expressed ignoring them can also be expressed by just deleting the unwanted conditions. Pragmatically, the SQL generation is made much easier if they are ignored; thus, on pragmatic grounds alone, in version 1.0 of InfoAssistant these conditions are ignored.

Thirdly, bag functions are not easily expressible as relational operations. So we postpone the treatment of the semantics of bag functions until the next section.

3.2 Bag Comprehension Based Semantics

Alternatively, a ConQuer query may be interpreted as specifying the contents of a bag, via bag comprehension. For example, the query 'Which cars are red?' (see Q8) would correspond to the expression:

$$\lbrack\!\lbrack\, x : \mathrm{Car} \mid \exists\, y : \mathrm{Color};\, z : \mathrm{ColorName}\, (\, x\ \mathrm{has}\ y \wedge y\ \mathrm{has\ colorname}\ z \wedge z = \text{'red'}\,)\,\rbrack\!\rbrack .$$

In general, a ConQuer query corresponds to the straightforward translation of the query into first-order logic with the ticked object types quantified over by the bag comprehension operator and the non-ticked object types by an existential quantifier. Note that conceptual nulls can never occur so there is no need to use Lukasiewicz's (or any other) three valued logic.

Q8   ☑Car
    └ has Color 'red'

Care must be taken in interpreting the "maybe" operator. Expressions of the form "maybe α", where α is some path expression, should be translated as:

$$\alpha' \vee (\neg\, \alpha \wedge x_1 = \square \wedge x_2 = \square \wedge \dots \wedge x_n = \square)$$

where α' is the translation of α (with restrictions removed); $x_1, x_2, \dots, x_n$ are the selected object types in α; and $\square$ is a blank in the result set (relationally a null).

A semantics for the bag (aggregate) functions of ConQuer can be given as follows. Construct a labeled bag expression corresponding to the ConQuer query where all expressions involving aggregate functions have been elided and object types with ticked aggregate function are treated as if they are themselves ticked.

For example, consider the query "What are the branches and total salary costs of branches with a total salary cost of more than $1 000 000?", which may be expressed in ConQuer as Q9:

Q9 ☑ Branch
    └ employs Employee
        └ earns ☑ **total**(Salary) > 1 000 000

Query Q9 would generate the following labeled bag:

$$\textbf{let } S = [\![\, x : \text{Branch}, y : \$\text{value} \mid \exists\, z : \text{Employee}; w : \text{Salary} \,(}$$

$$x \text{ employs } z \wedge z \text{ earns } w \wedge w \text{ has } \$\text{value } y \,)]\!].$$

The effect of the aggregate functions can then be expressed by a bag comprehension like:

$$[\![\, x : \text{Branch}, u : \Re \mid \langle x \rangle \in S_1 \wedge u = (\textstyle\sum_{\langle x', y\rangle \in S} y \mid x = x') \wedge u > 1\,000\,000 \,]\!]$$

where $\Re$ is the set of reals; $S_{i,\, j,\, \dots,\, k}$ is a set of tuples made up of the i'th, j'th, ..., k'th entries in each tuple of the bag S; and $(\sum_{\langle x,\, y,\, \dots,\, z\rangle \in S} \alpha \mid \rho)$ is, for each $\langle x, y, \dots, z \rangle$ in of the bag S, the sum of every α such that ρ holds.

In general, each ticked object type and ticked aggregate function will be quantified over by the bag comprehension, a conjunct will link selected object types to the corresponding elements of S, a series of conjuncts will specify the value of each aggregate function and a series of conjuncts will correspond to any conditions involving aggregate functions.

4 Conclusion

This paper has discussed ConQuer, a new conceptual query language based on ORM that enables end users to formulate queries in a natural way, without knowledge of how the information is stored in the underlying database. A basic version of ConQuer is supported in a commercial tool that reverse engineers existing relational schemas to an ORM schema, which can then be queried directly. The benefits of a conceptual, and more specifically an ORM-based approach, to queries were highlighted and a formal semantics provided.

Currently the language is undergoing major improvements to both the language architecture and the user interface, which will appear in a subsequent release. Moreover, the FORML language used for ORM modeling is being unified with ConQuer. While the current ConQuer architecture and mapping algorithms were developed by the authors, they would like to acknowledge the contributions of Erik Proper in formalizing an alternative version of the language and in suggesting the name "ConQuer".

References

1. Auddino, A., Amiel, E. & Bhargava, B. 1991 'Experiences with SUPER, a Database Visual Environment', *DEXA'91 Database and Expert System Applications*, pp.172-178
2. Date, C.J. 1996, 'Aggregate functions', Database Prog. & Design, vol. 9, no. 4, Miller Freeman, San Mateo CA, pp. 17-19.
3. Date, C.J. & Darwen, H. 1992, Relational Database: writings 1989-1991, Addison-Wesley, Reading MA, esp. Chs 17-20.
4. De Troyer, O. & Meersman, R. 1995, 'A logic framework for a semantics of object oriented data modeling', *OOER'95: Object-Oriented and Entity-Relationship Modeling*, Springer LNCS, no. 1021, pp. 238-49.
5. Halpin, T.A. 1995, Conceptual Schema and Relational Database Design, 2nd edn, Prentice-Hall, Sydney, Australia.
6. Halpin, T.A. & Orlowska, M.E. 1992, 'Fact-oriented modelling for data analysis', *Journal of Inform. Systems*, vol. 2, no. 2, pp. 1-23, Blackwell Scientific, Oxford
7. Halpin, T.A. & Proper, H.A. 1995, 'Subtyping and polymorphism in Object-Role Modeling', *Data and Knowledge Engineering*, vol. 15, Elsevier Science, pp. 251-81.
8. Halpin, T.A. & Proper, H. A. 1995, 'Database schema transformation and optimization', *OOER'95: Object-Oriented and Entity-Relationship Modeling*, Springer LNCS, no. 1021, pp. 191-203.
9. Hofstede, A.H.M. ter, Proper, H.A. & Weide, th.P. van der 1993, 'Formal definition of a conceptual language for the description and manipulation of information models', *Information Systems*, vol. 18, no. 7, pp. 489-523.
10. Jarke, M., Gallersdörfer, R., Jeusfeld, M.A., Staudt, M., Eherer, S., 1995, *ConceptBase—a Deductive Object Base for Meta Data Management*, Journal of

Intelligent Information Systems, Special Issue on Advances in Deductive Object-Oriented Databases, vol. 4, no. 2, 167-192.

11. Lawley, M. & Topor R. 1994, 'A Query Language for EER Schemas', *ADC'94 Proceedings of the 5th Australian Database Conference*, Global Publications Service, pp. 292-304.

12. Meersman, R. 1982, 'The RIDL conceptual language', Research report, Int. Centre for Information Analysis Services, Control Data Belgium, Brussels, Belgium, 1982.

13. Mylopoulos, J., Borgida, A., Jarke, M. & Koubarakis, M., 1990, *Telos: a language for representing knowledge about information systems*, ACM Transactions Information Systems vol. 8, no 4.

14. Parent, C. & Spaccapietra, S. 1989, 'About Complex Entities, Complex Objects and Object-Oriented Data Models', *Information System Concepts—An In-depth Analysis*, Falkenberg, E.D. & Lindgreen, P., Eds., North Holland, pp. 347-360

15. Proper, H.A. & Weide, Th. P. van der 1995, 'Information disclosure in evolving information systems: taking a shot at a moving target', *Data and Knowledge Engineering*, vol. 15, no. 2, pp. 135-68, Elsevier Science.

16. Rosengren, P. 1994, 'Using Visual ER Query Systems in Real World Applications', *CAiSE'94: Advanced Information Systems Engineering*, Springer LNCS, no. 811, pp. 394-405.

17. Staudt, M., Nissen, H.W., Jeusfeld, M.A. 1994, *Query by Class, Rule and Concept*. Applied Intelligence, Special Issue on Knowledge Base Management, vol. 4, no. 2, pp. 133-157

18. Wintraecken, J.J.V.R. 1990, *The NIAM Information Analysis Method: Theory and Practice*, Kluwer, Deventer, The Netherlands.

Using Structural Recursion as Query Mechanism for Data Models with References

WOLFRAM CLAUSS

Brandenburg Technical University
Department of Computer Science
PO Box 101344, D–03013 Cottbus

Abstract. Despite the fact that nearly all important data models include a concept for (explicit) references or referencial integrity, a database query language that directly supports this kind of structures has not been presented yet. This paper proposes an algebraically well-founded query technique that allows generic functional queries and updates on complex data models with references. We use structural recursion on the algebraic representation of data structures as the basic tool to achieve that goal. Before approaching the case of references, we will investigate previous solutions for data models that do not include them. The generalization of these models directly leads to this new proposal.

1 Motivation

Operational Aspects in Database Design

Operational aspects are an integral part of modern database application design. The close coupling of static and dynamic properties of regularly structured data objects suggests that database systems should offer a range of generic operators in order to support this part of the design process. This support does only rudimentarily exist, though.

The idea of nested transactions as a means to define the behavior of complex structures is well-known. Given a small set of generic operators, the programmer defines the dynamic properties of the system. This technique leaves the task to identify the relating dynamic aspects of the existing data structures entirely to the application implementor.

This paper proposes a mechanism that automatically produces the inherent operators of complex data types. These operators are still generic, offering the parametric adaptation to the specific application. This mechanism is significantly less expressive than Turing-complete languages, which are usually employed for transaction (or trigger etc.) design. Its distingushing property is the automatism and genericity.

Models with References

References are one of the most important tools for the structuring of data. In the absence of references, a hierarchy (or tree) is the only available topology for the layout of data.

The majority of successful database models includes the concept of referencing. The Entity-Relationship model [7] and each of its derivatives has explicit references, the relational data model [8] knows referential integrity (which Codd [9] claims to be a decisive part of his proposal), object-oriented models (e. g., the ODMG model [5]) have object identity, to name only a few important examples.

Some of these models carry their own query language(s). With the exception of Turing-complete programming languages in some object-oriented models, all "real" query languages in this group lack the ability to produce results including arbitrary, though schema-conform, references. There is no query language for functional updates on structures with references.

Most of the available languages are even unable to navigate along references. Expressions in relational algebra and related logical languages, for example, are totally ignorant of the existence of referential integrity constraints.

Interestingly, many data exchange formats as opposed to "real" database models do *completely* lack support of referencing. The reason for this situation is possibly that query languages that respect referencing are not available. The lack of efficient access languages for formats including references appears even worse than the lack of expressiveness resulting from omitting them. On the other hand, real database interoperability requires the exchange formats and, therefore, the query languages on top of them, to have at minimum the expressive power of the original data models. New developments at least recognize references in static structures [6, 16].

Our approach to this problem starts at the investigation of a simple but relatively powerful programming mechanism for lists and a number of similar data types. The underlying principles of this mechanism directly lead to an abstraction which is a universal query tool that does not depend on any specific data model. We are at this point able to choose an arbitrary representation of structures with references and employ the developed tool for querying.

2 A Well-Known Technique

Structural recursion is the abstraction of a very common programming technique. Recursive functions traversing tree data structures belong to this class. The usual form of processing lists in functional and logical programming languages is another example. Even the mathematical proof technique of induction is based on structural recursion.

The technique as presented here in addition intensively uses the typed λ-calculus without recursion (although we often omit the types if they are derivable). This calculus has the advantage of strict termination, which is a desirable property for database query languages. In addition, it has a clear and well-accepted semantics [12, 15].

The Insert Representation of Lists

A typical example of this technique is the recursive definition of a function computing the length of a list. The input list is given in a head-tail format (or *insert representation*, as $[.|.]$ is an operator that inserts a single element into a list).

$$\text{length}([]) = 0$$
$$\text{length}([Head|Tail]) = 1 + \text{length}(Tail)$$

It has been observed that a lot of relevant functions on lists can be defined in a very similar way.

$$\text{function}([]) = e$$
$$\text{function}([Head|Tail]) = i(Head, \text{function}(Tail))$$

We shall denote this function, *structural recursion on the insert representation of a list*, as sri-list(e, i) or, if the context permits the omissions, sr(e, i). In addition, we frequently use currying to improve readability of expressions. Our previous example now has the appearance:

$$\text{length} = \text{sr}(0, \lambda xy.1 + y)$$

The type of the polymorphic function "sr" is apparently

$$\text{sr} : S \times (T \times S \to S) \times \text{List}(T) \to S$$

where T, the type of the list elements, and S, the result type, are type parameters. The abstraction of structural recursion itself has occured in the literature on functional programming and database query languages under some pseudonyms (e. g., "fold" [18]).

This technique can be syntactically transformed to similar finite collection types, such as multisets (bags) and sets. Libkin and Wong [14] compare a number of structural recursion based query languages for sets and bags.

Further Representations

Instead of using the functions $[] : \text{List}(T)$ and $[.|.] : T \times \text{List}(T) \to \text{List}(T)$ to construct them, lists are often represented in a different way. One possibility is the *union representation*, consisting of $[] : \text{List}(T)$, $[.] : T \to \text{List}(T)$ (the unary list constructor), and $\circ : \text{List}(T) \times \text{List}(T) \to \text{List}(T)$ (list concatenation). Our standard example now looks accordingly.

$$\text{length}([]) = 0$$
$$\text{length}([x]) = 1$$
$$\text{length}(X \circ Y) = \text{length}(X) + \text{length}(Y)$$

Using the more abstract notation for structural recursion, here "sru-list" or short "sr", we consequently get

$$\text{length} = \text{sr}(0, 1, +),$$

with the polymorphic typing

$$\text{sr} : S \times (T \to S) \times (S \times S \to S) \times \text{List}(T) \to S$$

The generalization of "sru-list" to other collection types is, again, straightforward. Previous work has already suggested the implementation of structural recursion as selector function on these collection types and has shown the equivalence of insert and union representations [2, 3].

These representations are, however, not generally equivalent. For instance, although there is a union representation of binary trees, an insert form does not exist.

Another possible list representation (their number is, in fact, countably infinite) is the form of node-labeled binary trees. The corresponding notation of our example query would now be (leaving the details of the definition to the intuition of the reader):

$$\text{length} = \text{sr}(0, \lambda xyz.x + 1 + z).$$

On Uniqueness

Functions on the basis of structural recursion are not necessarily well-defined. For instance, the attempt to define the cardinality of a finite set in a similar way as the length of a list,

$$\text{card} = \text{sru-set}(0, 1, +),$$

leads to undesirable results. This problem becomes obvious in

$$1 = \text{card}(\{a\}) = \text{card}(\{a\} \cup \{a\}) \stackrel{\text{sr}}{=} \text{card}(\{a\}) + \text{card}(\{a\}) = 2.$$

The common solution is the restriction of the types that structural recursion may map onto (e. q., comprehension syntax [4] and the monoid calculus [10, 11]). Unfortunately, these approaches remove parts of the genericity and the expressive power of structural recursion. In particular, the ability to define new types and map onto them, fundamental to some contemporary (object-oriented and other) data models, is lost.

On the other hand, it indeed is possible to compute the cardinality of a set using structural recursion, as the following example shows.

```
set-to-bag = sri-set({||}, λxY.{|x|Y|})
in = λx.sri-bag(false, λx'y.if x = x' then true else y)
dupelim = sri-bag({||}, λxY.if in(x, Y) then Y else {|x|Y|})
length = sri-bag(0, λxy.1 + y)
card = set-to-bag ∘ dupelim ∘ length
```

The duplicate elimination in multisets is an equalizer of the ambiguous mapping from sets to multisets.

The next section will show that the problem of ambiguity is not at all located at the level of structural recursion. Instead, it is the semantics behind certain representations that is ambiguous.

3   Abstract Interpretation

Structural recursion is a very basic mathematical construction, as the following property suggests. Let $(\mathbf{M}, S)$ be the free many-sorted algebra over the finite signature S. Then for each sort $M \in \mathbf{M}$, the structural recursion function sr-M has a uniquely defined type and behavior.

This proposition is very important due to the fact that an abstract parametric operation as powerful as structural recursion can be derived immediately from the purely syntactic definition of a large number of frequently used data types. In other words,

structural recursion can be automatically generated for every type that is freely constructed.

Some examples of such types are records, unions, the Boolean type, natural numbers, lists, trees of fixed and variable arity, etc. The signature of our favorite example type, List(T), looks as follows.

$$[] : \text{List}(T) \qquad\qquad S\times$$
$$[.|.] : T \times \text{List}(T) \to \text{List}(T) \qquad (T \times S \to S)\times$$
$$\text{List}(T) \to S$$

The right hand side illustrates the formal derivation of the type of "sr" and suggests the generalization to other free types. The definition of the semantics has already appeared in the previous section.

Another interpretation of free types is that a context-free grammar generates the instances of the type. In this case, structural recursion is the corresponding generic attribute grammar. The idea of using attribute grammars to define some dynamic integrity constraints in databases has actually appeared much earlier than the abstract notation of structural recursion [17]. It recently has been proposed as a tool for querying (structured) text files [1]. This interpretation also makes it rather clear that the expressive power of structural recursion will suffice for most applications of database query languages.

The uniqueness problem outlined before is a consequence of the ambiguous transformation of semantic entities into syntactic objects. These ambiguities are exhibited if the parameter functions of structural recursion do not equalize the different possible representations, which is unfortunately undecidable for the general case. A solution, though it lacks the beauty of a purely syntactic technique, is to require a unique mapping between syntax and semantics. (An example is the unique representation of sets as ordered, duplicate-free lists.)

More than that, the type of structural recursion is well-defined for every many-sorted algebra, not only free ones. The behavior, although not unique for the (semantic) interpretation in some cases, is always unique for the (syntactic) representation and can be formally described based on pure syntax. Structural recursion can therefore serve as a

universal generic query language primitive

for any formally defined schema, whatever the underlying data model might be. As a consequence, the following sections on referencing just outline a special case of the general construction.

4   Local Referencing

It is an elementary fact that we cannot freely construct the instances of any sufficiently complex schema with references. The elements of a free algebra always have the form of term *trees*, while it is the distinguishing property of a schema with non-trivial references to be able to express different structures than just trees.

What we need to do to implement the concept of references is just to find a formal language (or signature) that describes all instances of the relevant schema. Then we have to give an interpretation to this formal language that assigns structures with references to term trees.

Layered Structures

The simplest case in which structures with references occur are data models with hierarchically organized schemas. If we ignore the existence of the typical cardinality constraints, most flavors of the entity-relationship model can serve as examples for this group (specifically all variants that classify relationships into layers where those of higher layers might only reference entities or relationships of lower layers).

Although a schema in these models is a tree, the data elements—whose layout defines the form of structural recursion—are not. Structural recursion in its trivial form does, therefore, not exist. It does, if we are able to find a suitable representation of the data.

As mentioned, the schema has the form of a tree. Legal elements of such a schema have a similar, but topologically different appearance. Basically, every node of the schema tree consists of a collection of data records that have multiple references along the original schema references to records of the corresponding schema node. The layering ensures that the result is a partially ordered set or, in other words, a collection of forward-chained trees.

The following representation implements such structures. Thus, it proves the appropriateness of structural recursion as a data access tool for this kind of models.

A Schema with Local References

Consider the following signature of a parametric data type $RFCT(T)$ of "multiple recursive forward-chained trees."

> leaf : $T \to RFCT(T)$
> join : $RFCT(T) \times RFCT(T) \to RFCT(T)$
> var : $Var \to RFCT(T)$
> let : $Var \times RFCT(T) \times RFCT(T) \to RFCT(T)$

As noted before, we have to assign the (static) semantics to each possible instance of the new type. The partial signature {leaf, join} defines the data type of binary, leaf-labeled trees of base type T. In addition, the type $RFCT(T)$ incorporates a constructor "var" that builds a leaf from an unspecified base type Var (free variables), interpreted as distinguishable leaves whose value is unknown, and a constructor "let", the binding of variables.

Note that the semantics of an expression without "let" is always a leaf-labeled binary tree. In particular, every such structure has a distinguished node, its root. The semantics of a data expression $let(x, y, z)$ is the graph that consists of the graphs y and z where each edge leading to a node labeled x is replaced by a node leading to the "root" of graph y. The "root" of this graph is recursively defined as the root of z.

A more common and, thus, rememberable syntax for "$let(x, y, z)$" might be "LET $x = y$ IN z". Despite the obvious similarity to a functional programming language construct, this expression is just a syntactic structure and has no operational meaning. In particular, LET $x = y$ IN z and $[y/x]z$ (the structure z where each occurence of x has been replaced by y) are completely different entities. We should remember that the functional representation of static objects does not create a dynamic semantics.

Example Queries

The following query computes the number of leaves in a $RFCT(T)$.

count : $RFCT(T) \rightarrow \mathbb{N}$
$= sr(\lambda x : T.1, \lambda x : Var.0, \lambda xy : \mathbb{N}.x + y, \lambda x : Var.\lambda yz : \mathbb{N}.y + z)$

As we can infer all types, this reduces to a more intuitive formula.

$= sr(1, 0, +, \lambda xyz.y + z)$

The function map(f) applies the function $f : T \rightarrow S$ to each leaf in a $RFCT(T)$ and produces a $RFCT(S)$ of the same structure.

map : $RFCT(T) \rightarrow RFCT(S)$
$= \lambda f : T \rightarrow S.sr(\lambda x : T.leaf(f(x)), \lambda x : Var.var(x),$
$\qquad \lambda xy : RFCT(S).join(x, y),$
$\qquad \lambda x : Var.\lambda yz : RFCT(S).let(x, y, z))$

If we add some syntactic sugar—a dot "."—to represent the frequently used function that just preserves the structure of a typed object, this expression becomes much simpler.

$= \lambda f.sr(\lambda x.leaf(f(x)), ., ., .)$

The last example is slightly more complicated. Imagine we want to replace all references with the values that are actually being referenced. In other words, we convert a structure with references into a—purely value-defined—tree. This operation must obviously produce nonsense on cyclic data structures because the results would be infinite trees. Nevertheless, since it explicitly produces all possible paths to the leaves of a non-cyclic structure, this operation is actually very useful.

$$\text{unref} : \text{RFCT}(T) \to \text{RFCT}(T)$$
$$= \text{sr}(.,.,.,\lambda xyz.\text{sr}(.,\lambda u.\text{if } u = x \text{ then } y \text{ else } . \text{ fi},.,.)(z))$$

This function consists of two nested structural recursions. The outer recursion just runs through the graph looking for local references. If found, it holds the reference identifier (x) and the refereed structure (y) and starts the inner recursion on the remaining structure (z). The inner recursion will replace all occurences of x by y in z. At this time all local references in z have already been replaced due to the bottom-up computing character of structural recursion.

Cyclic data structures will cause this function to produce results that contain free variables ("dangling pointers"), which have to be interpreted as representing the infinite trees that structural recursion is unable to unroll.

5   The General Case

Although quite powerful, the method of the previous section is unable to deal with general graph structures. This language only helps to define structures with references of limited range.

How can we consistently construct and query arbitrary typed (and even untyped) graphs? We will look at two (strongly related) methods. One possible method is based on the common tabular representation of graphs, another method "walks" on the graph to describe its data.

The Tabular Representation

We modify the "LET" syntax from above to allow multiple, mutually recursive bindings of variables. Since mutually recursive bindings are powerful enough to represent all graphs of given type (which is defined by the non-recursive operators of the signature), we can even drop the "IN" clause. The example illustrates again the case with an underlying $(2, 0)$-signature.

$$\text{leaf} : T \to \text{Tree}(T)$$
$$\text{join} : \text{Tree}(T) \times \text{Tree}(T) \to \text{Tree}(T)$$
$$\text{var} : \text{Var} \to \text{Tree}(T)$$
$$\text{letseq} : \text{Var} \times \text{Tree}(T) \times \text{Graph}(T) \to \text{Graph}(T)$$
$$\text{let} : \text{Var} \times \text{Tree}(T) \to \text{Graph}(T)$$

Structural recursion on this signature corresponds to the process of randomly selecting nodes of a graph and checking their immediate successors (or, more exactly spoken, references to these successors).

Although this signature still is a context-free grammar, the semantics of a structure of type $\text{Graph}(T)$ is, contrary to the previous examples, no longer independent of context. The reason is that multiple, contradicting definitions of the same node of the graph (within one data element) do not have a meaning. The structure defined in the following example illustrates this fact.

$$\text{letseq}(x, \text{leaf}(1), \text{letseq}(x, \text{leaf}(2), \text{let}(y, \text{join}(x, x))))$$

What is the meaning of this data description? In particular, is it a structure $(1, 1)$, or $(2, 2)$, or even $(1, 2)$ or $(2, 1)$, or none of these at all? A simple context assertion would correct this ambiguity. We could, for instance, declare that multiple occurences of the same variable are forbidden, or that the first (or last, or whatever) occurence is significant. Such an agreement, however, forces us to leave our context-free model of complex data types.

Note the similarity to the uniqueness problem we discussed earlier. Since the language is not powerful enough to define an isomorphic image, the semantic entities of a complex type map to multiple syntactic representations. As we have seen, using structural recursion on such objects is nevertheless possible at the price of the existence of multi-valued functions.

Another ambiguity, which we can ignore on the same basis, is the semantic equivalence of syntactic structures whose only difference is the name of one or more bound variables.

Unfortunately, the representation of general structures with references produces a second problem. The object

$$\text{let}(y, x)$$

is entirely undefined because of the appearance of a free variable. It does not correspond to any equivalence class in the semantic domain—be it either unique or multi-valued. This problem is completely different from the uniqueness of operations. Functions based on structural recursion might, therefore, be partial.

Although the previous example was bound to a specific representation, the depicted difficulty to model types with arbitrary references in a context-free setting are systematic:

A functional representation of general structures with references does not exist.

The reason is the necessity of an arbitrarily large number of different variables to distinguish any finite graph from all others up to isomorphism (a consequence of Karp's theorem). A context-free language obviously does not have the power to assert the boundedness of all variables.

The Walk Representation

We briefly look at a syntactically different but functionally equivalent representation of data with references. The proposition noted above is, of course, valid in this case as well.

Let us return to the signature of RFCT(T). Using the same context assumption as in the tabular representation (every variable is defined exactly once and is globally visible), the semantics now includes all graphs with appropriately typed nodes. Except that it allows local references to be expressed locally, which improves the modularity in data descriptions, this method is practically identical to the previous one.

The definition and applicability of structural recursion, which is based on pure syntax, remains unchanged.

6 Conclusion

Summary

Structural recursion is a powerful generic query mechanism for formally defined types. We have seen that the definition of structural recursion does not depend on the particular semantics behind type specifications. Instead, the semantics is explicitly given in the representational mapping. In order to implement new structures and their behavior, it is necessary to find an adequate syntactic representation.

The presented proposal for the treatment of types with references is, consequently, just an example of this method. This flexibility is one of the main advantages of the proposal. It does not only offer parametric operators—these operators are, in addition, automatically generated. A purely static description of the data, as typical for the data exchange in heterogeneous database environments, already carries the framework of its dynamic behavior.

In contrast to previous approaches specifically dealing with selected structures including references (e. g., recursive trees), this method leads from abstract type entities to concrete ones. An advantage is the integration of different complex data types and the resulting possibility for the creation of generic query and update operations.

The direct integration of referencing into model and language avoids the necessity for checking referential integrity. These constraints are part of the data type and are, therefore, inherently satisfied. On the other hand, we have seen that it is impossible to represent arbitrary references without context assertions. Hence, the integrity check has moved to an internal, type independent level.

Future Topics

The paper has already mentioned a number of interesting questions that have been left open. The following directions are potentially worth following in order to turn the proposal into use.

– One possible interpretation of structural recursion was based on attribute grammars. The context conditions in general structures with references are obviously asking for the same technique. Would the expressive power of structural recursion on references increase if both grammars (i. e., their attribute sets) are combined and the context values appear as parts of the parameters of structural recursion?

– A second approach to the problems of uniqueness and partiality could arise if the whole mechanism is shifted from the context-free to a context sensitive setting. A syntactic system based on this extended mechanism apparently builds a framework sufficient for the semantic mapping of the problematic structures we have seen.

The price is twofold. The mathematical basis of the given approach depends on the relationship between structural recursion, a general form of context-free attribute grammars, and algebraic structures. This relationship would disappear. The second drawback is the computational behavior of context sensitive systems. The identification of sufficiently powerful *and* efficient subclasses is necessary on this path.

– Another problem is the user-friendly representation of the mechanism in a query language. Although the paper has used some syntactic sugaring when it was near at hand, structural recursion still shows its descent from functional programming. It is certainly harder to communicate than descriptive style languages (comprehensions etc.).

Finally, the method presented in this paper is intended to become a part of a technology for the automatic support of database behavior design.

References

1. Serge Abiteboul, Sophie Cluet, and Tova Milo. Querying and updating the file. In *VLDB '93. International Conference on Very Large Databases*, pages 73–84, Dublin, Ireland, August 1993.
2. Val Breazu-Tannen, Peter Buneman, and S. Naqvi. Structural recursion as a query language. In *Proceedings of 3rd International Workshop on Database Programming Languages*, pages 9–19, Naphlion, Greece, August 1991. Morgan Kaufmann Publishers, Inc.
3. Val Breazu-Tannen, Peter Buneman, and Limsoon Wong. Naturally embedded query languages. In Joachim Biskup and Richard Hull, editors, *Database Theory— ICDT '92. 4th International Conference on Database Theory*, Berlin, Germany, October 1992. Lecture Notes in Computer Science, 646. Springer-Verlag.
4. Peter Buneman, Leonid Libkin, Dan Suciu, Val Tannen, and Limsoon Wong. Comprehension syntax. *SIGMOD Record*, 23(1):87–96, March 1994.
5. R. G. G. Cattell, editor. *The Object Database Standard: ODMG-93*. Morgan Kaufmann Publishers, Inc., San Francisco, CA, 1994.
6. Sudarshan Chawathe, Hector Garcia-Molina, Joachim Hammer, Kelly Ireland, Yannis Papakonstantinou, Jeffrey Ullman, and Jennifer Widom. The TSIMMIS project: Integration of heterogeneous information sources. In *Proceedings of the IPSJ Conference*, Tokyo, Japan, October 1995.
7. Peter P. S. Chen. The entity-relationship model: Toward a unified view of data. *ACM Transactions on Database Systems*, 1(1), 1976.
8. E. F. Codd. A relational model for large shared data banks. *Communications of the ACM*, 13(6), 1970.
9. E. F. Codd. *The Relational Model for Database Management: Version 2*. Addison-Wesley, Reading, MA, 1990.

10. Leonidas Fegaras. A uniform calculus for collection types. Technical Report 94-030, Department of Computer Science and Engineering, Oregon Graduate Institute, Beaverton, OR 97006-1999, 1994. Electronic version found at ftp://cse.ogi.edu/pub/crml/papers.html.

11. Leonidas Fegaras and David Maier. Towards an effective calculus for object query languages. *SIGMOD Record*, 24(2):47–58, June 1995.

12. Carl A. Gunter. *Semantics of Programming Languages: Structures and Techniques.* The MIT Press, Cambridge, MA, 1992.

13. Jan van Leeuwen, editor. *Handbook of Theoretical Computer Science.* Elsevier Science Publishers B. V., Amsterdam, The Netherlands, 1990.

14. Leonid Libkin and Limsoon Wong. Query languages for bags. Technical Report MS-CIS-93-36, University of Pennsylvania, School of Engineering and Applied Science, Computer and Information Science Department, Philadelphia, PA 19104–6389, March 1993.

15. J. C. Mitchell. Type systems for programming languages. In van Leeuwen [13].

16. Yannis Papakonstantinou, Hector Garcia-Molina, and Jennifer Widom. Object exchange accross heterogeneous information sources. In *IEEE International Conference on Data Engineering*, Taipei, Taiwan, March 1995.

17. Dzenan Ridjanovic and Michael L. Brodie. Defining database dynamics with attribute grammars. *Information Processing Letters*, 14(3):132–138, May 1982.

18. Tim Sheard and Leonidas Fegaras. A fold for all seasons. In *Proceedings of the 6th Conference on Functional Programming Languages and Computer Architecture*, pages 233–242, Copenhagen, Denmark, June 1993.

A Modular Design Strategy for a *Flexible* Graphical Database Design Environment: An Experimental Study *

Margita Altus

Computer Science Institute, Cottbus Technical University

Research Group Database and Information Systems

e-mail: altus @ informatik.tu-cottbus.de

Abstract. This paper informally introduces a modular design strategy embedded in our graphical database design environment underlying graph grammar formalism and demonstrates its systematic use by specifying two database modules of the library domain. The main idea is to consider an Entity-Relationship scheme as a set of nested graphs. Therefore, graph grammars can be applied to describe designs, design modules and design primitives based on the application of graph grammar productions.

1 Introduction

At present, graphical design systems hardly support the designer. Design systems of the future have to be flexible. Therefore, they have to be configurable and adaptable to the designer and to the application based on design rules. Designers prefer to reuse design modules and to construct new design modules on the basis of other modules. If this is not possible they need rules to start design module construction from the scratch. To support this style of working a design environment should include knowledge about designers, design expertise like knowledge about design strategies and the design model, global application knowledge, a complete, correct and minimal set of atomic design primitives, a library of design modules which have been constructed based on the atomic design primitives and design normalization. Furthermore, especially database design systems are considered to provide an interface between the database and the user/ designer of the database. It is proposed that for an interface to exist at any level of abstraction, there must be an operational framework which implements that level of abstraction [1].

The main purpose of this paper is to survey the atomic design primitives, the operational framework of our database design environment, *and* the way to construct design modules on the basis of atomic design primitives and construction rules or

---

* The paper is supported by the DFG project RADD (Th 465/2-1).

more precisely, the way to specify the content and the interface of database modules graphically. In the following, the term *unit* is used as synonym for database design module.

Design primitives are considered to be transformations on the design database. Scheme transformations and rearrangements have been deeply investigated in the literature (see, for instance, [19, 6, 18, 13, 17, 16, 12, 21]). They are motivated by different subproblems of scheme design like scheme evolution, scheme integration, scheme normalization, database reverse engineering, scheme translation and optimization.

A transformational approach for a correct database design using an entity relationship dialect can be based on graph replacement (see, for instance, [7, 10]). It has been accepted that the specification of databases should comprise the design of the static structure and the corresponding dynamic behaviour. The specification of the static structure can be based on a special kind of context-free graph grammar (e.g., [9, 15]) together with application conditions for each graph replacement rule or it is based on context-sensitive graph grammars (e.g. [7]). In this article the former approach is used to demonstrate the node rewriting system for a characteristical subset of atomic design primitives. The specification of the dynamic behaviour is demonstrated by programmed graph replacements based on attributed graph models for instance in [10, 20, 11]. In this article we concentrate ourselves on a characteristical subset of design primitives that is used to compose a modular database design strategy to support the *designer* in coping with consistency and correctness in scheme evolution and scheme integration with reference to the design of the static structure.

The next section describes salient aspects of the underlying extended entity relationship model in our database design environment (section 2). Afterwards, the use of a sequential *node* rewriting system is motivated (section 3.1) and node rewriting rules are used to present the characteristical subset of atomic design primitives (section 3.2, 3.3). The article then gives an informal introduction of the modular database design strategy based on our *graph grammar formalism* (section 3.4). The article continues with a running example from the library domain (section 4). Finally, the ideas and results of this paper are summarized (section 5).

2   Description of the EER Constructs and its Visualization

This section describes the salient design constructs of RADD design workbench's unified underlying data model (*R*apid *A*pplication and *D*atabase *D*evelopment, [2]) with emphasis on the static structural aspects. Our database design environment is a graphical database design system prototype. The collection of concepts and constraints below are considered to be a subset of the constituents encompassed in the *H*igher-order *E*ntity-*R*elationship *M*odel (HERM) that is defined in [23]. If time and space had been available, we would have included more static integrity constraints, as well as dynamic constraints and behaviour modelling based on the HERM-Methodology.

The EER begins with conventional entities, attributes, and relationships (with attributes, k-ary, whereby $1 \leq k \leq n$). It includes simple and nested attributes as well as first-order and higher-order relationships and clusters of them. *Nested attributes* are defined by the cartesian aggregation (tuple constructor) or by the set aggregation (set constructor). *Entity types* have a set of attributes that is called primary key or identifier. It is a non-empty subset of all attributes associated with this entity type. B is a key of the entity type E_1 if and only if the values of attributes in B uniquely identify the instance of E_1. One key of E_1 is declared primary, visualized by its name with an underline. All attributes of every key are null-not-allowed. Only attributes that do not belong to any key are null-allowed. *First-order relationship types* are defined to be associations between single entity types or clusters of them associated with a possibly empty set of attributes. *Higher-order relationship types (HoR)* are defined to have relationship types as components and possibly single entity types or clusters of both. They can also be associated with attributes. The key of relationship types is constructed by the primary key or any secondary key of its component types or by separate attribute types associated with this relationship type. The declaration of a key based on inclusion of keys of component types is visualized by an edge label (K). For each higher-order relationship an equivalent representation that contains only first-order relationships can be found. But, the latter representation introduces structural complexity to the scheme or it requires for an equivalent representation additional constraints.

Example of a HoR type (a): The entity type *'registered book'* is a component of the binary relationship types *'isA'* and *'is located at'*, Fig. 1. Since, its minimum and maximum participation for both relationships is one, the scheme can be simplified. In addition, we can observe that a book in general and a specific copy of a book needs the ISBN for identification. This requires an additional constraint. *'has'* is a value-determined relationship and represents a join path. Formally, *'has'* is value determined by matching attributes copy.ISBN and book.ISBN and consists exactly

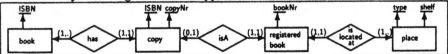

Fig.1 First-order relationship types and a redundant attribute type

the set of entity pairs (c,b) such that c[copy.ISBN] = b[book.ISBN]. The entity type *'copy'* was transformed to a relationship type reducing structural complexity and avoiding redundant attribute types and in consequence the type *'registered book'* changes to a HoR type in Fig. 12. Since, the Is-A (unary) relationship type can be generalized to n-ary relationship type [23] the attribute book.ISBN is inherited by the relationship type *'copy'* in Fig. 12. Thus, the primary key of *'copy'* is composed by book.ISBN and copy.copyNr.   □

Example of a HoR type (b): A person (user of a library) triggers a reservation for a lendable book if and only if this book is currently not available (it is borrowed): isBorrowed.lendableBook[bookNr] *includes* bookInAdvance.lendableBook[bookNr] (bookInAdvance.lendableBook[bookNr] ⊆ isBorrowed.lendableBook[bookNr]). Therefore, the type *'book in advance'* in Fig. 2 was transformed to a HoR type in Fig. 12.   □

Our notation of names is not case-sensitive and the so-called 'white spaces' (e.g.,

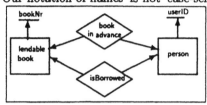

Fig.2

newline) are ignored. A *cluster* is a full union of types (entity or relationship type). There is an equivalent representation for clusters of types using Is-A relationship types and there is no syntactical difference between unary relationship types and Is-A relationship types.

Example of a cluster concept (b): The types *'student'* and *'employee'* are together covering the type *'university person'* and any person in the university is studying or working or both: student[userId] *does not exclude* employee[userId]. Since *'student'* and *'employee'* are at the same level in the generalisation hierarchy the constraints

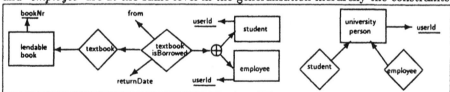

Fig.3 The cluster and generalisation concept

student.person[userId] ⊄ employee.person[userId] and employee.person[userId] ⊄ student.person[userId] are inherent in the representation using subtypes, but they are not inherent in the representation using clusters, Fig. 3. It is possible to group subtype and supertype in the same cluster. Only university persons have the permission to borrow textbooks. We omit the structural representation of this constraint in the sample design (section 4). Instead, we use an attribute type and assume that the constraint isBorrowed.lendableBook[type] ≠ "textbook" *or* isBorrowed.person[kind] ≠ "external user" is assigned to the type *'isBorrowed'* and it is inherited by the type *'book in advance'*.   □

Minimum and Maximum Participation: The entity type E_1 has minimum (maximum) participation of c (C) in the relationship type R if in each database state an instance e_1 from E_1 is related to at least (respectively, at most) c (C) instances e_2 from E_2. The entity type E_1 has *mandatory* participation in R if its minimum participation is greater than 0.

The notation $\boxed{E_1} \longleftarrow (c_1, C_1) - < R > - (c_2, C_2) \longrightarrow \boxed{E_2}$ is used to show the classical (min, max) participation by the entities on each side of relationship type R. For the classical case the maximum participation is visualized by a dot if it is greater than 1. The notation $\boxed{E_1} \longleftarrow \approx (a_1, A_1) - < R > - \approx (a_2, A_2) \longrightarrow \boxed{E_2}$ is used to show the *average* (min, max) participation by the entities on each side of relationship type R.

3   The Sequential *Node* Rewriting System

3.1   Motivation − Overview

The design process is accomplished by design steps. Each design step is a design decision and based on design primitives. Properties of design steps are content preservation, the preservation of the semantic of the application and minimality [18]. The RADD design workbench comprises mechanisms for modelling design steps using graph operations.

Such a formalism should define the *infinite* set of well-formed ER-diagrams and prevent a human designer from the creation of semantically doubtful or incorrect combinations using a *finite* set of rewriting rules. A sequential node/ graph rewriting system is a powerful tool for a meta-data representation of ER modeling rules [7]. Nevertheless, Breiteneder and Mück define in [7] a sequential graph rewriting system for ER diagrams that is too weak w.r.t. the kind of embedding relation and w.r.t. the application conditions of the graph productions. The *'identical embedding'* is *always* applicable since all productions are so designed that the left hand side of the rule is a partial graph of the right hand side, except the rule SGR3 (delete the start graph) and SGR11 (refinement of attributes). Therefore, only a special bottom-up design strategy is supported. The sets of application conditions include only structural restrictions. The sequential graph rewriting system in [7] is an instance of the *LEARRE* - graph grammar family and it is in all steps context-sensitive.

Graph operations have been adapted from the graphical kernel editor Graph[Ed] [14]. Graph[Ed] is an interactive editor for drawing and manipulating graphs and graph grammars (including graph parser, interpreter and graph constructor utilities). The possible graph constructs have been enriched by the semantic of the EER described in the previous section using a finite set of rewriting rules. Graph[Ed] can handle three types of graph grammars: NLC (Node Label Controlled), BNLC (Boundary-NLC) and 1-NCE (Neighbourhood Controlled Embedding for node rewriting system). The second and the third are special cases of the first graph grammar type which are also called NLC-like graph grammars [9]. All NLC-like graph grammars belong to the LEARRE graph grammar family *and* restrict the general case of graph rewriting to the case of *node rewriting*.

The way of rewriting a scheme graph S ([9]: the host graph) into a scheme graph S' is divided into five steps, the *LEARRE approach*: (1) The *L*ocate step finds a subgraph $\tilde{L}$ ([9]: the mother graph) in the scheme graph S that is an isomorphic graph to the left side of the production. (2) The second step establishes the *E*mbedding Area that includes the *identification* of nodes in the scheme graph S that are adjazent to nodes in the subgraph $\tilde{L}$ *and* which have a counterpart in the embedding relation of the rewriting rule. The elements of the embedding relation (connection relation) are called the *connection instruction* and they are of the form (α, β), where both are node labels. The meaning of such an instruction is that the embedding process should establish an edge between <u>each</u> node labeled α in the graph $\tilde{R}$ that is isomorphic the right side of the production ([9]: the daughter graph) and <u>each</u> node labeled β in the neighbourhood of the subgraph $\tilde{L}$ ([9], p.13). (3) The *R*emove step removes the subgraph $\tilde{L}$ from S that includes the removal of all edges that are incident with nodes in $\tilde{L}$. (4) The *R*eplace step creates a subgraph $\tilde{R}$ that is isomorphic to the right side of the production. (5) The *E*mbed step is the closing step and creates the edges identified in the second step. (Fig. 4)

The node-rewriting mechanism consists of one node at the left side of each production only, a "local unit" of the scheme graph S. Thus, if also the embedding is done in a "local" fashion (α and β of the embedding relation are adjacent), then a node rewriting step is a *local graph transformation*. The rewriting rules are the main constituent of the graph grammar, which is a *finite* specification of a graph/ node rewriting system, where each *rewriting rule* consists of one production and a finite number of connection instructions (that is different from the definition of a production in [15], p.19). [9]

Normally, the NLC framework rewrites undirected node-labeled graphs. Therefore, we use an easy adaptation the dNLC graph grammar, where d abbreviates 'directed' and *two* connection relations (embedding relations) are used to deal with the incoming and outgoing edges. In our dNLC approach "everything" is based on node labels, the rewriting process is completely local and a production is of the form $L \longrightarrow R$, where L is one node and R is a directed graph with a possibly empty set of nodes or edges (in [15] R is defined to be a weak connected graph). R is represented by a pair of sets (V_R, E_R), where V_R is the set of nodes of R and E_R is the set of edges of R. Each rewriting rule is represented by the tuple $(L \longrightarrow (V_R, E_R), C_{in}, C_{out})$.

Since the two embedding relations are defined to be *local* to each production this variant is known as RNLC grammar (rule dependent embedding node label controlled). Because of the unique name assumption in our EER every node label uniquely identifies a node. Thus, node labels in the connection instruction refer directly to nodes in the scheme graph. dNLC-like grammars with this type of connection instruction are called 1-dNCE (directed NCE and NLC).

3.2 Example: Node Rewriting Rule vs. Design Primitive

We use the graphical representation from [15] (with adaptations): Nodes of the right side and nodes of the embedding relation are drawn as cycles and the node of the left side are drawn as rectangle. *Example of the rewriting rule $p_{17'}$:* Let us consider a special case of the rewriting rule for the generic design primitive *split*: $p_{17'}$ (Figs. 4, 6). The marking of the left side a_0 appears in any corner of the rectangle. The right side is completely drawn inside of the rectangle (*instead* of writing $L ::= R$ [7]). The right side consists of two nodes marked b_0 and b_1 respectively without any edge. The meta-symbol "$*$" requires explicit that the *Replace* step creates a subgraph $\tilde{R}$ that is isomorphic to the right side of the production. The nodes marked d_0 and d_1 outside of the rectangle establish the embedding relation. Therefore, the rewriting rule for $p_{17'}$ contains one production and four connection instructions (outgoing edges only, the connection relation for the incoming edges is empty): $(a_0 \longrightarrow (\{b_0, b_1\}, \emptyset)$, $\emptyset, \{(b_0, d_0), (b_0, d_1), (b_1, d_0), (b_1, d_1)\})$. The connection relation for outgoing edges of this rewriting rule is a typical example for the *'identical embedding'*. □

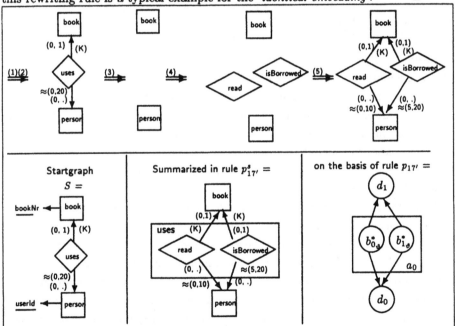

Fig.4 Split 'uses' $(p_{17'}^s)$

Semantic of the design primitive $(p_{17'})$: A relationship type is horizontally splitted. The new types together are covering the old type (total) and the new types are not necessarily disjunctive: $E_1 : a_0^s = b_0^{s+1} \cup b_1^{s+1}$, whereby it is *not* known that $b_0^{s+1} \cap b_1^{s+1} = \emptyset$. The concepts a_0^s, b_0^{s+1} and b_1^{s+1} model sets of entity pairs (e_0, e_1), where $e_0 \in d_0^s$ and $e_1 \in d_1^s$ and $\vartheta \in \{\times, \bowtie\}$ is the kind of operation used to determine the sets of entity pairs (e_0, e_1) and the concepts a_0, b_0 and b_1 do not exist concurrently emphasized by the design state s and $s + 1$ respectively. Thus, $E_2 : b_0^{s+1} \subseteq d_0^{s+1} \; \vartheta \; d_1^{s+1}$ and $E_3 : b_1^{s+1} \subseteq d_0^{s+1} \; \vartheta \; d_1^{s+1}$. It is obvious that $d_0^s = d_1^{s+1}$ and $d_1^s = d_1^{s+1}$ since d_0 and d_1 leave to be unchanged by the application of $p_{17'}$ Therefore, the expression E_0 for the relationship type a_0 exist: $a_0^s \subseteq d_0^{s+1} \; \vartheta \; d_1^{s+1}$.　　□

A design primitive is represented by the tuple:

$(L \longrightarrow (V_R, E_R), C_{in}, C_{out}, E_0, E_1, ..., E_n)$, **where** $n = | V_R \cup L |$.
Let us consider an instance $p_{17'}^s$, Fig. 4. The rule $p_{17'}^s$ summarizes a design step that transforms a scheme from a given design state s to a design state $s + 1$, where the placeholders $(a_0, b_0, b_1, d_0, d_1)$ of rule $p_{17'}$ are replaced by domain dependent node labels. The relationship type *'uses'* is splitted and it is replaced by the two relationship types *'read'* and *'isBorrowed'*. Thus, the following expressions have to be valid for a given database state t: $E_0 : uses^t \subseteq book^t \times person^t$, $E_1 : uses = read \; \cup \; isBorrowed$, $E_2 : read^t \subseteq book^t \times person^t$ and $E_3 : isBorrowed^t \subseteq book^t \times person^t$. Note, the set $isBorrowed^t$ is a true subset of the cartesian product $book^t \times person^t$. Later in the design process the expression E_3 will be extended by the expression: $\sigma_\omega (book^t \times person^t)$, where $\omega = (book[type] \neq$ *"textbook"* $or \; person[kind] \neq$ *"external user"*).　　□

Application conditions of the design primitive $p_{17'}^s$: The designer is supported with default assumptions using the expressions E_0, E_1, E_2 and E_3. The designer has to guarantee that these expressions are valid. In addition, it is assumed that the min/ max participation of d_0 and d_1 in b_0 and b_1 is equivalent to the min/ max participation in a_0. The rule $p_{17'}^s$ covers some changes with reference to the min/ max participation introduced by the designer. The unique name assumption requires that the domain dependent names for b_0 and b_1 do not exist in the current scheme of the design state $s + 1$.

The 1-dNCE methodology does not include application conditions for a *rewriting rule*. The replace step is for NLC grammars context-free, but the embed step is *not* context-free. A Church-Rosser-like property is valid for a sequence of design transformations. The 1-dNCE variant of graph grammar has the context-free property that the result of a derivation is independent of the order in which the productions are applied, a property that guarantees the existence of derivation trees (which embody the recursive nature of context-free grammars). A graph grammar that has this property is said to be *order-independent* or *confluent*. [10] Nevertheless, each design primitive is modelled by a graph grammar rule with an application condition that is called *context-sensitive supplementary condition*. User interaction/ selections are not avoidable even for a *scheme graph grammar approach*, but the designer can be supported with *default assumptions* about the current/ local application context and s/he is enforced to fullfill the application conditions. In addition, based on the analysis of several designer groups design patterns have been observed which are characterized by a restricted application order of design transformations represented by the rewriting rules. These design patterns represent the traditional approaches including top-down, bottom-up, and combined approaches.

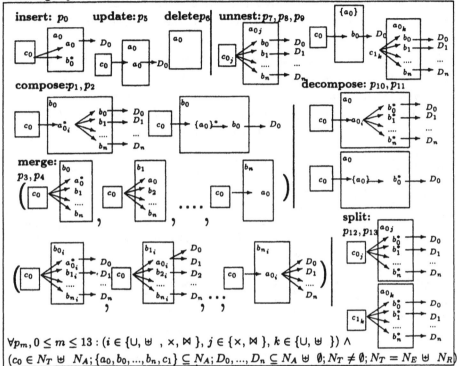

Fig.5 Rewriting rules for the attribute types.

3.3 Design Primitives

The set of design primitives was constructed based on the extended Entity Relationship Model (HERM). It can be divided in primitives for decomposition (top-down) and primitives for composition (bottom-up).

The consideration of the refinement, aggregate operations (omitting 'delete' and 'update') is sufficient since the design process is a revision process and is representable by backtracking to previous intermediary design results.

The picture of each generic graph operation is shown in the Fig. 5, 6. The nodes model complex design objects of different *kind* (attribute types, entity types and relationship types of order i). Constraint nodes are another possible kind of nodes, e.g. nodes which are aimed to vizualize explicit exclusion and inclusion constraints. They are omitted in this characteristical subset of design primitives, in Figs. 5, 6.

3.4 Composing the Modular Design Strategy

The application of a special design primitve *'initUnit'* is the start point of a unit design process. Their application procedure is different from the application procedure for the atomic design primitives (*LEARRE*). Only the 'Locate step' and the 'establish the Embedding Area step' is performed, the other steps are delayed until the unit design process is finished and the designer decides to integrate the unit with other units. At the unit initialisation time there is nothing to replace, the start node is created only. The sequential rewriting system is used to refine the right side of the **unit graph production**. The label of the node at the left side of each graph production is a path that contains the name of the unit (e.g. *'book'*, Fig. 10) and the label of the node that will be replaced or changed separated by a dot (e.g. *'book.author'*, Fig. 10).

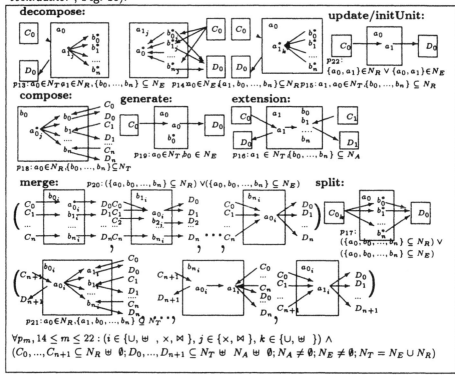

Fig.6 Rewriting rules for the entity and relationship types.

4 The Sample Design

The sample application is related to the library domain (the library of a university). Let us start with an informal description of the application. Suppose we have two units 'person' and 'book'. A skeleton models the relationships between these two units. Therefore, it includes information about booking in advance, the extension of the lending period, return and registration of books, the check of the return deadline using reminders. The design starts with the skeleton design and afterwards it continues with the refinement of each unit. The content of the different units is designed separately and a local interface is added to each database unit.

In more detail, the library database captures the following information: There are books which are registered. Each of them is identified by a unique book number. Furthermore, each registered book has a signature that is represented by two numbers: the field number and a serial number w.r.t. the field. A registered book *is a copy* of a book that is available in the library and to be found at a certain place identified by its type (e.g. reading room, archives) and a shelf number. In general, independent of the registration a book is identified by the ISBN and it is characterized by its publisher, the year of publication, the set of authors (for simplicity the order is omitted) and the title. Each book belongs to one or more fields of subject and there are at least one copy and approximately at most 30 copies of each book. A copy is identified by a serial number and the ISBN. For simplicity, the term *'book'* is used for anything that can be borrowed or used in the reading room of the library.

There are two kinds of books: books in the reading room which are not permitted to lend and books that are permitted to lend. Users of the library have the permission to borrow books for a lending period (normally 20 days). Furthermore, they have the allowance to extend this lending period at most three times. The extension of the lending period is not possible if another user of the library booked in advance the same book. There are three kinds of library user: students and employees of

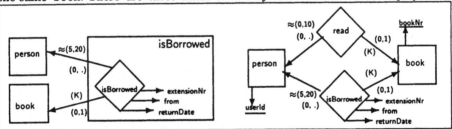

Fig.7 Extend 'isBorrowed' (p_{16}).

the university and other users (external users). Only students and employees of the university have the permission to borrow textbooks. Nobody has the allowance to extend the lending period for textbooks. Employees of the university are characterized by the name of their department and a phone number. Students are characterized by their number of immatriculation and their subject.

If a copy of the required book is not available then a user of the library has the possibility to book in advance. To book in advance requires the signature of the book and in addition, the user could order a copy that was published in a certain year (mainly the most recently publication is ordered). Each reservation is stored as relation between the user identification, the identification of the required book, the number of copies and a serial number to store the order of reservations for each book. At most nine reservations for each book are possible. If a copy of a book is returned then a message will be send off to the user who made the erliest reservation and in the following 10 days this book will not be lent to any other user. An extension of borrowing time for a copy will be canceled if a reservation is available for this book. In this case, one user with the highest number of extensions of the lending period w.r.t. the ordered copy has to return this copy.

The information about the sample application covered in the informal description is still incomplete. We descovered during the design process some additional information that is visualized in the final integrated scheme in Fig. 12. Nevertheless, the informal description contains already information about the dynamic behavior, but in this article we concentrate ourselves on the specification of the static structure of the database.

4.1 The Skeleton Design

The design construction process for the skeleton of the database is frequently realized using a pure top-down design strategy. The skeleton design demonstrated in this section covers some exceptions. The specification of attribute types may be required as intermediary design steps that are not the closing steps of the skeleton design. Furthermore, at the end of the skeleton design new relationship types may be introduced by the composition of existing entity or relationship types.

The start graph of our sample design is created by the composition of 'person' and 'book' introducing the relationship type 'uses', Fig. 4. Generic graph operations are applied until the skeleton contains all types that relate the units which have to be designed. At first, there is a high evidence to refine the skeleton by horizontally splitting the type 'uses' into the new types 'read' and 'isBorrowed' since the term 'uses' is too general and does not model its meaning in the context of the library, Fig. 4. Furthermore, it is likely that each of the new types models different inclusion dependencies. That means, the reason for the split operation may be that different subtypes of 'book' are components of the new types 'isBorrowed' and 'read'. Thus, the decomposition design primitive for the specialization is applied in the next design step, Fig. 8 since borrowing a book is only possible if the book is permitted to borrow, but reading any book is possible if it is not borrowed by another person. These two design steps, the split operation of a relationship type and the specialization of a component of the splitted relationship type, are followed very often by each other, but the order is not significant.

In the next step the designer decides to extend the relationship type 'isBorrowed' with attribute types, but the relationship type 'read' is not extended. This is an evidence that 'read' is less relevant for the library database. Finally, the designer introduces two relationship types to model the *'book in advance'* and the *'reminder'*, Figs. 8,9. During this design step the designer has to be supported in determining

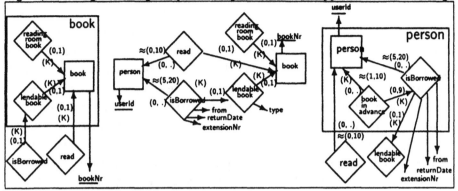

Fig.8 Decompose 'book' (p_{15}), compose 'book in advance' (p_{18}).

the correct components of the new relationship types since at this design state different subsets of *'book'* are already modelled. To be efficient the designer should consider at first the *smallest* subset, that means, a person reserves a book if and only if it is already borrowed by another person and a person receives a reminder for a book if and only if the same person borrowed this book and did not return it. Therfore, *'book in advance'* is composed by the components *'person'* and *'isBorrowed'* and *'reminder'* is composed by one component, *'isBorrowed'*. The following sections describe the design of the units 'person' and 'book'. Each design step is (meta-) modelled by a graph operation, examples are presented in the Figs. 4, 7, 8, 9, 10, 11. Assumptions about cardinalities (the average and the classical case) and primary keys are included by each design step.

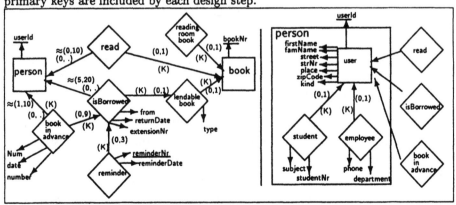

Fig.9 The complete skeleton, the complete unit 'person'.

4.2 The Design of the Unit 'person'

The unit 'person' with its local embedding relations is presented in the Fig. 9. The top-down design strategy is chosen by the designer for the design of the unit 'person'.

(1): The specialization step introduces two subtypes *'student'* and *'employee'*. Furthermore, the cardinality for each subtype is set to $(0, 1)$. Since *'userId'* is the primary key of *'user'* and belongs to the set of interface nodes, the primary key for each subtype is declared, (K). Thus, the primary key of *'user'* is inherited by *'student'* and *'employee'*. (2): The next design step extends *'user'* with attribute types common to both subtypes. (3): Finally, each subtype is extended with specific attribute types and the interface is checked (4). The embedding relation $\{($ *'user'*, *'userId'*$)$, $($ *'user'*, *'book in advance'*$)$, $($ *'user'*, *'is Borrowed'*$)$, $($ *'user'*, *'read'*$)\}$ did not change since the initialisation of the unit 'person' (Fig. 9). The order of the design steps is significant since the top-down design strategy was chosen. Between the first design step (initialisation of the unit) and the last design step (consistence check for the interface of the unit) possible incorrect and incomplete design states are allowed. The consistence check of the interface is the closing design step of a unit design and requires a complete and correct scheme graph at the right side of the **unit graph production**. Sometimes it includes possible changes of the local defined embedding relation since new entity and relationship types have been introduced. This case is demonstrated by the design of the unit 'book' in the next section.

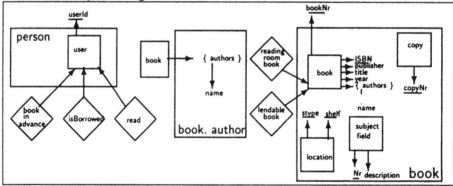

Fig.10 Init. of the unit 'person' (p_{22}), decompose 'author' (p_{11}), one design state of the unit 'book'.

4.3 The Design of the Unit 'book'

A modified bottom-up design strategy is chosen by the designer for the unit 'book'. The main steps of the design process of this unit and intermediary design states are presented in the Figs. 10, 11. The complete unit 'book' is shown in Fig. 11.

After the initialisation of the unit 'book' the design steps *generate 'copy'*, *'location'*, *'subject field'* are triggered. The next two design steps extend *'book'* with attribute types, whereby *'ISBN'* is declared as primary key and *'author'* is decomposed, Fig. 10. In Fig. 10 the unit 'book' is presented, whereby *'location'*, *'subject field'*, *'copy'* have been extended by attribute types and the primary keys have been declared. The type *'copy'* is extended by the entity type *'book'* in the next design step. That means, both concepts are related in the library domain by an (1:N) relationship and they are mandatory since for each book exists at least one copy in the library and each copy has a title, publisher, author(s) etc. Assumptions about the cardinalities are defined. Furthermore, *'book'* is declared as primary key component of *'copy'*, *(K)*. At the next design step the designer decides to model the association between a book and its subject field, Fig. 11 at the left, since the subject field of a book seems to be more relevant than the location and *determines* the shelf where the book will be placed after its registration. Afterwards, the association *'registered book'* is introduced by composing *'copy'* and *'location'*, and *'registered book'* is extended by additional attribute types, Fig. 11: *'serialNr'*, *'fieldNr'*.

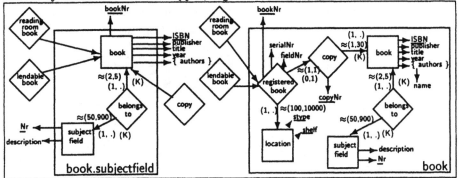

Fig.11 Compose 'belongs to' (p_{18}), the complete unit 'book' .

The consistence check of the interface requires changes of the local embedding relation $\{('book', 'reading\ room\ book'), ('book', 'lendable\ book'), ('book', 'bookNr')\}$. Since the intended semantic of the type labeled book has been changed by the introduction of new types. The type *'book'* represents the concept of a general book identified by the *'ISBN'*. The former intended semantic of book is modelled by the type *'registered book'* and *bookNr'* is the primary key of *'registered book'*. Copies in the reading room as well as all copies that are permitted to borrow are *included* in the library and the attribute type *'bookNr'* represents a unique book number for all copies in the library. Both of them are modelled by concepts which belong to the interface of the unit: *'reading room book'* and *'lendable book'*. Thus, the new embedding relation is $\{('registered\ book', 'reading\ room\ book'), ('registered\ book', 'lendable\ book'), ('regis-tered\ book', 'bookNr')\}$ and *'bookNr'* is inherited by *'reading room book'* and *'lendable book'*.

In Fig. 12 the result of the integration of unit 'person' and 'book' into the skeleton scheme graph is presented by the application of the two graph replacement operations 'person' and 'book'. The order of the application is not significant.

5 Conclusions

We have mentioned the relation between a modular design strategy and flexibility of design environments. We have argumented that database design needs an operational framework. The formal background of sequential node rewriting systems was demonstrated. Modular database design strategies can be based on a graph grammar formalism to support the designers during the database design process for a consistent development of well-formed ER-schemata of a special dialect (HERM, [23]). This kind of consistence enforcement is an internal support. To conclude the scheme graph can be considered to be a nested graph and the graph grammar mechanism can be applied recursively. The modular design strategy is composed by a set of atomic design primitives and a set of check points, e.g. check of the local embedding relations. We used in this article an empirical approach to demonstrate a modular database design strategy. At first, the items to be tested are identified, the atomic design primitives, and they are applied in an example from the library domain.

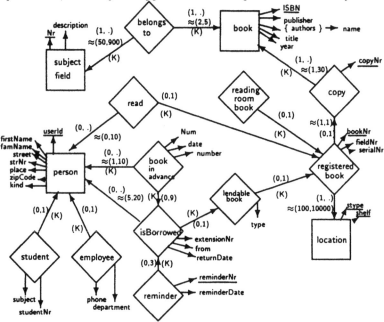

Fig.12 The integration of the units 'book' and 'person' into the skeleton of the library database

Acknowlegdements

The research described here was performed while the author was a scientific assistant at the University of Rostock in the Research Group Knowledge Representation and at the Technical University Cottbus in the Research Group Database and Information Systems of the Computer Science Institute and was supported by Prof.Dr.Bernhard Thalheim. Finally, the remarks of three unknown reviewers led to considerable improvements of this paper.

References

1. R.J.Abbott. On Interfaces. In: Journal of Systems Integration, 1, Kluwer Academic Publishers, Boston, Manufactured in The Netherlands, p.143-162, 1991.

2. M.Albrecht, M.Altus, E.Buchholz, A.Düsterhöft, and B.Thalheim, The rapid application and database development (RADD) workbench - A comfortable database design tool. In: Proc. of the 7th International Conference, CAiSE 95 (eds.: J.Ivari, K.Lyytinen, M.Rossi), LNCS 932, Jyväskylä, Finland, 1995, p.327–340 http://www.informatik.tu-cottbus.de/cs/dbis/radd/caise95/caise95.html.

3. M.Albrecht, E.Buchholz, A.Düsterhöft, B.Thalheim. An Informal and Efficient Approach for Obtaining Semantic Constraints using Sample Data and Natural Language Processing. In: Proc. of the Workshop on Semantics in Databases in Prague, January 13 - 16, 1995.

4. M.Altus, B.Thalheim. Strategy Support in RADD. In: Proc. of the Conference on Information Technique and Organisation - Planning, Economy and Quality, Ulm, 1995 (in German) http://www.informatik.tu-cottbus.de/~altus/node4.html.

5. P.Bachmann, W.Oberschelp, B.Thalheim, and G.Vossen. The design of RAD: Towards an interactive toolbox for database design. RWTH Aachen, Fachgruppe Informatik, Aachener Informatik-Berichte, 90-28, 1990.

6. C. Batini, S. Ceri, and S. Navathe, Conceptual database design, An entity-relationship approach. Benjamin Cummings, Redwood, 1992.

7. C.J.Breiteneder, T.A.Mück. Graph rewriting systems for the Entity-Relationship approach. In: Data & Knowledge Engineering, Volume 17, Number 3, December 1995.

8. H.Ehrig, H.-J.Kreowski, G.Rozenberg (eds.). Graph Grammars and Their Application to Computer Science. Proc. of the 4th International Workshop, Bremen, Germany 1990. LNCS 532, Springer-Verlag, Berlin, 1991.

9. J.Engelfried, G.Rozenberg. Graph Grammars Based on Node Rewriting: an Introduction to NLC Graph Grammars. In: [8] 1991.

10. G.Engels. Elementary Actions on an Extended Entity-Relationship Database. In: [8] 1990.

11. G.Engels, C.Lewerenz, W.Schäfer. Graph Grammar Engineering: A Software Specification Method. RWTH Aachen, Fachgruppe Informatik, Aachener Informatik-Berichte, 87-7, 1987.

12. J.-L. Hainaut, Catherine Tonneau, M.Joris, M.Chandelon. Transformation-Based Database Reverse Engineering. In: Proc. of the Entity-Relationship Approach, Arlington, Texas, USA, December 15-17 (Eds.: R.A.Elmasri, V.Kouramajian, B.Thalheim), LNCS 823,

13. T.Halpin, H.Proper. Database Schema Transformation and Optimization.. In: Proc. of the 14th International Conference on Object-Oriented and Entity-Relationship Modeling, LNCS 1021, Gold Coast, Australia, December 13-15 (Ed.: M.P.Papazoglou), Springer-Verlag, 1995, p.191–203.

14. M.Himsolt. Graph^{Ed} : An Interactive Tool for Developing Graph Grammars. In [8], 1990.

15. M.Kaul. Syntax Analysis of Graphs using Precedence Graph Grammars (in German). University of Passau, Faculty of Mathematics and Informatics, 1985.

16. R.Missaoui, J.-M.Gagnon, R.Godin. Mapping an Extended Entity-Relationship Schema into a Schema of Complex Objects. In: Proc. of the 14th International Conference on Object-Oriented and Entity-Relationship Modeling, LNCS 1021, Gold Coast, Australia, December 13-15 (Ed.: M.P.Papazoglou), Springer-Verlag, 1995, p.191–203.

17. O.Rauh, E.Stickel. Standard Transformations for the Normalization of ER Schemata. In: Proc. of the 7th International Conference, CAiSE 95 (eds.: J.Ivari, K.Lyytinen, M.Rossi), LNCS 932, Jyväskylä, Finland, 1995, p.313–326.

18. A. Rosenthal and D. Reiner. Tools and Transformations — Rigorous and Otherwise — for Practical Database Design. In: acm Transactions on Database Systems, Volume 19, Number 2, June 1994.

19. G.Santucci, C.Batini, G.Di Battista. Multilevel Schema Integration. In: Proc. of the 12th International Conference on the Entity-Relationship Approach, Arlington, Texas, USA, December 15-17 (Eds.: R.A.Elmasri, V.Kouramajian, B.Thalheim), LNCS 823, Springer-Verlag, 1993, p.364–375.

20. A.Schürr. PROGRESS: A VHL-Language Based on Graph Grammars. A revised version of: Technical Report no. 89-4: Introduction to PROGRESS, an Attribute Graph Grammar Based Specification Language. Auch in: [8], 1991.

21. T.J.Teorey, D.Yang, J.P.Fry. A Logical Design Methodology for Relational Databases Using the Extended Entity-Relationship Model. ACM Computing Survey 18,2 (June), 1986.

22. B.Thalheim. Database Design Strategies. Computer Science Institute, Cottbus Technical University, D-03013 Cottbus, 1993.

23. B.Thalheim. Fundamentals of Entity-Relationship Modelling. Computer Science Institute, Cottbus Technical University, 1995.

Graph Based Modeling and Implementation with EER/GRAL

J. Ebert, A. Winter, P. Dahm, A. Franzke, R. Süttenbach

University of Koblenz, Institute for Software Technology, Rheinau 1,
D-56075 Koblenz, email: ebert@informatik.uni-koblenz.de

Abstract. This paper gives a cohesive approach to modeling and implementation with graphs. This approach uses extended entity relationship (EER) diagrams supplemented with the $\mathcal{Z}$-like constraint language GRAL. Due to the foundation of EER/GRAL on $\mathcal{Z}$ a common formal basis exists. EER/GRAL descriptions give conceptual models which can be implemented in a seamless manner by efficient data structures using the GraLab graph library.
Descriptions of four medium size EER/GRAL-applications conclude the paper to demonstrate the usefulness of the approach in practice.

1 Introduction

Using graphs as a means for discussing problems, as a medium for formal reasoning, or as a paradigm for data structures in software is folklore in today's computer science literature. But most of the different approaches that use graphs are not used in a coherent way.

There are *different models* in use based on undirected or directed graphs, with or without multiple edges or loops. Sometimes graph elements are typed or attributed, sometimes they are not. Mathematical graph theory usually deals only with graph structure [Har72], whereas computer science usually uses graphs where vertices are distinguishable [Meh84]. In applications, graphs are often used *without a formal basis*. This leads to problems when assertions about the models have to be proved. Furthermore, graphs are frequently implemented using non-graph-based repositories that *do not match* the conceptual graph model exactly.

In this paper, we present a *coherent and consistent approach* to using graphs in a seamless manner

- as conceptual models,
- as formal mathematical structures, and
- as efficient data structures

without any discontinuity between these three aspects.

The approach, which is called the *EER/GRAL approach* throughout this paper, is based on extended entity relationship descriptions (EER diagrams, section 3.1) which are annotated by formal integrity conditions (GRAL assertions, section 3.2) in order to specifiy graphs, which are efficiently implementable by an appropriate C++ library (GraLab, section 4). A very general class of graphs is used (TGraphs, section 2) as basis.

As opposed to [EF95], where the theoretical basis is explained, the aim of this paper is to give an introduction into the approach with emphasis on its practical applicability.

Each of the applications sketched in section 5 has been described by technical reports which are publically available[1].

2 TGraphs

To make the approach as useful as possible a rather general kind of graphs has to be treated. *TGraphs* are used as the basic class of graphs. TGraphs are

- *directed*, i.e. for each edge one has a start vertex and an end vertex,
- *typed*, i.e. vertices and edges are grouped into several distinct classes,
- *attributed*, i.e. vertices and edges may have associated attribute-value pairs to describe additional information (where the attributes depend on the type), and
- *ordered*, i.e. the edges incident with a particular vertex have a persistent ordering.

All these properties are, of course, only optional. If a certain application only needs undirected graphs without any type, attribute or ordering, the respective properties may also be ignored.

2.1 Formal Definition

TGraphs as mathematical objects are specified using the $\mathcal{Z}$-notation [Spi92].

The basic *elements* of TGraphs are *vertices* and *edges*. With respect to a vertex an edge may have a *direction*, i.e. it may occur as an out-edge or as an in-edge. Graph elements may have a type and they may have attribute-value pairs associated.

$$ELEMENT ::= vertex\langle\!\langle N \rangle\!\rangle \mid edge\langle\!\langle N \rangle\!\rangle$$
$$VERTEX == \text{ran } vertex$$
$$EDGE == \text{ran } edge$$
$$DIR ::= in \mid out$$

$$[ID, VALUE]$$
$$typeID == ID$$
$$attrID == ID$$
$$attributeInstanceSet == attrID \nrightarrow VALUE$$

Using these basic definitions the *structure* of a TGraph consists of its vertex set, its edge set and an incidence function, which associates to each vertex v the sequence of its incident edges together with their direction.

---

[1] Most of them can also be found via http://www.uni-koblenz.de/~ist.

$$
\begin{array}{|l}
\hline
\underline{\quad TGraph}\ \rule{0pt}{0pt} \\
\quad V : \mathbb{F}\ VERTEX \\
\quad E : \mathbb{F}\ EDGE \\
\quad \Lambda : VERTEX \nrightarrow \mathrm{seq}(EDGE \times DIR) \\
\quad type : ELEMENT \nrightarrow typeID \\
\quad value : ELEMENT \nrightarrow attributeInstanceSet \\
\hline
\quad \Lambda \in V \rightarrow \mathrm{iseq}(E \times DIR) \\
\quad \forall\, e : E \bullet \exists_1\, v, w : V \bullet (e, in) \in \mathrm{ran}(\Lambda(v)) \wedge (e, out) \in \mathrm{ran}(\Lambda(w)) \\
\quad \mathrm{dom}\ type = V \cup E \\
\quad \mathrm{dom}\ value = V \cup E \\
\hline
\end{array}
$$

This class of graphs is very general and allows object-based modeling of application domains in an unrestricted manner.

The formal definition of TGraphs by a $\mathcal{Z}$-text admits an equally formal definition of all concepts described in this paper (e.g. the semantics of EER diagrams and GRAL) and gives the opportunity for reasoning about all kinds of properties of graphs in a common and powerful calculus.

2.2 Modeling using TGraphs

TGraphs can be used as formal models in all application areas that are subject to object-based modeling.

It is useful to adopt a general *modeling philosophy* for TGraph-based software development in order to exploit the full power of the approach. We propose to use the following rules ([EF95])

- every identifiable and relevant object is represented by exactly one vertex,
- every relationship between objects is represented by exactly one edge,
- similar objects and relationships are assigned a common type,
- informations on objects and relationships are stored in attribute instances that are assigned to the corresponding vertices and edges, and
- an ordering of relationships is expressed by edge order.

Of course, these rules require some modeling decisions (e.g. to decide what can be viewed as "relevant"). They help to achieve an appropriate formal graph model in the modeling process. Some examples will be shown later in this paper.

3 Graph Classes

The set of possible TGraph models for a given application is usually a subset of the set of all TGraphs, at least if the application domain has some sensible structure. This leads to the task of defining *classes of TGraphs* in a formal manner.

Here we propose to use extended entity relationship descriptions (EER diagrams) for this purpose. These diagrams may be annotated by additional restrictions (GRAL assertions).

3.1 EER Diagrams

EER diagrams are able to denote information about graph classes in a straight-forward manner:

- entity types denote vertex types,
- relationship types denote edge types,
- generalizations describe a vertex type hierarchy,
- incidences between relationship types and entity types describe restrictions on the incidence structure,
- attributes describe the attribute structure of vertices and edges, depending on their type, and
- higher-level modeling constructs like aggregation and grouping add additional structural information.

Example:
Fig. 1 shows the definition of a graph class *DFD* which gives the conceptual model of dataflow diagrams, i.e. it contains the metamodel for a dataflow language. The dataflow metamodel is used to generate an editor for dataflow diagrams [Drü96] with the KOGGE-Generator, described in section 5.2.

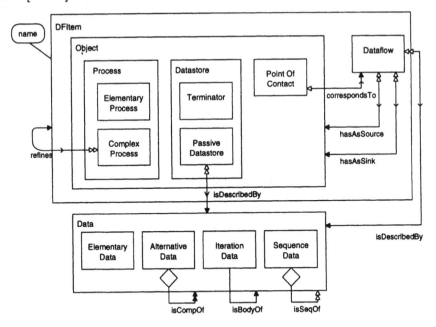

Fig. 1. EER diagram for dataflow diagrams

Dataflow diagrams describe procedural aspects through the main concepts *Process*, *Datastore* and *Dataflow*. These concepts are modeled as vertex types, which may be specialized. E.g. the concept *Process* is subdivided into *Complex Processes*, which are refined by further dataflow diagrams, and *Elementary Processes*. (Note, that specialization is depicted by inclusion of the respective rectangles of the vertex types, like in Venn diagrams.)

The relationships between these concepts are modeled using edge types. Each *Dataflow* connects exactly two *Objects*, its source and its sink. *Data* stored in *PassiveDatastores* or transported by *Dataflows* is described as regular structures in a datadictionary.

The refinement of *ComplexProcesses* by further *DFItems* is modeled using *refines*-edges. *PointOfContact*-vertices are used as surrogates for dataflows in a refinement. ∎

[CEW96] describes a complete *formal semantics* of EER diagrams in terms of the TGraph class which is specified by a given diagram. This is done by defining an appropriate TGraph for the EER diagram itself. The set *SchemaGraph* of those TGraphs which describe EER diagrams is the domain of the semantic function

$$graphSpecOf : SchemaGraph \rightarrow GraphSpec$$

which assigns a graph class specification to every instance of *SchemaGraph*. (This function is formally defined using $\mathcal{Z}$.)

For a given TGraph $g \in SchemaGraph$ the result $graphSpecOf(g)$ is a specification of the set of instance TGraphs of the EER diagram described by g. The TGraph class corresponding to $graphSpecTo(g)$ is the set of all graphs h, which fulfill the specification. E.g., the TGraph class *SchemaGraph* is itself the set of TGraphs corresponding to that graph specification which is the picture of (the graph of) some meta EER diagram under $graphSpecOf$.

Since EER diagrams in practical applications are used to model the concepts of the application domain, they are also called *concept diagrams* in the following.

3.2 GRAL Assertions

EER diagrams only allow to describe the local structure of TGraphs, i.e. the types and attributes and their incidences together with only a few additional properties, like e.g. degree restrictions. In applications one has often more knowledge about the models. This knowledge can be formalized as an extension of the corresponding EER diagram.

We propose to use the $\mathcal{Z}$-like *assertion language GRAL* (GRAph specification Language), which allows to formulate further restrictions on the graph class specified by a diagram. GRAL is described in detail in [Fra96a].

GRAL assertions refer to the formal $\mathcal{Z}$-definition of TGraphs given in section 2. A GRAL assertion corresponding to an EER diagram D has the format

for G **in** D **assert**
$pred_1; \ldots; pred_k$

Here, the predicates $pred_1; \ldots; pred_k$ may be all kinds of $\mathcal{Z}$-predicates restricted only in such a way, that GRAL predicates are efficiently testable on those TGraphs which suit to the corresponding EER diagram. This efficiency is achieved

- by restricting all quantifiers to finite domains and
- by using a library of basic predicates and functions which can be computed efficiently.

A feature of GRAL which extends $\mathcal{Z}$ in the direction of TGraphs is the use of *path expressions*. Path expressions are regular expressions of edge/vertex symbols, which allow the description of paths in graphs. They are used to derive sets of vertices and to formulate reachability restrictions.

Path expressions are

- either simple, consisting of an edge symbol ($\rightharpoonup, \leftharpoonup, \rightleftharpoons$), optionally annotated with an edge type (like in $\rightharpoonup_{writes}$) and followed by a $\bullet$ symbol which may itself be annotated with a vertex type (like in $\rightharpoonup_{reviews}\bullet_{author}$)
- or composite: given two path expressions p_1, p_2
  - the sequence $p_1 p_2$,
  - the iteration p_1^* or p_1^+, and
  - the alternative $(p_1 \mid p_2)$
  are regular path expressions.

Given a path expression p and two vertices v, w,

- $v\, p$ denotes the set of vertices reachable from v along paths structured according to p
- $p\, v$ denotes the set of vertices from which v is reachable along paths structured according to p
- $v\, p\, w$ denotes the predicate that w is reachable from v along a path structured according to p

The semantics of path expressions and their application to vertices is described formally using $\mathcal{Z}$ in [Fra96b]. Since GRAL is embedded in $\mathcal{Z}$, GRAL assertions also have a $\mathcal{Z}$-compatible semantics.

Example:

The graph class *DFD* defined in fig. 1 has further properties which are shown as a GRAL assertion in fig. 2:

for G **in** *DFD* **assert**

(1) $isDag(refines)$;

(2) $\{s_1, s_2 : Datastore \mid s_1 \leftharpoonup_{hasAsSink} \rightharpoonup_{hasAsSource} s_2\} = \varnothing$;

(3) $\forall\, p : ComplexProcess\ \bullet$

      $p(\leftharpoonup_{hasAsSource} \mid \leftharpoonup_{hasAsSink}) = p \leftharpoonup_{refines} \bullet_{PointOfContact} \rightharpoonup_{correspondsTo}$

(4) $\forall\, c : PointOfContact\ \bullet$

      $c \rightharpoonup_{correspondsTo} \rightharpoonup_{isDescribedBy} (\leftharpoonup_{IsCompOf} \mid \leftharpoonup_{isBodyOf} \mid \leftharpoonup_{isSeqOf})^*$

      $\leftharpoonup_{isDescribedBy} (\rightharpoonup_{hasAsSink} \mid \rightharpoonup_{hasAsSource}) c$

(5) $\forall\, d : Dataflow\ \bullet$

      $d(\rightharpoonup_{hasAsSource} \mid \rightharpoonup_{hasAsSink}) \bullet_{PassiveDatastore} \rightharpoonup_{isDescribedBy}$

      $(\leftharpoonup_{IsCompOf} \mid \leftharpoonup_{isBodyOf} \mid \leftharpoonup_{isSeqOf})^* \leftharpoonup_{isDescribedBy} d$.

Fig. 2. GRAL Assertion for Dataflow Diagrams

Refinement of processes by further dataflow diagrams has to be cyclefree (1) and dataflows are not allowed between datastores (2). Refinement has to be structurally balanced, i.e. it has to be assured that dataflows being incident to a refined process find their correspondence in the refinement (3) as a point of contact. If a dataflow is described by a regular data description, the corresponding point of contact has to have a conformant description (4). Accordingly, the regular descriptions of a data flow incident with a datastore, has to be conformant with the description of the datastore (5).

Balanced dataflow diagrams, an accompanying data dictionary entry and their TGraph-representation according to the graph class definition given in fig. 1 and 2 are shown in fig. 3.

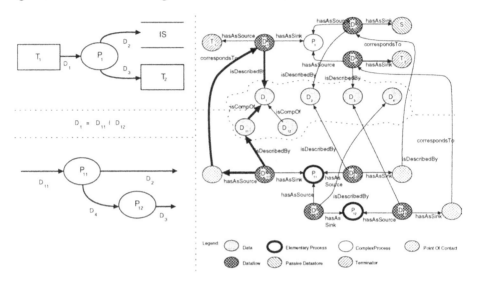

Fig. 3. Dataflow Diagram and its TGraph Representation

The emphasized arcs in the TGraph representation illustrate constraint 4 according to dataflow D_1. The other path expressions used in the integrity constraints could be followed analogeously. ∎

Experience shows that regular path expressions are a powerful means for describing TGraph properties in practical applications. Some examples will be given below.

3.3 Modeling using Graph Classes

The description languages given by EER diagrams and GRAL-assertions are two aspects of a common integrated approach to specifying graph classes. Due to the common semantic basis given by their $\mathcal{Z}$-description one may use both formalisms in a *seamless manner*. It is up to the user to decide which formalism to choose in expressing knowledge about the TGraphs. EER diagrams are very well suited for formalizing local ("context-free") properties, whereas GRAL-assertions have the power to formalize even global ("context-sensitive") aspects. But there are properties (e.g. degree restrictions), which may be formulated in either way.

The *EER/GRAL modeling approach* is suited for a modular modeling process: At first one defines EER/GRAL specifications for several (smaller) graph classes. Then, these specifications are integrated

- by melting vertex types which represent the same information,
- by generalizing vertex types which represent similar information, and
- by connecting vertex types in different graph classes with additional edge types.

The GRAL assertions of the submodels are conjugated (after renaming), and additional global information may be added by further GRAL predicates.

4   Implementation

All modeling concepts described upto here have to be implemented by concrete graph software, if seamlessness of the approach shall be achieved: The GraLab (*GRAph LABoratory*) software package ([DEL94]) makes a set of C++ classes available to implement TGraphs directly and exactly as specified by EER diagrams. It allows to transform graph class definitions into vertex and edge types and into C++ classes which implement the attributes.

GraLab provides an *interface* to efficiently use and manipulate graph structures, as well as the types and attributes assigned to vertices and edges. Inside GraLab TGraphs are represented as internal data structures by symmetrically stored forward and backward adjacency lists [Ebe87].

The *structure* can be accessed and manipulated via a simple interface which includes methods to

- create and delete vertices and edges,
- traverse graphs,
- retrieve start and end vertices of edges,
- relink edges,
- change order of incidences,
- count vertices and edges, and
- retrieve edges between vertices.

This interface includes control structures for graph traversal (in the form of C++ macros) which allow a high-level programming of graph algorithms, which is very near to pseudocode used for describing graph algorithms.

The type and attribute part of TGraphs is implementable as a *type system* using GraLab. The type system contains the connection between each vertex/edge type and its (application dependent) attribute class. Each attribute class is a C++ class whose instances contain all attribute values assigned to a graph element (vertex or edge) of the type given. Furthermore, the type system implements the type hierarchy.

Attribute values can be accessed and modified via pointers to the specific attribute object. Type casts on the pointers returned are necessary to access single attribute values.

Due to the internal datastructure most of these operations requires linear afford. Creating, deleting, relinking and finding (the next) incident edge or adjacent vertex can be done in $\mathcal{O}(1)$ and the traversal of graphs depends linearly on the number of edges resp. vertices ([Ebe87]). In the projects described below graphs with more than 100 000 graph elements were handled without efficiency problems.

The GraLab software package gives the necessary completion of the EER/GRAL modeling approach with respect to implementation. Thus, all EER/GRAL models may be directly implemented by graph structures in a seamless manner.

5 Applications

The approach described in the previous chapters was developed in strong conjunction to software engineering projects and has been successfully applied in several different application areas. In the following, four projects will be sketched shortly. Each of them is described in more detail in the references given.

The examples are chosen in such a way that the following aspects of the approach are expressed: EER diagrams and GRAL assertions are used for modeling, partial models are integrated into a larger common model, and algorithmic graph theory on models is used to get efficient software.

5.1 Application: Method Modeling

Software analysis and design methods (like e.g. the *Object Modeling Technique (OMT)* of [RBP+91]) usually contain lots of different pictures with some intuitively given semantics to describe models of software systems.

An OMT model consists of three logical parts describing different views of the system to be analyzed; the *object model* describes the structure of objects, the *dynamic model* is concerned with execution aspects, and the *functional model* shows the transformation of values in the system.

The visual languages used for these pictures usually lack a formal basis. But since visual documents may be abstracted in graphs, it is possible to define the *abstract syntax* of these languages by TGraph classes. Then, the EER/GRAL description of these classes permits an integration and comparison of different visual languages as well as a formal reasoning about them.

In [BES96] an EER/GRAL formalization for OMT is given. This formalization is an *OMT metamodel*, since its instances are OMT models. There, the elements of OMT descriptions are modeled by three different graph classes, one for each model. Furthermore, these three EER/GRAL descriptions are integrated into one overall abstract model for the whole OMT-approach by merging vertex types in different (sub)models and by introducing additional edge types. The resulting OMT-model consists of an EER-Diagram with about 50 strongly connected vertextypes and more than 20 GRAL consistency constraints. The inconsistencies and incompleteness of OMT were solved by decisions of the authors. Since the descriptions allow a deliberate and formally based discussion of alternatives, it is possible to discuss these decisions on a common basis.

5.2 Application: Tool Building

Describing real systems with visual languages without the support of tools is practically infeasable because of the complexity of the systems and the methods available for description. Such a tool must help the developer with regard to

- the underlying concepts, i.e. the abstract syntax,
- the notation used, and
- general functions to develop a description conformant to a method.

The metaCASE system KOGGE (*KOblenz Generator for Graphical Design Environments*)[2] was developed to generate graphical editors for visual languages on the basis of EER/GRAL descriptions of their abstract syntax ([EC94]).

A tool for a given language, which is generated by KOGGE, is called a *KOGGE tool.* There are several KOGGE tools in use, including one for dataflow diagrams (cf. section 3) and one for the object-oriented software development method BON [NW95]. The BON-KOGGE (*BONSAI*) [KU96] is used in Software Engineering education at University of Dortmund.

A KOGGE tool consists of the two physical parts – a tool description and the KOGGE base system.

The *base system* interprets the tool description at runtime in order to provide the user interface and to control its functions.

All KOGGE tools use the same base system, whereas the *tool description* is uniquely developed for any visual language. A tool description consists of three logical parts:

- an abstract syntax of the supported language,
- a set of statecharts, one for each tool operation, and
- a number of menu charts.

Since the abstract syntax inside KOGGE tools is described by EER diagrams, a KOGGE EER editor is used to specify and edit these diagrams. Analogously, a KOGGE statechart editor and a KOGGE menu editor are used to build the other parts of a tool description.

Inside KOGGE *TGraphs* are used for storing the tool specification and for representing the abstract syntax of the concrete documents, which are edited by the KOGGE tool. Both graphs are implemented using GraLab. One describes the tool itself according to the KOGGE meta EER specification, the other one represents the actual data according to the EER specification, which supplies the conceptual model of the language being edited.

An advantage of the KOGGE approach is that the abstract syntax of visual languages is given as an EER model. This allows to use the representation of an EER document inside the KOGGE EER editor as the tool specification graph of another KOGGE tool. Thus, one can develop KOGGE tools using KOGGE.

[2] The KOGGE Project was funded by the Stiftung Rheinland–Pfalz für Innovation, No. 8036-386261/112.

5.3 Application: Tour Planning

Schools for the handicapped have to organize a transportation service for their pupils who often are not able to reach the school by using e.g. public transport.

The aim of the MOTOS (*MOdular TOur Planning System*) project[3] is to develop a software component that supports *tour planning* for these schools. During the planning process, quite a lot of restrictions have to be considered that make tour planning a difficult task. Given geographical information and information on which pupils are waiting at which bus stop, MOTOS is meant to compute a set of tours that gets all pupils to their destinations while respecting all relevant constraints [GK96].

As in the other projects a TGraph class was defined in MOTOS. It is used as the (global) internal data structure for the tour planning algorithm, and represents the geographical data, the personal data, and the computed tours simultaneously.

Since MOTOS is part of a larger tour planning system, the interfaces to and from MOTOS had to be specified precisely. Basically, the MOTOS system consists of three modules:

- the *front end* that generates a MOTOS graph from the input data,
- the *planning component* that computes a suitable tour system, and
- the *back end* that hands the results over to the embedding system.

For the planning component different GRAL assertions are used: one for the initial state of the MOTOS graph, and one for the final outcome of the algorithm.

The MOTOS planning component uses well known graph algorithms like Dijkstra's shortest path algorithm, a traveling salesman algorithm for subgraphs, reachability algorithms etc. being confronted with specific aspects of the complex problem to be solved. The graph theoretical approach followed in MOTOS encouraged a kind of compositional algorithm design and enabled a quick solution quite fast. Thus, it was easy to experiment with different graph algorithms to find a good heuristic.

For MOTOS the EER/GRAL approach provided an adequate conceptual framework during the design phase. By using the GraLab, the designed data model could be implemented without much effort. Furthermore, graph theoretical concepts helped in finding a solution to the application problem which could be implemented without changing the view on the MOTOS data structure.

5.4 Application: Program Understanding

Maintenance and reuse of software requires a thorough understanding of software modules and their interdependence. It is impossible to predict all questions or classes of questions a reengineer might ask during the process of program understanding. Hence, a powerful program analysis facility is wanted which allows to answer any questions on user defined levels of granularity about programs written in different languages.

---

[3] The MOTOS project is a joint project of AED Süd, Meckenheim, Germany.

The GUPRO approach (*Generic Understanding of PROgrams*)[4] [EGW96], [EKW96] to program understanding is based on repositories which contain program information in graph data structures. The graph data structures can be consulted by a programming language independent analyzing mechanism.

The definition of the repository follows the modeling techniques described in this paper, namely EER/GRAL descriptions of TGraph classes are implemented by GraLab software. Thus, GUPRO is a generic approach, since EER/GRAL specifications can be used to adapt the system to different languages.

In the first part of the project an EER/GRAL specification of a heterogeneous software environment consisting of sources written in COBOL, CSP, PL/1, JCL, MFS, IMS-DBD and PSB was defined on a coarse grained level of granularity in tight cooperation with reengineers at Volksfürsorge [DFG⁺95]. The resulting model shows the main concepts of the different source languages and their interdependence which are used for supporting source code stocktaking. Here, GRAL assertions are used to specify additional edge types extending the abstract syntax, in order to simplify analysis.

In a first step, *isolated schemes* were defined representing the concepts of each single programming language on a fine grained level. In a second step, these single schemes were *integrated* into a common scheme by melting vertex types representing the same information, by generalization of vertex types representing similar information and by connecting vertex types with edge types.

The *GUPRO toolset* will consist of a parsing component and an analyzing component. It is implemented using GraLab functions.

The *parsing component* translates source codes into graph data structures matching the conceptual model in the EER diagram. It is generated from the programming language grammars, the user defined EER diagramms and their dependencies. The generated parser uses the GraLab library for creating instances of the conceptual model in the graph based repository [Dah95].

The *analyzing component* for language independent program analysis is also triggered by the conceptual model. An important part of the analyzing component is the query component, which allows any questions about the software stored in the repository according to the conceptual model. Retrieval of information from the repository uses a graph query language [Fra96b] suited to the graph based modeling approach described here.

Hence, GUPRO follows a closed approach of declarative conceptual program modeling using EER diagrams, storing program information in a repository using GraLab, and analyzing this repository using a query language in a consistent graph based manner.

---

[4] GUPRO is performed together with the IBM Scientific Center, Heidelberg, and the Volksfürsorge Unternehmensgruppe AG, (a german insurance company), Hamburg. GUPRO is supported by the Bundesminister für Bildung, Wissenschaft, Forschung und Technologie, national initiative on software technology, No. 01 IS 504.

6 Related Work

The main advantage of the EER/GRAL approach to graph based modeling is the coherent and consistent integration of several aspects, namely

- use of an EER dialect for declarative graph class specification,
- use of the GRAL extension of $\mathcal{Z}$ for specifying integrity constraints, and
- the efficient implementation of graphs using GraLab.

Formal semantics of ER-dialects have been defined by several authors. [Che76] already sketches a formal semantics of the basic entity relationship approach. Other sources are [NP80] and [Lie80]. An overview to the main concepts to EER Modeling including global considerations concerning derived schema components and (static) integrity constraints is given in [HK87]. [HG89] gives the semantics of a very general *EER-dialect*, which even allows entities to be attribute values. [TCGB91] discuss semantics for generalizations and specializations.

Older work on *integrity constraints* was done by [TN83]. [Len85] includes in his "semantic" entity relationship approach (SERM) integrity constraints into modells as rules. Constraints in first order logic are introduced by [Süd86] and [BT94]. Cardinality constraints are discussed by [Tha92].

Theoretical foundations for constructive *graph class descriptions* are laid by [Cou96], who uses monadic second order logic. Graph classes for concrete applications can also be specified by graph grammars (see [EK95]). PROGRES [Sch91], [SWZ95] is a language for specifying graph replacement systems, which can be used for this purpose. PROGRES also includes ER diagrams for specifying simple schemata. Thus, it includes also some declarative description elements, though they are weaker than those described here.

For the implementation of discrete structures as *internal structures* there exist efficient libraries like LEDA ([MN96]), though they are not directly adapted to such general graph types like TGraph e.g. directed an undirected graphs are stored differently, vertices are not typed, and the attribute structure is uniform for all vertices. For storing graphs persistently as *external structures* GRAS [KSW95] or PCTE [LW93] may be used. But then again TGraphs are not directly supported. Furthermore external storage leads to a tradeoff between the size of the graphs and the efficiency of graph traversals.

7 Conclusion

An overview on the EER/GRAL approach on graph based modeling was given. In order to define graph classes EER diagrams are used, which are extended by GRAL predicates. In conjunction with the GraLab C++-library this supplies a seamless way for modeling and implementation.

The modeling approach is formally based on $\mathcal{Z}$-specifications for the EER- and GRAL-definitions of TGraph classes. The approach has been successfully applied in various projects in different areas of information modeling.

Acknowledgement: The authors express their thanks for some help in compiling this paper to Ingar Uhe, Manfred Kamp, Bernt Kullbach, and Martin Hümmerich.

References

[BES96] F. Bohlmann, J. Ebert, and R. Süttenbach. An OMT Metamodel. Projektbericht 1/96, Universität Koblenz-Landau, Institut für Softwaretechnik, Koblenz, 1996.

[BT94] J. B. Behm and T. J. Teorey. Relative Constraints in ER Data Models. *R. A. Elmasri, V. Kouramajian, B. Thalheim (Eds.): Entity-Relationship Approach - ER'93, 12th International Conference on the Entity-Relationship Approach, Arlington, Texas, USA, December 15-17, 1993*, pages 46–59, 1994.

[CEW96] M. Carstensen, J. Ebert, and A. Winter. Entity-Relationship-Diagramme und Graphenklassen. to appear as Fachbericht Informatik, 1996, Institut für Softwaretechnik, Universität Koblenz-Landau, 1996.

[Che76] P. P.-X. Chen. The Entity–Relationship Model — Toward a Unified View of Data. *ACM Transactions on Database Systems*, 1(1):9–36, March 1976.

[Cou96] B. Courcelle. Graph structure definition using monadic second-order languages. *In: Proceedings of the Workshop on Finite Models and Descriptive Complexity, Princeton, New Jersey, January 14-17, 1996, to appear in: AMS-DIMACS Series in Discrete Mathematics and Theoretical Computer Science*, 1996.

[Dah95] P. Dahm. PDL: Eine Sprache zur Beschreibung grapherzeugender Parser. Diplomarbeit D-305, Universität Koblenz-Landau, Fachbereich Informatik, Koblenz, Oktober 1995.

[DEL94] P. Dahm, J. Ebert, and C. Litauer. Das EMS-Graphenlabor 3.0. Projektbericht 3/94, Universität Koblenz-Landau, Institut für Softwaretechnik, Koblenz, 1994.

[DFG+95] P. Dahm, J. Fricke, R. Gimnich, M. Kamp, H. Stasch, E. Tewes, and A. Winter. Anwendungslandschaft der Volksfürsorge. Projektbericht 5/95, Universität Koblenz-Landau, Institut für Softwaretechnik, Koblenz, 1995.

[Drü96] M. Drüke. Dokumentation für den Datenflußdiagramm-Editor. Studienarbeit S 429, Universität Koblenz-Landau, Fachbereich Informatik, Koblenz, Mai 1996.

[Ebe87] J. Ebert. A Versatile Data Structure For Edge-Oriented Graph Algorithms. *Communications ACM*, 30(6):513–519, June 1987.

[EC94] J. Ebert and M. Carstensen. Ansatz und Architekur von KOGGE. Projektbericht 2/94, Universität Koblenz-Landau, Institut für Softwaretechnik, Koblenz, 1994.

[EF95] J. Ebert and A. Franzke. A Declarative Approach to Graph Based Modeling. *in: E. Mayr, G. Schmidt, G. Tinhofer (Eds.) Graphtheoretic Concepts in Computer Science Springer, Berlin, Lecture Notes in Computer Science, LNCS 903*, pages 38–50, 1995.

[EGW96] J. Ebert, R. Gimnich, and A. Winter. Wartungsunterstützung in heterogenen Sprachumgebungen, Ein Überblick zum Projekt GUPRO. *in F. Lehner (Hrsg.): Softwarewartung und Reengineering - Erfahrungen und Entwicklungen, Wiesbaden*, pages 263–275, 1996.

[EK95]   H. Ehrig and M. Korff. Computing with Algebraic Graph Transformations - An Overview of Recent Results. *G. Valiente Feruglio and F. Rosello Llompart (eds): Proc. Colloquium on Graph Transformation and its Application in Computer Science. Universitat de les Illes Balears, 1995,* pages 17–23, 1995.

[EKW96]   J. Ebert, M. Kamp, and A. Winter. Generic Support for Understanding Heterogeneous Software. Fachbericht Informatik 3/96, Universität Koblenz-Landau, Fachbereich Informatik, Koblenz, 1996.

[Fra96a] A. Franzke. GRAL : A Reference Manual. to appear as Fachbericht Informatik, Universität Koblenz-Landau, Fachbereich Informatik, Koblenz, 1996.

[Fra96b] A. Franzke. Querying Graph Structures with G^2QL. Fachbericht Informatik 10/96, Universität Koblenz-Landau, Fachbereich Informatik, Koblenz, 1996.

[GK96]   S. Gossens and L. Kirchner. Projekt MOTOS Modellierung, Frontend und Backend. Studienarbeit S 410, Universität Koblenz-Landau, Fachbereich Informatik, Koblenz, Januar 1996.

[Har72]   F. Harary. *Graph theory.* Addison-Wesley, Reading, Mass., 3 edition, 1972.

[HG89]   U. Hohenstein and M. Gogolla. A Calculus for an Extended Entity-Relationship Model Incorporating Arbitrary Data Operations and Aggregate Functions. *C. Batini (Ed.): Entity-Relationship Approach: A Bridge to the User, Proceedings of the Seventh International Conference on Entity-Relationship Approach,* pages 129–148, 1989.

[HK87]   R. Hull and R. King. Semantic Database Modelling: Survey, Applications, and Research Issues. *ACM Computing Surveys,* 19(3):201–260, September 1987.

[KSW95]   N. Kiesel, A. Schürr, and B. Westfechtel. A Graph-Oriented (Software) Engineering Database System. *Information Systems, vol. 20, no. 1,* pages 21–52, 1995.

[KU96]   A. Kölzer and I. Uhe. Benutzerhandbuch für die KOGGE-Tool BONsai, Version 2.0. Projektbericht 4/96, Universität Koblenz-Landau, Institut für Softwaretechnik, Koblenz, 1996.

[Len85]   M. Lenzerini. SERM: Semantic Entity-Relationship Model. *P. P. Chen (ed.): Entity-Relationship Approach: The Use of ER Concept in Knowledge Representation, Proceedings of the Fourth International Conference on Entity-Relationship Approach, Chicago, Illinois, USA, 29-30 October 1985,* pages 270–278, 1985.

[Lie80]   Y. E. Lien. On the Semantics of the Entity-Relationship Data Model. *P. P. Chen (Ed): Entity-Relationship Approach to Systems Analysis and Design. Proc. 1st International Conference on the Entity-Relationship Approach,* pages 155–168, 1980.

[LW93]   J. Jowett L. Wakeman. *PCTE, The Standard for Open Repositories.* Prentice Hall, New York, 1993.

[Meh84]   K. Mehlhorn. *Data structures and algorithms,* volume 2. Graph algorithms and NP-completeness. Springer, Berlin, 1984.

[MN96]   K. Mehlhorn and S. Näher. LEDA. A Platform for Combinatorial and Geometric Computing. Technical report, Max-Planck-Institut für Informatik, 1996.

[NP80]   P. A. Ng and J. F. Paul. A Formal Definition of Entity-Relationship Models. *P. P. Chen (Ed): Entity-Relationship Approach to Systems Analysis and Design. Proc. 1st International Conference on the Entity-Relationship Approach,* pages 211–230, 1980.

[NW95]   J.-M. Nerson and K. Waldén. *Seamless Object-Oriented Software Architecture. Analysis and Design of Reliable Systems.* Prentice Hall, Englewood Cliffs, 1995.

[RBP+91] J. Rumbaugh, M. Blaha, W. Premerlani, F. Eddy, and W. Lorensen. *Object-Oriented Modeling and Design.* Prentice Hall, Englewood Cliffs, 1991.

[Sch91]   A. Schürr. *Operationales Spezifizieren mit Graph Ersetzungssystemen, Formale Definitionen, Anwendungsbeispiele und Werkzeugunterstützung.* Deutscher Universitaetsverlag, Wiesbaden, 1991.

[Spi92]   J. M. Spivey. *The Z Notation: A Reference Manual.* International Series in Computer Science. Prentice Hall, Hemel Hempstead, Hertfordshire, UK, 2 edition, 1992.

[Süd86]   N. Südkamp. Enforcement of Integrity Constraints in an Entity Relationship Data Model. Bericht 8607, Institut für Informatik und Praktische Mathematik, Christian Albrechts Universität, Kiel, September 1986.

[SWZ95]   A. Schürr, A.J. Winter, and A. Zündorf. Graph Grammar Engineering with PROGRES. *W. Schäfer (Ed.): ESEC '95, 5th European Software Engineering Conference,* pages 219–234, 1995.

[TCGB91] L. Tucherman, M. A. Casanova, P. M. Gualandi, and A. P. Braga. A Proposal for Formalizing and Extending the Generalization and Subset Abstractions in the Enity-Relationship Model. *F. H. Lochovsky (Ed.): Entity-Relationship Approach to Database Design and Querying, Proceedings of the Eight International Conference on Entity-Relationship Approach, Toronto, Canada, 18-20 October, 1989,* pages 27–41, 1991.

[Tha92]   B. Thalheim. Fundamentals of Cardinality Constraints. *G. Pernul, A. M. Tjoa (Eds.): Entity-Relationship Approach - ER'92, 11th International Conference on the Entity-Relationship Approach, Karlsruhe, Germany, October 7-9, 1992,* pages 7–23, 1992.

[TN83]   Y. Tabourier and D. Nanci. The Occurrence Structure Concept: An Approach to Structural Integrity Constraints in the Entity-Relationship Model. *P. P. Chen (Ed.): Proc. 2nd Int. Conf. on the Entity-Relationship Approach (ER'81),* pages 73–108, 1983.

On the Applicability of Schema Integration Techniques to Database Interoperation

Mark W.W. Vermeer and Peter M.G. Apers

Centre for Telematics and Information Technology
University of Twente, Enschede, The Netherlands
{ *vermeer, apers* } *@cs.utwente.nl*

Abstract. We discuss the applicability of schema integration techniques developed for tightly-coupled database interoperation to interoperation of databases stemming from different modelling contexts. We illustrate that in such an environment, it is typically quite difficult to infer the real-world semantics of remote classes from their definition in remote databases. However, defining relationships between the real-world semantics of schema elements is essential in existing schema integration techniques. We propose to base database interoperation in such environments on instance-level semantic relationships, to be defined using what we call object comparison rules. Both the local and the remote classifications of the appropriately merged instances are maintained, allowing for the derivation of a global class hierarchy if desired.

1 Introduction

Interoperation among pre-existing, heterogeneous, and autonomous databases has been an important research topic in the last few years. Recently, the trend in database interoperability research is moving towards architectures for interoperation of databases on a scale that goes beyond the context of a single organisation, exploiting the communication facilities offered by world-wide networks. The canonical model used is often an object-oriented one [1]. It has been recognised that such an environment requires flexible and scalable architectures, where users of the component databases are provided with tools to establish importation of information from remote data sources [2,3]. Tightly-coupled approaches, where the schemata of all component databases are unified into a single global schema by a central modelling authority possessing a helicopter view of all component databases [4], are generally agreed to be infeasible in such situations, if only because the component databases may be quite diverse, and no-one can be expected to grasp all information available in the interoperation environment.

Two main approaches towards a more loosely-coupled style of database interoperation can be distinguished. In the multidatabase approach [2], users are expected to define their information needs using a powerful query language with constructs for on-the-fly semantic reconciliation of heterogeneous data. It has been argued, however, that this puts an unacceptable burden on the user, to whom a single logical view of the interoperable databases is no longer presented.

An alternative is the federated approach [5], where a locally integrated schema is composed out of the schema of the local database and the import schema, which is a selection on export schemata of remote databases, by defining relationships between local and imported data. In this paper, we address the question to what extent schema integration techniques developed primarily for tightly-coupled environments are applicable in such environments.

One of the central problems with this approach is that the definition of relationships between local and imported data is far from trivial in a situation where information on the meaning of a remote schema is limited. In tightly-coupled architectures, the schema integrator is supposed to have a helicopter view of all databases, possibly obtained from intensive communication with the DBA's of the participating databases, but in our context a schema integrator must typically thrive on the remote class definitions and some limited additional information. Although many authors have advocated a more loosely-coupled approach to database interoperation, this issue has not been dealt with satisfactorily. Integrated data definition techniques used in federated architectures are usually directly based on schema integration techniques employed in tightly-coupled approaches [6], which in turn are often strongly similar to view integration techniques [7]. All these schema integration techniques require either explicitly or implicitly that (the relationship between) the real-world semantics of the classes to be integrated is known. This is a reasonable assumption in tightly-coupled approaches, but as we will illustrate in this paper, in a federation of databases from multiple modelling contexts this may be surprisingly difficult.

Instance integration [8] has been considered to logically succeed schema integration; i.e. once the relationship between classes defined in different schemata has been determined, the integration of the database instances becomes an issue. More recently, some work has emerged that explicitly considers instances in determining schematic relationships [9,10]. In this paper, we argue that in absence of full knowledge on the semantics of remotely defined classes, instance level semantic relationships form an appropriate basis for database interoperation. In essence, we maintain both the local and the remote classifications on a set of appropriately merged objects. Relationships between local and remote classes may then be derived from relationships between the objects they classify.

The remainder of this paper is organised as follows. In Section 2, we review some basic ideas of schema integration, illustrating that the semantic knowledge required by these techniques may not be available in loosely-coupled environments. In Section 3, we propose an instance-based approach to database integration. In Section 4, we discuss the derivation of integrated objects and classes from instance level relationships. Section 5 then illustrates that several schema-integration techniques are still applicable in our approach. Section 6 presents our conclusions.

2 Schema integration

In this section, we explain why traditional schema integration is not quite suited for federations where knowledge on the semantics of imported schemata is limited. Many techniques for schema integration exist [6]. We do *not* intend to discuss existing schema integration techniques in depth here; rather, we focus on some basic assumptions that do not apply to loosely-coupled federations.

2.1 Classes and entity types

The definition of a class is the result of conceptual modelling performed during database design, in which *entity types* [11] are distinguished. An entity type E is defined as a set of similar real-world objects. Each of the real-world objects grouped in an entity type is described by a set of *properties* associated with the entity type. In the database schema implementing the conceptual model, an entity type is represented by a class C, whose definition contains the properties associated with E. The entity type represented by a class C is called the *Real-World Semantics (RWS)* [12] of C. Moreover, the class may be populated with *database objects* representing some (not typically all) of the real-world objects grouped by the entity type. This set is called the *extension* of C.

As entity types are just sets of real-world objects, set relationships between entity types may exist. In this section, we will use the *subset* relationship as an example. [1] If an entity type E' contains a subset of the real-world objects represented by E, E' is called a *subentity* of E, or E' isa E. Let E' be represented in the database by a class C'. Within a database, we expect the following four statements to be equivalent: (1) C' is a subclass of C; (2) the RWS of C' is a subset of the RWS of C (E' isa E); (3) the extension of C' is a subset of the extension of C; (4) the set of properties describing C' is a superset of the set of properties describing C.

Example Consider a database DB containing classes **Person** and **Employee**, representing the entity types consisting of the set of persons resp. employees in the real world. Assuming that all employees are persons, Employee is a subentity of Person. Therefore each employee is described by the properties Name and Age, say, in his capacity as a person, and by the additional property Salary, which is used exclusively to describe employees. Moreover, to ensure the integrity of the database, every database object in the extension of **Employee** is contained in the extension of **Person** as well. Hence **Employee** isa **Person**. Figure 1a illustrates this situation, where C=**Person** and C'=**Employee**. □

2.2 View integration, database integration

Both view integration [7] and (tightly-coupled) database integration are concerned with reconciling multiple conceptual models. The difference is that the

---

[1] Throughout this section, we will make simplifying assumptions. Our goal here is not to discuss schema integration in depth, but rather to illustrate some features that limit the applicability of these techniques.

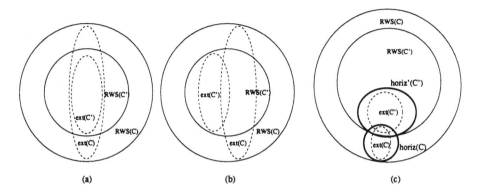

Fig. 1. Real-World Semantics, extensions, and modelling horizons

former is a design activity, whereas the latter deals with schemata that are already populated [6]. Existing work in both of these fields requires some kind of *integration assertions* postulating the relationship between the RWS of the schema elements to be integrated. We here illustrate this for database integration.

Let E be an entity type implemented in a database DB by a class C with properties $prop(C)$ and extension $ext(C)$. Let E' be an entity type implemented in a database DB' by a class C' with properties $prop(C')$ and extension $ext(C')$. Suppose we have the integration assertion $E' \subseteq E$. Note however, that due to modelling autonomy, $prop(C) \subseteq prop(C')$ does not necessarily hold, nor does $ext(C') \subseteq ext(C)$, as illustrated in Figure 1b. An integrated schema would then define virtual classes IC and IC', where $prop(IC') = prop(C') \cup prop(C)$ and $prop(IC) = prop(C)$. Moreover, the extensions of the virtual classes are defined as $ext(IC') = ext(C')$, and $ext(IC) = ext(C) \cup ext(C')$. Now it is assured that IC and IC' satisfy the four aspects of an **isa** relationship listed above.

Note however that whereas this settles things from a conceptual perspective, there are problems providing *values* for the properties of the integration classes. For example, IC'-objects, stemming from $ext(C')$ in DB', do not have values for $prop(C)$, as these properties are defined in the context of DB only. This is a known problem inherent to database integration.

2.3 Database integration in a loosely-coupled environment

So far, we tacitly assumed that set relationships between entity types stemming from different environments were discovered. In the view integration case, this assumption is quite realistic, as different user groups can be asked to provide precise definitions of the entity types they distinguish. The assumption may still be applicable for tightly-coupled database integration performed within a coherent context. However, if database interoperation is performed at such a scale that this kind of communication between database developer and database integrator is infeasible, an integrator is faced with the task of *inferring the entity type a class represents from the class definition only.* In this subsection, we discuss why this might be surprisingly difficult. We illustrate that, since conceptual modelling is always done within a particular *context* [12], one has to be extremely careful in postulating relationships between entity types from different conceptual models. The main problems we identify are *modelling horizons* and *subjectivity of classification.*

Example: Modelling horizons Suppose database DB is a university database. DB contains a class Employee, which is the implementation of an entity type Employee distinguished in its conceptual model. Let DB' be the database of the computer science department of this particular university. DB' contains a class Person implementing an entity named Person from its conceptual model. Given the general meaning of these terms, common sense may easily lead an integrator to conclude that Employee isa Person. This would be incorrect, however. Even though DB appears to implement the entity 'any employee', we know from the context of DB that this database is concerned with employees working for this particular university only. Moreover, DB' only regards persons as far as they have any connection to the CS-department, such as students and faculty. □

What we encounter here, is that the context in which conceptual modelling is performed introduces a *modelling horizon* to a conceptual model (this corresponds to the way in which the term 'context' is used in [13]). Whenever an entity type E is modelled, it is usually intended to mean 'E as far as it is of any concern to us'. Thus, instead of implementing E, a class C really implements an entity type $horiz(E)$, where $horiz(E) \subseteq E$.

Within a single database, or even within a tightly-coupled environment of databases, this horizon is usually of no importance, as all entity types are implicitly constrained by the *same* horizon. All relationships one expects to hold between entity types are valid. For example,

$$E \subseteq E' \Rightarrow horiz(E) \subseteq horiz(E')$$

When trying to deduce the entity types implemented by classes stemming from *different* modelling contexts and determining their relationships, however, this modelling horizon is quite relevant indeed, as it may invalidate obvious relationships between entity types. In other words,

$$E \subseteq E' \not\Rightarrow horiz(E) \subseteq horiz'(E')$$

Example As illustrated in Figure 1c, Employee (C') is not a subclass of Person (C) when their modelling horizon is taken into account. Even in this simple example, where the contexts of the different databases are quite closely related, deducing the relationships between the entity types represented by the classes from the class definition alone is far from trivial. If an integrator would have knowledge of the contexts of the databases, he would make the correct assertion that these classes have a common virtual superclass PersonAtOurUniversity. □

Some authors [14] explicitly disregard modelling horizons by introducing an 'equivalent domain assumption'. In our view, such an approach is infeasible in loosely-coupled database interoperation, where the modelling horizon can be regarded as an important semantic aspect of a class.

Subjectivity of classification Another important problem with inferring the RWS of remote classes is that conceptual modelling of a real-world domain is essentially a *classification* of 'similar' real-world objects into entity types. The problem with classifications is that they are inherently subjective, which hampers the definition of mappings between such classifications, as in [14,15]. Think of classifications like FederatedDBS versus MultiDBS, Hotel versus BudgetAccomodation, or even AmericanCar versus BeautifulThing. Many real-world examples of different classifications for identical real-world domains exist. It is then often very hard to precisely define the relationships between these classifications.

2.4 Our approach

In this paper, we present a possible alternative for the definition of integration assertions of the form above. In particular, instead of defining semantic relationships between different classifications for a similar real-world domain, we provide for the definition of semantic relationships among the classified *objects*. By applying *both* classifications on the set of appropriately merged objects, relationships between the different classes may then be derived. Note that such comparisons are also made in traditional integration approaches in the phase of *instance integration* [8], which is usually considered to logically succeed schema integration.

3 Instance-based integration

We treat interoperable databases as a collection of database objects, each representing a certain real-world object. Database objects are grouped into classes. Each class is assigned a set of properties by which the objects of that class are described. The set of properties determines the *structure* of an object. Each property has a *domain* from which its values are taken. For *referential* properties, this domain is a class. Each database object provides *values* for its properties. This set of values determines the *state* of a database object. We consider different databases describing a similar real-world domain in different ways.

Example Figure 2 shows a database *DB* which is used by a university department for purposes of reporting on its output. *DB* keeps track of publications and master's theses realised by the department. An example database instance is shown. The classification of the database objects reflects *DB*'s purpose. In this context, it is important to distinguish professional publications from scientific ones, and refereed publications from non-refereed ones, as each of these classes of publications have different status.

On the other hand, Figure 3 depicts a database *DB'* maintained within a certain research project, recording research publications realised within the project. Although the databases have similar application domains, they differ both in the objects distinguished and the classification for these objects, reflecting the different contexts in

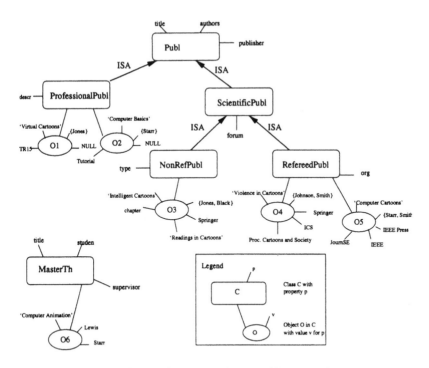

Fig. 2. The department's publications database

which the databases are used. Note that it would be far from easy to a priori define relationships between concepts such as **NonRefPubl** and **Paper**.

In the following, we assume that a user of the department database (the local database) wishes to create an integrated view of his own database and the project's database (the remote database). □

3.1 Object relationships

We now define a number of object relationships, which are basically the instance level equivalent of class relationships distinguished in traditional schema integration [6]. We do not only consider equality of a local object O [2] and a remote object O' [8], but also additional instance relationships, representing semantic relationships that are usually dealt with at the schema level. The following relationships are considered:

- O' may be *equal* to some locally observed object O. In the example, O'_6 is equal to O_4, 'Violence in Cartoons'. The local and remote database thus distinguish the same real-world object.

---

[2] The term 'object O' is to be interpreted as 'the real-world object represented by database object O' throughout this section. For clarity, a real-world object may also be referred to by the value of a key property.

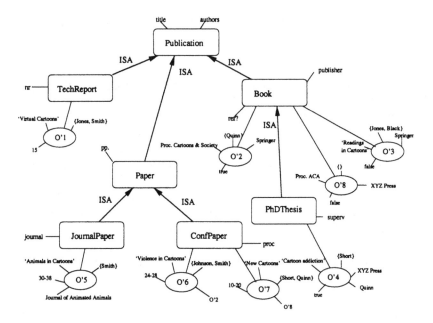

Fig. 3. A project's literature database

- O' may be *similar* to some set of locally observed objects $\{O_i, \ldots O_j\}$, collected in the local class C. We distinguish between strict and approximate similarity.

  Strict similarity occurs when O' logically belongs to C. That is, had O' been observed locally, it would have been classified under C. For example, had the department known about the publication of 'Animals in Cartoons' (O'_5), it would have been classified as a **RefereedPubl** (assuming all journals are refereed).

  Approximate similarity occurs when $C \cup \{O'\}$ is a meaningful class. That is, O' and the objects in C are sufficiently similar to group them into a new, more general class. In the example, a PhD thesis can be seen as approximately similar to a Master's thesis. That is, **MasterTh** $\cup \{O'_4\}$ would represent a meaningful class; let's call it **GradTh**.

- Locally O' would not be seen as an object in its own right, but rather as a set of property values used to describe another object O'', where O'' is equal or similar to a local object O. We say that O is *descriptive* of O''. For example, the object O'_2 is locally seen as a value of the 'forum' property of the object 'Violence in Cartoons'($O'' = O_4$).

- O' would locally be seen as a *constituent* of, or constituted by, an object O'' which is similar or equal to a local object O. That is, O' and O are observed at different levels of granularity. O' is an *aggregation* of O and some other objects, or vice versa. For example, O'_3 ('Readings in Cartoons') is a book containing a chapter by the editors, represented in DB (O_3). Note that we distinguish between aggregation and delegation. The former is used for composition of objects into a larger object, while the latter expresses relationships among objects.

To express these object relationships [3], we use the following predicates:

1. $Eq(A, B)$ holds iff object A is the same as the object represented by the modelling abstraction B. As illustrated above, B can either be an object (equal objects) or a set of properties (descriptive object).

2. $Sim(A, B[, NewCl])$ holds iff object A is similar to the objects represented by the modelling abstraction B. Again B may be an object or a set of values. If the similarity is approximate, $NewCl$ is the name of the new class classifying A and B.

3. $Aggr(A, B[, Role])$ holds iff the object represented by the modelling abstraction A is an aggregate of the object represented by the modelling abstraction B. A specific role played by B in A may be specified optionally.

Example For the databases of Figure 2 and 3, the relationships sketched above may be postulated as follows:

- Both databases describe technical report no. 15: $Eq(O_1, O_1')$.
- Proceedings are seen as separate objects in DB' and as values describing conference papers in DB: $Eq(O_2', O_4.\{\text{forum}\})$ and $Sim(O_8', \texttt{ConfPaper}.\{\text{forum}\})$.
- Book O_3' is a value describing O_3 in DB:$Eq(O_3', O_3.\{\text{forum}\})$.
- We might import Short's PhD thesis as something approximately similar to a master's thesis: $Sim(O_4', \texttt{MasterTh}, \texttt{GraduationTh})$.
- There are papers appearing in both databases: $Eq(O_6', O_4)$.
- The chapter by Jones and Black is contained in their book: $Aggr(O_3, O_3')$.
- A PhD thesis is refereed: $Sim(O_4', \texttt{RefereedPub})$.
- The journal paper is a refereed one: $Sim(O_5', \texttt{RefereedPubl})$.
- 'New Cartoons' did not appear in a refereed forum: $Sim(O_7', \texttt{NonRefPubl})$.
- 'JournSE' is a journal: $Sim(O_5, \texttt{JournalPaper})$.
- By default, we assume that all remote objects are similar to \texttt{Publ}.

□

3.2 Object comparison rules

Obviously, when integrating databases, the integrator cannot be expected to inspect individual objects in a pairwise manner to discover relationships between them. We therefore introduce *object comparison rules* as a means to specify conditions under which objects have a certain relationship with one another. For example,

$Sim(O' : \texttt{ConfPaper}, \texttt{RefereedPub}) \leftarrow O'.proc.ref? = true$

$Eq(O' : \texttt{ProfessionalPubl}, O : \texttt{TechReport}) \leftarrow occurs(concat(\text{'TR'}, O.nr), O'.descr)$

---

[3] A further relationship between O and O' may be distinguished: a *hidden relationship*, a relationship modelled in neither the local nor the remote database. For example, let O' be the object 'the Netherlands', then O_6 might be written in the Netherlands. Thus, O' might be the value of a new referential property 'written in' of O_6. In this paper, we do not consider such relationships between local and remote objects.

Comparable rules may be defined to specify the other relationships occurring in our example. Observe that such rules are able to deal with so-called *schematic discrepancies* [16], as they describe instances rather than classes. They distinguish themselves from the usual assertions used in schema integration [15] in that the sets of related objects that they define need not coincide with the class extensions of any of the schemata. Note that these rules extend the identity rules of [8] in that they allow for the definition of object relationships other than identity. We discuss these rules further in Section 5.

4 Integrated objects and classes

Having compared local and remote objects, a set of integrated objects and their classification must be determined. The problem that needs to be attacked here can be described as follows:

Given: (1) A set of local objects SL; (2) A classification CL for these objects; (3) A set of remote objects SF; (4) A classification CF for these objects; (5) Relationships between SL and SF;

Find: (1) A new set of objects SI (Subsection 4.1); (2) A classification CI for these objects (Subsection 4.2).

4.1 A new set of objects

Object-value conflicts To arrive at a set of integrated objects, first the local and remote view as to which aspects of the real world are modelled as objects must be reconciled. In particular, whenever an object O in database DB is found to be descriptive of an object O' in DB', i.e. $Eq(O, O'.Props)$ holds, it must be decided whether *Props* is to be expressed as an object (as in DB) or as a value (as in DB'). Such an *object-value conflict* is usually settled using a fixed strategy, such as 'settle every object-value conflict in favour of the local database', or 'settle every object-value conflict in favour of the object'.

To conform objects and values, *conformed object sets SLC* and *SFC* are created from SL and SF, respectively. This involves the creation of a *virtual object* from a value-set whenever an object-value conflict is settled in favour of the object, and the hiding of an object whenever an object-value conflict is settled in favour of the value.

Although we cannot treat object-value conflicts in depth here, we do remark that the creation of a virtual object gives rise to new object relationships. Let O'' be a virtual object created from the values of a property set PS of an object O based on the relationship $Eq(O.PS, O')$. This relationship is now replaced by $Eq(O'', O')$. Alternatively, let O''' be a virtual object created from the values of a property set PS of an object O based on the relationship $Eq(O''.PS, O')$, where $O'' \neq O$, but O and O'' both belong to the class C defining the properties PS. Then (approximate) similarity may hold between O''' and the class C' to which O' belongs. Such similarity relationships may be assumed by default or specified through additional rules.

*Example*Consider the relationships $Eq(O'_2, O_4.\{\text{forum}\})$ and $Eq(O'_3, O_3.\{\text{forum}\})$. Note that the strategy of settling all conflicts in favour of the local database would favour the value representation. We here assume that the object preference strategy is applied, however. Thus, virtual local objects O_7 and O_8 are created from the values 'Readings in Cartoons' and 'Proc.Cartoons and Society' of the forum property of O_3 and O_4. Moreover, a virtual object O_9 is created for the forum value 'TrSE' of O_5, as this object belongs to the class ScientificPubl in which the property forum is defined. All virtual objects belong to the virtual class Forum. The relationships $Eq(O_7, O'_3)$ and $Eq(O_8, O'_2)$ are deduced. □

Integrated objects Given the conformed object sets $SLC = \{O_1, O_2, \ldots, O_n\}$ and $SFC = \{O'_1, O'_2, \ldots, O'_m\}$, we generate an integrated object set $SI = \{O_{ij}|Eq(O_i, O'_j)\} \cup \{O_{i0}|\neg\exists j : Eq(O_i, O'_j)\} \cup \{O_{0j}|\neg\exists i : Eq(O_i, O'_j)\}$. Thus, the integrated object set is a merge of the adapted local and remote object sets, merging duplicate representations of the same real world object into a single integrated representation. Moreover, the aggregation relationship between integrated objects is derived from the aggregation relationship between local and remote objects by substituting the integrated equivalent of each of the related objects.

Example The set SI in our example is formed by

- Representations for real-world objects modelled as objects by both the local and the remote model: O_{11}, O_{46}.
- Foreign objects locally observed only virtually (i.e. as values): O_{73}, O_{82}.
- Virtual local objects not observed in the remote database: O_{90}.
- Objects observed only locally: $O_{20}, O_{30}, O_{50}, O_{60}$.
- Foreign objects not observed locally: $O_{04}, O_{05}, O_{07}, O_{08}$.

Furthermore, O_{73} is at a different level of aggregation than O_{30}. See also Figure 4. □

4.2 A new classification

In essence, we maintain both the local and the remote classification on the integrated object set. That is, initially the set of classes in the integration CI equals $\{\dot{C}|C \in CL\} \cup \{\dot{C}'|C' \in CF\}$, writing $\dot{C}$ to represent the integrated equivalent of the local class C. The set of integrated objects belonging to an integrated class is determined as follows:

- If a local object O_i belongs to a local class C, then the integrated object O_{ij} belongs to $\dot{C}$. (O_i may be virtual, in that case C refers to the corresponding virtual class)
- If a remote object O'_j belongs to a remote class C', then O_{ij} belongs to $\dot{C}'$. (O'_j may be virtual, in that case C' refers to the corresponding virtual class)
- If an object O'_j is strictly similar to a class C, then O_{ij} belongs to $\dot{C}$.
- If an object O'_j is approximately similar to a class C, then a *virtual superclass* CV is introduced. Both O_{ij} and all objects O_{kl} derived from objects in C belong to CV.

- If an integrated object O_{ij} belongs to $\dot{C}$ and $\dot{C}'$, where C and C' stem from different databases, and neither $\dot{C}$ isa $\dot{C}'$ nor $\dot{C}'$ isa $\dot{C}$ holds, then a *virtual subclass CV* is introduced. O_{ij} belongs to CV.

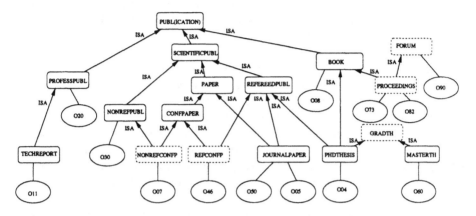

Fig. 4. Integrated objects and classes

Example In our running example, seventeen(!) integrated classes arise. Some examples: PAPER=$\{O_{46}, O_{50}, O_{05}, O_{07}\}$, JOURNALPAPER=$\{O_{50}, O_{05}\}$, CONFPAPER=$\{O_{46}, O_{07}\}$, the local virtual class FORUM=$\{O_{73}, O_{82}, O_{90}\}$, and integrated virtual classes such as REFCONFP=$\{O_{46}\}$ and PROCEEDINGS=$\{O_{73}, O_{82}\}$. The complete set of integrated classes is depicted in Figure 4. □

Although in principle the definition of integrated extensions for local classes is an appropriate basis for loosely-coupled database interoperation, in some situations it is desirable to derive an integrated class hierarchy describing the relationships between local and remote classes. Such class relationships follow from relationships between the integrated extensions. That is, the integrated class hierarchy is a consequence of relationships between local and remote objects rather than being defined explicitly. In particular, the following relationships between the integrated equivalent of a local class $\dot{C}$ and the integrated equivalent of a remote class $\dot{C}'$ may arise:

1. $\dot{C}$ isa $\dot{C}'$, i.e. $\forall O \in C \exists O' \in C' \mid Eq(O, O') \lor Sim(O, C')$ (or $\dot{C}'$ isa $\dot{C}$ etc.).
2. $\dot{C}$ and $\dot{C}'$ are identical, i.e. $\dot{C}$ isa $\dot{C}'$ and $\dot{C}'$ isa $\dot{C}$.
3. $\dot{C}$ and $\dot{C}'$ have a common virtual subclass CV, i.e. $\exists O \in C, O' \in C' \mid Eq(O, O') \lor Sim(O, C') \lor Sim(O', C)$.
4. $\dot{C}$ and $\dot{C}'$ have a common virtual superclass CV, i.e. $\forall O \in C, O' \in C' \mid Sim(O, C', CV) \lor Sim(O', C, CV)$.
5. $\dot{C}$ and $\dot{C}'$ have CV-generalisable elements, i.e. $\exists O' \in C' \mid Sim(O', C, CV)$ (or $\exists O \in C$ etc.). Here CV is a superclass of $\dot{C}$ and a virtual subclass CV' of $\dot{C}'$, where $CV' = \{O'|O' \in C' \land Sim(O', C, CV)\}$.

The class hierarchy for our example is depicted in Figure 4.

5 Specifying instance-based interoperability

5.1 Description overlap

Having determined a set of integrated objects and a corresponding classification, we turn to the discussion of structure and state of integrated objects. We touch upon this subject only briefly, as it has been treated exhaustively by existing schema integration methodologies.

In principle, we could simply define the structure and state of integrated objects as the merge of their local and remote counterparts. However, there is the possibility of *description overlap*; i.e. the local and the remote database contain descriptions of identical real-world properties. Description overlap may occur in any of the kinds of object relationships we distinguished. To establish the description overlap between objects stemming from classes C and C', *property equivalence assertions* between their properties must be defined. A property equivalence assertion states that a local and a remote property represent the same real-world property. In general, m properties of C may be equivalent to n properties of C'. That is, a property p of C derived from these m properties may be equivalent to a similar derived property p' of C'. Equivalent local and remote properties are merged into a single integrated property. Equivalent properties need not have identical *domains*, however. For integration purposes, a *conversion function* [17] between these domains must be defined. Even when domains of equivalent properties have been mapped to one another, different databases may disagree on the value chosen from that domain to represent a property p of a certain object O. Some *decision function* [18] is then applied.

Some additional observations can be made for *referential properties*. As the domain of a referential property is a class, conversion and integration of equivalent referential properties is influenced by the integrated class hierarchy. Conversion of a referential property is implicit; the integrated property refers to integrated objects instead of local objects. To infer an integrated delegation hierarchy, we again use an instance-based approach. That is, the domain of an integrated referential property is the most specific integrated class containing all referenced integrated objects.

Example Consider the integrated class REFCONFP. Local and remote objects merged in this class have the equivalent referential properties 'proc' resp. 'forum'. The domain class PROCEEDINGS is now inferred for the integrated referential property. □

5.2 Specification of database interoperation

A database interoperation specification consists of object comparison rules accompanied by property equivalence assertions. To express object relationship conditions, a tailored equality predicate $=_{prop}$ is used to compare values of equivalent properties, which is defined modulo any conversion function defined on the properties involved.

Object relationships and inheritance Let C be a local class and C_1', C_2' be remote classes such that C_2' **isa** C_1'. Then

$\forall O, O' \mid Eq(O : C, O' : C_2') \Rightarrow Eq(O : C, O' : C_1')$ and

$\forall O, O' \mid O' \in C_2' \wedge Eq(O : C, O' : C_1') \Rightarrow Eq(O : C, O' : C_2')$ and

$\forall O \mid Sim(O : C, C_2') \Rightarrow Sim(O : C, C_1')$

These laws can be used to derive additional object relationships from those defined directly by the object comparison rules. Equality is a stronger notion than similarity; hence equality rules are evaluated before similarity rules. A specifier may exploit these laws by defining equality rules on as general classes as possible, but similarity is defined on the most specific class.

The following requirements are made to ensure that Eq has the intended semantics. (1) Every equality rule defines a one-to-one mapping; and (2) the definition of equality rules of the form $Eq(O : C, O' : C') \leftarrow \psi$ when there also exists a rule $Eq(O : C_{sup}, O' : C'_{sup}) \leftarrow \phi$ where C **isa** C_{sup} or C' **isa** C'_{sup}, is allowed only if $\psi \not\Rightarrow \phi$. Furthermore, to avoid inconsistencies, the definition of similarity rules of the form $Sim(O : C, C') \leftarrow \psi$ is not allowed if there exists a rule $Sim(O : C, C'_{sup}) \leftarrow \phi$ where C' **isa** C'_{sup} and $\psi \Rightarrow \neg \phi$.

6 Discussion

The purpose of this paper has been to demonstrate the use of extensions in loosely-coupled database interoperation. We have argued that instance level relationship specifications can be the basis of a database interoperation mechanism. We believe that the information provided by the database extension can compensate for the decrease in knowledge of remote schemata and their modelling contexts, which is inherent to loose coupling. Thus, we avoid having to define class relationships, which we believe to be error-prone in view of modelling horizons and subjectivity of classification.

It may be observed that the use of object comparison rules is similar to works exploiting a query language for defining multidatabase mappings such as [19], and also [20]. Distinguishing features are the various object relationships we defined, leading to a style of specification which is suitable to loosely-coupled database interoperation, and the possibility of deriving a global class hierarchy. Note that in mediator systems aimed at interoperation of data not necessarily managed by a DBMS, instance-based approaches have been developed as well [21,22]. Compared to these contexts the schema information available in a federation of databases allows for the derivation of a schema for the integrated instances obtained through the interoperation mechanism.

Since we derive an integrated class hierarchy based on instance-level information, our approach is primarily targeted at relatively stable environments where discrepancies exist between the viewpoints of different databases containing related data. As in principle changes in the local extensions may result in changes to this integrated class hierarchy, our approach must be extended to also deal with dynamic environments where extensional relationships between classes are unstable. For example, a query mechanism capable of dealing with schema evolution at the integrated level could be devised. Alternatively, object comparison rules could be used in the context of import/export-based database interoperation [23], where a global hierarchy is not used at all. This is a subject of our current research.

We are also working on the inclusion of methods and constraints in our integration strategy. In particular, we are interested in the additional semantics that local methods and constraints provide for the local data structures, and the way in which this information can be used to detect inconsistencies in interoperation specifications. Some results in this direction can be found in [24].

References

[1] E. Pitoura, O. Bukhres and A. Elmagarmid, "Object orientation in multidatabase systems," *Comput. Surv.*, 27, no. 2, pp. 141–195, June 1995.

[2] W. Litwin, L. Mark and N. Roussopoulos, "Interoperability of multiple autonomous databases," *ACM Computing Surveys*, 22, no. 3, pp. 267–293, Sept. 1990.

[3] G. Wiederhold, "Value-added mediation in large-scale information systems," in *IFIP Data Semantics (DS-6), Atlanta, Georgia.* 1995.

[4] A. P. Sheth and J. A. Larson, "Federated database systems for managing distributed, heterogeneous and autonomous databases," *ACM Computing Surveys*, 22, no. 3, pp. 183–236, Sept. 1990.

[5] D. Heimbigner and D. McLeod, "A federated architecture for information management," *ACM Trans. Off. Inf. Syst.*, 3, no. 3, pp. 253–278, July 1985.

[6] C. Batini, M. Lenzerini and S. B. Navathe, "A comparative analysis of methodologies for database schema integration," *ACM Computing Surveys*, 18, no. 4, Dec. 1986.

[7] S. Spaccapietra and C. Parent, "View integration: A step forward in solving structural conflicts," *IEEE Trans. Knowl. & Data Eng.*, 6, no. 2, pp. 258–274, Apr. 1994.

[8] E-P. Lim, J. Srivastava, S. Prabhakar and J. Richardson, "Entity identification in database integration," in *Proceedings Ninth International Conference on Data Engineering, Vienna, Austria, Apr. 19–23, 1993.* Washington, DC: IEEE Computer Society Press, pp. 294–301, 1993.

[9] W-S. Li and C. Clifton, "Semantic integration in heterogeneous databases using neural networks," in *Proceedings of Twentieth International Conference on Very Large Data Bases, Santiago, Chile, Sept. 12–15, 1994*, J. Bocca, M. Jarke and C. Zaniolo, Eds. San Mateo, CA: Morgan Kaufmann Publishers, pp. 1–12, 1994.

[10] M. Garcia-Solaco, F. Saltor and M. Castellanos, "A structure based schema integration methodology," in *Proceedings Eleventh International Conference on Data Engineering, Taipei, Taiwan, Mar. 6–10, 1995.* Washington, DC: IEEE Computer Society Press, pp. 505–512, 1995.

[11] P. P. Chen, "The entity-relationship model - Towards a unified view of data," *ACM Trans. Database Syst.*, 1, no. 1, pp. 9–36, 1976.

[12] A. Sheth and V. Kashyap, "So far (schematically) yet so near (semantically)," in *IFIP Interoperable Database Systems (DS-5), Lorne, Victoria, Australia, 16–20 November, 1992.* Amsterdam: North-Holland, pp. 283–312, 1993.

[13] M. Garcia-Solaco, F. Saltor and M. Castellanos, "Semantic heterogeneity in multi-database systems," in *Object-oriented multidatabase systems*, O. A. Bukhres and A. K. Elmagarmid, Eds. Englewood Cliffs, NJ: Prentice-Hall, pp. 129–195, 1996.

[14] M. V. Mannino, S. B. Navathe and W. Effelsberg, "A rule-based approach for merging generalization hierarchies," *Inf. Syst.*, 13, no. 3, pp. 257–272, 1988.

[15] Y. Dupont, "Resolving fragmentation conflicts in schema integration," in *13th International Conference on Entity-Relationship Approach*. New York–Heidelberg–Berlin: Springer-Verlag, pp. 513–532, 1994.

[16] R. Krishnamurthy, W. Litwin and W. Kent, "Interoperability of heterogeneous databases with schematic discrepancies," in *Proc. First Intl. Workshop on Interoperability in Multidatabase Systems*. Montvale, NJ: IEEE Press, pp. 144–151, 1991.

[17] W. Kent, "Solving domain mismatch and schema mismatch problems with an object-oriented database programming language," in *Proceedings of Seventeenth International Conference on Very Large Data Bases, Barcelona, Spain, Sept. 3–6, 1991*, G. M. Lohman, A. Sernadas and R. Camps, Eds. San Mateo, CA: Morgan Kaufmann Publishers, pp. 147–160, 1991.

[18] U. Dayal and H-Y. Hwang, "View definition and generalization for database integration in a multidatabase system," *IEEE Trans. Software Eng.*, 10, no. 6, pp. 628–645, Nov. 1984.

[19] E. Kuehn and T. Ludwig, "VIP-MDBS: A logic multidatabase system," in *Proceedings of International Symposium on Databases in Paralleland Distributed Systems, Austin, Texas, Dec. 5–7, 1988*, S. Jajodia, W. Kim and A. Silberschatz, Eds. Montvale, NJ: IEEE Press, pp. 190–201, 1988.

[20] M. H. Scholl, H-J. Schek and M. Tresch, "Object algebra and views for multi-objectbases," in *Distributed object management*, M. T. Oszu, U. Dayal and P. Valduriez, Eds. San Mateo, CA: Morgan Kaufmann Publishers, pp. 353–374, 1994.

[21] H. Garcia-Molina, Y. Papakonstantinou, D. Quass, A. Rajaraman, Y. Sagiv, J. Ullman and J. Widom, "The TSIMMIS approach to mediation: Data models and languages," Stanford University, Stanford, CA, 1995.

[22] V. S. Subrahmanian, S. Aldali, A. Brink, R. Emery, J. J. Lu, A. Rajput, T. Rogers, R. Ross and C. Ward, "HERMES: A heterogeneous reasoning and mediator system," University of Maryland, Maryland, 1995.

[23] D. Fang, S. Ghandeharizadeh, D. McLeod and A. Si, "The design, implementation, and evaluation of an object-based sharing mechanism for federated database systems," in *Proceedings Ninth International Conference on Data Engineering, Vienna, Austria, Apr. 19–23, 1993*. Washington, DC: IEEE Computer Society Press, pp. 467–475, 1993.

[24] M. W. W. Vermeer and P. M. G. Apers, "The role of integrity constraints in database interoperation," in *Proceedings 22nd International Conference on Very Large Databases (VLDB'96), Bombay, India*. San Mateo, CA: Morgan Kaufmann Publishers, 1996.

Integration of Inheritance Trees as Part of View Generation for Database Federations

Ingo Schmitt & Gunter Saake

Otto-von-Guericke-Universität Magdeburg
Institut für Technische Informationssysteme
Universitätsplatz 2, D-39106 Magdeburg, Germany
E-mail: {schmitt|saake}@iti.cs.uni-magdeburg.de

Abstract. Schema integration is the basis for successfully building a database federation. Current proposals directly integrate the different schemata using a semantical powerful data model, for example an extended ER model or an object-oriented model. We propose instead to use for integration a semantical poor model and build semantically rich representations as external views only. This approach enables a flexible integration and derivation especially for inheritance trees. We present an algorithm enabling the derivation of different inheritance trees as external views onto an integrated schema. The resulting inheritance tree can be influenced by giving priorities to input classes or attribute combinations and satisfies several formalized quality criteria for external views.

1 Introduction

The integration of heterogeneous schemata and the derivation of views is an essential task in the area of multidatabase systems. Parts of local schemata have to be integrated and transformed to specific views of global applications. The data itself is integrated only virtually.

The main problem which arises during the integration of different schemata is how to correctly deal with the heterogeneity. Data model heterogeneity can be resolved by transforming each local schema into the canonical data model. After that schema heterogeneity has to be overcome. Many methodologies were proposed (e.g. [BLN86, LNE89, SPD92, Dup94, RPRG94, PBE95]) which describe various conflict resolution techniques.

In order to support logical data independence, different external schemata must be derivable from the integrated schema. In this work, we only consider external schemata, which present integrated views. From now on, we refer to such views as *external integrated schemata*. The generation of a view has to fit to the understanding of a specific user group. Users want to influence the generation of their external integrated schema.

There are different requirements attributed to an integrated schema (adopted from [BLN86, page 337]):

---

* This research is partially supported by the German Country Sachsen-Anhalt under FKZ: 1987A/0025 (Federating Heterogeneous Database Systems and Local Data Management Components for Global Integrity Maintenance).

- *Completeness and Correctness*: The integrated schema must contain all concepts present in any component schema correctly. The integrated schema must be a representation of the union of the application domains associated with the schemata.
- *Minimality*: If the same concept is represented in more than one component schema, it must be represented only once in the integrated schema.
- *Understandability*: The integrated schema should be easy to understand for the designer and the end user. This implies that among the several possible representations of results of integration by a data model, the one that is (qualitatively) the most understandable should be chosen.

These requirements and especially the support of different views are not sufficiently met by the proposed methodologies. Especially the integration of different inheritance hierarchies results in inheritance hierarchies which do not sufficiently fulfill the demand for minimality and understandability (cf. [TS93, GCS95]). Most of the proposed integration methodologies resolve semantical overlappings by introducing generalized classes (upward inheritance), e.g. [RPRG94, GCS95]. That is, the original inheritance hierarchies are subhierarchies of the resulting integrated hierarchy. Henceforth, the resulting hierarchy can become unnecessarily complex.

Most of the proposed schema integration techniques including view integration techniques (e.g. [MNE88, SL88, NEL86, SP94]) are based on a data model similar to the ER-model extended by subtype relationships. They take over the inheritance hierarchies from the local to the integrated schema level and adapt them to each other by adding new sub- or superclasses or deleting existing classes.

In our approach the original inheritance hierarchies can be completely restructured in order to support logical data independence. Therefore, we offer more flexibility to integrate hierarchies.

Our approach differs from most existing proposals in using a *semantically poor* canonical data model. The data model used for integration is based on a few orthogonal data structuring concepts, namely classes, attributes and object identification. To be used for the integration process, it supports fundamental integrity constraints capturing part of the semantics lost during the transformation towards a semantically poor data model. Our canonical data model does *not* support subtype relationships. Inheritance hierarchies must be decomposed into classes with disjoint extensions.

We will show that our approach allows the use of basic information on intensional (set of attributes) and extensional (set of possible objects) overlappings of original classes for an automatic integration and application specific view (or external schema) generation. Especially, the integration of *inheritance hierarchies* in object-oriented approaches is supported by a view derivation algorithm controlled by marking preferred classes. Classes which are marked as preferred will strongly influence the structure of the derived inheritance trees, that is, they will be located close to the roots of the derived inheritance trees. In this way users are able to influence the derivation of their external integrated schemata.

2 Generic Integration Model

The right choice of the canonical data model is essential to the design process of a federated database system (FDBS, cf. [SL90]). A discussion about the right canonical data model can be found in [SCG91]. The choice of the canonical data model influences the quality of the integration step, which is the most difficult step of the design process. Most of the recent proposals prefer an object-oriented data model (e.g. in [TS93, RPRG94, GCS95, PBE95, Bra93]). It is often argued that only a semantically rich data model can be the right canonical data model because no or only little semantics is lost during the transformation from an object-oriented local schema to the canonical data model (see also [SCG91]). On the other hand, a semantically rich data model causes more heterogeneity on the schema level than a semantically poor data model does. This heterogeneity on schema level in turn increases the complexity of the integration process. In our opinion, an object-oriented data model is very well suited to be a data model for *external* schemata rather than for a conceptual schema.

We propose the use of a canonical data model which is semantically poor. On the basis of the semantically poor data model *GIM*, abbreviation of *Generic Integration Model*, we propose an algorithm which generates external object-oriented schemata automatically. In this way we do not have the problem of semantical loss. A more detailed discussion about the advantages of a semantically poor canonical data model can be found in [Sch95].

Now we introduce the *Generic Integration Model* used for integration only. Because of space restrictions we are not able to describe GIM completely. We only describe some fundamental elements of our model[2].

In the following we use some mathematical conventions. A function is considered as a set of ordered pairs of elements which assigns to each element of the domain (abbreviated by *dom*) exactly one element of the range. A special function is a set function. Its range contains sets.

We assume that the set $\mathcal{D}at$ and the set function $\mathcal{D}omain$ are given. $\mathcal{D}at$ contains the names of elementary data types and the set function $\mathcal{D}omain$ is a function over $\mathcal{D}at$. $\mathcal{D}omain$ assigns to each data type name a set possible values.

- Class K:
  $K \stackrel{\text{def}}{=} (Kname, Att)$, $Kname$ is the name of the class and Att is a partial function from its defined attribute names into $\mathcal{D}at$ defining the intension of a class. Each class has an attribute Id which represents the object identifier. An object identifier is an integer value. Att can also contain reference attributes. Integrity constraints concerning reference attributes are not considered in this paper.
- Schema S:
  $S \stackrel{\text{def}}{=} (Sname, \mathcal{K})$, $Sname$ is the name of the schema and $\mathcal{K}$ is the set of classes $\{K_1, K_2, \ldots, K_n\}$.
- Extension $\mathcal{E}xt_K$ of class K:
  $\mathcal{E}xt_K$ is a set of functions. Each function represents an object and defines

---

[2] A complete formalization of GIM will be given in a forthcoming paper.

the attribute values for the given attributes. The object identifiers have to be unique.

$\forall f \in \mathcal{E}xt_K : f$ is a function over $dom(K.Att)$ and

$\forall x \in dom(f) : f(x) \in (\mathcal{D}omain(K.Att(x)) \cup \{NULL\})$ and

$\forall f_1, f_2 \in \mathcal{E}xt_K : f_1(Id) = f_2(Id) \Rightarrow f_1 = f_2$

- Extension $Ext_{Id,K}$ contains the identifiers of the extension of class K

$Ext_{Id,K} \overset{def}{=} \{f(Id) \mid f \in \mathcal{E}xt_K\}$.

- Database state $State_S$ is a set function over the classes $\mathcal{K}$ of schema S. To each class of the schema its extension is assigned.

$\forall K \in S.\mathcal{K} : State_S(K) = \mathcal{E}xt_K$ with

$\forall K_1, K_2 \in S.\mathcal{K} : Ext_{Id,K_1} \cap Ext_{Id,K_2} = \emptyset \vee Ext_{Id,K_1} = Ext_{Id,K_2}$.

The extensions of two classes have to be either equal or disjoint.

Due to the semantical poverty of the concepts listed above GIM should not function as interface to applications. In consequence, external schemata expressed in another data model than GIM have to be derived from the integrated schema. One way to do this is shown in Section 5.

3 Homogenization in GIM

In this section, we informally describe the process of transformation of object-oriented schemata to GIM and the resolving of extensional and intensional conflicts.

The original database schemata to be federated have to be transformed into GIM. This transformation is a complex task. For simplicity, we combine here the process of transformation to GIM and the process of integration into a GIM schema into one process. In general, the input database schemata are expressed in heterogeneous data models. Therefore, at first naming, attribute and constraint conflicts have to be detected and eliminated[3].

For our discussion, we use a very simplified example focusing on the problem of solving extensional and intensional overlappings. We assume that other conflicts are resolved (e.g. naming conflicts, meta conflicts [CL94] and attribute conflicts [LNE89]). Both example schemata are object-oriented, and attributes with identical name have identical semantics. The example schemata are taken from a library application and from a university administration, respectively (see Figure 1). The filled subclass-symbol denotes a non-exclusive specialization whereas an unfilled subclass-symbol denotes an exclusive specialization. In the second schema, a *bad guy* is a person who disregarded a library rule, e.g. he damaged a book.

Using this example, we will now discuss the integration process informally. A more detailed discussion of the following steps is given in [CHJ+96]. As a first step, we analyze the extensional overlappings of the five classes. This can be done for example using data inspection and key constraint analysis [ZHKF95]

---

[3] A taxonomy of conflicts is given in [SK93, Kim95].

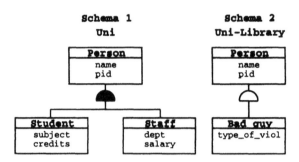

Fig. 1. Two input schemata

and must be assisted by an expert of the application domain. The result of the *analysis of class extensions* is shown in Figure 2. Each person of schema 1 is either a student or a staff member. There are persons which are both student and staff member. Each person of schema 2 is a person of schema 1. Only students can be registered as bad guys.

Based on the extension analysis, we then perform an *extension decomposition*. In this step, we generate a partition of all class instances based on all possible non-empty intersections of the input class populations. After performing this partition, we obtain eight disjoint partition classes as shown in Figure 2. For each of these partition classes we have a unique mapping to a combination of input classes and vice versa.

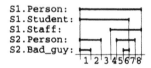

Fig. 2. Extensional overlappings and decomposition

Besides the extensional part, the *intensional* dimension has to be analyzed, too. As a result of the *intension analysis* we detect the intensional overlappings depicted in Figure 3.

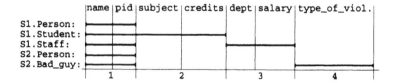

Fig. 3. Intensional overlappings and decomposition

The *intensional decomposition* results in the following attribute partition:

```
1: name, pid
2: subject, credits
3: dept, salary
4: type_of_viol
```

Now we are able to generate the integrated schema. The integrated schema is a GIM schema and not suited for global applications. Therefore, it is different to the integrated schema described in [SL90]. In order to emphasize that our integrated GIM schema is an intermediate schema for the derivation of external non-GIM schemata only, we use the term *normalized schema* instead.

An FDBS has to manage some schemata and mappings. Therefore, we introduce the superschema $\Sigma = (Cs, Map_{Cs}, Ns, \mathcal{E}s, Map_{\mathcal{E}s}, Sub_{\mathcal{E}s})$ with

- $Cs = \{S_{CS_1}, S_{CS_2}, \ldots\}$ is the set of component schemata in GIM,
- $Map_{Cs} = \{map_{CS_1,Ns}, map_{CS_2,Ns}, \ldots\}$
  for each component schema there exists a set function which assigns to each component class the respective classes of the normalized schema,
- Ns is the normalized GIM schema,
- $\mathcal{E}s = \{S_{ES_1}, S_{ES_2}, \ldots\}$ is the set of external schemata,
- $Map_{\mathcal{E}s} = \{map_{ES_1,Ns}, map_{ES_2,Ns}, \ldots\}$
  for each external schema there exists a set function which assigns to each external class the respective classes of the normalized schema,
- $Sub_{\mathcal{E}s} = \{sub_{ES_1}, sub_{ES_2}, \ldots\}$ with $sub_{ES_i} \subset S_{ES_i}.\mathcal{K} \times S_{ES_i}.\mathcal{K}$
  for each object-oriented external schema exists a binary relation on its external classes which defines the superclass-subclass relation

The normalized schema is the result of the transformation and integration steps. It can be derived from the extensional and intensional decompositions:

$$Ns = (\text{'NS'}, \mathcal{K}_{Ns}) \text{ with } \mathcal{K}_{Ns} = \{K_{Ns}^{1,1}, \ldots, K_{Ns}^{i,j}, \ldots\}$$

The indices i, j denote a pair of an extensional partition and an intensional partition. For each combination (i, j) of extensional partitions and intensional partitions which is occupied by an input class there exists a class $K_{Ns}^{i,j}$ of the normalized schema. The attributes of a class $K_{Ns}^{i,j}$ are defined by the intensional partition i. Its extension can be derived from the local classes which cover the extensional partition j.

In our example the normalized schema Ns contains the following classes:

$$\mathcal{K}_{Ns} = \{K_{Ns}^{1,1}, K_{Ns}^{1,2}, K_{Ns}^{1,4}, \ldots, K_{Ns}^{8,3}\}$$

The class $K_{Ns}^{1,3}$ cannot be a class of the normalized schema, because no input class covers the extensional partition 1 as well as the intensional partition 3.

The normalized schema can be represented by a matrix as shown in Figure 4. The horizontal dimension enumerates the eight partition classes resulting from the extensional decomposition. The vertical dimension is labeled by the four attribute partitions. The row 0 contains the indices of the extensional partitions and the column 0 contains the indices of the intensional partitions. We denote the value of a matrix element on column i and row j by $Mat^{i,j}$. The order of the rows and the order of the columns in the matrix is irrelevant. Only the index row and the index column must be the row 0 and column 0, respectively.

Fig. 4. Decomposed Schema

This notation can be directly used to derive view classes following the GIM notation. Each rectangle completely filled with crosses is a candidate for a view class. For example, the first row is a candidate for a class containing all instances and having the attributes name and pid.

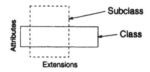

Fig. 5. Class and Subclass Candidates in GIM

Candidates for subclasses are rectangles, which are horizontally included in another class rectangle but vertically completely cover it. This is graphically depicted in Figure 5. With other words, a subclass contains a subset of the superclass instance population and a superset of the superclass attributes.

However, the order of both attribute and class labels in the diagrammatic notation is arbitrarily chosen. As a result, a different order of the labels may show different rectangles as candidates corresponding to different class hierarchies for external classes.

4 Criteria of Quality

The normalized GIM schema is the basis for the generation of external schemata. Because the normalized GIM schema cannot serve as integrated schema for global applications, we must be able to generate external schemata which meet the requirements attributed to the integrated schema (cf. [BLN86]). Therefore, we refer to such external schemata as external integrated schemata.

Classes of an external integrated schema are derived by composing classes of the normalized schema to greater ones. If an external schema is an object-oriented one then the external classes should be in subclass relation to each other.

Each external class can be defined by its mapping to classes of the normalized schema.

The problem is: *How* to compose normalized GIM classes to greater ones?

Before we can give a solution to this question, we sketch some criteria of quality attributed to an external schema S_{ES}. Our criteria are adopted from [BLN86] and adapted to our scenario.

Correctness

To all attributes of an object of the external class K_{ES} their values must be derivable. In graphically form this means: the area of the composed normalized classes must be a rectangle in at least one order of the extensional and intensional indices.

$$\forall i_1, j_1, i_2, j_2 : K_{\mathcal{N}_s}^{i_1, j_1} \in map_{ES, \mathcal{N}_s}(K_{ES}) \wedge K_{\mathcal{N}_s}^{i_2, j_2} \in map_{ES, \mathcal{N}_s}(K_{ES}) \Rightarrow$$
$$K_{\mathcal{N}_s}^{i_1, j_2} \in map_{ES, \mathcal{N}_s}(K_{ES})$$

The sub_{ES}-relations must be correct. Subclasses have a subset of the instance population and a superset of the attributes.

- $\forall (K_{ES}^1, K_{ES}^2) \in sub_{ES} : K_{\mathcal{N}_s}^{i,j} \in map_{ES, \mathcal{N}_s}(K_{ES}^2) \Rightarrow$
  $\exists k : K_{\mathcal{N}_s}^{k,j} \in map_{ES, \mathcal{N}_s}(K_{ES}^1)$
- $\forall (K_{ES}^1, K_{ES}^2) \in sub_{ES} : K_{\mathcal{N}_s}^{i,j} \in map_{ES, \mathcal{N}_s}(K_{ES}^1) \Rightarrow$
  $\exists k : K_{\mathcal{N}_s}^{i,k} \in map_{ES, \mathcal{N}_s}(K_{ES}^2)$

Completeness

Each normalized GIM class has to be a component of at least one external class.
$$\forall K_{\mathcal{N}_s}^{i,j} \in \mathcal{K}_{\mathcal{N}_s} : \exists K_{ES} \in \mathcal{K}_{ES} : K_{\mathcal{N}_s}^{i,j} \in map_{ES, \mathcal{N}_s}(K_{ES})$$

The sub_{ES}-relation must be complete. In order to formalize this requirement, we construct the transitive closure sub_{ES}^* from sub_{ES}. All external classes which can be in a subclass relation must be in the sub_{ES}^*-relation.
$$\forall K_{ES}^1, K_{ES}^2 \in \mathcal{K}_{ES} : (\forall K_{\mathcal{N}_s}^{i,j} \in map_{ES, \mathcal{N}_s}(K_{ES}^1) : \exists K_{\mathcal{N}_s}^{i,k} \in map_{ES, \mathcal{N}_s}(K_{ES}^2)) \wedge$$
$$(\forall K_{\mathcal{N}_s}^{i,j} \in map_{ES, \mathcal{N}_s}(K_{ES}^2) : \exists K_{\mathcal{N}_s}^{k,j} \in map_{ES, \mathcal{N}_s}(K_{ES}^1)) \wedge K_{ES}^1 \neq K_{ES}^2 \Rightarrow$$
$$(K_{ES}^1, K_{ES}^2) \in sub_{ES}^*$$

Minimality in view of completeness and correctness

Among complete and correct external schemata we prefer that schema with the minimal number of classes and subclass relations.

Understandability

Each object is a direct instance of exactly one most special class.
$$\forall K_{\mathcal{N}_s}^{i,j} \in \mathcal{K}_{\mathcal{N}_s} : \forall K_{ES}^1, K_{ES}^2 \in S_{ES}.\mathcal{K} : \forall (K_{ES}^{1'}, K_{ES}^1) \in sub_{ES} : \forall (K_{ES}^{2'}, K_{ES}^2) \in$$
$$sub_{ES} : K_{\mathcal{N}_s}^{i,j} \in map_{ES, \mathcal{N}_s}(K_{ES}^1) \wedge K_{\mathcal{N}_s}^{i,j} \notin map_{ES, \mathcal{N}_s}(K_{ES}^{1'}) \wedge$$

$$K_{\mathcal{N}_\delta}^{i,j} \in map_{ES,\mathcal{N}_\delta}(K_{ES}^2) \wedge K_{\mathcal{N}_\delta}^{i,j} \notin map_{ES,\mathcal{N}_\delta}(K_{ES}^{2'}) \Rightarrow K_{ES}^1 = K_{ES}^2$$

This is also required by the ODMG-93 standard.

In our opinion, exclusive specialization improve the understandability of an external schema:

$$\forall K_{ES}, K_{ES}^1, K_{ES}^2 \in S_{ES}.\mathcal{K} : \forall K_{\mathcal{N}_\delta}^{i,j} \in S_{\mathcal{N}_\delta}.\mathcal{K} : (K_{ES}^1, K_{ES}), (K_{ES}^2, K_{ES}) \in$$
$$sub_{ES} \wedge K_{\mathcal{N}_\delta}^{i,j} \in map_{ES,\mathcal{N}_\delta}(K_{ES}^1) \wedge K_{\mathcal{N}_\delta}^{i,k} \in map_{ES,\mathcal{N}_\delta}(K_{ES}^2) \Rightarrow K_{ES}^1 = K_{ES}^2$$

Similarity to a given local schema

A measure of similarity between a local class and an external schema is $Z_{K_{LS},ES}$ which specifies the number of external classes which are necessary to represent the extension of the local class. The similarity of an external schema to a local schema can be quantified by the following formula:

$$Z_{LS,ES} \stackrel{def}{=} \sum_{K_{LS} \in S_{LS}.\mathcal{K}} \frac{Z_{K_{LS},ES}}{|S_{LS}.\mathcal{K}|}$$

$Z_{LS,ES}$ should be minimal.

The proposed requirements have different priorities. Each external integrated schema has to be correct and complete (we do not consider incomplete external schemata here). However, the requirements for minimality and understandability are sometimes contradictory. Compromises must be made. Similarity of an external schema is sometimes necessary and can be quantified by the given formula.

With the criteria described above we are able to assess the quality of a given external schema.

5 Algorithm for Deriving External Schemata

A naive approach to generate the "best" external integrated schema is to generate all external classes by finding all possible compositions of normalized classes. After that all possible external schemata can be generated by computing the power set on the set of all external classes. By means of the quality criteria the "best" external schema can then be found. The disadvantage of this approach is its complexity. The complexity is exponentially dependent from the number of extensional partitions of the normalized schema.

A more practicable solution is given in this section. The steps of the algorithm are explained using our example. In our algorithm we transform the matrix in such a way that we are able to derive directly external classes from rectangles.

At the beginning of the algorithm some variables must be initialized. We need an empty external schema $S_{ES}.\mathcal{K} := \emptyset$, an empty map function $map_{ES,\mathcal{N}_\delta} := \emptyset$, and an empty subclass relation $sub_{ES,\mathcal{N}_\delta} := \emptyset$. New generated external classes will be inserted into $S_{ES}.\mathcal{K}$. We distinguish the new generated classes by giving them a consecutively numbered index which starts from zero. The index counter will be assigned to the external classes following their insertion order. Furthermore we need the variable $Sup := 0$ in order to generate subclass relations. ze is the number of rows and sp is the number of columns.

Step 1: Intensional and extensional sorting

We consider a row as a binary number and introduce a function on the present column order which computes to each row (without row 0) its row value:

$$\forall i \in [1 \dots ze - 1] : row(i) = \sum_{j \in [1 \dots sp-1]} Mat^{j,i} * 2^{sp-j-1}$$

We consider a column as binary number and introduce a further function on the present row order which computes to each column (without column 0) its column value:

$$\forall i \in [1 \dots sp - 1] : col(i) = \sum_{j \in [1 \dots ze-1]} Mat^{i,j} * 2^{ze-j-1}$$

The matrix has to be transformed by exchanging rows and exchanging columns so that the following both conditions are true:

$$\forall i \in [1 \dots ze - 2] : row(i) \geq row(i + 1)$$
$$\forall i \in [1 \dots sp - 2] : col(i) \geq col(i + 1)$$

Notice that an exchange of rows can change the computed column values and vice versa. Both conditions must be true basing on the current matrix order.

There is an algorithm which fulfills both conditions. First of all the rows have to be sorted in correspondence to their row values. Then the columns have to be sorted in correspondence to their column values. Since the column sorting changes the row values a row disorder is possible. Therefore, we continue both steps until the conditions are true. These both steps have to be repeated at most as often as different columns exist.

If we apply the row sort operation on the matrix of our example (left matrix depicted in Figure 6) then we obtain the middle matrix. The right matrix is the middle matrix sorted by column values. It fulfills both conditions mentioned above.

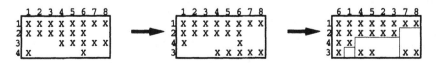

Fig. 6. Row and column sorting

Step 2: Deriving external classes

After the sorting steps have been carried out most crosses in the matrix are clustered in the left upper corner of the diagram building the shape of a triangle. This triangle can be interpreted as rectangles building a branch of a class hierarchy as depicted in Figure 7.

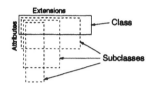

Fig. 7. Subclass candidates in triangle shape

As we can see in Figure 6 the diagonal of the triangle has some 'step corners' (at positions (8,1),(6,2),(2,3),(1,4) in our example). These 'corners' have to be detected. The sequence Cor_{Mat} contains these 'corners' in the order of their vertical position within the matrix that is the uppermost 'corner' is the first 'corner':

$$Cor_{Mat} = \langle(i_0, j_0), (i_1, j_1), \ldots, (i_{n-1}, j_{n-1})\rangle \text{ with:}$$

$$\forall k \in [0 \ldots n-1] : \forall ii \in [1 \ldots i_k] : Mat^{ii,j_k} = 1 \wedge (i_k + 1 \geq sp \vee Mat^{i_k+1,j_k} = 0) \wedge \forall jj \in [1 \ldots j_k] : Mat^{i_k,jj} = 1 \wedge (j_k + 1 \geq ze \vee Mat^{i_k,j_k+1} = 0) \wedge (k < n-1 \Rightarrow j_k > j_{k+1})$$

The sequence Cor_{Mat} can be generated as follows:

A cursor starts from the left upper position (1,1) of the matrix and moves to the right until the element at the right of the cursor is not set (0) or the right boundary is reached. If the matrix element directly below is not set (0) or the lower boundary is reached then the cursor position is a 'corner position' and must be inserted into the sequence. Then we start the same procedure at the next row starting from column 1 until the lower boundary is reached.

Now we set the variable $anz := | S_{ES}.\mathcal{K} |$.

From the sequence Cor_{Mat} we are able to generate external classes. From each 'corner' k we generate an external class which contains all normalized classes within the rectangle formed by column 1, column i_k, row 1 and row j_k. The order of the 'corners' within Cor_{Mat} builds the specialization order of the generated external classes:

for k:=0 **to** n-1
begin
$$S_{ES}.\mathcal{K} := S_{ES}.\mathcal{K} \cup \{K_{ES}^{anz+k} \mid (i_k, j_k) \in Cor_{Mat}\} \text{ with}$$
$$map_{ES,\mathcal{N}_s} = map_{ES,\mathcal{N}_s} \cup \{(K_{ES}^{anz+k};$$
$$\{K_{\mathcal{N}_s}^{m,n} \mid (o \in [1 \ldots i_k] : p \in [1 \ldots j_k] : m = Mat^{o,0} \wedge n = Mat^{0,p}) \vee$$
$$(Sup \neq 0 \wedge q \in [1 \ldots i_k] : m = Mat^{q,0} \wedge$$

$$K_{\mathcal{N}_s}^{m,n} \in map_{ES,\mathcal{N}_s}(K_{ES}^{Sup}))\})\} \text{ and}$$

$$sub_{ES,\mathcal{N}_s} = sub_{ES,\mathcal{N}_s} \cup \begin{cases} \{(K_{ES}^{anz+k}, K_{ES}^{anz+k-1})\} : k > 0 \\ \{(K_{ES}^{anz}, K_{ES}^{Sup})\} : Sup \neq 0 \wedge k = 0 \\ \emptyset : otherwise \end{cases}$$

end

The resulting external classes constitute a branch of an inheritance tree. The first class is the root of the inheritance tree. Extensions and intensions of the generated external classes can be derived from the information shown in Figures 3 and 2. Using these information, a designer has to find class names corresponding to the semantics of these derived classes. As result we obtain the following four classes from the right matrix of Figure 6:

Extension	Intension	Class
1,2,3,4,5,6,7,8	1	Person
1,2,3,4,5,6	1,2	Student
1,6	1,2,4	Bad_guy
6	1,2,3,4	Assisting_bad_guy

The intension *Att* of a generated external class can be derived from the map-functions and is not further considered here.

Step 3: Submatrices

After these steps have been carried out we may have some crosses left. In our example, left crosses are at positions (3,4), (4,4), (7,4), and (8,4). From such remaining crosses we construct the remaining branches of the inheritance tree by recursively applying our algorithm. The area below the triangle is partitioned by vertical lines starting from the 'corner' positions and ending at the lower boundary. Each resulting partitioned area can be considered as an isolated submatrix and if it contains at least one cross, it has to be transformed into triangle form by a further intensional and extensional sorting on the isolated submatrix. These triangles correspond to other branches of the constructed inheritance tree. They are located at specific positions in the diagram defined by the variable *Sup*.

Each partition constitutes a submatrix.

We generate from each 'corner' position (i_m, j_m) (with $\forall m \in [0 \ldots n-2]$) a submatrix Mat_{m+1} with number of columns $sp_{m+1} = i_m - i_{m+1} + 1$ and number of rows $ze_{m+1} = ze - j_m$:

- $\forall k \in [1 \ldots sp_{m+1} - 1] : Mat_{m+1}^{k+i_{m+1},0} = Mat^{k+i_{m+1},0}$
- $\forall k \in [1 \ldots ze_{m+1} - 1] : Mat_{m+1}^{0,k} = Mat^{0,k+i_m}$
- $\forall k \in [1 \ldots sp_{m+1} - 1] : \forall l \in [1 \ldots ze_{m+1} - 1] : Mat_{m+1}^{k,l} = Mat^{k+i_{m+1},l+j_m}$

In addition to these generated submatrices we generate a further submatrix Mat_n with number of columns $sp_n = sp - i_0$ and number of rows $ze_n = ze$:

- $\forall k \in [1 \ldots ze_n - 1] : Mat_n^{0,k} = Mat^{0,k}$
- $\forall k \in [1 \ldots sp_n - 1] : \forall l \in [0 \ldots ze_n - 1] : Mat_n^{k,l} = Mat^{k+i_0,l}$

In our example two non-empty submatrices are generated. The first submatrix contains two crosses at position (7,4) and (8,4) and the second one contains two crosses at position (3,4) and (4,4). This can be seen in Figure 6.

Step 4: Recursion

On each submatrix Mat_m generated by the previous step which is not empty, that is

$$\exists i \in [1 \ldots sp_m - 1] : \exists j \in [1 \ldots ze_m - 1] : Mat_m^{i,j} = 1$$

the steps starting from step 1 must be applied. The variable Sup_{new} has to contain the index of the superclass of the tree branch generated from the submatrix Mat_m and is defined by:

$$Sup_{new} = \begin{cases} anz + m - 1 : m \neq n \\ Sup_{old} : otherwise \end{cases}$$

If we apply this recursion to our example we obtain two further external classes:

Extension	Intension	Class
4,5	1,2,3	Assistant
7,8	1,3	Staff-Student

Step 5: Discriminants

In the last step, we have to analyze whether all columns are distinguished by their mapping to external classes. In order to avoid information loss we have to add an artificial *discriminant* attribute to the respective external class if some columns are not distinguishable.

In our example columns 7 and 8 are not distinguishable. Therefore we have to enhance the intension of the external class **Person** by a discriminant attribute which contains the column number (or a string with equivalent semantic meaning) of a given object. As result we obtain the external schema as depicted in Figure 8.

How are the criteria of quality of Section 4 fulfilled in our example?

It can be easily seen that an external schema generated by our algorithm is complete, correct and understandable. However, how can an external schema be generated which is similar to a given local schema? The priorities of the input extension order influence the results of the algorithm. If the extensional partitions of a local class have the highest priority (most left in the matrix) then there is exactly one external class in the resulting inheritance tree, which corresponds to the local class.

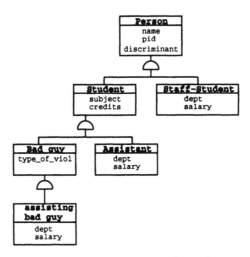

Fig. 8. External schema

As an example, we order the extensions in such a way, that all extensions (4,5,6,7,8) which correspond to Staff having the highest priority. The result of the sort steps is shown in Figure 9.

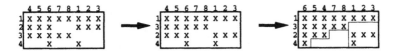

Fig. 9. Staff-oriented composition

The derived inheritance tree is depicted in Figure 10. It is different from the tree derived before (cf. Figure 8). In contrast to the first tree, all staff members are clustered in one branch of the inheritance tree.

Therefore, before our algorithm should be applied the designer has to order the extensional dimension by *priority*. The order of the extensional dimension influences the result of the derivation process: classes corresponding to extensions with higher priority will be located closer to the root of the inheritance tree of the resulting external schema.

Our algorithm generates a minimal, complete, correct, and understandable external schema. We demonstrated this using an example.

6   Conclusion and Outlook

We presented a framework for schema integration including a practicable algorithm to derive class hierarchies meeting the demand for minimality, correctness,

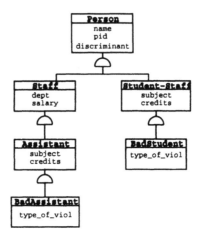

Fig. 10. Staff-oriented external schema

completeness and understandability. Whereas the derivation of an optimal inheritance tree is not tractable, our algorithm has the complexity of $O(t^4 * log(t))$ where t is the maximum number of rows and columns of the GIM representation (which corresponds to the number of attributes and disjoint class populations of the original input schemata). The result of the algorithm can be influenced by prioritizing extensional GIM classes.

Future work will concentrate on integrating more semantical assertions (e.g. integrity constraints) into the framework. Moreover, the aspect of multiple inheritance in derived inheritance trees has to be investigated. Other data models as target for external views have to be analyzed, too. The presented methods can be applied to scenarios different from the integration problem, e.g., for schema evolution, deriving views in object-oriented database systems, and classification problems.

A design tool supporting the presented methods and algorithms is currently under development. The presented work is part of a larger project on federating heterogeneous databases [CHJ+96]. In this context the integration of the presented methods into a larger design framework will be investigated. Especially, the role of constraints in federated database design is one focal point of the project.

Acknowledgements

The authors are grateful to Michael Höding, Can Türker and Stefan Conrad for helpful comments.

References

[BLN86]   C. Batini, M. Lenzerini, and S. B. Navathe. A Comparative Analysis of Methodologies for Database Schema Integration. *ACM Computing Surveys*, 18(4):323–364, December 1986.

[Bra93]   S.E. Bratsberg. *Evolution and Integration of Classes in Object-Oriented Databases*. Dissertation, The Norwegian Institute of Technology, University of Trondheim, June 1993.

[CHJ+96]   S. Conrad, M. Höding, S. Janssen, G. Saake, I. Schmitt, and C. Türker. Integrity Constraints in Federated Database Design. Preprint Nr. 2, Fakultät für Informatik, Universität Magdeburg, April 1996.

[CL94]   J. Chomicki and W. Litwin. Declarative Definition of Object-Oriented Multidatabase Mappings. In T. Özsu, U. Dayal, and P. Valduriez, editors, *Distributed Object Management*, pages 375–392. Morgan Kaufmann, 1994.

[Dup94]   Y. Dupont. Resolving Fragmentation Conflicts in Schema Integration. In P. Loucopoulos, editor, *Proc. ER'94* , pages 513–532. Springer, 1994.

[GCS95]   M. Garcia-Solaco, M. Castellanos, and F. Saltor. A Semantic-Discriminated Approach to Integration in Federated Databases. In S. Laufmann, S. Spaccapietra, and T. Yokoi, editors, *Proc. CoopIS'95* , pages 19–31, 1995.

[Kim95]   W. Kim, editor. *Modern Database Systems*. ACM Press, New York, 1995.

[LNE89]   J.A. Larson, S.B. Navathe, and R. Elmasri. A Theory of Attribute Equivalence in Databases with Application to Schema Integration. *IEEE Transactions on Software Engineering*, 15(4):449–463, 1989.

[MNE88]   M.V. Mannino, B.N. Navathe, and W. Effelsberg. A rule-based approach for merging generalization hierarchies. *Information Systems*, 13(3):257–272, 1988.

[NEL86]   S.B. Navathe, R. Elmasri, and J.A. Larson. Integration User Views in Database Design. In *Proc. IEEE ICDE'86*, pages 50–62. 1986.

[PBE95]   E. Pitoura, O. Bukhres, and A. K. Elmagarmid. Object Orientation in Multidatabase Systems. *ACM Computing Surveys*, 27(2):141–195, June 1995.

[RPRG94]   M. P. Reddy, B. E. Prasad, P. G. Reddy, and A. Gupta. A Methodology for Integration of Heterogeneous Databases. *IEEE Transactions on Knowledge and Data Engineering*, 6(6):920–933, December 1994.

[SCG91]   F. Saltor, M. Castellanos, and M. Garcia-Solaco. Suitability of Data Models as Canonical Models for Federated Databases. *ACM SIGMOD RECORD*, 20(4):44–48, December 1991.

[Sch95]   I. Schmitt. Flexible Integration and Derivation of Heterogeneous Schemata in Federated Database Systems. Preprint Nr. 10, Fakultät für Informatik, Universität Magdeburg, November 1995.

[SK93]   A. Sheth and V. Kashyap. So Far (Schematically) yet So Near (Semantically). In D. K. Hsiao, E. J. Neuhold, and R. Sacks-Davis, editors, *Interoperable Database Systems, Proc. DS-5* , pages 283–312. North-Holland, 1993.

[SL88]   A.P. Sheth and J.A. Larson. A Tool for Integrating Conceptual Schemas and User Views. In *Proc. IEEE ICDE'88*, pages 176–183. 1988.

[SL90]   A. P. Sheth and J. A. Larson. Federated Database Systems for Managing Distributed, Heterogeneous, and Autonomous Databases. *ACM Computing Surveys*, 22(3):183–236, September 1990.

[SP94]   S. Spaccapietra and P. Parent. View Integration:A Step Forward in Solving Structural Conflicts. *IEEE TKDE*, 6(2):258–274, 1994.

[SPD92]   S. Spaccapietra, C. Parent, and Y. Dupont. Model Independent Assertions for Integration of Heterogeneous Schemas. *The VLDB Journal*, 1(1):81–126, 1992.

[TS93]   C. Thieme and A. Siebes. Schema Integration in Object-Oriented Databases. In C. Rolland, F. Bodart, and C. Cauvet, editors, *Proc. CAiSE'93* , pages 55–70. LNCS 685, Springer 1993.

[ZHKF95]   G. Zhou, R. Hull, R. King, and J.-C. Franchitti. Using Object Matching and Materialization to Integrate Heterogeneous Databases. In S. Laufmann, S. Spaccapietra, and T. Yokoi, editors, *Proc. CoopIS'95* , pages 4–18, 1995.

A Formal Basis for Dynamic Schema Integration[1]

Love Ekenberg
lovek@dsv.su.se

Paul Johannesson
pajo@dsv.su.se

Logikkonsult NP AB
Swedenborgsgatan 2
S-118 48 STOCKHOLM, SWEDEN
and
Department of Computer and Systems Sciences
Royal Institute of Technology and
Stockholm University
Electrum 230
S-164 40 KISTA, SWEDEN
Telefax: +46-8-703 90 25

Abstract. We construct a framework for determining when two schemata can be meaningfully integrated. Intuitively, two schemata can be integrated if the rules of one of the schemata together with a set of integration assertions do not restrict the models of the other schema. We formalise this concept using the notion of *conflictfreeness* and shows how it can be used to ensure that the merging of two schemata results in an integrated schema with the same information capacity as the original ones. The problem of conflictfreeness is undecidable, and we outline how it can be addressed for finite domains and determine its complexity properties in this case. Our approach takes into account static as well as dynamic aspects of a schema, where the dynamics is modelled by means of the event concept. We introduce correspondence assertions for events that can be used to specify the equivalence of event combinations.

1 Introduction

Interoperability is becoming a critical issue for many organisations today. An increasing dependence and cooperation between organisations has created a need for many enterprises to access remote as well as local information sources. Further, even a single enterprise may have several independent information bases as a result of departmental autonomy. Thus, for many organisations it becomes important to be able to interconnect existing, possibly heterogeneous, information systems. An essential part of this activity is database integration, i.e., the process of constructing a global schema from a collection of existing databases. Database integration is similar to

---

[1]This work was partly performed within the project SDeLphi at Telia Research AB. It was also partly supported by the NUTEK project CISIS.

view integration, a process in classical database design, which derives an integrated schema from a set of user views. A generic term, *schema integration* [3], has been introduced to refer to both processes.

The schema integration process can be divided into three phases: schema comparison, schema conforming, and schema merging. *Schema comparison* involves analysing and comparing schemata in order to determine correspondences, in particular different representations of the same concepts. *Schema conforming* involves modifying one or both of the schemata to be integrated until each phenomenon in the Universe of Discourse (UoD) is represented in the same way in both schemata. *Schema merging* involves superimposing the schemata in order to obtain one integrated schema.

The most difficult part of the schema integration process is schema comparison. The fundamental problem here is that a UoD can be modelled in many different ways. The same phenomenon can be seen from different levels of abstraction, or represented using different properties. More precisely, three types of differences between schemata modelling the same UoD can be identified: differences in terminology, differences in structure, and differences in focus.

In an earlier paper [5], we tried to determine when two static schemata can be meaningfully integrated and claimed that this is the case if the rules of one of the schemata together with a set of integration assertions do not restrict the models of the other schema. We expressed this in terms of *conflictfreeness*. The main issue of the current paper is to investigate how the concept of conflictfreeness can be generalised to the dynamic case, and an important contribution of the paper is that it shows how previous work on schema integration, which has considered only static and structural aspects, e.g., [4], can be extended to also handle general dynamic aspects of a schema. We formalise the dynamics by means of the event concept and show that our results on schema integration for the static case naturally extends to the dynamic one.

The paper is organised as follows. In section 2, we introduce a first-order logic framework for conceptual schemata and define basic notions for schema integration. We also extend the framework by taking into account dynamic aspects, which are modelled by the event concept. In section 3, we show how new events can be constructed by combining events into sequences and define the concepts of conflictfreeness and dominance. In section 4, we introduce dynamic integration assertions that define events in terms of other events. In section 5, we discuss a procedure for determining when schemata can be integrated, and in the final section we summarise the work.

2 Preliminaries

We give a short overview of the basic concepts used in the sequel. An extended treatment of the various concepts can be found in [5].

In the definitions below, we assume an underlying *language* L of first order formulas. By a *diagram for* a set R of formulas in a language L, we mean a Herbrand model of S, extended by the negation of the ground atoms in L that are not in the Herbrand model. Thus, a diagram for L is a Herbrand model extended with classical negation.

2.1 Schema Properties

A *schema* S is a structure <R,ER> consisting of a *static part* R and a *dynamic part* ER. R is a finite set of closed first order formulas in a language L. ER is a set of *event rules*. Event rules describe possible transitions between different states of a schema and will be described below. *L(R)* is the *restriction of L to R*, i.e., L(R) is the set {p | p ∈ L, but p does not contain any predicate symbol, that is not in a formula in R}. The elements in R is called *static rules* in L(R). A *static integration assertion expressing the schema S_2 in the schema S_1* is a closed first order formula:

$\forall x \, (p(x) \leftrightarrow F(x))$, where p is a predicate symbol in L(S_2) and F(x) is a formula in L(S_1).[2] S_i below denotes a schema. Fig. 2.1 shows a graphical representation of the static part of a schema.

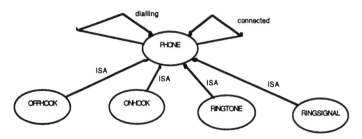

Fig. 2.1

The labels on the ellipses specify the unary predicate symbols, and those on the arrows specify the binary ones. The graph also depicts domain and range constraints, as an example the arrow between Person and Vehicle represents the formula:

$\forall x \forall y (\text{connected}(x,y) \rightarrow \text{Phone}(x) \wedge \text{Phone}(y))$.

The arrows labelled ISA represent generalisation relationships, e.g.,

$\forall x (\text{Offhook}(x) \rightarrow \text{Phone}(x))$.

Fig. 2.2 shows a schema that represents similar information as the previous one.

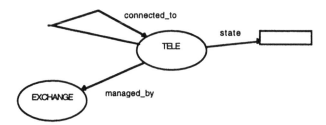

Fig. 2.2

The following is a set of static integration assertions that expresses the schema of Fig. 2.2 in the schema of Fig. 2.1:

$\forall x (\text{Tele}(x) \leftrightarrow \text{Phone}(x))$
$\forall x \forall y (\text{connected\_to}(x,y) \leftrightarrow \text{connected}(x,y))$
$\forall x (\text{state}(x, \text{passive}) \leftrightarrow \text{Onhook}(x) \wedge \neg \text{ringsignal}(x))$
$\forall x (\text{state}(x, \text{active}) \leftrightarrow \text{Offhook}(x) \vee \text{ringsignal}(x))$

---

[2]We can without loss of generality, in the definitions below, assume that the set of predicate symbols in L(S_1) and L(S_2) are disjoint.

2.2 Event Messages, Event Rules, and Basic Events

We define the concept of basic events, event messages, and event rules. Intuitively, a basic event gives rise to a transition from one diagram to another one, and is the result of an event rule together with an event message. Below, L denotes a language and B denotes the alphabet underlying the language L.

Def: An *event message* in L is a vector **e** of constants in the alphabet B.

Def: An *event rule* in L is a structure $<z, P(z, w), C(z, w)>$. $P(z, w)$ and $C(z, w)$ are first order formulas in L, and **z** and **w** are vectors of variables in B.[3]

Three examples of event rules of the schema of fig. 2.1 are:

lift1
<t,
(onhook(t) ∧ ¬(ringsignal(t))),
offhook(t) ∧ ¬onhook(t)>

lift2
<t,
(onhook(t) ∧ ringsignal(t) ∧ dialling(S, t)),
(offhook(t) ∧ ¬onhook(t) ∧ connected(S,t) ∧ ¬(ringsignal(t) ∧ ¬(dialling(S,t))))>

dial
<<t1, t2>,
(offhook(t1), onhook(t2)),
(ringtone(t1), ringsignal(t2), dialling(t1, t2))>

An example of an event rule of the schema of fig. 2.2 is:

connect
<<t1, t2, ex>,
(passive(t1) ∧ passive(t2) ∧ managed_by(t1, ex)),
(connected_to(t1, t2))>

Def: A *basic event* for a schema <R, ER> is a tuple (σ, ρ), where σ and ρ are diagrams for R, and

  (i) $\rho = \sigma$, or
  (ii) there is a rule $<z, P(z, w), C(z, w)>$ in ER, and an event message **e**, such that σ is a diagram for $P(e, w)$ and ρ is a diagram for $C(e, w)$. In this case we will also say that (σ, ρ) *results* from the event rule and the event message.

In the definition of an event rule, $P(z, w)$ can be thought of as a precondition and $C(z, w)$ as a post condition. Note that an event rule is non-deterministic, i.e. if a diagram σ satisfies the precondition of an event rule then any diagram ρ satisfying the event rule's post condition will give rise to a basic event (σ, ρ) resulting from the event rule.

   Thus, our approach to the dynamics of a schema differs from the traditional transactional approach in the database area, where an event deterministically specifies a minor modification of a state [2].

---

[3]The notation A(x,y) means that x and y are free in A(x,y).

A description of a schema is a structure consisting of all diagrams for a schema, together with all possible transitions that are possible with respect to the basic events for the schema.

Def: The *description of a schema S* is a digraph <M, A>, where M is the set of all diagrams for S, and A is the set of all basic events for S.[4]

Fig. 2.3 illustrates how a description of a schema can look. The arrows in the figure represent basic events and the dots represent the different diagrams for the schema.

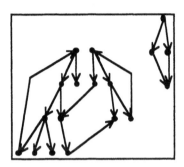

Fig. 2.3

3 Events, Event Instances and Dominance

In this section, we will investigate how new event rules can be constructed by combining the basic event rules of a schema. We will also investigate how these constructed event rules affect the concept of weak dominance.

3.1 Sequential Combinations of Event Rules and Event Instances

Next, we define a sequential combination of event rules. Below, the *concatenation* of the vectors z_1 and z_2 is denoted by $z_1; z_2$.

Def: Given a schema <R, ER>. The *sequential combination* of V_1, V_2, ..., V_{k-1} and V_k is denoted by
$$<z_1; ...; z_k, [P_1(z_1, w_1), C_1(z_1, w_1)] ; ...; [P_k(z_k, w_k), C_k(z_k, w_k)]>,$$
or shorter, $V_1 \nabla ... \nabla V_k$.
($\{V_1, V_2, ..., V_k\} \subseteq ER$, and $z_1, ..., z_k$ are vectors of variables.)

We introduce the concept of a instances of event rules and event messages.

Def: Let $S = <R, ER>$ be a schema, $V = <z, P(z, w), C(z, w)>$ be an event rule in ER and e a non empty event message (containing at least one constant).
The *basic instances of V and e*, denoted $\Lambda(S, V, e)$, is the set of pairs (σ, ρ), such that both σ and ρ are diagrams for R, and $P(e, w) \in \sigma$ and $C(e, w) \in \rho$, for some w. If e is the empty event message (denoted []), then $\Lambda(S, V, e) = \{(\sigma, \sigma) \mid \sigma \in L(R)\}$.

---

[4]Consequently, events are arcs between elements in M.

Consider the schemata in fig 2.1 and 2.2. An example of an element in the basic instance of the event rule lift1 and the event message <p1> is

({phone(p1), onhook(p1), ¬offhook(p1), ¬ringsignal(p1), ¬ringtone(p1)},
<{phone(p1), ¬onhook(p1), offhook(p1), ¬ringsignal(p1), ¬ringtone(p1)})

Def: Given a schema $S = <R, ER>$, a set $\{e_1, ..., e_k\}$ of event messages and a set $\{V_1, ..., V_k\}$ of event rules in ER. The *combined instances of $V_1 \nabla ... \nabla V_k$ and $e_1; ...; e_k$* is defined by:

(i) $\Lambda(S, V_1 \nabla ... \nabla V_k, e_1; ...; e_k) = \{(\sigma, \rho) \mid$ there is a τ, such that $(\sigma, \tau) \in \Lambda(S, V_1 \nabla ... \nabla V_{k-1}, e_1; ...; e_{k-1})$ and $(\tau, \rho) \in \Lambda(S, V_k, e_k)\}, k \geq 2$.

The *combined instances of $V_1 \nabla ... \nabla V_k$* is defined by:

(ii) $\Lambda(S, V_1 \nabla ... \nabla V_k) = \{(\sigma, \rho) \mid$ there is a $e_1; ...; e_k$, such that $(\sigma, \tau) \in \Lambda(S, V_1 \nabla ... \nabla V_k, e_1; ...; e_k)\}$.

The *combined extension of S* is defined by:

(iii) $\Lambda(S) = \{(\sigma, \tau) \mid$ there is $\{V_1, ..., V_k\} \subseteq ER$ and $e_1, ..., e_k$ such that $(\sigma, \tau) \in \Lambda(S, V_1 \nabla ... \nabla V_k, e_1; ...; e_k)$.

An event is either a basic event instance or a combined event instance.

Def: Given a schema $S = <R, ER>$, a set $\{V_1, V_2, ..., V_k\} \subseteq ER$ and a set of event messages $e_1, ..., e_k$. An *event* for S is a tuple $(\sigma, \rho) \in \Lambda(S)$.

3.2 Conflictfreeness and Weak Dominance

Next, we define the concept of conflictfreeness. Intuitively, two schemata are in conflict w.r.t. a set of static integration assertions if one of them together with the integration assertions restrict the set of diagrams for the other one.

Def: Let IA be a set of static integration assertions expressing S_2 in S_1, and let $<M_1, A_1>$ and $<M_2, A_2>$ be the descriptions of S_1 and S_2, respectively (i.e. A_1 and A_2 are sets of basic events). *S_2 and S_1 are conflictfree w.r.t. IA* iff for each diagram σ in M_1, there exists a diagram τ in M_2, such that $\sigma \cup \tau$ is a diagram for IA. Otherwise *S_2 and S_1 are in conflict w.r.t. IA.*

We combine two schemata by taking the union of them.

Def: Let IA be a set of static integration assertions expressing S_2 in S_1. The first level combined schema, *$\chi_1(S_1, S_2, IA)$*, is the schema: $<R_1 \cup R_2 \cup IA, ER_1 \cup ER_2>$.[5]

The concept of weak dominance intuitively expresses that the combined schema, in some sense, at least as much information as its components. Note that this should also be the case with respect to the combined extensions of the schemata.

---

[5]The definition of combination can be refined to eliminate various kinds of redundancies. This is more thoroughly described in [5], and a treatment of the details is omitted here.

Def: Let $S_1 = <R_1, ER_1>$ and $S_2 = <R_2, ER_2>$ be two schemata, and let IA be a set of static integration assertions expressing S_2 in S_1. S_2 *weakly B-dominates S_1 w.r.t. IA* iff there is a total injective function ξ such that for each $(\sigma, \rho) \in \Lambda(S_1)$, $(\xi(\sigma), \xi(\rho)) \in \Lambda(S_2)$, and $\sigma \cup \xi(\sigma)$ and $\rho \cup \xi(\rho)$ are diagrams for IA.

The dominance concept we introduce is similar to previous concepts of dominance and information capacity equivalence in the literature, [4, 6, 8]. A major problem with these concepts is that they are too liberal, i.e., there exist schemata that are equivalent according to these concepts although there is no intuitive relationship between them. Our definition of dominance overcomes this problem by being more restrictive than previous definitions. We define dominance and equivalence not as an absolute relationship between schemata; instead we state that a schema dominates another one only relative to a set of static integration assertions that provides an intuitive relationship between the schemata. We also require that there should be a total injective function from the dominated schema to the dominating one. This function expresses that the behaviour of the dominated schema is completely reflected in the dominating schema. We may now use the concept of conflictfreeness do determine whether the combined schema weakly B-dominates its components.

Theorem 1: Let $S_1 = <R_1, ER_1>$ and $S_2 = <R_2, ER_2>$ be two schemata, and let IA be a set of static integration assertions expressing S_2 in S_1. If S_2 and S_1 are conflictfree w.r.t. IA then $\chi_1(S_1, S_2, IA)$ weakly B-dominates S_1 w.r.t. IA.

Proof: When only basic events are considered in the definition of weak B-dominance, we call this weak dominance. To easier grasp the ideas behind the proof we first perform it with respect to weak dominance. Assume that the two schemata S_1 and S_2 are conflictfree with respect to a set of static integration assertions, IA, and that $<M, A>$ is a description for $\chi_1(S_1, S_2, IA)$. First, we need to show that there is a total injective function ξ between the description $<M_1, A_1>$ of S_1 and the description $<M, A>$, such that $(\xi(\sigma_i), \xi(\sigma_j))$ is in A if (σ_i, σ_j) is in A_1, i.e., the set of all basic events for S_1. For all basic events (σ_i, σ_j) in A_1, there are event rules $<z, P(z, w), C(z, w)>$ in ER_1, and event messages e, such that σ_i is a diagram for $P(e, w)$ and σ_j is a diagram for $C(e, w)$, if $\sigma_i \neq \sigma_j$. By the conflictfreeness of S_1 and S_2, there is an extension of σ_i to $\sigma_i \cup \sigma_i'$ and an extension of σ_j to $\sigma_j \cup \sigma_j'$, such that the extensions are diagrams for $R_2 \cup IA$. If σ_i is a diagram for $P(e, w)$, $\sigma_i \cup \sigma_i'$ is a diagram for $P(e, w)$, and if σ_j is a diagram for $C(e, w)$, $\sigma_j \cup \sigma_j'$ is a diagram for $C(e, w)$. Consequently, we can define the function ξ by letting $\xi(\sigma_i)$ be equal to $\sigma_i \cup \sigma_i'$, for every state description σ_i of S_1. It is also obvious that the function ξ has the property that for each σ_i in M_1, $\sigma_i \cup \xi(\sigma_i)$ is a diagram for IA, since $\xi(\sigma_i)$ is a diagram for IA.

We can now easily show that S weakly dominates S' with respect to IA iff S weakly B-dominates S' with respect to IA. Assume that S weakly dominates S' with respect to IA, and assume that $(\sigma_i \sigma_j) \in \Lambda(S')$ and $(\sigma_j, \sigma_k) \in \Lambda(S')$. Then $(\sigma_i, \sigma_k) \in \Lambda(S')$. Define a function $\omega((\sigma_i, \sigma_k)) = ((\xi(\sigma_i), \xi(\sigma_k))$. By the weak dominance, for all diagrams σ (σ_i, σ_j and σ_k), $\sigma \cup \xi(\sigma)$ is a diagram for IA. It is also clear that the weak dominance implies that ω defined in this way is a total injective function. The proof of the converse is immediate, since the basic events of a schema S is a subset of $\Lambda(S)$. ∎

3.3 Event Paths

As a consequence of the semantics for sequential combinations above, we only considered the events resulting from such a combination. However, if an event (σ, ρ) results from a combination, it could sometimes be useful also to include all diagrams between σ and ρ that the event traverses.

Def: Let $S = <R, ER>$ be a schema, $V = V_1 \nabla \dots \nabla V_k$ be a sequential combination of event rules in ER, and let $e = e_1; \dots; e_k$ be a concatenation of event messages. An *event path for V and e*, $\Pi(S, V, e)$, is a set of sequences of diagrams for S, $(\sigma_1, \sigma_2, \dots, \sigma_{k+1})$, such that (σ_i, σ_{i+1}) is an event resulting from V_i and e_i.

Fig. 3.1 exemplifies an event path. The dots represent diagrams and the arrows represent basic events. The labelled basic events in the leftmost graph corresponds to the labelled sequence in the rightmost graph.

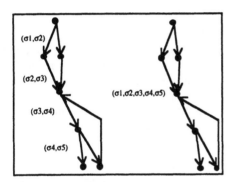

Fig. 3.1

Def: Let $S = <R, ER>$ be a schema, and let $V = V_1 \nabla \dots \nabla V_k$ be a sequential combination of event rules in ER. The *event path for V*, $\Pi(S, V)$, is the union of $\Pi(S, V, e)$ for all event messages e (including the empty event message). The *event path extension for S*, $\Pi(S)$, is the union of $\Pi(S, V)$ for all sequential combination V of event rules in ER.

Next, we introduce a new concept of dominance, which requires event paths to coincide. At first inspection one might believe that this dominance concept is stronger than our earlier ones, but the theorem below shows that this is not the case.

Def: Let $S_1 = <R_1, ER_1>$ and $S_2 = <R_2, ER_2>$ be two schemata, and let IA be a set of static integration assertions expressing S_2 in S_1. S_2 *weakly C-domi nates S_1 w.r.t. IA* iff there is a total injective function ξ, such that for each $(\sigma_1, \sigma_2, \dots, \sigma_n) \in \Pi(S_1)$, $(\xi(\sigma_1), \xi(\sigma_2), \dots, \xi(\sigma_n)) \in \Pi(S_2)$, and $\sigma_i \cup \xi(\sigma_i)$ is a diagram for IA, for all σ_i.

Theorem 2: Let $S_1 = <R_1, ER_1>$ and $S_2 = <R_2, ER_2>$ be two schemata, and let IA be a set of static integration assertions expressing S_2 in S_1. S_2 weakly B-dominates S_1 w.r.t. IA iff S_2 weakly C-dominates S_1 w.r.t. IA.

Proof: If $(\sigma_1, \sigma_2, ..., \sigma_n) \in \Pi(S_1)$, then, for all $1 \leq i < j \leq n$, $(\sigma_i, \sigma_j) \in \Lambda(S_1)$. Assume that S_2 weakly B-dominates S_1 with respect to IA, then there is also a total injective function ξ, such that for each $(\sigma, \rho) \in \Lambda(S_1)$, $(\xi(\sigma), \xi(\rho)) \in \Lambda(S_2)$, and $\sigma \cup \xi(\sigma)$ and $\rho \cup \xi(\rho)$ are diagrams for IA. Thus if $(\sigma_i, \sigma_j) \in \Lambda(S_1)$, then $(\xi(\sigma_i), \xi(\sigma_j)) \in \Lambda(S_2)$. By this we have that if $(\sigma_1, \sigma_2, ..., \sigma_n) \in \Pi(S_1)$, then, for all $1 \leq i < j \leq n$, $(\xi(\sigma_i), \xi(\sigma_j)) \in \Lambda(S_2)$.
Consequently, $(\xi(\sigma_1), \xi(\sigma_2), ..., \xi(\sigma_n)) \in \Pi(S_2)$. The proof of the converse is immediate, since $\Lambda(S)$ of a schema S is a subset of $\Pi(S)$. ∎

Thus by testing for conflictfreeness with respect to a set of static integration assertions, we get substantial information about the properties in the combined schemata. These properties are expressed as weak dominance is equivalent to weak B-Dominance, which in turn is equivalent to weak C-Dominance. Next, we extend the framework to include dynamic integration assertions.

4 Dynamic Integration Assertions

Before, we have considered a set IA of static integration assertions, i.e., a set of equivalences expressing predicates in one schema in terms of predicates in another one. In this section, we will introduce the dynamical counterpart to these, i.e., assertions expressing event rules in terms of other event rules. Thus, this section generalises the results from the earlier sections, by giving semantics for dynamic integration assertions, and investigates how this affects the concepts of conflictfreeness and weak dominance.

4.1 General Dynamic Integration Assertions

First, we introduce more general types of dynamic integration assertions, i.e., assertions expressing sequences of event rules in terms of sequences of other event rules. In section 4.2 we specify this a bit further to receive a more operationally meaningful concept.

Def: Let $S_1 = <R_1, ER_1>$ and $S_2 = <R_2, ER_2>$ be two schemata. A *dynamic integration assertion expressing the schema S_2 in the schema S_1* is an expression $([V_1, ..., V_k], [U_1, ..., U_n])$, where $V_1, ..., V_k$ are event rules in ER_2 and $U_1, ..., U_n$ are event rules in ER_1.

The intuition behind a set of dynamic integration assertions is that it expresses that some parts of a schema have a similar dynamic behaviour as some parts of another one, with respect to sequences of basic events. This intuition is formalised in the following definition.

Def: Let $S_1 = <R_1, ER_1>$ and $S_2 = <R_2, ER_2>$ be two schemata, and DIA be a set of dynamic integration assertions expressing the schema S_2 in S_1. DIA is *satisfied* by the events $(\sigma, \rho) \in \Lambda(S_1)$ and $(\sigma', \rho') \in \Lambda(S_2)$, if for all $([V_1, ..., V_k],$ $[U_1, ..., U_n]) \in$ DIA, $(\sigma, \rho) \in \Lambda(S_1, U_1 \nabla ... \nabla U_n, e_1; ...; e_n)$ for some event message $e_1, ..., e_n$ iff $(\sigma', \rho') \in \Lambda(S_2, V_1 \nabla ... \nabla V_k, f_1; ...; f_k)$, for some event message $f_1, ..., f_k$. If DIA is satisfied by the events (σ, ρ) and (σ', ρ'), we will also say that (σ, ρ) (and (σ', ρ')) is *compatible* with DIA.

In order to handle dynamic integration assertions when combining schemata, we first define a common structure for schemata w.r.t a set of integration assertions.

Def: Let $S = <R, ER>$ be a schema, and let DIA be a set of dynamic integration assertions expressing S in S. The *restriction of S w.r.t. DIA* is a structure $<R, ER, DIA>$.

The description of the restriction of a schema is similar to the description of the schema, but we include some events in $\Lambda(S)$ and exclude the events that are not compatible with a set of dynamic integration assertions.

Def: Let $S = <R, ER>$ be a schema, and let DIA be a set of dynamic integration assertions expressing S in S. The *description of the restriction of S w.r.t. DIA* is a digraph $<M, A>$, where M is the set of all diagrams for S. A is the set of all events for S minus the events that are not compatible with DIA.

We need a new notion of conflictfreeness and weak dominance to take the dynamic correspondence between schemata into account.

Def: Let $S_1 = <R_1, ER_1>$ and $S_2 = <R_2, ER_2>$ be two schemata, and DIA be a set of dynamic integration assertions expressing the schema S_2 in S_1. Also, let IA be a set of static integration assertions expressing the schema S_2 in S_1.
S_1 and S_2 are *E-conflictfree* w.r.t. IA and DIA, if for each event (σ, ρ) in $\Lambda(S_1)$, there is an event (σ', ρ') in $\Lambda(S_2)$, such that

(i)   DIA is satisfied by (σ, ρ) and (σ', ρ'), and

(ii) $\sigma \cup \sigma'$ and $\rho \cup \rho'$ are both diagrams for IA.

Def: Let $S_1 = <R_1, ER_1>$ and $S_2 = <R_2, ER_2>$ be two schemata, and DIA be a set of dynamic integration assertions expressing the schema S_2 in S_1. Also, let IA be a set of static integration assertions expressing the schema S_2 in S_1. S_2 *weakly E-dominates* S_1 w.r.t. IA and DIA, if there is a total injective function ξ, such that

(i)   for all diagrams σ in M_1, $\xi(\sigma)$ is in M_2 and $\sigma \cup \xi(\sigma)$ is a diagram for IA, and

(ii) for all events (σ, ρ) in $\Lambda(S_1)$, DIA is satisfied by (σ, ρ) and $(\xi(\sigma), \xi(\rho))$.

Theorem 3: Let $S_1 = <R_1, ER_1>$ and $S_2 = <R_2, ER_2>$ be two schemata, and DIA be a set of dynamic integration assertions expressing the schema S_2 in S_1. Also, let IA be a set of static integration assertions expressing the schema S_2 in S_1. Assume that S_1 and S_2 are E-conflictfree w.r.t. IA and DIA. Then, the restriction of $\chi_1(S_1, S_2, IA)$ w.r.t. DIA E-dominates S_1 w.r.t. IA and DIA.

Proof: Since S_1 and S_2 is E-conflictfree, for each event (σ, ρ) in $\Lambda(S_1)$, there is an event (σ', ρ') in $\Lambda(S_2)$ such that DIA is satisfied by (σ, ρ) and (σ', ρ'), and $\sigma \cup \sigma'$ and $\rho \cup \rho'$ are both diagrams for IA. We define a function $\xi: \Lambda(S_1) \rightarrow \Lambda(\chi_1(S_1, S_2, IA))$, such that for each event (σ, ρ) in $\Lambda(S_1)$, $\xi(\sigma) = \sigma \cup \sigma'$ and $\xi(\rho) = \rho \cup \rho'$. By the same argument as in the proof of theorem 1, both $\sigma \cup \xi(\sigma)$ and $\rho \cup \xi(\rho)$ are diagrams for IA. Since DIA is satisfied by (σ, ρ) and (σ', ρ') this function also has the property that DIA is satisfied by (σ, ρ) and $(\xi(\sigma), \xi(\rho))$. ∎

Reducing the number of event rules in a schema is often a desired goal when integrating schemata, but E-conflictfreeness does not generally allow us to this. Thus, the result above is somewhat limited from an operational viewpoint, why we restrict the dynamic integration assertions a little bit in the next section.

4.2 Identifying Dynamic Integration Assertions
Assume that we, for instance, want to compare a requirement and a design specification. Usually the latter one is conceptually richer and treats details that not are important from a conceptual point of view. Therefore, in addition to identification of sets of static integration assertions, we want to identify event sequences for the design specification that correspond to basic events for the requirement specification.

Def: Let $S_1 = <R_1, ER_1>$ and $S_2 = <R_2, ER_2>$ be two schemata.
An *identifying dynamic integration assertion expressing the schema S_2 in the schema S_1* is an expression $([V], [U_1, ..., U_n])$, where V is an event rule in ER_2 and $U_1, ..., U_n$ are event rules in ER_1.

Earlier we said that a set of dynamic integration assertions expresses that some parts of a schema have a similar dynamic behaviour as some parts of another schema. We may also restrict this semantic a little bit more as in the following definition.

Def: Let $S_1 = <R_1, ER_1>$ and $S_2 = <R_2, ER_2>$ be two schemata, and $ID = ([V], [U_1, ..., U_n])$ be an identifying dynamic integration assertion expressing the schema S_2 in S_1. *ID is adequate for S_1, S_2, and IA*, if:
(i) For all $(\sigma', \rho') \in \Lambda(S_2, V)$, there is a sequence of events $(\sigma_1, \sigma_2, ..., \sigma_n, \sigma_{n+1}) \in \Pi(S_1, U_1 \nabla ... \nabla U_n)$, such that $\sigma_1 \cup \sigma'$ and $\sigma_{n+1} \cup \rho'$ are both diagrams for IA.
(ii) For all $(\sigma_1, \sigma_2, ..., \sigma_n, \sigma_{n+1}) \in \Pi(S_1, U_1 \nabla ... \nabla U_n)$, there is an event $(\sigma', \rho') \in \Lambda(S_2, V)$, such that $\sigma_1 \cup \sigma'$ and $\sigma_{n+1} \cup \rho'$ are both diagrams for IA.

If only (i) above is fulfilled, then we will say that ID is *semi-adequate* for S_1, S_2 and IA. When $(\sigma_1, \sigma_2, ..., \sigma_n, \sigma_{n+1})$ and (σ', ρ') correspond in the way described in (i) or (ii), they are called *compatible* with ID.

An example of an identifying dynamic integration assertion, based on the schemata in section 2, is ([connect(t1, t2)], [lift1(t1), dial(t1, t2), lift2(t1)]). It is easy to verify that this assertion is adequate for the schemata and the static integration assertions of section 2.

In Fig. 4.1 below, $(\sigma_1, \sigma_2, \sigma_3, \sigma_4) \in \Pi(S_1, U_1 \nabla ... \nabla U_4)$ corresponds to the event $(\sigma', \rho') \in \Lambda(S_2, V)$.

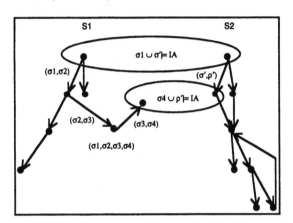

Fig. 4.1

We modify our earlier definition of conflictfreeness and weak dominance and incorporate the requirement of adequacy by the following definitions.

Def: Let $S_1 = <R_1, ER_1>$ and $S_2 = <R_2, ER_2>$ be two schemata. Also, let IA be a set of static integration assertions expressing the schema S_2 in S_1, and let D be a set of IDs. S_1 and S_2 are *D-conflictfree* w.r.t. IA and D, if:

(i) S_1 and S_2 are B-conflictfree w.r.t. IA.

(ii) S_2 and S_1 are B-conflictfree w.r.t. IA.

(iii)   All the IDs in D are semi-adequate for S_1, S_2, and IA.

A problem with our earlier schema combinations is that even if the combined schema dominates its components, we still have more events than we like to have. The concept of combination can be further developed to reduce the set of events, but still maintaining dominance.

Def: Let $S_1 = <R_1, ER_1>$ and $S_2 = <R_2, ER_2>$ be two schemata, and IA be a set of static integration assertions expressing the schema S_2 in S_1. Also let D be a set of IDs expressing the schema S_2 in S_1.
Assume that D = {([<x, $P_1(x)$, $C_1(x)$>], [<x, $P_{11}(x)$, $C_{11}(x)$>, ..., <x, $P_{1k_1}(x)$, $C_{1k_1}(x)$>]), ..., ([<x, $P_n(x)$, $C_n(x)$>], [<x, $P_{n1}(x)$, $C_{n1}(x)$>, ..., <x, $P_{nk_n}(x)$, $C_{nk_n}(x)$>])}. The combined schema, $\iota_1(S_1, S_2, IA, D)$, is the schema: <$R_1 \cup R_2 \cup IA$, $ER_1 \cup ER_2 - \{<x, P_1(x), C_1(x)>$, ... <x, $P_n(x)$, $C_n(x)$>}.

From theorem 1 follows that if S_1 and S_2 are conflictfree w.r.t. IA, then $\iota_1(S_1, S_2, IA, D)$ weakly B-dominates S_1 w.r.t. IA. This is the case since ER_1 is not affected by the combination. However the following theorem says that $\iota_1(S_1, S_2, IA, D)$ also weakly dominates S_2 w.r.t. IA if S_1 and S_2 are D-conflictfree w.r.t. IA and D.

Theorem 4: Let $S_1 = <R_1, ER_1>$ and $S_2 = <R_2, ER_2>$ be two schemata, and D be a set of IDs expressing the schema S_2 in S_1. Also, let IA be a set of static integration assertions expressing the schema S_2 in S_1. Assume that S_1 and S_2 are D-conflictfree w.r.t. IA and D. Then, $\iota_1(S_1, S_2, IA, D)$ weakly dominates S_2 w.r.t. IA.

Proof: Consider Fig. 4.1 again. Assume that an event rule V on the leftmost side in an identifying dynamic integration assertion D for S_1 and S_2 and that $U_1, ..., U_4$ are on the rightmost side in D. If we combine the schemata S_1 and S_2, the event $(\sigma_1 \cup \sigma', \sigma_4 \cup \rho') \in \Lambda(<R_1 \cup R_2 \cup IA, ER_1 \cup ER_2>, V)$ corresponds to the event $(\sigma', \rho') \in \Lambda(S_2, V)$. But, this is true even if we take the event rule V away, provided that there really is a sequence of diagrams whose first element is $\sigma_1 \cup \sigma'$ and whose last element is $\sigma_4 \cup \rho'$. It is also clear that there is such a sequence in $\Lambda(<R_1 \cup R_2 \cup IA, ER_1 \cup ER_2>, U_1, ..., U_4)$ if also the diagrams σ_2, and σ_3 can be extended to diagrams for $R_1 \cup R_2 \cup IA$. This is the case if S_1 and S_2 are D-conflictfree w.r.t. IA. Thus, if the sequence can be extended in such a way, it 'survives' in the combined schema. More generally, we need to show that there is a total injective function ξ, such that $(\xi(\sigma_i), \xi(\sigma_j))$ is in $\Lambda(\varepsilon_1(S_1, S_2, IA, D))$ if (σ_i, σ_j) is in $\Lambda(S_2)$. Assume that $([V], [U_1, ..., U_n])$ is an identifying dynamic integration assertion for S_1 and S_2. Since S_1 and S_2 are D-conflictfree, there is a sequence of diagrams $(\sigma_1, \sigma_2, ..., \sigma_n, \sigma_{n+1}) \in \Pi(S_1, U_1 \nabla...\nabla U_n)$, such that $\sigma_1 \cup \sigma'$ and $\sigma_{n+1} \cup \rho'$ are both diagrams for IA, for all $(\sigma', \rho') \in \Lambda(S_2, V)$. Thus, $(\sigma_1 \cup \sigma')$ and $(\sigma_{n+1} \cup \rho')$ are diagrams for $<R_1 \cup R_2 \cup IA, ER_1 \cup ER_2>$ as well as for $\varepsilon_1(S_1, S_2, IA, D)$. Also if the event $(\sigma_1 \cup \sigma', \sigma_4 \cup \rho')$ for $<R_1 \cup R_2 \cup IA, ER_1 \cup ER_2>$ results from the event rule V, this event also results from $U_1, ..., U_n$ in $\varepsilon_1(S_1, S_2, IA, D)$, provided that there are descriptions for $\varepsilon_1(S_1, S_2, IA, D)$ that are extensions of $\sigma_2, ..., \sigma_{n-1}$, and σ_n. The latter follows from that D-conflict-freeness implies that S_1 and S_2 are conflictfree w.r.t. IA. Consequently, since $<R_1 \cup R_2 \cup IA, ER_1 \cup ER_2>$ weakly dominates S_2 (by theorem 1 and that S_2 and S_1 are B-conflictfree w.r.t. IA), $\iota_1(S_1, S_2, IA, D)$ weakly dominates S_2. ∎

4.3 Internal and External Events

The requirement of adequacy can be made a bit stronger by the requirement that every event message should induce a similar behaviour in two different schemata.

Def: Let $S_1 = <R_1, ER_1>$ and $S_2 = <R_2, ER_2>$ be two schemata, and ID = ([V], [U_1, ..., U_n]) be an identifying dynamic integration assertion expressing the schema S_2 in S_1. ID is *message-adequate* for S_1, S_2, and IA, if:
  (i)   For all event messages **f**, and for all events $(\sigma', \rho') \in \Lambda(S_2, V, \mathbf{f})$, there is a concatenation of event messages $\mathbf{f};\mathbf{e_2};...;\mathbf{e_n}$ and an event $(\sigma_1, \sigma_2, ..., \sigma_n, \sigma_{n+1}) \in \Pi(S_1, U_1 \nabla...\nabla U_n, \mathbf{f};\mathbf{e_2};...;\mathbf{e_n})$, (where $(\sigma_1, \sigma_2) \in \Lambda(S_1, U_1, \mathbf{f})$), such that $\sigma_1 \cup \sigma'$ and $\sigma_{n+1} \cup \rho'$ are both diagrams for IA.

(ii) For each concatenation $(f;e_2;...;e_n)$ of event messages $(\sigma_1, \sigma_2, ..., \sigma_n, \sigma_{n+1}) \in \Pi(S_1, U_1 \nabla...\nabla U_n, f;e_2;...;e_n)$, there is an event $(\sigma', \rho') \in \Lambda(S_2, V, f)$, such that $\sigma_1 \cup \sigma'$ and $\sigma_{n+1} \cup \rho'$ are both diagrams for IA.

We call the elements $(\sigma_2, \sigma_3), (\sigma_3, \sigma_4), ..., (\sigma_n, \sigma_{n+1})$ above, *internal events*. (σ_1, σ_2) and (σ', ρ') are *external events*. $U_2, ..., U_n$, are *internal event rules*.

By substituting the requirement of message-adequacy for adequacy in our earlier sense, we get a similar dominance result as in theorem 4.

5 A Procedure for Determining Adequacy

In this section, a procedure for determining whether an identifying dynamic integration assertion is adequate for two schemata, considering only finite domains, is presented. Also the computational complexity of the procedure is investigated.[6] For simplicity, we describe the procedure using an example. The general case is very similar.

Assume that we have two schemata S_1 and S_2, a set of integration assertions IA and an identifying dynamic integration assertion ID = $([<x, A(x), B(x)>], [<x, C(x), D(x)>, <x, E(x), F(x)>])$. Also, there is no loss of generality to assume that the only possible event messages are e_1 and e_2.

Let $H(S_1)$ be the Herbrand expansion of the rules in S_1. Make three copies of $H(S_1)$ and index all the predicate symbols in the first copy by b, in the second copy by m, and in the third copy by a. We then denote the copies by $H_b(S_1), H_m(S_1)$, and $H_a(S_1)$, respectively. Also define $H_b(IA), H_a(IA), H_b(S_2)$, and $H_a(S_2)$ analogously. Consider the set $H_{bma}(ID) = \{([<e_1, A_b(e_1), B_a(e_1)>], [<e_1, C_b(e_1), D_m(e_1)>, <e_1, E_m(e_1), F_a(e_1)>]), ([<e_1, A_b(e_1), B_a(e_1)>], [<e_1, C_b(e_1), D_m(e_1)>, <e_2, E_m(e_2), F_a(e_2)>]), ([<e_2, A_b(e_2), B_a(e_2)>], [<e_2, C_b(e_2), D_m(e_2)>, <e_1, E_m(e_1), F_a(e_1)>]), ([<e_2, A_b(e_2), B_a(e_2)>], [<e_2, C_b(e_2), D_m(e_2)>, <e_2, E_m(e_2), F_a(e_2)>])\}$. This is the set of the possible variants of the ID, when the event combinations are instanced in all possible ways.

We can now observe that ID is semi-adequate for S_1 and S_2 if for all diagrams σ for $H_b(S_2) \wedge H_a(S_2) \wedge [(A_b(e_1) \wedge B_a(e_1)) \vee (A_b(e_2) \wedge B_a(e_2))]$, there is a diagram τ for $H_b(S_1) \wedge H_m(S_1) \wedge H_a(S_1) \wedge [(C_b(e_1) \wedge D_m(e_1)) \vee (C_b(e_2) \wedge D_m(e_2))] \wedge [(E_m(e_1) \wedge F_a(e_1)) \vee (E_m(e_2) \wedge F_a(e_2))]$, such that $\sigma \cup \tau$ is a diagram for $H_b(IA) \wedge H_a(IA)$.

Since we have no restriction of the formulas in a schema (except that they are first order formulas) the general problem of determining adequacy is undecidable. However, if we restrict our attention to languages with a finite number of constants, we have a problem in second order propositional logic that is Π_2^P-complete. This can be realised from the observation that the criteria is an expression in second order logic.[7] The treatment of E-conflictfreeness is very similar.

---

[6]The complexity properties for determining conflictfreeness are investigated in [5].

[7]A detailed treatment of the polynomial hierarchy is provided in [7].

6 Concluding Remarks

When integrating two schemata, there must exist a natural mapping between the integrated schema and the original ones. In this paper, we have formalised this requirement by means of the dominance concept. With respect to this, we have also identified various aspects of a condition, called conflictfreeness, that two schemata and a set of integration assertions must satisfy in order to be mergeable.

As pointed out in [1], there are essentially three ways of restricting a user to update a database:

a) Specify constraints (static as well as dynamic) that the database must satisfy and reject any update that leads to a violation of the constraints.

b) Restrict the updates themselves by only allowing the use of a set of prespecified update rules.

c) Permit users to request essentially arbitrary updates, but provide an automatic mechanism for detecting and repairing constraint violations.

In this paper, we have considered the first two ways of restricting updates by introducing static and dynamic rules as well as the event concept. Option c) above is studied in the emerging field of active databases [9]. An active database supports the automatic triggering of updates as a response to events. One possible extension of our work on schema integration is to investigate how this form of automatic updates can be incorporated into the proposed framework. Another research direction is to change the event concept used in this paper. Our event concept is deliberately weak and it could be argued that it does not capture common intuitions about events, in particular our approach implies that from a given state infinitely many states can be reached by means of one and the same event rule and event message. To remedy this situation, it is straightforward to introduce an alternative event concept, by means of an information processor that obeys some form of a frame rule. This would render our event concept more similar to traditional transactional update approaches in the database area, where updates are provided by means of transactions composed of sequences of insertions, deletions, and modifications [2].

References

[1]   S. Abiteboul, R. Hull, and V. Vianu, *Foundations of Databases*: Addison-Wesley, 1995.

[2]   S. Abiteboul and V. Vianu, "Equivalence and Optimization of Relational Transactions," *Journal of ACM*, vol. 35, pp. 130–145, 1988.

[3]   C. Batini, M. Lenzerini, and S. B. Navathe, "A Comparative Analysis of Methodologies for Database Schema Integration," *ACM Computing Surveys*, vol. 18, pp. 323–364, 1986.

[4]   J. Biskup and B. Convent, "A Formal View Integration Method," Proceedings of International Conference on the Management of Data, 1986.

[5]   L. Ekenberg and P. Johannesson, "Conflictfreeness as a Basis for Schema Integration," Proceedings of CISMOD-95, pp. 1–13, 1995.

[6]   R. Hull, "Relative Information Capacity of Simple Relational Database Schemata," *SIAM Journal of Computing*, vol. 15, pp. 856–886, 1986.

[7] D. S. Johnson, "A Catalogue of Complexity Classes," in *Handbook of Theoretical Computer Science: Volume A*, J. van Leeuwen, Ed. Amsterdam: Elsevier, 1990.

[8] R. Miller, Y. Ioannidis, and R. Ramakrishnan, "Schema Equivalence in Heterogeneous Systems: Bridging Theory and Practice," *Information Systems*, vol. 19, 1994.

[9] E. Simon, J. Kiernan, and C. de Mandreville, "Implementing High Level Active Rules on Top of a Relational DBMS," Proceedings of International Conference on Very Large Data Bases, pp. 281–290, 1992.

Graphical Entity Relationship Models: Towards a More User Understandable Representation of Data

Daniel Moody

Abstract. The Entity Relationship Model was originally proposed as a way of representing user requirements in a way that non-technical users could understand. However anecdotal evidence and empirical studies both indicate that users have major difficulties understanding Entity Relationship models in practice. This paper proposes a number of modifications to the Entity Relationship Model to make it more understandable to business users. These include the use of an enhanced graphical representation, levels of abstraction and the use of business scenarios. This method has been used successfully in a wide range of organisational contexts, and has been particularly successful at the corporate level, where understandability of models has been found to be a major barrier to their acceptance and use. In addition, an automated tool has been developed to support the technique, which allows users to interact directly with the model and understand how it works through the use of animation.
t>

1. INTRODUCTION

The Entity Relationship Model: A User Oriented Representation of Data?

The Entity Relationship Model was originally proposed as a way of defining information requirements in a business-oriented rather than a technical way (Chen, 1976). By defining user requirements in terms of real world concepts such as objects, people, events and the relationships between them, it was believed that it would provide a common language between business specialists and technical specialists (ISO, 1987; Kent, 1986; Date, 1986). This would enable users to directly participate in the development of models and verify their correctness.

A major advantage of the Entity Relationship model compared to other representational techniques is its graphical form (Feldman and Miller, 1986). Diagrams have significant advantages over textual specifications for the purposes of communication. They are also more effective for communicating with users because they put information in a form which is more palatable for non-technical people (Page-Jones, 1980).

According to the literature, the Entity Relationship Model is:

- Simple and easily understood by non-specialists (Konsynski, 1979);
- Highly intuitive and provides a very natural way of representing a user's information requirements (Brodie et al, 1984);
- Suitable for computer-naïve end-users (Berman, 1986).

Indeed, according to some authors, the Entity Relationship model is so natural and intuitive that users can develop models themselves, without the assistance of technical experts (Finklestein, 1989):

> "As data analysis began to be applied by more and more organisations ... it was found that users without a knowledge of computers were also able to apply this technique. In fact, in some cases, they developed logical database designs that were more correct than those of either the analyst or the DBA ... The search for user-driven methods was beginning to bear fruit"

Experience In Practice With The Entity Relationship Model

While this is fine in theory, what evidence is there in practice for the effectiveness of Entity Relationship models in communicating with users? In the author's experience as a consultant in a wide range of organisations, users generally do not consider data models as business oriented specifications. Because of this, many professional data analysts do not show data models to users directly, but verify them by translating them into natural language sentences. A number of CASE tools can do this automatically. This seems to contradict the widely held assertion that diagrams are easier to understand than text.

A number of empirical studies have recently found that users have difficulty understanding Entity Relationship models in practice. Goldstein and Story (1990) found that educators find the Entity Relationship model difficult to teach, which contradicts assertions made about the "naturalness, inutitiveness and general ease of use" of the Entity Relationship model. Hitchman (1995) found that analysts and clients do not find data models intuitive and that data models are not generally developed with direct client involvement. This study also found that many *practitioners* did not understand many of the concepts in the Entity Relationship model properly.

The problem is summarised by Hitchman (1995):

> "Information from the survey gives very strong evidence to support the assertions that data modelling is poorly understood by analysts and especially by clients. This seems to contradict the widely held academic proposition that data models are easy to build and understand..."

The understandability of Entity Relationship models is especially a problem at the corporate level. Corporate Data Models are significantly more complex than application level models, and so comprehension difficulties are multiplied many times over (Moody, 1991). Shanks (1996) found that the understandability of Corporate Data Models was a major barrier to their acceptance and use in practice.

Objectives Of This Paper

This paper argues that the Entity Relationship Model has never achieved its promise of providing a common language for communication between users and application developers. While it has proven very effective as a technique for database design, it has been far less effective for communication with users. Empirical studies and anecdotal evidence show that in general, users do not understand Entity Relationship models and are not actively involved in developing these models.

The communication properties of data models are of critical importance so that users can directly participate in the development of the model and verify its correctness (Moody and Shanks, 1994). This paper proposes a more "user friendly" way of representing the concepts of the Entity Relationship model, so that users can actively participate in the process. This method has evolved as a result of experience in practice, and has been used successfully in a wide range of industrial contexts.

2. WHY ARE ENTITY RELATIONSHIP MODELS DIFFICULT TO UNDERSTAND?

Entity Relationship Models "Look" Technical

There can be little doubt that data models look quite technical to the untrained user. The representation of the Entity Relationship model shown in Figure 1 is neither "friendly" to look at nor intuitively obvious in its meaning. This is the most commonly used representation in practice and is supported by most modern CASE tools.

Figure 1. Entity Relationship Model

In particular, the cardinality properties of Entity Relationship Models (indicated by "crows feet" and mandatory/optional symbols) are difficult to understand for business specialists (Batini, Ceri and Navathe, 1992). In practice, users need to be constantly reminded as to what the symbols mean and which direction they are read in.

To the average user, Entity Relationship models do not look very different to other technical diagrams used in the systems development process. For example, network communications diagrams, database structure diagrams and system architecture diagrams all have a similar structure to Entity Relationship diagrams—they consist of geometrical shapes connected by lines. Like these other types of diagrams, Entity Relationship models are rather lifeless looking technical diagrams. For this reason, they should more correctly be called "schematic" rather than graphical.

The Entity Relationship Model Does Not Handle Complexity Well

One of the most serious limitations of the Entity Relationship model in practice is its inability to cope with the size and complexity of data models encountered in real world situations (Moody, 1991). Feldman and Miller (1987) argue that data modelling techniques have not reached their full potential in practice primarily because of their inability to cope with complexity. With large numbers of entities, Entity Relationship models become difficult to understand and maintain (Simsion, 1989). The problem becomes unmanageable at the enterprise level, where models often consist of hundreds of entities.

When a data model gets too large, it becomes a barrier to communication because of its size and complexity (Simsion, 1989). Psychological evidence shows that due to limits on short term memory, humans have a strictly limited capacity for processing information—this is estimated to be "seven, plus or minus two" concepts (Miller, 1956; Newell and Simon, 1972). If the amount of information exceeds these limits, information overload ensues and comprehension degrades rapidly (Lipowski, 1975).

It is here that the diagrammatical representation of data models actually becomes a disadvantage. Textual descriptions, which are naturally sequential, can extend over as many pages as necessary without losing their meaning. However data models, because of their network structure, have no inherent ordering and must be perceived as a whole (Martin, 1987). As a result, Miller's limit is soon reached and their complexity quickly becomes overwhelming.

Users Find Entity Relationship Models Abstract and Difficult to Relate To

Classification is an abstraction used to group real world instances into classes or concepts. This is the mechanism used to create entities in the Entity Relationship technique. Entities represent classes of things (eg. Customer, Product) rather than actual instances. However users often find abstract representations of requirements difficult to relate to, and need concrete examples to understand what they mean (Moody, 1996).

Generalisation is the mechanism used to create more abstract concepts based on similar properties (attributes or relationships) of more specific entities (Batini, Ceri and Navathe, 1992). Subtypes and supertypes are used to represent generalisation in the Entity Relationship model. In the example below (Figure 2), Car and Truck are subtypes of Vehicle, while Vehicle is the supertype of Car and Truck.

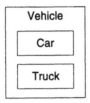

Figure 2. Representation of Subtypes and Supertypes

However users often find highly generalised representations of data difficult to understand (Moriarty, 1993a). At the enterprise level in particular, highly generalised models are often developed which lose all sense of the business. The level of abstraction of these models is a major barrier to their acceptance and understanding in practice, both by users and application developers (Shanks, 1996).

Entity Relationship Models Are Focused on Design Rather Than Analysis

What the Entity Relationship Model does most effectively is to define the technical aspects of data, for the purposes of database design. Campbell (1992) concluded that current data modeling representations are primarily focused on effective design rather than effective analysis. The Entity Relationship model has been used successfully to design relational and network schemas for two decades (Teory et al, 1986). Using this technique, analysts with little knowledge of database design are able to design databases that are comparable to those produced by experienced DBAs (Finklestein, 1989).

However this raises an important question: for whose benefit are data models anyway? For the technicians or users? The raison d'être of the Entity Relationship model was to represent information requirements in a way that could be easily understood by users. It was not meant to describe the way in which data would be stored in the computer (Elmasri and Navathe, 1989).

3. PREVIOUS RESEARCH

Data Modelling Research

The area of data modelling has attracted considerable research interest in the literature. A large amount of this research effort has been directed towards the development of new and semantically "richer" modelling notations (Batra and Davis, 1992). Many new data modelling techniques have been proposed, each with its own capabilities of capturing more meaning about the problem domain (see Peckham and Maryanski, 1988; Hull and King, 1987; ISO, 1987 for a review of models proposed).

In most cases, this has required the introduction of new constructs and symbols to provide additional semantics. For example, the Extended Entity Relationship Model (Figure 3) extends the standard Entity Relationship model to include a number of additional constructs: subtypes, composite attributes, multi-valued attributes and derived attributes:

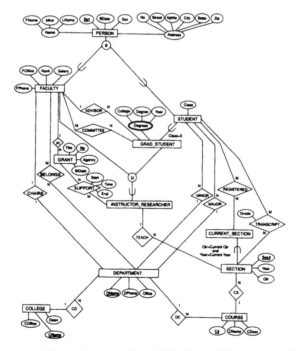

Figure 3. Extended Entity Relationship (EER) Model (Elmasri and Navathe, 1989)

In looking at the results of this research, the general effect seems to have been to enrich the representation from the data modeller's point of view, but make it even *more* incomprehensible for non-technical people. A large variety of different modelling constructs enables a more comprehensive representation of the real world, but makes it more difficult for people to understand (Batini, Ceri and Navathe, 1992). If, as Hitchman (1995) showed, people have difficulty understanding the standard Entity Relationship model, what chance will they have with these new methods?

In this respect, research into improved representation methods for Entity Relationship models seems to have missed the point. As discussed earlier, the original purpose of data modelling was to reduce the gap between user perceptions of reality and the technical representation. Instead however, the research seems to be taking data modelling even further away from the grasp of the average business user. To improve understanding, representational methods should be made simpler rather than more complex.

Focus of Data Modelling Research

Research in Entity Relationship modeling seems to have focused primarily on the "back end" of the data modelling process (see Figure 4). Most research effort has been expended on improving the transformation of a data model into a database design by making the representation more rigorous and complete, rather than the "front end", which is about making data models more understandable to users.

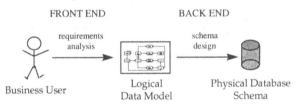

Figure 4. Database Design Process

To a large extent, this seems to run counter to the needs of practice. Empirical research shows that the real problems are not in transforming specifications to design but in getting specifications right to start with (Butler Cox, 1987). Industry studies show that over 50% of errors in the systems development process are the result of inaccurately defined requirements (Martin, 1989). According to Swatman and Swatman (1992), improving the requirements determination and specification process is the most important area for improving software development productivity.

Lessons From Other Disciplines

In trying to develop a more user friendly representation for data models, a natural place to start is to look at techniques used in other design disciplines. All design disciplines face a similar problem: how to make design specifications understandable to the customer as well as serving as the basis for construction of an artifact (man-made object) that will meet their requirements (Simon, 1982). In the case of Entity Relationship modelling, the artifact is a physical database.

Architecture

In architecture, architects produce technical drawings with detailed specifications and measurements that are used as a basis for construction of a building. However customers often have difficulty visualising the final result based on these drawings alone. To address this problem, Computer-Aided-Design (CAD) packages allow three-dimensional simulations of the buildings to be produced using computer graphics software. Using this software, customers can experiment with a range of alternative designs and "see" the result. The benefit of this is a design that is better customised to customer requirements, and much reduced risk of a mismatch between customer perceptions and the delivered product.

Soft Systems Methodology

The Soft Systems Methodology (SSM) uses a variety of techniques to define user requirements. One of the techniques used early on in the problem definition process is the "rich picture" (Figure 5). A rich picture is a pictorial representation of the problem situation, which summarises of all that is known about the situation (Checkland, 1981; Checkland and Scholes, 1990). The rich picture represents an agreed common understanding between the analyst and client as to what the problem is, which is used as a starting point for further analysis (Wood-Harper et al, 1992).

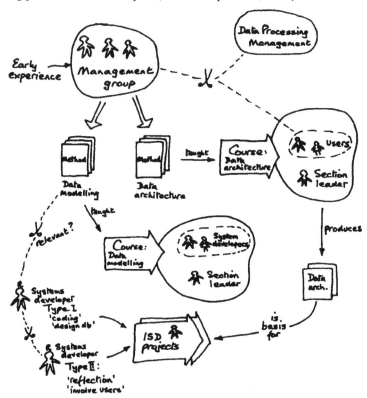

Figure 5. Example of a Rich Picture (Wood-Harper et al, 1992)

The rich picture often contains cartoon characterisations of the situation (eg. crossed swords to indicate conflict), and is a much more graphic and amusing form of diagram than more traditional techniques like Data Flow Diagrams (Lewis, 1992). Data Flow Diagrams consist of circles and arrows and are therefore *schematic,* while rich pictures contain more direct representations of concepts (eg. stick figures for people) and are therefore *graphical.*

Graphical User Interfaces (GUI)

The software development industry has undergone a major revolution with the widespread adoption of graphical user interface (GUI) technology. Instead of using text based menus or command driven interfaces, commercial software is being almost exclusively built nowadays using GUI techniques. Graphical user interfaces have become the predominant paradigm for designing systems over the last five years.

Graphical user interfaces involve the use of graphical "icons" and mouse-based ("point and click") navigation of the system and selection of options. Research has found that graphical user interfaces are more intuitive to use, more visually appealing and generally quicker than going through multi-level menus. Graphical user interfaces have been found to be particularly effective for untrained users.

4. GRAPHICAL ENTITY RELATIONSHIP MODELS

This section describes a more "user friendly" way of representing Entity Relationship models so they can be easily understood by non-technical users. The technique is based on the following concepts:

- The use of graphical images instead of geometrical shapes to represent entities. This makes models more vivid and lifelike, and less threatening for users;
- The use of levels of abstraction to deal with the complexity of data models. This helps to cope with limitations of human information processing;
- The use of scenarios to show the application of the model to the business environment. This helps to instantiate the model, and show how it works.

Use of Graphical Images

A major innovation of this technique is to use graphical images to represent entities instead of boxes as in traditional Entity Relationship diagrams. While this seems like quite a simple change, it has been found in practice to dramatically improve the value of models as a user communication tool.

Context Data Model

In any problem situation, a top level or Context Data Model should be produced which summarises the data in the area under study on a single page. The top level model should show the core business concepts and the relationships between them in the form of a picture.

On the Context Data Model, graphical images or "icons" are used to represent entities, with relationships shown using arrows. Relationships are labelled by the meaning of the relationship, with the direction of the arrows indicating the direction in which the relationship should be read. Figure 6 shows the context level diagram of a Corporate Data Model for an airline:

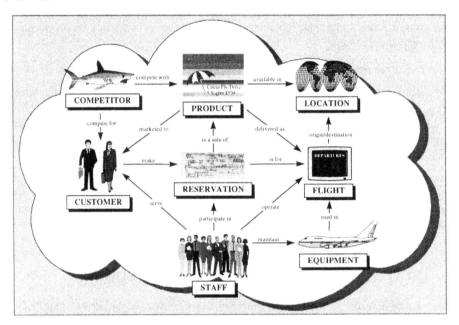

Figure 6. Top Level (Context) Data Model For An Airline

The Context Data Model should consist of a maximum of nine entities, following the "seven, plus or minus two" principle. This limit applies to both application data models and Corporate Data Models. Limiting the model to a maximum of nine concepts forces the analyst to focus on the central business concepts, and ensures that the model can be easily shown on a single page.

It is not necessary to show all relationships between the entities on the Context Data Model, only the most important ones from a business viewpoint. The top level diagram is meant purely as a communication tool, a high level sketch of the situation rather than a rigorous specification.

Choosing Appropriate Images

For communication effectiveness, it is important to find concrete and immediate icons for each concept, so it is immediately obvious what they represent. One way to do this is to find an "exemplar" of the concept—something that is highly representative and immediately recognisable to most people. For example, in Figure 6, an aircraft is the most easily identifiable item of equipment for an airline.

The use of metaphor is also effective in getting concepts across—for example in Figure 6, a shark is used to represent competitors. In general, colour and humour should be used whenever possible to liven up the diagram and make it more appealing to non-technical people. Artistic ability is a help but not essential. Images may be hand-drawn, scanned in, or drawn using computer graphics software. "Clip Art" libraries are available which contain a large variety of ready-made images.

The discipline of having to find a graphical image for each concept forces the analyst to use concepts that can be easily visualised and understood, and avoids the use of abstract concepts that do not correspond to reality. If a concrete representation cannot be found for an entity, this may indicate that the entity has not been well defined.

Introducing graphical images and colour into Entity Relationship models in this way makes them much more vivid and life-like to business users. They appear "three dimensional" rather than lifeless drawings on a page. Effectively, the graphical representation provides a "GUI" front end to the Entity Relationship model, without changing its underlying meaning.

Levels Of Abstraction

In order to manage the complexity of the model, it is represented at different levels of abstraction, following the technique described in Moody (1991). The diagram below (Figure 7) shows the structure of a Graphical Entity Relationship Model.

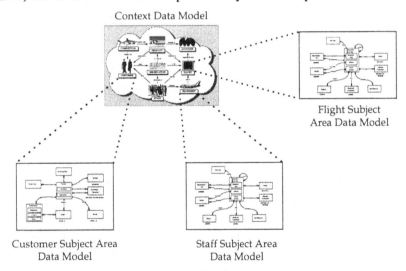

Figure 7. Levels of Abstraction

At the top level, the Context Data Model defines the core business concepts and relationships between them in graphical form. At the next level down, each of these graphical images "explodes" into a detailed Entity Relationship diagram. The hierarchical structure of Graphical Entity Relationship Models is similar to the use of levelling in Data Flow Diagrams (De Marco, 1978).

There are two basic rules used in partitioning a model into subject areas:

1. Each primitive level entity should be assigned to one and only one subject area (non-overlapping subsets)

2. Each subject area should consist of a maximum of nine entities.

Limiting each subject area to less than ten entities ensures that complexity is manageable at each level (7+/-2 entities), and that each subject area can be shown on a single page. With very large data models, this will mean that the model will need to be represented using more than two levels of abstraction.

Relationships Between Subject Areas

An important consideration in partitioning data models is to preserve relationships which span multiple subject areas. This is done through the mechanism of *foreign entities* (Moody, 1991). Whenever an entity on one subject area has a relationship to an entity on another subject area, the second entity is shown as a foreign entity. Foreign entities are shown as shaded boxes, with their primary subject area in brackets. Foreign entities act as cross-references between different subject areas of the model.

For example, a Person (which belongs to the Person subject area) is the subject of a Court Order (which belongs to the Result subject area). Figure 8 shows how this relationship would be shown on the Person subject area:

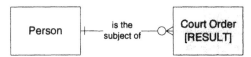

Figure 8. Foreign Entity Reference

Relationships which cross subject area boundaries should be shown on both subject areas to simplify navigation between subject areas. This means that on the Result Subject area, the same relationship would be shown as follows:

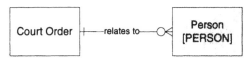

Figure 9. Foreign Entity Reference (reverse direction)

While an entity must be assigned to one and only one subject area (its primary subject area), it may appear on any number of subject areas as a foreign entity. Similarly, any number of foreign entities can appear on a Subject Area Data Model (these are *not* included in the count of entities for the subject area). Foreign entities provide a simple and intuitive mechanism for navigating between different parts of the model, which mirrors the use of foreign keys in the relational model (Moody, 1991).

Use of Aggregation

The levelling technique described here uses the mechanism of *aggregation* to create higher level entities (subject areas) from the primitive entities and relationships in the data model. This is precisely the same mechanism used to group attributes into entity types, and so is a natural extension to the Entity Relationship approach.

It is also natural from the point of view of human information processing, since it is the same mechanism used by humans to deal with large amounts of information. Miller (1956) showed that the number of "chunks" humans can hold in short term memory and process effectively is strictly limited ("the magical number, seven plus or minus two"). Once Miller's limit is reached, people reformulate information into larger and larger chunks, each containing more information and less detail (Uhr et al, 1962). The ability to recursively develop information saturated chunks is the key to man's ability to deal with complexity on a day to day basis (Flood and Carson, 1987).

Scenarios

A good way to make a data model easier for people to relate to their own experience is through the use of *scenarios* (Moriarty, 1993b; Mittermier et al, 1982). Scenarios are real life or fictitious examples which show how actual business situations may be represented using the concepts of the model. They are particularly useful for testing out the implications of the model in real life situations, and for showing how the model "works" as a whole. Scenarios are referred to "use cases" in the Object Oriented literature (Jacobson, 1992; 1995).

It is important to get a wide variety of scenarios to test the model, from simple to complex. Scenarios can be represented in the form of an English narrative, with the names of entities embedded in sentences. Figure 10 shows an example of a scenario to support a simple model.

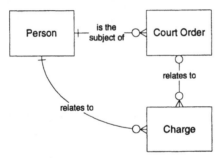

John Robertson (*Person*) was given an imprisonment order of three months (*Court Order*) for three counts of burglary *(Charge)*, and a fine of $1,000 (*Court Order*) for driving without a licence *(Charge)*.

Figure 10. Scenario Example

Users from different business areas can be asked to think up scenarios to test that the model works. These can be tested against the model dynamically, as part of a workshop session. Scenarios provide a good way of increasing user participation in the data modelling process, since they require no familiarity with data modelling techniques.

5. AUTOMATED SUPPORT FOR THE TECHNIQUE

An automated tool has been built to support the representational method described in this paper. This allows the user to interact directly with the model and see how it works. The graphical representation of the model lends itself naturally to implementation using a graphical user interface (GUI) system, with the top level model as the opening screen. The example used in this section to illustrate the use of the tool is a Corporate Data Model, but it is equally useful for representing application level data models.

Top Level Diagram

The opening screen of the system shows the top level or Context Data Model.

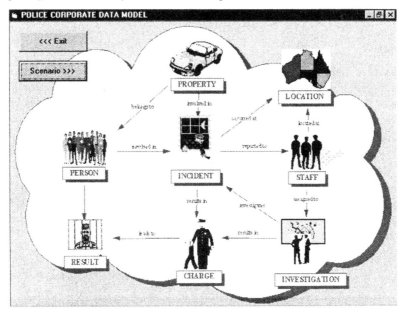

Entity Definitions

Clicking on any of the graphical icons shown on the top level model brings up a business definition for that entity.

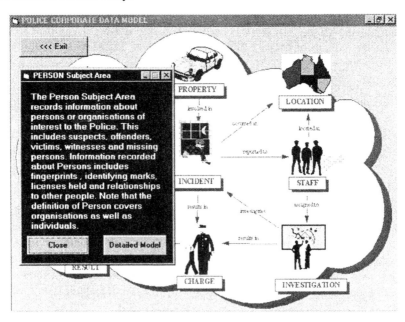

Subject Area Diagrams

If the user clicks on the "Detailed Model" button on the previous screen, the icon "explodes" to a detailed Entity Relationship model. This shows the subject area in full detail. The entities shown in green represent cross-references to other subject areas (foreign entities). Clicking on any of these entities will take the user to the adjoining subject area. The tool thus supports horizontal (subject area to subject area) as well as vertical (between levels) navigation of the model.

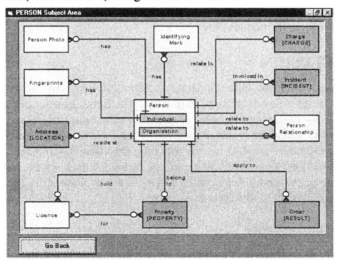

Scenarios

Clicking on the scenario button on the opening screen "plays out" a number of different business scenarios on the model, using the technique of animation. Each button on this screen shows a step in the process, and how it relates back to the concepts on the model. The example below shows the Burglary scenario.

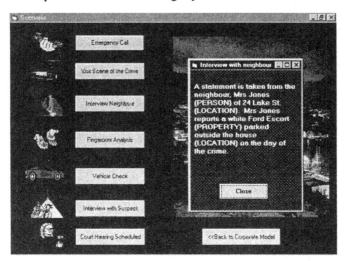

Use of the Automated Tool

The automated tool has been mainly used as a presentation tool to conduct user walk-throughs and review sessions. However it has also proven useful in practice for distributing the model electronically. The automated version of the model can be sent to people via electronic mail or on disk, rather than in document form. Data models are most commonly distributed in paper form, which is slow and cumbersome. Traditional CASE tools do not lend themselves to distributing copies of models because they are not easy to use for untrained users, and the software is generally not easily available throughout the organisation.

6. CONCLUSION

This paper argues that the understandability of Entity Relationship models to users is largely a myth and is unsubstantiated in practice. The Entity Relationship model is an excellent tool for designing database schemas, but never was and never will be suitable for direct consumption by business users. This paper has proposed a more "user friendly" representation for data models which incorporates visual images, colour and levels of abstraction. Importantly however, the technique does not change the underlying meaning of the Entity Relationship Model, but puts a user-friendly "front end" on it to make it more palatable for users.

Summary of the Technique

The rules of the technique are summarised below. There are just seven rules (following the seven, plus or minus two principle).

1. A Context Data Model should be produced which summarises the area under study. Each high level concept should be represented by a graphical image or icon.
2. The Context Data Model should consist of a maximum of nine entities, which represent the core business concepts.
3. Relationships should be shown on the Context Data Model as arrows connecting the icons, labelled by the meaning of the relationship. Arrows indicate the direction in which the relationship should be read.
4. Each entity on the Context diagram should "explode" to a detailed Entity Relationship model at the next level (Subject Area Data Model). Subject Area Data Models are shown in standard Entity Relationship form.
5. Each primitive level entity should be assigned to one and only one subject area, and each subject area should consist of a maximum of nine entities (excluding foreign entities).
6. Foreign entities should be used to show cross-references between Subject Area Data Models. These are shown as shaded boxes, with the name of their primary subject area in brackets.
7. A variety of business scenarios, from simple to complex, should be produced to demonstrate how the model works in the business environment.

Figure 11. Rules For Representing Graphical Entity Relationship Models

Benefits In Practice

The technique described in this paper has been applied in a wide variety of organisations, both in the public and private sector. It has been used primarily for representing Corporate Data Models, because this is the area where the author works. It is also at this level that problems of understandability are most difficult to overcome. However the technique is equally applicable at the application level.

A number of benefits of using this technique over traditional Entity Relationship models have been found as a result of experience in practice.

Overcoming Barriers To User Involvement

It is often difficult to get users involved in data modelling because it is perceived as a technical task. As a result, models are often developed without the involvement of the people who know most about the data. The use of Graphical Entity Relationship Models can help to break down these barriers. Models represented in this form are much less threatening to non-technical people. The concepts are the same, but they are presented in a much more user friendly way.

Maintaining Enthusiasm In Data Modelling Sessions

Using the technique described in this paper, data models are brought to "life" through the use of colour, humour and graphics. Representing models in this way has novelty value and immediate visual impact. This can help make the data modelling process "fun" rather than boring and technical. The importance of this is often underestimated in practice. Experience shows that users are much more likely to review models when they are presented in this format, simply because they look interesting.

Encouraging Creative Thinking

Creative thinking is an important part of the data modelling process. In order to get the best result, it is necessary to consider alternative ways of representing requirements (Moody, 1996). To be most effective, thinking should involve both sides of the brain (De Bono, 1989). The left hemisphere primarily focuses on verbal information, while the right hemisphere deals with images. The use of colour and graphics can help stimulate right brain activity in data modelling sessions and get people thinking in different ways. The injection of humour can also be helpful, presenting information in a novel way that stimulates open and revealing discussion (Lewis, 1992).

Acknowledgements to Tas Osianlis of Simsion Bowles and Associates, who developed the automated tool described in this paper.

REFERENCES

1. Batini, C., Ceri, S. and Navathe, S.B., *"Conceptual Database Design: An Entity Relationship Approach"*, Benjamin Cummings, Redwood City, California, 1992.
2. Berman, S., "A Semantic Data Model As The Basis For An Automated Database Design Tool", *Information Systems*, Vol 11, No. 2, 1986.
3. Brodie, M.L., Myopolous, J. and Schmidt, J.W. (Eds), *On Conceptual Modelling*, Springer-Verlag, New York, 1984.

4. Butler Cox Foundation, *Requirements Definition: The Key to Systems Development Productivity*, Position Paper No. 4, Butler Cox and Partners Limited, London, November, 1987.

5. Campbell, D., "Entity Relationship Modelling: One Style Suits All", *Database*, Summer, 1992.

6. Checkland, P.B. and Scholes, J., *Soft Systems Methodology in Action*, Wiley, Chichester, 1990.

7. Checkland, P.B., *Systems Thinking, Systems Practice*, Wiley, Chichester, 1981.

8. Chen, P.P., The Entity-Relationship Model: Towards a Unified View of Data, *ACM Transactions on Database Systems,* 1, 1976.

9. Date, C.J., *Relational Database: Selected Writings*, Addison-Wesley, 1986.

10. De Bono, Edward, *De Bono's Thinking Course*, BBC Books, London, 1989.

11. De Marco, T., *Structured Analysis and System Specification*, Yourdon Press, 1978.

12. Dumpala, S.R. and Arora, S.V., Schema translation using the Entity-Relationship Approach, In Chen, P.P. (ed.) *The Entity-Relationship Approach to Information Modelling and Analysis*, North-Holland, 1983.

13. Elmasri, R., and Navathe, S.B., *"Fundamentals of Database Systems"*, Benjamin Cummings, Redwood City, California, 1989.

14. Feldman, P. and Miller, D., Entity Model Clustering: Structuring a Data Model by Abstraction, *The Computer Journal*, Vol. 29, No. 4,1986.

15. Finklestein, C., *"An Introduction to Information Engineering: From Strategic Planning to Information Systems"*, Addison-Wesley, Singapore, 1989.

16. Flood, R.L. and Carson, E.R., *Dealing With Complexity: An Introduction to the Theory and Application of Systems Science*, Plenum Press, 1988.

17. Goldstein, R.C. and Storey, V.C., "Some Findings On The Intuitiveness of Entity Relationship Constructs", In *Entity Relationship Relationship Approach to Database Design and Querying"*, Lochovsky, F.H. (ed.), Elsevier Science, Amsterdam, 1990.

18. Hawryszkiewycz, I.T., *"Database Analysis and Design"*, Science Research Associates, 1984.

19. Hitchman, S., "Practitioner Perceptions On The Use Of Some Semantic Concepts In The Entity Relationship Model", *European Journal of Information Systems,* 4, 31-40, 1995.

20. Hull, R. and King, R. Semantic Data Models, *ACM Computing Surveys*, September, 1988.

21. ISO, *Information Processing Systems: Concepts And Terminology For The Conceptual Schema And The Information Base*. ISO Technical Report 9007, 1987.

22. Jacobson, I., *"Object Oriented Systems Engineering"*, Addison-Wesley, New York, 1992.

23. Jacobson, I., *"The Object Advantage"*, Addison-Wesley, New York, 1995.

24. Kent, W. The Realities Of Data: Basic Properties Of Data Reconsidered. In Steel, T.B. And Meersman, R. *Data Semantics*. North-Holland, 1986.

25. Koestler, A., *The Act of Creation*, Dell, 1964.

26. Konsynski, B.R., *Database Driven Systems*, University of Arizona Press, 1979.

27. Lewis, P.J., "Rich Picture Building in the Soft Systems Methodology", *Journal of Information Systems*, Vol. 1, No. 5, 1992.

28. Lipowski, Z.J., Sensory and Information Inputs Overload, *Comprehensive Psychiatry*, Vol. 16, 3, May/June, 1975.

29. Martin, J., *"Recommended Diagramming Standards For Analysts and Programmers: A Basis for Automation"*, Prentice-Hall, Englewood Cliffs, New Jersey, 1987.

30. Martin, J., *Strategic Data Planning Methodologies*, Prentice Hall, 1989.

31. Miller, G., The magical number seven, plus or minus two: Some limits on our capacity for processing information, *The Psychological Review*, March, 1956.

32. Mittermier, R.T., Hsia, P. and Yeh, R.T., "Alternatives to Overcome the Communication Problem of Formal Requirements Analysis", in Galliers, R. (ed), *Information Analysis: Selected Readings*, Sydney, Addison-Wesley, 1987.

33. Moody, D.L. and Shanks, G.G., "What Makes A Good Data Model? Evaluating the Quality of Entity Relationship Models", *Proceedings of the Thirteenth International Conference on the Entity Relationship Approach*, Manchester, England, December 14-17, 1994.

34. Moody, D.L., "A Practical Methodology for the Representation of Large Data Models", *Proceedings of the Australian Database and Information Systems Conference*, University of N.S.W., Sydney, Australia, February, 1991.

35. Moody, D.L., "The Seven Habits of Highly Effective Data Modellers", *Database Programming & Design*, October, 1996.

36. Moriarty, T., "Testing from the Top", *Database Programming and Design*, August, 1993b.

37. Moriarty, T., "Where's The Business?", *Database Programming and Design*, July, 1993a.

38. Newell A., and Simon, H.A., *Human Problem Solving*, Prentice-Hall, 1972.

39. Page-Jones, M., *A Practical Guide to Structured Systems Design*, Yourdon Press, 1980.

40. Peckham, J. and Maryanski, F. Semantic Database Modelling: Survey, Application and Research Issues, *ACM Computing Surveys*, September, 1987.

41. Shanks, G.G., "Enterprise Data Architectures: An Empirical Study", *Monash University Working Paper*, Monash University, Melbourne, Australia, August, 1996.

42. Simon, H.A. *Sciences of the Artificial*, MIT Press, 1982.

43. Simsion, G.C, A Structured Approach to Data Modelling, *The Australian Computer Journal*, August, 1989.

44. Simsion, G.C., *Data Modelling Essentials: Analysis, Design and Innovation*, International Thomson Computer Press, New York, 1994.

45. Swatman, P.A. and Swatman, P.M.C., "Formal Specification—An Analytic Tool For Management Information Systems", *Journal of Information Systems*, April, 1992.

46. Teory, T.J., Yang, D. and Fry, J.P., A Logical Design Methodology for relational databases using the extended Entity Relationship Model, *ACM Computing Surveys*, 18, 2, 1986.

47. Uhr, L., Vossier, C., and Weman, J., Pattern Recognition over Distortions by Human Subjects and a Computer Model of Human Form Perception, *Journal of Experimental Psychology*, 63, 1962.

48. Wood-Harper, A.T., Antill, L., Avison, D.E., *Information Systems Definition: The Multiview Approach*, Blackwell Scientific Publications, Oxford, 1985.

Benefits and Quality of Data Modelling - Results of an Empirical Analysis

Ronald Maier

University of Regensburg, Dept. of Business Informatics III, D-93040 Regensburg, Germany, E-Mail: ronald.maier@wiwi.uni-regensburg.de

Abstract. In this paper the results of an empirical study about benefits and quality of data modelling are presented. The main questions addressed are: How big is the share of companies that use data models? Who is responsible for data modelling? What are the main application areas for data modelling? How should data modelling projects be organised in order to make a profit? What is the size of project, departmental and enterprise data models actually in use? How can we tell a „good" from a „bad" data model? Based on the results of the empirical study a new quality concept for data modelling is motivated which focusses on the design of the organisational context of data modelling. This is seen as the single most important success factor regarding data modelling efforts.

1 Introduction and Motivation

During the past 25 years data modelling has changed dramatically, especially with regard to its goals and purposes as well as the way modelling methods have been used. In the beginning supporting the design of data base systems was the sole point of interest. This was due to a rapid development of data base technologies. Today data modelling is regarded as a proven method for structuring data in the MIS literature. Data modelling has become a solid basis for enterprise modelling. Its positive effects are hardly questioned.

Despite the large number of papers in the field of data modelling there is hardly an author who went to the trouble of conducting an empirical analysis. There are some empirical studies in related areas that deal with the (structural) organisation of data administration or data management respectively (e.g. [4, 6, 7, 10, 17, 22]) as well as with methods and tools supporting data modelling (e.g. [3, 5, 8, 18, 21, 24]). However, up to now only a few experiences concerning the application of data modelling are documented (e.g. [1, 9, 16, 19, 23]) and apparently there are no studies on the organisation of data modelling, the actual (not hypothetic!) application fields and especially the quality aspects of data models. This is also true for the more recent developments with regard to object oriented and business processes modelling.

The term **data model** represents different concepts in the relevant literature (for a review of definitions for the terms „model" and „data" see [12]). Here, data model stands for the results of the application of a data modelling method (e.g. the actual data structures of company X in ER-notation): A data model is a structured image of the data elements in a certain application domain (i.e. a part of the perceived reality), which is relevant to applications and/or users, along with the relations between these elements.

The starting point of this paper is the fact that there is little documented knowledge about the use of data modelling within companies. This is somewhat contradictory to the perceived ubiquity of this method. Thus, I will address the following questions: In which fields is data modelling actually applied and in which areas should it be used? How should data modelling in the various application fields be organised? Which criteria do companies take into account and which process is used for managing and evaluating the quality of data modelling?

In chapter two the research design is presented and the sample is described. Chapter three comprises the results of the empirical study. Chapter four summarizes the research findings, motivates a new approach to the quality of data modelling and gives an outlook to future developments.

2 Research Design and Sample

The study was conducted in two phases. The first phase comprised the evaluation of the state of the art of data modelling in German companies (late 1994). In addition to a questionnaire, personal interviews with experienced practitioners were conducted. Four interviews were used to improve the questionnaire and to clarify the research problem. Another four interviews were conducted after the questionnaire (in spring 1995) in order to gain more knowledge about the state of the art of data modelling.

The second phase focused on the development of a concept for managing and evaluating the quality of data modelling. In further interviews the approaches to managing and evaluating quality of data models were discussed.

On the whole the sample consists of 580 German companies and five Austrian companies. The selection was based on the hypothesis that so far only big companies, software houses, consultants and universities have sufficient experience with data modelling to take part in this study. 324 companies with over 5.000 employees and 261 software houses and consulting companies with over 50 employees were approached. 89 filled out the questionnaire (rate of return 15,21%). More than 50% of the answering companies belong to the industrial sector (51,7%), 47,2% belong to the service sector. 31,5% were software houses or consulting companies.

In the following, some important results of the study are presented. The theoretical background of the hypothesis tested is described in [15] and the results of the study are compared to results of other studies.

3 Results of the Study

3.1 Share of Companies Using Data Models

45 of the 89 companies that filled in the questionnaire did not use data modelling methods at all (50,6%). This figure is very high given the fact that the sample

comprised only big companies and software houses. There are good reasons for assuming that data modelling is even less used within the almost 85% of the companies that did not answer the questionnaire. However, since it takes much more time to fill in the questionnaire when the company actually uses data modelling (14 pages) compared to the time a non-user has to invest (1 page), it could also be the case that the percentage of companies not using data modelling is lower or as high as the figure computed here. Nevertheless, one can conclude that data modelling is not the state-of-the-art method used in almost all companies, as many authors would like to make their readers believe.

The relative majority (17 companies) of the companies had medium-sized to large DP departments (100 - 499 employees). 8 companies had more than 500 DP-employees, 7 companies had between 20 and 99 DP-employees. In 5 companies the DP departments consisted of less than 20 employees.

Fig. 1. Number of employees that use data modelling (absolute)

In the context of this paper we are interested in the degree to which data modelling has penetrated companies. As shown in figure 1 less than 100 employees deal with data models (70,3%) in most of the companies. In about a third of the companies less than 10 employees use data modelling methods.

The regression analysis is used to test the hypothesis that there is a relation between the number of DP employees and the number of employees who use data modelling. The null hypothesis (no relation between the two variables) could be rejected at a significance level of 0,99. One can give a rough estimation of the number of employees using data models when the number of DP employees is known by using the following equation:

$$EMPLOYEES\_DAT.MOD = -2,47 + 0,36 * DP\_EMPLOYEES$$

Thus, on average, about one third of the DP employees use data modelling (the relevant t-test is significant at a test level of 0,99). The small constant suggests that this share is relatively independent of the size of the DP department (though the results of the relevant t-test show no significance).

The (organisational) positions of the persons answering the questionnaire show no great surprise. There is a high concentration of the data modelers in the DP department most of which work within a data management group (app. 36% of all), a group dealing with methods, processes, tools (21%) and the application development (12%).

3.2 Application Fields for Data Models

In the questionnaire the application fields had to be scaled with regard to their importance (5=very important, 1= not important) in two ways: The (hypothetic) importance of a certain application field for the person answering (target value) was distinguished from the estimated „real" benefit for the organisation the person works for (actual value). In the following the means of the target and the actual values per application field as well as the differences between these two figures are ordered, compared and interpreted in short. The 64 application fields in the questionnaire were aggregated to 12 application areas (for detailed results see [14, 15]).

Table 1 shows the means of the target values. Note that data modelling turns out to be more important as an organisation instrument outside the DP department than within it. The value of „means for improving communication" is surprisingly low. When reviewing the application fields in detail, it turns out that the value for „communication within the project team" is very high (4,12) whereas the value for „communication to managers, to external persons and to other organisations" is low (3,22).

application area	target mean
basis for data base design or physical data organisation respectively	4,17
instrument for standardization	4,17
basis for management information systems (MIS)	4,05
basis for the integration within the DP department	3,98
basis for the development of application systems	3,96
organisation instrument outside the DP department	3,83
means for reduction of maintenance costs	3,79
basis for the use of standard software	3,69
means for improving communication	3,68
basis for the use of application systems in functional departments	3,62
means for improving motivation/acceptance	3,39
organisation instrument in the DP department	3,18

Tab. 1. Means of target values

Table 2 shows the means of the actual values. Note that also in the case of „communication" the value „within the project team" was high whereas the values „to managers, to external persons and to other organisations" were low. Again, the persons answering are of the opinion that functional departments profit more from the use of data models as an organisation instrument than the DP department. The low value for „basis for the use of standard software" is not surprising. I believe that data modelling has great potentials in this area. Table 2 shows that in the view of the persons answering significant benefits are gained in several different application areas by the use of data modelling.

application area	target mean
basis for data base design or physical data organisation respectively	3,19
basis for the development of application systems	3,02
instrument for standardization	2,94
means for reduction of maintenance costs	2,70
basis for the integration within the DP department	2,69
basis for management information systems (MIS)	2,67
means for improving communication	2,56
means for improving motivation/acceptance	2,53
organisation instrument outside the DP department	2,42
basis for the use of application systems in functional departments	2,39
basis for the use of standard software	2,25
organisation instrument in the DP department	2,20

Tab. 2. Means of actual values

Table 3 shows the differences between the means of target and actual values.

application area	differences between means
basis for the use of standard software	1,44
organisation instrument outside the DP department	1,41
basis for management information systems (MIS)	1,39
basis for the integration within the DP department	1,29
instrument for standardization	1,23
basis for the use of application systems in functional departments	1,23
means for improving communication	1,12
means for reduction of maintenance costs	1,10
organisation instrument in the DP department	0,99
basis for data base design or physical data organisation respectively	0,98
basis for the development of application systems	0,94
means for improving motivation/acceptance	0,86

Tab. 3. Differences between the means of target versus actual values

These could be interpreted as indicators for the potentials of data modelling in different application areas. Note that there is a significant difference between the use of data models as an organisation instrument within the DP department versus outside of it. I believe that the potentials of data modelling in this area are becoming increasingly important, especially in connection with business process modelling.

description of variable [related application area]	signifi-cance	difference of mean values
creating a basis for further developments [ENTW]	,00780 **	1,49 ***
command of the DP-technical complexity of the data system (e.g. heterogeneous system environ.) [DBEN]	,00799 **	1,02 *
standardized user interfaces (e.g. identical data structures-> identical design of screen dialogues) [STAN]	,00803 **	1,63 **
instrument for project planning (e.g. classification, prioritization, planning of order) [ORDV]	,01180 *	0,22
avoiding unintended side-effects in connection with subsequent changes in the data system [WART]	,01417 *	1,26 ***
instrument for project controlling (e.g. survey of the current projects, control of the project status) [ORDV]	,01678 *	0,73 +
increased stability of data base design [DBEN]	,01718 *	0,73 +
reduced training effort when changing responsibilities during the application life-cycles [WART]	,02622 *	0,89 *
improved DP experts' acceptance of the process of application development [MOTI]	,03481 *	0,25
reduction of the time required for development of DB definitions [DBEN]	,03668 *	0,96 **
improved documentation of the application system [ENTW]	,04983 *	0,88 **
supporting re-engineering [WART]	,05475 +	1,16 **
integration of (operative) application systems with MIS [INTE]	,06104 +	-0,19
basis for the integration of standard software into the existing application systems environment [STSW]	,06262 +	0,69
introduction of „data standards" for EDI [STAN]	,06288 +	1,28 **
improved communication between application functions [ENTW]	,07176 +	0,55 *
standardized procedure of application development [STAN]	,07351 +	1,11 **
command of the functional complexity of the data system [DBEN]	,08020 +	0,59
optimizing use of available data bases by supporting a precise understanding of data structures [NUTZ]	,09468 +	0,09
automatic generation of parts of the (application) system [ENTW]	,09768 +	0,96 +

Tab. 4. Relation between application fields and the form of project organisation

In the following some relations between the organisation of data modelling and the actual benefit gained by the use of data models are investigated. The abstract concept „organisation of data modelling" is given shape by certain organisational dimensions: structural organisation, members of project teams, use of enterprise-wide data models and the project organisation:

With the data of the questionnaire only weak relations between the dimensions structural organisation, team members and use of enterprise modelling can be shown. However, the relation to the form of the project organisation is significant (for a detailed description of the testing procedure see [15]).

As to the form of project organisation companies that use data modelling on a permanent basis (data modelling as a task on its own, e.g. in the sense of a permanently valid enterprise-wide data model) are distinguished from companies that use data modelling only within certain projects (e.g. for application development). Table 4 shows the statistical significance and the differences between the mean values for those application fields for which the mean values change significantly depending on the form of the project organisation (note that these are the detailed factors, not the aggregated application areas as depicted above).

The values for the application areas „basis for the development of application systems" (ENTW), „basis for data base design or physical data organisation respectively" (DBEN), „instrument for standardization" (STAN) and „means for reduction of maintenance costs" (WART) are all higher for those companies that regard data modelling as a permanent task.

3.3   Organisation of Data Modelling

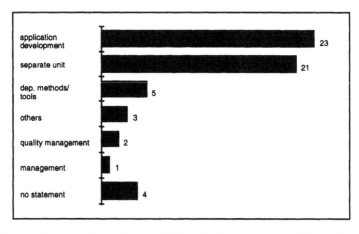

Fig. 2. Structural organisation of data modelling (absolute values, multiple replies possible, basis: 40 companies)

Figure 2 shows the structural organisation of the employees who deal with data modelling. The organisational position of the separate organisational units is interesting. In almost all companies these units (in most cases called „data administration" or „data management") are placed within the DP-department. Only in two companies these units can be found in the department for organisation. However, in the larger companies of this sample data modelling is rarely used only in one department. Most often several organisational units deal with data modelling from different points of view.

The question of a separate task „data modelling" which is somehow independent of other DP-tasks is often discussed in the relevant literature (see e.g. [19]). Here in over 90% of the companies data modelling is used as a method to support projects focussing on other goals (most often application development). However, in about a quarter of the companies data modelling represents a separate and independent task which is conducted either on a permanent basis or as a data modelling project (e.g. enterprise-wide data modelling).

Furthermore the question of responsibility for certain tasks in the context of data modelling was investigated. Figure 3 shows the responsibility areas defined. The questionnaire required the naming of the organisational unit in charge of each responsibility area. Apart from the option „no responsibility defined" the questions were open. Figure 3 shows the shares of responsibility of data administration, application development, functional departments as well as other units.

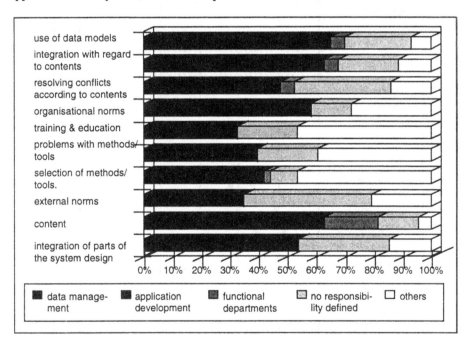

Fig. 3. Responsibility for data modelling tasks according to selected organisational units

Note the very small share of responsibility attributed to the functional departments. Even regarding the contents of data models it is the department responsible for the development of applications which is responsible in far more cases than the functional departments. In none of the companies in this sample the functional departments were responsible for norms (specific to the organisation as well as external norms), education and training as well as problems with methods and tools. Most of the time the main task of the data administration is the integration process with respect to the contents of the data models and the resolving of conflicts about contents (e.g. between different functional departments). The main areas of responsibility attributed to the application development team are the content of the data models (!) and the integration of the individual parts of the system design (e.g. the functional decomposition, the data flow diagram and the entity relationship model). Note that a substantial share of companies have not defined responsibilities for such central areas as content of data models or the selection of methods and tools to be used.

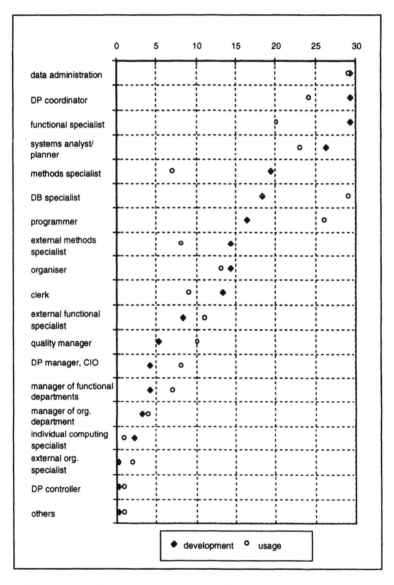

Fig. 4. Job positions of the persons which are involved in the development or use of data models (absolute values, basis: 42 companies)

Figure 4 shows the different job positions of the people who deal with data modelling. A distinction is made between the development and the use of data models. The job positions were adapted from a Swiss dictionary describing DP jobs (see [25]). Note that different job positions are involved in the development as opposed to the use of data models. Data base specialists, programmers, quality managers as well as the managers of all departments (DP, functional and organisational) seem to be much more involved in the use than in the development of data models. The opposite is true for DP coordinators, functional specialists, clerks and methods specialists. This could cause severe trouble concerning the motivation of staying in a data modelling project team, especially in the case of functional specialists and clerks. Note also that quality managers seem to focus on the product (in this case: on the use of the data models) rather than on the process of development. The main data model developers can be found generally at the middle hierarchical level (functional specialists, DP coordinators, systems analysts/planners, data administrators), whereas the management on the one side and clerks, data base people and programmers on the other have much less to do with data modelling.

3.4 Enterprise-Wide Data Models

element	mean	median	stand. dev.
entity types	535,8	159	631,5
relationship types	971,4	338	1.142,4
attributes	4.397,9	1.293	7.936,9

Tab. 5. Size of enterprise-wide data models

17 out of 41 answering companies (41,5%) have developed an enterprise-wide data model. A Chi^2-test was used to check the relation between the variables „industry or sector respectively" and „development of enterprise-wide data models". The relation is significant at a test level of 95%. In the service sector a greater portion of companies develops enterprise-wide data models than in the industrial sector. Software and systems houses as well as consultants were not tested as their customers could be both, in the service and the industrial sector.

group of data models	entity types	relation-ship types	attri-butes	ent.types : attributes	rel. types : attributes	num-ber
small EDMs without attributes	7-50	20-70	0	-	-	3
medium-sized EDMs with few attributes	70-130	200-280	200-470	1:3,350	1:1,396	2
medium-sized EDMs with many attributes	56-185	173-376	814-1.600	1:9,091	1:4,005	3
large EDMs	650-2.000	920-3.500	2.500-30.000	1:8,431	1:4,744	6
average	535,8	971,4	4.397,9	1:8,208	1:4,528	-

Tab. 6. Classification of enterprise-wide data models

The following can be concluded about the size of the enterprise-wide data models: the numbers of entity types, relationship types and attributes vary considerably from company to company. Table 5 gives an overview over mean value, median and standard deviation. Due to a few very big data models the differences between means and medians are quite big.

Due to the huge differences it is not possible to say what an enterprise-wide data model looks like „on average". Thus the data models were classified according to four sizes (see table 6). The distinction within medium-sized data models was made using a ratio between entity type and attribute of 1:5.

3.5 Project Data Models and Departmental Data Models

Each of the 32 companies answering the quesion about project or departmental data models had on average 28,8 data models. Again the values varied considerably: between 0 and 180 data models with a standard deviation of 35,8. All in all the 55 data models were described by the number of entity types, 47 by the number of relationship types and 49 by the number of attributes. Table 7 shows the means, medians and standard deviations for these measures.

element	mean	median	standard deviation
entity types	95,0	60	111,1
relationship types	169,0	100	217,4
attributes	1.053,6	380	2.809,7

Tab. 7. Size of project data models and departmental data models

In table 8 the data models are classified according to their size. Compared with enterprise-wide data models these models are substantially smaller.

entity types		relationship types		attributes	
≥ 100	27,3%	≥ 200	27,7%	≥ 1000	16,3%
50 - 99	30,9%	100 - 199	23,4%	500 - 999	22,4%
20 - 49	32,7%	30 - 99	42,5%	100 - 499	53,1%
≤ 19	9,1%	≤ 29	6,4%	≤ 99	8,2%

Tab. 8. Classification of project data models and departmental data models

3.6 Quality and Cost-Benefit-Analysis

In this paper the term „quality of data models" denotes „the degree to which the data model corresponds to the requirements of the users (of the data model) regarding the defined application areas for data models. Therefore quality criteria generally can only be set up in response to a company's application scenario (for examples of application scenarios and a more detailed description of this approach see [15]).

Consequently when developing general quality criteria one must take into account the application scenario in which the data models will (should) be used.

In response to the question „what do you think matters when you consider quality of data models" 34 persons answered making 98 statements. The number of statements suggest that the companies are extremely interested in the topic. This impression is strongly supported by the authors' experiences gained from the interviews. The individual statements can be grouped into 14 quality criteria (number of statements classified in parenthesis): structure (13); communicability/understandability (10); benefit/usability (10); clearness/readability (10); relation to the domain modeled (9); treatment of redundancies (7); consistency (6); modelling process (6); standardisation (6); explanations/examples (5); relation to implementation (e.g. data base system) (5); element-based criteria (e.g. treatment of business objects) (4); denomination (4); modelling scope (3).

As opposed to the great number of suggestions the persons answering made to the question above the companies seemed not to have very much experience with quality management of data models and with the evaluation of data models. The suggestions made were vague. They neither took into account the application scenario nor can they be regarded as a quality concept for data models.

Another area, which has been neglected in the relevant literature to date, is the cost-benefit-analysis of data modelling. Still, 41,9% of the companies answering to the questionnaire track costs of data modelling. However, in most cases only the time spent by data modelling specialists is recorded. The costs of the involvement of functional specialists or application developers are not recorded at all.

As opposed to the cost side, only a small portion of the companies keeps track of the benefit side (4,8). But the benefit analysis consists only of reports (experience reports, project reports) or simply slides that show the (hypothetical) advantages of data modelling. In other words, the companies are not able to quantify or even just estimate the benefits which they gain from the use of data modelling. The reasons for that lack of information are - according to the persons answering - the high effort that would have to be put forward to establish cost-benefit-controls and the expected obstacles to a quantification of benefits. Moreover, they complain about a lack of (cost) awareness on the side of the functional departments. Others claim that the recording of benefits reduces the acceptance of the method. The latter argument reflects the massive scepticism still present in many companies about wether or not to use data modelling.

4 Conclusion and Outlook on Future Developments

In the following the core research findings described above are summarized and an outlook to future developments concerning the quality of data modelling is given.

4.1 Summary of Research Findings

Today, in most cases data modelling is used as an instrument for the design of data bases, for the development of application systems and for standardisation. Data modelling seems to bear great potentials for additional benefits in other application areas. This applies especially to the use of data models as a basis for the use of standard software, as an organisation instrument outside the DP area and as a basis for the development of MIS.

There are several interdependencies between the application areas and the organisation of data modelling. Relations between the benefits realised and the form of the project organisation could be shown. The structural organisation of (full-time) data modelers, the education and organisational position of members of data model project teams, the intensity of the participation of functional departments and the use of enterprise models seem to have little influence on the perceived success of data modelling efforts.

The alternative organisational positions of (full-time) data modelers do not consider the application scenario. On the contrary the data modelers seem to be regarded somewhat automatically as DP personnel, in most cases belonging to application development and/or a separate organisational unit „data administration". Individual data modelling projects are the exception and focus on the development of an enterprise-wide data model, enterprise-wide standardisation, the establishment of norms and rules and the integration of data. Normally, however, data modelling is used as an instrument to support projects concerning the development of applications.

The two organisational units „application development" and „data administration" share the main responsibility for data modelling. In some cases the employees who are in charge of methods and tools as well as data base administrators are responsible for certain aspects of data modelling. The functional departments are rarely in charge of data modelling. It is interesting that frequently responsibility is not assigned at all, especially in the responsibility areas „resolving conflicts regarding contents", „integrating parts of the system design", „external norms" and „use of data models". Furthermore, in many companies the responsibility for data modelling tasks is shared among several organisational units, especially in the responsibility areas „use of data models", „content" and „selection of methods and tools". In many companies the responsibility for data modelling is ambigous. A clear definition of responsibility areas would help to reduce unnecessary „organisational redundancies" (e.g. double work, endless debates about terms and names).

The employees in the functional departments (functional specialists, DP coordinators and clerks) are much more involved in the development process than in the use of data models. In the case of data base specialists, programmers and managers (DP, functional departments) it is the other way round.

Considering the enormous differences in the sizes of project data models, departmental data models and enterprise data models it is clear that the companies' perceptions of data modelling vary greatly. In many companies even different groups of employees have a different conception of data modelling.

The situation concerning cost-benefit-analysis seems to be rather unsatisfying. Frequently there is no cost transparency. At best the benefits are estimated on the basis of subjective reports of experiences.

4.2 A New Approach to the Quality of Data Modelling

The results of the empirical study show that practitioners in data modelling are in need of a thoroughly defined quality concept for data models. This approach must take into account the actual situation in practice as described above which is not the case in most of the approaches documented in literature (for a detailed review of the literature see [15]). In addition to the existing approaches the following factors have to be taken into account:

• different **application scenarios** of data modelling in the companies;
• the **organisational design** of data modelling;
• quality of data **modelling** is not the same as quality of data **models**.

As the results of the questionnaire show, the application scenarios for data modelling vary greatly from company to company. Almost every company has its own understanding of „data modelling". In some of the companies even different groups of employees have quite different views about data modelling (especially concerning benefits, procedures, involved employees and tools). Thus it is not possible to make a general statement about what is „good" and „bad" in data modelling. This depends to a great extent on the application scenario in a certain company. Therefore one cannot assume that a quality concept exists which is suitable for all application scenarios. The different application scenarios have to be considered in the concept.

There is a lot of literature about methods and tools for the development of data models. There is, however, considerable uncertainty about how to design the organisational frame of data modelling which is the single most important factor influencing the success of data modelling efforts in a company.

Quality of data modelling is not the same as quality of data models. The existing approaches almost exclusively deal with the product quality (i.e. the quality of data models). This is all the more an obstacle to the improvement of quality management as some authors warn against the negative consequences of trying to „check quality into already completed data models" (cf. e.g. [20], p. 19). The results of the empirical study suggest that quality of data modelling depends much more on the processes of developing and using data models than on the quality of the models themselves.

Data modelling as it is understood in most of the companies today should help the different parties involved in application development to agree upon the terms, names and data structures that are to be used. In this way the individual perceptions and insights about the „reality" of all people involved should be brought together. Krogstie et al. speak of „externalisation" of the „local reality" of an individual social actor. The "externalisation" results in the construction of an „organisational reality" (cf. [11], p. 5). In this sense data modelling is an instrument for the documentation of organisational knowledge (see [13]).

It is obvious that certain rather „technical" or „syntactical" criteria for data modelling (e.g. the correct use of a method or the complete description of all data elements in a data dictionary) have to be met. However, the results of the empirical study suggest that these criteria do not help distinguish a successful data modelling effort from a poor one. Quality of data modelling therefore cannot be evaluated by just analysing the product.

4.3 Future Developments

In the short history of data modelling technical problems predominated at first (e.g. the development and integration of data modelling tools). Today these problems seem to be overcome. Data modelling is a powerful method which is sufficiently supported by a number of tools.

Recently the literature and many conferences focused more on object oriented modelling and business process modelling than on data modelling. The discussions circle around the question which method suits the requirements better, but at the same time many companies do not even know anything about the (promised) benefits of data modelling. To my mind the time has come to shift the focus from a technical consideration of enterprise (or „information") modelling to a more organisational one. Along with that shift the application scenarios have to be taken into account.

What will happen with data modelling? First, I expect that more and more companies will use data models. This trend is backed by a steadily growing and improving supply of data modelling tools and reference models. Additionally, many suppliers of standard software provide comprehensive data models as a part of their systems documentation. In this context the re-use of data models will be an important issue.

In the future companies will have to concentrate on the design of an organisational frame for data modelling which suits the process of modelling in a more efficient way and which takes advantage of the enormous potentials of data modelling.

5 Bibliography

1. Batra, D., Davis, J. G.: Conceptual Data Modelling in Database Design: Similarities and Differences Between Expert and Novice Designers, in: International Journal of Man-Machine Studies, Vol. 37, 1992, 83-101
2. Elmasri, R., Kouramajian, V., Thalheim, B. (ed.): Entity-Relationship Approach - ER '93, Proceedings of the 12th International Conference on the Entity-Relationship Approach in Dallas-Arlington, Texas, USA, Berlin et al. 1994
3. Finlay, P. N., Mitchell, A. C.: Perceptions of the Benefits From the Introduction of CASE: An Empirical Study, in: MIS Quarterly, December 1994, 353-368
4. Gemünden, H. G., Schmitt, M.: Datenmanagement in deutschen Großunternehmen - Theoretischer Ansatz und empirische Untersuchung, in: Information Management, Vol. 6, No. 4, 1991, 22-34
5. Gesellschaft für Mathematik und Datenverarbeitung, St. Augustin, Consiglio Nazionale delle Ricerche, Roma: Der Einsatz von Data Dictionaries: eine Umfrage, im Rahmen eines gemeinsamen Projekts "Auswahl und Einführung von Datanbanksystemen", St. Augustin, Germany 1981
6. Gillenson, M.L.: The State of Practice of Data Administration - 1981, in: Communications of the ACM, Vol. 25, No. 10, 1982, 699-706
7. Gillenson, M.L.: Trends in Data Administration, in: MIS Quarterly, Vol. 9, No. 4, 1985, 317-325

8. Grover, V., Teng, J.: An Examination of DBMS Adoption and Success in American Organizations, in: Information & Management, Vol. 23, 1992, 239-248

9. Hitchman, S.: Practitioner Perceptions on the Use of Some Semantic Concepts in the Entity-Relationship Model, in: European Journal of Information Systems, Vol. 4, 1995, 31-40

10. Kahn, B. K.: Some Realities of Data Administration, in: Communications of the ACM, Vol. 26, No. 10, 1983, 794-799

11. Krogstie, J., Lindland, O.I., Sindre, G.: Defining Quality Aspects for Conceptual Models, in: ISCO 3 - Proceedings of the International Conference on Information System Concepts - Towards a Consolidation of Views, Marburg, Germany 1995

12. Lehner, F., Hildebrand, K., Maier, R.: Wirtschaftsinformatik - Theoretische Grundlagen, Munich, Vienna 1995

13. Lehner, F., Maier, R.: Can Information Modelling be Successful Without a Common Perception of the Term „Information"? - Comparison of definitions and use of terms -, in: Kangassalo, H., Fischer Nilsson, J. (ed.): Proceedings of the 6th European - Japanese Seminar on Information Modelling and Knowledge Bases, Hornbaek, Denmark 1996

14. Maier, R.: Quality of Data Models, in: Ross, M., Brebbia, C.A., Staples, G., Stapleton, J. (ed.): Software Quality Management III - Vol. 1 - Quality Management, Proceedings of the third International Conference on Software Quality Management in Sevilla, Spain, Southampton et al., 207-218, 1995

15. Maier, R.: Qualität von Datenmodellen, Wiesbaden, Germany 1996

16. Marche, S.: Measuring the stability of data models, in: European Journal of Information Systems, Vol. 2, No. 1, 1993, 37-47

17. McCririck, I.B., Goldstein, R.C.: What Do Data Administrators Really Do?, in: Datamation, August 1980, 131-134

18. Myrach, T.: Die Nutzung von Data Dictionaries. Ergebnisse einer empirischen Untersuchung, in: Information Management, Vol. 9, Nr. 4, 1994, 52-61

19. R&O Software-Technik GmbH: Datenmodellierung in der Praxis - Eine Marktanalyse über die Anwendung einer Methodik, Planegger Straße 16-18, 82110 Germering, Germany 1992

20. Reingruber, M. C., Gregory, W. W.: The Data Modeling Handbook. A Best-Practice Approach to Building Quality Data Models, New York, 1994

21. Sankar, C.S., Marshall, T.E.: Database Design Support: An Empirical Investigation of Perceptions and Performance, in: Journal of Database Management, Vol. 4, No. 3, Summer 1993, 4-14

22. Schlögl, C.: Datenmanagement auf dem Prüfstand: am Beispiel der steirischen Großindustrie, dissertation at the faculty of social and economic sciences at the Karl-Franzens-University Graz, Austria 1995

23. Srinivasan, A., Te'eni, D.: Modeling as Constraint Problem Solving: An Empirical Study of the Data Modeling Process, in: Management Science, Vol. 41, 1995, 419-434

24. Sumner, M.: Factors Influencing the Success of Computer-Assisted Software Engineering, in: Information Resources Management Journal, Vol. 8, No. 2, 1995, 25-31

25. SVD - Schweizerische Vereinigung für Datenverarbeitung, VDF - Verband der Wirtschaftsinformatik-Fachleute (ed.): Berufe der Wirtschaftsinformatik in der Schweiz, Zurich 1993

Normative Language Approach
A Framework for Understanding

Erich Ortner
Technische Hochschule Darmstadt
Wirtschaftsinformatik 1 - Entwicklung
von Anwendungssystemen
Hochschulstraße 1, D-64289 Darmstadt

Bruno Schienmann
Universität Konstanz
Informationsmanagement
Postfach 5560, D-78434 Konstanz

Abstract. The development of information systems often presents communication problems between developers and users, because the languages used by both groups are too different. While users communicate in their ordinary language, developers make use of artificial, constructed languages (e.g. diagram languages) for the development of a specialised problem solution. However, an intensive communication between both groups is necessary, as users determine the system requirements. Furthermore, the expert knowledge of the field of application constitutes the decisive resources, which usually only users are able to contribute.This paper proposes to solve the language problem by introducing a regulated language (normative language).

1. Introduction

If the language gap in the development process between natural grown (ordinary) and artificial, constructed languages can be bridged, information systems will be constructed more effectively and economically. Several approaches to close this language gap between developer and user in the process of system design can be distinguished into:

- use of *diagram languages* for the communication between user and developer,
- determining of the relevant requirements of software solutions through *rapid prototyping*,
- *democratisation* of the requirements analysis with the users by establishing workshops and conferences (e.g. so-called data conferences which aim at a co-ordination of expert concepts (terms) within companies),
- methodical building up of a *normative expert language* with clarified, compulsory expert terms of the users.

This paper proposes to solve the language problem by introducing a normative language. In contrast to a naturally grown language, this language should have a reduced grammar (sentence patterns) and lexicon (expert terminology), but still should appear to be natural. The language should be constructed in such a way as to make it easy for users to accept the restrictions in grammar and lexicon, while at the same time it remains hidden to them that the language aims at an easier formalisation of the results in the following development phases. This aim is supposed to motivate developers to take part in cooperation with the users in an organised and methodical construction of expert languages, which have a standardised syntax (grammar) and a standardised terminology (lexicon). This concept of a gradual and controlled *construction* of a language is a process well known to the theory of science [Lorenzen87], which can be varied following Gethmann [Gethmann79] as shown in figure 1:

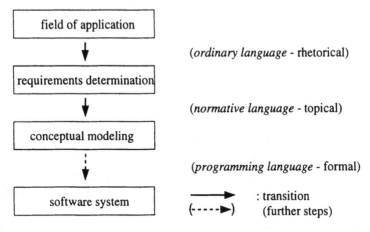

Fig. 1: Development of a software system

The development work reaches for the gradual differentiation of the parts of the solution of an information system from the *fields of application* (*universe of discourse* UoD) of the users with different languages. Gethmann [Gethmann79] divides them up into the categories *rhetorical languages* (dependent on persons and referring to topics), *topical languages* (referring to topics but not dependent on persons) and *logical languages* (not dependent on topics and persons). While rhetorical and topical languages can be called *material languages* (languages with an expert vocabulary referring to topics and persons), logical languages are defined as *formal* (structure words), which means that the statements made with them are deductible and can be proofed due to their structure. Formal (logical) languages do not have an „expert vocabulary" concerning the specific fields of application in information processing.

The differentiation (figure 1) of the information systems solution starts in the users' rhetorical (expert) language, which is in use as an *ordinary language* and leads from the requirements determination to the *requirements specification*. The ordinary languages which are characterised by the use of the same linguistic expressions by the language users are in contrast to the explicitly theoretical (for computers implement-technical) purposes and to the formal languages (e.g. logical languages or programming languages), which are not used for any „conventional" (natural) communication. The assessments made in an ordinary language can only be seen *rhetorically* (dependent on persons and topics). In a second step the (rhetorical) requirements for a conceptual system design are carried out. A topical (expert) language (normative language) is built up by reconstructing the relevant specific terms of the field of application, which are invariant to persons but referring to topics. The result is a conceptual model of the system solution (conceptual system design). In a last step of the differentiation the existing results are transferred into structures, which have only formal characteristics, which means they are complete, they can be derived and proofed. In software engineering this step is finished by using a programming language, where in a preceding logical design step with the help of a diagram language or a pseudo code the efficient structuring (algorithmication) of the system takes place. The result is a *software system* which can be used in the fields of application for the computer based execution of specific tasks like salary balancing, stores supervision, ordering and accounting.

2. Linguistic methods for information systems development - an overview

Several approaches which deal with the development of information systems based on linguistic criticism are existing (e.g. [Wedekind81; Abbott83; Saeki89; Rolland92; Kristen94; Tjoa94; Sykes95; Burg95; Düsterhöft96]). Their main characteristic is that they do not only use artificial languages (e.g. diagram languages) but also natural languages (e.g. user expert languages) for the construction of information systems. The different approaches can be split up by answering the question, whether an existing (natural) language is used to develop information systems or whether for this purpose a quasi-natural language is newly built up in cooperation with users of the information systems. Linguistic developmental methods of the first type can be called empirical approaches, linguistic methods of the latter type can be called constructive approaches. As for the empirical approaches one can differ between empirical-analytical and empirical-experimental methods.

Empirical-analytical methods in the development process do exactly represent users' statements on the facts in an application area by artificial formal means (e.g. with mathematical languages, diagram languages or a logical language). In *empirical-experimental* projects circumstances of communication as they appear in an office environment are simulated by recorded speech acts. The language use hereby recorded (and empirically simulated) builds the basis for the modelling of information systems.

As for the empirical-analytical approaches, the developed systems are interpretatively worked out from the *intension* of the (users') expert terms. With empirical-experimental approaches primarily the *extension* of (users') expert terms leads to the design of a system.

Constructive methods in the development of information systems aim at the construction of a new, quasi-natural, regulated expert language (normative language), which is complementary to the existing expert languages in a field of application. It should be reconstructed together with the users in such a way as to make it possible to represent the facts which are crucial for the development of an application clearly, obviously and „literally" (with a standardised terminology). Therefore constructive methods are mostly based on a material language approach. The reconstructed (material) language used for the development of information systems consists of a grammar (standardised sentence construction rules) and an expert lexicon of standardised expert terms (normative terminology).

The aim of this paper is to introduce an approach [Ortner95; Schienmann96; Ortner96] with the following characteristics:

- The approach is not based on formal languages but on *material* languages.
- The development results are not worked out method-specifically but method-*neutrally*.
- The (Re-) construction language is not a natural or diagram language but a *normative language*.

In the following paragraphs the terms material language, method-neutrality and normative language are explained more clearly. It will not be denied that other approaches have similar objectives.

3. Material versus formal system development

The view taken by today's theory of the development of application systems often is: programming languages are based on formal systems. The „material part" of a software solution (expert terms from the application areas), which is reconstructed in the development of an application, is only added in the development process and belongs to the application. On the other hand practical projects like STEP (Standard for the Exchange of Product Model Data) or EDIFACT (Electronic Data Interchange for Administration, Commerce and Transport) rather justify a *material* construction-language-approach for application systems. In both projects expert terminologies (e.g. determined by data models) as well as exchange formats for specific application areas are defined, towards which application software systems have to be oriented.

We can call a position in the development of information systems *formalistic* if its activities are concentrated in the area of formal systems (languages) and if the expert terminologies (their construction) used in the fields of application of the formal systems have no scientific importance. The tasks of such an approach consist of the development of sentence construction rules (calculi), independent of the question which expert terms are to be substituted for the symbols (variables) in sentence structures generated with these rules. First, a syntax is developed. The semantics, developed after the syntax, is the translation (verbalisation) of the calculus symbols with the help of a metalanguage. Natural languages can be used as metalanguages , including the terminologies in software application areas.

Usually this „translation" (verbalisation) is empirically supported, i.e. partly agreed to by system users. It can, however, be proved to be correct merely with regard to its structure - measured by the (formal) development system employed. Not universally accepted from the formalistic position in the development of application systems is a somewhat wider concept of the accuracy of a software solution which is based on the correspondence of the expert termini with their reconstructed and standardised usage (normative terminology) put down in a lexicon (as a part of the development system).

A complete language (grammar *and* expert terminology) on the one hand and linguistic products (development results, applications) on the other hand are in comparison an important feature of the *material language approach* for software development. The relevant difference towards formal development systems lies in the two components *grammar* (sentence construction rules) and *lexicon* (controlled vocabulary) which are parts of a material development system (construction language) for application software. Due to the development system, the specialised software solution (application) must not only fit into formal sentence structures (grammar), but also provide for a material vocabulary of the application area (expert terms), reconstructed so far and contained in the lexicon. The development process can be called „construction through built up", because it can be compared to development processes in traditional engineering disciplines. By connecting the reconstructed expert concepts (in the lexicon) the specialised software solution is not only analysed but, in fact, constructed (built up).

4. Methodically-neutral conceptual modeling

In conceptual modeling (see e.g. [Brodie84; Sowa84; Sowa91; Spaccapietra93]) the conceptual model for a planned application is developed based on the results of the preceding examination. This conceptual model should be exclusively problem-oriented and independent of the target system, i.e. it should only describe the features of an application which are necessary in the particular field of application (the *system essence* [McMenamin84]). This requirement for target-system-independence of the expert design can be expanded by the requirement for neutrality towards the design method [Ortner95]. Neutrality towards the design method means that the description of the facts in the field of application must not be determined by the expressive abilities of a software-technical design method with its respective representation constructs and the methods which underlie these solution paradigms. The description of things and occurences in the field of application should as far as possible be neutral towards a software-technical solution paradigm - e.g. the structured or the object-oriented paradigm, in order to avoid that expert statements and requirements are filtered too early with regard to a particular application systems solution and the development process becomes restricted too early to the requirements of system developers.

Woodfield, Embley and Kurtz emphasise the risks which lie in the formulation of the tasks of an application area in method-specific categories:

> Unfortunately, most software analysts view the world through 'programmer-colored glasses'. Most started as programmers, then became designers, and finally became analysts. As analysts try to record what is being expressed by non-computer scientists, they use concepts and representations learned when they were designers and programmers. This programmer-orientation can cause communication problems.[...] Their programmer-oriented paradigms prevent them from understanding and describing all aspects of a problem being stated by a user. [Woodfield90:441]

Blum takes a similar position: „One of the limits of formal methods is that their linguistic constructs may offer little insight into the application domain problem to be solved. [...] That is, the formalism masks our understanding of the application intent" [Blum93:228]. Even if the complex relation between recognition and language has not been completely clarified by now and different opinions are held about the way recognition is determined by language, at least, the studies by Sapir and Whorf prove that language and its expressive ability have an important influence on the respective recognition ability of the subject [Whorf56].

If the requirements of an application are described directly in categories like *data flow*, *function*, *data store* or *terminator* according to structured methods, there is a risk that the facts of the application area, which cannot be expressed directly in these categories, are not perceived and specified. Although it is often claimed that object-oriented methods allow a more „natural" system development as stated by Meyer`s classic assertion „The objects are just there for the picking!" [Meyer88:51], it has been shown in empirical studies [Barros92; Vessey94; Moynihan94; Opdahl94:211f] that this is not the case. Cook and Daniels put this criticism in a nutshell: „The world does not consist of objects sending each other messages, and we would have to be seriously mesmerised by object jargon to believe that it does" [Cook94:6].

The approach introduced in this paper is to carry out the description of an application not in software-technical categories but in a normative language, which makes distinctions of parts of speech and sentence construction rules based on a natural language. In accordance with this approach (figure 2), the conceptual modeling can be distinguished into one phase which reconstructs the terminology of a field of application neutral towards methods and another phase, in which the specification of the expert concept is carried out method-specific. The division of the conceptual modeling into a reconstruction phase and a specification phase is based on the transition of the design process from the level of the users and their specific terminology to the level of the information systems with their relevant description categories which are determined by the requirements of a specific software (similar distinctions into *problem-oriented/computer-oriented* and *application domain/implementation domain* can be found in [Hagelstein88:211; Blum93:223]).

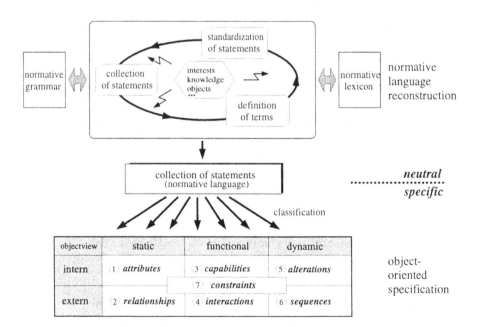

Fig. 2: Methodically-neutral and methodically-specific conceptual modeling

The phase of method-neutral reconstruction (figure 2) includes the steps collection of statements, the definition of terms and the standardisation of statements. The collection of statements is mainly *pragmatic-intentional*, while the second phase serves the *semantic-material* determination of the meaning of the terms. The third phase wants to bring out the *syntactic-formal* determination of statements. According to Carnap´s observation „pragmatics is the basis for all of linguistics" [Carnap48:13], all morphological, syntactic as well as semantic determinations of terms and statements are traced back to the (linguistic) practice of a particular field of application. The permanent repetition of these three steps must not be understood as a circle but as a (hermeneutic) spiral movement on a detailed level of description. In a process of building an approximate agreement the different views and opinions and the diverging expectations are gradually standardised and led to a mutual description of the expert knowledge in the form of a collection of statements based on a normative language.

On the basis of this collection of statements a conceptual model is developed in the following phase of specification. This expert concept puts down the structure and behaviour of an application system in a form which is suitable for the following system design. The single statements made in a normative language are classified with regard to the description aspects of a specification framework and transferred into the method-specific construction elements of a software-technical solution paradigm.

Figure 2 depicts in its lower part a specification framework for object-oriented application development [Schienmann95]. In order to secure and distinguish the complete specification of an object-oriented application system from the single descriptions, an *internal* and an *external* level for the description of the intra- and the inter-object-view are inserted into the specification frame in a right angle to the perspectives *static*, *dynamic* and *functional*. The static view describes the internal construction of the objects with their attributes (①) and the relations between the application objects (②). The way the single objects function internally is determined by their abilities (methods, operations ③). The way they function generally without regard to the objects results from the interactions between objects (④) by sending messages. The possible transactions (⑤), i.e. the conditions and transitions of single objects together with the respective events which trigger them off and the resulting order of events or sequences (the internal and external control logic) (⑥), are put down into a dynamic view. The object scheme is completed by stating restrictions in the form of assurances, invariants or conditions (⑦) for the regulation of characteristics of the application objects and rules for the specification of limited actions. Restrictions are put down comprehensively, they are able to connect variable parts of the description.

The following part intends to show, how, starting from a reconstruction of the expert terminology of a field of application, it is possible to specify on the basis of a normative language an object-oriented conceptual model.

5. Normative language and object-oriented specification

By reconstructing the terminology of a field of application it is intended to develop the conceptual model of a planned application system in a systematic and constructive way. The methodological basis for this reconstruction builds the linguistic-critical approach of constructivism [Kamlah84; Lorenzen87a]. Linguistic criticism in this context means the gradual and controlled transformation of statements made in colloquial language about circumstances in a field of application into statements in a normative language where the normative language functions as a model language for the reconstruction of statements made in colloquial language.

A normative language, which should basically be intelligible to all persons participating in the development process, is built up gradually by reconstructing meanings and standardising the ordinary language used in the application area. In contrast to other terminology-based approaches in application development in this linguistic-critical, (re-)constructive approach insecurities in the design process, which are caused by ambiguity, vagueness, inconsistencies or incompleteness of statements, can be ruled out in an early phase by reconstructing and standardising. Inadequate rulings of language in the fields of application are not taken over, but *reconstructed* (repaired) in a linguistic-critical way.

5.1 Reconstruction in a normative language

The reconstruction in a normative language starts with the collection of relevant statements concerning the facts in the respective application area. If the statements from the specific departments are examined, it becomes obvious that they often are ambiguous, incorrect and inconsistent. E.g. the statement »John borrows the copy with the pass« is syntactically ambiguous, because the prepositional phrase »with the pass« could either be an independent constituent of the verbal phrase or an attribute of »the copy« (see [Buchholz94:6]). However, before this syntactical ambiguity can be clarified and ruled with the help of a normative language, the meaning of the expert terms (predicators) contained in the statements has to be determined and put down. What is a *pass*? What kinds of library users can be distinguished? The answers to these questions and the determination of the meaning of the expert terms contained in the statements take place in three steps:

① Exemplary introduction

② Predicator rules

③ Explicit definition

The *exemplary introduction* helps the system analyser to practise together with an expert first, unknown predicators with illocutionary acts empractically (i.e. in non-linguistic acts) in a common acting context. Learning the unknown predicators can be supported by demonstrative gestures, by showing, by picking out an object or by demonstrating an action. An expert could, for example, explain the use of the predicator »CD-ROM« by taking up several objects that are present while assigning or not assigning them certain properties: »This object is a CD-ROM« or »This object is not a CD-ROM«. With »ε« and »ε'« as copulae for the assigning or not assigning of a certain property (read: »is« and »is not«), »ι« as demonstrator (read: »this«), »o« for »object« and »Q« for thing-predicators, these elementary predicators follow the form (of the sentence construction rules) »ι o ε Q« and »ι o ε' Q«.

With the help of this exemplary introduction the linguistic differentiations are traced back to non-linguistic actions. It is obvious that it is not possible in the course of the application development to enact empractically (exemplary) all situations which are necessary for the construction of the normative language. The language use has to be fixed by actions only in so far as it is necessary for the „Marking of first steps" [Mittelstraß89:273] and to arrive at a common understanding between all participants and this understanding cannot be achieved by linguistic means alone.

The usage of explicitly introduced predicators becomes further stabilised in a second step and regulated by predicator rules. Predicator rules determine linguistic standards for the usage of predicators by standardising relations (transitions). The usage of predicators becomes defined in relation to the usage of other predicators. Predicator rules correspond to Carnap`s *meaning postulates* [Carnap52]. Like these meaning postulates predicator rules are restrictions in a material language for the semantic description of predicators. They make it possible to standardise the meaning of predicators in a material-analytical way without reverting to the level of metalanguage. Different forms of predicator rules are, for example:

- *subordination:* $x \, \varepsilon$ employee $\Rightarrow x \, \varepsilon$ person
- *contrariety:* $x \, \varepsilon$ lending-out-copy $\Rightarrow x \, \varepsilon'$ reference-copy
- *synonymous:* $x \, \varepsilon$ pass $\Leftrightarrow x \, \varepsilon$ library card

The rule arrow »$\Rightarrow$« (read: »pass over to«) allows the transition from the statement standing on the right side, the antecedens, to the statement standing on the left side, the succedens. The first predicator rule states a subordination relation between »employee« and »person«. The second predicator rule establishes a contrarity between »ending-out-copy« and »reference-copy«. The third rule allows the transition in both directions, i.e. »pass« and »library card« are synonymous predicators. All kinds of sense relations can be expressed by predicator rules and combined to complex statements. A (reciprocal) contrariety between the cohyponems »person« and »institution« with regard to the hyperonym »user« is expressed by the following rules:

$$x \, \varepsilon \text{ person} \vee x \, \varepsilon \text{ institution} \Rightarrow x \, \varepsilon \text{ user}$$
$$x \, \varepsilon \text{ person} \Rightarrow x \, \varepsilon' \text{ institution}$$
$$x \, \varepsilon \text{ institution} \Rightarrow x \, \varepsilon' \text{ person}$$

The determination of predicators by predicator rules should be carried out axiomatically, i.e. all possible usages of words in sentences is analytically derived from a selected subset of predicator rules.

Starting with exemplary introductions and predicator rules it can be proceeded in a last step to introducing new predicators by explicit definitions and putting them down in a lexicon in normative language. Similar to predicator rules, explicit definitions help to agree on the usage of a term - the definiendum - in dependence on already settled terms - the definiens. In contrast to predicator rules, however, this agreement is complete and concluded, i.e. definiendum and definiens are equivalent and interchangeable (see [Rescher64:30ff; Suppes66:154]).

With »$\stackrel{\text{def}}{=}$« as definition symbol an explicit definition of »person« can be expressed as follows:

$$x \; \epsilon \; \text{person} \; \stackrel{\text{def}}{=\!=} \quad x \; \epsilon \; \text{user} \wedge x \vee \text{user number} \wedge x \; \gamma \; \text{borrow copy} \wedge \;....$$

If an object is assigned to the predicator »person«, it can be assigned to the predicator »user«, too. It is also valid for these objects that they have got a user number and the ability to take out copies of books; the ability copula in normative language is »γ«. It expresses that the object »x« can make topical the event »borrow copy«. The copula for characteristics »$\vee$« (read: »has«) implies that persons possess a user number. The term »person«, which has to be introduced, on the left hand side (definiendum) is determined unambiguously by the terms on the right hand side (definiens). However, all terms to be found in the definiens have to be introduced already. The circularity of definitions is excluded by tracing them back to predicator rules and predicators which have been introduced by way of example.

After the importance of predicators (expert terms) has been emphasised, in a last step of reconstruction the statements are standardised syntactically and brought into shape which ensures that the object classification of a described situation can be inferred from the structure of a statement. The standardisation is to be effected with the help of given sentence patterns, which serve as construction rules for putting together relevant expert sentences from the existing expert terms (sentence pattern is used synonymous to sentence construction plan, sentence construction rule or sentence form). The statement »John borrows the copy with the pass« can serve as an example for standardisation:

- *ordinary language*   [John borrows the copy with the pass]
- *standardised form:*   [John | π | borrow | ι copy | pass-with]
- *sentence pattern*   [N | π | P | Q_1 | Q_2^I]

A person which is called »John« carries out the act »borrow« of a copy by using a pass or library card. »N« is hereby a variable for a proper name, »π« symbolises the deed copula (read »does«). For the naming of the deed itself »P« is used as a variable for deed predicators. »ι« is the demonstrator for »this«; »Q_1« and »Q_2« are variables for object predicators. »pass« is an indirect object to »borrow« according to the main-predicator, which is put together with the case morpheme „with", in order to name the object which is needed for the act. Lorenzen calls this instrument-case (or *instrumentalis*, see [Fillmore68]) and chooses a superscripted »I« - therefore »Q_2^I« - in order to distinguish other cases [Lorenzen87:47].

Aside from singular statements, general (particular existence-quantified or universal all-quantified) statements and statements which are abstracted from these general statements on the scheme level, are interesting, as well. The general statement »$\forall x$ (x ϵ periodical $\rightarrow$ x ϵ collection)« or the corresponding predicator rule »$x \; \epsilon$ periodical $\Rightarrow$ $x \; \epsilon$ collection« lead to the scheme statement (concept relation) »PERIODICAL $\sqsubseteq$ COLLECTION« when they are abstracted with regard to synonym predicators. The symbol »$\sqsubseteq$« represents a subordination relation between the expert terms »PERIODICAL« and »COLLECTION«. When this statement is paraphrased into the sentence »A periodical is a collection« it resembles again the depiction of this fact in ordinary language, where the symbol »⊑« is replaced by the phrase »A ... is a ... «, which means the same thing.

This »is_a«-relation between expert terms can be distinguished into a static »is_kind_of«-relation - represented by » ⊑ «, the extension of the subsumable concept is here a subset of the extension´s generic term - and a dynamic »is_role_of« -relation - represented by » ⫤ « , the extension of the role concept and the generic term have the same scope (see [Wieringa95a:72]). Examples:

INSTITUTION ⊑ USER ∧ PERSON ⊑ USER

EXTERNAL ⫤ PERSON ∧ EMPLOYEE ⫤ PERSON ∧ STUDENT ⫤ PERSON

The extension of »INSTITUTION« and »PERSON« is a subset of »USER«. The extension of the role concepts »EXTERNAL«, »EMPLOYEE« and »STUDENT« are, in contrast, identical to the extension of »PERSON« (the extension of a concept includes all potential instances). Furthermore all extensions of a role concept can change through the migration of the instances of these role concepts without the extension of »PERSON« changing. »is_kind_of«-relations do not have this property. Similar to the subordination relation described above the statements in normative language for these kinds of relations can be paraphrased into ordinary language. The symbol » ⊑ « could be replaced by the phrase »A...is a kind of...«, the symbol » ⫤ « by the phrase »A ... is a role of...«. Additional inflections of the phrase words can hereby facilitate legibility. The paraphrased statements could be, for example: »An INSTITUTION is a kind of USER«, »A PERSON is a kind of USER«, »An EXTERNAL is a role of PERSON«, »An EMPLOYEE is a role of PERSON« and »A STUDENT is a role of PERSON«.

5.2 Object-oriented specification

After all statements, which are relevant to the specific field and neutral towards methods, have been collected and standardised in the reconstruction phase, the development of an object-oriented expert draft can follow in the specification phase. The statements in normative language are classified and modified with regard to the individual aspects of description of the specification framework (see figure 2). Then they are transformed into the construction elements of the used object-oriented design language (diagram language, specification language). The transitions between the individual languages, from the ordinary language to the normative language and from there to a diagram language and specification language, are depicted in figure 3 (as a diagram language, the *Object Modeling Technique OMT* [Rumbaugh91], for instance, may be chosen, as a specification language the *Conceptual Modeling Language LCM 3.0* by Feenstra and Wieringa [Feenstra93] can serve).

First, statements in ordinary language concerning the relevant facts in the fields of application are reconstructed in normative language. After this reconstruction in normative language has taken place, the object-oriented specification in a diagram language or formal specification language is carried out. In order to avoid the problems of common transformation approaches, where problems with controlling the design modification and inconsistencies between different representations can occur, and in order to make sure the seamlessness of the development results and the reversibility of the design process, it should be possible to reconstruct in a normative language every statement, which has been formulated in another language or diagram technique. Translations or transformations from a design language into another language are not carried out directly but are only translated further after a reconstruction and consolidation in normative language where a normative language which is neutral towards methods functions as an interlanguage [Schnelle73] .

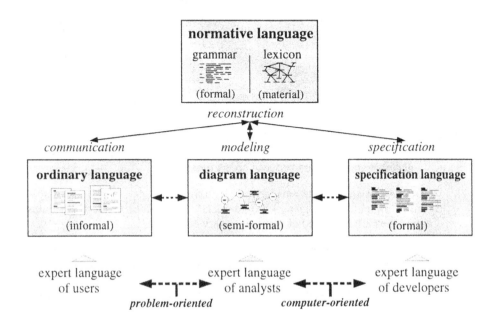

Fig. 3: Languages in conceptual modeling

As these different languages are based on different object classifications (method-neutrality - method-specialisation) and, of course, possess a different ability of expression - *LCM* in version 3.0, for example, does not have dynamical subtypes or roles -, these transformations often cannot be carried out automatically, i.e. only on a syntactical level. As no 1:1 mapping of the statements is given, such transformations are actually based on the system analyser's design decisions. While these design decisions always remain implicit in other design methods, the normative language approach allows their explication including their control and their comprehensibility.

The following example is supposed to make this even clearer: Library copies can be partitioned according to their type of media (type of media is the partition criterion) into books, magazines, computer discs, maps etc. In a normative language »COPY« would be reconstructed as generic term for »BOOK«, »MAGAZINE«, etc. In an object-oriented specification language this subordination relation could, for example, be expressed in the following different ways (see figure 4, the three alternatives are shown in the *OMT*-notation [Rumbaugh91]):

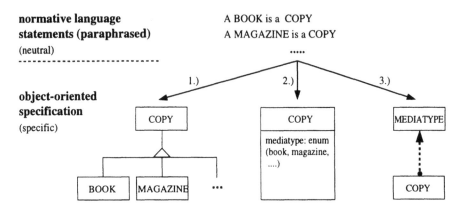

Fig. 4: Transition to object-oriented specification

① »COPY« becomes supertype of »BOOK«, »MAGAZINE« etc. This corresponds to a transcription of the subordination relations between expert concepts into a generalisation relation between object types.

② In »COPY« an attribute »mediatype« with the range of values (book, magazine, computer disk, map...) is introduced. Expressions of these attributes give the particular kind of media for every copy.

③ An independent object type »MEDIATYPE« is introduced. Every object of this object type describes one particular media type. Between the object types »MEDIATYPE« and »COPY« an *instantion-relation* [Wieringa95:59] is claimed, i.e. every instance of »COPY« is instance of an instance of »MEDIA-TYPE«.

Which transformation to choose depends for once on the abilities of the specification language itself - LCM 3.0 and Troll do not support the instantion-relation - and on the use of modification rules on which these design decisions are based. Possibility ①, for example, should be chosen if the resulting subtypes are to be described by further different characteristics and expressions of these characteristics are relevant for the application itself. Possibility ② can be chosen if some copies have to be assigned to only one media type. The third modification (③) should be chosen if different media types are to be described by identical characteristics but different types of characteristics and if these expressions of characteristics are identical for all assigned instances of »COPY« (see [Rescher64:52ff]) and especially the *principle of informativeness*).

6. Conclusion

The conceptual modeling of an application system can be seen as a process of linguistic (re-) construction. The development of a field of application which is to be modelled as well as specification and the following use of an application system is carried out in linguistic acts. The things and actions of the respective field of application are the objects of this speaking and acting. The order of these things and actions within the frame of the information-processing activities of a field of application is determined by the introduced expert terminology. If the development of applications is considered to be a gradual process of construction and transformation of linguistic expressions, a sound foundation of the conceptual model within the systematic reconstruction of the expert terms of a field of application can be achieved.

In this paper different solutions of a normative language approach for the conceptual modeling of information systems have been proposed. The conceptual modeling has been divided into a phase of reconstruction and a phase of specification. In the phase of reconstruction main emphasis is put on examination of the field of application and the commonly used expert terms in the context of information-processing activities. Aim of this phase is the materially (i.e. with regard to the practice of the expert language) founded reconstruction in normative language of those expert concepts which control information processing in an application area. In the following phase of specification these expert concepts or the reconstructed statements are used for the method-specific specification of the expert draft.

The advantages of the proposed approach can be summarised as follows:

- An implementation of the development work for information systems in an engineering-like way becomes possible from the beginning on, even in the early stages.

- The transition to a material-language approach can make the development of information systems more efficient, because the expert terminology is not distributed redundantly across the applications but is managed in a controlled way out of a development system (with a lexicon).

- Through the help of the method-neutral expert design the users of software drafts are not bothered anymore with concepts like »class«, »data type«,»transaction«, »data flow«, »message« or »workflow«.

- Normative languages can lead to advantages in competition between companies because they can not only be used in the computing field but can also serve as complementary languages to user expert languages (as standardised business or market language).

The project KASPER [Ortner94] tries to support the development process described above by tools. It is planned to build up a development environment for the design of information systems in normative language.

References

[Abbott83] Abbott, R.J.: Program Design by Informal English Descriptions. In: Communications of the ACM 26 (1983) 11, pp 882-894.

[Barros92] Barros, P.A.: The Nature of Bias and Defects in the Software Specification Process. Technical Report CS-TR-2822. Maryland: University Press 1992.

[Blum93] Blum, B.I.: Formalism and Prototyping in the Software Process. In: Colburn, R.T.; Fetzer, J.H. (eds.): Program Verification. Dordrecht: Kluwer Academic Publishers 1993, pp 213-238 (Printed from: Information and Decision Technologies 15 (1989), pp 327-341).

[Boehm79] Boehm, B.W.: Software Engineering: R&D Trends and Defense Needs. In: Wegner, P. (ed.): Research Directions in Software Technology. Cambridge: MIT Press 1979, pp 44-86.

[Brodie84] Brodie, M.L.; Mylopoulos, J.; Schmidt, J.W. (eds.): On Conceptual Modelling. Perspectives from Artificial Intelligence, Databases, and Programming Languages. New York: Springer 1984.

[Buchholz94] Buchholz, E.; Düsterhöft, A.; Thalheim, B.: Exploiting Knowledge Gained from Natural Language for EER Database Design. Technical Report I-10/94. Cottbus: Technische Universität 1994.

[Burg95] Burg, J.F.M.; Riet, van de R.P.: Syntax, Semantics and Pragmatics of COLOR-X Event Models: Specifying the Dynamics of Information and Communication Systems. Technical Report IR-392. Amsterdam: Vrije Universiteit 1995.

[Carnap48] Carnap, R.: Introduction to Semantics. Cambridge: Harvard University Press 1948.

[Carnap52] Carnap, R.: Meaning Postulates. In: Philosophical Studies 3 (1952), pp 65-73.

[Cook94] Cook, S.; Daniels, J.: Designing Object Systems. Object-Oriented Modelling with Syntropy. Englewood Cliffs: Prentice Hall 1994.

[Düsterhöft96] Düsterhöft, A.: Zur interaktiven natürlichsprachlichen Unterstützung im Datenbankentwurf. PhD Thesis. Cottbus: Brandenburgische Technische Universität Cottbus 1996.

[Feenstra93] Feenstra, R.B.; Wieringa, R.J.: LCM 3.0. A Language for Describing Conceptual Models. Technical Report. Amsterdam: Vrije Universiteit 1993.

[Fillmore68] Fillmore, C.J.: The Case for Case. In: Bach, E.; Harms, T.R.(eds.): Universals in Linguistic Theory. New York: Holt, Rinehardt & Winston, pp 1-118.

[Gethmann79] Gethmann, C.F.: Protologik. Untersuchungen zur formalen Pragmatik von Begründungsdiskursen. Frankfurt: Suhrkamp 1979.

[Hagelstein88] Hagelstein, J.: Declarative Approach to Information Systems Requirements. In: Knowledge Based Systems 1 (1988) 4, pp 211-220.

[Kamlah84] Kamlah, W.; Lorenzen, P.: Logical Propaedeutic. Lanham: University Press of America 1984.

[Kristen94] Kristen, G.: Object Orientation. The KISS Method. From Information Architecture to Information System. Wokingham: Addison-Wesley 1994.

[Lorenzen87] Lorenzen, P.: Lehrbuch der Konstruktiven Wissenschaftstheorie. Mannheim: BI-Wissenschaftsverlag 1987.

[Lorenzen87a] Lorenzen, P.: Constructive Philosophy. Amherst: University of Massachussetts Press 1987.

[McMenamin84] McMenamin, M.; Palmer, J.F.: Essential Systems Analysis. Englewood Cliffs: Prentice Hall 1984.

[Meyer88] Meyer, B.: Object-Oriented Software Construction. Englewood Cliffs: Prentice Hall 1988.

[Mittelstraß89] Mittelstraß, J.: Der Flug der Eule. Von der Vernunft der Wissenschaft und der Aufgabe der Philosophie. Frankfurt: Suhrkamp 1989.

[Moynihan94] Moynihan, T.: An Experimental Comparison of Object-Orientation and Functional-Decomposition as Paradigms for Communicating Systems Functionality to Users. In: Zupancic, J.; Wrycza. S. (eds.): Proc. of 4th Int. Conf. Information Systems Development - ISD'94, Bled 1994. Kranj: Moderna Organizacija 1994, pp 605-613.

[Opdahl94] Opdahl, A.L.; Sindre, G.: A Taxonomie for Real-World Modelling Concepts. In: Information Systems 19 (1994) 3, pp 229-241.

[Ortner94] Ortner, E.: KASPER - Ein Projekt zur natürlichsprachlichen Entwicklung von Informationssystemen. In: Wirtschaftsinformatik 36 (1994) 6, pp 570-579.

[Ortner95] Ortner, E.: Elemente einer methodenneutralen Konstruktionssprache für Informationssysteme. In: Informatik Forschung und Entwicklung 10 (1995), pp 148-160.

[Ortner96] Ortner, E.; Schienmann, B.: Normsprachlicher Entwurf von Informationssystemen - Vorstellung einer Methode. In: Ortner, E.; Schienmann, B.; Thoma, H. (Hrsg.): Natürlichsprachlicher Entwurf von Informationssystemen. Grundlagen, Methoden, Werkzeuge, Anwendungen. Proc. GI/EMISA-Workshop 1996, Tutzing. Konstanz: Universitäts-Verlag 1996, pp 109-129.

[Rescher64] Rescher, N.: Introduction to Logic. New York: St. Martin's Press 1964.

[Rolland92] Rolland, C.; Proix, C.: Natural Language Approach to Conceptual Modeling. In: Loucopoulos, P.; Zicari, R. (eds.): Conceptual Modeling, Databases, and Case. An Integrated View of Information Systems Development. New York: Wiley 1992, pp 447-463.

[Rumbaugh91] Rumbaugh, J.; Blaha, M.; Premerlani, W. et al.: Object-Oriented Modeling and Design. Englewood Cliffs: Prentice Hall 1991.

[Saeki89] Saeki, M.; Horai, H.; Enomoto, H.: Software Development Process from Natural Language Specification. In: Proc. of the 11th International Conference on Software Engineering. Washington: IEEE Computer Society Press 1989, pp 64-73.

[Schienmann95] Schienmann, B.: Objektorientierte Spezifikation betrieblicher Informationssysteme. In: König, W. (eds.): Wirtschaftsinformatik '95. Heidelberg: Physica 1995, pp 151-168.

[Schienmann96] Schienmann, B.: Objektorientierter Fachentwurf. Ein terminologiebasierter Ansatz für die Konstruktion von Anwendungssystemen. PhD Thesis. Konstanz: Universität 1996.

[Schnelle73] Schnelle, H.: Sprachphilosophie und Linguistik. Prinzipien der Sprachanalyse a priori und a posteriori. Hamburg: Rowohlt 1973.

[Sowa84] Sowa, J.F.: Conceptual Structures: Information Processing in Mind and Machine. Reading: Addison-Wesley 1984.

[Sowa91] Sowa, J.F.: Toward the Epressive Power of Natural Language. In: J.F. Sowa (Hrsg.): Principles of Semantic Networks. Explorations in the Representation of Knowledge. San Mateo: Morgan Kaufmann 1991, pp 157-189.

[Spaccapietra93] Spaccapietra, S.; Parent, C.; Sunye, M. et al.: Object Orientation and Conceptual Modeling. In: Mayr, H.C.; Wagner, R. (eds): Objektorientierte Methoden für Informationssysteme. Proc. GI/EMISA-Fachtagung 1996, Klagenfurt. Berlin: Springer 1993, pp 3-17.

[Suppes66] Suppes, P.: Introduction to Logic. Princeton: Van Nostrand 1966.

[Sykes95] Sykes, J.A.: English grammar as a sentence model for conceptual modelling using NIAM. In: Falkenberg, E.D.; Hesse, W.; Olive, A. (eds.): Information Systems Concepts. Towards an consolidation of views. London: Chapman & Hall 1995, pp 161-167.

[Tjoa94] Tjoa, A M.; Berger, L.: Transformation of Requirements Specifications Expressed in Natural Language into an EER Model. In: Elmasri, R.A.; Kouramajian, V.; Thalheim, B. (eds.): Entity Relationship Approach - ER '93, Proceedings. Berlin: Springer 1994, pp 206-217.

[Vessey94] Vessey, I.; Conger, S.A.: Requirements Specification: Learning Object, Process, and Data Methodologies. In: Communications of the ACM 37 (1994) 5, pp 102-113.

[Wedekind81] Wedekind, H.: Datenbanksysteme I. Eine konstruktive Einführung in die Datenverarbeitung in Wirtschaft und Verwaltung. 2. Auflage. Mannheim: BI-Wissenschaftsverlag 1981.

[Whorf56] Whorf, B.L.: Language, Thought and Reality. New York: Wiley 1956.

[Wieringa95] Wieringa, J.R.: A Method for Building and Evaluating Formal Specifications of Object-Oriented Conceptual Models of Database Systems. Technical Paper IR-340. Amsterdam: Vrije Universiteit 1995.

[Wieringa95a] Wieringa, J.R.; de Jonge, W., Spruit, P.: Using Dynamic Classes and Role Classes to Model Object Migration. In: Theory and Practice of Object Systems 1 (1995) 1, pp 61-83.

[Woodfield90] Woodfield, S.N.; Embley, D.W.; Kurtz, B.D.: Extending Analysis Paradigms. In: 9th Annual Int. Phoenix Conf. on Computers and Communications, Phoenix. Los Alamitos: IEEE Computer Society Press 1990, pp 441- 446.

Improving Quality in Conceptual Modelling by the Use of Schema Transformations

Petia Assenova and Paul Johannesson

Department of Computer and Systems Sciences
Stockholm University
Electrum 230, S-164 40 Kista, Sweden
email:<petia,pajo>@dsv.su.se

Abstract. The quality of the results produced in the early phases of systems development is a major factor in determining the overall quality of an information system. Therefore, an important task for research in conceptual modelling and requirements engineering is to clarify the concept of quality and develop methods for improving the quality of conceptual schemas. In this paper, we propose an approach for improving schema quality, which is based on a systematic use of schema transformations to incrementally restructure schemas. We introduce a number of schema transformations as well as a set of quality criteria for conceptual schemas, and we show how the transformations affect these quality criteria.

1 Introduction

Database management systems have been available for more than two decades, mainly in the form of the hierarchical, network, and relational schemas. In the mid 1970s the development of semantic database models was initiated. These were introduced primarily as schema design tools, meaning that a schema should first be designed in a high level semantic model and then translated into one of the traditional models for implementation.

The conceptual schema expressed in a semantic data model shall serve two different purposes. First, the schema shall serve as a vehicle for communication between users and systems analysts. Secondly, the schema shall provide a basis for constructing and implementing a computer supported information system. In order to satisfy these requirements, the schema must be of good quality. An important task for research in conceptual modelling and requirements engineering is, therefore, to clarify the concept of quality and develop methods for improving the quality of schemas. In the literature, many methods for this purpose have been suggested, [Lindland94]; basic techniques used in these methods are inspection, structured walk-through, computer supported visualisation, explanation, and simulation facilities. In this paper, we propose a complementary approach for improving schema quality, which is based on a systematic use of schema transformations to incrementally restructure schemas. The purpose of the paper is to analyse how such a restructuring influences quality aspects of conceptual schemas.

The paper is organised as follows. In Section 2, we introduce the notion of schema transformations and briefly survey how transformations have been used in database design and requirements engineering. In Section 3, we describe the modelling formalism and notation to be used in the rest of the paper. In Section 4, we discuss the concept of quality for conceptual schemas and suggest a number of quality criteria. In Section 5, which is the main section of the paper, we introduce a number of schema transformations and determine how they influence the quality criteria of Section 4. We also discuss how the order of applying the transformations affect the quality of the resulting schema. In the final Section, we summarise the paper and suggest directions for further research.

2 Schema Transformations

A schema transformation is a function that maps a conceptual (or data) schema into another schema. Most work on schema transformations has been carried out in the context of the relational model. All the first normal form transformations, the third, Boyce-Codd, the fourth, and projection normal form decompositions are examples of schema transformations,[Fagin79], [Ullman88], [Troyer93]. A central concern in this work has been to prove that the schema transformations are lossless (information preserving), and several notions of equivalence between relational schemas have been proposed,[Kobayashi86], [Hull86]. Informally, most of these proposals define two schemas as being equivalent if there exists a bijection between the instances of the schemas. Another important issue has been to show how to transform different types of rules and constraints associated with a relational schema, such as functional dependencies and inclusion dependencies, [Kobayashi86]. This work has been extended by research on transformations in the context of semantic data schemas, such as the ER schema [Chen76], and extensions of the ER schema [ElMasri85]. In this research, [Halpin90], [Hainaut91], also more general types of constraints have been taken into consideration, e.g. cardinality constraints and exclusion constraints.

Schema transformations have been used in many different contexts, for example in constructing database views, where users require to view specific portions of a database. Schema transformations have also been used to translate schemas in interoperable information systems, where separately developed systems need to interoperate, [Sheth90]. In the area of schema integration, schema transformations can be used to standardise the structure of schemas, [Johannesson94], [Miller94]. Schema transformations have also been proposed as tools for improving schema quality, [Batini88], [Eick91], which is also the purpose of this paper. What distinguishes our approach from previous ones is mainly that we provide a more fine-grained analysis of schema quality aspects, which gives a better basis for assessing the advantages and drawbacks of particular schema transformations.

3 Modelling Concepts and Notation

The basic concept in conceptual modelling approaches is the object (entity); objects judged as being similar are grouped together into object types, such as Employee and Department. Associations between objects are represented by means of attributes. In our graphical notation, see Schema 3.1, entity types are depicted by ellipses and attributes by labelled arrows. The arrow points from the domain to the range of the attribute. We distinguish between non-lexical and lexical objects, the latter are also called data values and include strings, integers, booleans, etc. Lexical object types are represented by rectangles. Attributes whose ranges are lexical types are called lexical attributes. We assume that it is possible to specify constraints in the schema that express propositions which should hold true in each state of the Universe of Discourse. The graphical notation can only represent domain and range constraints, shown by the direction of the arrows; generalisation relationships, shown by arrows labelled Isa; and cardinality constraints. The cardinality constraints specify for each attribute if it is single-valued, injective, total, or surjective. In the graphical notation, cardinality constraints are represented by a quadruple next to an attribute. The first component of the quadruple indicates whether the conceptual relation is single-valued or not. When single-valued, this component is set to 1, otherwise m. The second component of the structure indicates whether the conceptual relation is injective, in which case the component is set to 1, otherwise m. The third component indicates the totality of the conceptual relation. An attribute is total when each instance of its domain is associated with at leas one instance of the attribute's range. A t indicates totality, a p partiality. The fourth component indicates the surjectivity of the conceptual relation. When surjective, this component is set to t, otherwise p.

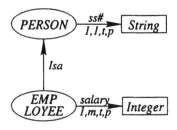

Schema 3.1

4 Quality Criteria

In the area of software engineering, quality properties of software products have been studied extensively. Software metrics, [Davis90], are used to assess the quality of code and other design products. In requirements engineering and conceptual modelling, however, the notion of quality is still poorly understood. Most of the literature on quality in this area only provides unstructured lists of desirable properties of conceptual schemas. More structured approaches to quality in conceptual modelling are rare, the most elaborate work on this topic so far seems to be [Lindland94]. The approach in this paper is to evaluate the quality of schemas along three dimensions - syntax, semantics, and pragmatics. Syntactic quality means that a schema should adhere to the grammar of the language it is expressed in. Semantic quality has to do with the degree of correspondence between the schema and the domain it describes. The schema should be *valid*, i.e., it should only contain true statements about the domain, and it should be *complete*, meaning that it should contain all true statements about the domain. Finally, pragmatic quality concerns the correspondence between the schema and the users' interpretation of it, that is the degree to which the schema has been understood.

The main purpose of this paper is to argue that schema transformations are useful for improving the quality of conceptual schemas, but it should be realised that they cannot improve quality along all the three dimensions introduced above. Syntactic quality cannot be improved by means of schema transformations, since the application of a schema transformation requires that the schema is already syntactically correct - transformation of a syntactically incorrect schema is not well defined. Neither can we hope to improve the semantic quality by means of schema transformations, at least not by using information preserving transformations. An information preserving schema transformation should not change the representational capacity of a schema, and it can therefore influence neither the validity nor the completeness of the schema. Thus, schema transformations can only be used to improve the pragmatic quality of a schema, in particular the following aspects:

Explicitness: Explicitness means that information about the Universe of Discourse (UoD) should be represented on the type level, not on the instance level.

Size: The size of a schema is the number of its object types and attributes. Large size is usually considered to be a disadvantage, but using additional object types and attributes can facilitate good naming conventions. So an increased size of a schema can be beneficial in certain situations.

Rule simplicity: Rule simplicity means that as many rules as possible are expressed by simple types of constraints in the schema, e.g., cardinality constraints.

Rule uniformity: Rule uniformity means that cardinality constraints should be uniform. Attributes with a non-lexical range should be (1,m,t,t), and attributes with a lexical range should be (1,1,t,p). The standardized cardinality constraints make the semantics for the attributes uniform. Moreover the required totality for the attributes ensures that all instances of an object type are similar to each other.

Query simplicity: Query simplicity means that it should be possible to retrieve simple information about the UoD through simple queries on the schema.

Stability: Stability means that when small changes in the UoD occur, it should only be necessary to make small changes to the schema in order to obtain a schema of good quality that reflects the UoD.

Some of these definitions are admittedly vague, but they will be made more precise in the following sections, where we show how the pragmatic quality of schemas can be improved by schema transformations. However the concept of quality is inherently somewhat vague due to the human ability to perceive phenomena in different ways.

5 Quality Effects of Schema Transformations

In this section we summarise a number of transformations found in the literature, [Halpin90], [Johannesson94], and introduce some new transformations. We restrict our attention to lossless transformations. Each transformation is described and then assessed according to how it satisfies the quality criteria described in the previous section. The final subsection discusses some of the problems depending on the order in which transformations are applied.

5.1 Transforming Partial Attributes

This transformation is applied in order to change partial attributes into total attributes. If an attribute in a schema is partial, the schema is transformed by introducing a new subtype and changing the domain of the attribute to this new type. As a result of this transformation the attribute becomes total. An example is shown in Schema 5.1.1 where the partial attribute *salary* gives rise to the introduction of a specialisation type so that the attribute *salary* in Schema 5.1.2 becomes total. The new object type is called *EMPLOYEE* [1]. Observe that the range of the partial attribute to be transformed does not need to be a lexical type as it is in this particular example, it can be a non-lexical type.

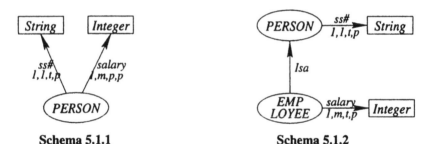

| Schema 5.1.1 | Schema 5.1.2 |

By introducing the object type *EMPLOYEE* the size of the schema increases. Furthermore after applying the transformation, all attributes become total, which shows that the transformation increases the rule uniformity in a schema.

The introduction of the entity *EMPLOYEE* to the schema also increases its stability. For instance Schema 5.1.2 can be extended with information for different categories of employees, by introducing a lexical attribute *employee category* with domain *EMPLOYEE* as shown in Schema 5.1.4. Similarly extending Schema 5.1.1 with the same information can be done by adding a lexical attribute *employee category* with domain *PERSON*, which results in Schema 5.1.3. This schema does not fit the quality criteria for rule simplicity, which the Schema 5.1.4 does.

Moreover there is a relationship between the attributes *salary* and *employee category*:

---

1. For the sake of clarity we will in the rest of the paper give appropriate names to all object types and attributes introduced by any transformation. However we do not consider naming in this situation as schema enrichment, since the purpose of it is to only make examples understandable.

if a person does not have salary than he/she will not have an employee category either, and vice versa. This relationship can be represented in Schema 5.1.3 by an integrity constraint. However in Schema 5.1.4 we do not need such an integrity constraint since the relationship is represented by the cardinality constraints for the attributes *employee category* and *salary*, which are both total. Consequently Schema 5.1.4 satisfies the criterion for rule simplicity, whereas the Schema 5.1.3 does not satisfy this criterion. Consequently enlarging the Schema 5.1.1 by transforming it into Schema 5.1.3 does not result in a satisfactory schema. Extending it in other ways requires more than the addition of only one attribute, which is more complicated than extending Schema 5.1.2 to make Schema 5.1.4. Therefore Schema 5.1.2 is considered more stable than Schema 5.1.1.

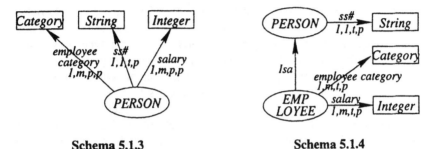

        Schema 5.1.3   **Schema 5.1.4**

5.2 Transforming Non-surjective Attributes

The transformation of partial attributes is limited to just these, and it does not concern non-surjective attributes. A parallel situation to the occurrence of partial attributes is the occurrence of non-surjective attributes. A partial and surjective attribute that is not lexical, becomes total by exchanging the domain and range of the attribute. An example of this is the partial and surjective attribute *employed at* with domain *PERSON* and range *COMPANY* in Schema 5.2.1. The same relation between these objects can be represented by a total and non-surjective attribute *employees* with domain *COMPANY* and range *PERSON* as shown in Schema 5.2.2. To make the transformation insensitive to the representation of an attribute we are suggesting a transformation of non-surjective attributes the range of which is a non-lexical type. The transformation of a non-surjective attribute changes a schema by introducing a new object type. This new object type is a specialisation of the former range of the attribute and becomes its new range. The result of the transformation is depicted in Schema 5.2.3. The attribute *employs* from Schema 5.2.2 becomes surjective through the introduction of the object type *EMPLOYEE* and by changing the range for employees to *EMPLOYEE*.

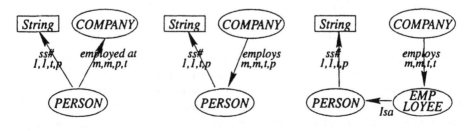

  Schema 5.2.1   **Schema 5.2.2**   **Schema 5.2.3**

Similar to the transformation of partial attributes the transformation of non-surjective attributes increases the size of the schema by introducing a new object type. It affects the cardinality constraints so that the resulting schema becomes rule uniform with respect to surjectivity. The separation of the concept employee from the concept person makes the schema more stable.

5.3 Transforming Partial Attributes which are Total in Union

The transformation of partial attributes is applicable in most but not all cases where there are partial attributes. A situation in which it is more suitable to apply other transformations is where an object type is the domain of a set of partial attributes, but where the union of those attributes is total. Consider the Schema 5.3.1. A restriction exists specifying that a head teacher must be responsible for at least one undergraduate course, or at least one graduate course, or several courses the type of which is immaterial. The attributes *responsible UC* and *responsible GC* are both partial, since there may be head teachers who are responsible for only one kind of course. However, the combination of the attributes is total because all courses have a head teacher. An alternative way of modelling the same UoD is shown in Schema 5.3.2, where a supertype *COURSE* to the object types *UNDERGRADUATE COURSE* and *GRADUATE COURSE* is introduced. In this situation the partial attributes *responsible UC* and *responsible GC* are replaced by a total attribute *responsible for* with domain *HEAD TEACHER* and range *COURSE*.

Generalising object types makes it possible to generalise their common attributes. This can by made by replacing the common attributes for the subtypes with correspond-ing attributes with the introduced supertype as domain. However, this refinement of the transformation requires semantic enrichment by adding information about which attributes are common for the generalised object types. Since in this paper only lossless transformation are considered, the last refinement is left aside.

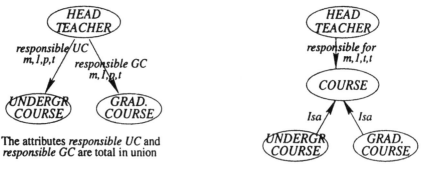

The attributes *responsible UC* and *responsible GC* are total in union	
Schema 5.3.1	**Schema 5.3.2**

Note that, in the example given above, the ranges of the attributes are not lexical types. An analogous situation occurs when the ranges of the partial attributes are lexical types. An example of this case is given in Schema 5.3.3 which can be transformed to Schema 5.3.4. A situation where some of the ranges are object types and some of them are lexical types is also possible and we generalise their transformation as follows. If the range for a partial attribute, which is total in union is a lexical type, an object type that corresponds to the lexical type is introduced and the correspondence is represented by an attribute. Then the transformation replaces the partial attributes which are total in union. A new (total) attribute is introduced, whose range is a new object type that is a generalisation of the ranges of the partial attributes.

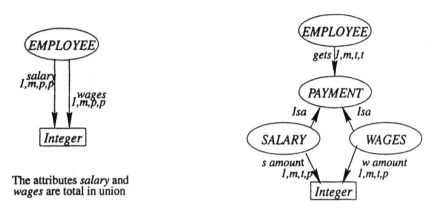

The attributes *salary* and *wages* are total in union

Schema 5.3.3   **Schema 5.3.4**

The new entities increase the size of the schema. The transformation increases the rule simplicity of the schema, since rules governing which attributes are total in union are represented explicitly in the schema by the introduced attribute, which is a generalisation of the attributes that are total in union. The transformation also increases the rule uniformity in a schema with respect to totality. The stability of the schema also increases. For instance if the schema need to be expanded with information about the object type *COURSE*, then a set of attributes with domain *COURSE* can be created in Schema 5.3.2, whereas two sets of attributes must be created in Schema 5.3.1: one with the domain *UNDERGRADUATE COURSE* and one with the domain *GRADUATE COURSE*.

However, this transformation has a negative effect on the criterion for query simplicity, since after the transformation some of the queries become more complex. For example a query for the head teachers of graduate courses in the untransformed schema is written *headTeacher GC(R,GC)* and in the transformed schema *responsible-for(R,GC),graduate course(GC)*.

5.4 Transforming Non-surjective Attributes which are Surjective in Union

A set of non-surjective attributes that are total in union becomes a set of partial attributes that are also total in union. This is done by exchanging the domain and the range of those attributes,

To guarantee the independence of the set of suggested transformations from the direction of the attributes, a transformation of non-surjective attributes which are jointly surjective is introduced. This transformation is analogous to the transformation of partial attributes which are total in union.

For example if the domain and range for each attribute are exchanged in Schema 5.3.1 then the attributes become surjective in union and the transformation can be applied. The result is the same as in Schema 5.3.2 except that the domain and range of the attribute *responsible for* should be exchanged. Obviously the quality criteria influenced by the transformation of attributes that are surjective in union, are the same criteria as those satisfied by the transformation for the attributes that are total union.

5.5 Transforming m-m Attributes

The transformation of m-m attributes (attributes which are neither single-valued nor injective) is applied in order to decompose m-m attributes. If an m-m attribute occurs in a schema, it is transformed by introducing a new object type and two single valued attributes, which connect the new object type with the domain and the range of the m-m attribute being transformed. The transformation is exemplified in Schema 5.5.1 and Schema 5.5.2 where the m-m attribute *employed* is replaced by a new object type *EMPLOYMENT* with the single valued attributes *at* and *for*.

| Schema 5.5.1 | Schema 5.5.2 |

Since the transformation introduces a new object type, the size of the schema will increase. The cardinality constraints for the introduced attributes make the schema rule uniform with respect to single valuedness.

The resulting schema is also more stable. For instance it is common for people to change their employment. To extend the schema so that it maintains the history of the various employments of an employee can be achieved in the Schema 5.5.2 by introducing a single lexical attribute *date* with the domain *EMPLOYMENT*. However, the introduction of a single attribute in the Schema 5.5.1 would not be enough to maintain this information.

This transformation negatively affects query simplicity. For instance, using Prolog, a query addressed to Schema 5.5.1 for finding people employed at Stockhom University, would be written with only one predicate *employed(stockholms_university,E)*. The same query addressed to schema 5.5.2 would require two predicates:
at(Emp,stockholms_university), for(Emp,E).

5.6 Transforming Lexical Attributes

If a schema contains an attribute with a lexical type which is not 1-1 (single valued and injective) then the schema is transformed by introducing a new object type, which becomes the range of that attribute. For example, in Schema 5.6.1 the fact that a company is geographical located in a city is modelled as an association between the object type *COMPANY* and the lexical type *City*, whereas in Schema 5.6.2 the same fact is modelled as an association between the objects *COMPANY* and *CITY*.

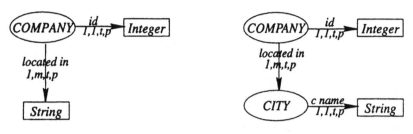

Schema 5.6.1   **Schema 5.6.2**

Introducing a new object type increases the size of the schema. Having changed the domain of the lexical attribute the new cardinality constraints make the schema rule uniform with respect to single valuedness and injectivity of the lexical attributes. The transformed schema is more stable, since it is easier to add extra attributes for cities. Some of the queries after the transformation become more complex, because their derivations cover a larger network of objects.

5.7 Transforming Attributes with Fixed Ranges

Lexical attributes are transformed when their domain is a lexical type with a finite extension. In this case the lexical attribute is replaced by a set of new object types which are specialisations of the domain of the attribute, and which correspond to the values of the range of the lexical type. For example the lexical attribute *employee category* in Schema 5.7.1 is used to categorise an employee as an administrator, a teacher, or a researcher. It is replaced in Schema 5.7.2 by the object types *ADMINISTRATOR, TEACHER*, and *RESEARCHER*, which are subtypes of the entity type *EMPLOYEE*.

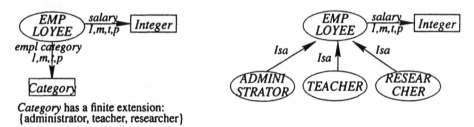

Category has a finite extension:
{administrator, teacher, researcher}

Schema 5.7.1   **Schema 5.7.2**

This transformation is an example of how a schema can be transformed so that the resulting schema is more explicit, i.e. the information is represented by types instead of instances. In Schema 5.7.1 the different categories of an employee are represented by the values of the lexical type *Category*. In Schema 5.7.2 the same information is represented by the object types *ADMINISTRATOR, TEACHER*, and *RESEARCHER*.

The Schema 5.7.2 is also more stable than the Schema 5.7.1. If information about the responsibilities of a teacher needs to be added, this can be done in Schema 5.7.2 by introducing an attribute *teacher's responsibility* with the domain *TEACHER*. In Schema 5.7.1 the attribute *teacher's responsibility* can be introduced with the domain *EMPLOYEE*, which necessitates a rule stating that *teacher's responsibility* only concerns the category teacher. The extra rule means that the schema does not satisfy the criterion for rule simplicity and several transformations will be necessary to attain rule simplicity.

As before, when introducing new object types the size of the schema increases. In contrast to others, this transformation does not affect the query simplicity of the schema, since the length of questions in the schema before and after the transformation is unchanged. The reason for this is that the introduced objects replace the already existing values of the lexical type. In this sense the introduced object types are not completely new concepts. For instance, a query asking for teachers' salaries would be written *salary(E,S),empl category(E,teacher)* in the untransformed schema and *salary(E,S), teacher(S)* in the transformed schema. Both queries consist of two predicates and so have equal simplicity.

5.8 Transformation to Lattice Structures

If two types are not disjoint, a common subtype is introduced. The extension of the common subtype is a subset of the intersection of the extensions of its supertypes. Obviously, the transformation is not applied to two non-disjoint types where one is a specialisation or generalisation of the other. For example, in Schema 5.8.1 the object types *RESEARCHER* and *TEACHER* are not disjoint. In Schema 5.8.2 a new object type *SCHOLAR* is introduced, which is specialisation of both *RESEARCHER* and *TEACHER*.

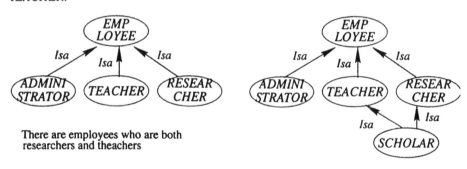

| **Schema 5.8.1** | **Schema 5.8.2** |

This transformation increases the size of a schema. The transformation satisfies the criterion for rule simplicity because after the transformation, the rules that show which types are not disjoint are not needed, as they are explicitly represented in the schema. At type level rather than instance level it can also be seen that some employees are both teachers and researchers which means that the transformation increases the explicitness of the schema.

Some of the queries become easier after transformation. For instance a query asking for all teachers who are researchers would be written *researcher(R), teacher(R)* in Schema 5.8.1, and only *scholar(R)* in Schema 5.8.2.

5.9 Transforming Non-unary Attributes

A situation in which an attribute represents two different concepts occurs in some schemas, as exemplified in Schema 5.9.1, where the attributes *sales Jan, sales Feb... sales Dec* all represent both sales and months. Since the represented concepts are the same and the attributes have the same domain and range, the schema can be transformed so that the concepts represented by these attributes are represented by the object types *SALES* and *MONTH* as depicted in Schema 5.9.2. The idea of this transformation is that an attribute in a conceptual schema must only represent a single and simple concept and not a combination of concepts. This transformation differs from the other transformations discussed in this section since it cannot be applied automatically without an understanding of the semantics in the schema.

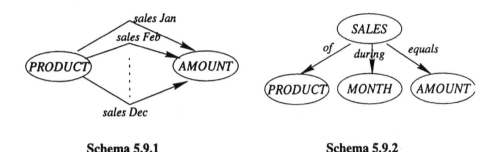

Schema 5.9.1   **Schema 5.9.2**

This is yet another example of a transformation in which additional object types improve the stability of a schema. The representation in Schema 5.9.1 is clearly very unstable. If we were to keep track of sales over a number of years, we would be forced to add a large number of new attributes. The representation in Schema 5.9.2 is much more stable, because if we wish to keep track of sales over a number of years, only a single attribute needs to be added.

A unique characteristic of this transformation is that it sometimes increases and sometimes decreases the query simplicity of a schema.

For instance the query asking for the sales for February of a certain product would be written *sales Feb(P,A)* in Schema 5.9.1. The simplicity of this query decreases in Schema 5.9.2 and becomes *during(S, february), off(S, P), equals(S, A)*.

However the query asking Schema 5.9.1 for the sales of a certain product over a period of a year would be written *sales Jan(P, AJ), sales Feb(P, AF), ... sales Dec(P, AD)*. The simplicity of this query increases in Schema 5.9.2 and becomes *off(S,P), equals(S,X)*.

5.10 The Order of the Transformations

The order in which transformations are applied is important since they are not commutative. For example, the result of applying the transformation of attributes with fixed ranges before applying the transformation of lexical attributes which are not 1-1, is different from applying them the other way round. Applying the transformation of fixed ranges to Schema 5.10.1 results in Schema 5.10.2, a schema to which the transformation of lexical attributes is not applicable. However, by first applying the transformation of lexical attributes which are not 1-1 to Schema 5.10.1 the resulting Schema 5.10.3 can continue to be decomposed using the transformation of fixed ranges, which results in Schema 5.10.4. This last schema is very unnatural, since the object types *TRUE* and *FALSE* only consist of one instance each. This demonstrates how applying the transformation of fixed ranges after the transformation of non-1-1 attributes yields unsatisfactory results.

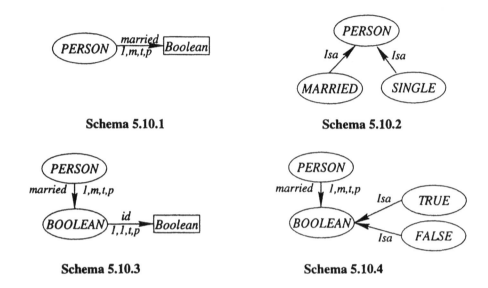

Schema 5.10.1	Schema 5.10.2

Schema 5.10.3	Schema 5.10.4

6 Concluding Remarks

This paper summarises a set of quality criteria for a conceptual schema. It focuses on how different schema transformations influence the quality of a schema according to these criteria. The proposed transformations are lossless and can improve the pragmatic quality of a schema. However, they can not improve its syntactic qualities, since transformations are defined for syntactically correct schemas. Neither can they improve a schema's semantic qualities, since they do not provide any additional semantics.

The influence of the transformation on the quality criteria is summarised in the table below. The positive effects of a transformation are marked with a plus sign, the negative with a minus sign. Note that some transformations affect some criteria both positively and negatively; these are marked with +/-. Furthermore, the increase of the size of a schema may be desirable for some reasons and undesirable for others, as discussed in Section 4. As a consequence of this, the transformations do not necessarily produce a schema which is "better" or more intuitively appealing than the original one. The application of a transformation must, therefore, always be at the discretion of the individual user. This fact may seem disappointing if a completely algorithmic approach for quality improvement is expected. However, such an approach is impossible to achieve, as different quality criteria may be in conflict with each other. The best one can hope for is, therefore, a set of rules of thumb that can assist a systems developer in choosing between different design alternatives. The advantage of the approach presented in this paper is that it provides a systematic way of generating design alternatives and thereby makes a developer aware of these different alternatives and their impact on quality.

	Total in Union/ Surjective in Union Attributes	Partial/ Non-surjective Attributes	m-m Attributes	Attribubes with Fixed Ranges	Lexical Attributes	Lattice Structures	Non-unary Attributes
Explicitness				+		+	
Size	+	+	+	+	+	+	
Rule uniformity	+	+	+		+		
Rule simplicity	+			+		+	
Query simplicity	-		-		-	+	+/-
Stability	+	+	+	+	+	+	+

An interesting observation is that most of the transformations increase the size of a schema. In addition all transformations increase the stability of schemas. The reason for this being that all transformations introduce new object types, which makes it easier to add future information to the schema. Finally most of the transformations which affect query simplicity affect it negatively. The reason for this is also due to the increased size of the schema. Consequently some queries become more complex because their derivations cover a larger network of objects.

We are currently constructing a tool for managing schema transformations as part of a larger tool for schema integration, [Hakkarainen95]. This tool provides extensive user interaction and allows users to roll back previous transformations. These features are needed in order to satisfy the requirement that a user must decide which transformations to apply - this cannot be decided automatically.

The schema transformations proposed in this paper are not meant to be exhaustive, and a direction for future work is to identify additional transformations. A promising approach here seems to be to investigate transformations that create schemas satisfying dynamic constraints. For example, one could require that destructive updates be forbidden in the transformed schema, which would amount to creating a temporal deductive schema based on an operational schema, [Olivé89].

References

[Batini88]   C. Batini and G. D. Battista, "A Methodology for Conceptual Docu-
                mentation and Maintenance", *Information Systems*, vol. 13, no. 3, pp.
                297-318, 1988.

[Chen76]   P. P. Chen, "The Entity-Relationship Model - Toward a Unified View
                of Data", *ACM ToDS*, vol. 1, no. 1, pp. 9-36, 1976.

[Davis90]   A. Davis, *Software Requirements: Analysis and Specification*, Pren-
                tice Hall, 1990.

[Eick91]   C. Eick, "A Methodology for the Design and Transformation of Con-
                ceptual Schemas", in *17th Conference on VLDB*, pp. 25 - 34, 1991.

[ElMasri85]   R. ElMasri, J. Weeldryer and A. Hevner, "The Category Concept: An
                Extension to the Entity-Relationship Model", *Data and Knowledge
                Engineering*, vol. 1, no. 1, 1985.

[Fagin79]   R. Fagin, "Normal Forms and Relational Database Operators", in
                ACM SIGMOD, pp. 153-160, 1979.

[Hainaut91]   J.-L. Hainaut, "Entity Generating Schema Transformations", in *10th
                International Conference on Entity-Relationship Approach*, San
                Francisco, 1991.

[Hakkarainen95] S. Hakkarainen and M. Bergholtz, "VINCI - a Tool for Schema Inte-
                gration", Department of Computer and Systems Sciences, Stockholm
                University, 1995.

[Halpin90]   T. Halpin, "A Fact-oriented Approach to Schema Transformations",
                in *Mathematical Foundations of Database Systems,* Springer, 1990.

[Hull86]   R. Hull, "Relative Information Capacity of Simple Relational Data-
                base Schemata", *SIAM Journal of Computing*, vol. 15, no. 3, pp. 856-
                886, 1986.

[Johannesson94] P. Johannesson, "Schema Standardization as an Aid in View Integra-
                tion", *Information Systems*, vol. 19, no. 3, 1994.

[Kobayashi86]   I. Kobayashi, "Losslessness and Semantic Correctness of Database
                Schema Transformations", *Information Systems*, vol. 11, no. 1, 1986.

[Lindland94]   O. Lindland, G. Sindre, et al. "Understanding Quality in Conceptual
                Modeling." *IEEE Software*, March: pp. 29- 42, 1994.

[Miller94]   R. Miller, Y. Ioannidis and R. Ramakrishnan, "Schema Equivalence
                in Heterogeneous Systems: Bridging Theory and Practice", *Informa-
                tion Systems*, vol. 19, no. 1, 1994.

[Olivé89]   A. Olivé, "On the Design and Implementation of Information Sys-
                tems from Deductive Conceptual Models", in *VLDB89*, Amsterdam,
                1989.

[Sheth90]   A. P. Sheth and J. A. Larson, "Federated Database Systems for Man-
                aging Distributed, Heterogeneous, and Autonomous Databases",
                ACM Computing Surveys, vol. 22, no. 3, 1990.

[Troyer93]   O. D. Troyer, "On Data Schema Transformations", PhD, Katholieke
                Universiteit Brabant, 1993.

[Ullman88]   J. Ullman, *Principles of Database and Knowledge-base Systems*,
                Computer Press, 1988.

An Approach to Maintaining Optimized Relational Representations of Entity-Relationship Schemas[*]

Altigran S. da Silva[1] Alberto H. F. Laender[2] Marco A. Casanova[3]

[1] Departamento de Ciência da Computação
Universidade do Amazonas
69077-000 Manaus AM, Brasil
alti@dcc.fua.br
[2] Departamento de Ciência da Computação
Universidade Federal de Minas Gerais
31270-901 Belo Horizonte MG, Brasil
laender@dcc.ufmg.br
[3] LAHESC
IBM Brasil
22960-900 Rio de Janeiro RJ, Brasil
casanova@vnet.ibm.com

Abstract. This paper presents a redesign method for maintaining optimized relational representations of entity-relationship schemas. This method is based on the generation of a transient virtual database state that is used to construct the new database state and that can be obtained without modifying the current relational representation. It also provides means to collect additional data and to integrate them to the the current database state, as well as to check for new integrity constraints.

1 Introduction

The traditional process of designing a relational database usually starts with the definition of an entity-relationship schema (ER schema) from requirements of the real world and proceeds by mapping this schema into a relational representation which will be implemented by a relational DBMS. This process has been extensively discussed in the literature over the past years and a number of design methodologies has been proposed to support it (see, for example, [1, 7, 11, 13]).

Now let us consider the following situation. Suppose that, due to changes in the real world and after the database has been created, the ER schema is modified. This implies that the corresponding relational representation must also be modified to accommodate such changes and that the current database state must be adapted to this new situation. This problem, called the *redesign problem*, is illustrated in Fig. 1 and is described in what follows.

---

[*] This work was partially funded by the Brazilian Ministry of Education agency CAPES and by the Brazilian National Research Council (CNPq) under grant 300959/85-0.

Let S_E be an ER schema. In the logical design phase, this schema is mapped (1) into a relational representation S_R. The database is then populated (2) to create a consistent database state σ. Suppose now that, according to changes in the real world, the ER schema S_E is modified generating (3) a new ER schema S'_E. The redesign process consists in modifying S_R to generate (4) a new relational representation S'_R and in mapping (5) σ to a new database state σ' that must be consistent with S'_R (7).

In [3, 4], a *redesign method* was proposed to address this problem. The method accepts as input (1) a list of redesign commands, specifying changes to the original ER schema, (2) the relational representation of the original ER schema, and (3) the current database state, and produces as output a *redesign plan*, which consists of commands written in a relational DDL/DML, to restructure the original database accordingly.

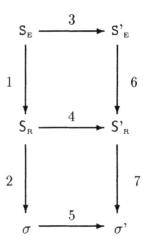

Fig. 1. Redesign process

In this paper, we review this redesign method and present a new approach to restructuring the database [12]. This new approach, which addresses some open problems left in [3, 4], is based on the generation of a transient virtual database state that is used to construct the new database state and that can be obtained without modifying the current relational representation. It also provides means to collect additional data and to integrate them to the the current database state, as well as to check if all the new integrity constraints are satisfied.

In the context of this paper, database redesign can be seen as the problem of how to reflect in the relational representation evolutions occurred in the conceptual schema. Conceptual schema evolution has been the subject of many works in the literature (see, for example, [5, 8]), but these works have focused on how to specify the evolution requirements rather than on how to reflect the changes on the database. Proposals for maintaining the logical representation of a database and to adapt the corresponding database state accordingly have also been presented in [9] and [10], but their approaches differ substantially from ours since the former is based on a diagrammatic notation used to specify schema derivations and to support the construction of views for the schema versions whereas the later uses a calculus-oriented ER notation to express database state mappings.

The rest of the paper is organized as follows. Section 2 presents some basic concepts and the terminology used throughout the paper. Section 3 presents an overview of the redesign method. Section 4 discusses the generation of the new ER schema. Section 5 addresses the generation of the new relational representation. Section 6 describes the aspects related to the generation of the new database state. Section 7 discusses the generation of the redesign plan. Finally, Section 8 discusses our main results and presents some conclusions.

2 Basic Definitions

2.1 Entity-Relationship Schemas

In this work, we use the concepts of ER schema, entity schemes, relationship schemes and specialization. We also use the standard integrity constraints usually associated with the notion of relationship and specialization [6, 7, 12].

An *entity scheme* has a name, a set of attributes with their respective domains and, optionally, a primary key. An instance of an entity scheme E is called an E-instance. A key is a subset of the entity scheme attributes whose values uniquely identify the E-instances in a set. At least one of the attributes of the entity scheme must be a *discriminating attribute* [12], an attribute whose value is never null. We use this feature to indicate the existence of an entity (instance). The primary key attributes are always discriminating attributes.

An entity scheme may be *specialized* into one or more entity schemes and may also *specialize* one or more entity schemes. We assume that if an entity scheme E specializes an entity scheme F, then every E-instance is also an F-instance. We also say that F is a generic of E.

If a given entity scheme does not specialize any other scheme, the definition of a primary key for this scheme is mandatory. We say that an entity scheme *inherits* the attributes and keys of its generics and we distinguish these attributes and keys, called *inherited* attributes and keys, from those defined in the scheme itself, called *native* attributes and keys. Also, we can define alternate keys to an entity scheme.

A *relationship scheme* has a name and may optionally have an attribute list. The instances of a relationship scheme R, also called R-instances, are elements from the Cartesian product of the set of instances of the entity schemes that are participants of R. To each participant is given a *role* that must be unique in each relationship scheme.

Let $\{E_1, \ldots, E_n\}$ be a subset of participants of R with roles $N_1, \ldots, N_n$, respectively. The set $\{N_1, \ldots, N_n\}$ is called an identifier of R if every combination of instances of $E_1, \ldots, E_n$ is unique in the set of R-instances. If $n = 1$ we say that R is *functional* on E_1. We also say that R is *total* on an entity scheme E with role N if every E-instance participates with role N in at least one R-instance.

Entity schemes and relationship schemes are also called *ER-object (ERO)* schemes in this paper.

An *ER schema* is a pair $S_E = \langle \mathcal{E}, \mathcal{R} \rangle$, where $\mathcal{E}$ is a set of entity schemes and $\mathcal{R}$ is a set of relationship schemes. A state σ_E of an ER schema S_E assigns to each ER-object O in S_E a set of O-instances. The state is *consistent* if all associated semantic constraints are satisfied by the instances of its entity and relationship schemes. A more precise definition may be found in [12]. We assume in this paper that every attribute has a unique name in an ER schema. This assumption is not actually needed, as explained in [12], but it will be used here to simplify the examples.

Fig. 2 shows the definition of the ER schema Company 1 which will be used as our running example in this paper. Since the schemas that we will present here are quite simple, we will omit the description of the syntax used to define them.

- define entity E (Employee)
  attributes Id   char(4) not null,
         Salary decimal(8,2)
  key   Id
- define entity S (Stock-Holder)
  attributes Code   char(4) not null,
         Stocks integer
  key   Code
- define entity P (Project)
  attributes Name   char(20) not null,
         Contractor char(20)
  key   Name

- define entity R (Researcher)
  attributes Degree char(4) not null
  specialization of E
- define entity A (Administrative)
  attributes Job_Desc char(40) not null
  specialization of E
- define entity M (Manager)
  attributes Title char(40) not null
  specialization of S, A
- define relationship W (Work) over R,P
  attributes Hours integer not null,
  identifier R

Fig. 2. ER schema Company 1

A graph $g = (V, A, l)$ of an ER schema S_E (or simply an *ER graph*) is a directed multi-graph, partially labeled by l, where every vertex in V corresponds to an ERO scheme of S_E and an arc $(S, T) \in A$ iff S specializes T or T participates in S with role N, being $l((S, T)) = N$. We say that (S, T) is a *total arc* if S is total on T. Fig. 3(a) shows the ER graph for the ER schema Company 1.

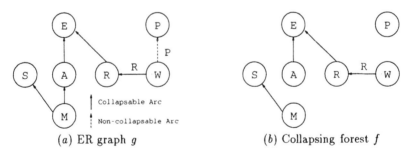

(a) ER graph g (b) Collapsing forest f

Fig. 3. ER graph and collapsing forest of the ER schema Company 1

2.2 Relational Schemas

A *relational schema* is a triple $S_R = \langle T, V, C \rangle$, where T is a set of relation schemes, V is a set of view schemes and C is a set of integrity constraints. A state σ for S_R assigns to each relation scheme R in T a relation r in the usual way. To stress that r is associated with R, we sometimes use the notation $r(R)$ in what follows.

A *relation scheme* has a name, an attribute list (each attribute has a respective domain), a primary key and, optionally, one or more alternate keys. We can also specify that a certain attribute may not assume null values. A null value is represented here by the symbol λ. A *primary key* is a list of attributes that must not assume null values and an alternate key is any list of attributes. Any view scheme in $\mathcal{V}$ is defined over relation schemes in $\mathcal{T}$ or others view schemes in $\mathcal{V}$.

The integrity constraints in $\mathcal{C}$ may be of two types: inclusion dependencies [2] and null dependencies [12].

Let $\mathcal{T}$ be a set of relation schemes. An *inclusion dependency (IND)* is an expression of the form $T_1[X_1] \subseteq T_2[X_2]$ where, for $j = 1, 2$, T_j is a relation scheme in $\mathcal{T}$ and X_j is a sequence of distinct attribute names of T_j such that X_1 e X_2 have the same number of attributes and that the k-th attribute of X_1 and the k-th attribute of X_2 have the same domain. An inclusion dependency is satisfied by the relations $t_1(T_1)$ and $t_2(T_2)$ of the same state σ iff, for each tuple t of $t_1(T_1)$, there is a tuple u of $t_2(T_2)$ such that $t[X_1] = u[X_2]$. We also allow the definition of INDs over view schemes.

A *null dependency (NUD)* is an expression of the form

$$R : A_1, A_2, \ldots, A_n \rightsquigarrow B_1, B_2, \ldots, B_m,$$

where $A = \{A_1, A_2, \ldots, A_n\}$ and $B = \{B_1, B_2, \ldots, B_m\}$ are two subsets of the set of attributes of a relation scheme R in $\mathcal{T}$. A null dependency is satisfied by a relation $r(R)$ iff, for every tuple u of $r(R)$, if some attribute A_i is null, then all B_j must necessarily be null $(i = 1, \ldots, n, j = 1, \ldots, m)$. We say that there exists a null dependency from B to A. In the DDL of many relational DBMS, it is possible to specify that an attribute will never assume a null value. In the context of null dependencies, this can be expressed by the notation $A_k \rightsquigarrow \square$, for an specific attribute A_k.

A *mutual null dependency* is an expression of the form $R{:}[C_1, C_2, \ldots, C_n]$, where $C = \{C_1, C_2, \ldots, C_n\}$ is a subset of the set of attributes of a relation scheme R in $\mathcal{T}$. A mutual null dependency is satisfied by a relation $r(R)$ iff, for every tuple u of $r(R)$, if some attribute C_i is null, then all the attributes in C are also null. We say that there is a mutual null dependency among the attributes of C, that is, the value of all the attributes of C must be either null or not null in a tuple.

An example of an relational schema is presented in Fig. 4. The syntax used to define this schema is also quite simple and will not be described.

2.3 Optimized Relational Representations of ER Schemas

A relational schema S_R is a *relational representation* of an ER schema S_E if the definition of S_R is such that every consistent state σ_E of S_E may be represented by a consistent state σ_R of S_R, and every consistent state σ_R represents a consistent state of S_E [12].

A straightforward method to obtain a relational representation of an ER schema is to generate a relation scheme (with appropriate attributes) to represent each ERO scheme and to use INDs to capture the semantics of the arcs of the corresponding ER graph. Despite its simplicity, this method potentially produces a large number of INDs that are expensive to check for violation [3, 4].

- define relation E•
attributes	Id	char(4) not null,
	Salary	decimal(8,2),
	Job_Desc	char(40),
	Degree	char(4),
	Hours	integer,
	Name	char(20)
key	Id	

- define view E
attributes	Id	char(4) not null,
	Salary decimal(8,2)	
key	Id	
  as E•[Id,Salary]

- define view A
attributes	Id	char(4) not null,
	Job_Desc char(40) not null	
key	Id	
  as E•[Job_Desc ≠ λ][Job_Desc,Id]

- define view R
attributes	Id	char(4) not null,
	Degree char(4) not null	
key	Id	
  as E•[Degree ≠ λ][Degree,Id]

- define relation S•
attributes	Code	char(4) not null,
	Stocks	integer,
	Title	char(40),
	Id	char(4)
key	Code	
key	Id	

- define view S
attributes	Code	char(4) not null,
	Stocks	integer
key	Code	
  as S•[Code,Stocks]

- define view M
attributes	Code char(4) not null,
	Id char(4) not null,
	Title char(40) not null
key	Code
key	Id
  as S•[Title ≠ λ][Title,Code,Id]

- define relation P•
attributes	Name	integer not null,
	Contractor char(40)	
key	Name	

- define view P
attributes	Name	char(20) not null,
	Contractor char(40)	
key	Name	
  as P•[Name,Contractor]

- define view W
attributes	Id	char(4) not null,
	Name char(20) not null,
	Hours integer not null
key	Id
  as E•[Hours ≠ λ][Hours,Id,Name]

- INDs: M[Id] ⊆ A[Id], W[Name] ⊆ P[Name]
- NUDs: S•:[Title,Id], E•:[Hours,Name], E•:Degree ↝ Hours,Name

Fig. 4. Relational representation of the ER schema Company 1

To reduce the number of INDs of a relational representation, a fairly common heuristic is to collapse into an entity scheme E the relationship schemes that are functional on a role that E plays, as well as the entity schemes that specialize E, and to represent them as a single relation scheme. In this way, several INDs can be removed and some may be replaced by NUDs, which are cheaper to check. We call a relational representation obtained using this strategy an *optimized relational representation* [3, 4, 12].

An optimized relational representation is constructed based on a structure called a *collapsing forest* [3, 4]. A collapsing forest f of an ER schema S_E is a set of trees containing the same vertices as the ER graph of S_E, but in which only the *collapsible* arcs of g are present. An arc (S,T) in g is collapsible when it has no label or it is labeled with a label N and S is functional on its participant T with role N.

In an optimized relational representation, for each root R in the collapsing forest f, we generate a relation scheme R*, called a *collapsing scheme*, such that R* represents all the ERO schemes corresponding to the vertices in the tree whose root is R. The generation of this scheme may be seen as the result of a function $\mu(f, R)$. Additionally, we generate a view scheme for each vertex V of the collapsing forest f. Each of these view schemes is used to individually represent an ERO scheme in the forest and is defined over the collapsing scheme into which the ERO scheme has been collapsed. We call these view schemes *representation schemes*. The generation of a representation scheme of an ERO scheme V may be seen as the result of a function $\nu(f, V)$. With respect to the integrity constraints, for each arc (S,T) of g that is not in f, we generate an IND from the representation of T to the representation of S. If (S,T) is a total arc, we also generate an IND in the inverse direction. For each arc (S,T) that is both in f and g, we generate a NUD from the attributes of T to the attributes of S. If (S,T) is a total arc, we also generate a NUD in the inverse direction. An exception to the former rule occurs when T is a root in the collapsing forest. A NUD is additionally generated to define a mutual null dependency involving the discriminating attributes of every ERO scheme that does not correspond to a root in the collapsing forest.

The design method outlined above is discussed in [3, 4]. In [12] we prove that it generates correct relational representations of ER schemas.

The relational schema Company 1 (Fig. 4) is an optimized relational representation of the ER schema Company 1 (Fig. 2).

3   The Redesign Method

Let S'_E be an ER schema that is the result of modifying an ER schema S_E. If a relational schema S_R is a relational representation of S_E, we must modify S_R in such a way that it becomes a new relational schema S'_R which is a relational representation of S'_E.

In general, the collapsing forest f of S_E is not an adequate collapsing forest for S'_E and we have to generate a new collapsing forest f'. By comparing the differences between f and f' (the new roots, internal vertices, arcs, etc) and the differences between the schemes associated with the vertices in both forests, we can produce S'_R.

We must also consider that S_R is possibly populated with data, that is, its corresponding relations form a consistent database state σ. Therefore we must map σ into a new database state σ' consistent with S'_R. In some cases, this goal can only be achieved by introducing additional data to satisfy new constraints added to the new relational representation, although sometimes even the addition of new data does not make the mapping possible.

The redesign method we propose accepts as input a sequence of *redesign commands* that specify changes to the original ER schema S_E to produce a new ER schema S'_E. The aim of the method is to generate a sequence of commands in a relational DDL/DML that, when executed, will transform the original relational representation S_R into a new relational representation S'_R and will map the original database state σ into a new database state σ', which must be consistent with S'_R. The method also checks σ to determine whether or not this mapping is possible. We call this sequence of commands the *redesign plan*.

In our redesign method, we have three main tasks to perform: (1) **Generation of the new ER schema** – In this task, the redesign commands are applied to the original ER schema producing a new ER schema and generating the corresponding graph and collapsing forest; (2) **Generation of the new relational representation** – This task addresses the modification of the original relational representation based on the comparison of the original graph and collapsing forest with the new ones; (3) **Generation of the new database state** – This task maps the original database state into a new one, possibly collecting some additional data to satisfy new integrity constraints and checking whether or not the mapping is possible.

Our method executes task (1) directly and generates a redesign plan whose commands must be executed in order to perform tasks (2) e (3). In the next sections, we describe, with the help of an example based on the ER schema of Fig. 2, how these three tasks are performed according to our redesign method. A more detailed discussion can be found in [12] where the algorithms for generating the commands that compose a redesign plan are described.

4 Generation of the New ER Schema

Given an ER schema, its graph, and its collapsing forest, the method applies a number of redesign commands, issued by the database designer, to transform the original ER schema into a new one. The redesign commands must be such that, after applying all of them, the resulting ER schema is a correct one. For example, we cannot issue a command to remove an entity scheme E if we do not also issue another command to remove the participation of E in all relationship schemes where E is a participant. We also assume that the list of participants in a relationship scheme cannot be changed.

Consider the ER schema Company 1 in Fig. 2 and the list of redesign commands presented in Fig. 5. If we apply this list of commands to the ER schema Company 1, we generate a new ER schema Company 2, whose ER graph and collapsing forest are shown in Fig. 6. Fig. 7 shows the new definition of the ERO schemes affected by these commands.

Although in this paper we use a simple set of redesign commands, which are defined in [12], we realize that a more elaborated and powerful set of transformation commands is needed to offer more facilities to the database designer. We refer the reader to [5, 8] where this topic is more deeply discussed.

- **add** "S specialization of E"
- **remove** "M specialization of S"
- **remove** "identifier R from relationship W"
- **add** "total P on relationship W"
- **remove** "key {Name} from P"
- **add** "attribute Num integer not null to P"
- **add** "key {Num} to P"

Fig. 5. Redesign commands to transform the ER schema Company 1

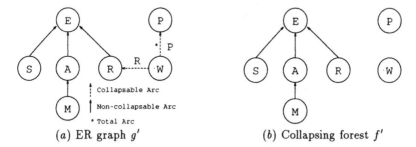

(a) ER graph g' (b) Collapsing forest f'

Fig. 6. ER graph and collapsing forest of the ER schema Company 2

5   Generation of the New Relational Representation

The transformation of the original relational representation into a new one is achieved by comparing the original and the new collapsing forests and the schemes of the corresponding vertices of both forests. Based on this comparison, the method issues commands that can be grouped into three types [12]: (1) **Expansion commands** – create collapsing schemes, representation schemes and new integrity constraints, and add new attributes and keys to relation schemes; (2) **Contraction commands** – remove collapsing schemes, representation schemes, integrity constraints, attributes and keys; (3) **Refreshing commands** – alter the representation schemes of ERO schemes when they are modified or their position in the collapsing forest is changed.

Fig. 8 presents expansion, contraction and refreshing commands (written in a informal syntax) that, if applied in this order to the relational schema of

- define entity S (Stock-Holder)
  attributes Code   char(4) not null,
             Stocks integer
  key   Code
  specialization of E

- define entity M (Manager)
  attributes Title char(40) not null
  specialization of A

- define entity P (Project)
  attributes Num   integer   not null,
             Name   char(20) not null,
             Contractor char(20)
  key   Num

- define relationship W (Work) over R, total P
  attributes Hours integer not null

Fig. 7. New definition of the ERO schemes affected by the redesign commands

Fig. 4, will generate the relational schema Company 2, shown in Fig. 9, which is the relational representation of the ER Schema Company 2. Note from Fig. 6(*b*) that, in our example, a new root W was created and that E now has S as a new child. Also note that the representation schemes of P and W now have new attributes. Thus, the commands shown in Fig. 8 reflect exactly these changes.

EX1. create W^* according to $\mu(f', W)$.
EX2. add Code,Stocks and Title to E^*
EX3. add an alternate key {Code} to E^*
EX4. create NUD E^*:Job_Desc $\leadsto$ Title
EX5. add Num to the primary key of P^*
EX6. create IND W[Num] $\subseteq$ P[Num]
EX7. create IND P[Num] $\subseteq$ W[Num]
EX8. create IND W[Id] $\subseteq$ $\bar{R}$[Id]

(*a*) Expansion commands

CT1. remove collapsing scheme S^*
CT2. remove IND W[Name] $\subseteq$ P[Name]
CT3. remove Hours,Name from E^*
CT4. remove Name from the primary key of P^*

(*b*) Contraction commands

RF1. rebuild S according to $\nu(f', S)$
RF2. rebuild M according to $\nu(f', M)$
RF3. rebuild W according to $\nu(f', W)$
RF4. rebuild P according to $\nu(f', P)$

(*c*) Refreshing commands

Fig. 8. Commands to transform the original relational representation

6 Generation of the New Database State

In this section, we describe how the method generates a database state σ', consistent with the new relational representation S'_R, from the original database state σ. This is performed by mapping σ into σ', that is, by adapting σ to S'_R. However, the new state will be consistent only if all integrity constraints in S'_R are satisfied by the parts of σ that remain in σ'. Thus, for any integrity constraint, we have three situations: (1) the integrity constraint is satisfied; (2) the integrity constraint is not satisfied; and (3) the integrity constraint cannot be checked because the values of the attributes to which it refers are not present in σ.

The third situation occurs, for example, when a new discriminating attribute is created in the new ER schema. To deal with this situation, the method provides means to: (1) collect additional data and integrate them to the database; and (2) verify if all integrity constraints in S'_R are satisfied in the *transient state*, i.e, the database state that corresponds to the data in σ integrated with new collected data. The additional data is collected through relations created by the method and that must be populated accordingly. This type of relation is called a Δ-*relation*. To integrate the new collected data to the database, the method

- define relation E*
  attributes Id   char(4) not null,
         Salary   decimal(8,2),
         Job_Desc char(40),
         Degree   char(4),
         Code   char(4),
         Stocks   integer,
         Title   char(40),
  key   Id
  key   Code

- define view E
  attributes Id   char(4) not null,
         Salary decimal(8,2)
  key   Id
  as E*[Id,Salary]

- define view A
  attributes Id   char(4) not null,
         Job_Desc char(40) not null
  key   Id
  as E*[Job_Desc $\neq \lambda$][Job_Desc,Id]

- define view R
  attributes Id   char(4) not null,
         Degree char(4) not null
  key   Id
  as E*[Degree $\neq \lambda$][Degree,Id]

- define view M
  attributes Id   char(4) not null,
         Title char(40) not null
  key   Id
  as E*[Title $\neq \lambda$][Title,Id]

- NUD: E*:Job_Desc $\rightsquigarrow$ Title
- INDs: W[Num] $\subseteq$ P[Num], P[Num] $\subseteq$ W[Num], W[Id] $\subseteq$ R[Id]

- define view S
  attributes Code char(4) not null,
         Stocks integer
         Id   char(4) not null
  key   Code
  key   Id
  as E*[Code $\neq \lambda$][Code,Stocks]

- define relation P*
  attributes Num   integer   not null,
         Name   char(4)   not null,
         Contractor char(40)
  key   Num

- define view P
  attributes Num   integer   not null,
         Name   char(20) not null,
         Contractor char(40)
  key   Num
  as P*[Name,Num,Contractor]

- define relation W*
  attributes Id   char(4), not null,
         Num   integer, not null,
         Hours   integer, not null
  key   Id,Num

- define view W
  attributes Id   char(4) not null,
         Num   integer not null,
         Hours   integer not null
  key   Id,Num
  as W*[Id,Num,Hours]

Fig. 9. Relational representation of the ER schema Company 2

creates a set of view schemes, called *transient representation schemes*, which will be used to generate the new database state σ'.

Note that some integrity constraints may not be satisfied by the new state. For example, let A be an entity scheme that participates in a relationship scheme B, and suppose that in the state σ we have an A-instance participating in more than one B-instance. If, in the new ER schema S'$_E$, A is functional on B, we have no means of adapting this state to S'$_E$ without loss of information, since only one of these B-instances would be allowed to exist in the new database state. In this case, we say that σ is not adequate to S'$_E$; otherwise, we say that σ is adequate to S'$_E$.

We divide the operations to generate the new database state into two groups: (1) operations to determine whether the original database state is adequate to the new ER schema; and (2) operations to map the original database state (possibly integrated with additional data) into a new state. The method adds these operations to the redesign plan by examining the current database state and the new constraints added to correctly represent the new ER schema.

Although some integrity constraints can be verified before data collection, in our method all the new constraints are checked after new data is collected and integrated to compose the transient state.

6.1 Adjusting the Original Database State to the New ER Schema

We will now illustrate how the redesign method proceeds to adjust the original database state, i.e., to adjust the current state of the original relational representation to the the new ER schema. Our aim is to show how additional data are collected and integrated to the current database state and how the transient state is used to check if all the new integrity constraints are satisfied.

Collecting and Integrating Additional Data. In our redesign method, data collection is performed basically to satisfy new integrity constraints. Thus, we have only to determine values for the discriminating attributes because all integrity constraints considered, i.e., key constraints, INDs and NUDs, are defined on such attributes.

Consider the transformation of the relational representation of the ER schema **Company 1** into the relational representation of ER the schema **Company 2**. We notice that new discriminating attributes have been introduced to the representations of S, P and W, as we can see by comparing Fig. 4 and Fig. 9.

The attribute **Num** is a new native discriminating attribute of P, so it must have a not null value for all P-instances. To deal with this situation, the method creates the relation P_Num(Name, Num), which is a Δ-relation that must be populated to associate a value of Num with each P-instance identified by the value of the attribute Name, the original key of P. Fig. 10(*b*) shows a possible instance for this relation. To associate the defined values for this new native discriminating attribute with the values of pre-existing attributes, the method generates the view $\overrightarrow{P}$, shown in Fig. 10(*c*), which is obtained by joining P_Num and the current instance of the original representation scheme P of P, shown in Fig. 10(*a*).

P	Name	Contractor
1	X	Comp.A
2	Y	λ
3	Z	Comp.C

(*a*)

P_Num	Name	Num
1	X	1
2	Y	2
3	Z	3

(*b*)

$\overrightarrow{P}$	Num	Contractor	Name
1	1	Comp.A	X
2	2	λ	Y
3	3	Comp.C	Z

(*c*)

Fig. 10. Collecting data for P

To determine the values of Num for W-instances, we must verify the values of Num in the corresponding P-instances. This is necessary because we have a previous association of P-instances and W-instances in the original ER schema. These values are determined by the relational algebra expression (W[Id, Name] $\bowtie$ $\overrightarrow{P}$)[Id, Num]. If we consider the relation W shown in Fig. 11(a) as the current state of the representation scheme of W, the result of this expression is the relation WxP, shown in Fig. 11(b).

W	Id	Name	Hours
1	E4	X	10
2	E6	Y	20
3	E5	Z	15

(a)

WxP	Id	Num
1	E4	1
2	E6	2
3	E5	3

(b)

S_Id	Code	Id
1	S2	E1
2	S5	E6

(c)

SxE	Id	Code
1	E3	S1
2	E1	S2
3	E4	S3
4	E5	S4
5	E6	S5

(d)

Fig. 11. Collecting data for W and S

In the representation of S, the new attribute Id is introduced to associate S-instances with E-instances, since S is now a specialization of E. Looking at the ER graph g in Fig. 3(a), we can see that some S-instances may be already associated with E-instances, because S and E have the entity scheme M as a common descendent. Based on this, the method generates the relational algebra expression S*[Title $\neq$ λ][Code, Id] to determine the values of Id that are already associated with some S-instance. In the relation that results from this expression, each tuple represents, by the value of the key Code of S, an S-instance. Note that, for S-instances that are not represented in this relation, the corresponding values of the attribute Id must be collected. For this purpose, the method creates a Δ-relation S_Id(Code, Id). A possible instance of this relation is shown in Fig. 11(c). Note that there will be an IND to be checked afterwards and that guarantees that this relation instance is correct. The method also generates the relational algebra expression S*[Title $\neq$ λ][Code, Id] $\cup$ S_Id, whose resulting relation SxE is shown in Fig. 11(d). This relation integrates the collected values of Id to those in the current database state σ. We assume that tuples 1, 3 and 4 show the pre-existing associations between S-instances and E-instances.

The sequence of commands generated by the method for performing this task is shown in Fig. 12. Note that commands VL2 and VL3 create INDs that guarantee that a value must be supplied for the attribute Num for every P-instance.

This simple example illustrates the basic aspects of the data collection strategy of our redesign method. A more detailed discussion of this topic can be found in [12].

Checking the New Integrity Constraints. Before we discuss how the new integrity constraints are checked, we introduce the concept of a *transient representation scheme*. A transient representation scheme of an ERO scheme O is a view scheme $\tilde{O}$ defined over its original representation scheme O and whose tuples correspond

VL1. create relation P_Num(Name,Num), key Name
VL2. add IND P_Num[Name] ⊆ P[Name]
VL3. add IND P[Name] ⊆ P_Num[Name]
VL4. include tuples in P_Num
VL5. create relation S_Id(Code,Id), key Code;
VL6. include tuples in S_Id

Fig. 12. Commands to collect data

to the O-instances that will compose the new database state according to its new representation scheme [12]. If new discriminating attributes have been added to O, the defining expression of $\widetilde{O}$ will involve the Δ-relations and additional relations (such as WxP and SxE shown in Fig. 11) generated to associate existing instances in the current database state. Otherwise, the defining expression of $\widetilde{O}$ will be a trivial relational expression on the original representation scheme O of O. Note that the tuples of $\widetilde{O}$ include at least the values of the discriminating attributes in the new relational representation and that such values are associated with the key of O in the original representation.

Fig. 13(a) shows the definition of the transient representation schemes for S, P and W ($\widetilde{S}$, $\widetilde{P}$ and $\widetilde{W}$, respectively). The corresponding views generated according to the relations and views previously presented are shown in Fig. 13(b).

define view $\widetilde{S}$
attributes Code   char(4),
          Stocks integer,
          Id   char(4)
as S[Code, Stocks] ⋈ SxE

$\widetilde{S}$	Code	Stocks	Id
1	S1	10000	E3
2	S2	5000	E1
3	S3	7000	E4
4	S4	8000	E5
5	S5	-	E6

define view $\widetilde{P}$
attributes Name   char(20),
          Contractor char(40),
          Num   integer
as P[Name, Contractor] ⋈ $\overrightarrow{P}$

$\widetilde{P}$	Name	Contractor	Num
1	X	Comp.A	1
2	Y	Comp.B	2
3	Z	Comp.C	3

define view $\widetilde{W}$
attributes Id   char(4),
          Hours integer,
          Num   integer
as W[Id, Hours] ⋈ WxP

$\widetilde{W}$	Id	Num	Hours
1	E4	1	10
2	E6	2	20
3	E5	3	15

(a)   (b)

Fig. 13. Transient representation schemes $\widetilde{S}$, $\widetilde{P}$ and $\widetilde{W}$

The transient representation schemes aim at: (1) integrating the additional data with the pre-existing data; (2) facilitating the checking of new integrity constraints; and (3) facilitating the generation of the new database state. Aim (1) is obviously fulfilled. Aims (2) and (3) will be discussed in what follows.

We call attention to the fact that a transient state can be viewed as a set of instances of transient representation schemes and that this state is in fact the initial state of the new relational representation. Note that this state can be obtained without modifying the original relational representation, that is, we can "virtually" generate the new relational representation and the new database state.

In order to discuss how the new integrity constraints are checked, let us consider that the new integrity constraints added to the new relational representation in our example are the following: (1) Keys {Id} of S, {Num} of P, and {Id,Num} of W; and (2) INDs S[Id] $\subseteq$ E[Id], P[Num] $\subseteq$ W[Num] and W[Num] $\subseteq$ P[Num].

As we said, the transient state will be used as the initial state of the new relational representation. These integrity constraints will be satisfied by this initial state iff they are satisfied by the transient state. Thus, we must check the following situations in the transient state: (1) if {Id}, {Num}, and {Id,Num} have unique values for the tuples of $\widetilde{S}$, $\widetilde{P}$ and $\widetilde{W}$, respectively; and (2) if the INDs $\widetilde{S}$[Id] $\subseteq$ $\widetilde{E}$[Id], $\widetilde{P}$[Num] $\subseteq$ $\widetilde{W}$[Num], and $\widetilde{W}$[Num] $\subseteq$ $\widetilde{P}$[Num] are satisfied.

If all new integrity constraints are satisfied in the transient state, we say that the current state of the original relational representation is *adequate* to the new ER schema. This means that we can generate a transient state, consistent with the relational representation of the new ER schema, from the current state of the original relational representation. Note that these two states co-exist in the database. Thus, we only have to check if the new integrity constraints are satisfied by the transient state, since all pre-existing integrity constraints are already satisfied and the current database state is considered consistent. The redesign method issues the commands to check these new integrity constraints.

6.2 Mapping the Transient Database State into the New State

Once the transient state is ready and checked, we must "materialize" it in order to generate the new database state. This is carried out by assigning values to the new relation attributes, i.e, by correctly filling the new attributes created by the expansion operations.

When an ERO scheme O is collapsed into a new collapsing scheme R* in the new relational representation, the O-instances (if there is any) must be "moved" to the tuples of the relation R*. This situation can be detected by examining the new and the original collapsing forests. Note that we guarantee that the state of a new relational representation is valid by taking the O-instances from the view defined by $\widetilde{O}$, the transient representation scheme of O. If, instead, O remains collapsed in the same collapsing scheme, we must check if new attributes have been included in its representation and also get the values of these attributes from $\widetilde{O}$.

In our example, the entity scheme S is a new child of E in the collapsing forest f'. This caused the expansion of E* with the attributes that represent S-instances. Also, we created a new root W, as well as a new collapsing scheme

W$^\bullet$, and expanded P$^\bullet$ with the new attribute of P. Fig. 14 shows the command sequence that must be executed to assign correct values to the new attributes.

ME1. update E$^\bullet$ set Code=λ, Stocks=λ
ME2. update E$^\bullet$ set Code=$\tilde{S}$[Code], Stocks=$\tilde{S}$[Stocks] where E$^\bullet$[Id] = $\tilde{S}$[Id]
ME3. update P$^\bullet$ set Num=λ
ME4. update P$^\bullet$ set Num=P[Num] where P$^\bullet$[Name] = $\tilde{P}$[Name]
ME5. insert W$^\bullet$(Id, Num, Hours) from $\tilde{W}$[Id, Num, Hours]

Fig. 14. Commands to assign values to new attributes

7 Generation of the Redesign Plan

To correctly generate the new relational representation and the new database state, we must execute the commands required to restructure the database in such an order that each operation is successfully executed. For example, we cannot execute a command to assign values to a new attribute of a relation before expanding its scheme accordingly. Moreover, these values must be firstly collected before this operation can be executed. This requirement is trivially satisfied if we generate the commands in the following order: (1) commands to collect new data needed for the new database state; (2) commands to generate the transient representation views; (3) commands to verify if the transient state is adequate to the new ER schema; (4) commands to expand the current relational representation (expansion commands); (5) commands to map the transient state into the new database state; (6) commands to alter the current representation schemes (refreshing commands); (7) commands to contract the current relational representation (contraction commands).

Thus, any sequence of commands in this order is a possible redesign plan. Note that a plan generated in this way is not necessarily optimal with respect to execution time, number of operations or additional space required, what means that some optimization strategy may be applied to it in order to improve its execution.

8 Conclusions

In this paper, we reviewed the database redesign method proposed in [3, 4] and presented a new approach to maintaining optimized relational representations of ER schemas which addresses some open problems left in those papers. This new approach is based on the generation of a transient virtual database state that is used to construct the new database state and that can be obtained without modifying the current relational representation. This allows the database designer to assess the impact of the conceptual changes without actually restructuring the database.

At the moment, we are implementing this redesign method as part of a database design/redesign tool for a specific commercial relational database management system. This tool generates the redesign plan entirely in terms of commands of the DDL/DML of the target system.

As a future work, we intend to extend the set of redesign commands proposed in [12] in order to offer more facilities to the database designer. We also intend to address the problem of optimizing the generation of the redesign plan. A possible strategy to address this problem may be to adapt the approach proposed in [5], which considers the problem at the conceptual schema level, to the relational representation level.

References

1. Batini, C., Ceri, S. and Navathe, S. *Conceptual Database Design: An Entity-Relationship Approach*, Benjamin Cummings (1992).
2. Casanova, M.A., Tucherman, L., Furtado, A.L. and Pacheco, A. "Optimization of relational schemas containing inclusion dependencies". *Proc. 15th Int. Conf. on Very Large Data Bases*, Amsterdam, Holland (1989).
3. Casanova, M.A., Tucherman, L. and Laender, A.H.F. "Algorithms for designing and maintaining optimized relational representations of entity-relationship schemas", in Kangassalo, H. (ed.), *Entity-Relationship Approach: The Core of Conceptual Modelling*, North-Holland (1991).
4. Casanova, M.A., Tucherman, L. and Laender, A.H.F, "On the design and maintenance of optimized relational representations of entity-relationship schemas", *Data and Knowledge Engineering 11*,1 (1993).
5. Castilho, J.M. "A State-Space Approach for Database Redesign", in Elmasri, R.A., Kouramajian, V. and Thalheim, B. (eds.), *Entity-Relationship Approach - ER'93*, Springer-Verlag (1994).
6. Chen, P.P., "The entity-relationship model: toward a unified view of data", *ACM TODS 1*, 1 (1976).
7. Elmasri, R. and Navathe, S. *Fundamentals of Database Systems*, 2nd ed. Benjamin Cummings (1994).
8. Hainaut, J-L., Tonneau C., Joris M. and Chandelon M. "Schema Transformation Techniques for Database Reverse Engineering", in Elmasri, R.A., Kouramajian, V. and Thalheim, B. (eds.), *Entity-Relationship Approach - ER'93*, Springer-Verlag (1994).
9. Liu, C.T., Chang, S.K. and Chrysanthis, P.K. "Database Schema Evolution using EVER Diagrams", *Proc. of the Workshop on Advanced Visual Interfaces*, Bari, Italy (June 1994).
10. Markowitz, V.M. and Makowsky, J.A. "Incremental Reorganization of Relational Databases", *Proc. 13th Int. Conf. on Very Large Data Bases*, Brighton, England (Sept. 1987).
11. Markowitz, V.M. and Shoshani, A. "Representing extended entity-relationship structures in relational databases: a modular approach", *ACM TODS 17*, 3 (Sept. 1992).
12. Silva, A.S. *A Contribution to the Problem of Maintaining Optimized Relational Representations of Entity-Relationship Schemas*, MSc Dissertation, Department of Computer Science, UFMG (1995). (in Portuguese)
13. Teorey, T.J., Yang, D. and Fry, J.P. "A logical design methodology for relational databases using the extended entity-relationship model", *ACM Computing Survey 18*, 2 (June 1986).

Transforming Conceptual Models to Object-Oriented Database Designs: Practicalities, Properties, and Peculiarities

Wai Yin Mok and David W. Embley

Brigham Young University, Provo, Utah, USA
email: {wmok, embley}@cs.byu.edu

Abstract. More work is needed on devising practical, but theoretically well-founded procedures for doing object-oriented database (OODB) design. Besides being practical and having formal properties, these design procedures should also be flexible enough to allow for peculiarities that make applications unique. In this paper, we present and discuss an OODB design procedure that addresses these problems. The procedure we discuss is practical in the sense that it is based on a common family of conceptual models and in the sense that it does not expect users to supply esoteric, difficult-to-discover, and hard-to-understand constraints (such as multivalued dependencies), nor does it make hard-to-check and easy-to-overlook assumptions (such as the universal relation assumption). At the same time, the procedure is well-founded and formal, being based on a new theoretical result that characterizes properties of interest in designing complex objects. It is also flexible and adaptable to the peculiarities of a wide variety of applications.

1. Introduction

Database design has had a long history. Object-oriented database design is more recent and "clearly needs more work" [11]. Over the long history of database design, many ad-hoc and empirical techniques have been used. There has also been a flurry of theoretical research that has provided us with some interesting insights, but has sometimes disappointed us in terms of practical realities. How can we bring together and extend the best of this work for use in designing object-oriented database systems?

Addressing this topic is an arduous task, and we do not pretend to have all of the answers. Nevertheless, we present here a point of view that builds on and extends past successes, is practical, has a formal foundation with provable properties of interest, and makes adjustments for several types of application peculiarities. In doing so, we do not provide a broad, superficial coverage of this vast area, but rather succinctly provide our contributions in the form of some specific model transformations and algorithms for scheme and method-signature generation, and in the form of several specific adjustments based on insights about application peculiarities and theoretical anomalies.

Succinctly stated, our procedure is as follows. We use as a foundation a particular type of conceptual model that is sufficiently rich for modeling applications of interest, but not so esoteric as to be unusable by analysts and designers with ordinary abilities.[†] Based on this conceptual model, we characterize and consider a restricted

---

[†]As anecdotal evidence on this usability point, we and others have successfully used the model we discuss here in hundreds of hours of work with employees of the Utah Division of Family Services for analyzing their Child Welfare System.

set of model instances, namely those from which we can derive a particular type of acyclic hypergraph and from which we can automatically extract the constraints we need.[†] Based on the hypergraph properties and on the extracted constraints, we present an algorithm to generate initial schemes with formal properties such as elimination of potential redundancy with respect to the constraints extracted. We then make adjustments for application characteristics such as large objects, update frequencies, and computations, and we generate a final set of schemes and method-signatures for OODB designs.

To bring this all together in a single paper, we build here on some earlier work we have done. The conceptual model we use is described elsewhere [6], as are the basic ideas we use for hypergraph generation and for design transformations [5]. We say enough here about the model, hypergraph generation, and design transformations to make the paper self contained, but we minimize this discussion to leave room for discussing the unique contributions of this paper. These include (1) a precise characterization of a restricted set of model instances from which we can generate designs, (2) a scheme generation algorithm that yields an initial set of schemes with some expected formal properties of interest for design, (3) a set of adjustments to tailor these initial designs for particular application characteristics, and (4) a way to do method placement for object-oriented designs.

Our contributions differ from those of others who have addressed these problems. The procedures presented in some recent books [2,9,16] show how to derive database designs from conceptual models. However, their models are different, as is the theoretical basis for their procedures, and their main focus is on standard database design rather than on OODB design.

We proceed with the development of our approach as follows. In Section 2, we present a running example and use it to illustrate our approach to conceptual modeling, hypergraph generation, and design transformations. We also define the particular type of hypergraph we need for our restricted set of model instances. In Section 3, we give our basic scheme-generation algorithm, show that it has the properties we expect. In Section 4, we augment our algorithm to take application characteristics into account. We summarize and conclude in Section 5.

2. Model Instances and Model-Instance Properties

The conceptual model we use is *OSA* — *Object-oriented Systems Analysis* [6]. Figure 1 shows the OSA model instance we use as a running example in this paper. The rectangles in the OSA diagram in Figure 1 are *object sets* and the labeled connections among object sets (with or without a diamond) are *relationship sets*. Dashed rectangles represent a set of *lexical* objects, whose representations are strings or specialized strings such as integers or percentages, or are images of various types. Solid rectangles represent a set of *non-lexical* objects, whose representations are object identifiers (OIDs). Role names, if given, are object sets representing the subset of objects participating in a relationship set. Numbers and number-pairs on relationship sets are *participation constraints*, which constrain the number of times an object in the connecting object set participates in a relationship set — 1 for exactly once, 1:* for one or

---

[†]We, and others [7], believe that most real-world applications satisfy these restrictions. When these restrictions do not hold, knowing what to do is application dependent, but resolvable based on time-space arguments. Lack of space prevents us from exploring these application-dependent, time-space arguments here.

more, and 0:* for zero or more. Constraints of the form $A_1, ..., A_n \rightarrow B_1, ..., B_m$ are *co-occurrence* constraints, which are (generalized) functional dependencies (FDs) that constrain the cardinality of objects co-occurring in tuples of objects in an *n*-ary relationship set. OSA also has a behavioral component that lets users specify both the individual behavior of objects and the interaction among objects, but this is not of concern to us here.

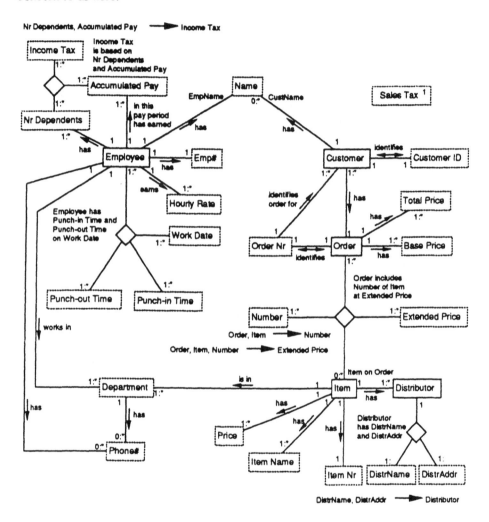

Figure 1. Sample OSA model instance.

OSA is similar to and can be classified as a member of the family of conceptual models commonly referred to as Object-Role Models (e.g., [9]). An important feature that distinguishes this family of models from the family of Entity-Relationship Models (e.g., [16]) is that there are only two types of basic sets — entity sets (or object sets as we call them in OSA) and relationship sets. This feature allows us to translate ORM model instances directly to hypergraphs, which are used so prevalently in relational theory. Basically, each object set is a node and each relationship set is an edge. Since we can convert all model instances from the ORM family to the type of hypergraph view of a model instance we present here, all the remaining results follow directly. Thus, with minor variations, what we say and illustrate here for OSA also holds for all members of the ORM family of models.

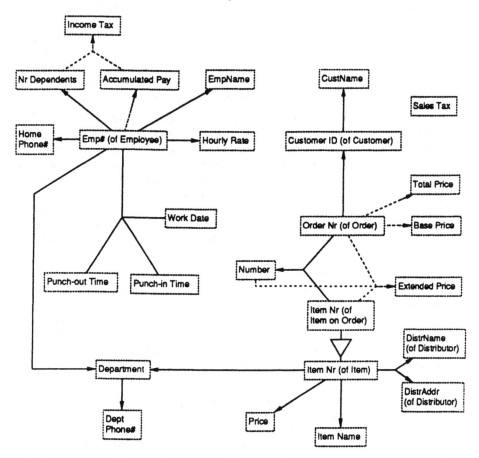

Figure 2. Design hypergraph for the OSA model instance in Figure 1.

For the OSA diagram in Figure 1, we can derive the hypergraph in Figure 2. Although relatively straightforward, the full details of the derivation are extensive. Moreover, we not only translate an OSA diagram to a hypergraph, but we also reduce the hypergraph through information-preserving and constraint-preserving transformations, for example, by removing redundant edges and edge components, consolidating connections, and converting n-ary edges to lower-degree edges. These transformations are similar to the transformations in [9]. We have reported the details of both converting an OSA diagram and reducing the resulting hypergraph in a previous ER conference [5]; here we only discuss the highlights of the translation of Figure 1 to Figure 2. To be specific in our discussion, we call the hypergraph we are deriving a *design hypergraph.*

A central idea in the initial creation of a design hypergraph is the extraction and representation of FDs. A 1 participation constraint yields an FD. For example, the 1 in the *Department has Phone#* relationship set in Figure 1 means that a department has only one phone. Thus, we have the FD *Department → Phone#*, which we can directly represent in a design hypergraph by a directed edge from *Department* to *Phone#*. When a relationship set has more than one 1 participation constraint, we obtain more than one FD. From the *Employee has Emp#* relationship set, for example, we obtain both *Employee → Emp#* and *Emp# → Employee*. Co-occurrence constraints directly represent FDs embedded in some *n*-ary edge of an OSA diagram. The *Order includes Number of Item at Extended Price* relationship set, for example, has two FDs: *Order, Item → Number* and *Order, Item, Number → Extended Price*. We put both of these directed edges in our design hypergraph.

One of the reduction transformations we can apply is called lexicalization, which lets us reduce a diagram by representing a non-lexical object set by a lexical object set with which the non-lexical object set has a one-to-one correspondence. We may for example represent employees by employee numbers. When we lexicalize in this way, we keep track of the original non-lexical object-set name in a parenthetical of-clause. Thus when we lexicalize the object set *Employee* by *Emp#*, we obtain *Emp# (of Employee)* as Figure 2 shows. In a variation of this lexicalization transformation, we have the pair *DistrName (of Distributor)* and *DistrAddr (of Distributor)* which, as a pair, are in a one-to-one correspondence with *Distributor*, and can thus replace the *Distributor* object set.

In another transformation, we can specifically introduce object sets for roles. Thus, for example, we have object-set rectangles for *EmpName* and *CustName*. Roles are specializations, which we denote by a triangle whose apex connects to a generalization and whose base connects to one or more specializations. In Figure 2, for example, *Item Nr (of Item on Order)* is a specialization of *Item Nr (of Item)*. If the union of the specialization object sets is equal to the generalization object set and there are no other connections to the generalization object set, we can discard the generalization. Thus *Name* does not appear as an object set in Figure 2.

As we transform an OSA diagram to a design hypergraph, we discard redundant edges and edge components. We base these reductions on classical reductions such as right reduce and left reduce as discussed in [12]. For example, since *Order Nr → Order* and *Order → Customer*, *Order Nr → Customer* is redundant. Like [13], however, we do not assume that the universal relation assumption holds [10,17]. Thus, when we find a potential reduction based on an implied FD, we must check its meaning before we make the reduction. For example, we see from Figure 1 that we have the derived FDs *Employee → Department* and *Department → Phone#*, which imply the FD *Employee → Phone#*. However, the *Employee has Phone#* relationship set is redundant only if it has the same meaning as the join and projection over the relationship sets *Employee works in Department* and *Department has Phone#* — in other words, if the employee's department phone number is the same as the employee's phone number. This may be true, but is not true if, as we assume here, the *Employee has Phone#* relationship set represents an employee's home phone number. The resolution in this case is not to remove the relationship set, which in fact is not redundant, but to add the roles, *Dept Phone#* and *Home Phone#*. Then, similar to the transformation for names, we add object-set rectangles for specializations and then, since we

314

realize that the union of the two phone-number object sets constitutes all the phone numbers of interest in the application, we discard the *Phone#* object set.

Design hypergraphs that are fully reduced by reduction transformations such as these are called *reduced design hypergraphs*. In particular, a design hypergraph is *reduced* if it is non-redundant, right reduced, left reduced, JD-edge reduced, lexicalized, and minimally consolidated. We have illustrated several of these reductions here. In [5] we describe all of them.

Not yet discussed are the dashed edges in the design hypergraph in Figure 2. These represent computations. Given value(s) from the tail-side object set(s), there exists a function that computes a value for the head-side object set. We can, for example and as we suppose here, compute an *Income Tax* value given an *Accumulated Pay* value and a *Nr Dependents* value. Sometimes, we need additional information obtainable from the tail-side objects by a query to do the derivation. We compute an *Accumulated Pay* value for an employee, for example, based on the employee's hourly rate and the information in the employee's punch-in/punch-out work record.

As we explained in the introduction, we are interested in a restricted set of model instances and hypergraphs. We call the type of design hypergraph we seek a *restricted reduced design (RRD) hypergraph*. An *RRD hypergraph* is a reduced design hypergraph, which, after discarding any generalization/specialization edges and removing any computed object sets from their respective edges, satisfies the following two conditions: (1) the hypergraph is γ-acyclic [8], and (2) every edge of the hypergraph is in BCNF [4].

The notion of γ-acyclic has been defined elsewhere [8], but we discuss its definition here for the sake of completeness. We first define what it means for two nodes in a hypergraph to be connected. A *path* from node s to node t is a sequence of $k \geq 1$ edges $E_1, ..., E_k$ such that (1) s is in E_1, (2) t is in E_k, and (3) $E_i \cap E_{i+1}$ is nonempty if $1 \leq i < k$. Two nodes are *connected* if there is a path from one to the other. Similarly, two edges are connected if there is a path from one to the other. A set of nodes or edges is connected if every pair is connected. A *connected component* is a maximal connected set of edges. Two edges E and F are *incomparable* if $E \not\subseteq F$ and $F \not\subseteq E$. A hypergraph is γ-*cyclic* if it has a pair (E, F) of incomparable, nondisjoint edges such that in the hypergraph that results by removing $E \cap F$ from every edge, what is left of E is connected to what is left of F. A hypergraph is γ-*acyclic* if and only if it is not γ-cyclic. By Theorem 14 in [3], γ-cyclicity can be checked in polynomial time.

The definition for BCNF is well known. A scheme R is in *BCNF* if for every nontrivial FD $X \to Y$ (given or implied) such that $XY \subseteq R$, $X \to R$. We adapt this to a restricted design hypergraph by letting directed edges be the FDs and by considering each edge to be a scheme whose attributes are the object-set names of the object sets in the edge.

3. A Scheme-Generation Algorithm

We base our fundamental scheme-generation algorithm on Nested Normal Form (NNF), which we have recently defined [14]. NNF precisely characterizes potential redundancy with respect to a given set of FDs and multivalued dependencies (MVDs) for nested relation schemes that are consistent with the given FDs and MVDs.[†] We do

---

[†] Note, by the way, that in Section 2 we said nothing directly about MVDs. Indeed, with our procedure, a designer need

not reproduce the definition of NNF here nor the lengthy set of preparatory definitions. Instead, since a consistent nested relation scheme S is in NNF if and only if S has no potential redundancy, we explain what NNF is by discussing redundancy in nested relations. Along the way, we also introduce the vocabulary necessary for giving our algorithm for producing NNF schemes from RRD hypergraphs.

We can graphically represent a nested relation scheme by a tree, called a *scheme tree*. If U is a given set of attributes and T is a scheme tree constructed from the attributes in U, then the nodes in T are nonempty subsets of U. We denote the set of attributes that appear in T by $Aset(T)$. We further stipulate that the nodes in T are pairwise disjoint and that their union is $Aset(T)$. In a scheme tree T, if N is a node in T, $Ancestor(N)$ notationally denotes the union of attributes in all ancestors of N, including N. Figure 3 shows a scheme tree T along with $Aset(T)$ and $Ancestor(C)$. Figure 4 shows a possible nested relation for T. For NNF, we require PNF (Partition Normal Form) [15], so that in a nested relation there can never be distinct tuples that agree on the atomic attributes of either the nested relation itself or of any nested relation embedded within it. The nested relation in Figure 4 is in PNF.

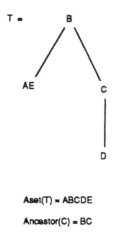

Aset(T) = ABCDE

Ancestor(C) = BC

Figure 3. Scheme tree, Aset, and Ancestor examples.

The scheme in Figure 4 (equivalently the scheme tree in Figure 3) may or may not be in NNF depending on the given set of FDs and MVDs. As examples, it is in NNF for $\{B \twoheadrightarrow AE,\ C \rightarrow B,\ C \twoheadrightarrow D\}$, but not for $\{B \twoheadrightarrow AE,\ D \rightarrow C\}$ nor for $\{B \twoheadrightarrow AE,\ C \twoheadrightarrow D\}$ [14]. Note that the nested relation in Figure 4 is not valid with respect to the first set of dependencies since it violates $C \rightarrow B$ (4 is associated with both 1 and 9). However, it is valid with respect to $\{B \twoheadrightarrow AE,\ D \rightarrow C\}$ or $\{B \twoheadrightarrow AE,\ C \twoheadrightarrow D\}$ and both of these two sets of dependencies cause it to have redundant data values. A data value in a nested relation r is redundant if it is uniquely

---

never specify MVDs! They are implied and can be automatically extracted from an RRD hypergraph [12]. We observe, however, that a designer does need to be able to individually consider an *n*-ary relationship set for $n > 2$ and determine whether it can be losslessly reduced to a lower-degree relationship set. This is what we mean by JD-edge reduced, as mentioned above and as described in [5].

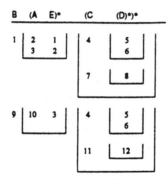

Figure 4. A sample nested relation.

determined by a constraint and the other data values in r. When the FD $D \rightarrow C$ holds for T, both 4's are individually redundant, for if either one were another value, $D \rightarrow C$ would not hold. Likewise, when the MVD $C \twoheadrightarrow D$ holds for T, both 5's and both 6's are individually redundant, for if any one were another value or were missing, $C \twoheadrightarrow D$ would not hold.

We are now ready to present our basic scheme-generation algorithm, which we give as Algorithm 1. In essence, the algorithm first creates a single-node scheme tree from a chosen edge in the given hypergraph. Since every edge is in BCNF, a single-node scheme tree created from an edge is in NNF vacuously. The algorithm continues to extend an existing scheme tree by adding other edges in the hypergraph as long as the scheme tree satisfies the conditions set forth. Intuitively, these conditions ensure that a scheme tree follows the natural hierarchical structure of the hypergraph — that is, we can continue adding as many one-one and one-many relationship edges as we wish, but we must stop as soon as we encounter many-one or many-many edges. Since each edge is included in only one tree, the algorithm runs in polynomial time with respect to the number of edges.

Theorem 1. Algorithm 1 generates NNF schemes.[†]

Theorem 2. For OSA model instances that correspond to RRD hypergraphs, the design process we have defined here is constraint-preserving and information-preserving.[†]

4. Application-Dependent Adjustments for Generated Schemes

In this section, we augment Algorithm 1 in several ways. The objective here is to show that we do not want to just blindly apply the algorithm for every application. There are application-dependent factors we need to consider as well. In the following subsections, we discuss some important additional factors that we should take into account when we generate nested relation schemes from a conceptual model.

[†] Proofs for these theorems are in a longer version of this paper available on the World Wide Web, URL: http://osm7.cs.byu.edu/HomePage.html.

Algorithm 1

input: An RRD hypergraph H. (Recall that this means that H is reduced, is γ-acyclic, has each edge in BCNF, has no generalization/specialization edge, and has no computed object set. The hypergraph in Figure 2 is an RRD hypergraph if we remove all computed edges — dashed edges — all the computed nodes — the object sets pointed to by dashed edges — and the generalization/specialization edge — the edge with a triangle.)

output: A set of scheme trees, each of which is in NNF with respect to the FDs and MVDs derived from H.

Repeat until all edges have been marked:

> Select an unmarked edge R in H and let the nodes in R be the set of nodes in the root of a new scheme tree T. Mark R as USED.
>
> While there is an unmarked edge R in H (i.e., not marked USED or DO_NOT_USE) such that $R \cap Aset(T) \neq \emptyset$, do:
>
>> If there is a node N in T such that $Ancestor(N) \subseteq R^+$ (the closure of R with respect to the FDs in the given RRD hypergraph) and $(R - Ancestor(N)) \cap Aset(T) = \emptyset$,
>>
>>> Extend T by adding a new node $N' = (R - Ancestor(N))$ as a child of N. If $Ancestor(N) \to A$ where $A \in N'$, move A up to N. If N' becomes empty, delete N' from T. Mark R as USED.
>>
>> Else T cannot be extended without violating NNF. Thus:
>>
>>> Mark R as DO_NOT_USE so that in this time through the while-loop, R will not be considered again.
>
> For each edge R that is marked DO_NOT_USE, unmark R.

For each object set S that is not involved in any edge in H, create a single-node scheme tree whose only node is S.

4.1. Chosen Roots

Algorithm 1 leaves an important question unanswered, namely, "What are the best roots for the nested relation schemes?" Since, in general, this depends on the semantics of the application, we cannot provide an answer in advance. However, we can provide some guidelines.

One of the purposes of having complex objects in OODBs is to have hierarchies of subobjects attached to these complex objects. Therefore, if we know which objects are important in the application, these object sets should be the roots of the nested relation schemes.

Sometimes, however, we may not know which objects are the most important, or after having generated a few trees, we may not know what is most important from what is left. In this case, we should probably choose roots that will give large scheme trees since normally we want to cluster as much data together as we can. Algorithm 2 explains how to choose roots so that Algorithm 1 will yield large scheme trees.

Algorithm 2

input: The same input as Algorithm 1.

output: A set of large NNF nested relation schemes.

(1)   For each edge E in the RRD hypergraph H, find the closure E^+ of E with respect to the FDs in H.

(2)   List the edges in H in the order $E_1, ..., E_n$ where if E_i^+ is a proper subset of E_j^+, then $i < j$. (Note that there may be more than one ordering of edges. In this case, we arbitrarily choose one possible ordering.)

(3)   Select the first edge in the list as the edge to start running Algorithm 1. As each edge E in H is marked USED in Algorithm 1, remove E from the list. For the next root, repeat this step by choosing the first edge left on the list, and so forth until the list is empty.

As an example, consider the RRD hypergraph in Figure 2, (i.e., hypergraph in Figure 2 after removing all computed edges, the computed nodes, and the generalization/specialization edge). Running Algorithm 2 yields the edge *Department has Dept Phone#*. When we then run Algorithm 1 starting with this edge, we obtain the scheme tree in Figure 5a. After eliminating all edges marked by Algorithm 1, we again run Algorithm 2, and this time we obtain the edge *Customer ID (of Customer) has Cust-Name*. When we then run Algorithm 1 starting with this edge, we obtain the scheme tree in Figure 5b. At this point, only the lone object set *Sales Tax* remains. Thus this object set becomes a scheme by itself as Figure 5c shows.

4.2. Flexibility in Edge Configurations

Algorithm 1 is more tightly specified than it needs to be. In particular, the initial root need not be an entire edge. We can create a single-branch scheme tree T from the chosen edge so long as for every node N in T, if $Ancestor(N) \to Y$ holds for T with respect to the given MVDs and FDs, $Y \subseteq Ancestor(N)$. The reminder of the algorithm is the same, and we can still guarantee NNF. This gives us some additional flexibility, which we can use to adapt Algorithm 1 to specific applications.

As an example, consider the RRD hypergraph in Figure 6. The FDs and MVDs implied by this hypergraph are equivalent to $\{B \twoheadrightarrow AE, C \to B, C \twoheadrightarrow D\}$. We stated above that the scheme tree in Figure 3 is in NNF with respect to $\{B \twoheadrightarrow AE, C \to B, C \twoheadrightarrow D\}$. Using the current form of Algorithm 1, however, we cannot generate the scheme tree in Figure 3 because we cannot have a single node in the root. Observe also, that if we make ABE the root, then we cannot attach D, and if we make BC the root, we cannot attach either A or E. With our new modification here, however, we can derive the NNF scheme tree in Figure 3. Suppose we initially select the edge BC. Now, since $B^+ = B$ and $C^+ = BC$, if we create a single-branch scheme tree with B as the root and C as the child, then when $Ancestor(N) \to Y$ holds for T with

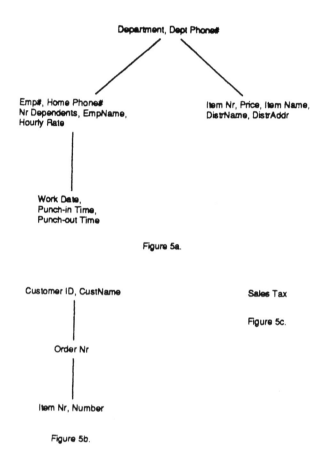

Figure 5a.

Figure 5b.

Figure 5c.

Figure 5. Generated scheme trees.

respect to the given MVDs and FDs, $Y \subseteq Ancestor(N)$. Note, however, that we could not have C as the root and B as the child because then we would have $Ancestor(C) = C, C \rightarrow B$, but $B \not\subseteq C$. We can now complete Algorithm 1 as written to obtain the scheme tree in Figure 3.

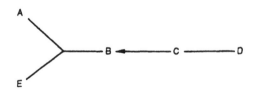

Figure 6. Design hypergraph for the scheme tree in Figure 3.

This idea of a single-branch scheme tree applies to subtrees as well as to the root. We can thus further modify the algorithm and gain even more flexibility. For example, in the scheme tree in Figure 3, we can either place A below E or E below A and still satisfy NNF.

Two heuristics guide the development of edge configurations within a scheme tree. (1) We should generally place attributes as high as possible in a scheme tree, and (2) we should generally include as many attributes as possible in a scheme tree. Unfortunately, these two guidelines conflict with one another. For our example here, if we attempt to place attributes as high as possible by choosing ABE as the root, there can be no child node, and thus we have not included as many attributes as possible in the scheme tree. Choosing either BC or CD as the root also does not work because either one prevents us from including both A and E as attributes in the scheme tree. We leave a resolution of this problem of finding best edge configurations and the potential problems of NP-completeness it may involve to future research.

4.3. Large Objects

Suppose our sample application in Figure 1 has pictures for items (images that can be displayed on-line). Each item is in some picture and many items can be in the same picture. Thus, we would have a new object set *Picture* and a new FD *Item* $\rightarrow$ *Picture* in the generated design hypergraph in Figure 2.

Now, when we run Algorithm 2 as we did before, *Picture* would be placed into the node that contains *Item Nr* in the scheme tree in Figure 5a. There is no NNF violation. However, the large size creates two problems that we can ignore for small atomic objects such as a name or a dollar amount, but should not ignore for large objects such as images. (1) Since many items may share the same picture, it would be unwise to replicate the picture many times for different items, and (2) the natural clustering would likely be lost because of interspersing large images among small objects. To solve these problems, we should replace *Picture* in the scheme tree by *Picture*↑, which is a set of pointers or OIDs that reference the pictures in *Picture*, and we should make *Picture* a single-node scheme tree by itself.

4.4. No Updates

Theoretically, NNF is a necessary and sufficient condition to characterize data redundancy caused by FDs and MVDs in nested relations whose schemes are consistent with the given FDs and MVDs. Thus, if a nested relation scheme is in NNF, we can guarantee that there will be no instance for the scheme that will have data redundancy caused by FDs and MVDs. We should not forget, however, that our goal is not to reduce redundancy(!), but to make applications efficient. Reducing redundancy usually helps us achieve the goal of making applications efficient because it generally reduces both the time to process updates and check integrity constraints and the space to store the data. However, if there are no or only a few updates, and if we are not concerned about space for a particular application, data redundancy and the corresponding update anomalies are not a problem. In this situation, we may want to violate NNF and create larger nested relation schemes for the chosen roots.

One way to create larger schemes (which may not be in NNF) is to relax the condition of the if-clause in the while-loop of Algorithm 1. We may replace "If there is a node N in T such that $Ancestor(N) \subseteq R^+$ and $(R - Ancestor(N)) \cap Aset(T) = \emptyset$" by "If there is a node N in T such that $(R - Ancestor(N)) \cap Aset(T) = \emptyset$." We keep everything else in Algorithm 1 the same. With this modification to Algorithm 1, it is possible to extend an existing scheme tree until we exhaust all the edges in a connected component of an RRD hypergraph. Of course, the designer may choose to stop earlier.

As an example in Figure 2, consider explicitly inheriting the object sets *Price* and *Item Name* from *Item Nr* (*of Item*) through the generalization/specialization to *Item Nr* (*of Item on Order*). Now, with the FDs *Item Nr* (*of Item on Order*) → *Price* and *Item Nr* (*of Item on Order*) → *Item Name*, if we run Algorithm 1 as we did before, we would *not* be able to include these two edges in Figure 5b. By relaxing the algorithm as just explained, however, we could include *Price* and *Item Name* in the leaf node in Figure 5b with *Item Nr* and *Number*. In our application, this would redundantly store the price and item name in a customer order of every item on order. For this application, however, this may be exactly what we want. We would not expect orders, once they are placed, to be updated. We would expect, however, that we may want to retrieve them to fill and ship orders and to check orders. This retrieval operation would be much faster with the redundant items stored than would be an operation that would have to join the nested relations for the scheme trees in Figures 5a and 5b so that the price and item name could be displayed with an order.

4.5. Computed Objects

Since computed object sets contain objects that are not stored, they cannot cause data redundancy and thus NNF should not apply to them. We can use our NNF algorithms, however, to properly group methods with schemes.

If S_c is a functionally computed object set that depends on object sets $S_1, ..., S_n$, $n \geq 1$, then there is an FD $S_1 ... S_n \rightarrow S_c$. It is possible that some of the S_i's are also computed object sets. For a generated scheme tree T, we can use the FDs that have computed object sets to determine which computed object sets are functionally determined by $Aset(T)$. If $Aset(T) \rightarrow S_c$ by using the RRD hypergraph FDs plus the FDs that have computed object sets that appear on either on the left- or right-hand sides, S_c becomes a method of T.

Note that it is also possible that a computed object set may not be associated with any generated scheme tree. For this case, we can generate a virtual scheme for the method — virtual in the sense that it does not have an extent. Thus, for the FD $S_1 ... S_n \rightarrow S_c$ we would have the flat virtual scheme $S_1 ... S_n, S_c$. We could also store other methods with this virtual scheme whose left- and right-hand side attributes are in the closure $(S_1 ... S_n S_c)^+$.

Applying these ideas to our RRD hypergraph in Figure 2, we can obtain the classes (scheme and method combinations) for our OODB in Figure 7. For illustration we have used an O_2-like syntax [1]. We have also added appropriate types for our attributes and methods. We could have introduced these types initially in our conceptual model and carried them through our discussion, but they would have been ignored until this point. Further, we have added the bulk type list. Buckets generated by our NNF algorithms are bulk types, which by default are sets of tuples, but can alternatively be organized as arrays or lists or as any other appropriate bulk type.

```
class SalesTax public: real end; name SalesTaxValue: SalesTax;

class Picture public: image end; name Pictures: set(Picture);

type EmployeeRecord: tuple(
    EmpNr: string,
    HomePhoneNr: string,
    NrDependents: integer,
    EmpName: string,
    HourlyRate: real,
    WorkRecord: list(tuple(
        WorkDate: Date,
        Punch-outTime: integer,
        Punch-inTime: integer))
    ); class Department public tuple(
    Department: string,
    DeptPhoneNr: string,
    Employee: set(EmployeeRecord),
    Item: set(tuple(
        ItemNr: string,
        Price: real,
        ItemName: string,
        Pict: Picture,
        DistrAddr: string,
        DistrName: string))
    ) method
    public AccumulatedPay(employeeRecord: EmployeeRecord): real,
    public IncomeTax(nrDependents: integer, accumulatedPay: real): real end; name Departments: set(Department);

type OrderRecord: tuple(
    Number: integer,
    ItemNr: string,
    ItemName: string,
    Price: real
    ); type CustomerOrder: tuple(
    OrderNr: string,
    IncludedItem: list(OrderRecord)
    ); class Customer: public tuple(
    CustomerID: string,
    CustName: string,
    Order: list(CustomerOrder)
    ) method
    public ExtendedPrice(orderRecord: OrderRecord): real,
    public BasePrice(customerOrder: CustomerOrder): real,
    public TotalPrice(basePrice: real, salesTax: SalesTax): real end; name Customers: set(Customer);
```

Figure 7. Classes for our application.

5. Concluding Remarks

We presented an approach for designing classes (schemes and methods) for OODBs. Our approach is based on OSA, a conceptual model in the ORM family. In our approach, we first transform an OSA model instance into a design hypergraph. We then reduce the hypergraph according to some model transformations and determine whether it is an RRD hypergraph, which we defined here as being reduced and γ-acyclic and as having each edge in BCNF. Algorithm 1, which we presented here, takes an RRD hypergraph as input and generates schemes that are in NNF. This guarantees that there is no potential redundancy for the generated nested relation schemes.

We explained that blindly applying Algorithm 1 for an application may not generate the schemes we want for our design. We therefore listed several ways to augment Algorithm 1 or adjust the results to better suit an application. These included (1) choosing the right roots, (2) using the allowed flexibility in edge configurations to create better design schemes, (3) placing large objects in a scheme by themselves, (4) allowing for redundancy when the data for some schemes is expected to be static after it is established, and (5) determining the proper placement of methods.

References

1. F. Bancilhon, C. Delobel, and P. Kanellakis (eds.), *Building an Object-Oriented Database System: The Story of O_2*, Morgan Kaufmann Publishers, San Mateo, California, 1992.

2. C. Batini, S. Ceri, and S.B. Navathe, *Conceptual Database Design*, The Benjamin/Cummings Publishing Company, Inc., Redwood City, California, 1992.

3. J. Biskup, "Database schema design theory: achievements and challenges," *Proceedings of the 6th International Conference, CISMOD'95. The proceedings appeared as Lecture Notes in Computer Science #1006*, pp. 14-44, Bombay, India, November 1995.

4. E.F. Codd, "Recent investigations in relational database systems," *Proceedings of the 1974 IFIP Conference*, pp. 1017-1021, 1974.

5. D.W. Embley and T.W. Ling, "Synergistic database design with an extended entity-relationship model," *Proceedings of the 8th International Conference on Entity-Relational Approach*, pp. 118-135, Toronto, Canada, October 18-20, 1989.

6. D.W. Embley, B.D. Kurtz, and S.N. Woodfield, *Object-oriented Systems Analysis: A Model-driven Approach*, Prentice-Hall, Englewood Cliffs, New Jersey, 1992.

7. R. Fagin, A.O. Mendelzon, and J.D. Ullman, "A simplified universal relation assumption and its properties," *ACM Transactions on Database Systems*, vol. 7, no. 3, pp. 343-360, September 1982.

8. R. Fagin, "Degrees of acyclicity for hypergraphs and relational database schemes," *Journal of the ACM*, vol. 30, no. 3, pp. 514-550, July 1983.

9. T.A. Halpin, *Conceptual Schema & Relational Database Design, 2nd Edition*, Prentice-Hall, Sydney, Australia, 1995.

10. W. Kent, "Consequences of assuming a universal relation," *ACM Transactions on Database Systems*, vol. 6, no. 4, pp. 539-556, December 1981.

11. W. Kim, "Editorial Directions," *ACM Transactions on Database Systems*, vol. 20, no. 3, pp. 237-238, September 1995.

12. D. Maier, *The Theory of Relational Databases*, Computer Science Press, Rockville, Maryland, 1983.

13. V.M. Markowitz and A. Shoshani, "Representing extended entity-relationship structures in relational databases: a modular approach," *ACM Transactions on Database Systems*, vol. 17, no. 3, pp. 423-464, September 1992.

14. W.Y. Mok, Y.K. Ng, and D.W. Embley, "A normal form for precisely characterizing redundancy in nested relations," *ACM Transactions on Database Systems*, vol. 21, no. 1, pp. 77-106, March 1996.

15. M.A. Roth, H.F. Korth, and A. Silberschatz, "Extended algebra and calculus for nested relational databases," *ACM Transactions on Database Systems*, vol. 13, no. 4, pp. 389-417, December 1988.

16. T.J. Teorey, *Database Modeling & Design: The Fundamental Principles, 2nd Edition*, Morgan Kaufmann Publishers, San Francisco, California, 1994.

17. J.D. Ullman, "The U.R. strikes back," *Proceedings of the ACM Symposium on Principles of Database Systems*, pp. 10-22, Los Angeles, California, March 1982.

Representing Partial Spatial Information in Databases

Thodoros Topaloglou and John Mylopoulos

Department of Computer Science, University of Toronto
Toronto, Ontario, M5S 1A4, Canada

Abstract. In this paper we present a spatial data model which facilitates the representation of and reasoning with various forms of qualitatively and quantitatively incomplete spatial information. The model is founded on a combination of object-oriented and constraint-based data modeling facilities and provides for representations of variable precision and granularity. We identify four basic reasoning tasks required for query processing operations and outline algorithms for each task. Finally, we discuss extensions of the model and outline an implementation based on the Telos knowledge base management system extended with an appropriate constraint reasoning component.

1 Introduction

Storing and manipulating spatial information is important for many database applications, including geographic information systems [MP94], vehicle navigation [Ege93], image retrieval [SYH94], protein structure prediction, environmental studies and many others. Existing spatial data models can generally be classified into two broad categories. The first category includes models that focus on explicit representations of space usually in terms of a *quantitative* formalism such as a map or a digitized array. We call these models *complete* since they represent the entire modeling space (see for example, [OM88], [RFS88], [GS95]). The second category includes models that focus on the representation of spatial features that are essential and are expressed in terms of a *qualitative* formalism such as symbolic arrays [GP92] or spatial relations [Her92]. These models are capable of reasoning about *partial* spatial information but, by-and-large, ignore quantitative spatial information and performance concerns.

This paper presents a spatial data model intended to accommodate both qualitatively and quantitatively partial spatial information. The expressiveness of the model is further enhanced by the provision of facilities for dealing with granularity and scale within a single framework. The formal tools employed in the paper include a conceptual modeling language, where the features of the proposed spatial data model are embedded, and a constraint-based language that is suitable for representing partially specified spatial information.

What are the sources of partial spatial information and what problems can it raise? Consider as an example a computerized system intended to coordinate first-aid vehicles that cover a geographic region (say, Metropolitan Toronto or Metro, for short). The region is divided into sections, which are further subdivided into subsections. For the coordinator and the vehicle drivers, *landmarks* serve as "constants" whose locations are precisely known by all concerned. Other spatial information is represented relative to landmarks. Each vehicle, V, has a range of activity, denoted by $scope(V)$, which is the area that it can reach within, say, 2 minutes from its current position. Each vehicle reports its position to the coordinating station in imprecise terms (for example, "moving east", "at Queen's Park", etc.). Hence, the vehicle position is represented by an *indeterminate* point. The scope of a vehicle is also partly known and is therefore represented by a rectangular region with an indeterminate boundary. Finally, the location of the trouble spot is reported by the coordinating station in imprecise terms, often through a reference to the nearest street intersection, and is represented by yet another indeterminate point. The reader should notice that indeterminate spatial objects in the example (vehicle positions, vehicle scopes and trouble spots) can be thought of as spatial variables which can take as value a spatial object within some spatial region. Moreover, indeterminate spatial objects are specified in varying degrees of precision, while for some of them only qualitative relationships may be known.

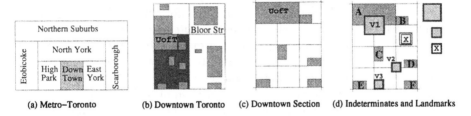

(a) Metro–Toronto   (b) Downtown Toronto   (c) Downtown Section   (d) Indeterminates and Landmarks

Fig. 1. An example map at different scales

Figure 1(a) depicts the Metro region divided into sections. This information can be extracted from a city map and can be as precise as desired. To keep the example manageable, we focus on the downtown section which is further subdivided into subsections (see Figures 1(b-c)). The dividing lines are major streets of downtown Toronto. In Figure 1(d), the different drawing styles distinguish between landmark objects (denoted by A,B,...,F) and indeterminate objects, i.e, the scopes vehicles V_1, V_2 and V_3 and a trouble spot X.

A frequent task for the first-aid coordinator is to determine at any time which aid vehicle will serve a call, taking into account information about the relative positions of vehicles and the trouble spot. The problem is obviously dynamic, since the position and the scope of vehicles change over time, and a solution to the coordinator's query involves resolving efficiently a set of variably "grained" constraints. The primitive operations that a back-end spatial database needs to support to accommodate such queries are various topological (e.g., overlaps and contains), directional (e.g., north/south, left or above) and distance-based (e.g., within 1Km) predicates between operands with mismatched degrees of precision. It would also be desirable to be able to evaluate queries which receive an intentional answer such as "the places that can be served equally well by two given vehicles V_1 and V_2".

The rest of this paper is organized as follows. Section 2 includes an informal presentation of the features of the proposed spatial data model using the running example. Section 3 integrates the proposed features with the conceptual modeling language Telos. Section 4 presents a formalization of the spatial constraint language employed by the data model and outlines the algorithmic complexity of the query processing operation. Section 5 discusses related work and investigates directions in which the proposed model can be extended. Finally, Section 6 summarizes the contributions of the paper and briefly discusses future research.

2 Partial Information in Spatial Representations

This section first introduces the notions of scale and grain as basic concepts emerging from the example of the introductory section and then presents two fundamental constructs of the proposed spatial data model: the *spatial envelope* and the *map* structure.

2.1 Basic Concepts

A *spatial object* is a symbol structure representing a point or region of space. *Spatial Object Types.* As suggested by the example, spatial objects can be either *landmarks*, in which case there is complete information about the point or region of space being represented, or *indeterminate* objects (or indeterminates, for short), for which there is only partial information about the point or region being represented. Indeterminates are related to landmarks through constraints expressed in a qualitative constraint language.

Scale. In a representation space, a scale is a system of ordered marks used as a reference standard in determining the relationships between representations. For metric domains, a scale is defined as an ascending set of point values which differ by a fixed interval, called *grain* (or *unit*), denoting distance from a fixed constant of the system. In qualitative domains a scale is defined as a fixed order between landmarks which may differ by a variable size qualitative interval.

Scale Hierarchy. A scale hierarchy is an ordered set of scales, $S = \{s_1, s_2, \ldots, s_n\}$, such that for each spatial object α at scale s_i there exists a container object $container(\alpha)$ at scale s_{i-1} that contains α, i.e., $inside(\alpha, container(\alpha))$, for $i = 2 \ldots n$. The existence of a unique container requires that the scales are not overlapping and that scale s_{i-1} is "coarser" than s_i. The coarser relation is a total order. The ordered set $\{city, section, division\}$ of the above example, defines such a scale hierarchy.

Haze. Haze is a region which encloses an indeterminate spatial object (point or region) and models its indeterminacy. The size of the haze area accounts for the degree of indeterminacy associated with the object. In the example, assume that the position of V_2 is specified as "at University Ave. and Queen St." where V_1 is said to be "near College and St. George St.". In effect, V_2's position is specified more precisely than that of V_1. Consequently, the haze size for V_1 is greater than the haze size for V_2.

2.2 Spatial Constraints

Constraints have been shown to be very successful in representing qualitative and quantitative temporal information [vB90], [KL91], [Kou94b]. This section considers a particular class of *spatial constraints*, which provide a convenient syntactic facility for expressing partial and relative information about spatial objects.

Spatial constraints are conjunctions of atomic formulas expressed in a constraint language such as the one developed in Section 4 that relates indeterminates and landmarks in one or two-dimensional space. In Section 4, we also define a set of higher level topological and directional spatial relations which can serve as basic vocabulary for the constraint language. For example: "*close*($V2$, "University Ave. and Queen St.")", or "*south_side*($V1$, "UofT") $\land$ *east_of*($V1$, "Spadina Ave.")".

The discussion in the rest of this section is restricted to constraints on a single dimension, that are conjunctions of the following two types of atomic constraints: $x\ R\ c$, and $x - y\ R\ c$; where x, y are variables representing indeterminates, c is a constant representing a landmark, and R is one of $\{=, <, \leq\}$.

2.3 Spatial Envelopes

Spatial constraints can be used to define arbitrary types of spatial indeterminacy. *Spatial envelopes* provide a convenient mechanism for defining a useful and often-occurring type of spatial indeterminacy. In particular, spatial envelopes constrain an indeterminate spatial object to fall within a rectangular region. If x is an indeterminate spatial object, its spatial envelope is denoted by $env(x)$. The spatial envelope of a two-dimensional object is a rectangle characterized by two one-dimensional envelopes. A one-dimensional envelope constrains the exact position of an indeterminate spatial interval.

one–dimensional envelope   two–dimensional envelope

Fig. 2. Spatial Envelopes

Indeterminacy in one-dimension is formulated as follows. Let I be an indeterminate interval whose (partly known) start and end points are denoted respectively by I_S and I_E. The length of I is denoted by some constant c, defined with respect to the scale of the metric domain of I. The envelope interval of I, $env(I)$, is a pair of point envelopes, $env(I_S)$, $env(I_E)$ (see Figure 2 for a graphical illustration). In a discrete domain, each point envelope, $env(P)$, is represented by two points, P_L and P_U which impose lower and upper bounds on the position of point P. Assuming that the size of the haze is g, then points P_L and P_U are related by the constraint $0 \leq P_U - P_L \leq 2g$, and the envelope definition $P_L \leq P \leq P_U$

for some point P. For interval envelopes, the length of the interval poses an additional metric constraint, i.e., $I_E = I_S + c$. As a result, the one-dimensional *interval envelope*, $env(I)$, can be characterized by four variables, $I_{S_L}, I_{S_I}, I_{E_L}$, and I_{E_I}, related by the following constraints:

$$\{\, 0 \le I_{S_I} - I_{S_L} \le 2g,\; 0 \le I_{E_I} - I_{E_L} \le 2g,\; I_{S_L} \le I_S \le I_{S_I},\; I_{E_L} \le I_E \le I_{E_I},\; I_E - I_S = c \,\}$$

2.4   The Map Structure

The *map* structure is a logical data structure used to define a collection of spatial objects and their inter-relationships. Formally, a map structure m is a quintuple

$$m = \langle\, L,\; I,\; C,\; s,\; g\, \rangle$$

where L is a finite set of landmarks, I is a finite set of indeterminate spatial objects, C is a set of spatial constraints and s and g are its scale and grain, respectively. As is often the case, the same block of space may be represented by multiple maps of variable granularity.

Example 2.4.1 Figure 1(d) defines a map m with $L = \{A, B, C, D, E, F\}$, $I = \{V_1, V_2, V_3, X\}$ at "city-division" scale and grain size g_m. The constraints of m are discussed in the next two examples. □

A valid map definition must be such that its grain size can accommodate the haze size of its indeterminates. More formally, if *haze* is a function returning the haze size of an indeterminate and g_m is the grain size of map m, then the condition is written as: $g_m \le min\{haze(i)|i \in I\}$.

The construction of a map involves two phases: First, the set of landmarks of the map are represented, followed by a definition of the map indeterminates. For the first phase, we assume that the input is a "segmented image", e.g., an $n \times m$ occupancy array, containing a set of landmarks, L. The grain, g, for the map is captured by the size of the array cells. A set of X and Y constraints can then be defined so that each one contains all the known order and distance relationships between landmarks along the X and the Y axes, respectively. Indeterminacy can now be circumscribed for map indeterminates through spatial envelope constraints.

Example 2.4.2 This example shows a constraint representation created for the static part of Figure 1(d). As indicated earlier, landmarks are approximated by their minimum bounding rectangle; we therefore need four parameters for representing them, namely, $A_{S_X}, A_{S_Y}, A_{E_X}$ and A_{E_Y}. For some grain g, the landmarks in the map are represented by the following two sets of equality constraints (i.e., the X and Y axis projections of its array representation):

$\{E_{S_X}{=}0, A_{S_X}{=}0, E_{E_X}{=}3, C_{S_X}{=}5, C_{E_X}{=}7, A_{E_X}{=}9, B_{S_X}{=}9, F_{S_X}{=}11, D_{S_X}{=}11, B_{E_X}{=}12, D_{E_X}{=}15, F_{E_X}{=}15\}$
$\{E_{S_Y}{=}0, F_{S_Y}{=}0, E_{E_Y}{=}2, F_{E_Y}{=}2, D_{S_Y}{=}5, D_{E_Y}{=}7, C_{S_Y}{=}7, C_{E_Y}{=}10, A_{S_Y}{=}15, B_{S_Y}{=}15, B_{E_Y}{=}17, A_{E_Y}{=}20\}$
□

Indeterminates are introduced next. According to the earlier discussion, a two-dimensional indeterminate is represented by a spatial envelope which consists of two coordinate one-dimensional envelopes. Each one-dimensional interval (resp. point) envelope is specified by four (resp. two) parameters, which are related by a fixed set of constraints as presented in Section 2.3. The notion of envelope parameters used here (in **courier** font) is similar to Koubarakis' *e(xistential)-variables* [Kou94a], intended to represent values which are not completely known but for which a global constraint exists. The indeterminate parameters (in *italics* style) are also *e-variables* since they name a specific indeterminate and their possible values are bounded by envelope constraints.

Example 2.4.3 The insertion of a rectangular indeterminate into the above map is demonstrated next: Let $V1 = \langle V1X_S, V1X_E, V1Y_S, V1Y_E \rangle$, $grain(V1) = g_1$, $size(V1) = c_1$; c_1 is a constant that denotes the size of $V1$'s scope. As for the discussion of Section 2.3, constraints 1-10 become available. In addition, the position of $V1$ in the representation space is specified by constraints 11-14 (on the envelope parameters):

1. $0 \leq \text{V1X}_{S_\text{r}} - \text{V1X}_{S_\text{L}} \leq 2g_1$
2. $0 \leq \text{V1X}_{E_\text{r}} - \text{V1X}_{E_\text{L}} \leq 2g_1$
3. $\text{V1X}_{S_\text{L}} \leq V1X_S \leq \text{V1X}_{S_\text{r}}$
4. $\text{V1X}_{E_\text{L}} \leq V1X_E \leq \text{V1X}_{E_\text{r}}$
5. $V1X_E - V1X_S = c_1$
6. $0 \leq \text{V1Y}_{S_\text{r}} - \text{V1Y}_{S_\text{L}} \leq 2g_1$
7. $0 \leq \text{V1Y}_{E_\text{r}} - \text{V1Y}_{E_\text{L}} \leq 2g_1$
8. $\text{V1Y}_{S_\text{L}} \leq V1Y_S \leq \text{V1X}_{S_\text{r}}$
9. $\text{V1Y}_{E_\text{L}} \leq V1Y_E \leq \text{V1X}_{E_\text{r}}$
10. $V1Y_E - V1Y_S = c_1$
11. $(E_{EX} = \text{V1X}_{S_\text{L}}) \wedge (\text{V1X}_{S_\text{r}} < C_{SX})$
12. $(C_{EY} < \text{V1Y}_{S_\text{L}}) \wedge (\text{V1Y}_{S_\text{r}} < A_{SY})$
13. $(C_{SX} < \text{V1X}_{E_\text{L}}) \wedge (\text{V1X}_{E_\text{r}} = C_{EX})$
14. $(B_{EY} = \text{V1Y}_{E_\text{L}}) \wedge (\text{V1Y}_{E_\text{r}} < A_{EY})$

Constraints 1, 2, 11, and 13 are integrated into the X constraint set of the earlier map and similarly, constraints 6, 7, 12 and 14 are integrated into its Y constraint set. Constraints 3, 4, 5 and 8, 9, 10 are local to object $V1$. □

3 Modeling Space in Telos

This section describes the integration of the proposed features for representing spatial information with the conceptual modeling language Telos [MBJK90]. This integration endows the resulting spatial data model with abstraction mechanisms such as generalization, classification and attribution, inherited from Telos, as well as facilities for expressing meta-concepts and for asserting constraints and rules.

Integration of spatial modeling facilities into Telos is accomplished through a library of meta-classes and meta-attributes that capture the semantics of the features presented in the previous section. The central class of the model is the **Map** class. Spatial information is attached to physical objects through the attribute mechanism of Telos. A spatial object participates in one or more maps that may vary in scale, grain and implementation. This becomes possible due to the capacity of Telos to handle multi-valued attributes. Its practical importance is that the resulting spatial data model can facilitate multiple representations of space. Finally, scale and scale transitions are modeled using the Telos assertional language.

It is assumed that the world being modeled includes, among other things, physical objects, which might have a temporal and a spatial aspect [Hay85]. The class **PhysicalObjClass** is a metaclass whose instances include physical object classes such as the class of vehicles, and the class of buildings or parks. All these classes are also specializations of **PhysicalObject**, which is also an instance of **PhysicalObjClass**. In addition, we introduce the metaclass **SpatialObjClass**, whose instances are spatial object classes such as **Street**, **Lot**, **Parcel** etc. These classes are also specializations of **SpatialObject**, which is an instance of **SpatialObjClass**. Physical objects can have an associated spatial object, about which information is represented in terms of one or more maps.

```
CLASS PhysicalObjClass IN M1_CLASS      CLASS SpatialObject IN SpatialObjClass
  WITH                                    WITH
    necessary,single                        attribute
      when:TemporalClass                      in-space:SpatialObject
      where:SpatialClass                      in-map:Map
      what:OrdinaryClass                  END SpatialObject
    attribute
      feature:AttributeClass            CLASS UofT-Lot IN SpatialObject
      time-feature:TemporalAttrClass      WITH
      space-feature:SpatialAttrClass      in-space
END PhysicalObject                          s1:division-City-Toronto-Parcel
                                          in-map
CLASS PhysicalObject IN PhysicalObjClass    m1:map1;
  WITH                                      m2:map2;
    where                                   m3:map3
      place:SpatialObject ...           END UofT-Lot
END PhysicalObject
```

According to these definitions, the **place** attribute of **PhysicalObject** is declared to be an instance of the **where** meta-attribute of **PhysicalObjClass**. A spatial object has an **in-space** attribute, which provides a spatial context, and zero or more associated maps that give information about the object. The next two definitions introduce different classes of spatial relationships. [1]

```
CLASS In-Map IN SpatialAttrClass        CLASS In-Space IN SpatialAttrClass
  WITH                                    WITH
    components                              components
      from:SpatialObject                      from:SpatialObject
      label:in-map                            label:in-space
      to:Map                                  to:SpatialObject
    attribute                               attribute
      rtype:RepresentationType                stype:SpatialType
END In-Map                              END In-Space
```

According to these definitions, **in-map** attributes have an associated attribute which specifies the representation type (landmark or indeterminate) of an object in a map. [2] Note that the same spatial object may have different types in different maps, i.e., be a landmark in one map and an indeterminate in another. Likewise, **in-space** associates a spatial type (region, point,...) to every spatial object / spatial context association. Again, the definition implies that a spatial object may have different types in different contexts.

A spatial object that serves as context for another object is itself described in terms of one or more maps. For example, the spatial token **UofT-Lot** is part of a division of the city of Toronto parcel, another spatial object, and participates in maps **map1, map2** and **map3** through relationships **m1, m2** and **m3**. The two types of spatial object types supported in our model are declared as instances of **RepresentationType**. Analogously, the geometric types of objects (i.e., point vs. region) are defined as instances of **SpatialType**.

---

[1] Telos does not have a built-in distinction between attributes and relationships.

[2] In Telos, all relationships are represented by a three-tuple, ⟨from, label, to⟩, which is called *proposition*. Intuitively, a proposition can be thought of as a link.

```
CLASS Map IN SpatialObjClass
  WITH
    single,necessary
      grain: Grain
      scale: Scale
    attribute
      X-constraint: ConstraintSet
      Y-constraint: ConstraintSet
    deductiveRule
      R1:indeterminate(ThisClassInstance,X):-
             instance(X,SpatialObject), instance(Y,In-map),
             proposition(X,Y,ThisClassInstance), rtype(Y,Indeterminate).
      R2:landmark(ThisClassInstance,X):-
             instance(X,SpatialObject), instance(Y,In-map),
             proposition(X,Y,ThisClassInstance), rtype(Y,Landmark).
    integrityConstraint
      :indeterminate(ThisClassInstance,X) and X.haze>ThisClassInstance.grain
END Map
```

The **Map** class models the principal data structure of our spatial data model. A map is characterized by its **grain** and **scale** attributes and the set of objects it inter-relates. **X-** and **Y-constraint** attributes take as values object inter-relationships, where the objects included in a map are retrieved by deductive rules. [3] Additional integrity constraints specify properties that any **Map** instance needs to satisfy. Granularity and scale are modeled in a similar fashion.

4 Spatial Constraints

This section presents a formalization of the proposed spatial constraint language and derives some of its formal properties. The section ends with an enumeration of four spatial reasoning tasks and a discussion of algorithms for solving each one of them.

4.1 A Language for Spatial Constraints

$\mathcal{L}_{\mathcal{H}}$ is intended as a language for specifying qualitative and quantitative constraints in one-dimensional space. $\mathcal{L}_{\mathcal{H}}$ is defined as a sorted predicate calculus with two sorts: hazy points, denoted by H, and exact points, denoted by E; $x, y, z, ..$ are variables of sort H, $c_1, c_2, c_3, ..$ are constants of sort E, and g is a designated constant also of sort E. The predicate symbols of $\mathcal{L}_{\mathcal{H}}$ include $\approx$, $\prec$ relating objects of sorts $H \times H$ and $H \times E$, and predicate symbols $=$, $<$ relating objects of sorts $E \times E$. $\mathcal{L}_{\mathcal{H}}$ also has a the function symbol "$-$" of sort $H \times H \to E$. An atomic formula of $\mathcal{L}_{\mathcal{H}}$ has one of the following forms: $x \approx y$, $x \prec y$, $c_1 = c_2$, $c_1 < c_2$, $x \approx c_i$, $x \prec c_i$, $y - x = c_i$, and $y - x < c_i$.

The well-formed formulas of $\mathcal{L}_{\mathcal{H}}$ are build up from the atomic formulas using logical connectives ($\neg$, $\vee$ and $\wedge$) and quantifiers ($\exists, \forall$) whose variables have to be of sort H.

The terms of $\mathcal{L}_{\mathcal{H}}$ are interpreted over the domain of integers. g is interpreted as the integer constant g. Each constant c_i of the sort E is interpreted as the integer

---

[3] For simplicity, deductive rules R1 and R2 are specified in Prolog notation.

i. Symbols $<, =$ and $-$ receive the standard interpretation of order, equality and subtraction over integers. Each variable x of sort H is interpreted as an integer $\mathbf{x}$ that ranges in the interval $[\mathbf{x}^* - \mathbf{g}, \mathbf{x}^* + \mathbf{g}]$, where $\mathbf{x}^*$ is some integer. Intuitively, $\mathbf{x}^*$ denotes the median of x's interpretation. Predicate symbols $\approx$ and $\prec$ are interpreted by the relations $R(\mathbf{x}, \mathbf{y}) = \{(\mathbf{x}, \mathbf{y}) : |\mathbf{x} - \mathbf{y}| \leq 2\mathbf{g}\}$ and $S(\mathbf{x}, \mathbf{y}) = \{(\mathbf{x}, \mathbf{y}) : \mathbf{y} - \mathbf{x} > \mathbf{g}\}$, respectively. The notions of truth and satisfaction are defined in the usual way [End72].

It should be noted that $\mathcal{L}_\mathcal{H}$ does not use constants to name a specific element of sort E; instead, it uses unbound variables which receive as interpretation the specific element of E in any particular model of its theory.

Moreover, if in an interpretation g is assigned to the value 0, then $\approx$ and $\prec$ have "exact" meaning (i.e., same as $=$ and $<$), and $\mathcal{L}_\mathcal{H}$ becomes the language of discrete point order constraints. Discrete point order constraints have been employed in Section 2 to express spatial envelope constraints. Note that envelopes have already "compiled away" spatial indeterminacy.

Example 4.1.1 This example elucidates the meaning of the terms of $\mathcal{L}_\mathcal{H}$. Assume that $\mathbf{g}{=}2$ throughout the example. Let v be an interpretation which assigns y to $\mathbf{y}^*{=}6$, then $\mathbf{y}$ can be one of $\{4,5,6,7,8\}$. If $x \approx y$, then the image of x has to be within at most 2 points from a $\mathbf{y}$, i.e., $\mathbf{x}$ can be one of $\{2,3,4,5,6\}$ if $\mathbf{y} = \mathbf{4}$ and so on.

In the same model, $x \prec y$ means that $\mathbf{x}^* < 4$ if $\mathbf{y}^*{=}6$. The meaning of the terms $c_1 = c_2$ and $c_2 < c_1$ is the obvious one. The (hazy) equality between a hazy point and an exact constant, $x \approx c_i$, means that $\mathbf{i} - \mathbf{g} \leq \mathbf{x} \leq \mathbf{i} + \mathbf{g}$, i.e., if $\mathbf{i}{=}8$ then $\mathbf{x}$ can be one of $\{6,7,8,9,10\}$. Analogously, in the same model, x for $x \prec c_8$ is interpreted by an integer which is less than 6.

The subtraction operator "$-$" is used to define a notion of distance between hazy points; "$-$" returns an exact quantity. [4] Let, for instance, $\mathbf{x}$ be interpreted in $\{1,2,3,4,5\}$ and $\mathbf{y}$ in $\{7,8,9,10,11\}$, the term $y - x = c_6$ means that $\mathbf{x}$ and $\mathbf{y}$ are now restricted to be exactly 6 units apart, i.e., the following five pairs $\{(1,7),(2,8),(3,9),(4,10),(5,11)\}$ are the only allowable interpretations for the pair x, y. $\qquad\qquad\square$

The language of one-dimensional hazy-point space is extended to a language where one can state relationships between two-dimensional hazy points and rectangles. To do so we use the technique of independent combination introduced in [Top94]. Independent combination views each dimension in a multi dimensional space independently. For the two-dimensional case, for instance, it requires that each two-dimensional point is a pair of two one-dimensional points, and each two-dimensional rectangle is a pair of two two-dimensional points. The intuition behind independent combination is that any operator between two spatial objects in k-dimensions is written as a conjunction of k expressions involving only primitive one-dimensional operators over the projected coordinates. In [Top96] we proved that the satisfiability of a formula with the independent combination property is reduced to the satisfiability of its one-dimensional counterparts. Hence,

---

[4] A subtraction operator "$\sim$" which returns a hazy quantity is also defined but not included in this presentation.

we are able to generate a calculus on two-dimensional spatial objects which has the computational properties of its one-dimensional coordinate calculi. Moreover, we are able to compose a solution for a two-dimensional constraint satisfaction problem by combining solutions of its coordinate problems.

Independent combination imposes some limitations to the expressiveness of the constraint language for multi-dimensional space. One limitation is that it assumes orthogonality of space. However, this is a well-founded assumption in reality. Moreover, the resulting language is expressive enough to cover an interesting set of spatial relationships encountered in geographic information systems [Pap94a] and picture retrieval systems [SYH94]. Another less restrictive limitation is that we consider two-dimensional spatial objects to be either points or rectangles. This limitation is opted for presentation purposes as, in Section 5, we show that the language can be extended to model objects of arbitrary shape. In the next section, we discuss sets of spatial relations that are expressible in our formalism.

4.2 Spatial Relations

Egenhofer's [Ege91] eight fundamental topological relations for two planar regions is the most popular set of topological spatial relations in spatial databases. One advantage of this proposal is its clean topological semantics. In our work, we offer an alternative semantics for these relations based on the ontology of hazy points. The novelty of our approach is that it considers spatial relationships between objects with vague boundaries. In addition, a measure of precision appears as a parameter in the relations' definition, thus making reasoning about imprecise spatial information possible.

Figure 3 shows a graphical presentation of topological relations. Their formal definition requires the definition of the helping relations in_0, in_1 and $close$. In the following, P, $P1$ and $P2$ are two-dimensional points and R, $R1$, $R2$ are rectangular regions. Subscript $_i$ denotes the projection coordinate: $_i$ is either x or y. R_S and R_E denote the bottom-left and the top-right points of R, respectively.

$$in_0(P, R) \equiv (R_{S_X} \prec_X P_X \wedge P_X \prec_X R_{E_X}) \wedge (R_{S_Y} \prec_Y P_Y \wedge P_Y \prec_Y R_{E_Y})$$
$$in_1(R1, R2) \equiv (R2_{S_X} \prec_X R1_{S_X} \wedge R1_{E_X} \prec_X R2_{E_X}) \wedge (R2_{S_Y} \prec_Y R1_{S_Y} \wedge R1_{E_Y} \prec_Y R2_{E_Y})$$
$$close(P1, P2) \equiv (P1_X \approx_X P2_X) \wedge (P1_Y \approx_Y P2_Y)$$

disjoint   tangent_t   overlaps   inside_i   inside_t   equal

Fig. 3. Hazy topological relations

$$\mathtt{disjoint}(R1, R2) \equiv \neg\exists P(in_0(P, R1) \wedge in_0(P, R2))$$
$$\mathtt{tangent}_1(R1, R2) \equiv \exists P1, P2(in_0(P1, R1) \wedge in_0(P2, R2) \wedge close(P1, P2))$$
$$\mathtt{overlap}(R1, R2) \equiv \exists P(in_0(P, R1) \wedge in_0(P, R2))0$$
$$\mathtt{inside}_i(R1, R2) \equiv in_1(R1, R2)$$
$$\mathtt{inside}_t(R1, R2) \equiv R2_{S_X} \preceq_X R1_{S_X} \wedge R1_{E_X} \preceq_X R2_{E_X} \wedge R2_{S_Y} \preceq_Y R1_{S_Y} \wedge R1_{E_Y} \preceq_Y R2_{E_Y}$$

$$\text{contain}_t(R1, R2) \equiv \text{inside}_t(R2, R1)$$
$$\text{contain}_i(R1, R2) \equiv \text{inside}_i(R2, R1)$$
$$\text{equal}(R1, R2) \quad \equiv close(R1_S, R2_S) \wedge close(R1_E, R2_E)$$

[5] The notion of tangency as defined above, is "loose" tangency in the sense that two rectangles share a point of their haze. If the size of the haze decreases, a tangent relationship will change to disjointness.

Many researchers developed sets of directional relations exploring either characteristic points of the participant objects [PS94], [Her92] or the order relation of the underlying domain [SYH94]. Our directional relations definition is closely related to the approach of [SYH94]:

$$\text{left\_of}(R1, R2) \equiv R1_{E_X} \prec_X R2_{S_X} \quad \text{right\_of}(R1, R2) \equiv \text{left\_of}(R2, R1)$$
$$\text{above}(R1, R2) \quad \equiv R2_{E_Y} \prec_Y R1_{S_Y} \quad \text{below}(R1, R2) \quad \equiv \text{above}(R2, R1)$$

Finally, and as a result of the independent combination property, our model can handle relationships between one-dimensional and two-dimensional point or region objects. Space limitation do not allow us to list them here.

4.3 Reasoning

A map structure is represented in terms of two constraint sets, $Xcon$ and $Ycon$, each of which is a conjunction of $x \ R \ c$ and $x - y \ R \ d$ atomic constraints, where x, y are variables representing the parameters of a spatial envelope, R is one of $\{=, <, \leq\}$, d is a grain parameter, and c is a constant corresponding to a landmark parameter. Any map with an envelope representation for its indeterminate objects can be placed in this simple normal form. Note that the set of variables in the two sets is disjoint (except for d's). The reader should also recognize that the deployed language in the map constraints is the language of linear order constraints on integers as resulted from the compilation of indeterminates into envelope constraints.

The fundamental reasoning problems addressed in a constraint representation of a map structure are as follows:

P1. *Given the $Xcon$ and $Ycon$ constraint sets, decide if the constraint sets are satisfiable, i.e., there is an assignment for variables that satisfies every atomic formula in the $Xcon$ and $Ycon$ set.*

P2. *Given the $Xcon$ and $Ycon$ constraint sets, compute an assignment for all variables that satisfies every atomic formula in the $Xcon$ and $Ycon$ set.*

The type of the d parameters plays a pivotal role in the determination of the complexity of the above problems. If d's are integer constants (fixed grains) then both problems are straight-forward to solve in polynomial time. For instance, problem **P1** could be solved using one of several path consistency algorithms proposed in [Mac77], [DMP91], [KL91], [Kou94b]. The complexity of path consistency algorithms for the type of constraints considered, is $O(n^3)$ where n is the number of variables in the constraint set. In the database literature, the classic results of [RH80] offer another alternative with the same complexity. The second reasoning problem, is closely related to the first one. In fact, a solution for

---

[5] Notation: $x_i \preceq_i y_i \equiv x_i \prec_i y_i \vee x_i \approx_i y_i$.

P2 implies a solution for **P1**. Plethora of solutions is available for **P2**, including the above-mentioned path consistency algorithms as well as the dual method involving variable elimination algorithms (see [LM88], [Kou92]).

The two problems change complexity if d's are taken to be integer variables. Then for a single d value efficient algorithms are still possible , since computing a solution involves solving a system of linear inequalities, a known polynomial complexity problem. For more than one d values, on the other hand, the problem of computing a minimal solution becomes intractable since it is equivalent to integer programming [Pap94b]. Our on-going work attempts to identify efficient special cases for the last problem.

In addition to **P1** and **P2**, there are two derivative spatial reasoning problems which require attention:

P3. *Given a consistent and minimal constraint set, $Xcon \cup Ycon$, of a map structure m, and i, an indeterminate of m, find the strongest possible bounds for the parameters of i.*

A solution to **P3** involves, first, projecting a solution of **P2** to the variables of i's envelope and, second, applying a path consistency algorithm on the selected set of constraints conjoined with i's local constraints. Both steps are realized in polynomial time. Note that, to determine the consistency of a map, m, we need to test **P3** for all of its indeterminates.

P4. *Given a consistent and minimal constraint set, $Xcon \cup Ycon$, of a map structure m, and g', a new grain value (resolution) for m, recompute problem **P2** with grain value g'.*

Problem **P4** involves recomputing the constants for the landmark parameters in the $Xcon$ and $Ycon$ constraint sets and then computing **P2**. The first step is solved in linear time. Assume that $g = r * g'$, $r > 1$, i.e., resolution is refined. Then each $P = v$ conjunct in the $Xcon$ and $Ycon$ constraint set is replaced by the constraint $(r * (v - 1) \leq P) \wedge (P \leq r * v)$. Similarly, if $g' = c * g$, $c > 1$, i.e., resolution coarsens, then each term $P = v$ is replaced by with $P = \frac{v}{s}$. [CCMSP93] presents an elaborate framework for scale-related granularity which is relevant to the above problem.

5   Discussion

This section completes the presentation of the proposed spatial data model by pointing at some of its expressive features but also discussing directions in which it can be extended.

The proposed spatial data model integrates ideas from object-oriented knowledge representation [MBJK90], constraint-based data models [KKR90], spatial knowledge representation [PS94], quantitative and qualitative temporal reasoning [KL91], and granularity modeling [CCMSP93]. In result, our spatial data model covers wide range of features, such as indeterminate spatial objects, multiple scales, granularity and spatial relations.

Our spatial data model may be atypical of other proposals, however it complies with general structure of spatial data models. Guting [Gut94] identifies four desirable abstractions of space that need to be represented in a database. Our spatial model matches features from three of these abstractions, namely, organizes the underlying space on a geometric basis (represented by constraints), offers a spatial relation-based language, and, integrates geometric types into the data model. Until now, our model has limited spatial data types support, points and rectilinear regions, but as we show bellow, the integration of lines and polygons is straight forward.

Our work is related also to temporal databases where the issues of granularity, scale and partially specified information have received considerable attention (e.g., [Kou94a], [DS93], [WJS93]) in the last few years.

Work on "undetermined" boundaries [Had95], and multiple representations of space [PD95], [RS95] are also related to this work. In fact, our model agrees with the proposal of [Had95] which suggests that undetermined boundaries can be founded on stochastic space, given that a haze area that surrounds a point space essentially represents the uniform distribution of the probability that this point can be found inside the area. Consequently, our model sets up a formal and computational base to address issues emerging from this proposal.

The ability to reduce the resolution of a map is called in Geography the map generalization operation [PD95]. Reasoning operation **P4** is essentially an instance of the map generalization operation in the context of minimum boundary rectangle representations of spatial data such as the one studied in [PTSE94].

An obvious, and for many practical reasons useful, extension of our data model, is to provide facilities for the representation of arbitrary complexity objects. This can be accomplished by defining a line to be a pair of two points, called endpoints. A chain is then defined to be a sequence of connected lines, and a polygon to be a closed polygon. A polygon in a plane defines two regions the interior and the exterior. Since the points used in these definitions have a haze, the defined geometric types are inheritedly "haze". The representational model is now extended with construction operators such as $line(P_1, P_2)$ which constructs a line out of two points, etc. Relations between objects can now be defined either in terms of Egenhofer's 3-intersection model [Ege91] or by relating characteristic points of objects [Pap94a]. A necessary extension to the underlying computational model is the redefinition of the primitive $point\_to\_polygon$ operation as a 3-valued operation (i.e, to return as answer yes/no/maybe). This change affects only reasoning with topological relations using the 3-intersection model. The proposed constraint-based reasoning model based on two one-dimensional projections and minimum bounding rectangle (mbr) approximations is still applicable. In addition, further non-mbr based computations using the one-dimensional projections are possible provided that a new mapping between two-dimensional relations and their one-dimensional projections is defined.

An implementation of the proposed data model is achieved by first expressing the non-spatial data concepts using an existing data model (e.g., an object-based or a relational system), then integrating the proposed spatial features and finally implementing a constraint-based inference engine for spatial constraints.

To-date, there is no generally accepted way for implementing large constraint databases. Logic programming is an obvious alternatives with serious limitations regarding its scalability to large datasets. Constraint-based reasoners is another option. This work follows the last option. Our proposed solution to the scalability problem is to explore the scale and grain features in order to partition large chunks of space into many small maps.

The first part of our prototype implementation integrates the proposed features for representing spatial information using the conceptual modeling language Telos [MBJK90]. This is accomplished through a library of meta-classes and meta-attributes as has already been discussed in Section 3. The integrated system is then put together using the framework developed in the Telos knowledge base management project [MCP+96]. Figure 4 displays part of the knowledge base that implements the spatial data model using the Telos system browser.

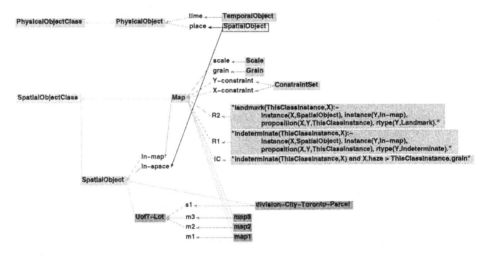

Fig. 4. Implementing Spatial Information in Telos

The second part of our implementation involves implementation of constraint reasoning in the context of haze orders and integrating it with the object model. Our accomplishment to date include the implementation of algorithms for supporting the reasoning tasks **P1** and **P2** presented in Section 4.3. A description of the algorithms and their implementation appears in [Top96].

The implementation will be completed with the development of a third component which will be responsible for answering queries with spatial and non-spatial qualifications. To date, this component is not available.

6 Conclusions and Future Research

We have presented a spatial data model which facilitates the representation of and reasoning with various forms of qualitatively and quantitatively incomplete spatial information, including indeterminate objects, multiple scales and granularity. Representation of incomplete spatial information is accomplished through a spatial constraint language with built-in notions for representing partial spatial information. Reasoning with such representations is addressed by identifying four classes of reasoning tasks and offering efficient processing algorithms for each class. Our proposal accommodates object-orientation by embedding the proposed model within Telos and exploiting the meta-modeling facilities of the latter.

A number of research issues remain open and will be addressed in the future:

- A thorough case study using an application domain with varying granularity and imprecise data which can be a source for implementation ideas; Genome and crystallographic databases are two promising applications for this study.
- A query language facility that can accommodate spatial and non-spatial qualifications. Although a logic-based language is the most obvious alternative, its inefficiencies suggest that a better alternative, possibly graphical, must be sought.
- The extension of the model to accommodate Datalog [BCW93] type of rules. Beyond advancing the expressive power of the formalism, this would also make it more usable.

References

[BCW93]   M. Baudinet, J. Chomicki, and P. Wolper. Temporal Deductive Databases. In *Temporal Databases: Theory, Design, and Implementation*, pages 294–320. Benjamin/Cummings, 1993.

[CCMSP93] E. Ciapessoni, E. Corsetti, A. Montanari, and P. San Pietro. Embedding Time Granularity in a Logical Specification Language for Synchronous Real-time Systems. *Science of Computer Programming*, 20:141–171, 1993.

[DMP91]   R. Dechter, I. Meiri, and J. Pearl. Temporal Constraint Networks. *Artificial Intelligence*, 49:61–95, 1991.

[DS93]   K. Dyreson and R. Snodgrass. Valid Time Indeterminacy. In *Proceedings of the 9th International Conference on Data Engineering*, 1993.

[Ege91]   Max Egenhofer. Reasoning about Binary Topological Relations. In *Second Symposium on Large Spatial Databases (SSD'91)*, pages 143–160, 1991.

[Ege93]   Max Egenhofer. What's Special about Spatial: Database Requirements for Vehicle Navigation in Geographic Space. In *Proc. of ACM/SIGMOD Conf.*, pp. 398–402, 1993.

[End72]   H. Enderton. *A Mathematical Introduction to Logic*. Academic Press, 1972.

[GP92]   J. Glasgow and D. Papadias. Computational Imagery. *Cognitive Science*, 16:355–394, 1992.

[GS95]   R-H. Guting and M. Schneider. Realm-Based Spatial Data Types: The ROSE Algebra. *The VLDB Journal*, 4:243–286, 1995.

[Gut94]   Ralf H. Guting. An Introduction to Spatial Database Systems. *The VLDB Journal*, 3(4):357–399, 1994.

[Had95]   Thanasis Hadzilacos. On Layer-Based Systems for Undetermined Boundaries. In P.A. Burrough and A. Frank, editors, *Geographic Objects with Undetermined Boundaries*. Taylor & Francis, 1995.

[Hay85]   Pat Hayes. The Second Naive Physics Manifesto. In J. Hobbs, R. Moore: *Formal Theories of the Commonsense World*. Ablex Publishing, 1985.

[Her92]   Daniel Hernandez. *Qualitative Representation of Spatial Knowledge*. PhD thesis, Faculty of Informatics, Technical University of Munich, 1992.

[KKR90]   P. Kanellakis, G. Kuper, and P. Revesz. Constraint Query Languages. Long version. Also appearred in *Proc. of 9th ACM PODS*, 1990.

[KL91]   H. Kautz and P. Ladkin. Integrating Metric and Qualitative Temporal Reasoning. In *Proceedings of AAAI-91*, pages 241–246, 1991.

[Kou92]   Manolis Koubarakis. Dense Time and Temporal Constraints with $\neq$. In *Proceedings of KR-92*, pages 24–35, 1992.

[Kou94a]   Manolis Koubarakis. Database Models for Infinite and Indefinite Temporal Information. *Information Systems*, 19(2):141–173, March 1994.

[Kou94b]   Manolis Koubarakis. *Foundations of Temporal Databases*. PhD thesis, National Technical University of Athens, 1994.

[LM88]   P. Ladkin and R. Maddux. Representation and Reasoning with Convex Time Intervals. Technical Report KES.U.88.2, Kestrel Institute, 1988.

[Mac77]   A.K. Mackworth. Consistency in Networks of Relations. *Artificial Intelligence*, 8(1):99–118, 1977.

[MBJK90]   J. Mylopoulos, A. Borgida, M. Jarke, and M. Koubarakis. Telos: A Language for Representing Knowledge About Information Systems. *ACM Transactions on Office Information Systems*, 8(4):325–362, 1990.

[MCP$^+$96] J. Mylopoulos, V. Chaudhri, D. Plexousakis, A. Shrufi, and T. Topaloglou. Implementing Knowledge Management Systems . *The VLDB Journal (to appear)*, 1996.

[MP94]   C.B. Medeiros and F. Pires. Databases for GIS. *ACM SIGMOD Record*, 23:107–115, 1994.

[OM88]   J. Orenstein and F. Manola. PROBE: Spatial Data Modelling and Query Processing in an Image Database Application. *IEEE Transactions on Software Engineering*, 14(5):611–629, 1988.

[Pap94a]   Dimitris Papadias. *Relation-based Representations for Spatial Databases*. PhD thesis, National Technical University of Athens, 1994.

[Pap94b]   Christos Papadimitriou. *Computational Complexity.* Addison-Wesley, 1994.

[PD95]   E. Puppo and G. Dettori. Towards a formal model for multiresolution spatial maps. In *Proc. of SSD'95*, pages 153–169, 1995.

[PS94]   D. Papadias and T. Sellis. Qualitative Representation of Spatial Knowledge in Two-Dimensional Space. *The VLDB Journal*, 3(4):479–517, 1994.

[PTSE94]   D. Papadias, Y. Theodoridis, T. Sellis, and M. Egenhofer. Topological Relations in the World of Minimum Bounding Rectangles: A Study with R-trees. In *SIGMOD-95*, 1994.

[RFS88]   N. Roussopoulos, C. Faloutsos, and T. SellisAn Efficient Pictorial Database System for PSQL. *IEEE Transactions on SE*, 14(5):639–650, 1988.

[RH80]   D. Rozenkrantz and H. Hunt. Processing Conjunctive Predicate and Queries. In *VLDB-80*, pages 64–72, 1980.

[RS95]   P. Rigaux and M. Scholl. Multi-Scale Partitions: Applications to Spatial and Statistical Databases. In *Proc. of SSD'95*, pages 171–183, 1995.

[SYH94]   P. Sistla, C. Yu, and R. Haddad. Reasoning about Spatial Relationships in Picture Retrieval Systems. In *VLDB-94*, 1994.

[Top94]   Thodoros Topaloglou. First Order Theories of Approximate Space. In *AAAI-94 Workshop on Spatial and Temporal Reasoning*, pages 47–53, 1994.

[Top96]   Thodoros Topaloglou. *On the Representation of Partial Spatial Information in Knowledge Bases*. PhD thesis, Department of Computer Science, University of Toronto, 1996.

[vB90]   Peter van Beek. Exact and Approximate Reasoning About Qualitative Temporal Relations. TR/CS 90-29, University of Alberta, 1990.

[WJS93]   X.S. Wang, S. Jajodia, and V.S. Subrahmanian. Temporal Modules: An Approach Towards Federated Temporal Databases. In *Proceedings of ACM/SIGMOD Conference*, pages 227–236, 1993.

Specification of Calendars and Time Series for Temporal Databases

Jae Young Lee, Ramez Elmasri, and Jongho Won

Department of Computer Science and Engineering
The University of Texas at Arlington, Texas 76019-0015
{jlee, elmasri, won}@cse.uta.edu

Abstract. Most temporal data models have concentrated on describing temporal data based on versioning of objects, tuples, or attributes. The concept of time series, which is often needed in temporal applications, does not fit well within these models. The goal of this paper is to propose a generalized temporal database model that integrates the modeling of both version-based and time-series based temporal data into a single conceptual framework. The concept of calendar is also integrated into our proposed model. We also discuss how a conceptual Extended-ER design in our model can be mapped to an object-oriented or relational database implementation.

1 Introduction

Most temporal data models have concentrated on describing temporal data based on versioning of objects, tuples, or attributes [18, 15, 11, 22, 10]. The concept of time series, which is often needed in temporal applications [17], does not fit well within these models. In this paper, we propose a generalized temporal data model that integrates the modeling of both version-based and time-series data into a single conceptual framework. The concept of calendar [4, 13, 3, 20] is also integrated into our proposed model since it is required in modeling of time series. We also discuss how time-series can be mapped to relational or object-oriented databases for implementation purposes.

To integrate time series into temporal data models, we represent time series as attributes of entities or objects. The entity may have other version-based temporal attributes as well as some immutable attributes. For example, a $STOCK$ entity may have immutable attributes StockNumber, CompanyName, and temporal attribute Dividend, and a time-series attribute StockPrice, which is a time series with daily temporal values, and with data values $< High, Low, Ticks >$ recording the daily stock price information: the high price, low price and a sequence of all price changes during the day.

The paper is organized as follows. Section 2 gives an overview of the conceptual temporal data model that we extend to handle time series data. Section 3 gives an overview of time series. Section 4 describes modeling of calendars. Section 5 presents the integrated data model. Section 6 describes how time series data can be mapped to an object-oriented database, and Section 7 shows how it can be mapped to a relational database.

2 Overview of Temporal Data Model

Research in temporal models has moved in two directions. The work in [18, 15] supports object versioning; whereas that in [11, 10] supports attribute versioning. Many previous representations are limited to the relational model and mainly address the issue of adding temporal capabilities to the query language. We review the two representations below:

- Object versioning: Each object is augmented with two chronons t_l and t_u, which specify a time interval $[t_l, t_u)$ during which an object version is valid (see Fig.1). Each temporal real-world object is represented by a number of object versions in the database.
- Attribute versioning: Each attribute is represented as a list of (*value, interval*) pairs, where the interval $[t_l, t_u)$ is associated with each version of an attribute value rather than with a complete object version (see Fig.2). Each temporal real-world object is represented by a single complex (nested) database object.

Name	Title	Salary	Time-Interval
Smith	Engineer	35K	9/94 - 9/95
Smith	Engineer	48K	9/95 - *now*
Brown	Analyst	32K	8/93 - 6/94
Brown	DBA	40K	6/94 - 1/96
Brown	DBA	46K	1/96 - *now*
Jones	CEO	80K	1/95 - *now*

Fig. 1. Object versioning

Name	Title	Time-Interval	Salary	Time-Interval
Smith	Engineer	9/94 - *now*	35K	9/94 - 9/95
			48K	9/95 - *now*
Brown	Analyst	8/93 - 6/94	32K	8/93 - 6/94
	DBA	6/94 - *now*	40K	6/94 - 1/96
			46K	1/96 - *now*
Jones	CEO	1/95 - *now*	80K	1/95 - *now*

Fig. 2. Attribute versioning

While much research for modeling a temporal database is based on the relational model, there have been some proposed temporal object-oriented models [16, 22, 8]. [16] extends the *ER* model into a temporal object-oriented model and incorporates temporal structures and constraints in the data model, and [22] proposes the OODAPLEX model, with temporal extensions to the DAPLEX functional data model.

The model we use is the temporal *EER* (*TEER*) model [10] based on attribute versioning. The *TEER* extends the EER model [9] to include temporal information on entities, relationships, superclasses/subclasses, and attributes. It uses a *temporal element* (or *valid time element* [21]) for a time representation, and adapts it to the requirements of the *EER* model constructs. Readers may refer to [10] for description of the TEER model. We assume that readers are familiar with the basic concepts of the *EER* model [9].

3   Overview of Time Series

Time series [4, 5, 17, 6, 19, 2] is a powerful abstraction mechanism to handle collections of data that possess observed values at regular periods, or intervals. Collection and analysis of financial data and scientific data are examples that can be modeled with time series. Such applications have special properties that distinguish them from other temporal applications [5]:

- Such applications usually involve large volumes of data.
- The change of values of a data item is tightly associated with a predefined, specific time pattern.
- Manipulation of data puts more emphasis on aggregation operations on a collection of data rather than on individual data items.

Accordingly, to model such applications, different abstraction mechanisms than those used to model usual, version-oriented temporal data are needed.

One such abstraction mechanism is the concept of *time series*. There has been limited research reported in the literature on time series [4, 5, 17, 6, 19, 2]. Here, we briefly review the general concept of a time series based on the CALANDA time series management system, which is an application-specific DBMS for time series management currently under development at the Union Bank of Switzerland [6]. A time series is a collection of observations made sequentially over time. It consists of a sequence of events. An *event* is an ordered pair consisting of a *temporal value* and an associated list of *data values*. A typical time series will have the following format: { $(t_1, < data\_value_{11}, data\_value_{12}, \ldots >), (t_2, < data\_value_{21}, data\_value_{22}, \ldots >), \ldots$ }. Many time series have single values rather than lists, and hence would have the following format: { $(t_1, data\_value_1), (t_2, data\_value_2), \ldots$ }. Here, $data\_value_{ij}$ (or $data\_value_i$) is the value of a data item from the corresponding domain of possible values. Each data item can be of an atomic data type or a structured data type, such as record, list, array, etc. This provides flexibility in modeling various types of complex data items. The sequence of temporal values $(t_1, t_2, \ldots)$ is based on a *calendar* [4, 13, 7, 3, 20] that determines the granularity and period of events associated with a time series. Since time series in different applications can have different types of temporal values for their events, there are possibly many different types of calendars that can be utilized. Calendars play crucial roles in time series management and, hence, we will discuss this issue in detail in the next section. An example of time series for closing daily stock prices of a bank is shown in Fig.3.

temporal value	data value
2/15/96	120
2/16/96	125
2/20/96	127
2/21/96	129
2/22/96	124

Fig. 3. An example time series

It is customary to store only the sequence of data values in a time series, because the corresponding temporal values can be determined from the associated calendar.

4 Calendar System

A calendar is a human abstraction of the physical time space [20], and the measurements of time vary in different calendar systems that are used in different cultural environments. Some familiar calendar systems are the Gregorian, Islamic, and Oriental-lunar calendars. We mainly discuss the Gregorian calendar but our concepts can be applied to other calendar systems. We first discuss the time representation used in modeling calendars, then discuss calendar specification and user-defined calendars appropriate for time series management.

4.1 Time Representation

The physical time space is considered as a hierarchy of totally ordered sets of time intervals. The smallest, indivisible time unit is called *chronon*, and the set of chronons is at the lowest level in the hierarchy. It is assumed, in this paper, that *second* is chronon. The successive levels are the sets of *minutes* (level 2), *hours* (level 3), and *days* (level 4). Each level (except level 1) is a partition of the next lower level with conventional meaning, such as 1 minute corresponds to 60 consecutive seconds. Figure 4 shows the bottom two levels where *minute* partitions *second*. This is similar to Temporal Universe in [1] except that *month* and *year* are not included in our model, because these are specific to the Gregorian only while the four levels (or more than four levels if a time unit smaller than second is chosen as a chronon) are universal to any calendar systems. The time units

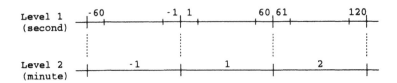

Fig. 4. Partition of seconds by minutes

used at each of the four levels are called *basic granularities*, and they are denoted by *Second, Minute, Hour* and *Day*. Time units at each level are modeled as iso-morphic to integers (without zero). Consequently, all the operations defined on integers are also applicable to time units at the same level. Operations on time units at two different levels can also be performed after the time units of the higher level is converted to that of the lower level according to the relationship between the corresponding granularities. In what follows, we use *nGranularity* to denote a time duration and *Granularity n* to denote a time unit, where *n* is an integer. For example, *3Minute* denotes the time duration of 3 minutes and *Minute 3* denotes the third time unit at level 2 time space. The granularity in the latter may be omitted if it is obvious in the context.

Time at each level is represented by a temporal element that is a finite union of time intervals [11]: $\{I_1, I_2, ...\}$ where I_i is a time interval. A time interval is an ordered pair of time units represented by $[t_l, t_u]$. A time unit can be represented by [t,t] (we will use [t] instead for brevity). Since our model does not have the notion of a *time point*, we do not use the notation for an *open* interval, "(" or ")", which is used in section 2. For example, an interval [1,6] with a granularity of *minute* is simply an ordered set $\{1,2,3,4,5,6\}$ in terms of minute or an ordered set $\{1, 2, ..., 360\}$ in terms of second.

4.2 Calendar Specification

A calendar is modeled as a totally ordered set (sequence) of intervals with ad-ditional semantics and represented by a tuple < *granularity, pattern, period, start time, end time*>, where

- *Granularity* is the smallest time unit allowed in a calendar.
- *Pattern* is a subsequence of time units expressed as a temporal element. If a calendar is periodic, the pattern with respect to one period is specified. Otherwise, the whole sequence of a calendar is specified. If there is more than one possible pattern, they are separated by "|" which means *or*.
- *Period* is the length of a time interval at which *pattern* occurs repeatedly. It is expressed in terms of the number of time units of a particular granularity in that period. It may be specified with the name of a periodic calendar. In this case the period of the calendar being specified is identical to the period of the other calendar. The *period* of an aperiodic calendar is specified by ∞.
- *Start time* is the time unit from which a calendar starts.
- *End time* is the time unit at which a calendar ends.

With this definition, the physical time space can be modeled by the following four *basic calendars*:

Calendar Seconds
  <granularity: chronon,
  pattern: {[1]},
  period: 1,
  start time: $-\infty$,
  end time: ∞ >

Calendar Minutes
  <granularity: Second,
  pattern: {[1, 60]},
  period: 60,
  start time: $-\infty$,
  end time: ∞ >

Calendar Hours
  <granularity: Minute,
  pattern: {[1, 60]},
  period: 60,
  start time: $-\infty$,
  end time: ∞ >

Calendar Days
  <granularity: Hour,
  pattern: {[1, 24]},
  period: 24,
  start time: $-\infty$,
  end time: ∞ >

4.3 Modeling of Gregorian

It is assumed that the Gregorian calendar system is well defined on the physical time space starting with a default start time. It is also assumed that different time measures, such as second, minute, hour, day, week, month, and year together with their relationships at the start time are also defined. For example, the start time is Year 1, Month 1, Day 1, Hour 1, Minute 1, and Second 1 (corresponding to a conventional notation 1/1/1, 01:01:01), and the first day is Monday. Note that the time unit for the start time (for all granularities) is not 0. This makes the model closer to real world calendars and human perception of the calendars. For historical data management, we can define the start time with a negative integer denoting BC (0 is not included in this case too). Due to the irregularity of the Gregorian (the lengths of months are not all identical and there are 97 leap years in every 400 years (leap second needs to be adjusted too)), it is not easily modeled with mathematical abstraction. Instead, we introduce the concept of *abstract granularities* and *abstract calendars* to eliminate the irregularities from the model. The three abstract granularities of the Gregorian are Week, Month, and Year. Week is defined to be 7Day. Month is defined to be 28, 29, 30, or 31Day (this is called *variable span* in [20]). Year is defined to be 12Month. The corresponding 3 abstract calendars are:

Calendar Weeks
    <granularity: Day,
      pattern: $\{[1,7]\}$,
      period: 7,
      start time: Default,
      end time: ∞ >

Calendar Months
    <granularity: Day,
      pattern: $\{[1,28]\}|\{[1,29]\}|\{[1,30]\}|\{[1,31]\}$,
      period: 28,29,30,or 31 (variable),
      start time: Default,
      end time: ∞ >

Calendar Years
    <granularity: Month,
      pattern: $\{[1,12]\}$,
      period: 12,
      start time: Default,
      end time: ∞ >

Here, *Default* in the start time denotes the default start time as defined in the Gregorian. These 3 abstract calendars together with 4 basic calendars provide a basis on which various user-defined calendars are derived using calendar operations described next. It is straightforward to transform time values from a lower-granularity calendar to a higher-granularity one (see Appendix).

4.4 Calendar Operations

The following high level calendar operations are defined and used to derive various user-defined calendars. All the operations are performed on time units at a certain level and, therefore, they can be implemented using basic set theoretic operations on time units. If calendars involved in an operation have different granularities, one or both need to be converted to a calendar(s) with the *greatest common granularity* before the operation is performed.

- $select_{gr}(C, i, j, ref)$: From each period of a calendar C, select j time units starting from the ith time unit. If ref is *begin*, it counts from the first time unit in a period, and it counts from the last time unit if ref is *end*. The result is represented in terms of the granularity gr.
- $intersect(C_i, C_j)$: Intersection of two calendars C_i and C_j.
- $union(C_i, C_j)$: Union of two calendars C_i and C_j.
- $Exclude(C_i, C_j)$: Exclude the whole sequence of a calendar C_j from that of a calendar C_i.

Note that operations *intersect* and *union* are commutative and associative, so for notational convenience, we allow more than two arguments. The followings are examples of user-defined calendars derived using these operations:

Example 4.1:

1. Calendar of all Novembers:
    Novembers $= select_{Day}(Years, 11, 1, begin) = select_{Day}(Years, 2, 1, end)$
2. Calendar of all Thursdays:
    Thursdays $= select_{Day}(Weeks, 4, 1, begin)$

3. Thanksgiving (the fourth Thursday of November every year):
   Thanksgiving $= select_{Day}(intersect(Novembers, Thursdays), 4, 1, begin)$
4. Christmas: /* assume a calendar Decembers is defined */
   Christmas $= select_{Day}(Decembers, 25, 1, begin)$
5. Holidays: /* assume calendars MemorialDay, LaborDay, and July4 are defined */
   Holidays $= union(MemorialDay, July4, LaborDay, Thanksgiving, Christmas)$
6. All weekends:
   Weekends $= select_{Day}(Weeks, 6, 2, begin) = select_{Day}(Weeks, 1, 2, end)$
7. All work-days:
   WorkDays $= Exclude(Years, union(Holidays, Weekends))$
8. 5 work-days a week:
   WorkDaysAWeek $= Exclude(Weeks, Weekends)$
9. 5 work-days a week excluding all holidays: /* same as 7, but with Week as period */
   BusinessWeek $= Exclude(WorkDaysAWeek, Holidays)$

User-defined calendars can also be specified explicitly without using calendar operations. For example, a calendar of 8 work hours per day is:

Calendar WorkHours
    <granularity: Hour,
     pattern: $\{[9, 11], [13, 17]\}$,
     period: 24,
     start time: 4/1/96,
     end time: ∞ >

5   Integrated Temporal Data Model

In this section, the proposed temporal database model that includes time series concepts is described. Update operations for the model are also presented.

5.1 Model Description

The integrated temporal database model is developed by adding the concept of time series to the conceptual TEER model [10], but the concepts can also be applied to extend other temporal data models. One goal here is a *seamless extension* of the TEER model. In other words, all the properties of the TEER are preserved and additional syntax and semantics should be minimized. To achieve this goal, we model time series as an attribute that is treated with similar semantics as other attributes, but with some extensions to handle characteristics of time series. Such an attribute is called a *time series attribute*.

Since time series attribute can have complex data values, type constructors [14] can be used. A composite attribute corresponds to utilization of the tuple constructor, whereas a multivalued attribute may be of a list, set, or bag data type, and corresponds to the list, set, or bag constructs. The data values of a time series can hence be complex structures created by the nesting of type constructors (tuple, set, list, bag, array, etc.). Since the basic EER model provides graphical notations only for tuple and set constructors (as composite and multi-valued attributes), we extend the notations as shown in Fig.5, which shows the notation for a time series attribute as well as tuple, list, set, bag, and array constructors. Notice that these constructors can be nested graphically to provide attribute structures of arbitrary complexity if needed.

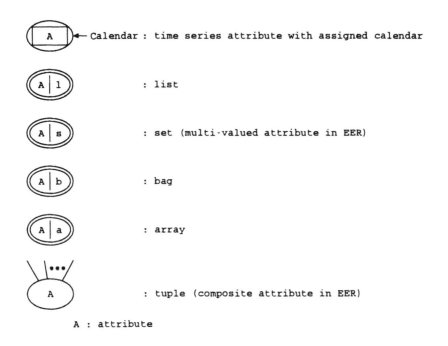

Fig. 5. Extended graphical notations

Associated with each time series attribute is a calendar. The calendar provides the temporal domain of values for the corresponding time series, and also acts as a constraint on the time series with regard to the validity of temporal values that can be associated with the data values.

Like other attributes in TEER model, temporal values of a time series attribute of an entity e, $TS(e)$, is a temporal assignment, that is a partial function $TS(e) : CALENDAR(TS) \rightarrow dom(TS)$, where $CALENDAR(TS)$ is the temporal domain of TS determined by the calendar associated with TS. Figure 6 shows an example database schema for a bank. The attribute *Price* is a time series attribute and is distinguished by a rectangle inside an oval. Its data values are complex, made up of three data items: *high, low,* and *ticks* denoting the daily high price, daily low price and a list of all prices per day, respectively. Assuming the calendar BusinessWeek of Example 4.1, a possible set of attribute values of an entity of type *Stock* is (note that Feb. 17 and Feb. 18 are weekends and Feb. 19 is a holiday in 1996 in the USA):

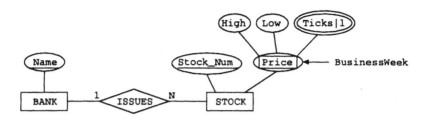

Fig. 6. An example database schema of a bank model

$SURROGATE(e) = \{[1/1/96, now] \rightarrow surrogate\_id\}$ /* system generated */
$stock\_num(e) = \{[1/1/96, now] \rightarrow ABC123456\}$
$price(e) = \{[2/15/96] \rightarrow < 130, 85, < 91, 85, ...130, 120 >>,$
$\quad\quad\quad [2/16/96] \rightarrow < 125, 81, < 81, 90, ...123, 125 >>,$
$\quad\quad\quad [2/20/96] \rightarrow < 132, 125, < 130, 132, ...125, 127 >>$
$\quad\quad\quad [2/21/96] \rightarrow < 142, 120, < 142, 140, ...120, 129 >>,$
$\quad\quad\quad [2/22/96] \rightarrow < 132, 124, < 132, 130, ...125, 124 >>\}$

5.2 Update Operations

Seven basic update operations on the TEER model are introduced in [10]:

- INSERT_ENTITY
- ADD_TO_RELATIONSHIP
- ADD_TO_SUBCLASS
- DELETE_ENTITY
- REMOVE_FROM_RELATIONSHIP
- REMOVE_FROM_SUBCLASS
- MODIFY_ATTRIBUTE

Since time series attributes are treated with the same semantics as other attributes, we can use these basic operations for time series attributes with little
modification in the integrated model. The modification must reflect the facts that
the temporal domain of a time series attribute is a calendar that is a sequence
of temporal values and that the calendar constraint should be enforced when the
values of time series attributes are modified. The following shows the modifications to three of the basic operations. Other operations are not affected. The
modifications are written in bold face characters. Recall that the events of a time
series can be alternatively represented as a list of tuples each of which consists of
temporal_value and a (possibly complex) *data_value*. We use this representation
in the following. We also define a term *legal temporal value* for concise operation
specifications. A *legal temporal value* with respect to a time series is a temporal
value that can exist within the calender specification associated with the attribute. We assume that when an entity is first created, any time series attributes
are empty. Time series events are then appended to the time series attribute by
using the modify operation based on the associated calendar.

- $INSERT\_ENTITY\,(E, attribute\_values, valid\_start\_time)$: A new entity of type E is created having a unique, system-defined surrogate key value and with the specified attribute values. Temporal elements for the entity and all its attributes, *except time series attributes*, will be $[valid\_start\_time, now]$.
  For a time series attribute:
  - If $valid\_start\_time$ is smaller than $starting\_value$ of the associated calendar, the creation of the entity is rejected.
  - Otherwise, an empty time series with no tuples is created.
- $DELETE\_ENTITY\,(E, e, valid\_end\_time)$: (Note that this is a "logical delete", which leaves the entity history intact.) The temporal element of entity e is updated so that now is changed to $valid\_end\_time$. The same change is made to the temporal elements of all attribute values of e *except for time series attributes*.
  For a time series attribute:
  - The time series attributes are not affected by the delete operation.
- $MODIFY\_ATTRIBUTE(E, e, A, new\_value, valid\_change\_time)$: The temporal assignment of attribute A, *except for time series attributes*, of entity e is changed so that now is changed to $valid\_change\_time - 1$ and a new entry $[valid\_change\_time, now] \rightarrow new\_value$ is added to the temporal assignment of $A(e)$.
  For a time series attribute:
  - A tuple $< change\_time, new\_value >$ is appended as the last tuple of the temporal value of the time series attribute , where $change\_time$ is $valid\_change\_time$ if it is a legal temporal value, or the smallest legal temporal value larger than $valid\_change\_time$ otherwise (this allows for different granularity between the time series calendar and the value of $valid\_change\_time$). The temporal value *must be the next legal temporal value* in the time series based on the associated calendar.

6 Mapping to Object-oriented Databases

Mapping of time series attribute in the integrated model to an OO data model involves two issues: mapping of a time series attribute itself and the association of a calendar with it. One may attempt to map a time series attribute to an attribute in the class definition of its associated class. This approach, however, does not provide an effective way to specify many specific time-series operations inside the associated class. Hence, we map each time series attribute into a separate class in the OO data model, and specify its operations in the class. If there are many time series in an application, we can organize their classes into a superclass/subclass hierarchy. There can be a system defined root class for all time series together with typical time series subclasses such as stock prices, weather data, etc. Then, a user can define application-specific time series subclasses based on their specific characteristics.

There are at least two alternatives to deal with a calendar. A simple way is to define a data type $CALENDAR$ using the calendar specification of section 4, and to declare various calendar variables of $CALENDAR$ type (see Fig.7). Then we can associate the calendar variables with time series with different calendar characteristics. If an application requires many sophisticated calendars, then we can define a separate calendar class hierarchy. For example, we first define a root calendar class and then several base calendar subclasses such as Gregorian, Islamic, Lunar, etc. Under these subclasses, users can define various calendars inheriting basic properties from the base calendars. For brevity, in this paper, we show the former approach, and assume the Gregorian calendar.

```
type CALENDAR: tuple(granularity: granularity_type,
                     pattern: pattern_type,
                     period: period_type,
                     start_time: time_unit,
                     end_time: time_unit) ;

/* declaration of calendar variables */
BusinessWeek, WorkHours: CALENDAR ;
/* initialization of these variables must follow */

class StockPrice inherit Security /* security is a superclass */
  type tuple(BusinessWeek: CALENDAR,
             StockValue: list
             (DailyValue: tuple(high: integer,
                                low: integer,
                                ticks: list(tuple (time: time_unit,
                                                   val: integer)))))

  method
    average(week: Week): real, /* stock average price for week */
    closing(day: Day): real, /* stock closing price for day */
    ...
end

class Stock
  type tuple (stock_num: string,
              price: StockPrice)
  method
    ...
end
```

Fig. 7. OO class definitions of a bank example

The mapping scheme is summarized below:

1. A class hierarchy of time series is defined. In this hierarchy, various specific time series are specified as subclasses as needed. Inside each class definition, application specific operations are defined as methods.

2. A calendar data type $CALENDAR$ is defined, and various variables of the type (such as a calendar of BusinessWeek, a calendar of WorkHours, etc) are declared and properly initialized.

3. All time series class definitions include an attribute of $CALENDAR$ type which is one of the calendar variables already declared (this establishes the association between a time series object and a calendar object).

4. A time series attribute itself remains as an attribute in the class definition of its associated class. The value of this attribute is the reference to an object instance of the corresponding time series class.

5. If a time series attribute is a complex attribute and one of its component attributes is also a time series attribute, it is dealt with in the same way as described above (nested time series).

A mapping from the EER database schema of Fig.6 to an OO data model is shown in Fig.7 that uses O_2 notations [14]. Note that the data types *granularity_type*, *pattern_type*, *period_type*, and *time_unit* must be defined separately, and calendar variable *BusinessWeek* must be properly initialized. It is assumed in Fig.7 that the attribute *ticks* is a regular temporal attribute as modeled in the TEER. If, however, stock ticks are sampled regularly it can be modeled as a nested time series. If we assume that it is sampled every hour except during the lunch time, then we can associate it with the calendar *WorkHours* (see Fig.8).

```
/* a new class for stock ticks is defined */
class StockTicks
  type tuple (WorkHours: CALENDAR,
              HourlyPrice: list(val: integer))
  method
        ...
end

/* class definition of StockPrice is changed */
class StockPrice inherit Security /* security is a superclass */
  type tuple(BusinessWeek: CALENDAR,
             StockValue: list
                 (DailyValue: tuple(high: integer,
                                    low: integer,
                                    ticks: StockTicks)))
  method
        ...
end
```

Fig. 8. Mapping of a nested time series

7 Mapping to Relational Databases

When we consider mapping our model into a relational model, we have to consider the ordering of the time series. Unfortunately, traditional relational databases do not have ordering. This is one major disadvantage of mapping our model into a relational database. The general mapping procedure of $TEER$ model into a relational model is provided in [12], and we describe only the mapping of time series attribute $TS =< T, D >$ of an entity type E, where T is a temporal value, and D is a list of data attributes. The list of attributes in D can include simple-data item attributes SD and multi-valued attributes MD. A multi-valued attribute can be one of list, array or bag, and they can also be a multi-valued attribute, thus creating nested structure.

1. For a list of atomic attributes, SD, of a time series TS of an entity type E, we create a temporal relational schema $R(SK, T, SD)$, where SK is the (foreign) key of the entity type E, T is a temporal value, and SD is the list of simple-data item attributes. T can be used as an ordering attribute for the time series since the relational model does not have any ordering. The primary key of the relation R is: (SK, T). The values of T will be derived from the associated calendar.

2. For each list-valued attribute MD_i, $1 \le i \le n$, of a time series TS, we create a temporal relational schema $R(FTK, O, MD_i)$, where FTK is the (foreign) key of the time series TS and O is an additional ordering attribute. The primary key of the relation R is : (FTK, O).

The rules for mapping time series and multivalued attributes may need to be applied recursively if complex attribute structure with arbitrary nesting exists. A mapping from the EER database schema of Fig.6 to a relational data model is shown in Fig.9.

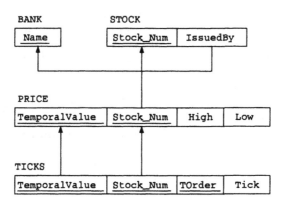

Fig. 9. A relational schema for a bank model

8 Conclusion

In this paper, we presented an integrated data model that handles both traditional, version-based temporal data, as well as time series temporal data within a single framework. Time series is modeled as an attribute that is associated with a calendar, and the calendar provides the temporal values for the time series. The attribute domain provides the data values for the time series, which may have arbitrarily complex structure based on applying the well-known type constructors: tuple, set, list, bag, array, and so on.

We also showed how time series attributes can be mapped to object-oriented and relational databases for implementation purposes. The mapping of version-based temporal data has been discussed in [12], so the mapping described in this paper completes the mapping process for our integrated model.

References

1. J. Clifford and A. Rao, "A Simple, General Structure for Temporal Domains," Temporal Aspects in Information Systems, C. Rolland, F. Bodart, and M. Leonard (Ed.) (1988) 17–28
2. R. Chandra and A. Segev, "Managing Temporal Financial Data in an Extensible Database," Proc. 19th Int'l Conf. on VLDB, (1993) 302–313
3. R. Chandra, A. Segev, and M. Stonebraker, "Implementing Calendars and Temporal Rules in Next Generation Databases," Proc. 3rd Int'l Conf. on Data Engineering (1994) 264–273
4. W. Dreyer, A. K. Dittrich, and D. Schmidt, "An Object-Oriented Data Model for a Time Series Management System," Proc. 7th Int'l Working Conf. on Scientific and Statistical Database Management (1994) 186–195
5. W. Dreyer, A. K. Dittrich, and D. Schmidt, "Research Perspectives for Time Series Management Systems," ACM SIGMOD Record, Vol. 23, No. 1 (1994) 10–15
6. W. Dreyer, A. K. Dittrich, and D. Schmidt, "Using the CALANDA Time Series Management System," Proc. ACM SIGMOD Int'l Conf. (1995) 489
7. C. E. Dyreson and R. T. Snodgrass, "Timestamp Semantics and Representation," Information Systems, 18, No. 3 (1993) 143–166
8. R. Elmasri, V. Kouramajian, and S. Fernando, "Temporal Database Modeling: An Object-Oriented Approach," CIKM 93, Proc. 2nd Int'l Conf. on Information and Knowledge Management (1993)
9. R. Elmasri, S.B. Navathe, "Fundamentals of Database Systems" 2nd Edition, Benjamin/Cummings (1994)
10. R. Elmasri, G. Wuu, "A Temporal Model and Query Language for ER Database," In IEEE Data Engineering Conference (1990)
11. S. Gadia, and C. Yeung, "A Generalized model for a temporal relational database," In ACM SIGMOD Conference (1988)
12. V. Kourmajian and R. Elmasri, "Mapping of 2-D Temporal Extended ER Models into Temporal FNF and NFNF Relational Models," Proc. 10th International Conference on the Entity-Relationship Approach (1991)
13. A. Kurt and M. Ozsoyoglu, "Modeling Periodic Time and Calendars," Proc. Int'l Conf. on Application of Databases (1995) 221–234

14. C. Lecluse, P. Richard, and F. Velez, "O_2, an Object Oriented Data Model," Proc. ACM SIGMOD Conference (1988)
15. S. Navathe, and R. Ahmed, "A Temporal Data Model and Query Language," In Information Sciences (1989)
16. E. Rose and A. Segev, "TOODM - A Temporal Object-Oriented Data Model with Temporal Constraints", Proc. 10th International Conference on the Entity-Relationship Approach (1991)
17. D. Schmidt, A. K. Dittrich, W. Dreyer, and R. Marti, "Time Series, a Neglected Issue in Temporal Database Research?," Proc. Int'l Workshop on Temporal Databases (1995) 214–232
18. R. Snodgrass, "The Temporal Query Language TQUEL," In ACM TODS 12(2) (1987)
19. A. Segev and A. Shoshani, "Logical Modeling of Temporal Data," Proc. ACM SIGMOD Int'l Conf. (1987)
20. M.D. Soo and R.T. Snodgrass, "Multiple Calendar Support for Conventional Database Management," Technical Report TR 92-07, Dept. of Computer Science, University of Arizona, USA
21. A. Tansel et al., Editors "Temporal Databases: Theroy, Design, and Implementations," Database System and Applications Series. Benjamin/Cummings (1993)
22. G. Wuu and U. Dayal, "A Uniform Model for Temporal Object-Oriented Databases," Proc. 8th International Conference on Data Engineering (1992)

Appendix: Relationship among Calendars and Granularities

Relationship among calendars and granularities are described by the following granularity conversion procedures. The conversion procedures use two integer operations $div(i,j)$ and $rem(i,j)$, which return the quotient and remainder, respectively, when i is divided by j.

1. Minute from Second: $Minute = div(Second, 60) + 1$
2. Hour from Minute: $Hour = div(Minute, 60) + 1$
3. Day from Hour: $Day = div(Hour, 24) + 1$
4. Week from Day: $Week = div(Day, 7) + 1$
5. Month from Day

   Due to leap years, the conversion procedure is complicated. Leap years are defined as: {set of all years divisible by 4} - {set of all years divisible by 100 but not divisible by 400}. The conversion procedure is:

   $r_1 = rem(Day, (1461 * 100 - 3)); \ d_1 = div(Day, (1461 * 100 - 3));$
   $r_2 = rem(r_1, (1461 * 25 - 1)); \ d_2 = div(r_1, (1461 * 25 - 1));$
   $r_3 = rem(r_2, 1461); \ d_3 = div(r_2, 1461);$
   $r_4 = rem(r_3, 365); \ d_4 = div(r_3, 365);$
   $Month = (d_1 * 400 + d_2 * 100 + d_3 * 4 + d_4) * 12 + get\_month(r_4);$

   Here, r_4 is the number of days from the beginning of the year, to which the given day belongs, up to (and including) the day. The get_month function returns the month the day belongs to, based on knowledge of month lengths and leap years. If $r_4 = 0$, then $get\_month(r_4)$ returns 12.

6. Year from Month: $Year = div(Month, 12) + 1$

View-Centered Conceptual Modelling

An Object Oriented Approach

Klaus-Dieter Schewe[1], Bettina Schewe[2]

[1] Technical University of Clausthal, Computer Science Institute, D-38678
Clausthal-Zellerfeld
[2] MICOS GmbH, D-26127 Oldenburg

Abstract. Information systems for highly skilled clerical workers present
themselves as a collection of window-based processes with underlying procedures accessing databases. It is left to the users to continue or interrupt
a certain piece of work or to switch from one application to another. Such
system can be supported by three layers: a database layer, a dialogue layer
and a presentation layer.
In this paper an integrated object oriented model with a distinction between
types and classes is outlined. In this model views on the datamodel can be
extended to dialogue classes which enable a smooth integration of dialogue
objects with the underlying datamodel. The only remaining task for the
presentation layer consists of suitable ergonomic presentations of dialogue
objects on the screen by means of a general UIMS.

1 Introduction

Conceptual modelling for information systems depends on the intended application.
In case of the work of highly skilled clerical workers to be supported we must be
aware that they do not follow a monotone working scheme. E.g., consider agencies
of a health insurance company with emphasis on the service for clients, who behave
different from one another, demand for optimal service and information without
delay, address their demands to the agents either personally, by phone or by fax, ap-
preciate not to be burdened with complicated terminology and forms etc. Therefore,
a supporting information system must support workflow beyond strict regularity
permitting its users to examine additional circumstances, write specialized letters
instead of using forms, escape or interrupt processes etc.

As a consequence such information systems have to be composed of several independently usable dialogues leaving to the user the decision which one to use in
a concrete situation. The dialogue system has to offer many quickly reachable dialogue objects without forcing its users to reach them in a specific way. Furthermore,
it must offer a good overview about a client's situation as context to the special
data to be actually processed. On the other hand, such systems must handle large
amounts of data, hence should be supported by a well-designed database system
without bothering the users with database details.

From a conceptual modelling point of view the description of dialogues can be divided into two major components. The first one comprises the pure representational
aspects concerning windows, field, menues, shortcuts etc., and its design is basically
concerned with a UIMS and ergonomic criteria [4]. The second one deals with the
abstract data contained in the dialogue objects.

The nature of the intended applications of being data-intensive makes (conceptual) database design a central task in their development. This task is governed by general requirements concerning the quality of databases, which must be free of redundancies, flexible with respect to future extensions, not limited to specific applications and achieve highly increased performance. However, the data processed in the dialogues is far from satisfying these criteria, but give rise to views.

The development process has to be understood as a learning process, where not all requirements are known at the beginning. This requires the participation of the users, because they are the only ones who can judge about the usefulness of proposed solutions. As a consequence the dialogue objects and hence the views on the data defined by them become the driving force in conceptual modelling. This should not be taken as an accident, but as a challenge.

In this paper we present an integrated model on the basis of the object oriented datamodel (OODM) in [10]. This datamodel has been defined in the spirit of Beeri's fundamental idea concerning the conceptual separation of values and objects [2]. Values are provided by the means of type systems consisting of base types and constructors [6]. Objects are provided by the means of classes which combine complex value and reference structures, operations and inheritance. This approach to object orientation is quite different from the work in [3, 7] which focusses on methods for object oriented programming. In particular, it is easy to see that certain classes of OODM schemata with only flat acyclic reference structures are equivalent to schemata in the higher-order entity relationship model [13]. We give an outline of the datamodel in Section 2.

The OODM has been extended by dialogue classes in [8, 12] in order to support the development of information systems as characterized above. These dialogue classes are defined analogously to classes in the datamodel, i.e. they provide structural and behavioural abstractions of dialogue objects as well as inheritance. The dialogue objects can then be handled in the same way as objects in the database which turns the management of the dialogues into a database task. The relationship between the dialogue model and the datamodel is given by the means of views. We present the dialogue model in Section 3.

The development of user interfaces then reduces to the task of finding suitable representations of dialogue objects on the screen. For this purpose we propose the use of a general UIMS. In Section 4 we present a brief outline of representational means with respect to our integrated model.

To that end, the work reported in this paper continues our previous work in [12]. With respect to that paper we now achieve some simplification concerning the definition of dialogue classes. This definition was first given independently from the datamodel and led to several additional notions such as selection classes, actions and different kinds of operations (selection, navigation, invocation, processing) and we observed already the relationship to views on the datamodel. Now this relationship is directly incorporated in the definition of dialogue classes. Furthermore, selection is enabled by exploiting uniqueness constraints in the datamodel that were introduced in handling the identification problem in OODBs [10], and navigation can be supported by references between dialogue classes. Finally, the variety of different operations can be simplified using the distinction between hidden and visible operations which is already present in the OODM. Actions then correspond to the head of visible operations, while some of their characteristics are shifted to presentations.

With respect to the modelling method we think of a refinement-based approach as presented in [9, 11] for the OODM and extended to the dialogue model in [8], i.e. the data schema and the dialogue schema have to be developped in parallel taking care about their interrelationships. This is in contrast to the work in [1, 5], where the starting point for user interface design is a complete entity-relationship schema. This topic will be briefly sketched in Section 5.

2 The data layer

In the object-oriented datamodel (OODM) [10] we distinguish between objects and values. Whereas values are common abstractions identified by themselves, objects depend on the particular application context and have to be encoded by object identifiers. In the OODM each object consists of a unique, immutable *identifier*, a set of describing values of possibly different types, *references* to other objects and *operations* associated with the object.

2.1 Application-independent abstraction: types

Types are used to describe immutable sets of values with (type-)operations pre-defined on them. Type systems are prescriptions for the syntax and semantics of permitted type definitions. Consider a type system that consists of some *basic types*, *type constructors* and a *subtyping* relation. Moreover, *recursive types*, i.e. types defined by equations, and *predicative types*, i.e. types defined by restricting formulae, are included.

Base types used here are $BOOL, NAT, INT, FLOAT, STRING, ID$ or $\perp$, where ID is an abstract identifier type without any non-trivial supertype and $\perp$ is the trivial type that is a supertype of every type.

The *type constructors* used here are $e_1 \mid \cdots \mid e_n$ (enumeration), $(a_1 : \alpha_1, \ldots, a_n : \alpha_n)$ (record), $\{\alpha\}$ (finite set), $[\alpha]$ (list), (α) (bag) or $(a : \alpha) \cup (b : \beta)$ (union), where $\alpha_1, \ldots, \alpha_n, \alpha, \beta$ are already defined types, $e_1, \ldots, e_n$ are constant values and $a_1, \ldots, a_n, a, b$ are field selectors.

We may use base types and constructors to define new types by nesting. If there is no confusion, the field selectors in record or union types may be omitted.

The semantics of such types as sets of values is defined as usual. Moreover, we assume the standard operations on base types and on records, sets, bags, ... We omit the details here. A type T is called *proper* iff the number of its parameters is 0. T is called a *value type* iff there is no occurrence of ID in T. If T' is a proper type occurring in a type T, then there exists a corresponding *occurrence relation* $o : T \times T' \rightarrow BOOL$ with $o(v_1, v_2) = true$ iff v_2 occurs in v_1 at the position indicated by the position of T' in T.

A *subtype function* is a function $T' \rightarrow T$ from a subtype to its supertype ($T' \preceq T$) defined by the usual subtyping rules [6].

Predicative types are used to restrict the set of values given by some type definition to a subset. Formally, a *predicative type* T consists of an underlying type T' and a formula $\mathcal{P}$ with exactly one free variable **self** of type T'. Clearly, the inclusion then gives a subtype function. In order to avoid inflationary use of quantifiers, other variables are also allowed to occur freely in such a formula. They are assumed to be universally quantified.

EXAMPLE 1. We define a type $PERIOD$ and a predicative subtype $COURSE$ of $[PERIOD]$:

Type $PERIOD = (\text{begin} : DATE, \text{end} : DATE \cup \bot)$
  Where self.end $\neq \bot \Rightarrow$ **self**.begin $\leq$ **self**.end
End $PERIOD$

Type $COURSE = [\, PERIOD\,]$
  Where self $= \text{concat}(L_1, [P_1, P_2 \mid L_2]) \Rightarrow P_2.\text{end} \neq \bot \wedge P_2.\text{end} \leq P_1.\text{begin}$
End $COURSE$

L_1 and L_2 are lists with elements of type $PERIOD$, P_1 and P_2 are values of type $PERIOD$ and 'concat' is the concatenation of two lists. Informally, the formula requires for any two successive periods the begin date of the first one to be later than the end date of the second one. ☐

2.2 Combined structure and behaviour: classes

The *class* concept provides the grouping of objects having the same structure and behaviour. Structurally this uniformly combines aspects of object values and references. Behaviourally, this abstracts from operations on single objects including their creation and deletion. In the OODM objects usually belong to more than one class.

References between classes give rise to implicit referential constraints. In addition, subclasses (IsA-relationships) require each database instance to satisfy inclusion constraints on object identifiers. As usual in object oriented approaches *class operations* are used to model the database dynamics. In the OODM these are associated with classes.

Since identifiers can be represented using ID, values and references can be combined into a representation type, where each occurrence of ID denotes references to some other class. Therefore, we may define the structure of a class using parameterized types. Moreover, classes are arranged in IsA-hierarchies.

More formally, if T is a value type with parameters $\alpha_1, \ldots, \alpha_n$ and if the parameters are replaced by pairs $r_i : C_i$ with a reference name r_i and a class name C_i, the resulting expression is called a *structure expression*.

Then a *class* consists of a class name C, a structure expression S, a set of class names $D_1, \ldots, D_m$ (called *superclasses*) and a set of *operations*. We call r_i the *reference* named r_i from class C to class C_i. The type derived from S by replacing each reference $r_i : C_i$ by the type ID is called the *representation type* T_C of the class C. The type $U_C = (\text{ident} : ID, \text{value} : T_C)$ is called the *class type* of class C.

EXAMPLE 2. Let us consider a class INSURANT for an insurance application.

Class INSURANT $=$
  Structure (insurance_number: NAT, name: $NAME$, address: $ADDRESS$,
    course of insurance: [(kind : "self", begin : $DATE$,
      end : (date: $DATE$, reason: $STRING$) $\cup \bot$) $\cup$
    (kind : "fam", begin : $DATE$, end : $DATE \cup \bot$,

self : SELF INSURANT, relation: "child" | "spouse")])
   Operation ...
End INSURANT

Class SELF INSURANT =
   IsA INSURANT
   Structure (employed by : COMPANY , account no : NAT)
   Operation ...
End SELF INSURANT

A period of insurance in this example is of one of two possible kinds: Either the insurant is employed by a company and therefore pays his/her own fee or (s)he is a family member of the insurant without own income. □

2.3 Operations

The OODM distinguishes between visible and hidden operations on classes to emphasize those that can be invoked by the user. However, all operations on a class including the hidden ones can be accessed by other operations. The justification for such a weak hiding concept is due to two reasons:

- Visible operations serve as a means to specify (nested) transactions. In order to build sequences of database instances we only regard these transactions assuming a linear invocation order on them.
- Hidden operations can be used to handle identifiers. Since these identifiers do not have any meaning to the user, they must not occur within the input or output of a transaction.

Each operation on a class C consists of a *signature* and a *body*. The *signature* consists of an operation name O, a set of input-parameter/type pairs $\iota_i :: T_i$ and a set of output-parameter/type pairs $o_j :: T_j'$. The *body* is recursively built of the following constructs:

- *assignment* $x := E$, where x is the class variable C of type $\{U_C\}$ or a local variable (including the output-parameters), and E is an expression of the same type as x,
- *local variable declaration* Let $x :: T$,
- *skip* and *fail*,
- *sequencing* $S_1 ; S_2$ and *branching* IF $\mathcal{P}$ THEN S_1 ELSE S_2 ENDIF ,
- *operation call* $C' :- O'($in $: E_1', \ldots, E_j',$ out $: x_1', \ldots, x_i')$, where O' is an operation on class C' with compatible signature and
- non-deterministic *selection* of values $New.f(x)$, where f is a selector on the representation type of C; New_Id selects a new identifier.

An operation O on a class C is called *value-defined* iff all types occurring in its signature are proper value types. As already mentioned we require each visible operation to be value-defined. Subclasses inherit the operations of their superclasses, but overriding is allowed as long as the new operation is a *specialization* of all its corresponding operations in its superclasses, but we dispense with a formal discussion of operational specialization.

2.4 OODM schemata and instances

A database *schema* S is given by a finite collection of type and class definitions such that all types, classes and operations occurring within type definitions, structure definitions and operations are defined in S.

At any time, a class represents a finite set of objects. More precisely this is captured by the notion of an *instance* (or database state). For a closed schema S an *instance* $\mathcal{D}$ assigns to each class C a value $\mathcal{D}(C)$ of type $\{(ident : ID, value : T_C)\}$ such that the following conditions are satisfied:

- For each class C identifiers must be unique.
- The set of identifiers in a subclass C is a subset of the one in the superclass C'. Moreover, if $T_C \preceq T'_C$ with subtype function $f : T_C \to T'_C$, then $(i, v) \in \mathcal{D}(C) \Rightarrow (i, f(v)) \in \mathcal{D}(C')$ holds.
- For each reference r from C to D identifiers j occurring in a value v of an object in C with respect to the occurrence relation o_r, i.e.$(i, v) \in \mathcal{D}(C)$ and $o_r(v, j)$ hold, must occur in $\mathcal{D}(D)$.

Basic update operations, i.e. insertion, deletion and update of a single object into a class C, cannot always be derived in the object-oriented case, because the abstract identifiers have to be hidden from the user. However, in [10] it has been shown that for *value-representable* classes these operations are uniquely determined by the schema and consistent with respect to the implicit referential and inclusion constraints.

Value-representability of all classes in a closed schema is implied, if we have a (trivial) *uniqueness constraint* for each class. Such a constraint requires the values of type T_C in the class extension C to be unique.

3 The dialogue layer

Object orientation within dialogue systems means to enter or select values on the screen and to invoke actions on them. The dialogue system reacts by offering other data or by activating and deactivating entries in selection lists or possible actions in the action bar [4]. We call such a collection of data and possible actions a *dialogue object* (d-object). In graphical user interfaces d-objects are normally presented in a window.

Users invoke actions to change data in the database, to navigate to another possibly new dialogue object or to a modified presentation of the same dialogue object. Depending on selections or entries made in a d-object only a part of the possible actions are allowed. The processing of an action may require further preconditions depending on the state of the dialogue system especially on other user's d-objects.

A *dialog object* consists of a unique abstract identifier, a set of values v_i in associated fields $F_1, \ldots, F_n$ which correspond to describing values of objects, a set of references to other dialogue objects in order to allow a quick navigational access, a set of actions to change the data and to control the dialogue and a state with the values 'active' and 'inactive'. This means, that dialogue objects only exist as long as the dialogue object is visible on the screen. If a window is closed the corresponding dialogue object ist deleted.

The identifier serves to administrate the dialogue objects. It is not known to the user, cannot be used by him and is not visible. Only the active d-object allows manipulations of the represented data and only its actions can be invoked.

3.1 Views in the datamodel

Roughly spoken a *view* may be regarded as a stored query. In the relational datamodel queries can be expressed by terms in relational algebra. This can be generalized to the OODM using its type system. Then a *query* turns out to be represented by a term t over some type T such that the free variables of t represent the classes.

Since objects employ identifiers, we have to distinguish between queries that result in values and those that result in (collections of) objects. Therefore we distinguish in the OODM between *value queries* and general access expressions. For a value query the type T of the defining term t must be a value type.

This allows terms t to be built which involve only identifiers already existing in the database. Thus, such queries are called *object preserving*. If we want the result of a query to represent 'new' objects, i.e. if we want to have *object generating queries*, we have to apply a mechanism to create new object identifiers. This can be achieved by object creating functions on the type ID with arity $ID \times \ldots \times ID \rightarrow ID$ [10].

The idea that a view is a stored query then carries over easily. Thus, a *view* on the schema S consists of a view name $v \in N_C$ such that there is no class C with this name, a structure expression $S(v)$ containing references to classes in S or to views on S and a defining access expression[3] $t(v)$ of type $\{(ident : ID, value : T_v)\}$, where T_v is the representation type corresponding to $S(v)$.

EXAMPLE 3. Let us give a sample view on the schema of Example 2:

View COURSE OF INSURANT =
    Structure
        [(kind : "self", begin : $DATE$,
            end : (date: $DATE$, reason: $STRING$) $\cup \perp$,
            fams: { (id: INSURANT, name: $NAME$, relation: "child" | "spouse",
                begin : $DATE$, end : $DATE \cup \perp$) }) $\cup$
        (kind : "fam", begin : $DATE$, end : $DATE \cup \perp$,
            self : (id : INSURANT, name: $NAME$,
                    begin : $DATE$, end : $DATE \cup \perp$))]
    Definition
        { (i,course) | $\exists$ cou . (i,cou) $\in$ INSURANT $\wedge$
            course = [p || $\exists$ c $\in$ cou.course of insurance .
                p.kind = c.kind $\wedge$ p.begin = c.begin $\wedge$ p.end = c.end $\wedge$
                (c.kind = "self" $\Rightarrow$ p.fams = { (j,fam) | $\exists$ cou' .
                    (j,cou') $\in$ INSURANT $\wedge$ fam.name = cou'.name $\wedge$
                    ("fam", fam.begin, fam.end, i, fam.relation) =
                            cou'.course of insurance.first $\wedge$
                    p.begin $\leq$ fam.begin $\wedge$
                    (p.end $\neq \perp \wedge$ fam.end $\neq \perp \Rightarrow$ fam.end $\leq$ p.end)) $\wedge$

---
[3] Assume for the moment that view definitions do not contain recursive definitions.

$$(\text{c.kind} = \text{``fam''} \Rightarrow \exists \, (\text{k,cou''}) \in \text{INSURANT} \, . \, \text{c.self} = \text{k} \wedge$$
$$\text{p.self.name} = \text{cou''.name} \wedge \text{p.self.begin} \leq \text{p.begin} \wedge$$
$$(\text{``self''}, \text{p.self.begin}, \text{p.self.end}) \in \text{cou''.course of insurance} \wedge$$
$$(\text{p.self.end} \neq \perp \wedge \text{p.end} \neq \perp \Rightarrow \text{p.end} \leq \text{p.self.end})) \,] \, \}$$

End COURSE OF INSURANT

This view contains the course of insurance of one concrete insurant. Together with one period of kind 'self' in that course there are also the latest insurance periods of the family members. Together with one period of kind 'fam' there is also the period of the insurant to whose family the related insurant belongs.   □

3.2 Dialogue classes

Dialogue classes serve to group dialogue objects with the same structure and behaviour. As with objects we may use the type *ID* to represent identifiers of d-objects and combine values and references in a structure expression now containing also references to other d-classes. This can be described by a view as defined in the previous subsection. In addition, there should be a visual type which describes the data shown on the screen. This should be a supertype of the representation type corresponding to the structure expression of the defining view. Then the content of a d-object may be split over more than one d-class which leads to the introduction of super-d-classes. Actions can be expressed by d-operations.

Thus, a *dialogue class* (d-class) consists of a unique name DC, a set of names $DC_1, \ldots, DC_n$ of d-classes (called the *super-d-classes* of DC), a defining view with a structure expression DT'_{DC} and a content definition def_{DC}, a value type DT_{DC} which is a supertype of the representation type T'_{DC} corresponding to DT'_{DC} and a set of d-operations. We call DT'_{DC} the *content structure* , T'_{DC} the content type and DT_{DC} the *visual type* of the d-class DC.

EXAMPLE 4. We give a part of the formal definition of a d-class corresponding to the view in Example 3:

Dialogue class COURSE OF INSURANCE
   IsA IIP
   Visual
      [(kind: "self", begin: $DATE$, end: (date: $DATE$, reason: $STRING$) $\cup \perp$,
      fams: {(name: $NAME$, relation: "child" | "spouse", begin: $DATE$,
         end: $DATE \cup \perp$)}) $\cup$
      (kind: "fam", begin: $DATE$, end: $DATE \cup \perp$,
         self: (name: $NAME$, begin: $DATE$, end: $DATE \cup \perp$))]
   Content
      [(kind: "self", begin: $DATE$, end: (date: $DATE$, reason: $STRING$) $\cup \perp$,
      fams: {(id : INSURANT, name: $NAME$, relation: "child" | "spouse",
         begin: $DATE$, end: $DATE \cup \perp$)}) $\cup$
      (kind: "fam", begin: $DATE$, end: $DATE \cup \perp$,
         self: (id : INSURANT, name: $NAME$, begin: $DATE$, end: $DATE \cup \perp$))]
   Definition ...
   Operations ...
End COURSE OF INSURANCE

For the definition we refer to the view presented in Example 3. □

3.3 Operations on d-classes

If a user selects an action associated with an active d-object, (s)he initiates changes to that d-object including its deletion, the creation of a new d-object, modifications to the underlying database or switches to other d-objects. This is modelled by the d-operations on d-classes.

As with the datamodel we distinguish between *visible* and *hidden* d-operations. Only visible d-operations are accessible by user actions, whereas hidden d-operations can only be called from other d-operations. In contrast to the datamodel the access to (visible) d-operations may be restricted by preconditions that express the statusa of a d-object by means of selected or non-selected parts. Such preconditions are given by supertypes of the visual type DT_{DC} of the d-class DC.

Thus, a *d-operation* consists of a *signature*, a *selection type* and a *body*. The signature is the same as for classes in the datamodel. This also applies to the body with the differences that operations to be called can be d-operations on d-classes and operations on classes, whereas assignments are not allowed. In this way we circumvent the update problem for views.

Then by analogy to the datamodel we require visible d-operations to be value-defined. Sub-d-classes inherit d-operations from their super-d-classes, and overriding is restricted to specialization.

EXAMPLE 5. The following defines a d-operation on the d-class COURSE OF INSUR-ANCE of Example 5:

$New\_Insurant$ [(fams:(name:$NAME$)) $\cup$ (self:(name:$NAME$)) $\cup$ $\perp$]
            (in : $\perp$, out : $\perp$)
        SYSTEM :- *save* (in: **cont**) ;
        Let ins :: ID ;
        COURSE OF INSURANCE :- *Select* (in: **sel**, out: ins) ;
        COURSE OF INSURANCE :- *Delete* (in: **cont**.ident) ;
        COURSE OF INSURANCE :- *Invoke* (in: ins)
    End $New\_Insurant$

Here the selection supertype has been put into brackets. Furthermore, we used two standard variables **cont** of type (ident : ID, value : T'_{DC}) for the identifier/content pair of the current d-object and **sel** for the selected values with respect to the selection type.

This d-operation *New Insurant* stores the actual data in the database, retrieves the identifier of the selected insurant, deletes the current d-object and creates a new one associated with the course of insurance of the selected insurant.

For that purposes we used calls to a d-operation *save* defined on the d-class SYSTEM (assume this has been defined as a super-d-class of IIP) and to *generic* d-operations on COURSE OF INSURANCE for the deletion and creation of d-objects. We shall investigate genericity below. □

3.4 The dialogue management level

The notions of d-schema and d-instance generalize the corresponding notions for the datamodel. A *d-schema* is a finite collection of type, class and d-class definitions that do not contain undefined types, classes, operations, d-classes or d-operations occurring in structure expressions, references, superclasses, signatures or calls. In particular, each d-schema $\mathcal{DS}$ has an underlying OODM schema $\mathcal{S}$.

Then an instance $\mathcal{D}$ of $\mathcal{S}$ already defines the contents of the views underlying d-classes in $\mathcal{DS}$ and hence also the contents with respect to the visual types. For a d-class DC we write $\mathcal{D}(\text{DC})$ for the value of type $\{(\text{ident} : ID, \text{value} : T'_{\text{DC}})\}$ defined by the content definition part def_{DC} on the instance $\mathcal{D}$. We call $\mathcal{D}(\text{DC})$ the set of *possible* d-objects in d-clasd DC with respect to the instance $\mathcal{D}$.

However, we want to associate with a d-instance the set of *actual* (active) d-objects in d-class DC. This should lead to subsets of $\mathcal{D}(\text{DC})$ satisfying conditions analogous to those required for instances $\mathcal{D}$.

Thus, a *d-instance* $\mathcal{DD}$ for a d-schema $\mathcal{DS}$ consists of an instance $\mathcal{D}$ of the underlying OODM schema $\mathcal{S}$ and a mapping $\mathcal{D}_{\text{act}}$ which assigns to each d-class DC $\in \mathcal{DS}$ a set $\mathcal{D}_{\text{act}}(\text{DC})$ such that the uniqueness of identifiers, the inclusion integrity and the referential integrity (as defined for instances) hold.

3.5 The impact of genericity: selection, invocation, navigation, deletion

As for classes in the datamodel we may ask for generic operations on d-classes. Since possible d-objects are already determined by instances, generic operations for d-classes can only provide the *deletion* of actual d-objects or the *invocation* of another d-object. Note that the latter case comprises the navigation to an existing (active) d-object as well as the creation of a new one (in $\mathcal{D}_{\text{act}}(\text{DC})$) combined with a switch to it.

Since sets of actual d-objects behave like sets of ordinary OODM objects, we may exploit the identification theoty of the OODM in [10] to generate these generic operations. Even simpler, due to the definition via views we only need a *value identification* for d-objects.

Recall that such a value identification is given by *uniqueness constraints* for all classes. Since subtyping can be easily extended to structure expressions, such a uniqueness constraint on a class C with structure expression S_C is simply given by a super-structure-expression $\bar{S}_C$. If the representation type $\bar{T}_C$ of $\bar{S}_C$ is a value type, then this means to determine a unique object in $\mathcal{D}(C)$, i.e. its identifier, from a given value of type $\bar{T}_C$ (if such an object exists at all). If $\bar{S}_C$ contains a reference, we first have to identify a referenced object, i.e. to determine its identifier from a given value of some value type.

Thus value identification gives rise to a generic *select*-operation which may call *select*-operations on other classes. If there are several uniqueness constraints, we may combine the required input types using the union constructor.

EXAMPLE 6. For the class INSURANT in Example 2 we may obtain a *select*-operation with the signature

select (in : sel :: (Isn: NAT) $\cup$ (name: $NAME$, date_of_birth: $DATE$, address: $ADDRESS$), out: i:: ID)

Since the view in Example 3 is object preserving and the d-class in Example 4 is defined on top of this view, the operation carries over to a select operation for a d-objerct (used in Example 5). □

As seen in Example 6 value identification gives rise to a generic *select*-operation for d-classes defined by object preserving views. In this case the *delete-* and *invoke*-operations can be split into a selection part, i.e. a call to the *select*-operation and a simpler *delete-* or *invoke*-operation with an input of type ID (the identifier of the d-object).

In the case of an object generating view the new objects depend on others and we may obtain a generic *select*-operation by first selecting these other objects. E.g., in our insurance application this applies to a d-class in which each period of an insurant is turned into a separate object.

4 The presentation layer

The handling of a dialogue system is best performed using a User Interface Management System (UIMS). Such a system provides (among other features)

- windows and operations to open and close them, to move them on the screen, to scroll, to change their size etc.;
- several representations of data, such as selection lists or buttons, text entry fields etc.;
- a main menu where all dialogues start, often called the operation desk.

4.1 Presentation of dialogue classes

For each d-class there is at least one representation on the screen. Normally there are actions with which the representation of the d-class on the screen can be modified without changing the state of the d-class. The representation of the d-class is given by the UIMS. The concrete description therefore depends on its functionality.

Visual values are associated with *fields* consisting of a relation to a component of the content type of a d-class, field attributes like 'protected' / 'unprotected', 'normal' / 'emphasized', ..., the type of the field (text entry field, selection field, ...), a selection state with the values 'selected' and 'unselected', the information whether data have been entered in a field or not, the information where the cursor is placed and an optional name of the field.

Fields may be grouped together. Further properties of fields depend on the features of the UIMS. For each field there is at least one representation on the screen comprising a declaration of its length, its style of emphasis and its style of representation of protection. For each representation there is also a representation of the selection state of the field.

EXAMPLE 7. The presentation of a d-object in the class COURSE OF INSURANCE consists of three parts corresponding to the d-classes COURSE OF INSURANCE, IIP and SYSTEM (see Figure 1):

System History Options Windows						
Course of the Insurance						

1133557 Neumann, Luise				10.11.1948	273
+ more information about the insurant +					

Kind	Begin	End	Reason of End			
			Name	Relation	Begin	End
self	01.04.1979					
			Neumann, Marga	child	13.02.1984	
			Neumann, Horst	child	27.04.1986	
fam	10.11.1976	31.03.1979				
			Meier-Neumann, Fritz		01.01.1975	
self	01.10.1967	09.11.1976	Too old as student			
fam	10.11.1948	30.09.1967				
			Neumann, Wilhelm		01.01.1919	16.08.1990

Fig. 1. The presentation of a d-object

- The 'insurant information part (IIP)' is part of most d-objects and gives an overview about the insurant.
- Besides the IIP the d-object contains a list of insurance periods. Each period is represented by a group of lines of which the first line contains the kind (self or as family member of another insurant), the begin and the end of the period. For periods of kind 'self' several lines (maybe 0) follow with names of family members, the relation of the family member to the insurant and begin and end of the latest insurance period of the family member. For periods of kind 'fam' one line follows with the name and the insurance period of the insurant whose family the member belongs to.
- The last line is used for messages and originates from the d-class SYSTEM. □

Besides the d-classes which are invoked by the user there are *dialogue boxes*, in which data can be entered and processed [4]. Dialogue boxes are called by operations of d-classes, if further data are needed to finish an operation.

4.2   Presentation of actions

The user uses *actions* to change the data on the screen and to control the dialogue. These actions correspond to the d-operations in the d-classes of the d-object and therefore consist of a name used in the action bar, a shortcut symbol with which the action can be invoked alternatively and a selection criterium.

The name of the action is the name of the corresponding d-operation, but names of menus may be added if necessary. The selection criterium is given by fields that may or must be selected before invoking the action. It corresponds to the selection type of the corresponding d-operation. Invoking an action means to execute the body of the corresponding d-operation.

EXAMPLE 8. Let us explain some actions associated with the d-object in Figure 1:

- 'History' shows earlier states of the course of the insurance.
- 'System' and 'Options' are pull-down-menus (omitted in the example). E. g., 'System' contains the following actions: New Insurant, Save, Cancel (Esc), Save and Quit (F3), Scroll Forward (Bild↓), Scroll Back (Bild↑), Desk (Strg + F4).
- 'New insurant' saves the data on the screen and shows the course of insurance of another insurant which can be selected in the list of periods. If no insurant is selected a dialogue box with entry fields for the search for a new insurant is activated.
- 'Save' saves the changes of the data on the screen and shows the same dialogue object again.
- 'Cancel' deletes the dialogue object and returns to the one which was active before respectively to the desk. Changes made to the data are forgotten.
- 'Windows' is a pull-down-menu, containing the list of all existing dialogue objects. It is offered by the UIMS and not described here.   □

5 Development Methods

In the previous sections we presented an integrated data- and dialogue-model for conceptual modelling, but we did not investigate how to use this model in practice. Due to space limitations, the following presentation of development methods will be rather sketchy. We indicate the power of the chosen model on the basis of two scenarios. The first one captures the case of a new system to be designed, the second one handles the case of changing or extending a working application. In both cases, we concentrate on the conceptual level.

5.1 Designing a New Application

In designing a new application we have to define types, classes and d-classes from scratch. We assume that purely presentational aspects are captured by the use of a UIMS. The method we propose assumes an almost monotonic growth of application knowledge by means of interviews with the intended users and analysis of their working processes to be supported. The first goal will be to gather the basic activities of the users and to outline the corresponding dialogues. At this level, representational aspects naturally come into play by means of restrictions on screens, facilities of the UIMS and basic hard- and software.

From a more abstract point of view this means to start with dialogue objects and to abstract to dialogue classes without knowing the underlying datamodel schema. E.g., we could decide to have a presentation of dialogue objects and actions (grouped to menues) as in Figure 1. The simplest way to obtain a first conceptual data schema is to take the view definition as trivial, i.e., the content type of the view coincides with the representation type of a class. Note that references only occur, if we decided to split the data in the presentation among several dialogue objects.

As to the methods, we may either postpone them for later specification or define them on the basis of this first schema. The first alternative is generally recommended as long as the database schema is not stable. Thus, the first development step results in a schema with certain undefined types, classes and references and with redundancies concerning the data schema.

Usually there is not only one such dialogue class – otherwise we are done. Hence there will be several dependencies among the classes of the schema. The second step will be to make these dependencies explicit by the definition of constraints. Then the third step is to refine the schema in order to shift as much of theses dependencies as possible into structures. Refinement rules for this purpose have been extensively discussed in [8, 9, 11]. These comprise

- the splitting of classes thereby introducing references or IsA-relations,
- the introduction of new classes by specialization omitting the old class or introducing an IsA-relation,
- the extension of the schema by new types, classes, d-classes etc. and
- the completion of the schema adding definitions to undefined components.

All these refinement steps can be reversed. Applying one of them requires consequent changes to the constraints and the methods defined so far. Furthermore, each refinement guarantees that classes of the old schema become views on the new schema, which in turn shows how to achieve complete d-classes.

5.2 Changing an Existing Application

When there already exists a running application and we want to change or extend it, the processing method is quite similar. We analyse the new processes, detect the dialogue object and add d-classes to the schema. In addition, let the underlying views be trivial thereby introducing redundancies on the data layer. Thus, the first schema update is simply additive.

In the following steps redundancies have to be made explicit using constraints and these are shifted into structure definitions. As a result we obtain again the required view definition which can finally be flattened. We omit further details and refer to [8] for an extensive discussion of an application example.

6 Conclusion

In this paper we presented an object oriented model which integrates a datamodel and a dialogue model by the means of views. Objects are used as units of data in the database with describing values, references to other objects and operations. They are managed by an object oriented database management system.

In the same way d-objects define the basic units of dialogues. A d-object abstract from presentational issues at the user interface und hence provides a description of data and actions presented in dialogues. The data in the database and the dialogues are related by the means of views. This allows d-objects to be managed in the manner as objects. Only screen presentations are left to a supporting user interface management system.

The conceptual building blocks for objects and d-objects then follow the same principles. We use classes and d-classes to describe the abstract structural and behavioural aspects of both. Then a view on the database describes the possible contents of d-objects. Selection and creation correspond to uniqueness constraint that were introduced in connection with value-representability. In contrast to previous work the paper emphasizes just these relationships between the datamodel and the dialogue model. '

References

1. H. Balzert. Der JANUS-Dialogexperte: Vom Fachkonzept zur Dialogstruktur. *Softwaretechnik-Trends*, 13(3), August 1993.
2. C. Beeri. A formal approach to object-oriented databases. In *Data and Knowledge Engineering, Vol. 5*, 353 – 382. North Holland, 1990.
3. P. Coad and E. Yourdan. *Object-oriented analysis*. Prentice Hall, Englewood-Cliffs, N.J., 1991.
4. IBM (International Business Machines Corp.). *Systems Application Architecture Common User Access / Advanced Interface Design Guide*, 1991. Nr. SC34-4290.
5. C. Janssen, A. Weisbecker, and J. Ziegler. Generating user interfaces from data models and dialogue net specifications. In *Human Factors in Computing Systems (INTER-CHI)*, 418 – 423, Amsterdam, 1993. ACM.
6. J. C. Mitchell. Type systems for programming languages. In J. von Leeuwen, editor, *The Handbook of Theoretical Computer Science, Vol. B*, 365 – 458. Elsevier, 1990.
7. J. Rumbaugh, M. Blaha, W. Premerlane, F. Eddy, and W. Lorensen. *Object-Oriented Modeling and Design*. Prentice Hall, Englewood Cliffs, New Jersey, 1991.
8. B. Schewe. *Kooperative Softwareentwicklung – Ein objektorientierter Ansatz*. Deutscher Universitätsverlag, Leverkusen, 1996.
9. B. Schewe, K.-D. Schewe, and B. Thalheim. Objektorientierter Datenbankentwurf in der Entwicklung datenintensiver Informationssysteme. *Informatik - Forschung und Entwicklung*, 10 (3), 1995, 115 – 127.
10. K.-D. Schewe and B. Thalheim. Fundamental concepts of object oriented databases. *Acta Cybernetica, Szeged*, 11(1/2), 1993, 49 – 84.
11. K.-D. Schewe and B. Thalheim. Principles of object oriented database design. In H. Jaakkola, H. Kangassalo, T. Kitahashi, and A. Márkus, editors, *Information Modelling and Knowledge Bases V*, 227 – 242. IOS Press, Amsterdam, 1994.
12. B. Schewe and K.-D. Schewe. A user-centered method for the development of data-intensive dialogue systems – an object oriented approach. In E. D. Falkenberg, W. Hesse, A. Olivé, editors, *Information System Concepts*, 88 – 103. Chapman & Hall, 1995.
13. B. Thalheim. Foundations of entity-relationship modeling. *Annals of Mathematics and Artificial Intelligence*, 7, 1993, 197 – 256.

Reverse Engineering of Relational Database Physical Schemas

Isabelle Comyn-Wattiau** and Jacky Akoka*

* Ecole Supérieure des Sciences Economiques et Commerciales (ESSEC),
Av B. Hirsch, B.P. 105, 95021 Cergy, France, Email : P_Akoka@edu.essec.fr
Tel : (33)(1)34 43 30 77 Fax: (33)(1) 34 43 30 01
* * ESSEC and Laboratoire PRiSM, Université de Versailles,
45, avenue des Etats-Unis 78035 Versailles

Abstract. This paper seeks to present and illustrate essential aspects of database physical de-optimisation within the context of a reverse engineering method, called MeRCI. The latter provides a framework allowing us to achieve a reverse engineering of a relational database into an Extended Entity-Relationship schema. In this paper we focus mainly on a critical step of MeRCI leading to schema de-optimization that removes the non-semantic aspects of the physical and logical schemas. To achieve such a result, we reverse engineer the physical structures obtained by a database designer when using restructuring operations. Removing optimization structures requires to reverse the effect of both relational operators (join, restrict, project, etc) and non-relational operators such as the flattening operator. The de-optimization process requires the analysis of both the Data Description Language (DDL) and the Data Manipulation Language (DML) specifications and to perform a data mining process, thus allowing us to recover the structure of a database conceptual schema. The paper illustrates the de-optimization process by applying it to various examples. Finally, we discuss implications for further research pertaining to the logic and development of an efficient and complete reverse engineering method eliciting the semantics of a relational database.

1 Introduction

It is now widely accepted that information systems are an important enabling technology. They are seen as a strategic resource, a potential source of competitive advantage. However, to play a key role in entreprise strategy, information systems will have to incorporate organizational changes resulting from the changing environment that characterizes the entreprises today. Existing computer applications must be modified to meet new or changing user requirements. Both organization and environment changes create new information requirements. Because of the soaring costs of data processing personnel, the maintenance of existing applications has become a very expensive process. It has been shown that maintenance consumes more than 50 percent of software budgets. More than one half of the EDP professional staff is involved in maintenance [20]. This cost is increasing due to rapid changes in information technology organization's environment, and the growing role of information in the firm. In order to alleviate the strain put on organizations today, new kinds of engineering methodologies are required to incorporate efficiently organization changes and maintain existing computer applications. Reverse engineering and more precisely database reverse engineering can play a central role. Reverse engineering takes existing programs and database descriptions and converts them into corresponding design-level components such as entities, relationships, attributes and processes. These existing programs and database descriptions and converts them into corresponding design-level components such as entities, relationships, attributes and processes. These design-level components can then be used in two ways : to create new computer applications and to redesign existing databases.

Database reverse engineering can be seen as a part of the maintenance process that procures a sufficient understanding of existing systems and their application domains, allowing changes to be incorporated [9]. Its aim is to recover design specifications by understanding a domain's semantics about an existing database [6]. Relational database reverse engineering aims to produce the conceptual schema by analyzing one of the main sources of the semantics of a given relational database : the database schema, the application programs, the explicit integrity constraints, and application programs [12].

In most real-life relational systems, normalized relations are not always ideal structures for implementation. They are restructured in order to meet the performances required by the users. Performance considerations force a change of the logical schema in two phases : *a structural design* phase leading to the choice of record type structures and link types, and *a physical design* phase aiming at an implementable organization where the structures designed can operate according to the performance requirements of the system.

Relational database reverse engineering should therefore take into account these structural and physical design phases and perform a de-optimization process. However, an analysis of past work shows that most previous methods for translation from the relational to a conceptual model assume that the database relations are normalized (3NF). As a consequence, they ignore that for performance reasons, normalized relations are rarely used, but are transformed into denormalized relations. MeRCI and the de-optimization phase consider as a starting point the denormalized relations and propose appropriate rules for the reverse engineering process.

The remainder of this paper is organized as follows. In Section 2, we present a state of the art of database reverse engineering. A review of earlier work used in our approach is presented. In Section 3, we present and discuss our MeRCI methodology allowing us to perform a reverse engineering of a relational database. Section 4 describes in some details the de-optimization phase of this methodology. We present a process for schema de-optimization that removes the non-semantic aspects of physical and logical relational database schema. This process leads to a set of transformation rules offering a high level of automation. Section 5 is devoted to a complete example. Finally, we present in Section 6 our conclusions and some further research.

2 Database Reverse Engineering : A State of the Art

Prior research in database reverse engineering can be split into two main generations. The first generation consists of rather simple algorithms for reverse engineering of database schemas. The first generation itself falls in two major streams : one that that focuses on transformation of navigational database schemas (including conventional files systems, hierarchical and CODASYL-type database schemas) and another that seeks to recover conceptual schema of relational systems. For instance, Casanova and Amarel de Sa [4,5], Davis and Arora [10] and Nilsson [22] proposed reverse engineering methods for conventional files, mainly COBOL-type files. Navathe and Awong [21], Winans and Davis [30] demonstrated the usefulness of reverse engineering methods for hierarchical database systems. Batini et al. proposed a simple reverse engineering process for CODASYL-type database systems [3]. These studies have one common theme : the reverse engineering process was obtained through a systematic empirical analysis.

In the second stream, devoted mainly to relational and object databases, the reverse engineering process was empirically formalized through the definition and test of data on indicators that operationalize the relevant concepts. Many algorithms have been proposed for converting relational database schemas into conceptual schemas using the Entity-Relationship model. Batini et al. proposed a reverse engineering process allowing the analysis of the relations and their associated concepts using a semantic knowledge of the source relational schema [3]. This reverse engineering process is considered, at best, very simple. Fonkam and Gray presented a comparative study of three representative algorithms for converting relational schemas to conceptual models [12]. They derived a new algorithm that integrates the most important concepts of the previous algorithms and introduced new concepts to rectify their limitations. A major contribution of this new algorithm is its treatment of subtypes/supertypes, relationships and candidate keys. By treating the latter in the same way as primary keys, it became possible to identify the relationships embodied by these candidate keys.

Therefore, the first generation methods can be classified in two groups. The first group consists of automated methods for reverse engineering which assume strong hypotheses on database schemas. The second group contains non automated methods presenting mainly guidelines for the reverse engineer.

The second generation methods emerged by 1992. Hainaut highlighted the problem of semantic degradation inherent in the database design process [13,14]. A number of approaches have been proposed to allow a more systematic reverse engineering process :
- Premerlani and Blaha proposed a set of methods and techniques allowing them to recover the semantics of relational databases, leading to an OMT conceptual schema [25]. This approach is mainly empirical and benefits from wide real database explorations.
- Chiang et al. presented a process of reverse engineering of relational schemas into EER schemas with a high level of automation [6,7,8]. To achieve such a result, the reverse engineering process recovers domain semantics by analysis of the executable schema and data instances. However, this approach leads to results that cannot be considered as decidable. An interesting aspect is the performance evaluation of the algorithm and a clear explanation of user interaction.
- Hainaut et al. define the reverse engineering process as a schema transformation and thus unify all the database design processes (forward/reverse engineering, logical and physical design) [14,15,17]. Hainaut et al. proposed a database reverse engineering two-phase process consisting in recovering the data structures, then in recovering their semantics. This approach is DBMS-independent, allowing the translation of relational, CODASYL, hierarchical systems, as well as COBOL and file structures.
- Petit et al. [24] and Andersson [2] presented methods for extracting a conceptual schema from a relational database based on an analysis of data manipulation statements extracted from the application code. Attributes and possible keys are determined by an analysis of join conditions in queries and view definitions. The database extension is investigated in a selective manner. The main advantage of these approaches is that it makes possible to construct a conceptual schema using rudimentary information. The DREAM approach [24] performs a reverse engineering

process based on the data dictionary, SQL requests and the database extension. There is no hypothesis on attribute names. As a consequence two attributes having the same name in two different relations are not considered as equivalent. Petit et al. recommend to consider denormalized schemas. However they don't integrate this aspect in their rules. DREAM requires the SQL request to be correctly designed, in order to use the database.

- The cognitive approach proposed by Signore et al. [26] performs a reverse enginering process based on the identification of schema primary keys, SQL and procedural indicators that lead to the rebuilding of the conceptual schema. The methodology is implemented using a Prolog prototype, requiring a user interaction.

Finally let us mention the research conducted by Vermeer and Apers [29]. They described a method for translating database operations from a relational database to an object-oriented context. Two main reverse engineering techniques are described : a translation algorithm for embedded SQL, and the notion of object classes as shadow types of program variables.

To the best of our knowledge, few of the previous approaches deal with the problem of de-optimization :

- most papers consider that the database was implemented in 3NF relations.
- Chiang's algorithm supports non 3NF-relations only if functional dependencies are provided [6]. Thus the tool transforms the schema into a 3NF one using these functional dependencies. Vertical partitioning detection is mentioned as a refinement suggested by the user at the end of the reverse engineering process.
- Hainaut lists the most frequent optimization transformations and can detect the merging of two entity types linked by a one-to-many relation type into a single entity type if functional dependencies are given [15]. For other optimization transformations (computed attributes, horizontal and vertical partitioning, horizontal and vertical merging), the detection seems to be left to the reverse engineer.
- Premerlani and Blaha have found out are a number of optimization transformations in their experimentations leading to possible heuristics, but it is not clear if these heuristics are currently implemented [25]. They mention horizontal partitioning, redundant one-to-one relationship implementation and implementation artifacts.

In this paper, we concentrate on this de-optimization process, eliciting rules to detect the optimization transformations in the data dictionary, the DML specifications and in the data instances.

3 MeRCI : An Intelligent Reverse Engineering Method

MeRCI, a French acronym for Intelligent Reverse Engineering Method (Méthode de RétroConception Intelligente) aims at the transformation of a relational database physical and logical schemas into a conceptual schema starting mainly from the source codes of the application (DDL and DML). The study of the physical schema and its associated SQL programs allows us to identify appropriate informations translated into a knowledge base fact using the reverse engineering rule base. This intelligent translation process leads to a conceptual schema. Based on an expert system, it proposes alternative solutions to be validated at each reverse engineering phase by the database designer. Before briefly describing the method, let us stress the two following considerations :

- The aim of this paper is not to describe in a detailed way the different steps of MeRCI. Readers interested by the method are referred to [1].
- The aim of this paper is to describe, analyze and apply a de-optimization phase in the reverse engineering process. This phase ignored by most of previous approaches is critical to attain a sound conceptual schema. It starts with relational physical schema containing denormalized relations and proposes a set of rules to de-optimize the physical schema. This step is a fundamental step of MeRCI.

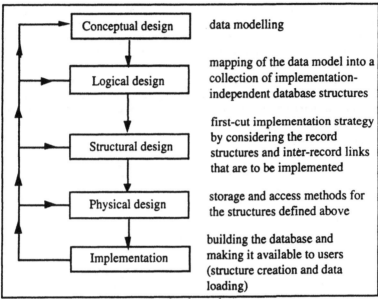

Fig. 1- The database design steps

MeRCI is a reverse engineering method based on the life-cycle database system development model. The latter generally involves five stages (Fig 1). MeRCI reverses the order of the five stages of the life-cycle model leading to an equivalent reverse engineering process described below (Fig 2). Let us mention that Hainaut already suggested to inverse the order of database design process by splitting the reverse engineering process into two phases [15]. The main steps of MeRCI are :

a) Extraction of the physical schema.

The aim of this step is to obtain a complete description of the physical schema. This result can be achieved by using the data dictionary, the DDL, the views, the sub-schemas and even by analyzing the content of users outputs or of the input screens. It may be necessary to consider the source codes in order to identify some hidden structures, non-declared structures and even lost specifications.

b) De-optimization of the physical schema

Starting from the physical schema obtained at the end of the preceding step, we apply a set of physical reverse engineering rules to de-optimize the physical schema. Since this process represents the major contribution of this paper, it is described in more details at Section 4.

c) Identification of entities, relationships and cardinalities

The entity, relationship and cardinality identification process is performed :
- using all the informations extracted from the de-optimized physical schema,

- examining the embedded SQL source code to determine identifiers (primary keys, unique columns, unique index and possible candidate keys),
- searching for synonyms and foreign keys,
- looking for referential integrity constraints.

MeRCI suggests meaningful indicators to fully identify entities, relationships and cardinalities, thus enriching Signore's propositions [26].

d) Detection of hierarchies

The aim of this step is to detect generalization/specialization. The transformation of EER generalizations into relations can be performed using three main rules [3]. This step seeks informations in DDL and DML specifications and by scanning data to detect a potential application of these three rules. The reverse process thus allows us to recover the generalization links, mainly by analyzing the DML specifications.

e) Conceptualization

Some of the informations defined in step c) can be used to identify multivalued attributes, decode tables and more generally the "spurious" relations. Some hypotheses can be formulated on the conceptual meaning of the entities and relationships obtained.

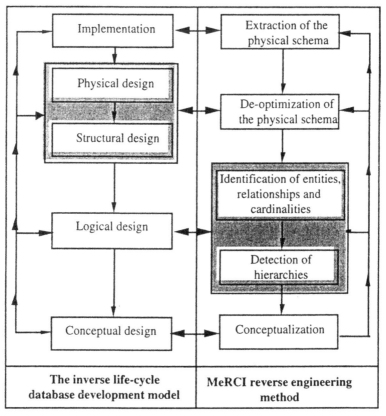

Fig. 2- MeRCI reverse-engineering process and the life-cycle database development

As it can be seen, MeRCI is a complete reverse engineering method, encompassing two important steps generally ignored by most previous approaches : extraction of physical schemas and de-optimization of the physical schemas. Of course, in the other steps, we borrow some reverse rules and heuristics from previous methods. The de-optimization phase plays a central role in the method and can be usefully incorporated into the other methods described in the literature (Section 2).

4 De-optimization of relational physical schema

The aim of this section is to propose a reverse engineering process allowing us to de-optimize a relational database physical schema. Optimization operations aim to avoid a non-useful flow of input/output or costly relational calculus.

In order to detect potential optimization operations which would have transformed the logical schema, we first examine the DDL specifications extracted from the database or deduced from the data dictionary. If we meet conditions allowing us to suspect an optimization operation, we then scan the DML specifications to confirm or infirm the first presumptions. In the case where both DML and DDL specifications meet the reverse engineering rule conditions, we perform a data mining process to validate the restructuring operations. This process is iterated as long as reverse engineering rules have to be tested. Finally a restructured logical schema is presented to the designer in order to validate the transformations. In this section, we describe the different rules applied to relational operators (join, project, restrict) and to non-traditional operators such as the flattening operator.

For each operation, we present the principle underlying the optimization, an example and the potential consequences on schema normalization. Then we describe the reverse operation and its detection process. Finally, we give the complete reverse engineering rules.

4.1 The join operation

a) Principle
The join operator is considered to be one of the most time-consuming and data-intensive operations in relational query processing. Since frequently used, the join operations must be performed efficiently. Physical database design requires that relations in a database must be such that any pair can be joined without loss of data. Several types of joins can be considered [23].

b) Example
Let Invoice and Customer be two relations with a common attribute Customer# :
Invoice (Invoice#, Customer#, Amount, Date).
Customer (Customer#, Customer_name, Address).
By joining the two relations we obtain a third relation :
Incust (Invoice#, Customer#, Amount, Date, Customer_name, Address).
Storing the join results instead of the two initial relations avoids costly relational calculus. In this example, we used an outerjoin in order to avoid the loss of data about customers without invoices.

c) Consequences on schema normalization
Depending on the situation, the join operator will not generate a denormalized schema or can transform a 3NF schema into a 2NF schema or can even transform a 2NF schema into a 1NF schema. More precisely, four different cases can be considered :

Case 1 : The join is performed on an attribute which is a primary key of the two relations.

$$R1(\underline{K}, C_1, C_2, ..., C_n) \ \& \ R2 \ (\underline{K}, D_1, D_2, ..., D_m)$$
$$=> \ R(\underline{K}, C_1, C_2, ..., C_n, D_1, D_2, ..., D_m)$$

This join operator can introduce a great number of null values. However, it does not have any consequence on the normalization. Therefore, if R1 and R2 are in 3NF, R will be in 3NF. This result holds even if K is a compound key.

Example : Employee (<u>Employee-number</u>, Rank, Salary).

Career (<u>Employee-number</u>, Arrival-date, First-Career-Job, Starting-Salary)

Case 2 : The join operator is performed on the primary key of the first relation and on the foreign key of the second relation.

$$R1(\underline{K1}, C_1, C_2, ..., C_n) \ \& \ R2 \ (\underline{K2}, D_1, D_2, ..., D_m, K1)$$
$$=> \ R(\underline{K2}, C_1, C_2, ..., C_n, D_1, D_2, ..., D_m, K1)$$

This join operation generates redundant data. Moreover it has an effect on the normalization process. If K1 is a primary key of R1, K1 will functionally determine $C_1, C_2, ..., C_n$. Therefore R contains functional dependencies between non-key attributes.

Example : Invoice (<u>Invoice#</u>, Customer#, Amount, Date)

Customer (<u>Customer#</u>, Customer-name, Address)

Case 3 : The join operator is performed on a primary key of the first relation and on an attribute of the compound key of the second relation.

$$R1(\underline{K1}, C_1, C_2, ..., C_n) \ \& \ R2 \ (\underline{K1, K2}, D_1, D_2, ..., D_m)$$
$$=> \ R(\underline{K1, K2}, C_1, C_2, ..., C_n, D_1, D_2, ..., D_m)$$

This join operation generates redundant data. Moreover, it has an effect on the normalization process. Since K1 is a primary key, it will functionally determine $C_1, C_2, ..., C_n$. Therefore, R will contain functional dependencies between the attribute of the compound key and non-key attributes ($C_1, C_2, ..., C_n$).

Example : Student (<u>Student#</u>, Name, Level)

Result (<u>Student#, Course#</u>, Grade)

Case 4 : The join operation is performed on non-key attributes of both relations.

$$R1(\underline{K1}, C_1, C_2, ..., C_n, NK) \ \& \ R2 \ (\underline{K2}, D_1, D_2, ..., D_m, NK)$$
$$=> \ R(\underline{K1, K2}, C_1, C_2, ..., C_n, D_1, D_2, ..., D_m, NK)$$

This join operation is seldomly performed. This is not a natural join since it does not link unrelated data mainly for normalization considerations. If R1 and R2 are in 3NF, R will contain redundant data. It will not be in 2NF since there exist functional dependencies between part of the key (for example K1) and non-key attributes such as $C_1, C_2, ..., C_n, NK$.

Example : Supplier (<u>Supplier#</u>, Name, Address, Headquarter-city).

Part (<u>Part#</u>, Part-name, Production-city)

If we wish to store the result relation by joining both relations on the criterion Headquarter-city = Production-city, we will be in the case of a join operation on non-key attributes.

d) The reverse operation

The reverse engineering process will be performed by suppressing the relation obtained by the join operation and replacing it by the input relations. The reverse join operation is the project operation. The four cases described in paragraph c) can be recovered :

Case 1 : $R(\underline{K}, C1, C2, ..., C_n, D_1, D_2, ..., D_m)$ where K is the key of the two relations.

Case 2 : R(<u>K2</u>, C1, C2, ..., C_n, D1, D2, ..., D_m, K) where K is the key of one of the two relations
Case 3 : R(<u>K1K</u>, C1, C2, ..., C_n, D1, D2, ..., D_m) where K is a key of one relation and an attribute of the compound key of the second relation
Case 4 : R(<u>K1.K2</u>, C1, C2, ..., C_n, D_1, D_2...D_m,K) where K is not a key.

e) The detection process

The detection of structures that have been modified and denormalized for performance consideration can be realized by successively examining the DDL and the DML specifications and by performing some data mining :
- Data Description Language : The join operator may generate a lot of null values. Therefore, we can detect very few (if not zero) NOT NULL clauses.
- Data Manipulation Language : Requests are mainly project operations on some attributes. In most cases, the project operations are performed on the same attributes of a relation.
- Data mining : Functional dependencies can be detected by analyzing the data which are in contradiction with the second and the third normal forms. In this case, several null values are found.

f) The reverse engineering rules

The rule Ru1 corresponding to case 1 can be interpreted as follows :

Given the relation R(K, C1, C2, ..., C_n, D1, D2, ..., D_m),

IF there is no attribute C_j or D_j defined as NOT NULL <u>and/or</u>
  there are several SQL requests with SELECT, WHERE, ORDER BY
  GROUP BY performed only on K and the C_j <u>and/or</u>
  there are several SQL requests with SELECT, WHERE, ORDER BY
  GROUP BY performed only on K and the D_j <u>and/or</u>
  there is no tuple in contradiction with the functional dependency :
  K -> C1,C2,...,C_n <u>and/or</u>
  there is no tuple in contradiction with the functional dependency :
  K -> D1,D2, ...,D_m <u>and/or</u>
  there are tuples having null values for all C_j <u>and/or</u>
  there are tuples having null values for all D_j
THEN MeRCI proposes the decomposition of R in two schemas
  R1(<u>K</u>, C1, C2, ..., C_n)
  R2(<u>K</u>, D1, D2, ..., D_m)

The other rules Ru_j are straightforward. Because of space limitations, we do not detail them.

4.2 The project operation

a) Principle

The project operator simplifies a relation by reducing its width. It can also be used to rename attributes of a relation, which is useful with the definition of join and/or to permute attributes of a relation, thus changing column ordering in a table.

b) Example

Employee (<u>Employee#</u>, Rank, Salary, Arrival-Date, First-career-job, Starting-Salary)
Two projections can be performed on Employee leading to two relations
Payroll (<u>Employe#</u>, Rank, Salary)
Career (<u>Employee#</u>, Arrival-Date, First-Career-Job, Starting-Salary).

As it can be seen, the projections are very powerful and allow the restructuring of one relation into two (or more) relations. This project operation minimizes input/output statements especially when frequent requests are performed on the same subset of attributes.

c) Consequences on schema normalization

Project operations can be performed without any loss of data. Each project output relation will keep the same key as the input relation. In this case, if the input relation is in 3NF, the output relations will also be in 3NF.

d) The reverse operation

The reverse engineering process will consist in suppressing the relations obtained by the project operation. These relations will be replaced by the initial relation containing all the attributes.

e) The detection process

Once again, the detection process will be performed using the DDL, DML and data mining :
- Data Description Language : Several relations with attributes being primary keys or unique, have the same name and are defined by the same data type.
- Data Manipulation Language : Some SQL requests are join operations between the keys of the two relations.
- Data mining : We verify that attributes having the same name and identifying all the relations correspond to the same values.

f) The reverse engineering rules

> Suppose two relations $R1(\underline{K1}, C1, C2, ..., C_n)$ and $R2(\underline{K2}, D1, D2, ..., D_m)$
> **IF** K1 and K2 have the same name <u>and/or</u>
>   K1 and K2 have the same data type <u>and/or</u>
>   there are one or several SQL requests with the clause WHERE containing an equality between K1 and K2 or a comparison of K1 and K2 with the operator IN <u>and/or</u>
>   the intersection of the values of K1 and K2 contains a great number of common values
> **THEN** MeRCI proposes the regrouping of R1 and R2 in one relation
> $R(\underline{K1}, C1, C2, ..., C_n, D1, D2..., D_m)$

4.3 The restrict operation

a) Principle

The restrict operator effect is to form a relation whose tuples correspond to those of the input relation, but which have been filtered through a restriction predicate or a condition. The algebra permits restriction predicates of arbitrary complexity making use of the conventional dyadic predicate constants ($=, \neq, <, >, \leq, \geq$) and the logical connectives (and, or, not).

b) Example

The relation Customer (<u>Customer#</u>, Customer-name, Address, Turnover) can be restricted to two relations Large_Customer (<u>Customer#</u>, Customer-name, Address, Turnover) and Small-Customer (<u>Customer#</u>, Customer-name, Address, Turnover) depending on the turnover amount (either larger or smaller than a given amount).

c) Consequences on schema normalization

Restrict operations can be performed without any loss of data. Therefore every output relation will keep the same schema as the initial relation. In this case, if the input relation is in 3NF, the resulting restricted relations will also be in 3NF.

d) The reverse operation

The reverse engineering process is achieved by suppressing the restricted relations. They will be replaced by the input relation containing all the tuples. The union operation is the reverse operation of the restrict operation.

e) The detection process

We examine the DDL and the DML specifications and perform a data mining process :
- Data Description Language : Several relations have the same schemas. The attributes which are primary keys or unique have the same name and are defined by the same data type. The other attributes have also the same names, the same data types, and possibly the same constraints (FOREIGN KEY, CHECK, etc...).
- Data Manipulation Language : Some SQL requests are union operations between the two (or more) relations.
- Data mining : we verify that columns which are identifiers and which have the same names, have a set of disjoint values.

f) The reverse engineering rules

Let $R1(K1, C1, C2, ..., C_n)$ and $R2(K2, D1, D2, ..., D_m)$ be two relations. IF K1 and K2 have the same data name <u>and/or</u>
   K1 and K2 have the same name <u>and/or</u>
   C_i and D_j have the same name and/or the same data type <u>and/or</u>
   there are one or several SQL requests with
   - one UNION between two SELECT performed respectively on relation R1 and relation R2 <u>and/or</u>
   - the WHERE clause containing one condition on K1 linked by an operator OR to the same condition on K2 <u>and/or</u>
   the intersection between the values of K1 and K2 is empty
 THEN MeRCI proposes to transform R1 and R2 into a unique relation $R(\underline{K1}, C1, C2, ..., C_n)$.

This set of rules allows us to reverse the consequences of a restrict operation. The latter is often used to minimize the number of searches in a relation.

4.4 The flattening operation

a) Principle

This operator is not a traditional operator. It allows the designer to move information from one representation to another, in this case from values to attributes names. It is applied only to attributes whose types are discrete and small in cardinality. It has the effect of flattening out such field type into the structure definition. This operator shows that information can equally well be represented as field values, as field names or as structure names. The combinatorial explosion in possible restructuring choices clearly presents design problems in the de-optimization phase.

b) Example

The relation Courseplanning (Course#, Course-Day, Course-Name, Course-Hour) can be flattened using *course-day*. The result is :

Course (Course#, Course-Name, Monday-Hour, Tuesday-Hour, Wednesday-Hour, Thursday-Hour, Friday-Hour, Saturday-Hour).

c) Consequences on schema normalization

Flattening operation is usually performed on an attribute belonging to a compound key. The result relation has a key that has been reduced. If the input relation is in 3NF, the flattened relation will be in 3NF.

d) The reverse operation

The reverse engineering process replaces several columns having the same type by a field which describes this type. If we proceed to the flattening of $R(\underline{K}, C1, C2, ..., C_n, D1, D2, ..., D_m)$ over the columns C_i, the reverse effect can be obtained by replacing R with $R1(\underline{K, K2}, C, D1, D2, ..., D_m)$.

e) The detection process

Both DDL and DML specifications are examined. Data mining is also performed :
- Data Definition Language : the flattened relation has several columns with the same type, and with a name which is partially common.
- Data Manipulation Language : some SQL requests use WHERE clauses having the same predicates on different columns of the same type.
- Data mining : we verify that the values of the columns with the same data type are identical.

f) The reverse engineering rules

Let $R(\underline{K}, C1, C2, ..., C_n, D1, D2, ..., D_m)$ be a relation.
IF C_i have part of their name common and/or
  C_i are defined by the same data type and/or
  there are one or several SQL requests whose WHERE clause or SET clause
  contains an identical condition on the different columns C_i and/or the intersection
  of C_i sets of values have common range values and several common values
THEN MeRCI proposes to transform R into R1 with $R(\underline{K, K1}, C, D1, D2, ..., D_m)$

The decision table for the additional operators (project, restrict, flattening) is presented below (Fig 3). It completes the reverse engineering rules allowing us to de-optimize a database relational physical schema. The decision table integrates the set of rules and the conditions under which they can be used to perform the translation of a physical schema into a logical schema. The rules rely on the examination of DDL and DML specifications and on a data mining process. The de-optimization process is a technical stage, and one that is difficult. However, it is very useful and even mandatory for a good and complete reverse engineering method. The example considered in the next section will illustrate its main rules.

			Ru5	Ru6	Ru7
C O N D I T I O N S	**D D L**	R1($\underline{K1}$ C_1 C_2 ... C_n)	X	X	
		R2($\underline{K2}$ D_1 D_2...D_m)	X	X	
		R($\underline{K}C_1C_2$...$C_nD_1D_2$...D_m)			X
		K1 and K2 have same names	X	X	
		K1 and K2 have same data types	X	X	
		C_i and D_j have same names	X	X	
		C_i and D_j have same data types		X	
		C_i have part of their name common			X
		C_i have same data types			X
	D M L	One or several SQL specifications with - a WHERE clause containing an equality between K1 and K2	X		
		- a comparison of K1 and K2 using the IN operator	X		
		- a UNION between two SELECT performed respectively on R1 and R2		X	
		- a WHERE clause containing a condition on K1 linked by OR to the same condition on K2		X	
	D A T A	- the intersection of the values of K1 and K2 contains a great number of common values	X		
		- the intersection between K1 and K2 values is empty		X	
		- the intersection of C_i sets of values has common range values and several common values			X
A C T I O N S		R($\underline{K1}$ C_1 C_2 ... C_nD_1 D_2... D_m)	X		
		R($\underline{K1}$ C_1 C_2 ... C_n)		X	
		R($\underline{KK1}$ C D_1 D_2... D_m)			X

Fig.3 - The decision table for project, restrict and flattening operations

5 Example

In this section, we will illustrate the de-optimization process using a fairly complex example containing an original set of restructured relations (adapted from [31]). Using the DDL specifications and the data dictionary, we have extracted the following relations (MeRCI phase 1). The underlined columns are those declared as primary keys or unique in the specifications :

American_countries(<u>country_code/char(6)</u>;country_name/char(30),restrictiveness/char(30))
Arrival(<u>flight_number/char(6)</u>;airport_code/char(6))
Asian_countries(<u>country_code/char(6)</u>;country_name/char(30),restrictiveness/char(30))

Arrival(<u>flight number/char(6)</u>;airport_code/char(6))
Asian_countries(<u>country code/char(6)</u>;country_name/char(30),restrictiveness/char(30))
Departure(<u>flight number/char(6)</u>;airport_code/char(6))
European_countries(<u>country code/char(6)</u>;country_name/char(30),restrictiveness/char(30))
Fares(<u>flight number/char(6),type code/char(4),conc class/char(30)</u>,single/decimal(6,2),
     return/decimal(6,2))
Flights(<u>flight number/char(6)</u>;aircraft/char(30),distance/integer,airline_code/char(3),
airline_name/char(30))
Int_Stops(<u>flight number/char(6),airport code/char(6)</u>;airport_name/char(30),
     country_code/char(6), stop_number/integer)
Restrictions(<u>country code/char(4), visa type/char(30)</u>; conditions/text)
Savers(<u>saver code/char(3)</u>; saver_name/char(30), saver_conditions/text)
Season(<u>season code/char(1)</u>; season_name/char(30), start_date/date, end_date/date)
Seat_Classes(<u>seat class code/char(1)</u>; seat_class_name/char(30))
Times(<u>flight number/char(6)</u>;mon_dep/decimal(4,2),mon_arr/decimal(4,2),
     tue_dep/decimal(4,2), tue_arr/decimal(4,2),wed_dep/decimal(4,2),wed_arr/decimal(4,2),
     thu_dep/decimal(4,2),thu_arr/decimal(4,2),fri_dep/decimal(4,2),
     fri_arr/decimal(4,2),sat_dep/decimal(4,2),sat_arr/decimal(4,2),
     sun_dep/decimal(4,2),sun_arr/decimal(4,2))
Types(<u>type code/char(4)</u>; seat_class_code/char(1), saver_code/char(3),
     season_code/char(1))

The relations *American_countries*, *European_countries* and *Asian_countries*
represent countries in which the various airlines operate. *Flights* is a relation which
defines a route flown by an airline. *Arrival* and *Departure* are two relations defining
the flights and their corresponding airports. Intermediate stops are represented by the
relation *Int_Stops*. First, business and economic classes are represented in the relation
Seat_Classes. Conditions for reduction are described in the relation *Savers* (APEX,
PEX, Budget, etc). The seasons during which flights are operated are described in
Seasons. The time tables are represented in the relation *Times*. The relation *Types*
represents the different seat types and is a compound of *Seat_Classes*, *Savers* and
Seasons. Finally, *Restrictions* represents the restrictions imposed by some countries
such as a visa. Clearly, since normalized relations are not always ideal structures for
implementations, some of the relations described above have been restructured for
mainly performance considerations. We now turn to the examination of the reverse
engineering rules that can be applied to the physical schema described above. To a
large extent, this examination requires a detailed knowledge of the application
requirements, its update and retrieval transactions. A sample of these transactions is
presented below. For lisibility reasons, we will present them in a litteral way and not
using the original DML specifications :
- update transactions :
     (1) add details of a new flight (that means, the flight number, its times, its stops and its
     fares)
     (2) remove details of a flight
     (3) modify flight times
- retrieval transactions :
     (4) list the fares for all types of ticket available, from any airline, to travel from airport
     A to airport B
     (5) times of departure and arrival of the flight F
     (6) airport names of intermediate stops for a given flight number F
     (7) entry restrictions applying to a country with name C
     (8) list the different countries and their continent names
     (9) list the different airports and their respective countries

(10) list the different airlines characteristics
(11) select the different flights realized with a given aircraft
(12) the distance covered by a given flight

The application of the reverse engineering rules leads to a rule/relation matrix where the columns represent reverse engineering rules and the rows represent the physical relations as illustrated in Fig 4. A mark is entered at the matrix position (i,j) if and only if rule j is applied to relation i. There are three types of marks :

X   means that the specified rule can be applied to the stated relation,
o   means that the specified relation meets only a few conditions of the stated rule,
-    means that the specified rule cannot be applied to its associated relation.

TABLE/RULE	Ru1	Ru2	Ru3	Ru4	Ru5	Ru6	Ru7
Am_Countries	-	-	-	-	o	X	-
Arrival	-	-	-	-	X	o	-
As_Countries	-	-	-	-	o	X	-
Departure	-	-	-	-	X	o	-
E_Countries	-	-	-	-	o	X	-
Fares	-	-	-	-	-	-	-
Flights	-	X	-	-	-	o	-
Int_Stops	-	-	X	-	-	-	-
Restrictions	-	-	-	-	-	-	-
Savers	-	-	-	-	-	-	-
Season	-	-	-	-	-	-	-
Seat_Classes	-	-	-	-	-	-	-
Times	-	-	-	-	-	o	X
Types	-	-	-	-	-	-	-

Fig. 4 - A rule/relation matrix

From the matrix described above, we can see that Ru7 can be applied to the relation *Times* since :
- the columns *mon_dep, ..., sun_dep and mon_arr, ..., sun_arr* have part of their names in common,
- these columns are defined by the same data type,
- there are DML specifications (requests 1,3,5 for example) whose WHERE clause or SET clause contains an identical condition in the different columns mon_dep, ..., sun_dep,
By exploring data instances, it seems that the columns *mon_dep,..., sun_dep* have common range values and even common values.
Ru7 transforms the structure of *Times*, suggesting the following restructurings :
Times(flight number, dep_arr; time) where dep_arr is a concatenation of common parts of columns names. In its current version, our system is not able to distinguish between the two subsets of columns {mon_dep, tue_dep, ..., sun_dep} and {mon_arr, tue_arr, ..., sun_arr}.

Ru6 can be applied to the three tables *European_Countries, Asian_Countries* and *American_Countries* because of the following facts :
- the three table keys have the same name,

- the three table keys have the same data type,
- the non-key columns have same name and same data type,
- there is a DML specification (request 8) performing a UNION operation between the three tables.

We can proceed to data mining showing that the intersection between the sets of key values of the three tables is empty.

Ru6 will transform the three relations into a unique relation :

Countries(country_code, country_name, restrictiveness, continent)

Let us now consider the relations *Departure* and *Arrival*.Their keys have the same name and the same data type. However, there is no DML specification allowing us to go further in this process. Therefore, Ru6 cannot be applied to these relations. The same reasoning can be used for the tables *Departure, Arrival, Flights, Times* which are considered together or two by two. They only meet the DDL conditions required by Ru6 but not the other conditions.

In the same way, Ru5 cannot be fired for the tables *Flights* and *Times* on the one hand, and *European_Countries, Asian_Countries* and *American_Countries* on the other hand. However, Ru5 can be applied to the tables *Departure* and *Arrival* due to the following observations :

- the table keys have the same names,
- the table keys have the same data types,
- there is one or several DML specifications (for example request 4) containing a comparison of the keys.

We can now perform a data mining and find out that the intersection of the key values contains a great number of common values (they are probably identical).

Ru5 will propose the regrouping of *Departure* and *Arrival* into one relation :

Dep_arr(flight_number; airport_dep, airport_arr).

Moreover, Ru3 can be applied to the relation *Int_stops* since :

- none of its columns is associated with the NOT NULL constraint,
- there are DML specifications including only *airport_code, airport_name, country_code* (such as request 9),

We can proceed to data mining and check that :

- no tuple contradicts the following functional dependency :
  airport_code -> airport_name, country_code,
- there exist tuples with null values for stop_number representing the airports where, at this date, no flight stops.

Ru3 suggests splitting *Int_Stops* into the two following tables :

Int_Stops(flight_number, airport_code; stop_number)
Airport(airport_code; airport_name, country_code).

Finally, rule Ru2 can be applied to the relation *Flights* for the following reasons :

- no attribute in *Flights* is defined with the NOT NULL constraint,
- there are DML specifications (such as request 10) performed only on the columns airline_code, airline_name,
- there are DML specifications performed only on the columns flight_number, distance (request 12) or flight_number and aircraft (see request 11),
  so we can proceed to the data mining, making sure that :
- no tuple contradicts the following functional dependency :
  airline_code -> airline_name,

- there exist tuples with null values for aircraft and distance to store the airlines which have no flight at that time.

Ru2 will split *Flights* into the two following tables :

Flights(flight number, aircraft, distance)

Airline (airline code, airline_name).

This first iteration of the rule set leads to the following logical schema :

Airline (airline code, airline_name)

Airport(airport code; airport_name, country_code)

Countries(country code/char(6);country_name/char(30),restrictiveness/char(30), continent)

Dep_arr(flight number; airport_dep, airport_arr)

Fares(flight number/char(6),type code/char(4),conc class/char(30),single/decimal(6,2), return/decimal(6,2))

Flights(flight number, aircraft, distance)

Int_Stops(flight number, airport code; stop_number)

Restrictions(country code/char(4), visa type/char(30); conditions/text)

Savers(saver code/char(3); saver_name/char(30), saver_conditions/text)

Season(season code/char(1); season_name/char(30), start_date/date, end_date/date)

Seat_Classes(seat class code/char(1); seat_class_name/char(30))

Times(flight-number, dep-arr ; time)

Types(type code/char(4); seat_class_code/char(1), saver_code/char(3), season_code/char(1))

A second iteration of the rule set allows us to trigger rule Ru5 on the tables *Flights* and *Dep_arr* leading to the following table structure :

Flights (flight number, aircraft, distance, airport_dep, airport_arr)

There is no remaining restructuring. Starting from the resulting logical schema, MeRCI leads us to the following conceptual schema (Fig 5).

This example shows how the different rules allow us to detect the optimization transformations operated on the original logical schema of the database. Of course, the restructurings proposed by the tool must be validated by the designer since they are mainly based on a heuristic approach. Empirically, we did not notice different results when the rules were applied in different orders. In the absence of any special statement of transaction priority, we can apply the reverse engineering rules in any order. However we plan to check this aspect further.

Another remaining work is to add rules for the other potential transformations, for example restructurings resulting from relational *divide* or *union* operations. However, we think that the transformations described in this paper are the most common ones.

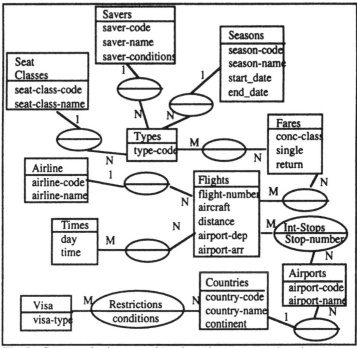

Fig. 5 - Conceptual schema resulting from the reverse engineering process

6 Conclusion

This paper sought to recover EER schemas from relational database physical schemas. We have derived a set of rules allowing us to de-optimize relational database physical schemas. This step is becoming increasingly important for an efficient reverse engineering process which does not assume that the relations are in 3NF. We highlighted how a set of conventional and non-conventional relational operators interact in physical schema design, leading to denormalized relations. We offered ways to detect their impact and several reverse engineering rules associated with each of them. The major implication focuses on how this de-optimization phase can be incorporated in reverse engineering methods. We have presented briefly one of these methods called MeRCI, based on the life-cycle (multi-stage) method of database system development.

De-optimization of relational database physical schemas and, more generally, relational database reverse engineering, remains an area of active research. New algorithms for extracting EER schemas from a relational database are being devised. They are usually variants or extensions of the basic methods reviewed in Section 2. It is clear that further research is needed, especially in devising reverse engineering methods applicable to operational databases not obtained by rigorous database design process.

In our approach, several aspects have to be refined and completed. There are three principal areas of improvements :
- Investigation of the effect of additional operators such as *divide* and *union*. We consider likely benefits from the various possible restructurings that stem from the applications of these operations.

- Analysis of the effect of different orderings when applying rules to the physical schema. We suspect that rules order has a minor effect on the final logical schema.
- The airline example illustrates the great fluidity of representation that is possible in database design : information can be represented as field values, as field names, and as structure names. This combinatorial explosion in possible restructuring choices presents reverse engineering design problems. Our MeRCI approach and especially the de-optimization phase should be robust to face this problem.

References

1. Akoka, J., Comyn-Wattiau, I., "MeRCI : Une Méthode de Rétroconception Intelligente des Bases de Données Relationnelles", CERESSEC W.P., 1996.
2. Andersson M., *Extracting an Entity Relationship Schema from a Relational Database through Reverse Engineering*, in Proceedings of the 13th Conf. on ER Approach, Manchester, UK, Dec 1994.
3. Batini C., Ceri S., Navathe S.B., *Conceptual Database Design : An Entity-Relationship Approach*, The Benjamin/Cummings Publishing Company, Inc., 1992.
4. Casanova M., Amarel de Sa J., *Designing Entity Relationship Schemas for Conventional Information Systems*, in Proc. of Entity-Relationship Approach, pp. 265-278, 1983.
5. Casanova M.A., Amarel de Sa J., *Mapping uninterpreted Schemes into Entity-Relationship diagrams : two applications to conceptual schema design*, IBM J. Res. & Develop., 28(1), January, 1984.
6. Chiang R.H.L., Barron T.M., Storey V.C., *Performance Evaluation of Reverse Engineering Relational Databases into Extended Entity-Relationship Models*, in Proc. of the 12th Int. Conf. on ER Approach, Arlington, USA, Décembre 1993.
7. Chiang R.H.L., Barron T.M., Storey V.C., *Reverse Engineering of Relational Database : Extraction of an EER model from a relationnal database*, Data & Knowledge Engineering 12, pp 17-142, 1994.
8. Chiang R.H.L., *A knowledge-based system for performing reverse engineering of relational databases*, Decision Support Systems 13, pp 295-312, 1995.
9. Chikofsky E.J., Cross J., *Reverse Engineering and Design Recovery, : a Taxonomy*, IEEE Software, January 1990.
10. Davis K.H., Arora A.K., *A Methodology for Translating a Conventional File System into an Entity-Relationship Model*, Proc. of the 4th Int. Conf. on ER Approach, Chicago, USA, Octobre 1985.
11. Davis K.H., Arora A.K., *Converting a Relational Database Model into an Entity-Relationship Model*, Proc. of the 6th Int. Conf. on ER Approach, New York, USA, Novembre 1987.
12. Fonkam M.M, Gray W.A., *An Approach to Eliciting the Semantics of Relational Databases*, Proc. of 4th Int. Conf. on Advance Information Systems Engineering - CAiSE'92, pp. 463-480, Springer-Verlag, 1992.
13. Hainaut J.L., *Database Reverse Engineering : Models, techniques and strategies*, Proc. of the Tenth International Conference on Entity-Relationship Approach, 1991.
14. Hainaut J.L., Cadelli M., Decuyper B., Marchand O., *Database CASE Tool Architecture : Principles for Flexible Design Strategies*, Proc. of 4th Int. Conf. on Advance Information Systems Engineering - CAiSE'92, Springer-Verlag, 1992.

15. Hainaut J.L., Tonneau C., Joris M., Chandelon M., *Schema Transformation Techniques for Database Reverse Engineering*, Proc. of the 12th Inter. Conf. on Entity-Relationship Approach, Arlington, Texas, Dec 1993.

16. Hainaut J.L., Tonneau C., Joris M., Chandelon M., *Transformation-based Database Reverse Engineering*, in Proc. of the 13th Int. Conf. on ER Approach, Manchester, UK, Dec 1994.

17. Hainaut J.L., Englebert V., Henrard J., Hick J.M., Roland D., *Requirements for Information System Reverse Engineering Support*, Proc. of the IEEE Working Conf. on Reverse Engineering, Toronto, Canada, IEEE Computer Society Press, July 1995.

18. Johannesson P., Kalman K., *A Method for translating Relational Schema into Conceptual Schemas*, Proc. of the Eighth International Conference on Entity-Relationship Approach, 1991, pp 231-246.

19. Kalman K., *Implementation and Critique of an algorithm which maps a relational database to a conceptual model*, Proc. of 3th Int. Conf. on Advance Information Systems Engineering - CAiSE'91, 1991.

20. Lientz B.P., Swanson, E.B., *Software Maintenance Management*, Reading Mass : Addison Wesley, 1980.

21. Navathe S.B., Awong A., *Abstracting Relational and Hierarchical Data with a Semantic Data Model*, Proc. of Entity-Relationship Approach : a Bridge to the User, Elsevier Science Publishers, pp. 305-333, 1988.

22. Nilsson E.G., *The Translation of COBOL Data Structure to an Entity-Rel-Type Conceptual Schema*, Proc. of Entity-Relationship Approach, October, 1985.

23. Mishra, P., Eich, M.H., "Join Processing in Relational Databases", ACM Computing Surveys, 24(1), March 1992.

24. Petit J.M., Kouloumdjian J., Boulicaut J.F., Toumouni F., *Using Queries to Improve Database Reverse Engineering*, Proceedings of 13th International Conference on ER Approach, Manchester, 1994.

25. Premerlani W.J., Blaha M.R., *An approach for Reverse Engineering of Relational Databases*, Communications of the ACM, Vol 37(5), pp 42-49, May 1994.

26. Signore O., Loffredo M., Gregori M., Cima M., *Reconstruction of ER Schema from Database Applications : a Cognitive Approach*, Proc. of the 13th Int. Conf. on ER Approach, Manchester, UK, Dec. 1994.

27. Springstell F.N, Kou C., *Reverse Data Engineering of E-R designed Relational schemas*, in Proc. of Databases, Parallel Architectures and their Applications, March 1990.

28. Tilley S.R., Müller H.A., Withney M.J., Wong K., *Domain-Retargetable Reverse Engineering*, Proc. of IEEE Working Conf. on Software Maintenance, 1993.

29. Vermeer, M.W.W., Apers, P.M.G., "Reverse Engineering of Relational Database Applications", Proc. of the 14th Conf. on object-Oriented and Entity-Relationship (OOER'95), Brisbane, Australia, 1995.

30. Winans J., Davis K.H., *Software Reverse Engineering from a Currently Existing IMS Database to an Entity-Relationship Model*, Proc. of Entity-Relationship Approach, pp. 345-360, Oct. 1990.

31. Wittington, R.P., *Database Systems Engineering*, Clarendon Press, Oxford, 1988.

Extracting N-ary Relationships
Through Database Reverse Engineering

Christian SOUTOU

Université de Toulouse II
IUT 'B', Laboratoire ICARE
1, Place Georges Brassens
31703 Blagnac, FRANCE
soutou@iut-blagnac.fr

Abstract. This paper presents an automatic process for reverse engineering the n-ary relationship tables from an operating relational database. This process performs the extraction of cardinality ratios by generating a set of SQL queries for each n-ary relationship table. We focus on realistic assumptions. We suppose that there are no constraints on the uniqueness of the key attribute names and the dependencies are not supposed to be known a priori. A PRO*C program has been implemented, it enables us to automatically build SQL queries via dynamic SQL. We also study the influence of the number of key attributes and the number of tuples upon the performance of our process.

1 Introduction

Database Reverse Engineering is a part of maintenance process that obtains a sufficient understanding of an existing information system to allow appropriate changes to be made. Legacy systems are characterized by old-fashioned architecture or lack of documentation and non-uniformity resulting from numerous extensions. These properties lead to inflexible systems and high maintenance costs. There are various reasons for applying reverse engineering to existing relational databases : semantic degradations, maintenance and redesign, integration of databases (integration process are often performed at the conceptual level.

Several researchers have provided some means for translating a relational schema into extended Entity Relationship models or object-oriented ones [5,9,11,12,16]. Most of these surveys are based on key inclusion dependencies. Some recent methodologies [1,3,4,13,14] use data instances and heuristics. Because the reverse engineering of relational applications is a very big and complex task, all existing approaches are conditionned by a set of restrictive hypotheses : the designer must specify semantic information schema (such as definition of candidate keys, foreign key, functional dependencies of various types, inclusion dependencies, and others) ; relational schemas are supposed to be in third normal form ; the key attributes are consistent named ; the relations are given without instances ;....

Moreover up to now methods do not clearly show how to extract n-ary relationships (n>2). [7] proposes generic transformation operations that could be used on n-ary relationships in practical design activities including database reverse engineering. [5] maps relations with two or more primary key fields to N:N relationships. We believe this statement is ambiguous because a relation having two attributes primary key may express 1:1, 1:N, or N:N relationship. [2] determine the nature of relationships through an analysis of inclusion dependencies. They state that if there is no indication concerning referential integrity (foreign key) in the schema, then inclusion dependencies must be extracted from data instances. They propose heuristics to reduce the set of possible dependencies. We believe that even though the relational schema contains informations about foreign keys, it is necessary to inspect data instances. [14] proposes heuristics to extract relationship but they do not deduce the kind of relationship. [4] identifies 1:N or 1:1 relationship from foreign keys and inclusion dependencies specified by the user, they state that if the foreign key contains unique values then the cardinality ratio is 1:1. They do not show how they extract this fact. Moreover, this methodology does not specify cardinality ratios for relationship types of degree higher than two.

To the best of our knowledge the automatic extraction of n-ary relationships (n≥2) from a relational database has never been studied. For more details about n-ary relationships see [6,8,10,15,18]. In this paper we present an automatic process resolving this problem. Our extraction is based on a snapshot of the database extension that we find at the beginning of the reverse engineering process. It does not tell us anything definite about the equivalent conceptual schema but it can facilitate the understanding of the semantic expressed by the n-ary relationships during a reverse engineering step. We focus on the realistics assumptions that there are no constraints on the uniqueness of the key attribute names and the dependencies are not supposed to be known a priori. Our process performs in an automatic way the deduction of cardinality ratios of n-ary relations by building and running a set of SQL queries on each of them.

The remainder of this paper is organized as follows. Section 2 describes the context. In section 3 we detail our process for automatically extracting cardinality ratios of n-ary relations from a relational database. Section 4 discusses the performance evaluation of reverse engineering n-ary relations according to the number of key attribute and the number of records. In the appendix we present results from a database example.

2 Context

This section is particulary important in understanding the context of the arguments made in this paper. The overall object of this research is to develop a process which can be include in a complete database reverse engineering methodology.

Definition : R[$a_1,a_2,...a_k,b_1\#,b_2\#,...b_j\#,p_1,p_2,...p_m$], denotes an n-ary relation n is called degree of the relationship, n=k+j such that :
- a_i : primary key attributes, note that a_i may be a foreign key, or may belong to a foreign key ;
- $b_i\#$: pure foreign key attributes ;
- p_i : non key attributes.

Statemeht 1 : At a given degree, an n-ary relationship table may have different number of primary key attributes.

Let us consider Fig. 2 a relational database schema written with a data definition langage (DDL) as SQL-92 inspired from [18]. Though this kind of schema contains a lot of information about semantic the relations, how determinate the semantic expressed by the relation assigned_to? Does two n-ary relations have the same meaning as they have the same structure? The response of these questions is obviously no. The semantic of n-ary relationships is provided by cardinality ratios.

```
create table employees
(emp_id number, name char(20), primary key(emp_id));

create table projects
(project_name char(12), budget number, primary key(project_name));

create table location
(local_name char(3), adress char(40), primary key(local_name));

create table assigned_to
 (emp number, proj char(12), loc char(3), primary key(emp,proj),
 foreign key(emp) references employees(emp_id),
 foreign key(proj) references projects(project_name),
 foreign key(loc) references location(local_name));
```

Fig. 1. : Example of data definition

See on the figure 2 the possible cardinality ratios for assigned_to. Cardinality ratio X:Y:1 indicates that for each pair of (emp,proj) there is one instance of loc, for each pair (loc,proj) there are X instance(s) of emp, for each pair (emp,loc) there are Y instance(s) of proj. Note that the connectivity N:N:N is not possible because the primary key is not composed of three attributes.

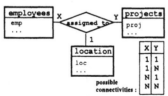

Fig. 2. : Possible connectivities

Statement 2 : As pure foreign key attributes involve a connectivity 1, an n-ary relationship table R[$a_1,a_2,...a_k,b_1\#,b_2\#,...b_j\#,p_1,p_2,...p_m$], may represent 2^k possible n-ary relationships.

Data schemas writen with SQL92 are more comprehensible than oldest ones. The constraints PRIMARY KEY, FOREIGN KEY, REFERENCES, UNIQUE, NOT NULL may provide a deduction of existing relationships but they do not give any information about cardinalities. Legacy database schemas are not likely to include any indication about foreign keys. If we envisage to apply this process to legacy DBMS where DDL or data dictionary doesn't support sufficient informations to deduce foreign key we have to test $2^{k+j}=2^n$ possible n-ary relationships.

The major drawback of this method is that the original intent of the designer may be to allow N:M relationship, but the current data cannot exhibit this freedom and our extraction can reveal cardinality ratio 1:N or 1:1. The solution is to run the process at different time and compare cardinality ratios. The greater cardinality must be kept in · the final conceptual schema.

3 Extracting Cardinalities

The first step of our process performs the automatic extraction of relations representing n-ary relationships [17]. The second step is described here. Each of these n-ary relations are affected by this step. We propose a database reverse engineering process which extracts current cardinality ratios of n-ary relations. This process is based on an automatic generation and execution of a set of SQL queries for each n-ary relation. These set of SQL queries do not exceed 2^n.

It must be noted that for a given relationship table, only one of the 2^n queries will be successful. When a generated query returns 'not found' then the process generates another one testing other cardinalities. When a generated query is succesful, it returns 'X:Y:Z Relationship Table' (X,Y,Z $\in$ {'1','N'}) according to its cardinalitites. The next step consists in extracting the name of the related entities from the data dictionnary. An example of result is given Fig. 3.

```
Relation : ASSIGNED_TO
N:1:1 Relationship Table
Cardinalities :
N      EMP          EMPLOYEES
1      PROJ         PROJECTS
1      LOC          LOCATION
```

Fig. 3. : Example of result

3.1   Body of the SQL Queries

Our process will examine n-ary relations $R[c_1,c_2, ...,c_n,p_1,p_2, ...p_m]$ (c_i : primary or foreign key attributes, p_i : non key attributes. At each combination of cardinality ratio we build a corresponding SQL query. Each query $q_{i=1, .. 2^n}$ is composed of n nested sub-queries (j sub-queries 'exists' n-j sub-queries 'not exists', j=0,..n).

Sub-queries 'exists' will give way to the detection of cardinalities "N". Sub-queries 'not exists' will give way to the detection of cardinalities "1". Each sub-query is either composed of n or n-1 predicates according to its option. No one of the sub-query is similar because each of them give way to the deduction of a cardinality from one key attribute (refered to an entity) to the rest of the set of key attributes. See Fig. 4 the composition of the generated SQL queries.

number of sub-queries j=0,n number of attributes in the clause	n-j	j
n-1	'not exists'	
n		'exists'

Fig. 4. : composition of a query q_i having j nested sub-queries

Sub-Queries 'exists'.
The sub-queries 'exists' require all the n key attributes.

Let R n-ary relationship table $R[a_1,a_2,...a_k,b_1\#,b_2\#, ...b_j\#,p_1,p_2, ...]$,

if : $(x_1,x_2...,x_{h-1},\alpha_h,x_{h+1}, ...,x_n) \in R$ and $(x_1,x_2...,x_{h-1},\beta_h,x_{h+1}, ...,x_n) \in R$, with $\alpha \neq \beta$ and $h \leq k$,

then the attribute a_h refer to a multivalued entity.

As an example, we apply this proposition to the relation assigned_to. If this query returns a result (at less one tuple), the entity 'employees' is multivalued.

```
select * from assigned_to t1, assigned_to t2
    where     t1.proj = t2.proj
    and       t1.loc = t2.loc
    and       t1.emp != t2.emp;
```

Sub-Queries 'not exists'.
The sub-queries 'not exists' require only n-1 key attributes.

Let R n-ary relationship table $R[a_1,a_2,...a_k,b_1\#,b_2\#, ...b_j\#,p_1,p_2, ...]$,

if : $(x_1,x_2..., x_{h-1},\alpha_h,x_{h+1}, ...,x_n) \in R$ and $(x_1,x_2..., x_{h-1},\beta_h,x_{h+1}, ...,x_n) \in R \Rightarrow \alpha=\beta$,

then the attribute a_h refer to a monovalued entity.

As an example, we apply this proposition to the relation assigned_to. If this query does not return a result (not found), the entity 'location' (identified by the missing key attribute 'loc') is monovalued.

```
select * from assigned_to t1, assigned_to t2
    where     t1.proj = t2.proj
    and       t1.emp = t2.emp
    and       t1.ROWID != t2.ROWID;
```

The predicate 'and t1.ROWID != t2.ROWID' appears in every sub-query 'not exists' because we do not compare the same pair of tuples. Without this predicate, theses sub-queries will always return false whatever the database contains.

3.2   Problems to be Solved

The reverse engineering process we propose for extracting the cardinality ratios of n-ary relationship tables generates no more than 2^n SQL queries for each n-ary table found in the database. We have to cover the whole range of cardinalities, and to care to not generate any incompatible or redundant query.

An incompatible query is a query which returns 'not found' whatever the database contains (sub-queries 'exists' and 'not exists' contradictory). A redundant query is a query which has some equivalent sub-queries ('exists' or 'not exists'). Since a generated query has n sub-queries, if two sub-queries are similar, it involves that one required would be missing.

incompatible query	redundant query

`select '1:...:N:...`
 `Relationship Table'`
 `from dual`
 `where not exists`
 `   (select * from R t1, R t2`
 `   where t1.a1 = t2.a1`
 `   and t1.a2 = t2.a2`
 `   and t1.ROWID != t2.ROWID)`
 `...`
 `and exists`
 `   (select * from R t1, R t2`
 `   where t1.a1 = t2.a1`
 `   and   t1.a2 = t2.a2`
 `   and   t1.a3 != t2.a3)`
 `...;`
	`select '1:...:1:...`
	 `Relationship Table'`
	 `from dual`
	 `where not exists`
	 `   (select * from R t1, R t2`
	 `   where t1.a1 = t2.a1`
	 `   and t1.a2 = t2.a2`
	 `   and t1.ROWID != t2.ROWID)`
	 `...`
	 `and not exists`
	 `   (select * from R t1, R t2`
	 `   where t1.a2 = t2.a2`
	 `   and t1.a1 = t2.a1`
	 `   and t1.ROWID != t2.ROWID)`
	 `...;`

Fig. 5. : improper queries

Solving Incompatible Queries. We avoid generating incompatible queries by assigning a rank for each key attribute. By this way, for a query r_j having n sub-queries (j sub-queries 'exists' and n-j sub-queries 'not exists'), an attribute is not affected by more than one sub-query for a same rank. In the previous example Fig. 5, the attributes a1 and a2 are affected by two sub-queries of the same rank (a1 at rank 1, a2 at rank 2).

We use a circular permutation between the key attributes. For each combination of consecutive n elements , an attribute is not affected more than once to the same rank. The data structure used is the chained list. The chained list results from the concatenation of the combinations. The combinations for each sub-query are given by reading this data structure.

As an illustration, this principle can be applied to the 4-ary relationship table R[a,b,c,d]. The chained list will be : 'a b c d b c d a c d a b d a b c'. The generated query will use each combination for each sub-query: {a b c d, b c d a, c d a b, d a b c}.

As the sub-queries 'not exists' require only n-1 key attributes, the last element of the combination is not taken into account inside such a nested sub-query. As the sub-queries 'exists' require the n key attributes, each element of the combination is taken into account inside such a nested sub-query. We give Fig. 6 the first and the last of the 2^4 queries that will be generated. Only one of them will be successful.

first generated query	...	last generated query
| ```
select '1:1:1:1 Relationship
Table' from dual
where not exists
    (select * from R t1,R t2
    where    t1.a = t2.a
    and      t1.b = t2.b
    and      t1.c = t2.c
    and t1.ROWID !=t2.ROWID)
and not exists
    (select * from R t1,R t2
    where    t1.b = t2.b
    and      t1.c = t2.c
    and      t1.d = t2.d
    and t1.ROWID !=t2.ROWID)
and not exists
    (select * from R t1, Rt2
    where    t1.c = t2.c
    and      t1.d = t2.d
    and      t1.a = t2.a
    and t1.ROWID !=t2.ROWID)
and not exists
    (select * from R t1,R t2
    where    t1.d = t2.d
    and      t1.a = t2.a
    and      t1.b = t2.b
    and t1.ROWID!=t2.ROWID);
``` | ... | ```
select 'N:N:N:N Relationship
Table' from dual
where exists
    (select * from R t1,R t2
    where t1.a = t2.a
    and   t1.b = t2.b
    and   t1.c = t2.c
    and   t1.d != t2.d)
and exists
    (select * from R t1, R t2
    where t1.b = t2.b
    and   t1.c = t2.c
    and   t1.d = t2.d
    and   t1.a != t2.a)
and exists
    (select * from R t1, R t2
    where t1.c = t2.c
    and   t1.d = t2.d
    and   t1.a = t2.a
    and   t1.b != t2.b)
and exists
    (select * from R t1, R t2
    where t1.d = t2.d
    and   t1.a = t2.a
    and   t1.b = t2.b
    and   t1.c != t2.c);
``` |

Fig. 6. : queries generated for R[a,b,c,d]

Solving Redundant Queries. We avoid generating redundant queries by using a binary tree with its height equal to n. By this way, each of the 2^n leaves represents a possible combination of cardinalities for an n-ary relationship (1:1:...:1, 1:1:...:1:N, ... so on until N:N:....:N). The use of the chained list previously defined for each leaf implies the non existence of redundant queries r_j since each combination of cardinalities is different and for each combination, the list of attributes used in the j sub-queries 'exists' and n-j sub-queries 'not exists' are different thanks to circular permutation.

3.3   Binary Tree of Queries

We test every combination of cardinality ratios by using a binary tree. For a given n-ary relation we generate no more than 2^n queries by assigning to the cardinality "1" a nested sub-query 'not exists' and by assigning to the cardinality "N" a nested sub-query 'exists'. When a generated query returns 'not found' then the process generates another one testing other cardinalities. When a generated query is succesful, it returns the corresponding cardinality ratio. Figure 7 illustrates the binary tree of queries generated for R[$c_1,c_2,...c_n,p_1,p_2, ...$]. Each query has j sub-queries 'exists' and n-j sub-queries 'not exists' according to the leaf it depends. Thanks to a circular permutation (*cp*), no sub-queries are redundant. As the sub-queries 'not exists' require only n-1 key attributes, the related circular permutation will deal with n-1 attributes (cp_j*). As the sub-queries 'exists' require the n key attributes, the related circular permutation will deal with n-1 attributes (cp_j).

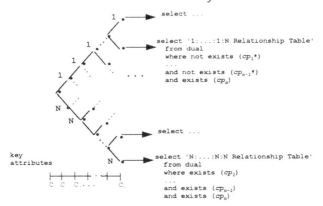

Fig. 7. : Binary tree of queries

We give in the appendix some results of our process. These queries are built in a PRO*C program and executed via dynamic SQL.

4 Experimental Measures

Thanks to these measures, we can quantify the running time of our program according to the volumes of tables (number of tuples) and to the number of key atttributes. Our test is composed of several 3-ary, 4-ary, 5-ary and 6-ary relationship tables. For each relationship family we automatically and randomly inserted some tuples (10, 100, 1000 and 10000 recordings). We briefly describe these relationship tables. This test was performed on an HP 9000/400 with Oracle version 6.0.30.

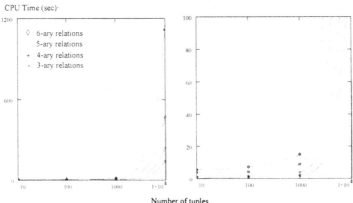

Fig. 8. : Measures

The graph Fig. 8 shows that the number of tuples is a proportional factor. For a 3-ary relationship table, we generate 2^3 queries, for a 4-ary relationship table, we generate 2^4 queries, etc.... The measures confirm that the time is approximately twice longer as the relationship table increases by one degree. Moreover, past a certain threshold (approximately 1000 recordings) CPU time increases in an exponential way. The reasons are first that the size of the query raises by $o(n^2)$ and second that the swaping time is induced by the number of rows processed. We can conclude that the number of records is more influential than the degree of an n-ary relationship table.

5 Conclusion

An automatic process for reverse engineering of n-ary relationship tables from operating relational database has been presented. Our extraction is based on a snapshot of the database extension that we find at the beginning of the reverse engineering process. It does not tell us anything definite about the equivalent conceptual schema but our process can facilitate the understanding of the semantic expressed by the n-ary relationships during a reverse engineering step. One of the goals of our methodology is to encompass an as large as possible relational schemas. We do not rely on the assumption that the schemas are well designed.

This work is based on the generation and execution of a set of SQL queries which not exceeds 2^n for each n-ary relationship table.. We use a binary tree having its height equal to n. By this way, each of the 2^n leaves represent a possible combination of cardinalities for a n-ary relationship ("1:1:...:1", "1:1:...:1:N", ...and so on until "N:N:...:N"). A PRO*C program querying an ORACLE database has been developed. Thanks to these measures, we can quantify the running time of our program according to the volume of tables (number of tuples) and to the number of key atttributes.

On the basis of this work we contemplate the optimization of this process. Because when we operate on old DBMS we observe that they support a DDL which do not enable us to deduce foreign key. Generating more than one set of SQL queries for each n-ary relationship table can be greatly inefficient. A solution could be supplied by using heuristics to reduce the human intervention and to prune the search tree.
Other open issues are the automatic detection of binary (resp. n-1 ary) relationships within ternary (resp. n-ary) relationships based on an analysis of functional dependencies. In our example dealing with manages, we can deduce the following dependencie: emp,proj→mgr. Suppose we extract in the database in another relationship table the dependencie proj→mgr. We can propose to losslessly decompose the ternary relationship into two binary relationships according to the suggested decompositions defined in [10].

References

1. M. Andersson, "Extracting an Entity Relationship Schema from a Relational Database through Reverse Engineering", Proceedings of the 13th Int. Conference on Entity-Relationship Approach, Springer Verlag, Vol 881,403-419, 1994.
2. M.Castellanos, "A Methodology for Semantically Enriching Interoperable Databases", Proceedings of the 11th British National Conference on Databases, 58-75, 1993.

3. R. Chiang, T. Barron, V. Storey, "Performance Evaluation of Reverse engineering Relational Databases into Extended Entity-Relationship Models", Proceedings of the 12th Int. Conference on Entity-Relationship Approach, Springer Verlag, Vol 823, 402-413, 1993.

4. R. Chiang, T. Barron, V. Storey, "Reverse engineering of relational databases : Extraction of an EER model from a relational database", Journal of Data and Knowledge Engineering, Vol 12, N°2, 107-142, 1994.

5. K.H. Davis, A.K. Arora, "Converting a Relational Database Model into an Entity Relationship Model", Proceedings of the 6th International Conference on Entity-Relationship Approach, 1987.

6. R. Elmasri, S.B. Navathe, "Fundamental of Database Systems", Benjamin Cummings, 1989.

7. J.L. Hainaut, C. Tonneau, M. Joris, M. Chandelon, "Transformation-based Database Reverse Engineering", Proceedings of the 12th Int. Conference on Entity-Relationship Approach, Springer Verlag, Vol 823, 364-375, 1993.

8. I.T. Hawryszkiewycz, "Database Analysis and Design", Macmillian Publishing, 1991.

9. P. Johanneson, K. Kalman, "A method for Translating Relational Schemas into Conceptual Schemas", Proceedings of the 8th Entity-Relationship Approach, Elsevier Science, 271-285, 1990.

10. T.H. Jones, I.Y. Song, "Binary Representation of Ternary Relationships in ER Conceptual Modeling", Proceedings of the 14 th Int. Conference on Entity-Relationship Approach, Springer Verlag, Vol 1021, 216-225, 1995.

11. K.M. Markowitz, J.A. Makowsky, "Identifying Extended Entity-Relationship Object Structures in Relational Schemas", IEEE, Transactions on Software Engineering, Vol 16, N°8, 777-790, 1990.

12. S.B. Navathe, H. Awong, "Abstracting Relational and Hierarchical Data with a Semantic Data Model", Proceedings of the 6th International Conference on Entity-Relationship Approach, 1987.

13. J.M. Petit, J. Kouloumdjian, J.F. Boulicaut, F. Toumani, "Using Queries to Improve Database Reverse Engineering", Proceedings of the 13th Int. Conference on Entity-Relationship Approach, Springer Verlag, Vol 881, 369-386, 1994.

14. O. Signore, M. Loffredo, M. Gregori, M. Cima, "Reconstruction of ER Schema from Database Application : a Cognitive Approach", Proceedings of the 13th Int. Conference on Entity-Relationship Approach, Springer Verlag, Vol 881, 387-402, 1994.

15. I.Y. Song, T.H. Jones, "Analysis of Binary Relationships within Ternary Relationships in ER Modeling", Proceedings of the 12th Int. Conference on Entity-Relationship Approach, Springer Verlag, Vol 823, 271-282, 1993.

16. C. Soutou, "Relational Database Reverse Engineering : Extraction of an IFO_2 Schema", Proceedings of the 6th Int. Conference on Database and Expert Systems (DEXA), Springer Verlag, Vol 978, 469-478, 1995.

17. C. Soutou, "Algorithms for Building SQL Queries to Improve Relational Database Reverse Engineering", submitted to publication.

18. T.J. Teorey, "Database Modelling and Design : The Fundamental Principles", Morgan Kaufmann, 1994.

Appendix

In the first step of our process [17] we automatically extract the n-ary relationship tables from an operating relational database. For each of them we only detail the successful SQL query according to examples of data instances. The next step consists in extracting the name of the related entities from the data dictionnary. An example of result is given Fig. 3. For each succesful query we give the corresponding relationship expressed in the ER model. We use a database example inspired from [18].

Appendix 1 : 1:1:N Relationship

```
create table employees (emp_id number, name char(20),
    primary key(emp_id));

create table projects (project_name char(12), budget number,
    primary key(project_name));

create table location (local_name char(3), adress char(40),
    primary key(local_name));

create table assigned_to
    (emp number, proj char(12), loc char(3), primary key(emp,proj),
    foreign key(emp) references employees(emp_id),
    foreign key(proj) references projects(project_name),
    foreign key(loc) references location(local_name));
```

SQL query successfully generated

```
select 'N:1:1 Relationship Table'
from dual
    where exists
        (select * from assigned_to as1,
        assigned_to as2
            where as1.proj = as2.proj
            and    as1.loc = as2.loc
            and    as1.emp != as2.emp)
    and not exists
        (select * from assigned_to as1,
        assigned_to as2
            where as1.proj = as2.proj
            and    as1.emp = as2.emp
            and    as1.ROWID != as2.ROWID)
    and not exists
        (select * from assigned_to as1,
        assigned_to as2
            where as1.loc = as2.loc
            and    as1.emp = as2.emp
            and    as1.ROWID != as2.ROWID);
```

Example of data instances

assigned_to

emp	proj	loc
48101	forest	B66
48101	ocean	E71
20702	ocean	A12
20702	river	D54
51266	river	G14
51266	ocean	A12
76323	hills	B66

ER Diagram

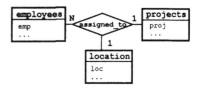

From this result we can deduce at this time the following facts :
- each employee assigned to a project works at only one location for that project, but can be at a different location for different projects ;
- at a given location, an employee works on only one project ;
- at a particular location, there can be many employees assigned to a given project.

Appendix 2 : 1:N:N Relationship

```
create table employees (emp_id number, name char(20),
   primary key(emp_id));

create table projects (project_name char(12), budget number,
   primary key(project_name));

create table managers (mgr_id number, salary number,
   primary key(mgr_id));

create table manages
   (emp number, proj char(12), manager number,
   primary key(emp,proj),
   foreign key(emp) references employes(emp_id),
   foreign key(proj) references projects(project_name),
   foreign key(manager) references managers(mgr_id));
```

SQL query successfully generated

```
select 'N:N:1 Relationship table'
from dual
   where exists
   (select * from manages m1,
    manages m2
      where m1.proj = m2.proj
      and   m1.manager = m2.manager
      and   m1.emp != m2.emp)
   and exists
   (select * from manages m1,
   manages m2
      where m1.emp = m2.emp
      and   m1.manager = m2.manager
      and   m1.proj != m2.proj)
   and not exists
      (select * from manages m1,
      manages m2
      where m1.proj = m2.proj
      and   m1.emp = m2.emp
      and   m1.ROWID != m2.ROWID);
```

Example of data instances

manages

emp	proj	manager
4106	alpha	27
4200	alpha	27
7033	beta	32
4200	beta	14
4106	gamma	71
7033	delta	55
4106	delta	39
4106	iota	27

ER Diagram

From this result we can deduce at this time the following facts :
- each engineer working on a particular project has exactly one manager ;
- a project may have many managers and an engineer may have many managers and many projects ;
- a manager may manage several projects.

Appendix 3 : 1:1:1 Relationship

```
create table projects (project_name char(12), budget number,
   primary key(project_name));

create table technicians (emp_id number, name char(20),
   primary key(emp_id));

create table notebooks (notebook_no number, brand char(20),
   primary key(notebook_no));

create table uses_notebook
   (emp number, proj char(12),notebook number,
   primary key(emp,proj),
   foreign key(emp) references technicians(emp_id),
   foreign key(proj) references projects(project_name),
   foreign key(notebook) references notebooks(notebook_no));
```

SQL query successfully generated

```
select '1:1:1 Relationship Table'
from dual
   where not exists
      (select * from uses_notebook u1,
      uses_notebook u2
         where u1.emp = u2.emp
         and    u1.notebook = u2.notebook
         and    u1.ROWID != u2.ROWID)
   and not exists
      (select * from uses_notebook u1,
      uses_notebook u2
         where u1.emp = u2.emp
         and    u1.proj = u2.proj
         and    u1.ROWID != u2.ROWID)
   and not exists
      (select * from uses_notebook u1,
      uses_notebook u2
         where u1.proj = u2.proj
         and    u1.notebook = u2.notebook
         and    u1.ROWID != u2.ROWID);
```

Example of data instances

uses_notebook

emp	proj	notebook
35	alpha	5001
35	gamma	2008
42	delta	1004
42	epsilon	3005
81	gamma	1007
93	alpha	1009
93	beta	5001

ER Diagram

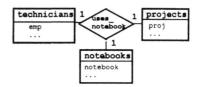

From this result we can deduce at this time the following facts :
- each technician uses exactly one notebook foe each project ;
- each notebook belongs to one technician for each project ;
- a technician may still work on many projects and maintain different notebooks for different projects.

Appendix 4 : N:N:N Relationship

```
create table employees (emp_id number, name char(20),
   primary key(emp_id));

create table projects (project_name char(12), budget number,
   primary key(project_name));

create table skills (skill_type char(10), domain char(30),
   primary key(skill_type));

create table skill_used
   (emp number, skill char(10), proj char(12),
   primary key(emp,skill,proj),
   foreign key(emp) references employees(emp_id),
   foreign key(proj) references projects(project_name),
   foreign key(skill) references skills(skill_type));
```

SQL query successfully generated

```
select 'N:N:N Relationship Table'
from dual
   where exists
      (select * from skill_used u1,
       skill_used u2
         where u1.skill = u2.skill
         and   u1.proj = u2.proj
         and   u1.emp != u2.emp)
   and exists
      (select * from skill_used u1,
       skill_used u2
         where u1.emp= u2.emp
         and   u1.proj = u2.proj
         and   u1.skill != u2.skill)
   and exists
      (select * from skill_used u1,
       skill_used u2
         where u1.skill = u2.skill
         and   u1.emp = u2.emp
         and   u1.proj != u2.proj);
```

Example of data instances

skill_used

emp	skill	proj
101	algebra	electronics
101	calculus	electronics
101	algebra	mechanics
101	geometry	mechanics
102	algebra	electronics
102	set-theory	electronics
102	geometry	mechanics
103	topology	mechanics

ER Diagram

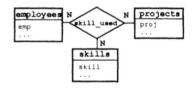

From this result we can deduce at this time the
following facts :
   - each employees can use different skills on any one of many projects ;
   - each project has many employees with various skills.

Inheritance as a Conceptual Primitive*

Roland Kaschek
Institut für Informatik
Universität Klagenfurt

Abstract

Inheritance is one of the central concepts of object-oriented programming (OOP). In object-oriented design therefore a part of the knowledge worked out during object-oriented analysis (OOA) is mapped onto inheritance structures. Thus at the conceptual level an analog to inheritance in object oriented programming languages is needed. Recent approaches offer generalization as such analog. In this paper a definition of inheritance as a conceptual primitive is proposed. It is shown that generalization, aggregation and instantiation are special cases of inheritance. The latter however is not covered by the former concepts and so it is offered as a new basic primitive.

1 Introduction

During OOA aggregation, generalization and instantiation are important concepts. Inheritance is one of the central concepts in object oriented programming ([9], p.60). Therefore most applications implemented in object oriented programming languages use inheritance. It specifies a transfer of knowledge concerning a so-called superclass to a so-called subclass. Usually inheritance is taken to implement generalization. We show that the mentioned knowledge transfer not only accompanies generalization but also aggregation and instantiation. Thus to employ the full power of inheritance at the conceptual level, a more general understanding of the concept is needed. Our problem related definition of inheritance is intended to provide for such understanding. We show that it generalizes the modeling primitives just mentioned but is not covered by them. Thus its introduction at the conceptual level improves the expressive power of languages for object oriented analysis.

We use the category Σ of sets with relations as morphisms and composition as the usual composition of relations as a framework to define the meaning of

---

*A draft version of this paper has been presented at the Workshop 'Semantics in Databases' in Prague, Řež, January 13-16, 1995.

the modeling notions. Σ was discussed in [36] where our basic idea to define the semantics of conceptual database schemas is also present.

In what follows in 2 we introduce into the topic , show that popular methods for object oriented analysis don't address our problem and discuss some approaches to inheritance. Then in 3 we give some examples indicating that inheritance is implied by aggregation, generalization and instantiation. After that in 4 we define the notion of conceptual database schema and the mentioned modeling primitives. Then we investigate Σ-morphisms and show that inheritance is implied but not covered by the other concepts. Finally in 5 some aspects of this paper are revisited.

2 Inheritance in Object Orientation

In the mid 80's object orientation not only as a language paradigm or programming style became important (see [38] p. 298f, [55] p. 206f). Object-oriented methodologies were elaborated to build applications.

2.1 Applying Inheritance at The Conceptual Level

The present paper contributes to an implementation independent and problem related view of inheritance. An attempt to view inheritance that way, e.g. is in [7], p.112. It there is stated that with respect to classes A and B the class A should not be a subclass of B, 'if A "is not a" kind of B'. In [48] p.207 however, because of the different realizations of object oriented concepts in the various object oriented languages, it is claimed that during OOA one needs to know about the intended implementation means. If that were true then a strict limitation to reuse of design documents during software development would follow. Our approach overcomes this limitation by offering an implementation independent and problem oriented approach to inheritance.

Methodologies for object-oriented software development should, as is the case in conventional database design, drive the developer to do a conceptual design (see [6] p.6). Then the methodology should drive its user to construct a series of models until the implementation is reached. This series reflects the fact that every program is a model of something ([33]). Results of software experiments (, i.e. carrying out some computation) may be applied to the modeled system. (As a source to systems theory work see [62].) We believe this **model-of relationship** to be fundamental. We thus take it as a model for our conceptual notion of inheritance. An instance of that relationship is said to take place if there is a relationship specification such that for any state of affairs within the UoD at hand the specified relation is a Σ-monomorphism.

It is reasonable to model the knowledge transfer from a superclass A to a subclass B (with extents A^e and B^e respectively) by means of a Σ-monomorphism because the existence of such $f \subseteq B^e \times A^e$ implies that certain equations concerning A^e only can be valid if corresponding equations concerning B^e hold.

This is a consequence of f's defining property that $fg = fh$ implies $g = h$ for all Σ-morphisms g, h.

In the theory of modules as well as in the theory of acts over monoids the concept of purity (see [18], p. 547) is used to lead back solvability of systems of linear equations in superstructures to the solvability within substructures. It could be the case that purity gives raise to a more general notion of knowledge transfer, i.e. inheritance, in the context of classes.

In category theory a certain equivalence class of monomorphisms is said to be a subobject (see [4], p42f.) of the target of one of its representatitves. Usually this morphism's source then is viewed as 'the' subobject of its target. As is well known his subobject concept generalizes the subset concept and so is (for some discussion see 3.1) related to generalization and inheritance.

If one tries to use an algebraic approach to objects then it is reasonable to formalize inheritance by means of the subalgebra concept. However this forces a method and its inherited version m to coincide as an input-output relation on the domain of m. This, due to side effects (, i.e. that a method's action might not be described sufficiently precise by its input-output relation, see ([48], p.202)), does not cover the full power of inheritance. It is well known that the categorical subobject concept generalizes the subalgebra concept. Thus it is reasonable to employ the category theory approach to overcome the limitations of the algebraic approach.

Papers viewing inheritance as an incremental modification mechanism are [63, 13, 9]. Because we are more interested in the ontology than in programming language theory we don't follow this work. Concerning subtyping we just note ([10, 9]) that it often can be viewed as a consequence of a subset relation.

Although, we here focus on the object oriented roots of inheritance, we point out that within this realm inheritance at least dates back to SDM ([25]), where it is dealt with as a consequence of subset inclusion (IsA).

2.2 Abstraction Concepts in Popular OOA-Methods

We present the set of abstraction concepts offered by some popular OOA methods and show that they focus on the classical concepts and don't address the problem to give a conceptual analog to inheritance. They either don't offer the full power of the inheritance or utilize programming language concepts or don't give sharp definitions.

- The **OMT** approach ([50]) offers aggregation, generalization and classification as abstraction concepts. Inheritance is dealt with as an implementation concept (p. 47,66). Thus no conceptual level definition of inheritance is given.

- As in OMT in **OOSE** ([28] the classical abstraction concepts are offered. Inheritance (p. 64 f.) should be used for the reuse of code, for subtyping, specialization of classes and subset inclusion for extents of classes. Clearly reuse of code and subtyping are not matters of the conceptual level. Subset inclusion of extents of classes may be seen as a consequence of generalization (see e.g. [50] p.38). So just specialization of classes is left. No real definition is given in OOSE for specialization.

- In **OOA/OOD** ([7] p.59) the ontological connection between the entities modeled in order to justify the application of inheritance is called 'is a kind of'. A definition of this connection is not given. But the examples given in the source (p. 59) seem to indicate that generalization is intended. It is not clear which degree or kind of similarity is supposed to exist for to justify the application of inheritance.

2.3 Further Remarks on Inheritance in OO-Literature

We now discuss some references dealing with the problem of inheritance semantics for OOA.

- A view of inheritance one can find (e.g. [48]) is the one of **derivation**. This means that one class is derived from another one by extending their attributes and methods by new ones. Also overriding and generalization by restriction is possible This view of inheritance however leaves too much freedom to the designer with respect to design of object behavior ([27]). No ontological connection between super class and subclass is assumed to exist.[1]

- If inheritance is to **preserve the behavior**, then it is natural to ask for the degree of preservation. For three different degrees of preservation and thus different degrees of restriction to modification of inherited methods see [63] p.62f. In the object database management system O_2 e.g. inheritance is restricted in such way that a method m and its inherited version $m\prime$ have to coincide (as an input output relation) on the domain of $m\prime$. ([30] p.73.) This is partial compatibility from [63]. As we pointed out in 2.1, this concept does not cover inheritance in full.

- Approaches to inheritance focusing on **compatibility of life cycles**, which are given by finite state machines or petri nets, are presented in [43, 29, 52]. This approaches make it possible not only to inherit the behavior i.e. the operations of a class of objects, but also the structure of this behavior i.e. the constraints put on the states or the operations. Although the approach is completely conceptual we don't follow it here because it is not clear what kind of life cycle compatibility one should prefer[2].

---

[1] In [57] problems are discussed which may rise in object oriented programming languages if one uses inheritance this way.

[2] In terms of graph theory ([21]) at least subgraphs, induced subgraphs, retracts and homeomorphic images are candidates for to describe the type of relationship intended by life cycle compatibility .

3 Some Examples

In what follows we present some examples. They indicate that the classical abstraction concepts of database design imply inheritance. Within each of the following examples we discuss some universe UoD. We shall argue, that a property is an inherited version of another one.

3.1 Generalization Relationship

According to [46] p. 155 generalization is the means by which differences among similar objects are ignored to form a higher level objects in which the similarities can be emphasized. Several authors view this intensional definition as a specification of a subset relationship, where instances of the specific object type are instances of the generic object type and have certain additional properties. In [33], p.85 this view of generalization is used to define the concept. In [50] no clear distinction is made between intensional and extensional aspects.

Let UoD be a university. Within UoD there are persons, which have specific properties such as a name or an address. Further there are staff members and students. They all have the properties persons have but the former also have a social security number and the latter a register number. The similarities between classes student and staff member can be addressed by a class person. Now that person can serve as model for student (as well as for staff member) one can view e.g. the name of student to be a property inherited from person.

The monomorphism employed in this example is the forgetful function which with respect to a student just remembers that the student is a person.

3.2 Aggregation Relationship

According to [46] p. 155 aggregation is the means by which associations between objects can considered to be a higher level object.

Let UoD be a car sellers shop. Let it consist of cars and customers. A car is mounted from components. One of them is the car's engine. Engines have the properties number of cylinders n and power p. Customers, which want to be informed about cars, view n and p as properties of the car and not just of the engine. In this sense one can say that e.g. power is inherited from engine to car[3].

The components can serve as abstractions of the higher level object. Thus a component e.g. the engine of a car can serve as a model of the whole. Therefore properties of the component apply to (i.e. are inherited by) the whole. The monomorphism in this example is the forgetful function that with respect to a car forgets everything else than its engine.

Whether complex objects inherit the attributes of their components, already was asked for in [22] p.167. As in [23], p.836 we claim that aggregation implies

---

[3]This is interesting also with respect to more sophisticated discussions which take into account that the cars engine output wattage is not the same as the wattage which effectively occurs between wheels and ground.

inheritance. Instead of speaking of inheritance in such situations in [33] p.81 the term hereditary property is used. In [34] p.120 f. (the source of the example) it is argued that a kind of inheritance appears with aggregation. It is assumed to be incomparable with the so-called subtype inheritance. We however show below that both types of inheritance are essentially the same.

The reference [31], claims to give two orthogonal aspects of aggregation. The first aspect is exclusiveness of being a component. however exclusiveness of playing roles defined in an associations context at least for generalization is discussed in the literature [6]. The other aspect is existence dependency, which together with identification dependency was discussed in [11, 12], where aggregation was not under investigation. Both aspects thus are not specific for aggregation.

For more detailed discussions on aggregation relationships see [58, 51, 24, 31, 42, 39].

3.3 Instantiation Relationship

According to [46] p. 156 classification is the means by which a collection of objects is defined to be a higher level object. Instantiation then is the means to denote that a certain entity belongs to the higher level object.

Let UoD be the world of fairy-tales. It contains a class raven, an instance of which is Abraxas. All properties which apply to raven apply to each instance of the class, especially to Abraxas. Thus it inherits the properties of raven e.g. has the property to sit on the shoulder of some witch.

The monomorphism relevant in this example is the identical inclusion of Abraxas into the extent of raven.

3.4 Model-Of Relationship

Let UoD be a mathematical universe containing the classes cylinder and pipe the instances of which are placed at a point c of $(x, y, 0)$-plane such that the center of one of the ground faces coincides with c. Because of mathematical purity cylinders are not pipes. Cylinders and pipes have the properties center c, diameter d, height h and volume v. Additionally pipes have an inner diameter i. It is the case that for each pipe, one of the cylinders the pipe is mapped onto, only is an image of the very pipe.

Now one would like to utilize the volume formula of cylinder for pipe. This can be achieved by introducing two abstractions. A pipe $p = (d, i, h, v)$ is related to two cylinders $c_1 = (d, h, v)$ and $c_2 = (i, h, v)$. Clearly we can state, that $p.v = c_1.v - c_2.v = h * \pi * (d^2 - i^2)/4$.

With help of this model-of relationship the volume formula from cylinder is inherited to pipe. The specific way each of the cylinders models the pipe explains the formula for the pipe volume we used above. Here we have a special case of the model-of relationship in that two cylinders each model a pipe. Both the models of a pipe are needed to inherit the volume formula from cylinder to pipe.

The monomorphism in this case is the relation μ which relates a pipe to the inner and outer cylinder which model the pipe. In 4.2.9 it will be shown that this relation indeed is a monomorphism.

3.5   Multiple inheritance

Up to some extent, inheritance -in the form of multiple inheritance- may be used to implement aggregation. A car e.g. could be said to consist of body, engine and so on. One can implement a class car in such way that it inherits from each of the car's component classes. In ([7], p. 127) with respect to mix-in inheritance the class multiply inheriting from mixins (abstract classes only defined for to inherit from them) is called *aggregate class*. In [50], p.58 it is emphasized that aggregation relates instances while generalization relates classes. Thus multiple inheritance if not based on mixins somehow is related to generalization as well as to aggregation.

3.6   Additional Abstraction Concepts

One could view a formula as a model of the set, i.e. the graph of the function given by the formula. Properties of the function can be derived from properties of the formula. So inheritance accompanies the lambda abstraction .

The experimental language K2 ([49]), has a fully elaborated module concept. In K2 there are module types, module variables and module instances. Subtyping of modules which is defined via module extension, i.e. a kind of generalization, implies inheritance.

Our model of relationship justifies the definition of properties of one object with respect to the properties of another one. Thus a definability relationship (see [15]) is introduced while employing the model of relationship.

4   Semantics of Conceptual Schemas

Several papers used category theory to define the semantics of conceptual database schemas or the object concept e.g. [40, 19, 54, 66, 59, 36]. Introductory texts into category theory are, e.g. [53, 4, 61].

Our approach to semantics of conceptual schemas also works for relational database schemas and implicitly is present in [45] but also is used in a categorical context in [36]. In contrast to [40, 59] we permit the unrestricted use of the cardinality notion.

4.1   Conceptual Database Schemas

A conceptual database schema $S = (V, E)$ is a labeled graph such that every vertex $v \in V$ either is a specification of a class or of an object. The respective subsets of V are denoted by $cls(S)$ and $obs(S)$. For each vertex v of S there is a description $d(v) = (att(v), met(v), sig(v), fsm(v), type(v))$. The components of $d(v)$ are called **attributes, methods, signature, dynamics** and **type** of v respectively. Each attribute is a pair (val, dom) consisting of value and domain - a set containing the value. The signature $sig(v)$ is a tuple $(s_1, \ldots, s_n)$ containing exactly one method signature s_i for the method m_i in $met(v) = (m_1, \ldots, m_n)$. The signature s_i is a pair (in_i, out_i). Therein in_i and out_i are value sets or subsets of V. The dynamics of v is a finite state machine.

The edges in E are pairs $((v_1, v_2), note)$, where v_1, v_2 are vertices of S and $note$ is a string. As value of $note$ besides IsA, IOf, POf and IMo every string may appear. The mentioned four strings specify that an instance of generalization, instantiation, aggregation or model of relationship occurs. All other occurrences of $note$ are treated as relationship names. No IsA-, IOf- or POf-cycle is allowed to exist in S.

Definition 4.1.1 *An interpretation of schema S, modeling the universe of discourse UoD, is a functor F from S into Σ such that the following properties hold:*

1. *$F(v)$ is a set of objects for each vertex v of S. Then, if $type(v) = object$ and v specifies an object f then $F(v) = \{f\}$. But if $type(v) = class$ and v specifies a class with extent $\{f_1, \ldots, f_p\}$ then $F(v) = \{f_1, \ldots, f_p\}$.*

2. *Let v be a vertex of S and $\{e_1 \ldots e_m\}$ the set of IsA-edges with target v then $F(v)$ is a coproduct object $\coprod_{i=1}^{m} F(v_i)$ of the sets $F(v_i)$ and $F(e_i)$ is the identical inclusion of $F(v_i)$ in $F(v)$, if $e_i = ((v_i, v), IsA)$, $\forall i \in \{1, \ldots, m\}$.*

3. *Let v be a vertex of S and $\{e_1 \ldots e_m\}$ the set of POf-edges with source v. If $e_i = ((v, v_i), POf), \forall i \in \{1, \ldots, m\}$ then the aggregate $F(v)$ is the set $\{x \in \mathcal{P}(\coprod_{i \in \{1, \ldots, m\}} F(v_i)| \exists$ an aggregation instance exactly associating the elements of $x\}$ [4]. Each edge e_i then is mapped onto $F(e_i) = \{(o, o_j^i)|o \in F(v), o_j^i \in o \cap F(v_i)\}$. We further assume the following conditions to hold*

   (a) *No two objects $o, o' \in F(v)$ may for any $i \in \{1, \ldots, m\}$ share any object in the $i - th$ component.*

   (b) *No object $o \in F(v)$ may have for any $i \in \{1, \ldots, m\}$ an empty ith component.*

4. *If v is a vertex of S and $\{e_1 \ldots e_m\}$ the set of IOf-edges with target v then $type(source(e_i)) = object$ and $F(v_i) \subset F(v)$, $\forall i$ and $F(e_i)$ is the identical inclusion of $F(v_i)$ in $F(v)$.*

5. *If $e = ((v, v'), IMo)$ is an IMo-edge then $F(e)$ is a monomorphism of $F(v)$ into $F(v')$.*

An interpretation F of a schema is called **admissible** if every assertion concerning the objects in the image of F are in coincidence with the state of affairs of the UoD.

---

[4] Note that according to 3.2 an aggregation is a certain kind of association.

Let the interpretation $F(v)$ of a vertex v in schema S is a singleton set. To distinguish whether v is a class specification or an object specification demands and only is possible by inspection of the value of $type(v)$.

As can be seen in the proof of 4.2.5 the coproduct in Σ is the disjoint union. We use this approach just because of technical simplicity. It is easy to see that the expressive power of a language which admits generalization to be specified as total or not and as overlapping or not has no more expressive power than a language within which generalization is assumed to be total and not overlapping, which are properties the coproduct in Σ has.

In Comparison with the terminology of [24] our POf relation is similar to the exclusive meronyme relation. Also the approach to aggregation taken in [20] seems to be rather similar since it defines the extent of the aggregate as a suitable subset of the cartesian product of the extension of the components, which is the product in the category of sets. Also in [1] the approach to aggregation is based on cartesian products (although the authors didn't use this term) as is true for the ER-model ([6]). Much more general POf relationships already have been discussed in linguistics ([14]).

A schema is intended to capture the meaning, which an UoD has to its designer. As is well known ([32] p.12) this meaning cannot be captured by only referencing object sets i.e. the extents of classes. Because of this a data dictionary (DD) is used to collect natural language definitions of the non generic things found in the UoD. The generic relationships are generalization, aggregation, classification, instantiation and model-of relationship. Other generic notions within our approach are, e.g. object, class, attribute, attribute domain, attribute value.

The treaty of links i.e. edges between vertices in a schema S as relations between the extensions of the vertices is inspired by the functional data model, [56] and the HIT data model, [65].

4.2 Properties of Σ

Throughout this paper we assume that for all problems related to connections of classes in object-orientation it suffices to study the category Σ. The category oppositional to Σ is denoted by Σ^*.

Let A, B be sets and $f \subseteq A \times B$ a (heterogeneous) relation. Then $\forall b \in B$ the **b-fiber** of f is the set $\{a \in A \mid (a, b) \in f\}$. It is denoted by $\phi(f)_b$. $\forall a \in A$ the **a-cofiber** or **a-image** of f is the set $\{b \in B \mid (a, b) \in f\}$. It is denoted by $\gamma(f)_a$. The **image** $im(f)$ and the **domain** $dom(f)$ of f respectively are the sets $\cup_{a \in A} \gamma(f)_a$ and $\cup_{b \in B} \phi(f)_b$. The transposition f^* of f is the set $\{(b, a) \mid (a, b) \in f\}$. f is called **surjective** or **total** if $im(f) = B$, f^* is surjective, respectively. Clearly for relations f, g we have $f = g$ iff $f^* = g^*$ holds. The identity relation on A will be denoted by 1_A. The powerset of A is denoted by $\mathcal{P}(A)$. f is said to be **epic** or **right invertible** if it is right cancellative or invertible with respect to the composition of relations. Similarly we define the concepts **monic** and **left invertible**.

The most obvious observation is:

Proposition 4.2.1 *The functor $T : \Sigma \to \Sigma^*$ which is the identity on sets and the transposition on relations is a contravariant, full and faithful bijector.*

Proof

The functor is contravariant because of the well known transposition property $(fg)^* = g^* f^*$ of relations. The other assertions hold trivially.●

Next we characterize monics and epics in Σ.

Proposition 4.2.2 *Let A, B be sets and $f \subseteq A \times B$. Then the following assertions are equivalent.*

   1. *f is epic,*

   2. *f is right invertible,*

   3. *$\forall b \in B \exists a \in \phi(f)_b \quad such \quad that \quad \gamma(f)_a = \{b\}$,*

   4. *f is surjective and $\forall M, N \subseteq B$ from $M \neq N$, it follows $\bigcup_{m \in M} \phi(f)_m \neq \bigcup_{n \in N} \phi(f)_n$.*

Proof

Obviously 2 implies 1 and 3 implies 2. Thus it suffices to show that 4 implies 3 and that 1 implies 4. For that let 4 hold true. Assume 3 not to hold true. Then $\exists b \in B \forall a \in \phi(f)_b$ such that $\gamma(f)_a \neq \{b\}$. Then the hypothesis and $B \neq B \setminus \{b\}$ imply that $\bigcup_{b' \in B \setminus \{b\}} \phi(f)_{b'} \neq \bigcup_{b' \in B} \phi(f)_{b'}$. But the right term of this inequality equals $dom(f)$. Therefore $\exists x \in dom(f) \setminus \bigcup_{b' \in B \setminus \{b\}} \phi(f)_{b'}$. But this implies that $x \in \phi(f)_b$ and $\gamma(f)_x = \{b\}$ holds in contradiction to the assumption.

    To show that 1 implies 4 let f be epic. At first we show that if f is not surjective then f is not epic. If f is not surjective then $\exists b \in B$ such that $\phi(f)_b = \emptyset$. Let $g = 1_B$ and $h = 1_{im(f)}$. Then $gf = f = hf$. Clearly $g \neq h$ and f is not epic. We now show that if subsets M, N of B exist such that $M \neq N$ and $\bigcup_{m \in M} \phi(f)_m = \bigcup_{n \in N} \phi(f)_n$ then f is not epic. Thus let M, N be such sets. Let $\{c\} = C$ and $g = \{(m, c) \mid m \in M\}$, $h = \{(n, c) \mid n \in N\}$. Then $gf = \{(a, c) \mid \exists b \in B s.t. (a, b) \in f, (b, c) \in g\} = \{(a, c) \mid \exists m \in M s.t.(a, m) \in f, (m, c) \in g\} = \{(a, c) \mid a \in \bigcup_{m \in M} \phi(f)_m\} = \{(a, c) \mid a \in \bigcup_{n \in N} \phi(f)_n\} = \{(a, c) \mid \exists n \in N s.t. (a, n) \in f, (n, c) \in h\} = hf$. Now that $g \neq h$ holds f is not epic. ●

Corollary 4.2.3 *Let A, B be sets and $f \subseteq A \times B$. Then the following assertions are equivalent.*

   1. *f is monic,*

   2. *f is left invertible,*

   3. *$\forall a \in A \exists b \in \gamma(f)_a \quad such \quad that \quad \phi(f)_b = \{a\}$,*

   4. *f is total and $\forall M, N \subseteq A$ from $M \neq N$, it follows $\bigcup_{m \in M} \gamma(f)_m \neq \bigcup_{n \in N} \gamma(f)_n$.*

Proof

The corollary follows from 4.2.1 and 4.2.2 with help of the observation, that a monic in Σ is epic in Σ^*.•

The equivalences of 1 and 2 in 4.2.2 as well as 1 and 2 in 4.2.3 were (with a somewhat different terminology) established in [36].

Corollary 4.2.4 *Let A, B be sets and $f \subseteq A \times B$. Then f is isic iff f is a bijective mapping.*

Proof

It suffices to show the necessity of the condition. Let f for this be isic. Then there $\exists g \subseteq B \times A$ such that $gf = 1_B$ and $fg = 1_A$. It leaves to show that then f is a mapping. For this assume f not to be a mapping. Then there are $a \in A$, $b, b' \in B$ such that $(a, b), (a, b') \in f$. Clearly this implies $(b, a), (b', a) \in g$. But then $(b, b') \in fg \neq 1_B$ and therefore f is a mapping.•

We now investigate products and coproducts in Σ.

Proposition 4.2.5 Σ *has coproducts.*

Proof

Let I be a set and $\{A_i\}_{i \in I}$ a family of sets. Let $\coprod_{i \in I} A_i$ be the set $\cup_{i \in I} \{i\} \times A_i$. For $i \in I$ let $e_i = \{(a, (i, a)) \mid a \in A_i\}$. Then $e_i \subseteq A_i \times \coprod_{j \in I} A_j$. Let X be a set and for $i \in I$ let $f_i \subseteq A_i \times X$. We have to show that there is a unique $f \subseteq \coprod A_j \times X$ such that $fe_i = f_i$ holds, $\forall i \in I$. Obviously for $f = \{((i, a), x) \mid i \in I, (a, x) \in f_i\}$ the equation $fe_i = f_i$ holds, $\forall i \in I$. Let f' be another relation $f' \subseteq \coprod A_j \times X$ such that $f'e_i = f_i$ holds, $\forall i \in I$. For to show that $f' = f$ holds we state the following chain of equivalences: $((i, a), x) \in f)$ iff $(a, (i, a)) \in e_i$ and $((i, a), x) \in f)$ iff $(a, x) \in f'e_i = fe_i$ iff $((i, a), x) \in f'$. Therefore coproducts in Σ exist.•

Corollary 4.2.6 Σ *has products. Any product object is isomorphic to any coproduct object with respect to families of isomorphic objects.* [5]

Proof

The assertion follows from 4.2.1 and 4.2.5.•

Remark 4.2.7 *It is shown in [36] that Σ has not all equalizers and that therefore Σ is neither complete nor cocomplete. This observation shows that in Σ one cannot define the semantics of an arbitrary query against a conceptual database schema as a limit of a diagram representing the query. Thus the idea from [59] to define a query language at the conceptual level as a set of (commutative) diagrams for Σ probably does not work.* •

Proposition 4.2.8 *Let $S = (V, E)$ be a conceptual database schema. Let further be $v \in V$ and $\{e_1, \ldots, e_m\}$ the set of POf-edges with source v. If F is an interpretation of S, then $F(e_i) \subseteq F(v) \times F(v_i)$ is monic.*

---

[5]This result was communicated to me by Elke Wilkeit from Oldenburg University.

Proof
The assertion follows from 3 in 4.2.3 and the formalization of aggregation in 4.1.1.•

Corollary 4.2.9 *Let P, C be sets of pipes and cylinders according to the hypothesis of 3.4 respectively. Let μ the relation defined in 3.4. Then μ is monic.*

Proof
The result follows immediately from 4.2.3 and the definition of the μ in 3.4.•

Proposition 4.2.10 *A mapping is monic in Ens iff it is monic in Σ.*

Proof
The result follows immediately from 3 in 4.2.3 and that mappings are assumed to be total.•

4.3   A Comparison of Modeling Notions

Now we apply our formalism to deduce the main results.

Definition 4.3.1 *Let $S = (V, E)$ be a conceptual database schema and $e = (v, v', note) \in E$ be an edge of S. Then we say that v inherits v' if for all admissible interpretations F of S the morphism $F(e)$ is monic in Σ.*

Proposition 4.3.2 *Let $S = (V, E)$ be a schema and $e = ((v, v'), note) \in E$ an edge in S. If $note \in \{IsA, IOf, POf\}$ then v inherits v'.*

Proof
Let F be an admissible interpretation of S. Then it follows from 4.1.1 that IsA and IOf edges map to identical inclusions in *SoRel*. Therefore 4.2.10 in this case implies the result. In case $note = POf$ 4.2.8 implies that e is mapped onto a monomorphism.•

Proposition 4.3.3 *Inheritance is not covered by aggregation, generalization and instantiation.*

Proof
It suffices to show that there is a monomorphism which is not the composition of any morphisms given by aggregation, generalization or instantiation. For that let $A = \{a, b, c\}$ and $B = \{x, y\}$. Let $f = \{(x, a), (x, b), (y, b), (y, c)\}$. Then f is not a product of morphism of types mentioned above because no morphism of that type can produce overlapping cofibers. Obviously f is monic and the proposition proved. •

Remark 4.3.4 *As 4.2.3 shows we could weaken our formalization of aggregation in 4.1.1 such that object sharing in components would be possible and that 4.2.8 still would hold. But then it could be a problem to prove 4.3.3. Our choice in 4.1.1 however seems to be close to literature.•*

5 Conclusion

We started with the observation that a conceptual analog to inheritance in object oriented programming languages is needed. We then studied how some prominent methods for object-oriented analysis deal with inheritance and found that their approach is not sufficient. After that we discussed some examples indicating that inheritance occurs in situations were typically aggregation, generalization or instantiation are applied. In terms of category theory we defined the semantics of the classical modeling notions as well as of inheritance. Then we investigated some elementary properties of the category Σ which we have chosen as a framework of our approach. We showed that inheritance is implied by each of the classical notions and finally argued that inheritance is not covered by the whole of them.

References

[1] Atzeni P., Torlone R.: A Metamodel Approach for the Management of Multiple Models And the Translation of Schemes. Information Systems 18,6(1993):349-362.

[2] Bancilhon F., Buneman P.(Eds.): Advances in Database Programming Languages. ACM Press. New York, N.Y.. 1990.

[3] Bancilhon F., Delobel C., Kanellakis P.: Building An Object-Oriented Database System. Morgan Kaufmann Publishers. San Mateo, Cal.. 1992.

[4] Barr M., Wells C.: Category Theory for Computer Science. Prentice-Hall. New York et al. 1990.

[5] Batini C.(Ed.): Entity Relationship Approach. Elsevier Science Publishers B.V.(North Holland). 1989.

[6] Batini C., Ceri S., Navathe S.: Conceptual Database Design. The Benjamin/Cummings Publishing Company, Inc..Redwood City, Cal.. 1992.

[7] Booch G.: Object-Oriented Analysis And Design. The Benjamin/Cummings Publishing Company, Inc.. Redwood City, Cal..1994.

[8] Bruce K.B., Wegner P.: An Algebraic Model of Subtype And Inheritance. In [2]. p.75-96.

[9] Cardelli L.: A Semantics for Multiple Inheritance. In [41], p.59-83.

[10] Chaudhuri S.: Database Types: A Plea for Simplicity. In [44]. p.165-181.

[11] Chen F.: The Entity-Relationship Model- Toward a Unified View of Data. ACM Transactions on Database Systems 1,1(1976):9-36.

[12] Chen P.: Database Design based on Entity and Relationship. In [64]:174-210

[13] Cook W.R., Hill W.L., Canning P.S.: Inheritance Is Not Subtyping. In Proceedings Of 17th. ACM Symposium On Principles Of Programming Languages. p.125-135.

[14] Cruse D.A.: On the transitivity of the part-whole relation. Journal of Linguistics 15(1979):29-38.

[15] Ebbinghaus H.-D., Flum J., Thomas W.: Einführung in die mathematische Logik. Wissenschaftliche Buchgesellschaft Darmstadt.1978.

[16] Eder J., Kalinichenko L.A.: East/West Database Workshop. Springer Verlag. Berlin et al..1995.

[17] Ehrig H., Mahr B.: Fundamentals of Algebraic Specification 1. Springer-Verlag. Berlin et al..1985.

[18] Eisenreich G.: Lexikon der Algebra. Akademie Verlag. Berlin. 1989.

[19] Fiadeiro J., Sernadas C., Maibaum T., Saake G.: Proof-Theoretic Semantics of Object-Oriented Specification Constructs. In: [44]. p.243-284.

[20] Furtado A.L., Neuhold E.J.: Formal Techniques for Data Base Design. Springer-Verlag. Berlin et al. 1986.

[21] Gould R.: Graph Theory. The Benjamin/Cummings Publishing Company, Inc.. Menlo Park, California et al..1988.

[22] Graham I.: Object Oriented Methods. Addison-Wesley Publishing Company. Wokingham, England et al.. 1991.

[23] Goldstein R.C., Storey V.C.: Materialization. IEEE Transactions on Data And Knowledge Engineering 6,5(1994):835-842.'

[24] Halper M., Geller J., Perl Y.: "Part" Relations for Object-Oriented Databases. In [47]. p.406-422.

[25] Hammer M., McLeod D.: Database Description with SDM: A Semantic Database Model. ACM Transactions on Database Systems 6,3(1981):351-386.

[26] Henderson-Sellers B.: A Book Of Object-Oriented Knowledge. Prentice Hall. New York, N.Y. et al.. 1992.

[27] Heuer A.: Objektorientierte Datenbanken-Dynamik ohne Grundlage?.In [35]. p.61-64.

[28] Jacobson I., Christerson M., Jonsson P., Övergaard G.: Object-Oriented Software Engineering. Addison-Wesley Publishing Company. Workingham, England et al.. 1992.

[29] Kappel G., Schrefl M.: Inheritance of Object Behaviour- Consistent Extension of Object Life Cycles. In:[16]:289-300.

[30] Kanellakis P., Lecluse C., Richard P.: Introduction to the Data Model. In [3] as Chapter 3, p.61-76.

[31] Kim W., Bertino E., Garza J.F.: Composite Objects revisited. ACM SIGMOD International Conference on the Management of Data. 1989. p.337-347.

[32] Klein H.K., Hirschheim R.A.: A Comparative Framework of Data Modelling Paradigms and Approaches. The Computer Journal 30,1(1987):8-15.

[33] Kristensen B.B., Østerbye K.: Conceptual Modeling and Programming Languages. ACM SIGPLAN Notices 29,9(1994):81-90.

[34] Liu L.: Exploring Semantics in Aggregation Hierarchies for Object Oriented Databases. Proceedings of the 8th. International Conference on Data Engineering. p.116-125. Febr. 2.-3.1992. Tempe, Arizona. IEEE.

[35] Lipeck U.W., Manthey R.(Eds.): Kurzfassungen des 4. GI-Workshops "Grundlagen von Datenbanken". technical report ECRC-92-13. 1992.

[36] Lippe E., ter Hofstede A.H.M.: A Category Theory Approach to Conceptual Modeling. Technical Report CSI-R9415, Computing Science Institute, University of Nijmegen. Nijmegen, The Netherlands. December 1994.

[37] Lipeck U., Vossen G. (Eds.): Formale Grundlagen für den Entwurf von Informationssystemen. GI-Workshop, Tutzing. 24.-26. Mai 1994.

[38] Louden K.C.: Programming Languages. PWS-KENT Publishing Company. Boston. 1993.

[39] Li X., Orlowska M.: A Generalized Approach to Modeling Complex Objects. In: Srinivasan, Zelesnikov (Eds.): Proceedings of the 2nd. Australien DB-IS Conference. p.29-44. Sydney, 4.-5. Febr. 1991.

[40] Lellahi S.K., Spyratos N.: Towards a Categorical Data Model Supporting Structured Objects and Inheritance. In: Proceedings of 1st. International East/West Database-Workshop, Kiev, Oct. 1990.:86-105.

[41] Maier D., Zdonik S.B.: Readings in Object-Oriented Database Systems. Morgan Kaufmann Publishers, Inc.. San Mateo, California. 1990.

[42] Mattos N.M.: Abstraction Concepts: The Basis for Data and Knowledge Modeling. In [5]. p.473-492.

[43] McGregor J.D., Dyer D.M.: Inheritance And State Machines. ACM SIGSOFT Software Engineering Notes. 18,4(1993):61-69.

[44] Meersman R.A., Kent W., Khosla S.(Eds.): Object-Oriented Databases: Analysis, Design And Construction (DS-4). Elsevier Science Publishers B.V. (North Holland). Amsterdam et al.. 1991.

[45] Paredaens J., De Bra P., Gyssens M., Van Gught D.: The Structure of the Relational Database Model. Springer Verlag. Berlin et al. 1989.

[46] Peckham j., Marjanski F.: Semantic Data Models. ACM Computing Surveys 20,3(1988):153-189.

[47] Pernul G., Tjoa A.M. (Eds.): ER-Approach-ER'92. Springer Verlag. Berlin et al.. 1992.

[48] Pomberger G., Blaschek G.: Grundlagen des Software Engineering. Carl Hanser Verlag München Wien. 1993.

[49] Radenski A.: Module Types, Module Variables, and Their Use as a Universal Encapsulation Mechanism. ACM SIGPLAN Notices 29,1(1994):3-8.

[50] Rumbaugh J., Blaha M., Premerlani W., Eddy F., Lorensen W.: Object-Oriented Modeling And Design. Prentice-Hall International, Inc.. Englewood Cliffs, N.J. et al.. 1991.

[51] Schienmann B.: Die Teil/Ganze Beziehung im objektorientierten Fachentwurf. In [37], p.43-62.

[52] Saake G., Hartel P., Jungclaus R., Wieringa R., Feenstra R.: Inheritance Conditions for Object Life Cycle Diagrams. In: [37], p. 79-88.

[53] Semadeni Z., Wiweger A.: Einführung in die Theorie der Kategorien und der Funktoren. BSB B.G. Teubner Verlagsgesellschaft. Leipzig. 1979.

[54] Sernadas A., Ehrich H.-D.: What is an Object, After All?. In: [44]. p.39-69.

[55] Sethi R.: Programming Languages. Addison-Wesley Publishing Company. Reading, Mass.. 1989.

[56] Shipman D.: The Functional Data Model And The Data Language DAPLEX. ACM Transactions on Database Systems. 6,1(1981):140-173.

[57] Snyder A.: Encapsulation and Inheritance in Object-Oriented Programming Languages. In: [41]. p.84-91.

[58] Storey V.C.: Understanding Semantic Relationships. VLDB Journal 2(1993):455-488

[59] Tuijn C., Gyssens M., Paeredaens J.: A Categorical Approach to Object-Oriented Data Modeling. In: Proceedings of 3rd. Workshop on Foundation of Models for Data and Objects. Aigen, Austria. 1991.:187-196.

[60] Wegner P.: Concepts and Paradigms of Object-Oriented Programming. ACM SIGPLAN OOPS Messenger 1,1(1990):7-87

[61] Walters R.F.C.: Categories And Computer Science. Cambridge University Press. 1991.

[62] Wymore A.W.: Theory of Systems. In: Vick C.R., Ramamoorthy C.V. (Eds.): Handbook of Software Engineering. Van Nostrand Reinhold. New York. 1984.p. 119-132.

[63] Wegner P., Zdonik S.: Inheritance as an Incremental Modification Mechanism or What Like is and Isn't Like. In Proceedings of The ECOOP'88, p.55-77.

[64] Yao S.B.:Principles of Database Design. Prentice Hall, Inc.. Englewood Cliffs, New Jersey.1985.

[65] Zlatuska J.: HIT Data Model, Databases From The Functional Point of View. Proceedings of VLDB 1985. p.470-477.

[66] Zamfir Bleyberg M.: A Categorical Entity-Relationship Model of Databases. In: Proceedings of the 1991 Symposium on Applied Computing. April 3-5, 1991. Kansas Ciy, Missouri.:156-166.

iO2
An Algorithmic Method for Building Inheritance Graphs in Object Database Design

A. Yahia[1], L. Lakhal[1], R. Cicchetti[2], and J.P. Bordat[3]

[1] LIMOS, Complexe Scientifique des Cézeaux, 63177 Aubière Cedex, FRANCE.
yahia@libd1.univ-bpclermont.fr
lakhal@ucfma.univ-bpclermont.fr

[2] Case 901, Faculté des sciences de Luminy, 163 Av. de Luminy, 13288 Marseille
Cedex9, FRANCE.
cicchetil@lim.univ-mrs.fr

[3] LIRMM, 161 rue ADA, 34392 Montpellier cedex 5 FRANCE.
bordat@lirmm.lirmm.fr

Abstract. This paper proposes a method, called iO2, for building the inheritance graph of an O2 database schema. The iO2 method is based on the Galois lattice data structure. It encompasses three steps: a (first) construction step, a (second) optimization step, and a (final) generation step. This paper focuses on the two first steps.
The construction step builds the Galois graph of the finite binary relation associating properties to entity and relationship types. A new algorithm is proposed for this first step. The optimization step builds the Galois inheritance graph from the Galois graph. A new algorithm is proposed for this second step in order to eliminate the redundancies. The generation step yields the O2 inheritance graph from the Galois inheritance graph. The transformation principles underlying this third step are given. The detailed generation algorithm is presented in [Yah96a].

1 Introduction

The schema of an object-oriented database has two dimensions. The first dimension (horizontal) is the class composition hierarchy which represents the aggregation relationship between a class and its attributes and the domains of its attributes. The second dimension (vertical) is the inheritance hierarchy which captures the generalization/specialization relationship between a class and its subclasses.

Inheritance has been studied under different facets including its semantics [Card90, Coo89], consistency which avoids conflicting specifications within an object database schema [For94], and conflict resolution for which many techniques have been proposed [Duc92], as well as consistent evolutions of class hierarchies [Del91, Pon93, Ami94]. These different aspects of inheritance are neither exhaustive nor independent one from each other. However, very few approaches attempt to provide methods and tools for designing inheritance graphs in object databases.

Indeed, when considering current conceptual modeling and design approaches [Rum91, Coa90, Boo91] no emphasis is placed on aiding the specification of inheritance graphs. Such a construction is a major issue for both modeling and design of object database schemas. It is likely to be more crucial during the design step since the process is no more driven by the real world vision but by optimization considerations. Nevertheless, in most conceptual modeling and design approaches the inheritance hierarchy construction is under the designer's judgment, *i.e.* based on his experience and good sense.

In this paper, we propose a method, called iO2, for building the inheritance graph of an O2 database schema.

The iO2 method is based on the Galois lattice of a finite binary relation. This lattice is also called the lattice of concepts [Wil92]. The Galois lattice data structure is usually used in Artificial Intelligence to build conceptual classifications [Wil82, Wil92, Carp93, God95a,b,c]. These approaches consider each element of the Galois lattice as a formal concept and the edges of the Galois graph (Hasse diagram of the Galois lattice) as a generalization/specialization relationship between concepts. The Galois lattice reveals itself to be well adapted for designing class hierarchies because:

(1) The elements of a Galois lattice (or nodes of the Galois graph) correspond to maximal factorizations of properties. Maximal factorizations of common properties between classes reduce non optimal and non natural class hierarchies [Coo92].

(2) The partial order relation (inclusive relation) of Galois lattices is in conformity with the inheritance relation of class hierarchies. The inheritance relation can be interpreted as an inclusion relation between sets [Bra83].

These two criteria are important for designing class hierarchies as mentioned in [God95a, Goh88, Kor92].

The iO2 method computes the inheritance graph of object database schemas through three steps. The first step constructs the Galois graph of the finite binary relation associating properties to Entity and Relationship types (ERs). The second step computes the Galois inheritance graph from the Galois graph. We define a new optimization algorithm which applies on the Galois graph and yields the Galois inheritance graph. The third step focuses on the O2 inheritance graph generation. We give a new generation process and algorithm for the construction of the O2 inheritance graph from the Galois inheritance graph.

Throughout the paper, the iO2 method is illustrated through an example inspired from [Adi93]; a travel agency application managing touristic information (for instance about hotels) and client reservations.

This paper is organized as follows: section 2 presents the proposed method and gives an outline of existing related methods. In section 3, we provide the preliminary definitions of the Galois lattice, its graph and the O2 inheritance graph. Section 4 illustrates the Galois graph of the finite binary relation ERs/properties. Section 5 defines the Galois inheritance graph, describes the optimization step and gives the optimization algorithm. Section 6 broadly presents the generation step of iO2. This step is described in detail in [Yah96a]. As a conclusion, the strong points of iO2 are emphasized and an outlook of future work is given.

2 Related Work and Proposal

Before presenting our approach and in order to highlight its contributions, it would be interesting to provide a brief survey of modeling and designing inheritance hierarchies.

Among existing approaches for designing inheritance graphs, there are two main trends:

(1) The first group involves extensional currents. They are based on conceptual clustering methods and taxonomic reasoning in knowledge representation systems for discovering ISA Links. Inspired from these techniques, the approach proposed in [Lie91] involves the automatic discovery of classes from example objects. [Ber92] introduces the formalism $\mathcal{FL}^*$, detects contradictory concepts and computes subsumption (ISA hierarchy) between classes by comparing their extensions.

(2) The second class encompasses intensional currents. They are relevant when exhibiting inheritance hierarchies by handling only structural elements (rather than extensions or objects), and are cost-less when compared to extensional methods. M. Missikoff and M. Sholl [Mis89] represent a conceptual-level class hierarchy as a Galois lattice (called M-Lattice) and define an algorithm to insert object types in this lattice, which can be seen as an incremental method for designing Galois lattices. R. Godin and H. Mili [God93] propose an approach in which classes and methods are considered. A so-called inheritance Galois lattice [God95b] is generated from the binary relation associating methods to classes for Smalltalk library construction. None of these approaches address the problem of generating the DAG (direct acyclic graph) representation of inheritance hierarchies in object databases.

The iO2 method belongs to the intentional currents. It is inspired from [God93] and [Mis89]'s research work, as it makes use of Galois lattices to generate analysis-level class hierarchies, but it places much more emphasis on defining algorithms yielding as an end result the DAG represenation of O2 inheritance hierarchies. iO2 encompasses three steps (fig. 1):

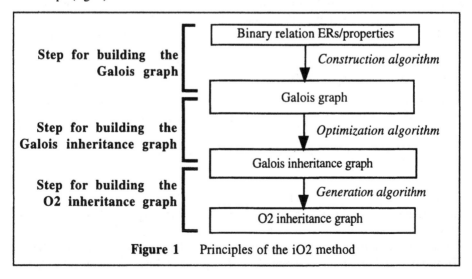

Figure 1   Principles of the iO2 method

(1) The first step computes the Galois graph. We propose a new algorithm for the construction of the Galois graph from the finite binary relation associating properties to entity or relationship types.

(2) The second step builds the Galois inheritance graph by removing the redundancies from the Galois graph. We define a new optimization algorithm which improves previous results.

(3) The third step generates the (O2) inheritance graph from the Galois inheritance graph.

The starting point of iO2 is the user defined binary relation between properties (attributes and operations/methods) and entity/relationship types (ERs) of the 'real world'. This binary relation captures for each property, the ERs in which it belongs. This knowledge is organized, in an automated way, through a Galois graph. This graph is handled by the second and the third steps which successively perform an optimization and a generation operations. The former removes the redundancies within the Galois graph, and the latter yields the end result which is the DAG representation of the O2 inheritance hierarchy.

3 Preliminary Defintions

In this section we provide definitions of the Galois lattice, the Galois graph and the O2 inheritance graph.

3.1 Galois Lattice and Galois Graph of a Binary Relation

Let G and M be any two finite sets of elements and I any finite binary relation defined on GxM. Let us consider the derived functions $f: 2^G \rightarrow 2^M$ and $g: 2^M \rightarrow 2^G$ defined by:

$f(X) = \{ y \in M / x I\ y, \forall\ x \in X\}$, for all $X \in 2^G$;

$g(Y) = \{ x \in G / x I\ y, \forall\ y \in Y\}$, for all $Y \in 2^M$.

The couples $(gf(X), f(X))$ where X belongs to 2^G, are maximal (w.r.t. inclusion) and are called maximal rectangles of I. The set of maximal rectangles of I, denoted by Trmax(I), is provided with the strict partial order *infmax* defined by:

$\forall\ (X,Y),(X',Y') \in$ Trmax, (X,Y) *infmax* $(X',Y') \Leftrightarrow X \subset X'\ (\Leftrightarrow Y' \subset Y)$.

Let's denote by *-inf*, the covering relation of *infmax* on Trmax(I), and let T be an indexed set representing Trmax(I).

Basic Theorem for Galois Lattices [Wil82]. (Trmax(I), *infmax*) is a complete lattice, called concept lattice of the context (G,M,I), for which minimum and extremum are defined as follows:

$$\bigwedge_{i \in T} (X_i, Y_i) = (\bigcap_{i \in T} X_i, fg(\bigcup_{i \in T} Y_i))\ \text{and}\ \bigvee_{i \in T} (X_i, Y_i) = (gf(\bigcup_{i \in T} X_i), \bigcap_{i \in T} Y_i).$$

(Trmax(I), *infmax*) is usually called Galois lattice of I. Indeed, f and g define a Galois connection (between the power sets of G and M), which expresses a natural duality between elements of G and those of M.

(Trmax(I), *infmax*) is graphically represented by its Hasse diagram, that is (Trmax(I),*-inf*). We call this diagram, the Galois graph of I and we denote it by G(I).

3.2 O2 Inheritance Graph

In an O2 database schema [Lec88], the inheritance graph (or class hierarchy) is a directed acyclic graph (DAG) whose nodes represent classes and where edges capture the inheritance relation (based on the subtyping relation [Card90]) between classes. The root node denotes a particular class (meta-class) named "Object" which is a super-class of all the other classes of the graph.

Definition [DEL91]. The inheritance graph is formally defined as a pair $(E_c, -<)$ where : • E_c is the set of *nodes*. Each node represents a class;

• $-<$ is the covering relation of the subclass partial order $(<)$ on E_c, with class Object as root.

For each couple of classes (x , x') belonging to E_c x E_c, $x' -< x$ represents an *edge* between x' and x, x being higher than x' in the hierarchy. Said otherwise, x is an immediate superclass of x'. More generally, $x' < x$ represents the existence of a path from x up to x' and denotes that x is a superclass of x'.

4 Building the Galois Graph

In this section we provide illustrations of the binary relation ERs/properties and the Galois graph.

4.1 Binary Relation ERs/Properties

Let' s denote by Ω the set of all entity and relationship types of the 'real world', by Φ the set of all properties of the 'real world', and by R the binary relation between Ω and Φ.

	cities	name	country	map	speciality	century	monument-city	place-country	tariff	invoice	reserve-tour	reserve-hotel	init	birth-date	age	address	city	salary	free	total-left	assign-reserv.	hotel	tour	discount
Country	1	1																						
City		1	1																					
Place								1																
Monument					1	1	1																	
Museum				1			1																	
Tour										1	1													
Hotel										1		1												
Employee													1	1	1	1	1	1						
Client													1	1	1	1	1			1	1	1		
Client-Employee													1	1	1	1	1	1	1	1	1	1		1
HotelReservation								1													1			
TourReservation								1															1	

Figure 2 Matrix of the binary relation ERs/properties

This binary relation specifies whether a property (attribute or method) is defined in an ER (entity or relationship type) or not. As shown in figure 2, R is represented through a matrix. For a given ER x and a particular property y, the associated element in the matrix is 1 if y is a property of x or 0 otherwise.

Example. Figure 2 shows the matrix capturing the binary relation between ERs and properties of the 'real world'. For instance, the ER Country (which is an entity type) has only two properties : "cities" which yields the list of cities in the country and "name" just giving the name of the considered country.

4.2 Galois Graph

As no confusion may occur and for brevity, we will call 'Galois graph' the 'Galois graph used in iO2' and we'll use Trmax to denote Trmax(R).

Definition. The (iO2) Galois graph is defined as the Galois graph of R and is denoted by $G(R)$. In other words, the galois graph is (Trmax, -inf).

In the Galois graph each node is composed of two elements. The first component is a sub-set of ERs, whereas the second consists of a sub-set of properties. The semantics of a node is the following: all its properties are defined in all its ERs, and it does not exist another property in the 'real world' which would be defined for all the ERs of the node. Furthermore, there is not another ER in the 'real world' containing all the properties of the considered node. Thus a node is defined by the cartesian product of its two components. The association between ERs and properties, captured in each node, is maximal and is called maximal rectangle. This means that these associations can not be included one in another (Cartesian product inclusion).

The Galois graph contains two terminal nodes: the extremum and minimum nodes. The extremum node groups all the ERs of the 'real world' and their common properties. In most cases, the sub-set of properties in this node is empty, else it includes properties which are shared by all the ERs of the 'real world'. In contrast, the minimum node contains all the properties defined in the 'real world' and their possible associated ERs. The set of ERs in this node is likely empty because such ERs must include all the properties defined in the 'real world'.

In the Galois graph, edges represent a strict partial order defined on Trmax (the set of maximal rectangles) and express a double inclusion relation between the nodes' components. The ER sub-set of a low-level node is included in the ER sub-set of its ancestors while the property sub-set of a high-level node is included in the property sub-set of its descendants. Ancestor and descendant are generic terms for nodes possibly related through several edges (and thus through intermediary nodes), we use the terms upper and lower if the inclusion relation (infmax) is direct (a single edge).

Example. Figure 3 shows the Galois graph generated from our matrix example (Figure 2). Let us consider the node labelled 1. Its property sub-set is included in the property sub-set of both the nodes labelled 2 and 3. The ER sub-set of these latter nodes is included in the ER sub-set of the node 1. In the extremum node, Ω stands for the set of all the ERs of the 'real world'.

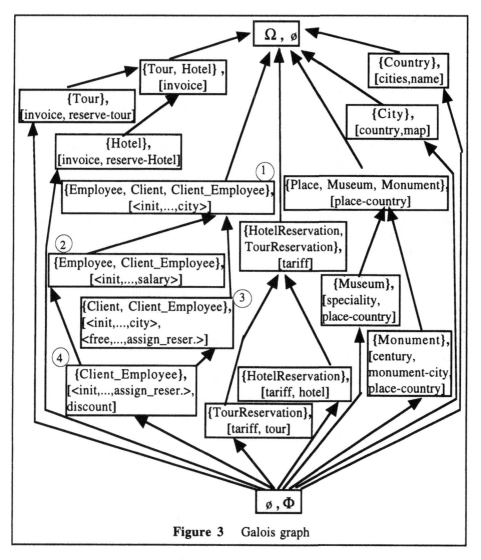

Figure 3   Galois graph

For the sake of clarity, we do not give, in Figure 3, the exhaustive list of properties. For instance, the property subset denoted by <init,....,city> stands for all the properties between columns "init" and "city" of the matrix in Figure 2. A maximal rectangle corresponds to the largest sub-set of ERs sharing the same greatest sub-set of properties. In figure 3, node 2 has [<init,...,salary>] as sub-set of properties and {Employee, Client_Employee} as sub-set of ERs. It depicts the fact that, there are no more than two ERs posessing each *at least* all properties in <init,...,salary>, and sharing *at most* these properties in common. Indeed, notice that node 1 which contains fewer properties than node 2 (property salary missing) has more ERs, and that property discount which applies to Client_Employee (in node 4) is not provided for Employee (in node 2).

In this example, the extremum (resp. the minimum) node has an empty sub-set of properties (resp. ERs). This means that there is no ER (resp. property), including (resp. defined for) all of the properties (ERs).

4.3 Construction Algorithm

In this section, we describe a new algorithm for building the Galois graph, adapted to our context from its first version in [Bor86]. For lack of space, the full text of the algorithm is not included. It can be found in [Yah96b].

Many algorithms deal with the problem of constructing the Galois graph of some binary relation. A synthesis of the majority of existing algorithms can be found in [Gue90]. They can be distinguished according to two directions:

• Algorithms which effectively build the Galois graph, and those which just enumerate the set of maximal rectangles. The latter have to be complemented with procedures for determining the partial order among maximal rectangles, as well as its minimal cover. Most existing construction algorithms belong to this second category.

• Algorithms which are batch (global), or else incremental. Batch algorithms operate on the binary relation as a hole. Incremental algorithms [Carp93, God95c] operate on an initial sub-binary relation, containing only one element (together with its associated *image* elements), and proceeds successively by adding one new element at a time, until the binary relation is entirely captured. In fact, incremental algorithms are update rather than construction algorithms.

Our algorithm builds the Galois graph and belongs to the batch category. To our knowledge, it is the only batch algorithm for building the Galois graph.

The algorithm is based on the notion of maximal parts of a maximal rectangle, which is defined below. A maximal rectangle can have 0 or several maximal parts. According to the following theorem, each maximal part defines one and only one immediately superior maximal rectangle, *w.r.t. infmax*. Thus, the issue of deriving upper nodes for a given node is reduced to determining the maximal parts of the corresponding maximal rectangle.

Definition. Let $S = R(W, Y)$ be the restriction of R to sets W, Y ($\Omega \supseteq W$, $\Phi \supseteq Y$) and s: $W \rightarrow Y$ the function defined by $s(w) = \{ y \in Y / w S y \}$. The sets defined by $\{ s(w) / w \in W \}$ which are maximal w.r.t. inclusion are called the maximal parts of S.

Theorem [Bor86]. For all (X, Y) and $(X_i, Y_i) \in Trmax$: (X_i, Y_i) covers (X, Y), *i.e.* (X, Y) -inf (X_i, Y_i), iff Y_i is a maximal part of $R(\Omega-X, Y)$. Then, X_i is the disjoint union of X and the set of elements w in $\Omega-X$ such that $s(w)=Y_i$.

Remark. By language misuse, we will call maximal parts of some maximal rectangle (X,Y), the maximal parts of the sub-relation $R(\Omega-X, Y)$.

The Galois graph is built up "in breadth-first order" starting with the minimum node. The minimum node corresponds to the maximal rectangle (Ω', Φ), where Φ is the set of all properties of the 'real world', and Ω' is equal to $g(\Phi)$, and represents the sub-set of all ERs which have every property of the 'real world'. Notice that the elements of

Ω' correspond to the lines fully filled with "1", in the matrix.

Given a node N_1 holding the maximal rectangle (X_1, Y_1), the maximal parts of the sub-relation $R(\Omega-X_1 x Y_1)$ are determined. For each computed maximal part, the corresponding maximal rectangle is generated.

Whenever a maximal rectangle is generated for the first time, a new node is created. In other cases, an edge is added to the lattice relating the node being processed to the node containing the generated maximal rectangle (either new or old).

The algorithm ends when all nodes have been processed. The last node to be processed is the extremum node, which corresponds to $(\Omega, f(\Omega))$. It represents the sub-set of those properties belonging to all ERs of the 'real world'.

Example. Let us illustrate the algorithm with the example (figure 3). Starting with $(\Omega' = g(\Phi) = \emptyset, \Phi)$, nodes are processed in breath-first order. The processing of one node determines its upper nodes. For example, let's consider node 4 = ({Client_Employee}, [<init,...,assign_reserv.>, discount]). The restricted relation $R(\Omega-\{Client\_Employee\}$, [<init,..., assign_reserv.>, discount]) has two maximal parts [<init,..., salary>] and [<init,...,city>, <free,...,assign_reser.>]. These are the second components of maximal rectangles, the which are the upper nodes of node 4. Since they have not yet been generated as upper nodes of some other node, they are created as new nodes: ({Employee, Client_Employee}, [<init,..., salary>]) and ({Client, Client_Employee}, [<init,...,city>, <free,...,assign_reser.>]).

5 Building the Galois Inheritance Graph

The second step of the iO2 method builds the Galois inheritance graph. In this section, we provide illustrations of its concepts and we define a new optimization algorithm which applies on the Galois graph and yields the Galois inheritance graph.

5.1 Galois Inheritance Graph

In the Galois graph, nodes are redundant from the viewpoint of both ERs and properties. The Galois inheritance graph preserves the nodes and the edges of the initial Galois graph. However, it does not contain any redundant information.

Informally, the Galois inheritance graph is a Galois graph without redundancies. It can be obtained through two successive operations. The first processing computes the ER set of each node while performing a bottom-up navigation through the graph, *i.e.* from lower to the upper nodes. For each node, an ER is preserved if it does not appear in the ER set of its descendants, else it is removed. The second step computes the property set of the nodes by performing a top-down navigation through the graph. For each node, a property is retained if it is not defined in the property set of its ancestors, else it is deleted. Thus, the new values of a node depends on its descendants and ancestors.

Example. By applying optimization, as described above, on the Galois graph of the example (Figure 3), we obtain the Galois inheritance graph illustrated in Figure 4. Let us examine the nodes labelled 1, 2, and 3.

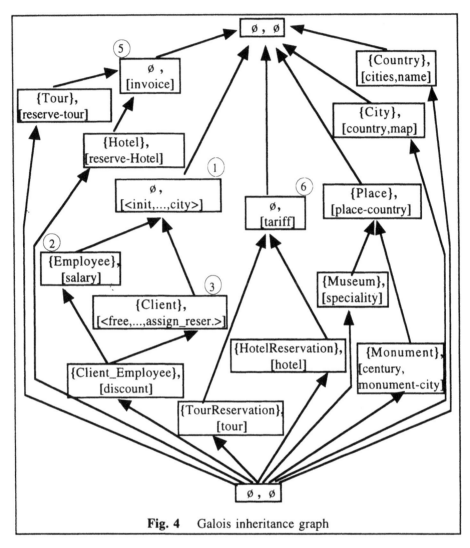

Fig. 4   Galois inheritance graph

Their common properties are defined in the high-level node (labelled 1), and have been removed from the low-level nodes (labelled 2 and 3). Conversely, common ERs have been discarded from the high-level node. The result is an empty ER component for node 1.

In this example, the minimum and the extremum nodes have no ERs. This means that there isn't any ER inheriting from all the other ERs and there isn't any ER from which all the other ERs inherit.

5.2 Optimization Algorithm

In this section, we propose a new corollary which improves a previous result of [Wil92] and [God93], and entails a new optimization algorithm. This algorithm optimizes the Galois graph without copying it and without considering its edges. The new content of each node is computed as a function of its old value (the corresponding maximal rectangle) and of the R binary relation. In our previous work [Yah96a], we introduce an other optimization algorithm which is built on a more traditional parse of the graph, but yet has similar computation time in the order of $|\text{Trmax}| * (|\Omega| + |\Phi|)$.

Proposition [Wil92], [God93].
The Galois inheritance graph $H(R)$ called the labelled Hasse diagram in [Wil92] and inheritance Galois lattice in [God93] is obtained by substituting in each node of $G(R)$, the maximal rectangle (X,Y) with the couple (X',Y') such that:
$$X' = \{ x \in \Omega \ / \quad f(x) = Y \};$$
$$Y' = \{ y \in \Phi \ / \quad g(y) = X \}.$$
Notice that $f(x)$ ($g(y)$ resp.) is a language misuse for writting $f(\{x\})$ ($g(\{y\})$ resp.).

In the following corollary, we give an improvement of this result by considering the sub-set cardinalities rather than the sub-sets themselves. It is more interesting (efficient) from an algorithmic point of view.

Corollary. The Galois inheritance graph $H(R)$ is obtained by substituting in each node of $G(R)$, the maximal rectangle (X,Y) with the couple (X',Y') where:
$$X' = \{ x \in X \ / \quad |f(x)| = |Y| \};$$
$$Y' = \{ y \in Y \ / \quad |g(y)| = |X| \}.$$

Proof. The proof is given in [Yah96b].

The corollary suggests a less constrained condition than the one given in the above proposition. As such, it defines a more efficient optimization algorithm.

Algorithm:

Input: $G(R)$
Output: $H(R)$
Notations: $H(R)$ is initialized with $G(R)$. A node N of $H(R)$ represents a maximal rectangle of Trmax. Its two components are denoted by N.ERs and N.properties.

Begin

    $H(R) \leftarrow G(R)$

    <u>for each</u> node N in $H(R)$ <u>do</u>

        $n_X = |\text{N.ERs}|$

        $n_Y = |\text{N.properties}|$

        $X' \leftarrow \emptyset, Y' \leftarrow \emptyset$

        <u>for each</u> $x \in$ N.ERs <u>do</u>   <u>if</u> $|f(x)| = n_Y$ <u>then</u> $X' \leftarrow X' + \{x\}$

        N.ERs $\leftarrow X'$

        <u>for each</u> $y \in$ N.properties <u>do</u>   <u>if</u> $|g(y)| = n_X$ <u>then</u> $Y' \leftarrow Y' + \{y\}$

        N.properties $\leftarrow Y'$

    <u>endfor</u>

End

5.3 Interpretation of the Galois Inheritance Graph

By its very nature, the Galois inheritance graph has some interesting properties relevant to the generation step (last step) of the iO2 method. For this reason, nodes are distinguished according to the cardinalities of their two component sub-sets. More precisely, three cardinalities are significant : zero, one and many. Nodes are called empty-, single-, or many-ER (property resp.) according to their number of ERs (properties resp.).

Single-ER Nodes. Property (P1) states that each ER and each property appears only once in the Galois inheritance graph. Thus, a single-ER node stands for a 'real world' ER having its own specific properties.

Empty-Property Nodes. Property (P2) states that apart from the extremum, an empty-property node has *at least* two upper nodes. Thus, an empty-property node expresses a specialization without 'specific' properties.

Empty-ER Nodes. Property (P3) states that except the minimum, an empty-ER node has *at least* two lower nodes. Thus, an empty-ER exhibits a generalization need. It corresponds to, either a missing ER which has not been initially mentioned by the user, or an artificial useful ER the user may wish to keep.

Empty-ER / Empty Property Nodes. Apart from the extremum and minimum, a node which is both empty-ER and empty-property represents a specialization and a generalization at the same time. It inherits all its properties which are also inherited by its lower nodes.

Edges. In the Galois inheritance graph, edges do not have the same semantics as in the Galois graph. They no longer capture a twofold inclusion relation between nodes, but instead they express an inheritance relation between nodes.

6 Building the O2 Inheritance Graph

The last step of the iO2 method, called generation step, yields the O2 inheritance graph. The detailed description of the principles underlying the generation process as well as the generation algorithm are given in [Yah96a].

In summary, the generation process destroys the lattice structure of the Galois inheritance graph by applying the following principles:

- Nodes having a single ER are kept as such.

- Nodes having zero ERs are either named or deleted according to the user preferences. This occurs when a generalization can be introduced for an improved sharing of properties.

- Nodes having more than one ER are split into as many new nodes.

- The extremum and minimum nodes are processed according to the above principles, with a slight modification.

The resulting reorganized graph is a DAG in which nodes contain each a single ER (entity or relationship type) together with its specific (not inherited) properties.

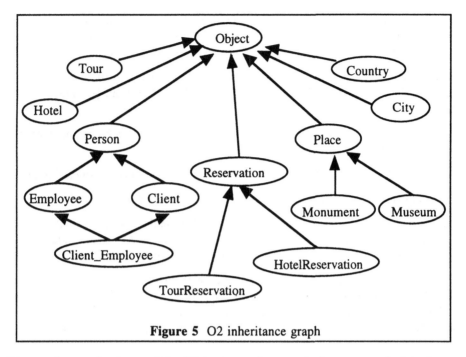

Figure 5 O2 inheritance graph

These nodes are the classes of the O2 database schema and edges capture the inheritance relation (-<) between classes.

Example. Figure 5 illustrates the O2 inheritance graph obtained when applying the final step on the Galois inheritance graph in Figure 4. In this graph, three nodes have an empty ER sub-set (nodes 1, 5, 6). In each case, a generalization need is expressed in order to share common properties between ERs, for example between "employee" (node 2) and "client" (node 3). The two artificial ERs corresponding to nodes 1 and 6 are preserved in the inheritance hierarchy and named "Person" and "Reservation" respectively. In the opposite, node 5 is not preserved (figure 4): it does not appear in the inheritance graph (figure 5).

In the Galois inheritance graph (figure 4), both the minimum and the extremum nodes are empty-ER/empty-property nodes. The former is deleted and the latter just named "Object" (figure 5).

7 Conclusion

In this paper, we have presented a method which provides designers with an aid for building up the inheritance graph of an O2 database schema by using a Galois lattice data structure. The Galois lattice approach was originally proposed to solve scheduling problems [Bap84] and conceptual classification in knoweledge representation and data analysis [Wil82, Wil92, Carp93, God95a,b,c]. We have shown, as in [Mis89] and [God93], that this approach provides an interesting basis for the construction of the inheritance hierarchy. From the Galois graph of the binary relation associating properties to ERs, iO2 performs the optimization of the graph and then reorganizes it through a generation step. Capturing additional semantics can be necessary and requires interactions with the user. When compared with our starting point: a set of ERs with their properties, iO2 exhibits ISA links between ERs, optimizes property sharing by detecting new ER requirements and reveals some modeling defects.

Our approach relates to those of [Mis89] and [God93] by using a Galois lattice as the formal tool for designing inheritance hierarchies. It differs from [God93] mainly because .

1) It is devoted to the design of the logical-level inheritance hierarchies rather than the conceptual-level inheritance hierarchies;

2) it integrates a new algorithm for the construction of the Galois inheritance graph;

3) it automatically generates the DAG representation of the O2 inheritance hierarchy.

In comparaison with [Mis89], our method is global while their is incremental. In fact, they have given an algorithm to insert object types in an M-lattice. Indeed, this algorithm can be seen as an incremental way for building the Galois graph.

We believe that our method could be combined with conceptual approaches, such as OMT [Rum91], OOA/OOD [Coa90], OOD [Boo91],.., for aiding designers in modeling specializations or generalizations but also all along the design step when the application schema is enriched with implementation-required classes (for instance, managing the user's interface [Coo92]).

To complement our method, we have defined update algorithms applying to the Galois graph on the one hand[Tao96], and to the Galois inheritance graph [Yah95] on the other hand. Update algorithms are crucial for they assist the designer to take into account real world evolutions or to rectify a part of his inheritance graph without redefining the whole. The major issue, when dealing with such reorganizations of the graph, is to guarantee its consistency. Another interesting aspect to be studied in more depth is the correctness of the generated inheritance hierarchies. We believe that ideas developped in [For94] could apply to iO2. Finally, we would like to use richer class descriptions (method signatures and attribute types), to fully take advantage of the expressive capabilities of OO models.

References

[Adi93]   M. Adiba, and C. Collet, "Objets et bases de données : le SGBD O2". Ed. Hermes, 1993.

[Ami94] E. Amiel, M. J. Bellosta, E. Dujardin, and E. Simon, "Supporting exceptions to behavioral schema consistency to ease schema evolution in OODMS". In Proceedings of the 20th International Conference on Very Large Databases-VLDB94., Chile 1994, pp. 108-119.

[Bap84] P. Baptiste, and J. Favrel, "Résolution de problèmes d'ordonnancement par les treillis de Galois et les graphes d'intervalle". RAIRO-Automatique/Systems Analysis and Control, 1984, Vol. 18, N° 4, pp. 405-416.

[Ber92] S. Bergamashi, and C. Sartori, "On taxonomic reasoning in conceptual design". ACM Transactions on Database Systems, Vol. 17, N° 3, September 1992, pp. 385-422.

[Boo91] G. Booch, "Object-oriented design with applications". Benjamin/ Cumming Company, 1991.

[Bor86] J. P. Bordat, "Calcul pratique du treillis de Galois d'une correspondance". Mathématiques et Sciences Humaines, N° 96, 1986, pp. 31-47.

[Bor92] J.P. Bordat, "L'algorithmique combinatoire d'ordres finis". Phd Thesis, Université de Montpellier II, 1992.

[Bra83] R. J. Brachman, "What ISA is and isn't". Analysis of Taxonomic Links in semantic Network, Computer N°10, 1983.

[Card90] L. Cardelli, "A semantics of multiple inheritance". Readings in Object-Oriented Database Systems, S. B. Zdonik and D. Maier (Eds.), 1990. pp. 51-67.

[Carp93] C. Carpineto, and G. Romano, "GALOIS: An order-theoretic approach to conceptual clustering". Proceedings of the Machine Learning Conference, 1993, pp. 33-40.

[Coa90] P. Coad, and E. Yourdon, " Object-oriented analysis". Yourdon Press Computing Series, 1990.

[Coo89] W. R. Cook, and J. Palsberg, "A denotational semantics of inheritance and its correctness". In proceedings of the International Conference On Object-Oriented Programming Languages and Applications- OOPSLA89, 1989, pp. 433-443.

[Coo92] W. R. Cook, "Interfaces and specifications for the smaltalk-80 collection class". In proceedings of the International Conference On Object-Oriented Programming Languages and Applications- OOPSLA92, 1992, pp. 1-15.

[Del91] C. Delcourt, and R. Zicari, "The design of an integrity consistency checker (ICC) for an object oriented database system". European Conference on Object Oriented Programming- ECOOP 91. LNCS N° 512, Geneva, Switzerland, July 1991. pp. 97-117.

[Duc92] R. Ducournau, M. Habib, M. Huchard, and M. L. Mugnier, "Monotonic conflict resolution mechanisms for inheritance". In proceedings of the International Conference On Object-Oriented Programming Languages and Applications- OOPSLA92, 1992, pp. 16-24.

[For94] A. Formica, and M. Missikoff, "Correctness of ISA hierarchies in object-oriented database schemas". In proceedings of the 4th International Conference on Extending Database Technology- EDBT 94, LNCS N° 779, Cambridge, United Kingdom, March 1994, pp. 231-244.

[God93] R. Godin, and H. Mili, "Building and maintaining analysis-level class hierarchies using Galois lattices". In proceedings of the International Conference On Object-Oriented Programming Languages and Applications- OOPSLA 93, 1993, pp. 394-410.

[God95a] R. Godin, G. Mineau, R. Missaoui, and H. Mili, "Conceptual clustering methods based on Galois lattices and applications". French Review on Artificial intelligence, Vol. 9, N° 2, 1995, pp. 105-137.

[God95b] R. Godin, G. W. Mineau, and R. Missaoui, "Incremental structuring of knowledge bases". In proceedings of the International KRUSE Symposium, Callifornia, 1995, pp. 179-193.

[God95c] R. Godin, R. Missaoui, and H. Alaoui, "Incremental concept formation algorithms based on Galois (concept) lattices". In Computational Intelligence, Vol. 11, N°2, 1995, pp. 246-265.

[Gue90] A. Guénoche, "Construction du treillis de Galois d'une relation binaire". Mathématiques et Sciences Humaines, N° 109, 1990, pp. 41-53.

[Goh88] R. Johnson, and B. Foote, "Designing reusable classes". Journal of Object-Oriented Programming, June/July, 1988, pp-22-35.

[Kor92] T. Korson, and J. D. McGregor, "Technical criteria for the specification and evaluation of object-oriented Libraries". Software Engineering Journal, March 1992, pp. 85-94.

[Lec88] C. Lécluse, P. Richard, and F. Velez " O2, an object-oriented data model". In proceedings of the ACM SIGMOD International Conference On Management of Data. June 1988, pp. 424-433.

[Lie91] K.J. Lieberherr, P.Bergstein, and I.Silvalep, "From objects to classes: algorithms for optional object-oriented design". Journal of Software Engineering. July 1991, pp. 205-228.

[Mis89] M. Missikoff, and M. Scholl, "An algorithm for insertion into a lattice: application to type classification". Foundations of Data Organization and Algorithms, 3rd International Conference-FODO89, Paris, France, June 1989, LNCS N° 367, pp. 64-82.

[Pon93] P. Poncelet, M. Teisseire, R. Cicchetti, and L. Lakhal, "Towards a formal approach for object-oriented database design". In Proceedings of the 19th International Conference on Very Large Databases- VLDB 93, Dublin, Ireland. August 1993, pp. 278-289.

[Rum91] J. Rumbaugh, M. Blaha, W. Premerlani, F. Eddy, and W. Lorensen , "Object oriented modeling and design". Prentice Hall, 1991.

[Tao96] R. Taouil, L. Lakhal, and J.P. Bordat, "Evolutive building of Galois lattices". Technical Report of LIMOS, Clermont-Ferrand University, Avril 1996.

[Wil82] R. Wille, "Restructuring lattice theory : An Approach Based on Hierachies of Concepts". In Ordered Sets, I. Rival (Eds.), 1982, pp. 445-470.

[Wil92] R. Wille, "Concept lattices and conceptual knowledge systems". Computers Math. Applications Vol. 23, No. 6-9, 1992, pp. 493-515.

[Yah95] A. Yahia, "Restructuring the Galois inheritance graph". Technical Report of LIMOS, Clermont-Ferrand University, September 1995.

[Yah96a] A. Yahia, L. lakhal, and R. Cicchetti, "Building inheritance graphs in object database design". DEXA' 96 Conference, Zurich, 9th-13th September 1996.

[Yah96b] A. Yahia, L. lakhal, R. Cicchetti, and J. P. Bordat, "Conceptual modelling and design of class hierarchies in object database design". In revision stage for The Computer Journal, 1996.

Workflow Evolution[*]

F. Casati, S. Ceri, B. Pernici, G. Pozzi

Dipartimento di Elettronica e Informazione - Politecnico di Milano
Piazza L. Da Vinci, 32 - I20133 Milano, Italy
ceri/casati/pernici/pozzi@elet.polimi.it

Abstract. A basic step towards flexibility in workflow systems is the consistent and effective management of *workflow evolution*, i.e. of changing existing workflows while they are operational. One of the most challenging issue is the handling of running instances when their schemata are modified: simple solutions can be devised, but they often imply loosing all the work done or failing in capturing the advantages offered by workflow modifications; this is unacceptable for many applications.

In this paper we address the problem of workflow evolution, from both a static and a dynamic point of view. We define a complete, minimal, and consistent set of modification primitives that allow modifications of workflow schemata and we introduce a taxonomy of policies to manage evolution of running instances when the corresponding workflow schema is modified. Formal criteria are introduced, based on a simple workflow conceptual model, in order to determine which running instances can be transparently migrated to the new version. A case study, relating the assembling of a desktop computer, will exemplify the introduced concepts.

1 Introduction

In recent times the need for reorganization and improvement of business processes and the advances in information technology created a huge market request for workflow systems. Modern workflow management systems (WFMSs) enable the design, enactment, and monitoring of workflows in a heterogeneous and distributed environment, allowing efficient process execution and management.

It is widely recognized that one of the basic characteristics that workflow system should provide is *flexibility* [7, 8, 9]. In a fast-changing environment, companies need to constantly refine their processes in order to effectively meet the constraints and opportunities proposed by new technology, new market requirements, and new laws. Furthermore, in particular in the first executions of a process, unplanned situations not considered in the design could urge for a modification of the workflow definition.

The problem of workflow evolution has two facets:

- *static workflow evolution* refers to the issue of modifying the workflow description. The WFMS must provide primitives to allow the progressive re-

---

[*] Research presented in this paper is sponsored by the WIDE Esprit Project N. 20280

finement of a workflow without rewriting it from scratch, and must guarantee that the new version of the workflow is syntactically correct;

- *dynamic workflow evolution* refers to the problem of managing running instances of a workflow whose description has been modified. The WFMS here should assist the designer in providing mechanisms to 'gently' bring running instances to meet the new requirements.

One of the most challenging issues in the modification of workflows is the management of executions started with the old workflow model. Simple solutions, such as letting the processes finish according to the old model or aborting them, are often inconvenient or impossible to be applied, depending on the notification of the change and the nature of the workflow. If, for instance, a new law forces a modification of a workflow, then running instances will need to respect the new constraints as well. Aborting running executions does not solve the problem, since this often implies the loss of great amount of work. Furthermore, in certain processes (in pharmaceutical and chemical industries, for example) it is impossible to stop the activities in order to organize the change.

This paper focuses on workflow modifications involving the *flow structure*, i.e. the definition of the sequence in which activities should be executed within a process. We do not consider changes applied to other workflow characteristics, such as assignment of tasks to agents, organizational schema within a company, access to external databases, and so on; most concepts introduced here are applicable, with minor improvements, to other workflow components. Modifications applied to a specific instance of a workflow in order to cope with exceptional, unplanned event, are also outside the scope of this paper.

In this paper we propose a set of primitives that allow generic modification of a workflow, preserving syntactical correctness criteria both when they are applied to a (static) workflow description and to (dynamic) workflow instances. We reuse concepts introduced in the analysis of schema evolution in object-oriented databases, since we recognize similar problems and similar solutions.

We then introduce a taxonomy that describes how running instances can be managed after a modification to the corresponding process description, defining in particular the constraints that these instances have to meet in order to continue their execution according to the new, modified model.

A case study, representing the assembling of a personal computer in a fully automated factory, will exemplify these concepts.

1.1 Previous Related Work

The problem of schema evolution has been widely addressed in the field of Object-Oriented Databases[3, 1, 12]. The first approach to this problem can be found in [1], where a complete taxonomy of schema modification operation is introduced. Rules are proposed to put constraints on schema evolution: these rules preserve *invariants* of the schema. A set of primitives to manage schema evolution in the O_2 object-oriented database system is described in [12]; the paper also proposes some consistency properties that should be maintained after a schema modification.

Little work has been done in addressing the problem of workflow evolution, particularly concerning the dynamic evolution problem. A notable contribution comes from [7], where a correctness criteria for workflow evolution is proposed, based on the definition of the set of all valid task sequences. The paper, however, restricts to a limited set of modifications and does not discuss the handling of instances that can not meet the correctness criteria. A theory for evolving application models is presented in [10]. The paper proposes concepts relating schema evolution which are independent on the particular modeling technique, be it Entity-Relationship, Extended-Entity-Relationship, or Object-Oriented; it defines a formalism able to describe all these models, and provides constraints and properties that should hold upon schema modifications, but does not deal with the problem of how instances should be managed.

1.2 Outline of the Paper

The outline of the paper is the following: Section 2 introduces a simplified version of our workflow model, focusing on aspects relevant to workflow evolution. Section 3 presents a bird eye's view on workflow modification primitives, defining their characteristics (a complete listing of syntax and semantics of the primitives can be found in the appendix); Section 4 introduces a taxonomy of case evolution policies, defining the possible strategies to be followed when managing evolution of running workflow instances; finally, Section 5 contains concluding remarks and future work.

2 Overview of Workflow Modeling and Enactment

This section contains a simplified workflow conceptual model in order to introduce evolution issues without defining a number of details irrelevant to our purpose. The complete model specification can be found in [4]. The model will be introduced by presenting a case study, that will be used throughout this paper to exemplify problems and possible solutions concerning workflow evolution.

2.1 The PC Assembling Case Study

The case study relates the assembling of desktop personal computers performed in the fully automated factory *AutoComp*. The case is actually much simplified with respect to the real process. Basically, the construction process begins by preparing a cabinet (see Figure 1). The cabinet may be either a *Tower* or a *Minitower*. At the same time the motherboard is prepared, by inserting the CPU and disk controller in it. When both the cabinet and the motherboard are ready, the motherboard is inserted into the cabinet. Then, step by step, all other components are inserted. After the FDD is inserted, a condition variable (set by the **Get_Cabinet** task) determines if the cd-rom must be inserted or not (AutoComp releases cd-roms only on tower models); the inserted cd-rom is a BestCD 4x. Finally, the hard disk and the video ram are inserted, and the workflow is completed. In the following of the paper, this workflow will be denoted as *AutoComp.I* (initial version of the AutoComp workflow).

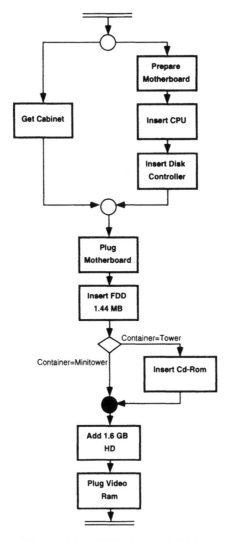

Fig. 1. AutoComp PC assembling WF schema, initial version (Autocomp.I)

2.2 Workflow Definition

Figure 1 introduces our graphical representation of a *WF schema* (i.e. a computer model of a process in the real world). In the figure, boxes represent *tasks*, that are units of work to be performed by a human or an automated agent. The other symbols represent *connectors*, and define the order in which the tasks must be executed.

We call *WF instance* (or *WF case*) any execution (enactment) of a WF schema. For instance, in the PC assemble workflow, a new WF case is created whenever a new computer begins being assembled. Normally, several WF cases of the same WF schema may be active at the same time.

WF cases have a state, which is identified by the set of running tasks and by *WF variables*. WF variables are local to a single case, and their lifespan is that of the case itself. The state of a case determines the path to be followed during case execution. Workflows may also access an external database (shared with other workflows) to store application data.

Sequences and dependencies among tasks can be specified in several ways: two tasks can be directly connected by an edge, with the intuitive meaning that, as soon as the former ends, the latter is ready for execution. In all other cases, connections among tasks are performed by two special-purpose routing tasks: *forks*, for initiating concurrent executions, and *joins*, for synchronizing after concurrent execution [2, 11]. The schema specification may include cycles, where the same task can be executed several times within the same WF instance.

Each **fork** is preceded by one task, called its *predecessor*, and followed by many tasks, called *successors*. Forks are classified as:

- *Conditional*: each successor is associated with a condition; after the predecessor ends, conditions are evaluated and only successors with a **true** condition are activated.
- *Total*: after the predecessor ends, all successors are activated. The total fork is equivalent to a conditional fork in which all successors have an always **true** condition.

A **join** is preceded by many tasks, called *predecessors*, and followed by one task, called *successor*. Joins are classified as:

- *Total*: the successor is activated only after the end of all its predecessors.
- *Iterative*: the successor is activated every time a predecessor ends.

Each WF schema has one start symbol and several stop symbols. WF connectors are represented in Figure 2.

A workflow graphical description could also contain direct links between connectors. The semantics of this is brought back to the one described above by ideally breaking the link with a *null task*. A null task is a task that performs no action, and finishes immediately after it starts; it is introduced only as a conceptual device to define the semantics of the WF diagram.

Formally, a workflow W is described by a quintuple $\Sigma^W = < Tasks^W$, $Vars^W$, σ^W, ς^W, $\theta^W >$, where $Tasks^W$ is the set of tasks of W, $Vars^W$ is the set of variables of W, σ is the *successor* function, associating to every task t in $Tasks^W$ a set of tasks of W (i.e. an element of the powerset of $Tasks^W$), ς is the *condition* function, associating to every task of $Tasks^W$ a condition, and θ^W is the *type* function, defining the type of link with a task's successors (i.e., direct, through

Fig. 2. Graphical representation of workflow items. From left to right: task, total fork, conditional fork, iterative join, start/stop symbol. The total join has the same symbol as the total fork.

a fork, through a total join, through an iterative join). The three functions σ, ς, and θ define the *flow structure*. Their meaning will be clarified when describing the workflow execution model. Intuitively, when a task t is completed, the set $\sigma(t)$ is considered; for every task p in that set, if $\varsigma(p)$ holds, then task p is started. θ^W is needed to distinguish iterative from total joins. A condition $\varsigma(t)$ is expressed by a set of pairs $< varName, value >$, and it yields a true value iff, for every pair in the set, the value of $varName$ is $value$. The domain and codomain of σ may also contain special tasks, signaling respectively the start and the end of the workflow.

Functions σ and ς have to meet certain constraints for Σ^W to be *legal*, i.e. syntactically correct. To formally define legality for workflow schemata and other concepts that will be used in the following, we introduce the following definitions:

- *Successor transitive closure*: the *transitive closure* of the successor function, denoted as σ^*, is defined as:
  $\sigma^*(t) = \{p: (p \in \sigma(t) \vee (\exists s: s \in \sigma(t) \wedge p \in \sigma^*(s))\}$
- *Reachability*: a task t is *reachable* iff $t \in \sigma^*('start')$
- *Predecessor function*: the *predecessor* function, denoted as $\pi(s)$, represents the set of tasks that have s as successor: $\pi(s) = \{t : s \in \sigma(t)\}$

A WF schema is *legal* iff all tasks in the flow structure (i.e. that are part of the domain or codomain of σ) are reachable. The above definition of reachability implies the existence of a path connecting the start symbol to every task in the workflow. However, this does not avoid the existence of tasks that will never be executed, regardless of the particular schema instantiation, due to badly placed conditions; for instance, some task conditions could be **false** in any case execution.

2.3 Workflow Execution

A case is executed by scheduling tasks and assigning them to the proper executing agent. The scheduling is performed by the *workflow engine*, that receives notification of tasks' completion, and determine the next task(s) to be executed, on the basis on the schema specifications and of the case state.

In our simplified model, we assume that:

1. a task, once scheduled from the WF engine, is immediately assigned to an agent and is ready for execution. The task is then executed by the proper agent, until it is completed;

2. the time spent by the engine in scheduling tasks is neglectable compared to task execution time;
3. two or more task executions cannot be completed at the same time. The engine will therefore process one event at a time.

Relating a case C (in execution) of a given workflow W, we introduce the following definitions and symbols:

- t_n denotes the n-th execution of a task t; n is called the *activation number*;
- $Active_C^W$ denotes the set of active tasks of case C of workflow W; the set evolves as case execution proceeds, being modified after every task completion. $Active_C^W(t_n)$ denotes the value of the $Active_C^W$ set after the completion of n-th execution of task t;
- $Vars_C^W$ denotes the set of values of the variables of C; it consists of a set of pairs <varName,value>, in which values are initialized to their (possibly NULL) default value when the case is started; $Vars_C^W(t_n)$ denotes the value of the $Vars_C^W$ set after the completion of n-th execution of task t (i.e. after the modifications made to WF variables by task t have been recorded in the $Vars_C^W$ set);
- $Completed_C^W$ denotes the set of completed task executions within case C. The set is initialized to the empty set when the case is started, while executions t_n are added as they are completed;
- $Completed_{C,n}^W$ denotes the set of all tasks for which an execution whose activation number was n has been completed;
- S_C^W denotes the *state* of a case: it is represented by the sets $Active_C^W$, $Vars_C^W$, and $Completed_{C,n}^W$ (for all n for which there has been at least one execution). $S_C^W(t_n)$ denotes the state of case C after the completion of n-th execution of task t, and is represented by the sets $Active_C^W(t_n)$, $Vars_C^W(t_n)$, and $Completed_{C,n}^W$.

Whenever a task execution t_n is completed, an event is generated signaling the task completion to the WF engine. Events are totally ordered (within a case C), since we have assumed that two or more task completions do not happen concurrently. When an execution t_n is completed, the following is performed by the workflow engine:

1. t is removed from the set of active tasks, t_n is inserted in the *Completed* set, and t is inserted in the $Completed_{C,n}^W$ set;
2. the effect of task t on case variables is registered (i.e. the set $Vars_C^W$ is modified according to the actions performed by t), and the next task(s) to be started is(are) scheduled in the following way:
   $\forall s, s \in \sigma(t),$
   if $((\pi(s) \subseteq \{Completed_{C,n}^W\}) \wedge (\varsigma(s) \subseteq Vars_C^W)) \vee \theta(t) = $ iterative_join
   then start the execution of s (and put s into the set of active tasks).

In the following, function $\eta(\Sigma^W, S_C^W(t_n), t_n)$ will denote the process (described by point 2 above) of scheduling tasks to activate after the completion of the n-th execution of task t in case C of schema W.

3 Schema Evolution Primitives

In this section we introduce the characteristics of the WFML (WorkFlow Modification Language) constructs that allow modification of a WF schema (a detailed description of syntax and semantics of primitives can be found in the appendix). Our goal is to define a set of primitives that is *complete, minimal*, and *consistent*.

Completeness refers to the possibility of transforming a generic WF schema in another generic WF schema. Minimality refers to the achievement of completeness with a minimal set of primitives, while consistency relates the problem of modifying schemata without causing compile-time or run-time errors. In particular, taking concepts typical of schema evolution in database systems [12], we introduce the notions of *structural consistency* and *behavioral consistency*.

Structural consistency refers to the static part of a WF, i.e. the schemata description. Structural consistency implies that after any sequence of modifications, the resulting schema is *legal*.

Behavioral consistency refers to the dynamic part of a WF, i.e. its population of running cases. Behavioral consistency implies that any set of primitives, when applied to a case in execution, results in a case (in execution) of a different schema and with a *legal* state. The state of a case C of a schema W is *legal* iff it can evolve without resulting in run-time errors, i.e. the behavior of the scheduler is always defined for every task completion in $Active_C^W$.

Behavioral and structural consistency in WFML are guaranteed for the application of every single primitive, thus implying the validity of these properties when a sequence of them is applied.

WFML primitives are divided in two parts:

- *declaration primitives* modify the declaration of WF variables and tasks: variables can be added or removed, their default value can be changed; tasks can also be added to the *Tasks* set, while tasks removal is automatically performed when tasks are no more part of the flow structure. The declaration primitives are *AddVar*(VarName v, DefaultValue d), *RemoveVar*(VarName v), and *AddTask*(Task t)
- *flow primitives* modify the flow structure of the schema, i.e. the sequence in which the task must be executed. The flow primitives are *AddSuccessor*(Task t, Task s) (adds or replaces, according to specified options, a successor to a task), *RemoveSuccessor*(Task t, Task s) (removes an element from the set of successor of a task), *ModifyType*(Task t, type T), (modify the type of connection between t and its successors), and *ModifyCondition*(Task t, Condition C) (changes the condition associated to a task activation).

Referring to the PC assembling workflow, suppose now that AutoComp management deals with NiceLabs Co., which offers the NiceSuite (cd-rom 4x and an audio card) at the same price and quality of the BestCD 4x.

AutoComp management decides then that all produced computers should carry the NiceLabs Suite, and therefore the assembling process must be modified according to this new requirement. The WF schema describing the new process

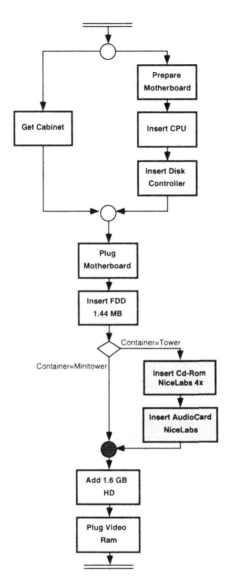

Fig. 3. AutoComp desktop assemble WF schema, final version (AutoComp.F). Newly inserted tasks are shadowed

is depicted in Figure 3 (newly inserted tasks are shadowed). This schema will be denoted in the following as *AutoComp.F* (final version of the AutoComp PC Assembling schema).

Modifications, in this example, involve only flow primitives, since variables and tasks characteristics have not been modified, while a task has been removed and two tasks have been added in the flow structure.

The WFML primitives that allow this evolution are:

AddSuccessor(Insert_Cd-Rom_BestCd_4x, Insert_Cd-Rom_NiceLabs_4x)
AddSuccessor(Insert_Cd-Rom_NiceLabs_4x, Insert_AudioCard_NiceLabs)
RemoveSuccessor(Insert_FDD_1.44_MB, Insert_Cd-Rom_BestCd_4x)

The first two primitives append the new tasks Insert_Cd-Rom_NiceLabs_4x and Insert_AudioCard_NiceLabs after task Insert_Cd-Rom_BestCd_4x, while the last instruction causes the task Insert_Cd-Rom_BestCd_4x to be skipped in case executions. WFML operations must be executed atomically and in the specified sequence in order to achieve the desired result.

The same primitives can be used for static and dynamic workflow evolution. If the modification primitives transform a schema W.I (initial workflow) into a schema W.F (final workflow), the same primitives applied to running cases of W.I *migrate* them into running cases of W.F. This is done by modifying the state of running cases in a consistent way. The migration of a case C is performed by atomically applying the transformation while C is running, and while therefore the engine is not considering the scheduling of case C. After the next completion of a task of C, the engine will then schedule the next tasks to be activated according to the new schema. Intuitively, the main problems are given by the RemoveSuccessor primitive, when it relates tasks t in execution. When this happens, the semantics of primitives is such that, depending on user's choice, either t is allowed to finish (but no more executions of t will be started) or t is suspended and its effect are rolled back (the semantics of the rollback is not discussed here: we assume that database operations can be automatically rolled back, while real-world operations must be undone in ad-hoc ways).

4 Taxonomy of Case Evolution Policies

This section describes the policies the workflow administrator (WFA) can adopt to manage running cases upon a modification τ of their schema, from schema W.I to schema W.F (where W.F represents the final *version* of schema W).

4.1 Case Evolution Policies

We have devised three main policies to manage case evolution:

- *Abort*: all WF cases of W.I are aborted, and the newly created cases will start following W.F;
- *Flush*: all existing cases are allowed to terminate following schema W.I. In the meantime, no new case of A will be started. When all cases of W.I are finished, new cases can start following schema W.F;
- *Progressive*: different decisions for different cases are taken, according to case state or case history. Multiple schema version may exists at the same time. Progressive policies will be detailed in the following of the section.

The first two solutions are the simplest from the WFMS point of view, since only one version of the schema exists at the same time, and all active cases therefore follow the same schema version. Referring to the PC assemble case study, the *abort* policy corresponds to interrupting the current production and assembling all computers according to the new specifications. Therefore, we know that from the moment in which the modifications are introduced, no PC will exit the production department if assembled with the old specifications (schema). The drawback with this policy is that some useful work can be lost, since existing cases are aborted.

A *Flush* policy in our case study would mean letting PCs in construction be assembled according to the old specifications before starting the production of PCs carrying the NiceLabs Suite. With this policy, no work is lost, but the solution could be unsatisfactory since letting existing cases finish according to the old schema could be inconvenient or impossible. In the case study, for instance, the management could decide that the improvements offered by the NiceLabs suite should be immediately adopted, since they offer high advantages.

The situation is even more critical when the modifications are caused by the introduction of a new law. Consider for example the process of building a train cab and suppose that the original design included an amianthus coating. If a new law states that amianthus is no longer allowed as coating, the train building WF will surely need to be modified. Running cases cannot simply continue with the old schema, since there is no chance for new train cabs to be homologated. In any case, the fact that no case is allowed to start until all existing ones are ended causes a reduced productivity when using a *flush* policy.

The inadequateness of the two previous policies in managing case evolution urges for better, more efficient solutions to this problem. These solutions are represented by the *progressive* policies.

4.2 Progressive Policies

Progressive policies allow a case dependent evolution management. Different decisions may be taken according to the case state or to the execution history of a case. Consider again the train cab building example. Progressive policies allow to gently bring old cases to follow the new schema, or at least to modify case execution in a way that allow us to build the cab according to the law without dropping all the work done.

Progressive policies are detailed as follows:

- **concurrent to completion**: cases in execution proceed according to their schema version, while new cases can start immediately following the new version. In our case study, this means that partially assembled computers will include the BestCD cd-rom, but the assembling of computers carrying the NiceLabs Suite can start immediately;
- **migration to final workflow**: existing cases are migrated to the new version. This is always syntactically and formally possible, since the modifications primitives allow the transformation (and the correspondent case migration) from any schema to any schema, and therefore the application of τ

to a running case C of W.I would migrate it to a running case of W.F. Unfortunately, although we are guaranteed that execution of C will proceed in the *future* according to W.F, nothing is said about its *past*. In the PC assemble workflow for instance, if in a WF case the task `Insert_Cd-Rom_BestCD_4x` has been executed, we can migrate the case to the new version, but this solution is not satisfactory, since the BestCD cd-rom has already been inserted. On the other hand, if the task `Insert_Cd-Rom_BestCD_4x` has not been executed (either because case execution is in its early stages or because the `Container` variable is set to `Minitower`), the migration to the new version would allow capturing full advantage from the modifications, since the Nice-Labs Suite would be inserted into the PC (if the cabinet is a tower). These examples suggest that only cases for which certain conditions hold can be effectively migrated to the new version. Intuitively, what it is required is that the execution of a case C of W.I can be seen as an instance of W.F, i.e. the scheduler of W.I and of W.F would have scheduled the same tasks in correspondence of every task completion occurred during C's execution. If this happens, then C can take full advantage from the modifications, since its execution has been like that of a case of W.F in the past, and the migration guarantees that the execution will proceed according to W.F in the future. Cases of W.I that have this property are said to be *compliant* to W.F. A formal definition of compliance is given in the appendix.

Migration to W.F is *unconditional* if C is compliant to W.F. This is the most desirable situation. If C is not compliant to W.F, but the WFA needs to bring it to follow the W.F model, then a *conditional* migration is required. With conditional migration, C undergoes some modification in order to become compliant to W.F. These modifications typically involve rollbacking (or undoing with compensating tasks, where defined) some task executions in order to satisfy the compliance condition. In the worst situation, the case will need to be rolled back to the beginning.

Every case C in which the task `Insert_Cd − Rom_BestCD_4x` has not been completed yet (i.e. $\mathtt{Insert\_Cd − Rom\_BestCD\_4x}_1 \notin Completed_C^{AutoComp.I}$) is compliant to the new schema (modifications involve the latter part of the schema, so in the first part the two scheduler behave in the same way). Cases in which the Cabinet variable is set to the Minitower value are also compliant to W.F, independently on their state, since the modifications do not affect any executed path. All these cases can therefore be migrated to the new version. Cases in which `Insert_Cd-Rom_BestCD_4x` task has been completed (i.e. $\mathtt{Insert\_Cd − Rom\_BestCD\_4x}_1 \in Completed_C^{AutoComp.I}$), can instead be brought to follow version 2 schema only through conditional migration. To be compliant with version 2, in fact, they must be rolled back to a situation in which the task `Insert_FDD_1.44_MB` has not been completed.

migration to ad-hoc workflow: In many situations it will not be necessary to roll back to a compliant state in order to achieve the (informally defined) WF goal according to the new specifications. In particular, the WFA may prefer to make case specific adjustment to reach the goal, however with a sub-optimal procedure (we assume that the optimal one is represented by W.F). This is obtained by defining new, hybrid, temporary schemata to handle specific cases; these cases will then be migrated to the newly created schemata. Again, this migration may be unconditional or conditional, with the same semantics of the previous policy. Considering the PC assemble example, if the last task (Plug_Video_Ram) is in execution, and the cabinet is of the tower type, it is not necessary to roll back to a compliant situation to satisfactorily solve the problem.. It could be more efficient to add at the end of the last task some other activities involving the removal of the cd-rom and the insertion of the NiceLabs Suite. This hybrid schema (called AutoComp.H_1) is depicted in Figure 5. A reasonable solution to the problem could therefore be to migrate some cases of AutoComp.I into AutoComp.H_1. Note that every case of AutoComp.I is compliant to AutoComp.H_1, since modifications involve the insertion of tasks at the end of the workflow.

- **abort**: the case is aborted. The semantics of abortion is dependent on the WF schema considered, and in particular on the transactional properties of the schema. In the highly automated AutoComp factory, we may assume that aborting a case means undoing all the tasks, i.e. disassembling the PC and re-stocking components.

4.3 Managing Case Evolution with Progressive Policies

When progressive policies are adopted to manage dynamic workflow evolution, The WFA should analyze running cases of W.I and, for each (group) of them, define which progressive policy should be adopted. This process leads to a segmentation of the set of running cases of W.I, as depicted in Figure 4. At the end of the evolutionary process, the population of W.I will be only composed of those cases for which the concurrent to completion solution was chosen, while the population of W.F will grow due to migrated cases.

The segmentation can be done on the basis of case states and case execution history. The system can assist the WFA in determining cases compliant to W.F, but for the others the choice is left to the WFA. The appropriate solution depends on the kind and extent of the modifications, the WF goal, the motivation that urged the change, and the case execution history. In our case study, segmentation of the population of version 1 could be done as follows:

- Segment 1 (unconditional migration to final workflow) includes cases in which the cabinet is a minitower or Insert_Cd − Rom_BestCD_4x$_1$ has not been completed yet (Insert_Cd − Rom_BestCD_4x$_1$ $\notin$ $Completed_C^{AutoComp.I}$). This property can be determined by the WFMS.
- Segment 2 (conditional migration to final workflow) includes cases in which the cabinet is a tower and Insert_Cd-Rom_BestCD_4x or Insert_1.6_GB_HD have been completed (Insert_Cd − Rom_BestCD_4x$_1$ $\in$ $Completed_C^{AutoComp.I}$ or Insert_1.6_GB_HD$_1$ $\in$ $Completed_C^{AutoComp.I}$). These could be rolled back to the Insert_FDD_1.4_MB task, without loosing useful work.

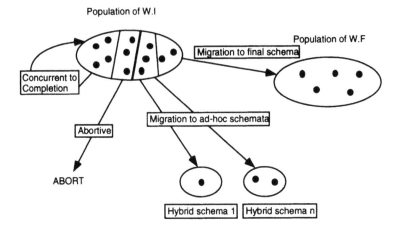

Fig. 4. Partitioning old schema population to manage evolving WF cases

- Segment 3 (migration to hybrid workflow) is composed of all cases in which the cabinet is a tower and the task **Plug_Video_Ram** is in execution. Since rolling back would imply loosing some work, then a set of tasks (see Figure 5) are added, to remove the cd-rom and insert the NiceLabs Suite.

5 Concluding Remarks and Future Work

This paper proposed an approach to the problem of static and dynamic workflow evolution. Our interest on this topic was risen during the kick-off meeting of the Esprit project WIDE, held in Toledo in November 1995; users from *Hospital General de Manresa* (Spain) and *ING bank* (The Netherlands) stressed the importance of an effective management of dynamic workflow evolution and case migration. Results achieved in this research will be used in the development of the WIDE project, to enrich the functionalities provided by the FORO WFMS.

In summary, we have defined a language that allows generic modification of a WF schema, respecting structural and behavioral integrity. We have also introduced a taxonomy that offers the WF designer a set of options to manage cases of modified workflow schemata, defining thereby a criteria (compliance) that, if met by a running case, allows its transparent migration to the new schema. Future work in this area includes the extension of the analysis to modification of other workflow characteristics, and the development of methodologies that allow the semi-automatic derivation, from a set of modification primitives applied to a schema, of ad-hoc workflow schemata that allow migration of non-compliant cases.

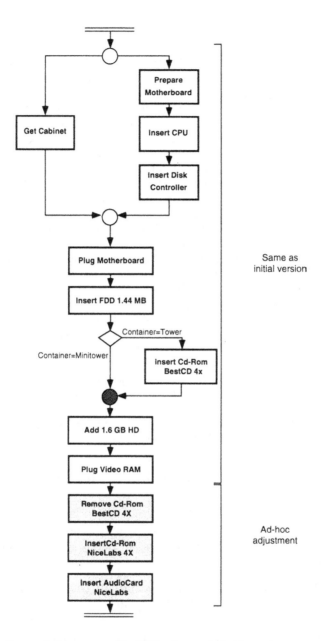

Fig. 5. AutoComp desktop assemble WF schema: hybrid version to cope with case specific situations (AutoComp.H_1)

References

1. Banerjee J.,Kim W., Kim H., Korth H., Semantics and Implementation in Object-Oriented databases, *Proc. of ACM SIGMOD Conference on Management of Data*, San Francisco, CA, May 1987.
2. Bandinelli S., Fuggetta A., Ghezzi C., Software Process Model Evolution in the SPADE Environment, *IEEE Transactions on Software Engineering*, December 1993.
3. Bertino E., Martino L.D., Object-Oriented Database Systems - Concepts and Architectures. Addison-Wesley International, 1993.
4. Casati F., Ceri S., Pernici B., Pozzi G., "Conceptual Modeling of Workflows", *Proc. of the Object- Oriented and Entity-Relationship Conf.*, Gold Coast, Australia, 1995.
5. Cohen B., Human Aspects in Office Automation, Elsevier, 1984.
6. Croft W.B., Lefkowitz L.S., Task Support in an Office System, *ACM Transactions on Office Information Systems*, July 1984.
7. Ellis S., Keddara K. and Rozenberg G., "Dynamic Change within Workflow Systems", *ACM Conf. on Organizational Computing Systems* (COOCS 95), 1995.
8. Hsu M., Kleissner C., ObjectFlow: Towards a Process Management Infrastructure, *Distributed and Parallel Databases*, 4, 1996.
9. Kappel G., Lang P., Rausch-Schott S., Retschitzegger W., Workflow Management Based on Object, Rules and Roles, *IEEE Data Engineering*, March 1995.
10. Proper H., Van der Weide T.P., A General Theory for Evolving Application Models, in *IEEE TKDE*, Dec. 1995.
11. Rusinkiewicz M., Sheth A., Specification and Execution of Transaction Workflows, in *Modern Database Systems: the Object Model, Interoperability, and beyond*, Kim W. (ed.), Addison-Wesley, 1994.
12. Zicari, R., A Framework for O2 Schema Updates, *Proceedings of the 7th Intl. Conference on Data Engineering*, Kobe, Japan, April 1991.

Appendix A: Detailed Description of Schema Evolution Primitives

This section introduces the WFML primitives, partitioned according to the criteria defined in Section 3. These primitives are clearly complete, minimal, and consistent, since:

1. Every WF schema can be developed by initially transforming it into a *null schema* (a schema that ends immediately after it starts);
2. Primitives deal with insertion or removal of distinct concepts;
3. Workflows are consistent, since after any primitive application they remain legal.

The set of WFML primitives we introduce here constitutes a basis for composing higher-level, user-friendly primitives to be used in schema modification tools.

We will denote with $\Sigma^{W.F}$ (and consequently *Tasks* $^{W.F}$, $Vars^{W.F}$, $\sigma^{W.F}$, $\varsigma^{W.F}$, $\theta^{W.F}$) the schema resulting from the application of a single WFML primitive τ to schema $\Sigma^{W.I}$ ($Tasks^{W.I}$, $Vars^{W.I}$, $\sigma^{W.I}$, $\varsigma^{W.I}$, $\theta^{W.I}$). The effect of the application of a sequence of primitives is the composition of the effects caused by a single primitive. The semantics will be defined both for static evolution (i.e. modifications on $\Sigma^{W.I}$) and for dynamic evolution (i.e. modifications on $S_C^{W.I}$). While static evolution is always performed, after the application of τ, generating a new workflow schema, the WFA can decide, according to the chosen policy, if running cases must be migrated to the new schema (i.e, whether to perform or not dynamic evolution).

Declaration Primitives

- *AddVar*(VarName v, DefaultValue d): it adds a variable to the schema declaration part. The formal semantics is:
  static evolution: **if** ($\not\exists x : < v, x > \in Vars^{W.I}$) **then** $Vars^{W.F} = Vars^{W.I} \cup \{< v, d >\}$
  dynamic evolution: **if** ($\not\exists x : < v, x > \in Vars^{W.I}$) **then** $Vars_C^{W.F} = Vars_C^{W.I} \cup \{< v, d >\}$
- *RemoveVar*(Var v): it removes a variable from the schema declaration part. The semantics is:
  static evolution: $Vars^{W.F} = Vars^{W.I} - \{< v, ds >\}$,
  dynamic evolution: $Vars_C^{W.F} = Vars_C^{W.I} - \{< v, dd >\}$
  where ds and dd are such that $\exists \{< v, ds >\} \in Vars^{W.I}$ and $\exists \{< v, dd >\} \in Vars_C^{W.I}$
- *AddTask*(Task t): it adds a task to the set of tasks of a schema. This operation has no effect on the flow structure and on dynamic evolution.
  static evolution: $Tasks^{W.F} = Tasks^{W.I} \cup \{t\}$, $\varsigma(t) = \oslash$

Flow Primitives Flow primitives only affect static evolution, since no operation is required on a case state in order to migrate the case. Square brackets denote optionality.

- *AddSuccessor*(task t, task s) ["FORK"]: it adds a successor s to task t. 'FORK' specifies that s must be added in parallel with existing successors of t.
  Formally, if 'FORK' is not specified, the following steps are executed in sequence:
  static evolution:
  1. $\forall p \in \pi^{W.I}(s), p \neq t, \sigma^{W.F}(p) = \{n1\}$, where n1 is a null task
  2. $\sigma^{W.F}(n1) = \{s\}$
  3. $\varsigma^{W.F}(n1) = \varsigma^{W.I}(s), \varsigma^{W.I}(s) = \oslash$
  4. $\sigma^{W.F}(t) = s$
  5. $\sigma^{W.F}(s) = \sigma^{W.I}(t) \cup \{n2\}, \varsigma^{W.F}(n2) = \oslash$, where n2 is a null task
  6. $\sigma^{W.F}(n2) = \sigma^{W.I}(s)$
  If instead 'FORK' is specified:
  static evolution:

1. $\forall p \in \pi^{W.I}(s), p \neq t, \sigma^{W.F}(p) = \{n3\}$, where n3 is a null task
2. $\sigma^{W.F}(n3) = \{s\}$
3. $\varsigma^{W.F}(n3) = \varsigma^{W.I}(s)$
4. $\sigma^{W.F}(t) = \{n1, n2\}$, where $n1$ and $n2$ are null tasks
5. $\sigma^{W.F}(n1) = \sigma^{W.I}(t)$
6. $\sigma^{W.F}(n2) = \{s\}$
7. $\varsigma^{W.F}(n1) = \oslash, \varsigma^{W.F}(n2) = \oslash$
8. if $\sigma^{W.I}(s) = \oslash$ then $\sigma^{W.I}(s) = $'end'

- *ModifyType* (task t, type T): sets the type of t to T; this primitive do not affect the case state (i.e., it is relevant only to static evolution). Formally: *static evolution*: $\theta(t) = T$
- *RemoveSuccessor* (task t, task s): this primitive has different effects, depending on $\pi^{W.I}(s)$ and on whether s is the stop symbol or not. If s is a task, and t was its only predecessor, then this primitive has a very simple semantics: it simply transforms s into a null task. This allow a very simple and effective handling of dynamic evolution, since the cases' state need not to be modified: if, in a case execution, the removed task s was active, this semantics allow the completion of s. When s is completed, the engine knows how to schedule the next task, since s is still part of the flow structure. Further executions of s are anyway inhibited (null tasks are only conceptual devices, and do not correspond to any action in the real world).
  static evolution: **if** $((s \neq \text{'end'}) \wedge (t = \pi^{W.I}(s))$ **then** transform_into_null(s)
  If, on the other hand, s had other predecessors, then it is removed from the list of successors of t provided that no task becomes unreachable and that t has a successor.
  static evolution: **if** $((s \neq \text{'end'}) \wedge (t \subset \pi^{W.I}(s))$ **then** $\sigma^{W.F}(t) = \sigma^{W.I}(t) \cup \text{'end'} - \{s\}$
  Again, this operation has no effect on dynamic evolution: s remains in the flow structure and therefore once again the engine knows how to schedule the next task after s's completion.
  Finally, if s is the end symbol, then it is removed from the set of successors of t. Formally:
  if $(s = \text{'end'}) \wedge (\exists p \neq t : p \in Tasks^{W.I} \wedge \text{'end'} = \sigma(p))$ **then** $\sigma^{W.F}(t) = \sigma^{W.I}(t) - \text{'end'}$
  Modifications caused by the *RemoveSuccessor* primitive are rolled back if either the resulting schema is not legal or there is no end symbol. By applying these primitives, it is possible to transform every schema in a null schema, by making all its task *null tasks*.
- *ModifyCondition*(task t, condition c): sets the condition of task t to c. This is allowed only if task t is not following a join, i.e. it has only one predecessor.
  static evolution: **if** $\exists$ p: $p = \pi^{W.I}(t)$ **then** $\varsigma(t) = c$

Compliance

After having introduced the semantics of WFML primitives, we can formally define compliance: a case C of a schema W.I is compliant to W.F iff,
$$\forall t_n, t_n \in Completed_C^{W.I}, \text{ is } \eta(\tau(\Sigma^{W.I}), \tau(S_C^{W.I}(t_n)), t_n) = \eta(\Sigma^{W.I}, S_C^{W.I}(t_n), t_n)$$

A Model for Classification Structures with Evolution Control

M. C. Norrie, A. Steiner, A. Würgler, M. Wunderli

Institute for Information Systems,
ETH Zurich, CH-8092 Zurich, Switzerland.
email: {norrie,steiner,wuergler,wunderli}@inf.ethz.ch

Abstract We present a general model for classification structures that supports object role modelling. Objects can be associated with many roles simultaneously in a way that provides multiple classification views over objects. Further, objects can change their roles through migration within a classification graph. Object migration is controlled through the structure of the classification graph and the types of the nodes, thereby restricting possible evolution paths. We show how the model can be generalised to classification structures over relationships. In addition, we consider approaches to constraint maintenance in the case of object and relationship evolution.

1 Introduction

Entities of application domains change their roles during the course of their lifetime. To reflect these role changes in the corresponding database application system, the system must have mechanisms to support and control the evolution of the objects which represent those entities. Support for object evolution requires an operation for object reclassification and this may involve changing the type of an object as well as the addition and removal of the object in various classification sets. Control over object evolution requires a means of restricting the reclassification of objects to ensure that only meaningful forms of evolution are possible.

Object evolution is a basic form of evolution and yet is not supported in most existing object-oriented database management systems. The importance of being able to model multiple and changing object roles has been recognised within the research community and there are now a number of proposed models for supporting some notion of object evolution, for example [GSR96, SLR+92, Pap91, RS91, Ghe90, Sci89]. Some proposals address the specific problem of how objects can evolve when the associated programming language and system do not provide a general mechanism for objects changing their type. For example, [GSR96] presents a solution to object role modelling in Smalltalk. Others, such as [SLR+92] and [Ghe90], propose a general semantic data model with mechanisms for object evolution, but do not address the issue of evolution control.

Proposed mechanisms for evolution control usually involve dynamic modelling of object life-cycles. In some cases, these life-cycles are encoded in object methods and therefore cannot be accessed or updated directly during system operation [Sch90]. Alternatively, they may be encoded either as scripts or rules [BMW84] which, while very powerful in terms of dynamic modelling, of course add an extra layer of complexity to a system.

In this paper, we propose a general model for object role modelling that can be used to provide a level of control over object evolution. The structure of the classification graph in terms of both the types of the nodes and the connection paths between nodes are used to restrict migration paths. While the approach may not be as expressive as other dynamic modelling approaches with respect to modelling object life cycles, it is both flexible and simple and is achieved with little overhead.

Our model for classification structures has three main features that contribute to support for object role modelling. First, the model separates the notions of classification from typing in a way that allows a very flexible means of modelling semantic groupings of objects and different classification views over objects. Second, the model partitions classification graphs into disjoint classification structures thereby distinguishing fundamentally different kinds of objects within a system. Third, we have two varieties of object classifications – kinds and roles – where the former represents fixed forms of classification and the latter represents those that may change over time.

The model presented has been incorporated into the OM object data model [Nor95, Nor93] and has been implemented in the OMS system [Wür95]. In the case of the OM model, two-way relationships between objects may be represented explicitly by an association construct. Classification structures over associations are also supported which means that relationships as well as objects may be classified into various roles. To show the generality of our approach to role modelling, we show how our model for classification structures and evolution control generalises to support the evolution of relationships as well as objects.

This model for classification structures has been used as a conceptual model for the design of systems implemented both on object-oriented and relational database management systems. Further, application systems have been developed on the OMS system directly.

In section 2, we present our basic model in terms of how objects are classified and how these classifications may be related through specialisations to form a set of classification structures. Section 3 extends the model for classification structures to represent kinds and roles and defines a migration operation for object reclassification.

In section 4, we introduce an association construct for modelling relationships between objects and show how the model for classification structures can be generalised to deal with both object and relationship classifications.

Object and relationship evolution, as with other forms of update, can lead to constraint violation. Section 5 discusses issues of constraint maintenance and update propagation specific to the migration operation and the approach currently adopted in our system OMS. Concluding remarks are given in section 6.

2 Classification Structures

Objects are classified according to the roles they adopt within an application system. A particular classification of objects is represented by a set of objects and an associated type definition which specifies the required properties of objects belonging to that set. If C is an object classification, we use $type(C)$ to denote the associated type.

An object belonging to the classification C may have additional properties as specified by one or more subtypes of $type(C)$. The type associated with the classification C may be regarded as a form of constraint that ensures that the classified objects have at least the set of properties specified by the type $type(C)$.

Note that we use the term classification as a general term for a semantic grouping of objects. In other models, the constructs class, collection, type extent or role may be considered equivalent. However, given the variety of uses of those terms, here we prefer to use a more neutral term since the notions introduced here are not dependent on the details of any particular type/data model.

An individual object may belong to several classifications simultaneously as long as it exhibits the properties required by each of the associated types. This corresponds naturally to the fact that an entity may hold several roles within an application domain simultaneously. For example, a person can be an employee, a manager, a husband and a tennis player. Some roles may be specialisations of other roles. For example, a manager may be a special kind of employee. Other roles, such as husband and tennis player, may be unrelated other than the fact that they are both roles of persons.

The flexibility of object role modelling in our model stems from the clear separation between typing and classification. Typing is concerned with representation, whereas classification is concerned with semantics. While in many

459

traditional data processing applications these may appear very closely related, there are other applications where the distinction is much clearer. For example, in a document management system, documents may be classified according to their semantic content or status. For example, we may have documents classified into **Drafts** and **Publications** as well as being classified according to the projects with which they are associated, e.g. **Project_X_Docs**, or the model they describe e.g. **OM_Model_Docs**. This classification of documents is independent of the form of the document which may be a LaTeX, Postscript or simple ASCII text document. The form of the document would be given by the type with the necessary methods specifying the operations for creating, editing and printing documents of that form. A detailed discussion of the benefits obtained by the separation of typing and classification is given in [Nor95].

Generally, if a classification C_2 is a specialisation of another classification C_1, an object which belongs to C_2 must also belong to C_1. In other words, a specialisation of entity roles implies a subset relationship between the associated sets of objects. It follows that all of the objects in C_2 have the properties defined by $type(C_2)$ in addition to those defined by $type(C_1)$. We can therefore consider $type(C_2)$ to be a subtype of $type(C_1)$. We use $C_2 \preceq C_1$ to denote that C_2 is a specialisation of C_1.

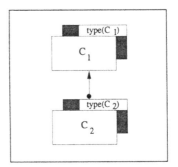

Figure 1. Classification Specialisation

In figure 1, we show our graphical notation for classifications and their specialisations. A classification is represented by a shadowed rectangle. The name of the classification is given in the rectangle and the associated type is specified in the shadow of the rectangle. A declared specialisation $C_2 \preceq C_1$ is represented by an arrow from the specialised classification C_2 to the more general classification C_1.

Object classifications together with specialisations form a classification graph as shown for example in figure 2.

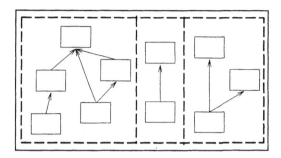

Figure2. Classification Graph

A *classification graph* is a directed acyclic graph $\langle \mathcal{U}, \mathcal{S} \rangle$ where $\mathcal{U}$ is the set of all classifications in the database and $\mathcal{S}$ is the set of edges. If $C_1, C_2 \in \mathcal{U}$, an edge from C_2 to C_1 indicates that C_2 is defined to be a specialisation of C_1, i.e. $C_2 \preceq C_1$. In general, a classification C can be a specialisation of arbitrarily many other classifications $C_1, C_2, ... C_n$.

A classification graph can be partitioned into a number of disjoint connected subgraphs. For example, the classification graph of figure 2 can be partitioned into three connected subgraphs as indicated by the dotted lines. We refer to a connected classification subgraph as a *classification structure*.

We use this partitioning of the classification graph into classification structures to separate out the fundamentally different kinds of objects within a system. Thus, as shown in figure 3, a system might have objects representing employees and objects representing projects. The classification **Employees** has two specialisations **Programmers** and **Managers**. It is possible to define constraints over specialisations. Here, we declare that **Programmers** and **Managers** are disjoint specialisations which means that no object in **Employees** can be in both **Programmers** and **Managers**. In the OM data model, disjoint, cover, partition and intersection constraints over specialisations are supported [Nor93]. As described, the classifications **Employees**, **Programmers** and **Managers** are part of a single classification structure.

Figure 3 shows a second classification structure comprising the classification **Projects** and its specialisation **ProposedProjects**. Note that here the types of the two classifications are the same which means that the objects in **ProposedProjects** have no additional properties.

As stated above, each classification structure should be used to model a fundamentally different kind of object and this is then used as a basic means of controlling object evolution. An object can migrate within a classification structure but cannot migrate to a different classification structure. In this way,

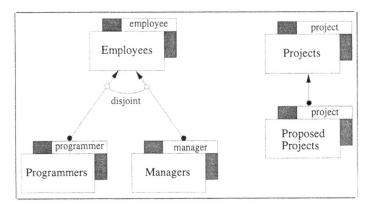

Figure3. Classification Structures

an object cannot evolve to a fundamentally different kind of object. For example, in figure 3, an object in **Employees** could not be reclassified in **Projects**.

In the next section, we examine object reclassification in detail and show how a slight refinement of our model for classification structures can be used to provide further controls over object migration within classification structures.

3   Object Reclassification

An object may be reclassified over time according to transitions of the corresponding entities in the application domain. For example, an employee is promoted and becomes a manager capable of leading projects, or, a man marries and is reclassified as a husband rather than as a bachelor. Thus, object reclassification may result in losing as well as gaining membership of classifications.

Some classifications will be more fixed than others. The classification of an entity as a person or document is fundamental and remains fixed, whereas the further classification of persons into trainee programmers is something that reflects a particular role adopted by that entity at a particular point in time and is subject to change. We distinguish those two forms of classification by referring to the former classification as a *kind* and the latter as a *role*. Generally, we then control the reclassification of objects so that an object may change its roles but not its kinds.

Then the set of all classifications $\mathcal{U}$ is partitioned into the set of kinds, $\mathcal{K}$, and the set of roles, $\mathcal{R}$; i.e. $\mathcal{U} = \mathcal{K} \cup \mathcal{R}$ and $\mathcal{K} \cap \mathcal{R} = \emptyset$.

In [Zdo87], Zdonik introduces a similar distinction by the introduction of *essential types* which are similar in their purpose to our notion of kinds in that they represent the fundamental classification of entities.

Object reclassification may require a metamorphosis of the object from one type to another. For example, the types of **Employees** and **Managers** are not the same. This means that an object migrated to **Managers** will retain all the properties of type **employee** and should gain properties that are specific to type **manager**. In our model, an object can attain the properties of a subtype by means of a *dress* operation. In the OMS interactive system, values for the additional properties can be supplied directly by the user at the time of object reclassification. An alternative approach is to employ some notion of default or null values. In the case of an object migration from **Managers** to **Employees**, an object may remain of type **manager**. However, in OM, we also provide a *strip* operation which can be used to remove type properties from an object when required.

In many object-oriented programming languages, objects have only one type and cannot change types which is a problem for object role modelling. In [GSR96], they discuss the problem in detail for the Smalltalk language and propose a role concept that allows objects to change roles and their associated properties.

We now consider in detail how distinguishing kinds and roles can be used to control object evolution. As stated above, each classification is declared to be either a kind or a role. A classification structure therefore comprises kinds and roles related through specialisation links. A given classification has a context within a classification structure. This context determines the general classification of its objects in terms of the sets of kinds and roles to which they must belong. For example, consider the classification structure for employees given in figure 4. The kinds are shaded black and the roles grey.

In figure 4, there are two kinds and three roles such that

$$\mathcal{K} = \{\texttt{Managers}, \texttt{SeniorProgrammers}\}$$

and

$$\mathcal{R} = \{\texttt{Employees}, \texttt{Programmers}, \texttt{TraineeProgrammers}\}$$

If an object is classified in the kind **SeniorProgrammers**, they will also be classified in the roles **Programmers** and **Employees**. We therefore consider the context of **SeniorProgrammers** to be the kind **SeniorProgrammers** (since it is part of its own context) and the roles **Programmers** and **Employees**.

Let $C \in \mathcal{U}$. We introduce the functions *kinds* and *roles* which together give the context of a classification as follows:

$$kinds(C) = \{C_i | C_i \in \mathcal{K} \wedge C \preceq C_i\}$$

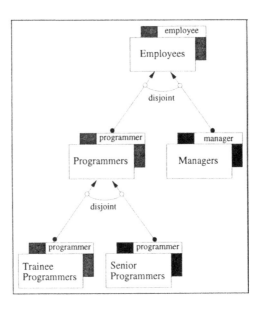

Figure4. Classification Structure with Kinds and Roles

$$roles(C) = \{C_i | C_i \in \mathcal{R} \wedge C \preceq C_i\}.$$

Now let us examine the interpretation of the designation of the various classifications as kinds and roles. The classification structure of figure 4 classifies employees within a software company. Since **Employees** $\in \mathcal{R}$, an object can lose this classification and be removed from the associated set. If **Employees** were specified as a kind, it would mean that once an object had been added to this classification, it could never be removed from it.

Employees has two specialisations - one designated a kind and the other a role. How should we interpret the situation of a role having a specialisation which is a kind? The interpretation used is that the kind represents a fixed classification in the context of the parent role. For example, if an employee object belongs to kind **Managers**, it must remain in that classification as long as it belongs to **Employees**. Similarly, an object classified in **SeniorProgrammers** can only lose this classification in the event that they are no longer classified in **Programmers**. This models a situation in which once a programmer becomes a senior programmer, they can lose that status only when they are no longer a programmer: they cannot be demoted. However, a programmer in **TraineeProgrammers** can be reclassified in **SeniorProgrammers**. Therefore our classification structure represents a company in which only promotion is allowed: a trainee programmer can be promoted to programmer, a programmer can be promoted to a senior programmer and a senior programmer can be promoted to a manager.

Having outlined the required operation of object evolution by consideration of the above example, we now specify it formally.

Let C_1 and C_2 be classifications and let $x \in C_1$. Then we specify the migration of x from C_1 to C_2 by the operation

$$x :: C_1 \rightarrow C_2$$

This operation is valid in the case that:

1. $\exists C \in \mathcal{U} . C_1 \preceq C \wedge C_2 \preceq C$
2. $\not\exists C \in \mathcal{U} . x \in C \wedge C \preceq C_1 \wedge C \not\equiv C_1$
3. $\forall C_i \in (kinds(C_1) - kinds(C_2)) . \exists C_j \in roles(C_i) . C_j \notin roles(C_2)$

The first condition ensures that an object can only migrate within a classification structure. Thus, it cannot migrate freely within the classification graph but only within connected subgraphs.

The second of these conditions checks that object x is not in any specialisations of C_1. Here, $C \not\equiv C_1$ specifies that C is not identical to C_1. In fact, the dependencies between classifications and their specialisations would ensure that an object could not be removed from C_1 unless it was also removed from all specialisations of C_1.

The third condition specifies that an object migration in which an object loses a kind is valid only in the event that the object also loses a role in terms of which that kind is defined. Thus if an object is deleted from a classification $C_1 \in \mathcal{K}$, it must also be deleted from some classification C_2 where $C_1 \preceq C_2$ and $C_2 \in \mathcal{R}$.

For example, given the classification structure of figure 4, consider the migration

$$x :: \textsf{SeniorProgrammers} \rightarrow \textsf{Managers}$$

We have

$$kinds(\textsf{SeniorProgrammers}) = \{\textsf{SeniorProgrammers}\}$$
$$roles(\textsf{SeniorProgrammers}) = \{\textsf{Employees}, \textsf{Programmers}\}$$
$$kinds(\textsf{Managers}) = \{\textsf{Managers}\}$$
$$roles(\textsf{Managers}) = \{\textsf{Employees}\}$$

Then

$$kinds(\textsf{SeniorProgrammers}) - kinds(\textsf{Managers}) = \{\textsf{SeniorProgrammers}\}$$

but

$$\textsf{Programmers} \in roles(\textsf{SeniorProgrammers}) \text{ and } \textsf{Programmers} \notin roles(\textsf{Managers})$$

therefore the migration operation is valid.

However the migration

$$x :: \texttt{Managers} \rightarrow \texttt{SeniorProgrammers}$$

would not be allowed since

$$kinds(\texttt{Managers}) - kinds(\texttt{SeniorProgrammers}) = \{\texttt{Managers}\}$$

and

$$roles(\texttt{Managers}) \subset roles(\texttt{SeniorProgrammers}).$$

The object x would lose its classification as kind **Managers** but would retain its contextual role **Employees** and the migration would therefore be disallowed.

A migration operation may lead to constraint violations. In section 5, we look at some of the ways in which constraints might be violated and approaches to update propagations to restore consistency.

4   Associations

In this section, we consider an extension to our model to support the direct representation of user-defined relationships between objects. We introduce the relationship classification construct which is used to represent relationships between members of object classifications. A member of a relationship classification is a pair of values representing the related objects. The member type of a relationship classification is a pair type consisting of the source and the target type of the relationship classification.

An association between classifications consists of a relationship classification, associated cardinality constraints and the links to the source and the target classifications. Note that in the OM data model, the source and the target classifications can themselves be relationship classifications [Nor93].

The introduction of relationship classifications is orthogonal to the classification constraints discussed in section 3, therefore allowing the construction of relationship classification structures with migration control as shown in figure 5. As with object classifications, relationship classifications can be divided into kinds and roles.

The notion of classification graph introduced in section 2 also generalises. As before, nodes of the graph are classifications – object or relationship – and edges are specialisations. For any two classifications C_1 and C_2, $C_1 \preceq C_2$ implies that either both C_1 and C_2 are object classifications or both are relationship classifications. Therefore, the classification graph for the example of figure 5 contains

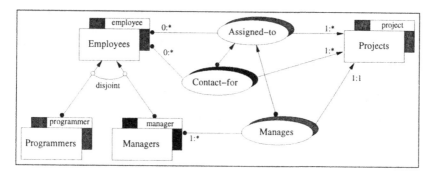

Figure5. Associations

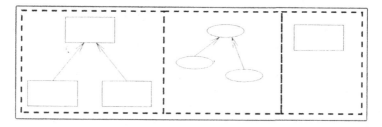

Figure6. Classification Structures with Associations

three classification structures, two object classifications and one relationship classification as shown in figure 6.

Let us concentrate on the relationship classification structure. Employees are assigned to projects. An employee may further be selected as a contact person for a project to which they are assigned. Since contact information is widely spread, employees will remain as contacts as long as they are assigned to the project. To guarantee that constraint, we model **Contact-for** as a kind. On the other hand, being assigned as the manager of a project may change and therefore we model **Manages** as a role.

Migration between relationship classifications is possible according to the same rules given in section 3. For example, we may migrate a relationship object of **Assigned-to** to **Contact-for**. However, migration in the opposite direction from **Contact-for** to **Assigned-to** is not possible since **Contact-for** is a kind.

Migration becomes more interesting in the case where migration in one classification structure effects other classification structures. For example, consider migrating a relationship from **Manages** to **Assigned-to**. This migration would be allowed if we consider the relationship classification structure isolated from the others. However, the migration involves an object in the classification **Managers** and the constraint that a manager must manage at least one project might also require reclassification of a manager object. We will discuss the aspect of migration induced propagation in detail in the next section.

5   Propagations under Evolution

In this section, we consider the issue of constraint maintenance in the case of the migration of objects and relationships within classification structures. A migration operation involves a number of addition and removal operations in classifications and, as with any form of update operation, they may lead to violations of consistency constraints. In the case of constraint violation, the general approach adopted in a particular system may be either to abort the transaction or to propagate update operations and restore consistency. A review of the approaches to constraint maintenance is given in [FP93].

In our system OMS, we adopt the policy of extending the semantics of addition, removal and migration operations to include limited forms of update propagation. For example, as shown in figure 7, when adding an object to a classification, the object is added to more general classifications as well. In the case of removing an object from a classification, it is removed from any specialised classifications automatically. Other forms of propagation may be specified by the user through the use of preference files to explicitly define update propagation operations.

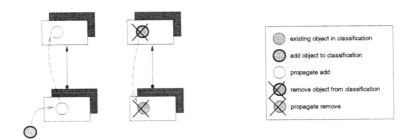

Figure7. Add and Remove Propagations for Specialisations

We now consider how the introduction of kinds and roles and a migration operation can effect constraint maintenance through update propagation.

The concept of kinds and roles for evolution control forms part of a general constraint mechanism. To show how the specification of a classification as either a kind or a role can influence the way in which consistency is restored, consider the example of figure 8. We illustrate the case of an object being added to the specialisation C_1 when it already resides in the other specialisation C_2, thereby resulting in a violation of the disjoint constraint. To restore consistency, the object must be removed from either C_1 or C_2. If both specialisations are roles, the object could be removed from either C_1 or C_2. In the case of the OMS system, the object will be removed from C_1, i.e. the addition is undone, unless otherwise specified in the preference file. If, however, C_2 is a kind and C_1 a role, these additional constraints would eliminate the choice and force removal from the role C_1.

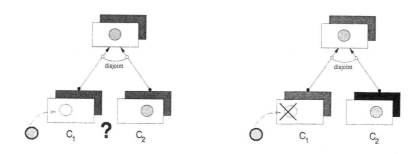

Figure8. Propagations in Disjoint Specialisations

Associations between classification structures also impose constraints as given by the specification of a source, a target and the associated cardinality constraints. Updates on associations could invoke update propagations in the three directly involved classification structures containing the source, target and relationship classifications.

Recall the example of figure 5 and consider the case of a programmer taking over the management of a project on which they are working. We could migrate the corresponding relationship from **Assigned-to** to **Manages**. However, the source of **Manages** is **Managers** rather than **Employees** and therefore the programmer object would also have to be migrated from **Programmers** to **Managers**. We illustrate the relationship migration together with the resulting propagated migration in figure 9. Generally, the evolution of relationships may invoke the evolution of the objects involved in that relationship.

Alternatively, we could first migrate the programmer object from **Programmers** to **Managers**. In this case, it is not clear which relationship in **Assigned-to** has to be migrated to **Manages** if the programmer is assigned to more than one project (see figure 10). In general, evolving objects in source and target classifications cannot lead directly to propagations in relationship associations.

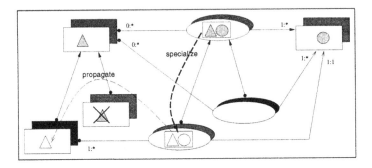

Figure9. Propagations for Relationship Migration

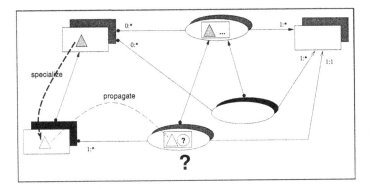

Figure10. Propagations for Object Migration

At first, one might consider using cardinality constraints to determine the propagation of the migration shown in figure 10 to the relationship classification structure. If a programmer is assigned to only one project and we then promote them to manager, does it imply that they become the manager of that project? It can be dangerous to assume semantics not specified by the user.

As another example, consider the situation where a relationship is removed from a classification **Assigned-to**. In the case where the referenced project object has no further employees assigned to it, the question arises as to whether the update should be propagated and the project object removed from **Projects**. This corresponds to the standard problem of maintaining referential integrity under update. In OMS, the default behaviour would be not to propagate and rather to disallow the removal of the relationship.

Next consider the scenario where someone starts in the company as a manager. If the relationship between the manager and the project they manage is inserted directly into **Manages**, the specialisation constraint causes a propagation which inserts the relationship into **Assigned-to**. Further propagations will cause the referenced manager object to be added to **Managers** and also to **Employees**.

If the relationship in **Manages** later needs to be removed, we cannot simply remove the referenced manager object from **Managers** in the event that the manager has no other projects to manage. The **Managers** classification is a kind and objects can only be removed according to the rules introduced in section 3.

As described in [FP93], update propagations can be triggered either when the updates are executed or when the constraints are checked before committing a transaction. The first possibility effectively extends the semantics of the update operation to include the propagations. As stated previously, this is the approach adopted in our OMS system where we have *enhanced migration operations* which specify the propagations indicated in the above examples.

The OMS system is an interactive system which supports the user by displaying the ways in which objects may evolve. After the selection of an object within a classification, a migration operation will list for selection only those classifications to which migration is allowed. The migration operation handles the necessary type metamorphosis, removal and addition of objects in classifications along the migration path. As described, certain limited forms of propagations will also take place.

6 Conclusions

We have presented a general model for classification structures that can be applied to both object and relationship classification. Classifications can be specialised and it is possible that an object or relationship belongs to many classifications simultaneously. In this way, the model supports a flexible and expressive means of both object and relationship role modelling.

Control over evolution of objects and relationships is achieved in two ways. First, classification graphs are partitioned into disjoint classification structures corresponding to fundamentally different kinds of entities or relationships and evolution is allowed only within a single classification structure. Second, classifications are further classified into kinds and roles according to whether they represent fixed or non-fixed classifications, respectively. In general, an object or relationship cannot lose a kind unless it also loses the contextual role of the kind.

The resulting model for classification structures is expressive in terms of object role modelling and we have used it both for the conceptual modelling of systems developed on other implementation platforms as well as for the development of application systems on OMS. The mechanisms for evolution control are very simple and require little overhead. Also, we have found such structural controls useful for many application scenarios where the life cycles of objects are not well-defined in terms of fixed object evolution paths as would be required in other models. We are currently investigating the different approaches to constraint maintenance under evolution. In particular, we are considering the use of triggered rules as a means of specifying required update propagations to restore consistency.

References

[BMW84] A. Borgida, J. Mylopolous, and H. K. T. Wong. Generalization/ Specialization as a Basis for Software Specification. In M. L. Brodie, J. Mylopoulos, and J. W. Schmidt, editors, *On Conceptual Modelling.* Springer-Verlag, 1984.

[FP93] P. Fraternali and S. Paraboschi. A Review of Repairing Techniques for Integrity Maintenance. In *Proc.1st Intl. Workshop on Rules in Database Systems*, Edinburgh, Scotland, 1993.

[Ghe90] G. Ghelli. A Class Abstraction for a Hierarchical Type System. In *Proceedings of 2nd Intl. Conf. on Database Theory, ICDT'90,* LNCS 470, pages 56–70. Springer Verlag, December 1990.

[GSR96] G. Gottlob, M. Schrefl, and B. Röck. Extending Object-Oriented Systems with Roles. *ACM Transactions on Information Systems,* 14(3), 1996.

[Nor93] M. C. Norrie. An Extended Entity-Relationship Approach to Data Management in Object-Oriented Systems. In *12th Intl. Conf. on Entity-Relationship Approach*, Dallas, Texas, December 1993.

[Nor95] M. C. Norrie. Distinguishing Typing and Classification in Object Data Models. In *Information Modelling and Knowledge Bases*, chapter 25. IOS, 1995.

[Pap91] M. Papazoglou. Roles: A Methodology for Representing Multfaceted Objects. In *Proc. Intl. Conf. on Database and Expert Systems Applications,* 1991.

[RS91] J. Richardson and P. Schwarz. Aspects: Extending Objects to Support Multiple, Independent Roles. In *Proc. Intl. Conf. on Management of Data*, 1991.

[Sch90] M. Schrefl. Behaviour modelling by stepwise refining behaviour diagrams. In *Proc. Entity Relationship Conference*, Lausanne, Switzerland, 1990.

[Sci89] E. Sciore. Extending Object-Oriented Systems with Roles. *ACM Transactions on Information Systems,* 7(2), 1989.

[SLR+92] M. H. Scholl, C. Laasch, C. Rich, H. J. Schek, and M. Tresch. The CO-COON object model. Technical report, Department of Computer Science, ETH Zurich, 1992.

[Wür95] A. Würgler. Object model system: An object database management system for the om data model. Master's thesis, Institute for Information Systems, ETH Zurich, 1995.

[Zdo87] S. B. Zdonik. Can Objects Change Type? Can Type Objects Change? In *Proceedings Workshop on Database Programming Languages, Altair, France,* 1987.

Integrating Versions in the OMT Models

E. Andonoff, G. Hubert, A. Le Parc, G. Zurfluh

Laboratoire IRIT, Université Toulouse III, 31062 Toulouse Cédex, France
Email : {ando,hubert,leparc,zurfluh}@irit.fr

Abstract. This paper shows how to extend the object, dynamic and functional models of the OMT method so that it integrates version modeling capabilities. Thus, this method will suit new database applications relevant to fields such as computer aided design, technical documentation or software engineering where managed data are time-dependant.

1 Introduction

The version concept has been introduced in database systems to describe evolution of real world data over time: different significant states of data are kept (neither only the last state as in classical databases nor all the states as in temporal databases); these states correspond to different versions. The concept of version is important in computer aided design, technical documentation or software engineering fields where managed data are time-dependent [2].

Most current object-oriented database systems implement the version concept in order to suit database applications relevant to these fields (e.g. Orion [7], Encore [20], Avance [4]...). However, current database design methods such as OMT [19], OOA [6]... do not take into account versions and consequently do not suit database applications relevant to the previous fields. Indeed, these methods do not give solutions to describe versions in the different models they propose. The version problem is only approached when implementing the database according to the model of the database system. Now, version modeling is an activity recovered from the design stage. From this stage, a designer must be able to tell if an entity or an entity class evolve over time. So, he must have tools to describe versions in the different models he defines.

This paper shows how versions can be modeled from the design stage of a database: it proposes solutions to extend the conceptual models (object, dynamic and functional ones) of the OMT method [19] in order to describe versions. OMT is chosen because it begins to be widely used in aeronautical industry in Toulouse where managed data are documentary or multimedia ones. So, this work extends the OMT method so that it integrates version modeling capabilities and consequently suits new database applications relevant to fields such as computer aided design, technical documentation or software engineering.

This paper is organized as follows. Section 2 outlines the works relating to the modeling of versions. Section 3 introduces the version concept. The following sections describe the OMT conceptual model extensions. Sections 4 presents the extensions provided to the object model in order to describe versions. It also studies the problems relating to the modeling of composition, relationship and inheritance links between classes according to their instances (objects or versions), and, the operations that the classes and their instances can perform. Section 5 describes the extensions provided to the dynamic and functional models. Section 6 is the conclusion.

2 Related works

Works relating to the modeling of versions are the matter for two modeling levels: the system level and the conceptual level.

Works which are the matter for the system level are numerous. In these works, versions are investigated at two abstraction levels: the object level and the class level. Some systems have studied versions at only one abstraction level. For example, CloSQL [17] or Clamen's works [5] have studied this concept at the class level while Ode [1] or OVM [11] have investigated it at the object level. Other systems, such as Orion [7], Encore [20], Iris [3], Avance [4] or Presage [21] have studied versions at the two abstraction levels. But they do not clearly explain the outcomes of both management of class and object versions. Moreover, they partially tackle the problem relating to the modeling of links between instances because they do not take into account each kind of instance (object and version) and each kind of link (composition, relationship and inheritance).

Works which are the matter for the conceptual level are less numerous. Current object-oriented database design methods such as OMT or OOA... do not provide version modeling capabilities. Only [9] and [10] have tried to extend the Entity-Relationship model to include version modeling capabilities. But these works do not tackle neither the problem relating to the modeling of composition, relationship or inheritance links between Entity-Relationship classes nor the dynamic and functional aspects of the database.

Our work is the matter for the conceptual level. As in [9,10], we consider that the version concept is a concept of the real world which can be modeled from the design stage of a database, as relationships or entity classes. Our work extends the object, dynamic and functional models of the OMT method in order to describe object and class versions. It particularly approaches the object model because it is the most important one when modeling database applications [19]. It tackles the modeling of composition, relationship or inheritance links between classes taking into account the different kinds of class instances. It also studies the operations that the classes and their instances can perform.

3 The Version Concept

This section first describes basic concepts for versions and then presents the object and class version concepts.

3.1 Basic Concepts

A real world entity has characteristics which may evolve during its life cycle: it has different successive states. In object-oriented database systems which provide version management, this entity is described by a set of objects called versions. A version corresponds to one of the significant entity states. Then, it is possible to manage several entity states (neither only the last one as in classical databases nor all the states as in temporal databases).

The entity versions are linked by a derivation link; they form a version derivation hierarchy [12]. When created, an entity is described by only one version. The definition of every new entity version is done by derivation from a previous one. Such versions are called derived versions [12] (e.g. E1.v1 is a derived version from E1.v0). Several versions may be derived from the same previous one. They are called alternatives [12] (e.g. E1.v2 and E1.v3 are alternatives derived from E1.v1).

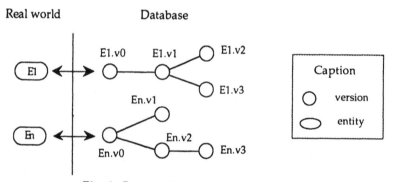

Fig. 1. Representing entities with versions

A version is either frozen or working. A frozen version describes a significant and final state of an entity. A frozen version may be deleted but not updated. To describe a new state of this entity, we have to derive a new version (from the frozen one). A working version is a version that temporarily describes one of the entity states. It may be deleted and updated to describe a next entity state. The previous state is lost to the benefit of the next one.

The default version of an entity [8] is a version pointed out as the most representative version of the entity. It is unique for each entity and may be chosen among the set of frozen or working versions.

3.2 Object and class versions

Evolution of entities may find expression in either value or schema evolution. One talks about object version when the entity evolution is a value evolution. One talks about class version when the entity evolution is a schema evolution. Value evolution consists in updating (in a partial or a total way) the attribute values of the considered object version. Schema evolution consists in adding new attributes, links (composition, relationship or inheritance links) or methods, in the considered class version. It also consists in updating or deleting existing attributes, links or methods. When value and schema evolution are available for an entity, the entity is described by a set of object versions belonging to different class versions. Note that only the version model of Presage [21] gives such a possibility.

Object or class versions are defined by deriving an object or a class version (derived or alternative). These object or class versions are linked by a derivation link; they form a version derivation hierarchy. The frozen, working and default version concepts are available for object and class versions.

4 Modeling Versions in the Object Model

This section first briefly summarizes the basic OMT object model and then shows how versions are taken into account.

4.1 Basic Object Model [19]

The class is the unique tool for modeling real world entities. A class contains a set of objects having the same schema. The class schema describes the structure and behaviour of its objects. The structure is represented by a set of (monovalued or multivalued) attributes whose domain is a predefined class (integer, real...) and the behaviour is defined through a set of methods described by their signature. Links which are inheritance, composition or relationship links can be defined between classes.

4.2 Extending the Basic Object Model with Versions: the Classes

The basic model is extended to integrate the object and class version concepts. Not versionable classes and versionable classes are introduced. Not versionable classes correspond to the basic model classes: only the last schema of the class is kept. Versionable classes are classes describing entity classes of which several schemas (class versions) are kept. The instances of these classes are objects or versions. Objects correspond to the basic model objects: only the last value of the object is kept. Versions are objects describing entities of which several values (object versions) are kept.

So, four cases of classes are conceivable:

- not versionable classes whose instances are objects (no version),
- not versionable classes whose instances are versions (only object versions),
- versionable classes whose instances are objects (only class versions),
- versionable classes whose instances are versions (both object and class versions).

Operations inherent to the introduction of versions are class operations and instance operations. Class operations permit us to create a new class deriving an existing one (derive), to modify the schema of an existing class (update), to delete an existing class (delete), to freeze an existing class (freeze) or to create (from scratch) an instance in an existing class (create). Instance operations enable us to create a new instance deriving an existing one (derive), to modify the values of an existing instance (update), to delete an existing instance (delete) or to freeze an existing instance (freeze).

The freeze operation enables us to keep the state of a class or an object version. This operation is either triggered at the class level (a class version is frozen) or at the instance level (an object version is frozen and the class it belongs to is automatically frozen). The derive operation for a class consists in defining a new class version from an existing one (which becomes frozen) and, in updating this derived class version using the update operation. This operation can only be performed to conventional classes or to unfrozen class version (versionable classes). Moreover, this operation can trigger a data conversion process (this process is not discussed in this paper; see [5,15,16,18] for further information). The derive operation for an object consists in defining a new object version from an existing one (which becomes frozen) and, in updating this derived object version using the update operation. This operation only consists in modifying the value of the considered object version. We can observe than that operation can only be performed on (conventional) objects or on unfrozen object versions.

4.3 Extending the Basic Object Model with Versions: the Links

This section addresses the problems relating to the modeling of composition, relationship and inheritance links between the four kinds of classes. This section also studies in detail the main operations for classes and instances according to their links.

4.3.1 Composition Links
Composition links are defined between versionable or not versionable classes containing either objects or versions. However, only four composition cases are put forward in the paper. Indeed, the constraints which are inherent to composition link cardinalities must only be taken into account at the instance level. So, it is useless to distinguish versionable classes from not versionable classes. The four composition cases are the following. Only the last three ones are novel and presented in the paper.

Case 1
- composition link between classes which contain objects (see [14]),
- composition link between a (composite) class containing objects and a (component) class containing versions,
- composition link between a (composite) class containing versions and a (component) class containing objects,
- composition link between classes which contain versions.

Case 2. Composition between a composite class containing objects and a component class containing versions. The cardinality is defined as follows (Fig. 2):

- from the composite class to the component class, one expresses a link from a composite object to one (monovalued link) or several (multivalued link) hierarchies of component versions,
- from the component class to the composite class, one expresses a link from a component version to one (exclusive link) or several (shared link) composite objects.

Composite objects   Composite objects

Component version hierarchies   Component version hierarchies

Fig. 2. Composition between objects and versions

Case 3. Composition between a composite class containing versions and a component class containing objects. The cardinality is defined as follows:

- from the composite class to the component class, one expresses a link from a composite version to one (monovalued link) or several (multivalued link) component objects,
- from the component class to the composite class, one expresses a link from a component object to one (exclusive link) or several (shared link) hierarchies of composite versions.

Case 4. Composition between classes containing versions. The cardinality is defined as follows (Fig. 3):

- from the composite class to the component class, one expresses a link from a composite version to one or several hierarchies of component versions,
- from the component class to the composite class, one expresses a link from a component version to one or several hierarchies of composite versions.

Composite versions   Composite versions

Component version hierarchies   Component version hierarchies

Fig. 3. Composition between versions

To the best of our knowledge, cases 2 and 3 are never approached in the literature. Case 4 is only really studied in Orion which proposes a different solution for the one we propose: when several derived versions have the same component version, only one of them is linked to the component version. The other ones are linked to the default version of the generic object corresponding to the component version. This solution (as in the one we propose) limits version duplication but information is lost when derived composite versions are linked to the default component ones instead of being directly linked to the chosen component ones (which are often different from the default ones). In the solution we propose, composite versions are directly linked with their component versions; indeed, we authorize a component version to be a part of several successive derived versions belonging to the same composite hierarchy.

Operations. Because of space limitation, this paragraph only details the create and derive operations for object versions. Only the most interesting cases are considered.

Create. The composition link semantics imposes to create a component instance only when creating a composite instance [14].

Case 2. Composition between a composite class containing objects and a component class containing versions. A new (created) composite object must be linked to one or several versions belonging to hierarchies of versions of the component class according to the composite class cardinality. These versions are:

- root versions of new hierarchies of component versions,
- versions belonging to existing hierarchies of component versions if the link is shared for the component class.

Case 4. Composition between classes containing versions. In this case, a new composite version must be linked to one or several versions belonging to hierarchies of versions of the component class according to the composite class cardinality. These versions are:

- root versions of new hierarchies of component versions,
- versions derived from a free leaf version of existing hierarchies of component versions,

- versions belonging to existing hierarchies of component versions if the link is shared for the component class.

A leaf version of a component hierarchy is free when it is not part of a leaf version of a composite hierarchy:

Composite version hierarchies

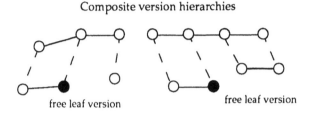

Component version hierarchies

Fig. 4. Free leaf versions

Derive. Derive is an operation which can only be performed on versions. Unlike create, derive can be performed either on composite or component versions.

Case 4. Composition between classes gathering versions. On the one hand, a derived composite version must be linked to one or several versions belonging to hierarchies of versions of the component class according to the composite class cardinality. These versions are:

- the same component versions as the composite version it derives from,
- versions derived from the component versions,
- root versions of new hierarchies of component versions,
- versions derived from free leaf versions of component hierarchies existing in the component class (Fig. 4).
- versions belonging to existing hierarchies of component versions if the link is shared for the component class.

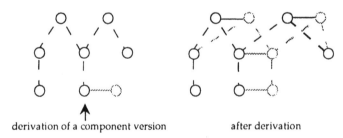

derivation of a component version   after derivation

Fig. 5. Derivation of a component version

On the other hand, a component version derivation triggers the derivation of the composite versions it composes (Fig 5). More precisely, it triggers the derivation of all the composite versions from the derived component version up to the root versions of all the composition hierarchies that the derived component version belongs to. The versions linked to versions belonging to the considered composition hierarchies are kept and not derived. Note that such a propagation process restricts useless version duplication as in Presage [21], Encore [20], or Katz's works [12].

4.3.2 Relationship Links

Relationship links are defined between versionable or not versionable classes. These classes contain either objects or versions. However, only three relationship cases are put forward in the paper. Indeed, the constraints which are inherent to relationship link cardinalities must only be taken into account at the instance level. So, it is useless to distinguish versionable classes from not versionable classes.

The three relationship cases are the following but only the last two ones are novel and presented in the paper:

- relationship link between classes which contain objects (see [6,19]),
- relationship link between a class containing objects and a class containing versions,
- relationship link between classes which contain versions.

Case 2. Relationship between a class which contains versions and a class which contains objects. The relationship cardinality is defined as follows:

- from the class which contains versions to the class which contains objects, one expresses a link from a version to one or several objects,
- from the class which contains objects to the class which contains versions, one expresses a link from an object to one (monovalued link) or several (multivalued link) current version hierarchies.

We distinguish current and past links between objects and versions. A current link is the last link defined between an object and a version. A past link exists because the previous versions of the considered version are also linked to the object. A current hierarchy for an object is a hierarchy having at least one version linked to the object with a current link.

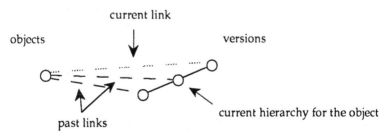

Fig. 6. Current links and current hierarchies

Case 3. Relationship between classes containing versions. The relationship cardinality is defined as follows: one expresses a link from a version to one (monovalued link) or several (multivalued link) hierarchies of versions. We note that a version linked to a hierarchy of versions can be linked to several versions which belong to the hierarchy and which are derived one from another.

Operations. Because of space limitation, this paragraph only details the create operation. Case 2 is the most interesting for this operation.

Case 2. Relationship between a class which contains versions and a class which contains objects. A new (created) version must be linked to one or several objects according to the version class cardinality. These objects are:

- new objects or free objects or existing objects which are not yet linked,
- existing objects if the link is shared for the object class.

A free object is an object which is not linked to a leaf of a hierarchy of versions.

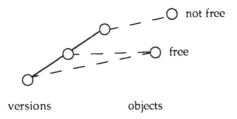

versions   objects

Fig. 7. Free object

When a new object is created, it must be linked to one or several versions belonging to hierarchies of versions according to the object class cardinality. These versions are:

- new root versions of new hierarchies,
- new versions derived from free leaf versions of existing hierarchies,
- existing versions of existing hierarchies which are not yet linked to objects,
- existing versions if the link is shared for the version class.

4.3.3 Inheritance Links

Inheritance links are defined between versionable or not versionable classes. However, with the aim of describing the class operation derive, only three cases are put forward:

- the superclass is a versionable class whereas the subclass is not versionable,
- the subclass is a versionable class whereas the superclass is not versionable,
- the subclass and the superclass are both versionable classes.

Operations. Only class operations must be considered with inheritance links. Because of space limitation, we only study the derive operation (which is the most interesting one). Two possibilities are conceivable: derivation of a superclass and derivation of a subclass.

Derivation of a superclass. The derivation of a superclass does not trigger the derivation of its subclasses. The derived class has the same characteristics as the class from which it derives: it is a versionable class and contains objects or versions (e.g. a versionable class containing objects derives a versionable class containing objects).

Derivation of a subclass. For this operation, two situations are possible according to the derivation. In both situations, the derived class has the same characteristics as the class from which it derives: it is a versionable class which contains either objects or versions.

Situation 1: if the derivation corresponds to a redefinition of inherited attributes or to an update of specific attributes belonging to the subclass, the derived class inherits from the same class as the class from which it derives.

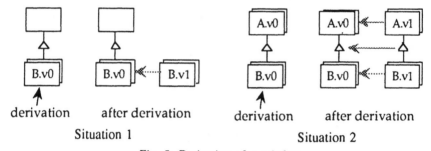

Fig. 8. Derivation of a subclass

Situation 2: if the derivation corresponds to an update of inherited attributes, deriving the subclass causes the derivation of its superclass. The derived subclass inherits from the derived superclass. We note that this situation is possible if the superclass is versionable.

5 Modeling Versions in the Dynamic and Functional Models

This section summarizes the basic features of the dynamic and functional models and shows how versions are combined with these basic models.

5.1 Basic Dynamic Model [19]

This model describes the database behaviour through the behaviour of its instances. This behaviour is described in state diagrams through events and states. These diagrams show how the state of an object changes when an event occurs (possibly if a condition is satisfied). States diagrams can be generalized in order to describe complex dynamic models.

5.2 Extending the Basic Dynamic Model with Versions

The proposed solution consists in introducing generalized state diagrams. Three generalized states diagrams are introduced: two for describing object versions and one for describing class version.

According to OMT, a state diagram is defined for each class (class version or simple class) of the database. This state diagram, called Class State Diagram (CSD), defines the behaviour of all the instances (objects or versions) of the class. Moreover, to express that an object version is either working or frozen, we define for each class which contains object versions, a state diagram which generalizes the CSD state diagram of the class. This state diagram, called Version State Diagram (VSD), is the following.

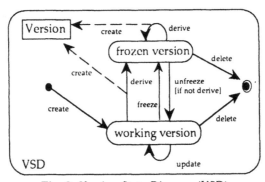

Fig. 9. Version State Diagram (VSD)

Version is a class describing object versions. The VSD diagram is the state diagram of that class. It nests the CSD one as follows:

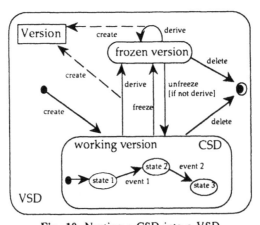

Fig. 10. Nesting a CSD into a VSD

The *working version* state is a generalization of all the states described in the state diagram (CSD) of the considered class. The *update* event is also a generalization of all the events described in the state diagram of the considered class. The *derive* event is an event which triggers the *create* event in the class Version.

A state diagram indicates how a version belonging to a class version can evolve to belong to another class version. The version states are the different VSD diagrams for each class version and *change* is the one and only existing event (a version is going to belong to another class). This state diagram, called VErsionable State Diagram (VESD), is the following:

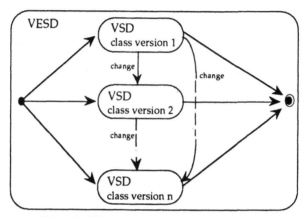

Fig. 11. VErsionable State Diagram (VESD)

Finally, a generalized state diagram is also defined to describe the behaviour of the class versions. Class versions are considered as instances of a meta-class and the state diagram of this meta-class indicates if a class version is working or frozen; this state diagram is the same as the VSD one.

5.3 Basic Functional Model [19]

This model consists of several data flow diagrams. A data flow diagram contains processes that transform data, data flows that move data, actors and data stores. Actors are active object which produce or consume values: they are attached to the inputs and outputs of the data flow diagram. Data stores are passive objects which store passively data. A data flow diagram shows the flow of values from external inputs, through processes and data stores, to external outputs.

5.4 Extending the Basic Functional Model with Versions

The proposed solution consists in introducing versionable actors and versionable data stores to take into account object versions. Class versions are taken into account through the data flow diagrams of the different class versions: there is as much data flow diagrams for a process as class versions.

A versionable actor is an active object version which produce or consume values (i.e. an actor which is an object version) whereas a versionable data store is a passive object which store object versions (i.e. a data store for object versions). Versionable actors and versionable data stores are represented as follows:

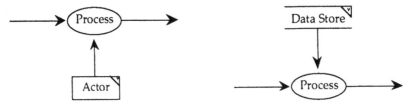

Fig. 12. Versionable actors and versionable data stores

6 Conclusion

This paper defends the idea that versions must be studied from the design stage of a database. Current database design methods do not propose solutions to describe versions in the different models they propose: versions are only taken into account when implementing the database according to the model of the database system. Now, version modeling is an activity recovered from the design stage. From this stage, a designer must be able to tell if an entity or an entity class evolve over time. The version concept must be considered as relationships or entity classes.

This paper has shown how versions can be modeled from the design stage of a database. It proposes solutions to extend the conceptual models (object, dynamic and functional ones) of the OMT method [19] in order to describe versions. Both object and class versions are considered through the three models. Our work particularly approaches the object model because it is the most important one when modeling database applications [19]. Notably it tackles the modeling of composition, relationship or inheritance links between classes taking into account the different kinds of instances of the classes (object and version). It also studies the main operations that the classes and their instances can perform.

To the best of our knowledge, such a study has never been done for conceptual models. However, it is partially approached for logical (database) models with regards to the object model. However, in these approaches, links and operations are not studied in details (inheritance, relationship and composition between objects and versions are not investigated in the literature).

This study has extended the OMT method so that it integrates version modeling capabilities and consequently suit new database applications relevant to fields such as computer aided design, technical documentation or software engineering. OMT has been chosen because it begins to be widely used in aeronautical industry in Toulouse where managed data are documentary or multimedia ones. However, this study can be re-used to extend the data models of current object-oriented database design methods.

Now, we carry on this work addressing the problem of the implementation of the modeled conceptual schemas into existing object-oriented database systems.

References

1. R. Agrawal, S. Buroff, N. Gehani, D. Sasha: Object Versioning in Ode. In: 7th International Conference on Data Engineering, Kobe (Japan), April 1991.

2. D. Batori, W. Kim: Modeling Concepts for VLSI CAD Objects. In: ACM Transaction On Database Systems, 10(3), 1985.

3. D. Beech, B. Mahbod: Generalized Version Control in an Object-Oriented Database. In: 4th International Conference on Data Engineering, Los Angeles (USA), April 1988.

4. A. Björnerstedt, C. Hultén: Version Control in an Object-Oriented Architecture. In: Object-Oriented Concepts, Databases and Applications, Edited by W. Kim, F. Lochovsky, Addisson-Wesley Publishing Company, 1989.

5. S. Clamen: Schema Evolution and Integration. In: Distributed and Parallel Databases Journal, 2(1), 1994.

6. P. Coad, Y. Yourdon: Object-Oriented Analysis. In: Yourdon-Press Publishing Company, 1990.

7. H.T. Chou, W. Kim: A Unifying Framework for Version Control in a CAD Environment. In: 12th International Conference on Very Large Databases, Kyoto (Japan), August 1986.

8. H.T. Chou, W. Kim: Versions and Change Notification in Object-Oriented Database System. In: 25th International Conference on Design Automation, Anaheim (USA), June 1988.

9. K. Dittrich, W. Gotthard, P. Lockemann: Complex Entities for Engineering Applications. In: Research Foundation in Object-Oriented and Semantic Database Systems, Edited by A. Cardenas, D. Mc Leod, Prentice-Hall Publishing Company, 1990.

10. J. Dijkstra: On Complex Objects and Versioning in Complex Environments. In: 12th International Conference on Entity-Relationship Approach, Arlington (USA), December 1993.

11. W. Käfer, H. Schöning: Mapping a Version Model to a Complex Object Data Model. In: 8th International Conference on Data Engineering, Tempe (USA), February 1992.

12. R. Katz: Toward a Unified Framework for Version Modeling in Engineering Databases. In: ACM Computing Surveys, 22(4), 1990.

13. W. Kim, H.T. Chou: Versions of Schema for Object-Oriented Databases. In: 14th International Conference on Very Large Databases, Los Angeles (USA), August 1988.

14. W. Kim: Composite Object Revisited. In: 14th ACM International Conference on Management of Data, Portland (USA), June 1989.

15. W. Kim, N. Ballou, HT. Chou, J. Garza, D. Woelk: Features of the Orion Object-Oriented Database System. In: Object-Oriented Concepts, Databases and Applications, Edited by W. Kim, F. Lochovsky, Addisson-Wesley Publishing Company, 1989.

16. B. Lerner, A. Habermann: Beyond Schema Evolution to Database Reorganisation. ACM SIGPLAN Notices, 25(10), 1990.

17. S. Monk, I. Sommerville: Schema Evolution in Object-Oriented Databases using Class Versioning. ACM SIGMOD Record, 22(3), September 1993.

18. D. Penney, J. Stein: Class Modification in the GemStone Object-Oriented Database System. In: International Conference on Object-Oriented Programming, Systems, Languages and Applications, OOPSLA 87, Orlando (USA), September 1987.

19. M. Rumbaugh, M. Blaha, W. Premerlani, F. Eddy, W. Lorensen: Object-Oriented Modeling and Design. Prentice-Hall Publishing Company, 1991.

20. A. Skarra, S. Zdonik. The Management of Changing Types in an Object-Oriented Database. In: International Conference on Object-Oriented Programming, Systems, Languages and Applications, OOPSLA 86, Portland (USA), September 1986.

21. G. Talens, C. Oussalah, M.F. Colinas: Versions of Simple and Composite Objects. In: 19th International Conference on Very Large Databases, Dublin (Ireland), August 1993.

22. S. Zdonik: Version Management in an Object-Oriented Database. In: International Workshop on Object-Oriented Databases, LNCS n° 244, Trondhein (Norway), June 1986.

Author Index

Akoka, Jacky	372	Maret, Pierre	89
Altus, Margita	146	Menzel, Ralf	28
Andonoff, Eric	472	Mok, Wai Yin	309
Apers, Peter M. G.	179	Moody, Daniel	227
Assenova, Petia	277	Mylopoulos, John	325
Bachman, Charles W.	1	Norrie, Moira C.	456
Biskup, Joachim	28	Orlowska, Maria E.	73
Bloesch, Anthony C.	121	Ortner, Erich	261
Bordat, Jean-Paul	422	Parc, Annig Le	472
Casanova, Marco A.	292	Pernici, Barbara	438
Casati, Fabio	438	Pinon, Jean-Marie	89
Ceri, Stefano	438	Polle, Torsten	28
Cicchetti, Rosine	422	Pozzi, Giuseppe	438
Clauß, Wolfram	134	Rajapakse, Jayantha	73
Comyn-Wattiau, Isabelle	372	Ravve, Elena V.	5
Dahm, Peter	163	Roland, Didier	42
Ebert, Jürgen	163	Saake, Gunter	195
Ekenberg, Love	211	Sagiv, Yehoshua	28
Elmasri, Ramez	341	Schewe, Bettina	357
Embley, David W.	309	Schewe, Klaus-Dieter	357
Englebert, Vincent	42	Schienmann, Bruno	261
Franzke, Angelika	163	Schmitt, Ingo	195
Hainaut, Jean-Luc	42	Silva, Altigran Soares da	292
Halpin, Terry A.	121	Soutou, Christian	392
Henrard, Jean	42	Steeg, Martin	105
Hick, Jean-Marc	42	Steiner, Andreas	456
Hofstede, Arthur H. M. ter	73	Süttenbach, Roger	163
Hubert, Gilles	472	Theodoratos, Dimitri	58
Johannesson, Paul	211, 277	Topaloglou, Thodoros	325
Kaschek, Roland	406	Vermeer, Mark W. W.	179
Laender, Alberto H. F.	292	Winter, Andreas	163
Lakhal, Lotfi	422	Won, Jongho	341
Lee, Jae Young	341	Würgler, Alain	456
Maier, Ronald	245	Wunderli, Martin	456
Makowsky, Johann A.	5	Yahia, Amina	422
Mannila, Heikki	27	Zurfluh, Gilles	472

Lecture Notes in Computer Science

For information about Vols. 1–1081

please contact your bookseller or Springer-Verlag

Vol. 1082: N.R. Adam, B.K. Bhargava, M. Halem, Y. Yesha (Eds.), Digital Libraries. Proceedings, 1995. Approx. 310 pages. 1996.

Vol. 1083: K. Sparck Jones, J.R. Galliers, Evaluating Natural Language Processing Systems. XV, 228 pages. 1996. (Subseries LNAI).

Vol. 1084: W.H. Cunningham, S.T. McCormick, M. Queyranne (Eds.), Integer Programming and Combinatorial Optimization. Proceedings, 1996. X, 505 pages. 1996.

Vol. 1085: D.M. Gabbay, H.J. Ohlbach (Eds.), Practical Reasoning. Proceedings, 1996. XV, 721 pages. 1996. (Subseries LNAI).

Vol. 1086: C. Frasson, G. Gauthier, A. Lesgold (Eds.), Intelligent Tutoring Systems. Proceedings, 1996. XVII, 688 pages. 1996.

Vol. 1087: C. Zhang, D. Lukose (Eds.), Distributed Artificial Intelliegence. Proceedings, 1995. VIII, 232 pages. 1996. (Subseries LNAI).

Vol. 1088: A. Strohmeier (Ed.), Reliable Software Technologies – Ada-Europe '96. Proceedings, 1996. XI, 513 pages. 1996.

Vol. 1089: G. Ramalingam, Bounded Incremental Computation. XI, 190 pages. 1996.

Vol. 1090: J.-Y. Cai, C.K. Wong (Eds.), Computing and Combinatorics. Proceedings, 1996. X, 421 pages. 1996.

Vol. 1091: J. Billington, W, Reisig (Eds.), Application and Theory of Petri Nets 1996. Proceedings, 1996. VIII, 549 pages. 1996.

Vol. 1092: H. Kleine Büning (Ed.), Computer Science Logic. Proceedings, 1995. VIII, 487 pages. 1996.

Vol. 1093: L. Dorst, M. van Lambalgen, F. Voorbraak (Eds.), Reasoning with Uncertainty in Robotics. Proceedings, 1995. VIII, 387 pages. 1996. (Subseries LNAI).

Vol. 1094: R. Morrison, J. Kennedy (Eds.), Advances in Databases. Proceedings, 1996. XI, 234 pages. 1996.

Vol. 1095: W. McCune, R. Padmanabhan, Automated Deduction in Equational Logic and Cubic Curves. X, 231 pages. 1996. (Subseries LNAI).

Vol. 1096: T. Schäl, Workflow Management Systems for Process Organisations. XII, 200 pages. 1996.

Vol. 1097: R. Karlsson, A. Lingas (Eds.), Algorithm Theory – SWAT '96. Proceedings, 1996. IX, 453 pages. 1996.

Vol. 1098: P. Cointe (Ed.), ECOOP '96 – Object-Oriented Programming. Proceedings, 1996. XI, 502 pages. 1996.

Vol. 1099: F. Meyer auf der Heide, B. Monien (Eds.), Automata, Languages and Programming. Proceedings, 1996. XII, 681 pages. 1996.

Vol. 1100: B. Pfitzmann, Digital Signature Schemes. XVI. 396 pages. 1996.

Vol. 1101: M. Wirsing, M. Nivat (Eds.), Algebraic Methodology and Software Technology. Proceedings, 1996. XII, 641 pages. 1996.

Vol. 1102: R. Alur, T.A. Henzinger (Eds.), Computer Aided Verification. Proceedings, 1996. XII, 472 pages. 1996.

Vol. 1103: H. Ganzinger (Ed.), Rewriting Techniques and Applications. Proceedings, 1996. XI, 437 pages. 1996.

Vol. 1104: M.A. McRobbie, J.K. Slaney (Eds.), Automated Deduction – CADE-13. Proceedings, 1996. XV, 764 pages. 1996. (Subseries LNAI).

Vol. 1105: T.I. Ören, G.J. Klir (Eds.), Computer Aided Systems Theory – CAST '94. Proceedings, 1994. IX, 439 pages. 1996.

Vol. 1106: M. Jampel, E. Freuder, M. Maher (Eds.), Over-Constrained Systems. X, 309 pages. 1996.

Vol. 1107: J.-P. Briot, J.-M. Geib, A. Yonezawa (Eds.). Object-Based Parallel and Distributed Computation. Proceedings, 1995. X, 349 pages. 1996.

Vol. 1108: A. Díaz de Ilarraza Sánchez, I. Fernández de Castro (Eds.), Computer Aided Learning and Instruction in Science and Engineering. Proceedings, 1996. XIV, 480 pages. 1996.

Vol. 1109: N. Koblitz (Ed.), Advances in Cryptology – Crypto '96. Proceedings, 1996. XII, 417 pages. 1996.

Vol. 1110: O. Danvy, R. Glück, P. Thiemann (Eds.), Partial Evaluation. Proceedings, 1996. XII, 514 pages. 1996.

Vol. 1111: J.J. Alferes, L. Moniz Pereira, Reasoning with Logic Programming. XXI, 326 pages. 1996. (Subseries LNAI).

Vol. 1112: C. von der Malsburg, W. von Seelen, J.C. Vorbrüggen, B. Sendhoff (Eds.), Artificial Neural Networks – ICANN 96. Proceedings, 1996. XXV, 922 pages. 1996.

Vol. 1113: W. Penczek, A. Szalas (Eds.), Mathematical Foundations of Computer Science 1996. Proceedings, 1996. X, 592 pages. 1996.

Vol. 1114: N. Foo, R. Goebel (Eds.), PRICAI'96: Topics in Artificial Intelligence. Proceedings, 1996. XXI, 658 pages. 1996. (Subseries LNAI).

Vol. 1115: P.W. Eklund, G. Ellis, G. Mann (Eds.), Conceptual Structures: Knowledge Representation as Interlingua. Proceedings, 1996. XIII, 321 pages. 1996. (Subseries LNAI).

Vol. 1116: J. Hall (Ed.), Management of Telecommunication Systems and Services. XXI, 229 pages. 1996.

Vol. 1117: A. Ferreira, J. Rolim, Y. Saad, T. Yang (Eds.), Parallel Algorithms for Irregularly Structured Problems. Proceedings, 1996. IX, 358 pages. 1996.

Vol. 1118: E.C. Freuder (Ed.), Principles and Practice of Constraint Programming — CP 96. Proceedings, 1996. XIX, 574 pages. 1996.

Vol. 1119: U. Montanari, V. Sassone (Eds.), CONCUR '96: Concurrency Theory. Proceedings, 1996. XII, 751 pages. 1996.

Vol. 1120: M. Deza. R. Euler, I. Manoussakis (Eds.), Combinatorics and Computer Science. Proceedings, 1995. IX, 415 pages. 1996.

Vol. 1121: P. Perner, P. Wang, A. Rosenfeld (Eds.), Advances in Structural and Syntactical Pattern Recognition. Proceedings, 1996. X, 393 pages. 1996.

Vol. 1122: H. Cohen (Ed.), Algorithmic Number Theory. Proceedings, 1996. IX, 405 pages. 1996.

Vol. 1123: L. Bougé, P. Fraigniaud, A. Mignotte, Y. Robert (Eds.), Euro-Par'96. Parallel Processing. Proceedings, 1996, Vol. I. XXXIII, 842 pages. 1996.

Vol. 1124: L. Bougé, P. Fraigniaud, A. Mignotte, Y. Robert (Eds.), Euro-Par'96. Parallel Processing. Proceedings, 1996, Vol. II. XXXIII, 926 pages. 1996.

Vol. 1125: J. von Wright, J. Grundy, J. Harrison (Eds.), Theorem Proving in Higher Order Logics. Proceedings, 1996. VIII, 447 pages. 1996.

Vol. 1126: J.J. Alferes, L. Moniz Pereira, E. Orlowska (Eds.), Logics in Artificial Intelligence. Proceedings, 1996. IX, 417 pages. 1996. (Subseries LNAI).

Vol. 1127: L. Böszörményi (Ed.), Parallel Computation. Proceedings, 1996. XI, 235 pages. 1996.

Vol. 1128: J. Calmet, C. Limongelli (Eds.), Design and Implementation of Symbolic Computation Systems. Proceedings, 1996. IX, 356 pages. 1996.

Vol. 1129: J. Launchbury, E. Meijer, T. Sheard (Eds.), Advanced Functional Programming. Proceedings, 1996. VII, 238 pages. 1996.

Vol. 1130: M. Haveraaen, O. Owe, O.-J. Dahl (Eds.), Recent Trends in Data Type Specification. Proceedings, 1995. VIII, 551 pages. 1996.

Vol. 1131: K.H. Höhne, R. Kikinis (Eds.), Visualization in Biomedical Computing. Proceedings, 1996. XII, 610 pages. 1996.

Vol. 1132: G.-R. Perrin, A. Darte (Eds.), The Data Parallel Programming Model. XV, 284 pages. 1996.

Vol. 1133: J.-Y. Chouinard, P. Fortier, T.A. Gulliver (Eds.), Information Theory and Applications II. Proceedings, 1995. XII, 309 pages. 1996.

Vol. 1134: R. Wagner, H. Thoma (Eds.), Database and Expert Systems Applications. Proceedings, 1996. XV, 921 pages. 1996.

Vol. 1135: B. Jonsson, J. Parrow (Eds.), Formal Techniques in Real-Time and Fault-Tolerant Systems. Proceedings, 1996. X, 479 pages. 1996.

Vol. 1136: J. Diaz, M. Serna (Eds.), Algorithms – ESA '96. Proceedings, 1996. XII, 566 pages. 1996.

Vol. 1137: G. Görz, S. Hölldobler (Eds.), KI-96: Advances in Artificial Intelligence. Proceedings, 1996. XI, 387 pages. 1996. (Subseries LNAI).

Vol. 1138: J. Calmet, J.A. Campbell, J. Pfalzgraf (Eds.), Artificial Intelligence and Symbolic Mathematical Computation. Proceedings, 1996. VIII, 381 pages. 1996.

Vol. 1139: M. Hanus, M. Rogriguez-Artalejo (Eds.), Algebraic and Logic Programming. Proceedings, 1996. VIII, 345 pages. 1996.

Vol. 1140: H. Kuchen, S. Doaitse Swierstra (Eds.), Programming Languages: Implementations, Logics, and Programs. Proceedings, 1996. XI, 479 pages. 1996.

Vol. 1141: H.-M. Voigt, W. Ebeling, I. Rechenberg, H.-P. Schwefel (Eds.), Parallel Problem Solving from Nature – PPSN IV. Proceedings, 1996. XVII, 1.050 pages. 1996.

Vol. 1142: R.W. Hartenstein, M. Glesner (Eds.), Field-Programmable Logic. Proceedings, 1996. X, 432 pages. 1996.

Vol. 1143: T.C. Fogarty (Ed.), Evolutionary Computing. Proceedings, 1996. VIII, 305 pages. 1996.

Vol. 1144: J. Ponce, A. Zisserman, M. Hebert (Eds.), Object Representation in Computer Vision. Proceedings, 1996. VIII, 403 pages. 1996.

Vol. 1145: R. Cousot, D.A. Schmidt (Eds.), Static Analysis. Proceedings, 1996. IX, 389 pages. 1996.

Vol. 1146: E. Bertino, H. Kurth, G. Martella, E. Montolivo (Eds.), Computer Security – ESORICS 96. Proceedings, 1996. X, 365 pages. 1996.

Vol. 1147: L. Miclet, C. de la Higuera (Eds.), Grammatical Inference: Learning Syntax from Sentences. Proceedings, 1996. VIII, 327 pages. 1996. (Subseries LNAI).

Vol. 1148: M.C. Lin, D. Manocha (Eds.), Applied Computational Geometry. Proceedings, 1996. VIII, 223 pages. 1996.

Vol. 1149: C. Montangero (Ed.), Software Process Technology. Proceedings, 1996. IX, 291 pages. 1996.

Vol. 1150: A. Hlawiczka, J.G. Silva, L. Simoncini (Eds.), Dependable Computing – EDCC-2. Proceedings, 1996. XVI, 440 pages. 1996.

Vol. 1151: Ö. Babaoğlu, K. Marzullo (Eds.), Distributed Algorithms. Proceedings, 1996. VIII, 381 pages. 1996.

Vol. 1153: E. Burke, P. Ross (Eds.), Practice and Theory of Automated Timetabling. Proceedings, 1995. XIII, 381 pages. 1996.

Vol. 1154: D. Pedreschi, C. Zaniolo (Eds.), Logic in Databases. Proceedings, 1996. X, 497 pages. 1996.

Vol. 1155: J. Roberts, U. Mocci, J. Virtamo (Eds.), Broadbank Network Teletraffic. XXII, 584 pages. 1996.

Vol. 1156: A. Bode, J. Dongarra, T. Ludwig, V. Sunderam (Eds.), Parallel Virtual Machine – EuroPVM '96. Proceedings, 1996. XIV, 362 pages. 1996.

Vol. 1157: B. Thalheim (Ed.), Conceptual Modeling – ER '96. Proceedings, 1996. XII, 489 pages. 1996.

Vol. 1158: S. Berardi, M. Coppo (Eds.), Types for Proofs and Programs. Proceedings, 1995. X, 296 pages. 1996.